For more than half a millennium the Mamluks – military slaves emanating from the steppes of southern Russia and later from the Caucasus and the Balkans – wielded power over Egypt. During this time they formed a remarkable political, military and economic elite, ruling as sovereigns from 1250 to 1517 and, after the Ottoman conquest of Egypt, regaining much of their former paramountcy under Turkish supremacy. In this collection of essays, Thomas Philipp and Ulrich Haarmann have brought together the research of some of the most distinguished scholars in the field to provide an accessible and coherent introduction to the structure of political power under the Mamluks and its economic foundations. The essays also offer a unique insight into the Mamluk households and their relationship with the indigenous Egyptian population.

Cambridge Studies in Islamic Civilization

The Mamluks in Egyptian politics and society

Cambridge Studies in Islamic Civilization

Editorial board
DAVID MORGAN (general editor)
VIRGINIA AKSAN MICHAEL BRETT MICHAEL COOK PETER JACKSON
TARIF KHALIDI ROY MOTTAHEDEH BASIM MUSALLAM CHASE ROBINSON

Titles in the series

STEFAN SPERL. *Mannerism in Arabic poetry: a structural analysis of selected texts, 3rd century AH/9th century AD–5th century AH/11th century AD*
*BEATRICE FORBES MANZ. *The rise and rule of Tamerlane*
AMNON COHEN. *Economic life in Ottoman Jerusalem*
PAUL E. WALKER. *Early philosophical Shiʿism: the Ismaili Neoplatonism of Abū Yaʿqūb al-Sijistānī*
BOAZ SHOSHAN. *Popular culture in medieval Cairo*
STEPHEN FREDERIC DALE. *Indian merchants and Eurasian trade, 1600–1750*
*AMY SINGER. *Palestinian peasants and Ottoman officials: rural administration around sixteenth-century Jerusalem*
MICHAEL CHAMBERLAIN. *Knowledge and social practice in medieval Damascus, 1190–1350*
*TARIF KHALIDI. *Arabic historical thought in the classical period*
REUVEN AMITAI-PREISS. *Mongols and Mamluks: the Mamluk–Īlkhānid war, 1260–1281*
LOUISE MARLOW. *Hierarchy and egalitarianism in Islamic thought, 1260–1281*
JANE HATHAWAY. *The politics of households in Ottoman Egypt: the rise of the Qazdağlis*
THOMAS T. ALLSEN. *Commodity and exchange in the Mongol empire: a cultural history of Islamic textiles*
DINA RIZK KHOURY. *State and provincial society in the Ottoman empire: Mosul, 1540–1834*

* Also published as a paperback

The Mamluks in Egyptian politics and society

Edited by

THOMAS PHILIPP

Institut für Politische Wissenschaft, Erlangen

and

ULRICH HAARMANN

Universität Kiel

CAMBRIDGE
UNIVERSITY PRESS

PUBLISHED BY THE PRESS SYNDICATE OF THE UNIVERSITY OF CAMBRIDGE
The Pitt Building, Trumpington Street, Cambridge CB2 1RP, United Kingdom

CAMBRIDGE UNIVERSITY PRESS
The Edinburgh Building, Cambridge CB2 2RU, United Kingdom
40 West 20th Street, New York, NY 10011–4211, USA
10 Stamford Road, Oakleigh, Melbourne 3166, Australia

First published 1998

Printed in the United Kingdom at the University Press, Cambridge

Typeset in 10/12pt Times [SE]

A catalogue record for this book is available from the British Library

Library of Congress cataloguing in publication data
The Mamluks in Egyptian politics and society / edited by Thomas
Phillip and Ulrich Haarmaan.
p. cm. – (Cambridge studies in Islamic civilization)
ISBN 0-521-59115 5 (hb)
1. Mamluks. 2. Egypt – History – 1250–1517. 3. Egypt–
History – 1517–1882. I. Philipp, Thomas. II. Haarmaan, Ulrich,
1942– . III. Series.
DT96.M2156 1997
962′.02′088355 – dc21 97-9821 CIP

ISBN 0 521 59115 5 hardback

Contents

Illustrations

Preface

Mamluk rule was the culmination of a long evolution of military slavery – an institution that seems to have been specific to, as well as, typical of Islamic societies. For centuries military slaves had played a role in the politics of the islamic lands. Occasionally leading individuals had established local dynasties. But usually the power of the military slaves, or rather their officer corps, was exerted from behind the scenes. Lacking the legitimization to rule on their own officers preferred to co-opt weak caliphs or other, more legitimate, rulers.

At the time of the demise of Ayyubid rule in Egypt in the middle of the thirteenth century the slave troops of the Ayyubids seem to have hesitated as to what structure and shape their political power should take. Testimony to their hesitation and embarrassment was the rise to power of the only (albeit for only eighty days) female sultan in Islamic history. As the mother of a predeceased Ayyubid son she seemed to possess at least a shred of dynastic legitimacy.

The solution that eventually evolved was unique. The Mamluks themselves took power, formally and publicly, and enthroned one of their own as sultan. Yet, firmly opposed to any dynastic claim to power and to any undue concentration of power in the hands of one person, they continued to reproduce themselves as a ruling elite by replenishing their ranks with fresh imports of slaves from beyond the realm of Islam. The newly bought slaves were integrated into the Mamluk elite by being attached to one of the Mamluk households where they not only received their training but also developed a fierce loyalty to their master and comrades-in-arms. The Mamluks' own children and descendants, the *awlād al-nās*, were more often than not pushed aside in favour of young Mamluks succeeding to the power and wealth of their Mamluk masters who had bought and raised them. The reproduction of the ruling class by recruitment from abroad prevented its assimilation into the local population and fostered a group consciousness and loyalty among the members of this elite.

The peculiarities of the surprisingly durable Mamluk ruling system and organization in Egypt are patent. Turkish and Circassian youngsters were recruited as military slaves in the Qipchaq steppes and in the northern Caucasus. In the Ottoman period their countries of origin were mainly

Georgia and the Balkans. All these were regions markedly different from Egypt, linguistically, anthropologically and culturally. The Mamluks were brought to the Arab Middle East, were purchased by local strongmen (during the sultanate in principle only Mamluks themselves were allowed to buy white slaves), were educated to be good Muslims, and were trained, before 1517, as lancers, bowmen and cavalrymen, in consistency with the rigorous traditions of the steppes. Eventually the young Mamluk was affranchised and – if he was good, crafty and lucky – he could ultimately be promoted to become, before 1517, a member of the military oligarchy or even sultan. In the battles of Marj Dābiq and al-Raydāniyya in 1516 and 1517 the Mamluk kingdom was destroyed; Egypt and Syria were annexed to the victorious Ottoman Empire. But as early as the end of the sixteenth century Mamluk influence gradually reasserted itself in Egypt. New Mamluk groupings came into being with a membership that was recruited from specifically Mamluk quarters, yet also attracted members of the Ottoman regiments stationed in Egypt. These so-called neo-Mamluk households enjoyed distinct social, political and economic privileges and legitimized themselves even with their proper myths of origin. The authority of the Ottoman sultan as the supreme head of the land, however, was never overtly, let alone successfully, challenged by Mamluk grandees; although, from the middle of the eighteenth century, they reasserted their actual control over Egypt.

The Mamluks had achieved very early on an aura of legitimacy for their regime when they succeeded in defending the realm of Islam against the Crusaders and the Mongols. Two-and-a-half centuries later the Mamluks' way of fighting proved to be obsolete against Ottoman firearms. Chivalrous and colourful as the Mamluks were, their military prowess turned out to be woefully inadequate against French infantry and field artillery another 250 years later. Early contemporaries of the Mamluks, both European Christian and North African Muslim observers, had clearly perceived the uniqueness of the system, its strengths, and its intrinsic contradictions. Their curiosity was aroused by the unusual arrangements of this ruling elite, whereby in the succession to power the elite's own descendants were passed over in favour of imported slaves and whereby the ruler was rather a *primus inter pares* than a dynastic monarch. It appeared that not the family, but rather the Mamluk household, was the focus of loyalty and power, and permanent ethnic separation from the ruled population was elevated to a principle. The Mamluk institution caused a lot of speculation and comment among pre-modern observers. But so thorough was the defeat of the Mamluks by Napoleon in 1798 and their subsequent liquidation by Muḥammad ʿAlī that for the following generations they remained a perhaps exotic but utterly inconsequential phenomenon.

The Mamluk period was infelicitously situated between what the European Orientalists revered as the classical age of Islam and that period Egyptian nationalists would consider the dawn of modern Egypt. Orientalists could only observe the sad decline from a time they considered the height of Islamic civilization; modern Egyptian historians always felt ambivalent about an elite which had admittedly led Egypt to cultural and political peaks but had never become part of the Egyptian nation.

Only some forty years ago did modern Mamluk studies receive a new impetus with the works of David Ayalon. Since then, thanks also to new approaches in social, economic and cultural history, a small but distinct number of historians have contributed considerably to the study of the Mamluks.

It was the purpose of a small conference held in Bad Homburg in December 1994 to bring together some of these scholars for an exchange of ideas and to form an impression of the 'state of the art' of Mamluk studies. The present volume is the result of this symposium. Certain questions seemed to play a major role in the discussions:

Was the uniqueness of this habit of permanently rejuvenating the ranks of the military leaders and of the virtual owners of the arable land from the outside at all perceived (and then justified) by the Mamluks and their Egyptian subjects? How real was the alleged non-heredity of power during the sultanate? Were the sons of Mamluks, the so-called *awlād al-nās*, really excluded from the political, social and economic prerogatives of their fathers, as has been often claimed in the existing scholarly literature; were they assimilated into the social environment and, if yes, in what ways? What was the rule of the Mamluk household? Another major theme is the comparison between the Mamluks under Ottoman rule and their independent predecessors in Egypt. Closely connected with this comparison is the question of the rise of the neo-Mamluks to near independence during the eighteenth century and their eventual collapse.

The contributions to the symposium can roughly be divided into two thematic parts. In the first, the struggle of members of the Mamluk elite for political and social influence *within* their own class and system is treated. We are informed about the gradual demise of the power of the sultan and then also of the leading amirs to the advantage of the rank-and-file Mamluks during the fourteenth and fifteenth centuries (Amalia Levanoni, Haifa); the self-perception and self-representation of Mamluk rulers in late medieval and early modern panegyrical historiography (Peter M. Holt, London); the principal career patterns of the sons of Mamluks before 1517 (Donald Richards, Oxford and Ulrich Haarmann, Kiel); the gradual genesis of 'neo-Mamluk households' joining Mamluks, sons of Mamluks and non-Mamluk clients together as common beneficiaries of political might and economic wealth under the Ottomans (Jane Hathaway, Columbus and Michael Winter, Tel Aviv); the limits of solidarity and loyalty among eighteenth-century Mamluks in times of crisis and affliction (Thomas Philipp, Erlangen); and finally, the capacity of the Mamluk institution in absorbing ethnic diversity in the Ottoman period (Daniel Crecelius, Los Angeles).

The second thematic part deals with the relations of the Mamluks' military establishment with its non-Mamluk environment. The following questions are tackled: were the Mamluks autonomous producers and patrons of culture? Here urbanization activities during the sultanate and the Ottoman period (Doris Behrens-Abouseif, Munich); educational aspects of the sultanate (Jonathan Berkey, Davidson) and of the Ottoman era (Nelly Hanna, Cairo) were dealt with. Is it possible to identify sciences that attracted the particular interest of Mamluks (David King, Frankfurt)? How did the civilian population, especially the jurists, react to the discriminating Mamluk monopoly on arms (Ulrich Haarmann, Kiel)? Were members of religious minorities and their immediate descendants used by the Mamluks as scapegoats because of their contested loyalties and their inherent vulnerability (Donald P. Little, Montreal)? Three papers, predicated upon three different scholarly disciplines (historiography, urban topography, cultural anthropology) cover both the early period of the sultanate and the era of Ottoman sway: what were the effects of the loss of political and cultural centrality on the historiographical discourse of Cairo after 1517 (Otfried Weintritt, Freiburg)? Was there any tangible relationship between social standing and the choice of residential quarters in Cairo (André Raymond, Aix-en-Provence)? What was the Mamluk contribution to the rich festive culture of pre-modern urban Egypt (Huda Lutfi, Cairo)? Finally, and now again restricted to a limited chapter in the history of Ottoman Egypt: were there any recognizable ethnic and racial barriers in the marriage patterns of eighteenth-century Mamluks (Afaf Lutfi al-Sayyid Marsot, Cairo)?

The two organizers of the symposium and editors of this volume owe cordial thanks to all those institutions and individuals who munificently helped us in achieving our goals. The Werner Reimers Foundation in Bad Homburg invited us to its mansion on the slopes of the Taunus mountains for three wonderful, sunny days in December 1994 and paid for part of the expenses of the participants. The sizeable remaining share was generously and unbureaucratically covered by a contribution from the Gerda Henkel Foundation in Düsseldorf. To both foundations and their trustees goes our gratitude.

Co-ordinating the diverse contributions towards this volume was no easy task. We emphatically thank Stefan Winter for helping with this and catching many stylistic flaws. His work was kindly supported by the Wissenschaftskolleg in Berlin. He also translated A. Raymond's paper from French into English and compiled the indices for this volume, a task completed by Stephen Conermann, Kiel. Special praise is due, last but not least, to Sibylle Appelt of the departmental office in Erlangen. She not only collected and standardized the various and at times rather heterogeneous contributions, but also typed them and thus created the neat manuscript that served as the basis for this publication.

Ulrich Haarmann, *Kiel*
Thomas Philipp, *Erlangen*

PART I

Mamluk rule and succession

CHAPTER 1

Literary offerings: a genre of courtly literature

P. M. HOLT

In *al-Sayf al-muhannad*, a work which will be discussed below, the author, al-ʿAynī, says that 'it has been customary in ancient and modern times to make an offering to kings and sultans of what God has placed within the power and capacity of everyone'.[1] He therefore makes his offering in the form of a book, presented to the sultan shortly after his accession. Seven such offerings form the subject of this chapter, five of them presented to Mamluk sultans, the sixth to the Ottoman Selim the Grim after the conquest of Syria and Egypt, and the seventh to a neo-Mamluk grandee of the eleventh/seventeenth century.

The first of these works is *al-Tuḥfa al-mulūkiyya fī 'l-dawla al-Turkiyya* by the Mamluk chronicler Baybars al-Manṣūrī (d. 725/1325).[2] It has generally been regarded as a chronicle of the Turkish Mamluk sultans to 711/1311–12. Ashtor described it as 'a first-hand report by a high ranking state dignitary . . . Baybars is interested only in political history',[3] and briefly discussed its relationship to Baybars al-Manṣūrī's chronicle of Islamic history, *Zubdat al-fikra fī ta'rīkh al-hijra.* Little calls it 'a compilation from the sections of *Zubdat al-fikra* that deal with the Turkish or Baḥrī dynasty'.[4] These descriptions overlook, however, the specific character of *al-Tuḥfa* as indicated by the author's life history, the time of the work's production, and its intended destination.

Although the sons and later descendants of Mamluks *(awlād al-nās)* played a very important part in the cultural history of Egypt and Syria, Baybars al-Manṣūrī, a first-generation immigrant, is almost unique among the chroniclers of the period. Ashtor, and still more strongly Wiet,[5] have emphasized his dependence on secretaries, but whatever their responsibility for the phraseology and style of *al-Tuḥfa*, it bears the impress of Baybars al-Manṣūrī's own personality and experience. He was in the service of Qalāwūn al-Alfī (from

1 Badr al-dīn Maḥmūd b. Aḥmad al-ʿAynī, *al-Sayf al-muhannad fī sīrat al-Malik al-Mu'ayyad,* ed. Fahīm Muḥammad Shaltūt (Cairo, 1387/1967), 6. (Hereafter, *sayf*).

2 Baybars al-Manṣūrī, *Kitāb al-Tuḥfa al-mulūkiyya fī 'l-dawla al-Turkiyya,* ed. ʿAbd al-Ḥamīd Ṣāliḥ Ḥamdān (Cairo, 1407/1987) (Hereafter *Tuḥfa).*

3 E. Ashtor, 'Some unpublished sources for the Baḥrī period', in Uriel Heyd (ed.), *Studies in Islamic History and Civilization* (Jerusalem, 1961), 13.

4 Donald Presgrave Little, *An Introduction to Mamluk Historiography* (Wiesbaden, 1970), 5.

5 Ashtor, *u.s.*, at 12 and n. 4.

whose royal title of al-Malik al-Manṣūr he obtained his *nisba*) by 664/1265–6. After Qalāwūn's death in 689/1290 he remained loyal to his son, al-Nāṣir Muḥammad, during whose first two (nominal) reigns he held the great office of *dawādār*. He played a part in the final restoration of al-Nāṣir Muḥammad, in 709/1310. When he ended *al-Tuḥfa* with the events of 711/1312 he had been appointed vice regent in Egypt, the highest office in the sultanate. With his master restored, and at last firmly established on the throne, and himself to all appearance the sultan's trusted lieutenant, the work could appropriately be closed, and placed in the royal library, for which (as he tells us in the colophon) it was intended.

Al-Tuḥfa, then, is not simply the abridgment of another chronicle but a deliberate presentation of the history of the early Mamluk sultans to do honour to Baybars al-Manṣūrī's former master, al-Manṣūr Qalāwūn, and to Qalāwūn's son, who had at last emerged victorious over his opponents and the usurpers of his throne. After an introduction in which Baybars describes his abridgement of the final bulky part of *Zubdat al-fikra*, and al-Nāṣir Muḥammad's gracious interest in the work, he opens his history with the death of the Ayyubid sultan, al-Ṣāliḥ Ayyūb, in 647/1249. The Baḥriyya rising like lions overthrew his unworthy son, Tūrān Shāh, and then disposed of the king of France and his soldiery. After this, Aybak al-Turkumānī was appointed *atābak al-ʿasākir* before being installed as sultan. In the annal for 650/1252–3 Qalāwūn makes his appearance with Baybars al-Bunduqdārī in command of an expedition against the Arabs of Upper Egypt. He is most significantly mentioned in 656/1258, when he and Baybars al-Bunduqdārī, both at that time exiles, visited a certain Shaykh ʿAlī al-Bakkā living in Hebron, who foretold that both of them would obtain the sultanate. Alleged prophecies of this kind are not unusual as devices of legitimization, and here as in some other instances one may suspect that Baybars alone originally figured in the incident, which was subsequently extended when Qalāwūn usurped the throne.

The presentation of Baybars al-Bunduqdārī as champion of Islam and sultan was in the circumstances a somewhat delicate operation. His importance in the history of the Mamluk sultanate could not be ignored; on the other hand he could not be allowed to overshadow Qalāwūn, whose usurpation equally required careful handling. A crucial episode was the battle of ʿAyn Jālūt in 658/1260, where credit for the victory over the Mongols is given to Baybars by his biographer and encomiast, Ibn ʿAbd al-Ẓāhir.[6] In *al-Tuḥfa*, however, Baybars is shown merely as being sent to pursue the fugitives from the battlefield, when (in an incident not mentioned by Ibn ʿAbd al-Ẓāhir) he is surprised by a relieving force of Mongols, who are defeated by the Mamluks. The subsequent annals to 676/1277–8, twenty-two folios in the original man-

[6] Muḥyī al-dīn b. ʿAbd al-Ẓāhir, *al-Rawḍ al-zāhir fī sīrat al-Malik al-Ẓāhir*, ed. ʿAbd al-ʿAzīz [b. ʿAbdallāh] al-Khuwayṭir, (Riyadh, 1396/1976), 64.

uscript, cover the reign of Baybars, and give a fair and straightforward account of his achievements. One may compare with this the less sympathetic revisionist biography of Baybars, completed a few years later (716/1316) by Shāfiʿ b. ʿAlī.[7] Baybars' death is ascribed to his accidentally drinking from a poisoned cup intended for an Ayyubid prince – a story which is not mentioned by Ibn ʿAbd al-Ẓāhir or Shāfiʿ, and which may be a romantic legend although it is found in other sources.[8]

Since usurpation and restoration form in a sense the central theme of *al-Tuḥfa*, it is instructive to compare Baybars al-Manṣūrī's treatment of two usurpations. The first is that of Qalāwūn, who in 678/1279 brought about the deposition of Baybars' son, Baraka Khān, and the installation of his infant brother, Salāmish, only to dethrone Salāmish three months later, and take the sultanate himself. In Baybars al-Manṣūrī's account of the course of events leading to the usurpation, he makes it clear that Qalāwūn exploited a power struggle between Baraka Khān's Mamluk household and his father's veterans, the Ẓāhiriyya, to secure the ascendancy of his own comrades, the Baḥriyya. Baybars al-Manṣūrī justifies this usurpation in a significant passage:

> Al-Ẓāhir [Baybars] was confident that the command would pass to him [Qalāwūn], and this was a reason for his establishing a connection by marriage with him.[9] The pious Shaykh ʿAlī al-Bakkā foretold his sultanate, as we have mentioned. Then after that one of his retinue had a dream of him, as if an unseen speaker said, 'This Qalāwūn will break Halāwūn [Hülegü].' When he was told of the dream, being yet an amir, he said, 'These are confused dreams.' But the matter was [divinely] recorded, and the dream was a foretelling; and the story of the dream spread in the talk of the people.[10]

So not only was the sultanate of Qalāwūn foretold by Shaykh ʿAlī al-Bakkā, and foreseen by Baybars, but he was promised in a dream that he would be the victor at ʿAyn Jālūt.

Very different is the presentation of the usurpation by Kitbughā al-Manṣūrī, who served as vice regent (*nā'ib al-salṭana*) to the infant al-Nāṣir Muḥammad at his first accession, then desposed him, and became sultan in Muḥarram 694/December 1294. Baybars al-Manṣūrī represents Kitbughā as being incited by conspirators seeking to obtain assignments (*iqṭāʿāt*) and promotion, and he comments: 'He thought that kingly rule was by way of being seated on the throne, and he did not know that it was by the coincidence of good fortune and the coming of good luck'.[11] He goes on to demonstrate that these tokens of legitimate kingship were lacking to Kitbughā, whose short and

7 Shāfiʿ b. ʿAlī al-ʿAsqalānī, *Ḥusn al-manāqib al-sirriyya al-muntazaʿa min al-sīra al-Ẓāhiriyya*, ed. ʿAbd al-ʿAzīz b. ʿAbdallāh al-Khuwayṭir, (Riyadh, 1396/1976). The *nisba* 'al-ʿAsqalānī' may be found in the notice of Shāfiʿ b. ʿAlī in al-Ṣafadī, *al-Wāfī bi'l-wafayāt*, ed. Wadād al-Qāḍī (Beirut/Stuttgart, 1982), 29 vols., vol. XVI, 77 (no. 97).

8 Peter Thorau, *The Lion of Egypt* (London, 1992), 241–3.

9 Baybars' son and immediate successor, Baraka Khān, was married to Ghāziya Khātūn, Qalāwūn's daughter; cf. *Tuḥfa*, 83.

10 *Ibid.*, 91. 'The people' (*al-nās*) probably signifies the Mamluks rather than the people generally.

11 *Ibid.*, 144.

luckless reign (694–6/1294–6) saw the dreaded traditional cycle of a low Nile, dearth, pestilence and high mortality; and who was himself ousted by another usurper, Lājīn al-Manṣūrī. Baybars al-Manṣūrī makes no special comment on this coup, nor on the enthronement of Baybars al-Jāshnikīr in 708/1309, when, according to some accounts, al-Nāṣir Muḥammad was not deposed but abdicated voluntarily.

Al-Tuḥfa al-mulūkiyya, then, presents the history of the Mamluk sultanate as proceeding to its glorious culmination in the third reign of al-Nāṣir Muḥammad b. Qalāwūn. His reign was indeed to be both long and successful – epithets which can by no means be applied to that of his son, al-Ṣāliḥ Ismāʿīl, to whom the second work now under consideration was addressed. Its full title is *al-Nūr al-lāʾiḥ waʾl-durr al-ṣādiḥ fī ʾstifāʿ mawlānā al-sulṭān al-Malik al-Ṣāliḥ*.[12] The author was one Shams al-dīn Ibrāhīm b. ʿAbd al-Raḥmān al-Qaysarānī, who died in 753/1352. He came from a Syro-Palestinian family; his great-grandfather, Khālid ibn al-Qaysarānī, was the vizier of Nūr al-dīn b. Zangī (d. 569/1174). He himself was a chancery clerk in Damascus, and subsequently in Cairo. The sultan for whom he prepared this offering, al-Ṣāliḥ Ismāʿīl, was the fourth of al-Nāṣir Muḥammad's sons to succeed to the throne in the two years following his death. The first two sons had been victims of the factional ambitions of the great Mamluk amirs. The third, al-Nāṣir Aḥmad, had withdrawn, after a few weeks' visit to Cairo, to his stronghold of al-Karak, against which eight expeditions were sent in al-Sāliḥ Ismāʿīl's reign. The last of these captured the great fortress, and the former sultan was put to death.

The enthronement of al-Ṣāliḥ Ismāʿīl, who bore a reputation for piety, may have seemed to promise better times, but he died after three years' reign (743–6/1342–5). His name, ʿImād al-dīn Abū ʾl-Fidāʾ Ismāʿīl, is identical with that of the Ayyubid ruler of Ḥamāh who was al-Nāṣir Muḥammad's favourite, and it may perhaps be surmised that he was born in 720/1320, when his namesake was granted the title of sultan.

In his opening pages al-Qaysarānī stresses the divine election of al-Ṣāliḥ Ismāʿīl as sultan, and proceeds to give his titulature at considerable length, including the historical style of 'Servitor of the Two August Sanctuaries' (*khādim al-ḥaramayn al-sharīfayn*), which was to pass in due course to the Ottoman sultans. He pays a remarkable tribute to al-Ṣāliḥ Ismāʿīl's piety by asserting that 'it is he who is sent to this [Islamic] Community (*hādhihi ʾl-umma*) at the end of these hundred years to renew its Faith'.[13] This salutation of a Mamluk sultan as a *mujaddid* is surely unique.

The body of the work follows the same lines as *al-Tuḥfa* but is a briefer and altogether feebler piece of historical writing. It opens with the statement that

[12] Ibrāhīm b. ʿAbd al-Raḥmān b. al-Qaysarānī, *al-Nūr al-lāʾiḥ waʾl-durr al-ṣādiḥ fi ʾstifāʾ mawlānā al-sulṭān al-Malik al-Ṣāliḥ*, ed. ʿUmar ʿAbd al-Salām Tadmurī (Tripoli, 1402/1982) (hereafter *Nūr*).

[13] *Ibid.*, 50. The hundred years referred to are the first century of the Mamluk sultanate not, as usually with this belief, a *hijrī* century.

from the start of the Mamluk sultanate to the death of al-Nāṣir Muḥammad is one hundred years; i. e. the period which was to be crowned by the coming of al-Ṣāliḥ Ismāʿīl as *mujaddid*. The period begins with al-Ṣāliḥ Ayyūb and closes with al-Ṣāliḥ Ismāʿīl; a neat literary turn, although a slight blurring of the chronology. Al-Qaysarānī does not, however, begin his narrative with al-Ṣāliḥ Ayyūb, but goes back to al-ʿĀdil Nūr al-dīn b. Zangī. This allows him to mention his two distinguished ancestors, Khālid b. al-Walīd, the Companion of the Prophet, and Khālid Ibn al-Qaysarānī, Nūr al-dīn's vizier. After dealing with the exploits of Saladin, and the accumulation of the Ayyubid territories by his brother, Sayf al-dīn, the author passes on to the formation of al-Ṣāliḥ Ayyūb's Mamluk household. At this point al-Qaysarānī says that he will give a brief list of the sultans with their dates, which he proceeds to do from Tūrān Shāh, al-Ṣāliḥ Ayyūb's son, to Salāmish, the son of al-Ẓāhir Baybars. This bald record enables al-Qaysarānī to leave unmentioned the violent circumstances in which some of these sultans gained or lost the throne. There is no mention of Baybars' exploits against the Mongols or Franks, although it is noted that he died of dysentery after eating coarse food and drinking much koumiss. Al-Qaysarānī finds space, however, to mention that his own grandfather was Baraka Khān's vizier in Syria.

The accession of Qalāwūn is introduced with no mention of his usurpation of the sultanate from Salāmish. To the roll of the sultan's titles al-Qaysarānī appends the information that his grandfather was continued in office as vizier, and subsequently transferred to a post in the royal chancery, which he held until his death. He goes on to stress that Qalāwūn was the founder of the hereditary sultanate, which at the time of writing had lasted for sixty-four years and ten months. The brief account of Qalāwūn's reign is chiefly concerned with his death when about to undertake a campaign against Acre. It is followed by an equally brief notice of al-Ashraf Khalīl, his evil vizier Ibn al-Salʿūs, and his fate. This impressionistic treatment continues in the presentation of al-Nāṣir Muḥammad, who is shown as reigning continuously for forty-nine years. The usurpations of Kitbughā, Lājīn and Baybars al-Jāshnikīr are disparagingly dismissed, and the bulk of al-Qaysarānī's notice of the reign is a series of encomia in rhymed prose, in which al-Nāṣir Muḥammad is improbably celebrated as a fighter in the Holy War: 'How many strongholds and cities did he conquer for Islam, plucking out castles and fortresses from the hands of the infidel? How many of his armies did he send to raid the idolaters in the midst of their country?'[14] The sultan's military exploits were in fact limited to two defensive campaigns against the Mongols who had invaded Syria, and these were moreover in his second reign, when he was still a youth under the tutelage of Salār and Baybars al-Jāshnikīr.

From the death of al-Nāṣir Muḥammad, which, we are told, caused universal grief, and which the author commemorates in an elegy, the work passes

[14] *Ibid.*, 63.

directly to the accession of al-Ṣāliḥ Ismāʿīl, omitting any reference to the three brothers who preceded him on the throne. He is hailed as ruler by hereditary right, 'the sultan, son of the sultan, son of the sultan; the imam, son of the imam, son of the imam',[15] who will bring in better times; 'he reassures the alarmed hearts of Islam, and gives stability to the distracted minds of men'.[16] In fact, al-Sāliḥ Ismāʿīl, whom Ibn Taghrībirdī describes as the best of al-Nāṣir Muḥammad's sons,[17] made little impression on the course of events in his short reign.

The period of the later Qalawunids from the death of al-Nāṣir Muḥammad in 741/1341 to the usurpation of the throne by al-Ẓāhir Barqūq, finally in 792/1390, was dominated by the Mamluk magnates, who controlled the financial resources of the state behind the façade of the sultanate. Barqūq's usurpation ended this charade. His own attempt to establish a hereditary sultanate failed when his son, al-Nāṣir Faraj, was overthrown in 815/1412. Thereafter the throne passed to a succession of war-lords, who had made themselves the first among the great amirs, their equals. A nominal sovereignty was frequently held by their sons until the emergence of the next successful usurper, but this was a device for administrative continuity and not a serious recognition of any hereditary principle. Two of the usurping sultans in the early ninth/fifteenth century were al-Mu'ayyad Shaykh (815–24/1412–21), the successor to al-Nāṣir Faraj after the brief and ineffectual rule of the caliph al-Mustaʿīn, and al-Ẓāhir Ṭaṭar (824/1421), who deposed al-Mu'ayyad Shaykh's infant son. To each of these in turn a literary offering was presented by Badr al-dīn Maḥmūd al-ʿAynī (762–855/1361–1451), a native of ʿAyntāb, who held the post of *muḥtasib* under Barqūq and his successors. His enjoyment of their somewhat capricious favour was assisted by his knowledge of Turkish.

Al-Sayf al-muhannad fī sīrat al-Malik al-Mu'ayyad,[18] al-ʿAynī's offering to Shaykh, can hardly be described as a *sīra*, a biography, in the usual sense. It is rather a work of encyclopaedic range, which in two separate blocks of narrative (chap. VI, sec.5; chaps. IX, X) narrows its focus to the events of his career and reign from 802/1400 to Jumādā II 819/August 1416, where it reaches its abrupt conclusion.

The first chapter ostensibly discusses al-Mu'ayyad Shaykh's origin and nationality (*fī aṣlihi wa-jinsihi*). It begins, in fact, with a survey of traditional Islamic cosmology. God has created 18,000 worlds, of which the earth is one. There are four orders of created beings: the angels, mankind, the *jinn* and the devils (*al-shayāṭīn*). Noah divided the earth among his three sons, from whom all nations are descended. The descendants of Japhet (*Yāfith*) include the

[15] The salutation of al-Ṣāliḥ Ismāʿīl (and also by implication his father and grandfather, al-Nāṣir Muḥammad and Qalāwūn) as imam is in line with a tendency in the Mamluk sultanate to transfer the caliph's prerogatives to the sultan. For an early instance, cf. W. Madelung, 'A treatise on the imamate dedicated to Sultan Baybars I', *The Arabist: Budapest Studies in Arabic*, 13–14 (n.d.), 91–102. [16] *Nūr*, 65.

[17] Ibn Taghrībirdī, *al-Nujūm al-zāhira* (Cairo, 1963–72), 16 vols., vol. X, 96. [18] *See n.* 1 above.

Franks, the Slavs, the Turks and the Mongols. Al-ʿAynī then expatiates on the Turkish tribes, and gives *inter alia* an account of Seljuq origins, from which he passes at a bound to Chingiz Khān, the Īlkhāns, and the Golden Horde. Turning to the Circassians, who are presented as 'from the people of the Turks' (*min ṭā'ifat al-Turk*), al-ʿAynī deals in detail with al-Mu'ayyad Shaykh's tribal origins. He was, we are told, a son of the fourth hereditary chief of the tribe of Karamūk, which claimed to be of partially Arab descent. According to tribal legend, when Jabala b. al-Ayham, the last Ghassanid ruler, renounced Islam, he and 500 of his men fled with Heraclius, and became Christians. When Byzantine power declined, they withdrew to the mountains of Circassia, and intermarried with its people. Al-ʿAynī notes the qualities, good and bad, which the Circassians share with the Arabs, amongst them being an inveterate tendency to the perpetuation of hostility and the vendetta. The chapter ends on a personal note. Al-Mu'ayyad Shaykh's mother was reputed to be Turkish, but the sultan assured al-ʿAynī that she was a Circassian. This, he says, was 'when I met with him on Monday, 10 Rabīʿ II 818 [19 June 1415] for the purpose of reading his history and biography'.[19] Apart from providing a date for at least the first draft of the work, the incident is reminiscent of the sessions, over a century previously, when Ibn ʿAbd al-Ẓāhir read his biography of al-Ẓāhir Baybars to the sultan.

The following chapters might be designated an exposition of the sultan's *manāqib*. They are in fact an elaborate and strained assertion of al-Mu'ayyad Shaykh's particular fitness for the throne he had usurped. Every possible significance is squeezed out of the sultan's personal name (Shaykh), his *kunya* (Abū 'l-Naṣr), and his *laqab* (al-Mu'ayyad), and all of these are made the occasion for encomia. He is even presented as an eschatological figure by reason of the letter *khā'* at the end of his name. Al-ʿAynī says that 'he is the last of the Turkish [*sic*] sultans according to the interpretation of a certain interpreter of symbols, and the goodness of the earth shall come by him, and after him shall the order of the world be corrupted'.[20]

These observations on al-Mu'ayyad Shaykh's nomenclature occupy the second, third and fourth chapters of al-ʿAynī's work. With the fifth he passes on to another subject, which enables him to display at length his historical knowledge. The dominant theme is the number nine. Al-Mu'ayyad Shaykh is, he says, 'the ninth of the Turkish sultans who were brought to Egypt',[21] i.e. the true *mamlūks*, not the sons of sultans, who were *awlād al-nās*. Al-ʿAynī's researches have shown him that there were nine great states before Islam, and nine great Islamic states. Each of these had nine great rulers, of whom the ninth was the best in every way. This leads him on to a lengthy excursus of almost 100 pages in the printed edition, in which he deals in turn with the nine pre-Islamic and Islamic dynasties, and the nine rulers of each, beginning with the kings of Persia, and ending with the Ayyubid sultan, al-Ṣāliḥ Ayyūb. He

[19] *Sayf*, 30. [20] *Ibid.*, 39. [21] *Ibid.*, 105.

concludes the chapter with a prayer that al-Mu'ayyad Shaykh's days may be as happy as the days of al-Ṣāliḥ Ayyūb. Can either the sultan or his encomiast have been unaware of the irony?

The sixth chapter of *al-Sayf al-muhannad* consists of ten sections demonstrating the various ways in which al-Mu'ayyad Shaykh is worthy of the sultanate. His age of about forty-four is the age of maturity, and al-ʿAynī notes that the Prophet was first inspired at the age of forty. Youthful sultans have done harm: 'Do you not see that a number of the sons of sultans have held the sultanate, and many evils have resulted from them?'[22] The defective sultans are then listed in order from ʿAlī b. Aybak to Ḥājjī b. Shaʿbān, the last of the Qalāwūnids, the implication being that Barqūq's usurpation of the sultanate was justified. Section 6 gives a detailed account of al-Mu'ayyad Shaykh's career from his first appointment as governor of Tripoli in 802/1400 to the overthrow of al-Nāṣir Faraj and the partition of the Mamluk dominions between Shaykh and his rival Nawrūz in 815/1412. The tenth section seeks to demonstrate his unique fitness for the throne, and disparages Nawrūz, who in fact was perfidiously taken and put to death on 21 Rabīʿ II 817/10 July 1414. The section ends with two prophetic dreams concerning al-Mu'ayyad Shaykh. These are specimens of a literary form favoured by the encomiasts of Mamluk sultans.

The two following chapters, the seventh and the eighth, are essentially essays in the genre of mirrors for princes. The first deals with what the sultan should and should not do; the second with appointments made by the sultan.

The ninth chapter returns to historical narrative, and is concerned with the accession of al-Mu'ayyad Shaykh to the sultanate. It picks up the story from the point reached in chapter 6, section 6, i. e. the entry of Shaykh into Cairo on 2 Rabīʿ II 815/12 July 1412. On 8 Rabīʿ II/18 July the caliph al-Mustaʿīn, the nominal sultan, conferred full powers on Shaykh, who was himself installed as sultan on 1 Shaʿbān/6 November. The installation ceremonies are described, and the account of the new ruler's royal ride from the stables into the Citadel ends with astrological predictions of a long and successful reign.

Bearing in mind al-ʿAynī's preoccupation with the number nine, shown (as mentioned above) in the long fifth chapter, this was probably the end of the original offering, bringing it to a satisfactory literary and historical conclusion. There is, however, a tenth chapter, which gives in a straightforward narrative the annals of the reign to 8 Jumādā II 819/3 August 1416. The abrupt end is followed by a note, written presumably by some person after al-ʿAynī's death, saying: 'The shaykh, the imam, the most erudite scholar, Badr al-dīn al-ʿAynī (may God have mercy on him) completed to this point the compilation with which he concerned himself. God grant blessing and peace to our Lord Muḥammad, his family and his Companions'.[23]

The sudden ending of *al-Sayf al-muhannad* was perhaps due to al-ʿAynī's loss of the sultan's favour. When, however, Shaykh's infant son was deposed

[22] *Ibid.*, 209. [23] *Ibid.*, 346.

by the powerful regent, Ṭaṭar al-Ẓāhirī, during an expedition to Syria in Shaʿbān 824/August 1421, al-ʿAynī was ready with an offering to the new sultan. Its title, *al-Rawḍ al-zāhir fī sīrat al-Malik al-Ẓāhir,*[24] was borrowed from Ibn ʿAbd al-Ẓāhir's great biography, to which this work bore otherwise little resemblance. Al-ʿAynī wrote his offering when the news of Ṭaṭar's usurpation reached Cairo on 9 Ramaḍān/7 September, i. e. before the arrival of the new sultan himself. It was, as he says, a preliminary sketch, to be expanded later if time and circumstances permitted. He had a model ready to hand in his own *al-Sayf al-muhannad*, the plan of which he follows closely, sometimes even plagiarizing himself, with of course such adaptation as was necessary to suit the new ruler. Al-ʿAynī had enjoyed closer relations with Ṭaṭar than with Shaykh, and in a significant passage at the start of *al-Rawḍ al-zāhir* he seeks the sultan's patronage on the grounds of their old acquaintance.

Al-Sayf al-muhannad, as indicated above, probably consisted originally of nine chapters, as befitted a work in honour of the ninth Mamluk sultan according to al-ʿAynī's reckoning. By the same reckoning al-Ẓāhir Ṭaṭar was the tenth sultan, and *al-Rawḍ al-zāhir* is accordingly divided into ten chapters. The first five of these deal with the same topics as the corresponding chapters of *al-Sayf al-muhannad.* The sixth chapter of the earlier work covers the same ground as the sixth and seventh chapters of *al-Rawḍ al-zāhir*, thus allowing a correspondence between the last three chapters of each book. *Al-Rawḍ al-zāhir* is on a much less ample scale than its prototype, so that historical and anecdotal excursuses like those that inflate *al-Sayf al-muhannad* here occupy much less space.

The individuality of *al-Rawḍ al-zāhir* appears particularly in three chapters. The first of these deals with Ṭaṭar's tribal origins. Like the corresponding chapter in *al-Sayf al-muhannad*, it outlines the traditional scheme of anthropology, presents the Circassians as akin to the Turks (*min jins al-Turk*), and repeats the legend of their partial descent from the Arabs of Ghassān. Unlike Shaykh, however, Ṭaṭar is not shown to be of illustrious Circassian origin, and his tribe is not mentioned. In the fifth chapter al-ʿAynī endeavours to show the significance of Ṭaṭar's being the tenth of the Mamluk sultans. He does not produce in evidence a roll-call of dynasties as in the corresponding chapter of *al-Sayf al-muhannad.* Instead, he presents the sultan as an eschatological figure. As we have seen, he had already presented Shaykh in this role, but here the theme is more fully developed. Some skilled in numbers, he says, assert that the sultanate in Egypt will close with the last Turkish ruler, who will inaugurate a golden age of justice and security. This prediction will be realized in the days of Ṭaṭar. One interpretation of the prophecy is that the eleventh sultan will not come from the Turks; another is that after the tenth sultan there will be a time of troubles, and the sultanate will effectively cease. Finally the tenth chapter of *al-Rawḍ al-zāhir*, corresponding to the ninth of *al-Sayf al-muhan-*

[24] Al-ʿAynī, *al-Rawḍ al-zāhir fī sīrat al-Malik al-Ẓāhir*, ed. Hans Ernst (Cairo, 1962).

nad, deals with Ṭaṭar's accession to the sultanate, and justifies his usurpation. His election in Damascus, and the rejoicing when the news arrived in Cairo, are described. A somewhat strained historical parallel between the caliphate of Muʿāwiya and the accession of Ṭaṭar in Damascus is seen as a favourable omen. The work ends with a statement that the consensus of those skilled in numbers is that his reign will be long and happy. Three months later Ṭaṭar was dead (4 Dhū 'l-Ḥijja 824/30 November 1421).[25]

There is some uncertainty about the authorship of the next work to be considered, *al-Badr al-zāhir fī nuṣrat al-Malik al-Nāṣir*.[26] An insertion on the title-page of the unique manuscript attributes it to 'Ibn al-Shiḥna'. This is the *nasab* of an old-established judicial family of Aleppine origin. The most probable author was Sarī al-dīn ʿAbd al-Barr b. Muḥammad Ibn al-Shiḥna (851–921/1477–8–1515–16).[27] He was the Ḥanafī judge in Aleppo and subsequently in Cairo. *Al-Badr al-zāhir* is unusual in two respects. In the first place it commemorates the achievements of a son of a sultan, al-Nāṣir Muḥammad b. Qāytbāy, who succeeded for a time in maintaining himself in power, and who in this respect was unique among the stop-gap sultans in the Circassian succession. In the second place the main body of the work marks a reversion to the tripartite form used by Ibn Shaddād in *al-Nawādir al-sulṭāniyya*, and by Ibn ʿAbd al-Ẓāhir in *al-Rawḍ al-zāhir*, the biographies respectively of Saladin and al-Ẓāhir Baybars. In all three works there is first an introductory section on the ruler's background and early history, second an interpolated encomium on his virtues, and third an account of his subsequent career. In *al-Badr al-zāhir* this is limited to a narrative of the deposition and restoration of al-Nāṣir Muḥammad b. Qāytbāy, i. e. it is an accession-offering that was never continued into a full biography. There is, however, a fourth chapter which has no counterpart in the biographies of Saladin and Baybars – a catena of sixteen dreams of supernatural aid given to al-Nāṣir Muḥammad, which predict his victory in the accession struggle. This section perhaps marks the final emergence of the dream as a form of literary political propaganda.

Turning now to the content of *al-Badr al-zāhir*, the first chapter describes

[25] These two offerings by al-ʿAynī, together with *Sukkardān al-sulṭān* of Ibn Abī Ḥajala, have recently been discussed by Otfried Weintritt, *Formen spätmittelalterlicher islamischer Geschichtsdarstellung* (Beirut, 1992), 183–200. Weintritt stresses that these works, like *Kitāb al-Ilmam* of al-Nuwayrī al-Iskandarānī (the main topic of the monograph), are essentially literary works, and should be judged as such, rather than by their sparse historical data. Following an indication by the present writer, Weintritt also emphasizes (at 185–6) the current political character of the works: 'ihre Hauptintention ist auf eine affirmative Rechtfertigung der Herrschaft der Sultane angelegt, um den Nachweis des berechtigten Anspruchs auf das Sultanat zu erbringen'.

[26] *Al-Badr al-zāhir fī nuṣrat al-Malik al-Nāṣir*. The text has been published twice in recent years:

1 Ed. ʿUmar ʿAbd al-Salām Tadmurī (Beirut, 1403/1983).
2 Ed. Richard T. Mortel, in *Majallat Kulliyyat al-ādāb (Jāmiʿat al-Malik Saʿūd*, 1407/1987), vol. XIV, 661–775.

[27] So Mortel, (ed.), *Majallat*, 664, 775. Tadmurī, however, attributes the probable authorship to ʿAfīf al-dīn Ḥusayn b. Muḥammad b. Muḥammad (d. 910/1504–5 or 916/1510–11).

the political situation at court in the last months of Qāytbāy's reign. The sultan was in his eighties, his health was poor, and he did not want his son to succeed him as a puppet of the great amirs. Among these were two rivals, each with his faction of supporters: Qānṣūh Khamsmi'a, who was already planning to seize the throne, and Aqbardī. The former obtained the upper hand, and Aqbardī's faction absconded. Qānṣūh obtained the formal deposition of Qāytbāy by the caliph, and on 26 Qaʿda 901/6 August 1496 installed al-Nāṣir Muḥammad (aged fourteen) as sultan. Qāytbāy died the next day, and Qānṣūh was effectively regent.

At this point the narrative breaks off, and Ibn al-Shiḥna eulogizes the virtues of the young sultan – his abolition of oppressive dues, his liberality, his soundness of judgement, and his phenomenal courage. When the account of events is resumed in the third chapter, Aqbardī has reappeared, but in distant Gaza, and there sees an opportunity of shaking off the control of the dominant faction. Matters come to a head in Cairo when an armed assembly at Qānṣūh's house recognize him as sultan and demand entry to the Citadel, which is held by al-Nāṣir Muḥammad with a handful of the Royal Mamluks. They mount artillery on the towers, and fire on their opponents in the city. Skirmishing takes place. Qānṣūh himself is wounded, and by the time of the Friday prayer on 30 Jumādā I 902/3 February 1497 the rebels have been defeated. Ibn al-Shiḥna added a chapter of dreams predicting the sultan's victory, and finished writing on 18 Jumādā II/15 February. *Al-Badr al-zāhir* thus provides a detailed eyewitness account of an important event in the political history of the Circassian Mamluk sultanate.

Unlike the works previously surveyed, which are all offerings to Mamluk sultans, *al-Durr al-muṣān fī sīrat al-Muẓaffar Salīm Khān*[28] is a tribute to the Ottoman sultan Selim the Grim, the conqueror of the Mamluk sultanate. The author was a certain ʿAlī b. Muḥammad al-Lakhmī al-Ishbīlī al-Maghribī al-Dimashqī, of whom nothing further is known, but whose *nasab* indicates an Arab family once settled in Seville, but subsequently taking the road of exile to North Africa, and finally to Damascus. No doubt he and other Muslims who had lost their ancestral homes in Andalusia saw in Selim a potential champion of Islam against Christendom.

Al-Durr al-muṣān consists essentially of a laudatory account of Selim's victories, first over Shāh Ismāʿīl at Chāldirān, then over the Mamluks at Marj Dābiq and al-Raydāniyya, which were followed by the *khuṭba* for Selim in Cairo. His enemies are depicted in the blackest colours. The Safavids are 'the apostates, the opponents of the party of the monotheists'. The vile Circassians, as al-Ishbīlī designates the Mamluks, 'have laid waste the land, plundered the people, corrupted the earth, abrogated the divine law of inheritance, and allowed the goods of orphans and legacies to be devoured'.[29]

[28] ʿAlī b. Muḥammad al-Lakhmī al-Ishbīlī [al-Maghribī al-Dimashqī], *al-Durr al-muṣān fī sīrat al-Muẓaffar Salīm Khān*, ed. Hans Ernst (Beirut, 1962) (hereafter *Durr*). [29] *Ibid.*, 7.

As a narrative of the Ottoman campaign against the Mamluks, the work has some value as a primary source, supplementing the accounts by Ibn Iyās and Ibn Ṭūlūn. Like *al-Badr al-zāhir* and other works, it has its complement of dreams and visions. Thus, some days before Marj Dābiq an unnamed person dreamt of two moons, one coming from the south, the other from Syria. They met, and the southern moon vanished, while the other, above the Umayyad mosque in Damascus, swelled into a full moon. Other visionaries saw Selim protected by angels and archangels on his way to Egypt. Another group of portents served as propaganda for the Ottomans during Selim's absence from Syria.

A central point of *al-Durr al-muṣān* is al-Ishbīlī's presentation of Selim. At the start a tacit contrast is drawn between the Mamluk sultanate and the hereditary Ottoman monarchy. After describing, as above, the evil rule of the Circassians, the author shows Selim as divinely commissioned to end their regime: 'For God, blessed and exalted be He, has willed that these august places should be purified, and that this oppression should cease from the divine lands. He has sent them one of His saints, a blessing from His worshippers and elect. He has moved him [Selim] to march on them, and after hesitation to proceed to them'.[30] Selim is not, however, merely a divinely chosen *mujāhid*. Throughout the work there are indications that he has a sacral quality, that he is indeed the rightful caliph. An encomium in the opening pages describes him as 'absolutely the king of the age, who deservedly mounts the throne of the caliphate'.[31] The allusion to the caliphate is picked up elsewhere. Selim is entitled 'the reviver of the traces of the Orthodox Caliphs'.[32] Of Ṭūmān Bāy it is said that 'his power did not rival the power of the caliphate'.[33] Finally, in one passage Selim is actually designated by the caliphal title of *amīr al-mu'minīn*.[34] It seems that here we have tentative propaganda for an Ottoman caliphate. It came to nothing at the time, but there may be an echo of it in the later legend that the last Abbasid ceded the caliphate to Selim.

I conclude this survey of literary offerings with a brief examination of a later work dedicated to a neo-Mamluk bey, who, it would seem, had aspirations to the sultanate of Ottoman Egypt in the eleventh/seventeenth century. Entitled *Qahr al-wujūh al-ʿābisa bi-dhikr nasab al-Jarākisa*[35] this is ostensibly a genealogical work, as its title indicates. It was offered to (or more precisely, commissioned by) Riḍwān Bey, who was *amīr al-ḥājj* almost uninterruptedly from 1040/1631 until his death in 1066/1656. The author does not give his name; indeed he is probably only the author to a very limited extent, since he claims that the bulk of his material is summarized from a treatise by an unidentified Shihāb al-dīn Aḥmad al-Ṣafadī, the imam of a mosque in Ak Şehir, who died in 980/1572/3.

[30] *Ibid.*, 7. [31] *Ibid.*, 2. [32] *Ibid.*, 3. [33] *Ibid.*, 13. [34] *Ibid.*, 6.

[35] For an early study of *Qahr al-wujūh* by the present writer, see his article, 'The exalted lineage of Riḍwān Bey: some observations on a seventeenth-century Mamluk genealogy', *BSOAS*, 22/2 (1959), 221–30. This was based on the MSS in the John Rylands Library, Manchester, and the British Library. For the present notice use has been made of the text printed in Cairo at the press of Muḥammad Efendi Muṣṭafā for Muḥammad Efendi Ḥāfiẓ al-Jarkasī al-Bājī in 1316/1898–9.

The first six chapers of the book deal with the legendary history of Mecca to the time of the Prophet. The seventh chapter mentions the account of the flight of Jabala b. al-Ayham with Heraclius to *bilād al-Rūm*, but does not go on to make the Ghassanids the legendary ancestors of the Circassians. Instead, a parallel legend is provided in which Kisā' b. 'Ikrima, the chief of Banū 'Āmir, a sub-tribe of Quraysh, flees with his people to *bilād al-Rūm* during the caliphate of 'Umar I, and ultimately settles in territory taken from the Armenians. This was the origin of the Circassians, *Jarākisa* or *Sarākisa*, so called because Kisā' fled by night (*sarā Kisā'*).

With the conclusion we come to the point of al-Ṣafadī's treatise. In it he deals with the return of the Banū 'Āmir to Islamic territory, and specifically with the inauguration of the Circassian Mamluk sultanate by Barqūq. The succession of sultans down to the Ottoman conquest of Egypt is rapidly reviewed. Thereupon, he says, some of the Circassians returned to their homeland, among them the amir Rustum, who is shown as a descendant of Barsbāy in the sixth generation. The genealogy is flawed. Rustum's grandfather is named as Yashbak b. Mahdī. This Yashbak was a historical personage, who played an important part during the sultanate of Qāytbāy until he was killed in 885/1480. He was not, however, <u>ibn</u> Mahdī, as the genealogist claims, but <u>min</u> Mahdī, i.e. a <u>mamlūk</u>, not a son of Mahdī. Al-Ṣafadī tells us that Rustum married a cousin, and was a king in his own country, and concludes with the names of Rustum's three sons. The anonymous author of *Qahr al-wujūh* links Riḍwān Bey with this questionable genealogy by asserting that he was the son of Jānibak 'Azīz, one of Rustum's sons. For this assertion there is no independent support. Indeed, far from his being of royal Circassian descent, there is some doubt that Riḍwān was a Circassian at all, since one of his biographers, the Syrian al-Muḥibbī (d. 1111/1699) specifically states that he was a Georgian – a nationality which played no part under the Mamluk sultanate.

So perhaps the whole edifice of Riḍwān's Circassian ancestry is a fable. Whether or not this is the case, it is constructed with two palpable political aims. The first is to demonstrate that Riḍwān's connection with Mecca extends far beyond his mere annual appointment by the Ottoman sultan as *amīr al-ḥājj*. As a descendant of Banū 'Āmir, a clan of Quraysh, he has an ancestral link with the Holy City from its earliest days. The second aim is to show him as the heir of the Circassian Mamluk sultans. Barsbāy was his ancestor, and Barsbāy was not only the *mamlūk* of Barqūq but (according to al-Ṣafadī) his cousin also. Thus a line of hereditary descent linked Riḍwān with the founder of the Circassian succession of sultans in Egypt, while Barqūq himself was a descendant in the fourteenth generation of Kisā', the founder of the Circassian nation. A dubious genealogy thus provided Riḍwān with the title-deeds to the sultanate of Egypt as well as a more illustrious ancestry than that of the Ottoman ruler, should circumstances favour his ambition. In the event he died as he had lived, a grandee of Egypt and the head of a powerful Mamluk household.

Although the seven works here considered vary considerably in the nature of their contents, and to some extent in their literary quality, they have some points in common. The five works addressed to Mamluk sultans were all produced at, or shortly after, the time at which the ruler assumed power. This is clear in the cases of *al-Nūr al-lā'iḥ, al-Sayf al-muhannad* (disregarding the tenth chapter, as suggested above), and *al-Rawḍ al-zāhir*, commemorating the accession of al-Ṣāliḥ Ismāʿīl, al-Mu'ayyad Shaykh and al-Ẓāhir Ṭaṭar respectively. *Al-Tuḥfa al-mulūkiyya* ends shortly after the second restoration of al-Nāṣir Muḥammad b. Qalāwūn, when at last he became the effective ruler. *Al-Badr al-zāhir* similarly marks the triumph of al-Nāṣir Muḥammad b. Qāytbāy over his opponents. Selim the Grim, the hero of *al-Durr al-muṣān*, had been the Ottoman sultan for several years before the book was written, but the occasion for al-Ishbīlī's writing was Selim's succession by conquest to the Mamluk sultanate in Egypt and Syria. They may also be seen as accession offerings, and it is tempting to surmise that *Qahr al-wujūh* was produced at an analogous stage in Riḍwān Bey's career; i. e. when he was first appointed *amīr al-ḥājj*.

Qahr al-wujūh was expressly commissioned by Riḍwān Bey, and the role of patronage, even of participation in the composition of some of these works, is indicated. *Al-Tuḥfa al-mulūkiyya* was, as we have seen, intended for the royal library, and that the sultan himself contributed information is suggested by Baybars al-Manṣūrī's description of it as 'a composition which was compiled with what he [the sultan] poured forth from the excess of his favour so that he might honour it by reading it'.[36] Al-ʿAynī read *al-Sayf al-muhannad* to al-Mu'ayyad Shaykh, who corrected him on at least one detail. Patronage of this kind was, of course, nothing new. One of the major works of courtly literature in the seventh/thirteenth century was Ibn ʿAbd al-Ẓāhir's biography of Baybars, the composition of which was, perhaps somewhat maliciously, described by the biographer's nephew, Shāfiʿ b. ʿAlī al-ʿAsqalānī:

> His eloquent secretary, Muḥyī al-dīn Abū 'l-Faḍl ʿAbdallāh b. Shaykh al-Islām Rashīd al-dīn ʿAbd al-Ẓāhir, disclosed his [i. e. Baybars'] days in an organized biography, in which he set down the chapters of his good works, chapter by chapter, and chronicled his acts which are written in the pages of his merits. He expatiated pleasantly, and delivered himself most delightfully. He completed the whole of his days, day by day, and indicated their unique quality. But circumstances required him to record both what was trivial and what was substantial, and to repeat the hyperbole with which he spoke to the ear of his sultan. Nevertheless he was truthful in this, he did not lie.
>
> When he had completed a section of it, the late sultan would take his seat, and bid him be seated so that he might hear him. He gave him good recompense with costly robes. How did he continue to requite him for his delightful and marvellous work![37]

[36] *Tuḥfa*, 24. [37] *Ḥusn al-manāqib* 26, 166.

CHAPTER 2

Rank-and-file Mamluks versus amirs: new norms in the Mamluk military institution

AMALIA LEVANONI

Mamluk sources of the fifteenth century contain frequent scenes of rank-and-file Mamluks – especially the *ajlāb* or *julbān*, the sultan's own Mamluk household – bluntly abusing their master, his amirs and his officials, and without hindrance committing crimes against the Cairene civilians. David Ayalon links the *julbān's* unbridled behaviour to a change in Mamluk factional solidarity, the *khushdāshiyya*, ensuing from the professional decline of the Mamluk army and the political and economic deterioration of the Mamluk sultanate. While in the Baḥrī period (648–784/1250–1382) *khushdāshiyya* 'tend[ed] to foster moderate competition among the various [Mamluk] units, stimulated the troops and prevented stagnation', in the Circassian period (784–922/1382–1517) it became one of the factors in the 'army's ruin' by opening the way for the Mamluk factions to act according to their selfish impulses and, towards the middle of the fifteenth century, led to the domination of the *julbān* over all the units of the army.[1]

In this chapter I intend to approach the rank-and-file Mamluks' breaches of discipline from a somewhat different angle, namely, to examine them in their sociological context. The domination by simple Mamluks in the army as we find it in the fifteenth century then appears as the final phase of what was actually a long process of change in the Mamluk elite's social stratification, going back as far as the third reign of al-Nāṣir Muḥammad ibn Qalāwūn (709–41/1310–41). Motivated by personal interests, al-Nāṣir Muḥammad initiated changes in those devices of the Mamluk system that till then had guaranteed the sultan's discrete status and the amirs' exalted position. In so doing, he was soon to blur the distance which earlier sultans had been careful to preserve between the amir class and these rank-and-file Mamluks. After al-Nāṣir Muḥammad's death, this process obviously continued, kindled even by his amirs who, in order to secure the Mamluks' support, proved increasingly ready to give in to the latter's ever-growing demands. The more they acquiesced in the simple Mamluks' demands, the more the amir class turned vul-

[1] D. Ayalon, 'Studies on the structure of the Mamluk army', *Bulletin of the School of Oriental and African Studies*, 15/2 and 3; 16/1 (1953, 1954), 210–13.

nerable and became dependent on them. Once rank-and-file Mamluks came to hold the key to factional consolidation, it was out of the amirs' control and gradually came to assert its grip on the political decision-making process. A shift in the army's foci of power and, with it, an upheaval in Mamluk social structure was inevitable – the once powerful status of the amir class eroded away, to be supplanted largely by that of the rank-and-file Mamluks.

The early Mamluk sultans, especially al-Ẓāhir Baybars (658–76/1260–77) and al-Manṣūr Qalāwūn (678–89/1279–90), whom the Mamluk sources considered the founding fathers of the Mamluk state, were described as powerful and authoritative sultans. Both maintained strict control over their Mamluk households through a rigid hierarchy in the training and advancement systems intended to channel a Mamluk's personal aspirations to be fulfilled within the Mamluk factional framework and thus affirming his *khushdāshiyya* bonds. The Mamluk's training period was long and extremely rigorous. It included various stages, from the moment of his purchase to his emancipation and recruitment into the army. A modest life style and stringent discipline were an indispensable part of the Mamluks' military training, foremost so as to foster a sense of respect for authority.[2] Baybars demanded strict discipline from his Mamluks while setting a personal example through his own behaviour.[3] Qalāwūn was described as 'a great influence on his Mamluks, one who put terror in their hearts, and who never allowed them to do repulsive deeds (*kāna dhū* [!] *saṭwa ʿalā mamālīkihi la yuḥsinu lahum fiʿl qabīḥ qaṭṭu*)'.[4]

After his emancipation, a Mamluk's advancement remained slow and gradual, clearly founded on Mamluk seniority and his military talents. Thus, for example, Amirs Balabān al-Rūmī al-Dawādār, Baybars al-Manṣūrī, Aydamur al-Shujāʿī, Aybak al-Mawṣilī, Arjuwāsh al-Jamdār, Bahādur al-Manṣūrī, Baybars al-Shujāʿī, Baktamur al-Ḥusāmī, Ḥusām al-dīn Ṭuruntāy

2 Aḥmad ibn ʿAlī al-Maqrīzī, *Kitāb al-Mawāʿiẓ wa-l-iʿtibār fī dhikr al-khiṭaṭ wa-l-āthār*, (Cairo, 1987), vols. I–II (hereafter *Khiṭaṭ)*, vol. II, 214; Shihāb al-dīn Aḥmad ibn ʿAbd al-Wahhāb al-Nuwayrī, *Nihāyat al-ʿarab fī funūn al-adab*, Leiden Library, MS. or no. 19B, 2N, 2M, 2O (hereafter al-Nuwayrī), 2N, fols. 44a–b; 2O, fol. 39b; Nāṣir al-dīn Muḥammad ibn ʿAbd al-Raḥīm ibn al-Furāt, *Tārīkh al-duwal wa-l-mulūk*, ed. Qusṭanṭīn Zurayq (Beirut, 1942) vols. VII–IX, (hereafter Ibn al-Furāt), vol. VIII, 105; D. Ayalon, 'l'Esclavage du Mamelouk', *Oriental Notes and Studies*, 1 (Jerusalem, 1951), 14–15, 47–8; A. Levanoni, *A Turning Point in Mamluk History, the Third Reign of al-Nāṣir Muḥammad ibn Qalāwūn, 1310–1341* (Leiden, 1995) (hereafter Levanoni), 14–27.

3 Ibn al-Furāt, vol. VII, 82; Aḥmad ibn ʿAlī al-Maqrīzī, *Kitāb al-Sulūk li-maʿrifat duwal al-mulūk*, ed. Muḥammad Muṣṭafā Ziyāda (Cairo, 1930–1972) vols. I–IV (hereafter *Sulūk*), vol. I, 528–9, 559, 568, 637; Muḥyī al-dīn ibn ʿAbd al-Ẓāhir, *al-Rawḍ al-zāhir fī sīrat al-Malik al-Ẓāhir*, ed. ʿAbd al-Azīz al-Khuwayṭir (Riyadh, 1976) (hereafter *Sīrat al-Ẓāhir)*, 238, 389, 401–2, 451.

4 Abū Bakr ibn ʿAbdallāh ibn Aybak ibn al-Dawādārī, *Kanz al-durar wa-jāmiʿ al-ghurar*, eds. Hans Robert Roemer, ʿAbd al-Fattāḥ ʿĀshūr, and Ulrich Haarmann (Cairo, 1960–1972), vols. VI–IX, (hereafter Ibn al-Dawādārī), vol. VI, 303; Nāṣir al-dīn Shāfiʿ ibn ʿAlī, *al-Faḍl al-maʾthūr min sīrat al-Sulṭān al-Malik al-Manṣūr*, Bodleian Library (Oxford) MS Marsh no. 424 (hereafter Shāfiʿ ibn ʿAlī), fols. 126–127a; Muḥyī ʾal-dīn ibn ʿAbd al-Ẓāhir, *Tashrīf al-ayyām wa-l-ʿuṣūr fī sīrat al-Malik al-Manṣūr*, ed. Murād Kāmil (Cairo, 1961) (hereafter, *Tashrīf al-ayyām), 24–6.*

and many others underwent long periods of service as Mamluks before they were awarded amirate rank.[5] Then they climbed, again step by step, the Mamluk rank echelon. The stratified granting of *iqṭāʿāt* in the Mamluk army was yet another expression of the military hierarchy because it reflected the economic power behind the ranks.[6]

Together with a consistent and strict adherence to these hierarchic training and advancement methods, a set of status symbols consolidated the Mamluk social and political framework. The standing of the amirs during the reign of Qalāwūn was distinguished by their dress, the different ranks each marked by a particular dress.[7] For example, we are told that the sash of a commander of one thousand cost 300 dinars and that of an amir of forty 200. Commanders of one thousand wore golden sashes on ceremonial occasions to emphasize their special status. In much the same way, at the annual ceremony of the allocation of horses, the sultan gave amirs of one hundred horses complete with saddle and harness while amirs of forty were provided with horses only. This was intended to 'make the prominent among them [the Mamluks] stand out from the rank-and-file (*tamyīz khāṣṣatihim ʿalā ʿāmmatihim*)'.[8]

It was quite natural for the amirs to guard jealously the essence and insignia of their status, thus reinforcing the distinction between their class and that of the rank-and-file Mamluks: 'And when the Mamluk attained a senior position and high rank, he knew its value . . . (*fa-idhā waṣala ilā manzila kabīra wa-rutba ʿāliya ʿarafa miqdārahā*)'.[9]

On attaining the sultanate for the third time (709/1310), determined to shore up his own position *vis-à-vis* the amirs who earlier had twice put an end to his rule, al-Nāṣir Muḥammad ibn Qalāwūn set about buying the Mamluks'

5 Al-Nuwayrī, 2O, fol. 51b; 2N, fols. 81b, 89b, 95a; *Sulūk*, vol. I, 671–2, 731; vol. II, 314; Ibn al-Furāt, vol. VII, 196; vol. VIII, 38, 181, 192; Rukn al-dīn Baybars al-Manṣūrī al-Dawādār, *Kitāb al-tuḥfa al-mulūkiyya fī al-dawla al-turkiyya*, ed. ʿAbd al-Ḥamīd Ṣāliḥ Ḥamdān (Cairo, 1987) (hereafter *Tuḥfa*), 84; Rukn al-dīn Baybars al-Manṣūrī al-Dawādār, *Zubdat al-fikra fī Tārīkh al-hijra*, British Library, MS Add. 23325 (hereafter *Zubda*), fols. 52a, 84a–b, 129a,b, 166b, 195b, 219b, 246b; K. V. Zettersteen (ed.), *Beiträge zur Geschichte der Mamlukensultane* (Leiden, 1919) (hereafter Zettersteen), 156–7; Shihāb al-dīn ibn Faḍl Allāh Aḥmad ibn ʿAlī ibn Ḥajar al-ʿAsqalānī, *al-Durar al-kāmina fī aʿyān al-miʾa al-thāmina* (Cairo, 1966) (hereafter *Durar*), 5 vols., vol. I, 439–40; vol. II, 16,33; vol. III, 325–6, 330–1, 348; Ṣalāḥ al-dīn Khalīl ibn Aybak al-Ṣafadī, *Kitāb al-Wāfī bi-l-wafayāt* (Wiesbaden, 1931–83), vols. I–XIX, XXI, XXII, XXIV (hereafter *Wāfī*), vol. XV, 477–8; Jamāl al-dīn Abū al-Maḥāsin ibn Taghrībirdī, *al-Nujūm al-zāhira fī mulūk Miṣr wa-l-Qāhira* (Cairo, 1963–72), vols. VII–XVI (hereafter *Nujūm*), vol. VII, 350, vol. VIII, 55; Jamāl al-dīn Abū al-Maḥāsin ibn Taghrībirdī, *al-Manhal al-ṣāfī wa-l-mustawfī baʿda ʾal-wāfī*, ed. Muḥammad Muḥammad Amīn (Cairo, 1985–90), vols. I–VI (hereafter *Manhal*). vol. III, 85–8. For further details see Levanoni, 19–25.

6 Shāfiʿ ibn ʿAlī, fol. 19b; *Sīrat al-Ẓāhir*, 159–60. See the cases of Sunqur al-Alfī and Lājīn al-Dawādār al-Darfīl: Ibn al-Furāt, vol. VII, 238; Faḍl Allāh ibn Abī al-Fakhr ibn al-Ṣūqāʿī, *Tālī kitāb wafayāt al-aʿyān*, ed. Jacqueline Sublet (Damascus, 1974) (hereafter Ibn al-Ṣuqāʿī), 52, 133.

7 *Nujūm*, vol. VII, 330–2; *Khiṭaṭ*, vol. II, 98–9, 216–17; Shihāb al-dīn Aḥmad al-Qalqashandī, *Kitāb ṣubḥ al-aʿshā fī ṣināʿat al-inshāʾ* (Cairo, 1913–19), vols. I–XIV (hereafter al-Qalqashandī), vol. IV, 39–41; Shihāb al-dīn Aḥmad ibn Yaḥyā ibn Faḍl Allāh al-ʿUmarī, *Masālik al-abṣār fī mamālik al-amṣār*, ed. Dorothea Kravulsky (Beirut, 1986) (hereafter *Masālik al-abṣār*), 99.

8 *Masālik al-abṣār*, 94–5; *Khiṭaṭ*, vol. II, 216.

9 *Sulūk*, vol. II, 525.

fealty. To this end he introduced far-reaching changes in the Mamluk training, advancement and remuneration systems. Al-Nāṣir Muḥammad's Mamluks were no longer subject to the austere lifestyle of apprenticeship and to the process of slow and gradual advancement, but on arrival were immediately given conditions their predecessors had enjoyed only at the peak of their military careers: 'On the day of their arrival he [al-Nāṣir Muḥammad] bestowed upon these Mamluks fine clothing, golden sashes, horses and grants to impress them (*ḥattā yudhishahum*)'.[10]

Rapid advancement and the discarding of objective military criteria soon made itself felt in al-Nāṣir Muḥammad's army. Many of his amirs attained the highest ranks in the Mamluk army with the full period of their military training left in doubt. Outstanding examples are Qawṣūn, Ṣūṣūn, Bashtāk and Maliktamur al-Ḥijāzī.[11] Many of al-Nāṣir's amirs such as Āqbughā ʿAbd al-Wāḥid, Bahādur al-Damurdāshī and Alṭunbughā al-Māridīnī were promoted to their high positions for reasons entirely divorced from professional military criteria.[12]

In his distribution of *iqṭāʿāt*, wages and grants throughout all sectors of the army, al-Nāṣir went beyond anything his predecessors had ever done. He did away with the gradual pay scale whereby the Mamluk's pay kept track with his slow military advancement – instead he introduced wages to the rank-and-file Mamluks that went 'beyond all limit'.[13] Al-Maqrīzī relates that al-Nāṣir 'did not preserve his father's custom . . . of advancing the Mamluks through all the stages of service . . . and gradually increase his [the Mamluk's] pay from three dinars a month to ten dinars, and later transfer him to a service post, but resolved to fill their [the Mamluks'] needs in one fell swoop with high wages (*wa-lam yurāʿi ʿādat abīhi . . . fī tanaqqul al-mamālīk fī aṭwār al-khidam . . . wa-fī tadrījihi min thalāthat danānīr fī 'l-shahr ilā ʿasharat danānīr thumma naqlihi min al-jāmakiyya ilā waẓīfa min waẓā'if al-khidma bal iqtaḍā ra'yuhu an yamla'a aʿyunahum bi-l-ʿaṭā' al-kathīr dafʿatan wāḥidatan*)'.[14]

By the same measure, the *iqṭāʿāt* and grants al-Nāṣir gave his closest amirs

[10] Ibid., 524.

[11] Al-Nuwayrī, 19B, fol. 119b–120a, 131a–132b; *Wāfī*, vol. X, 143, *Durar*, vol. II, 120; vol. III, 342, vol. V, 127–8; *Khiṭaṭ*, vol. II, 65–7, *Nujūm*, vol. IX, 89; vol. X, 184; *Sulūk*, vol. II, 288, 291, 451, 452–5, 466, 755; Shams al-dīn al-Shujāʿī, *Tārīkh al-Malik al-Nāṣir Muḥammad ibn Qalāwūn al-Ṣāliḥī wa-awlādihi*, ed. Barbara Schäfer (Wiesbaden, 1977), vol. I (hereafter al-Shujāʿī), 160, 219; Maḥmūd Badr al-Din, al-ʿAynī, *ʿIqd al-jumān fī tārīkh ahl al-zamān*, Topkapı Saray (Istanbul), MS Ahmet no. A2912/4 (hereafter *ʿIqd*), fol. 372b. For many other examples see Levanoni, 34–42.

[12] Al-Shujāʿī, 253; *Wāfī*, vol. IX, 204–5; vol. X, 299; *Nujūm*, vol. X, 105, 107; al-Nuwayrī, 19B, fol. 115b; Zetterstéen, 148; *Durar*, vol. II, 418. For other examples see *Nujūm*, vol. IX, 303; vol. XI, 292; *Durar*, vol. II, 324, 325; Zetterstéen, 164–5; al-Nuwayrī, 19B, fol. 117b; *Sulūk*, vol. II, 376; *ʿIqd*, fol. 342a; *Wāfī*, vol. X, 299; Mūsā ibn Muḥammad ibn Yaḥyā al-Yūsufī, *Nuzhat al-nāẓir fī sīrat al-Malik al-Nāṣir*, ed. Aḥmad Ḥuṭayṭ (Beirut, 1986) (hereafter al-Yūsufī), 212.

[13] Muḥammad ibn Shākir ibn Aḥmad al-Kutubī, *ʿUyūn al-tawārīkh*, Cambridge University Library, MS Add. no. 2923 (hereafter *ʿUyūn*), fol. 50b.

[14] *Khiṭaṭ*, vol. II, 214; *Sulūk*, vol. II, 524–5. For an example of salary from Qalāwūn's reign see al-Nuwayrī, 2O, fol. 26b.

were enormous in comparison with any granted before in the Mamluk state. For example, on Amir Bashtāk's death, his *iqṭāʿ* was found to equal seventeen *iqṭāʿāt* of amirs of forty, and was subsequently divided among eighty Royal Mamluks.[15]

Immediately upon his accession, al-Nāṣir made the award of special grants to his Mamluk bodyguard, the *khāṣṣakiyya*, the rule: 'And al-Nāṣir Muḥammad reached new heights with his munificence, generosity, benevolence and open-handedness that exceeded all bounds (*ghāya takhruju ʿan al-ḥadd*) and in a single day granted more than one hundred thousand gold dinars and did not cease to award his *khāṣṣakiyya* [grants] of some ten thousand dinars'.[16]

Al-Nāṣir's introduction of rapid advancement and easy access to material plenty together with permissive training methods soon had its repercussions on the hierarchical order of the Mamluk army. Signs of increasingly lax discipline became manifest even during his own period of rule in frequent breaches of discipline whereby both amirs and rank-and-file Mamluks openly flouted his authority.

As early as 718/1318, the officer in charge of discipline, *muqaddam al-mamālīk al-sulṭāniyya*, had to be reprimanded for dereliction of duty.[17] By 732/1331, because the need to restore discipline in the royal barracks (*al-ṭibāq*) had become urgent, al-Nāṣir Muḥammad saw himself forced to replace ʿAnbar al-Sakhartī, the eunuch in charge of the Royal Mamluks' discipline, with Amir Āqbughā ʿAbd al-Wāḥid, who was known as a stern disciplinarian.[18] Three years later, 735/1334, in the same circumstances, Āqbughā was again appointed to the position.[19]

It did not take long for al-Nāṣir Muḥammad's Mamluks to regard the easy material conditions they had been given as their right and on several occasions, in their efforts to hold onto them, they showed little restraint, putting into question their master's authority and their loyalty to him. In Ṣafar 721/March 1321, while al-Nāṣir Muḥammad was in his harem, 1,500 Mamluks gathered outside the palace gate to protest the delay in payment of their wages. Prior to their demonstration they had met Karīm al-dīn, *mushidd al-jaysh*, humiliated him with their abuse, and also ignored the orders of the *muqaddam al-mamālīk*. When word of this reached him, al-Nāṣir Muḥammad became greatly agitated and sent Amir Baktamur al-Sāqī, his

15 *Sulūk*, vol. II, 357, 563, 591, 592, 614, 615, 672; *Nujūm*, vol. X, 74, 75; al-Shujāʿī, 219; *Durar* vol. II, 11; *Wāfī*, vol. X, 142; ʿ*Uyūn*, fol. 39a, 59a–b; al-Yūsufī, 157, 159. For further examples of large *iqṭāʿāt* granted by al-Nāṣir Muḥammad, See Zetterstéen, 200; *Sulūk*, vol. II, 436, 463, 467, 493, 525; *Durar*, vol. V, 138.

16 *Sulūk*, vol. II, 535, see also *Tuḥfa*, 218; al-Nuwayrī, 2O, fol. 69a; 19B, fol. 119b–120a, 131a–132b; *Nujūm*, vol. IX, 89, 112, 119, 174, 211; vol. X, 105; al-Shujāʿī, 222, 266; *Sulūk*, vol. II, 82, 129, 131, 288, 365, 385, 432, 448, 535, 538, 539; *Wāfī*, vol. IX, 364; vol. X, 142, 144, 194, 299; *Durar*, vol. II, 10–12, 19, 20; vol. III, 342–4; vol. V, 127–8, 212; *Khiṭaṭ*, vol. II, 68.

17 *Sulūk*, vol. II, 183.

18 Al-Yūsufī, 230–1; *Sulūk*, vol. II, 341–2; *Nujūm*, vol. IX, 98–9.

19 *Sulūk*, vol. II, 377.

senior *khāṣṣakiyya*, to meet the protesters. They greeted him with scorn and said they refused to negotiate with anyone other than the sultan in person. Details in the sources on al-Nāṣir's reaction to this event made clear that not a single Mamluk who had taken part in the protest was executed. While 180 Mamluks were exiled to Syria and a further group was later housed outside the Citadel, the rest were placated over and above their stated demands.[20] This Mamluk protest did not remain an isolated incident, as it proved an effective means of exerting pressure on al-Nāṣir Muḥammad.[21]

A further crucial development came when the atmosphere of general laxity began eroding the hierarchical distance between the amir class and the rank-and-file Mamluks. Both amirs and Mamluks could now be found violating the rules of the Mamluk tradition that forbade congregation for any purpose.[22] Amir Maliktamur al-Ḥijāzī used to organize extravagant cruises on the Nile with a group of Sulṭānī Mamluks, enjoying the performance of local entertainers and the company of ladies of the town. In 738/1337, al-Nāṣir Muḥammad took Maliktamur to task and threatened him with execution should he refuse to desist. On the same day, thirty-six Mamluks were exiled and the next day another forty met with the same punishment for drinking wine. Al-Nāṣir used this opportunity to ban another form of Mamluk amusement, and ordered the archery butts dismantled and prohibited the manufacture and sale of archery equipment used for target shooting. The Mamluks had become so taken with this sport that they would leave the Citadel without the sultan's permission and stay overnight in Cairo in direct violation of his orders.[23]

Aware of the growing power of the rank-and-file Mamluks as a pressure group on the sultan, the amirs tried to harness them in support of their own interests. Common struggles of amirs and rank-and-file Mamluks worked to blur further the distance between the two levels and strengthened the latter's position.

In Rabīʿ al-Ākhir 727/March 1327 rank-and-file Mamluks were spurred on by the amirs to pressure the sultan into releasing their peers, Amirs Quṭlūbughā al-Fakhrī and Ṭashtamur Ḥummuṣ Akhḍar who, in an anonymous note, had been accused of wanting to murder him. Officeholders among the Sulṭānī Mamluks, joined by the Mamluks of the barracks in the Citadel, went on a hunger strike. Faced with the Mamluks' ultimatum, al-Nāṣir had no option but to release the two amirs. While Ṭashtamur was left in his post in Egypt, Quṭlūbughā was exiled to Syria even though it was he who had written the note – the idea had been to direct suspicion of authorship of the note onto Baktamur al-Sāqī and thus arouse the sultan's ire against him. And yet the punishment meted out to Quṭlūbughā appears light considering that what he had tried to do was foment disorder in the army. The sources are silent about

[20] Al-Nuwayrī, 19B, fols. 14a–b; *ʿIqd,* fols. 341b–342b; *Nujūm*, vol. IX, 73; *Sulūk*, vol. II, 229–30.

[21] For further examples of al-Nāṣir Muḥammad's acceding to the Mamluks' claims, see al-Yūsufī, 356–7; *Sulūk*, vol. II, 414; *ʿIqd*, fol. 375a; al-Shujāʿī, 52–3.

[22] *Khiṭaṭ*, vol. II, 213, 216.

[23] *Sulūk*, vol. II, 455; *Nujūm*, vol. IX, 73; *ʿIqd,* fol. 342a–b.

al-Nāṣir's reaction to the part played by the rank-and-file Mamluks of the barracks.[24] The latter came out of such confrontation with a certain measure of political power which they could use to advance their own claims.

Upon al-Nāṣir's death the process of increasing power of rank-and-file Mamluks took on its own dynamics. The amirs began taking advantage of the Mamluks' opportunism and quest for material plenty to win them over in their struggle for power behind the Qalāwūnid dynasty. By bribing the Mamluks with *iqṭāʿāt*, gifts and more money into shifting their loyalties, the amirs virtually lent legitimacy to the disintegration of the *khushdāshiyya* – the fealty of the Mamluks to their master and their solidarity with their peers – that had been the basis for Mamluk factional consolidation prior to al-Nāṣir Muḥammad's third rule. This was to be a crucial factor in changing the norms of intra- and interfactional consolidation, making the amir class increasingly dependent on the rank-and-file Mamluks.

Amir Qawṣūn's bid for power immediately after al-Nāṣir's death embodies the amirs' fragile situation *vis-à-vis* the rank-and-file Mamluks.[25] Ostensibly, Qawṣūn had the necessary military, economic and political power to rally the Sulṭānī Mamluks to his cause – the army initially supported him, he had 700 Mamluks of his own, was independently wealthy, had the state treasury at his disposal, and held the formal office of *nā'ib al-salṭana* which, in the absence of an independent sultan, accorded him wide governing power.[26] Six of the seven amirs who had gained power from the beginning of the Mamluk state to the rise of al-Nāṣir Muḥammad – Aybak, Quṭuz, Qalāwūn, Kitbughā, Lājīn and Baybars al-Jāshnikīr – had enjoyed conditions similar to Qawṣūn's. Prior to their rise to power, these sultans could still negotiate with Mamluk factions who had undergone traditional Mamluk military training, i.e., factions imbued with *khushdāshiyya*, who acknowledged the authority of the government and the loyalty they owed their leaders.[27] Qawṣūn, however, had to negotiate with al-Nāṣir's Mamluks. These Mamluks displayed such a large measure of fickleness in their loyalty that they offered to sell their support to the highest bidder. Qawṣūn bought their support in order to oust Abū Bakr, al-Nāṣir's son, by 'making them many promises'.[28] When Amir Ṭuquzdamur, who then held the post of *nā'ib al-salṭana*, reprimanded them for their betrayal of their master, they claimed: 'We have no master other than Qawṣūn. The son of our master ignores us . . .'[29] These same Mamluks, however, openly mutinied against Qawṣūn only two months later, Rabīʿ al-Ākhir 742/September 1341, saying: 'How can we abandon the son of our master and serve another?'[30]

24 al-Nuwayrī, 19B, fol. 117a, 117b; *Durar*, vol. III, 335.
25 For details on Qawṣūn's bid for power and his fall see Levanoni, 81–5.
26 *Sulūk*, vol. II, 569, 570–1, 572–3, 574; *Nujūm*, vol. X, 40; al-Shujāʿī, 141, 159, 183, 184.
27 See for example the Mamluk cohesion and solidarity between Sultan Baybars and Sultan Qalāwūn and their colleagues: *Zubda*, fols. 43a, 90a–b, 159b; *Sīrāt al-Ẓāhir*, 33, 73, 74, 79, 96; Ibn al-Furāt, vol. VII, 18, 74, 150, 168.
28 Al-Shujāʿī, 149–50; *Nujūm*, vol. X, 29–30.
29 *Sulūk*, vol. II, 569.
30 Ibid., 575; al-Shujāʿī, 149–50; *Nujūm*, vol. X, 25–6.

Their demands, as already under al-Nāṣir Muḥammad, were almost exclusively material. And indeed, soon after suppressing the mutiny, Qawṣūn granted the Sulṭānī Mamluks amirates and *iqṭāʿāt* with larger incomes, and outdid himself in looking after their well-being.[31] Even so, Qawṣūn's alliance with the Sulṭānī Mamluks was short lived. Despite the many grants he had received, Amir Quṭlūbughā al-Fakhrī abused the trust Qawṣūn had placed in him and joined al-Nāṣir's son Aḥmad, who claimed the sultanate and, based in al-Karak, formed an alliance with some *nuwwāb* from the Syrian provinces.[32] Quṭlūbughā had little difficulty in inflicting a heavy defeat on Qawṣūn's large forces in Syria led by Alṭunbughā al-Ṣāliḥī, the *nā'ib* of Damascus – he simply bribed large numbers of Mamluks to defect to his camp during the battle and indeed Alṭunbughā himself and a group of his closest amirs only just managed to escape with their lives.[33] In Cairo, the senior amirs who supported Qawṣūn, such as Aydughmish, his partner in government, despite the generous grants and *iqṭāʿāt* he distributed to them, decided to break the life-and-death oath they had made to him and deserted his camp, taking with them a large number of Sulṭānī Mamluks. The following day, totally isolated, Qawṣūn was defeated.[34]

Once the buying of the Mamluks' support had become standard practice, the amirs found themselves caught up in a vicious circle that forced them to pay an ever higher price for support which was growing progressively fragile.

Extortion and even violence became part of the accepted methods whereby Mamluks sought to realize their demands. Thus, for example, in 778/1376 Amir Ṭashtamur al-Laffāf was taken hostage by the Mamluks and threatened with death unless they were paid the promised reward for their participation in the rebellion against Sultan al-Ashraf Shaʿbān. Their demands were met and Ṭashtamur was released.[35]

While buying Mamluks' fealty may have been personally beneficial for some of the amirs in the short term, once established as a norm it eroded the position of the amir class in the long term, for they lost the key to factional consolidation to the rank-and-file Mamluks. The latter were quick to grasp the implications. No longer satisfied with mere material rewards in return for their

[31] *Sulūk*, vol. II, 577, 580; *Nujūm*, vol. X, 28.

[32] Al-Shujāʿī, 156, 159, 161–5, 175; *Sulūk*, vol. II, 581; *Nujūm*, vol. X, 33; ʿImād al-dīn Ismāʿīl Abū al-Fidā', *Kitāb al-makhtaṣar fī akhbār al-bashar* (Hyderabad, 1954–61) (hereafter Abū al-Fidā'), vol. IV, 135; Ismāʿīl ibn ʿUmar ibn Kathīr, *al-Bidāya wa-l-nihāya*, (Beirut, 1966) (hereafter *Bidāya)*, vol. XIV. 194.

[33] Al-Shujāʿī, 171, 179, 180, 181; *Bidāya*, vol. XIV, 195–7; *Sulūk*, vol. II, 583–5; *ʿUyūn*, fol. 56a; Zayn al-dīn ʿUmar ibn al-Wardī, *Tatimmat al-mukhtaṣar fī akhbār al-bashar*, ed. Aḥmad Rifʿat al-Badrāwī (Beirut, 1970) (hereafter Ibn al-Wardī), vol. II, 471–2.

[34] Al-Shujāʿī, 171, 174–5, 182–3, 184, 186–7, 189–90; *Sulūk*, vol. II, 586–91; *Nujūm*, vol. X, 38; Ibn al-Wardī, vol. II, 472.

[35] *Sulūk*, vol. III, 275, 278, 287, 288. For further examples see ibid., 33–4, 139, 141, 150, 152, 276; *Durar*, vol. I, 413; vol. II, 294; Shihāb al-dīn ibn Faḍl Allāh Aḥmad ibn ʿAlī ibn Ḥajar al-ʿAsqalānī, *Inbā' al-ghumr bi-abnā' al-ʿUmr fī 'l-tārīkh* (Hyderabad, 1967–75) (hereafter *Inbā'*), vols. I–VIII, vol. I, 235–6.

military support to the amirs' claims to power, they demanded a steadily growing part in the political decision making.

Prior to al-Nāṣir Muḥammad's third reign, candidates for rule had come from the ranks of the previous sultan's senior amirs and his closest confidants. With their colleagues and rank-and-file Mamluks closing ranks behind them, they created pressure groups which put up claims for their stake in government. It was in this way, for instance, that Quṭuz, Qalāwūn, Lājīn and Baybars al-Jāshnikīr had all risen to power.

Immediately after the demise of Qawṣūn in 742/1341 a group of Mamluks united and fought on behalf of Ramaḍān, one of al-Nāṣir Muḥammad's sons, in an effort to help him attain the sultanate, while not a single senior amir joined or led them.[36] Although they failed in their attempt, the very fact that they made claims to the sultanate without the benefit of the leadership of any of the amirs reveals that they were confident enough to demand a say in matters of rule. From this time onwards, the amirs were well aware that they could no longer ignore the Mamluks' part in the decision-making process and place a son of the House of Qalāwūn on the throne without securing the consent of the Mamluks. Thus, for example, when the amirs decided to remove al-Nāṣir Aḥmad from the sultanate (10 Muḥarram 743/22 June 1342), and hastily replaced him with his brother, al-Ṣāliḥ Ismāʿīl, two of the amirs made a somewhat apologetic approach the following day to the Sulṭānī Mamluks: 'We made him sultan while being unable to consult you. Now make up your minds and tell us what you think (*wa-mā kāna al-waqt mujtahid mashūratikum. Wa-l-ān fa-tabaṣṣarū ra'yakum aysh taqūlū*)'.[37] In 746/1345 the Mamluks were the deciding factor in installing al-Kāmil Shaʿbān as sultan.[38] After the murder of Sultan al-Muẓaffar Ḥājjī in 748/1347, the Mamluks exerted pressure on the amirs, even using threats of rebellion, to place Ḥusayn, one of al-Nāṣir's sons, on the throne. The amirs did not yield but they made a hasty and forced decision by nominating his brother al-Nāṣir Ḥasan.[39] In Rabīʿ al-Awwal 768/November 1366, when the Yalbughāwiyya Mamluks rebelled against their master, Yalbughā al-ʿUmarī, the idea of the rebellion had originated with the Mamluks. They were the ones who forced the senior amirs to join them, threatening those who would not unite with them with dire consequences. Following the success of the rebellion, the Mamluks insisted that the sultan, al-Ashraf Shaʿbān, hand over to them their defeated master whom they then murdered.[40] Normally this should have satisfied their demands and enabled a return to Mamluk obedience to government authority. But from the

[36] Al-Shujāʿī, 241–4; *Nujūm*, vol. X, 82–4, 85; *Durar*, vol. II, 203.

[37] Al-Shujāʿī, 230. See for another example *Sulūk*, vol. II, 680–1, 744; *Nujūm*, vol. X, 95, 173.

[38] *Sulūk*, vol. II, 680–1; *Nujūm*, vol. X, 95.

[39] *Sulūk*, vol. II, 744; *Nujūm*, vol. X, 173.

[40] *Sulūk*, vol. III, 130–1; *Nujūm*, vol. XI, 36. For further examples see *Nujūm*, vol. XII, 196–7; vol. XV, 234, 265; vol. XVI, 41, 356, 359; Ṣārim al-dīn Ibrāhīm ibn Muḥammad ibn Duqmāq, *Kitāb al-Jawhar al-thamīn fī siyar al-Khulafā' wa-l-salāṭīn*, ed. Muḥammad Kamāl al-dīn ʿIzz al-dīn ʿAlī (Beirut, 1985) (hereafter *al-Jawhar al-thamīn)*, vol. I, 228.

positions the Yalbughāwiyya Mamluks were accorded in the wake of the rebellion, it becomes clear that what they had been after was an active part in government. Four central government posts went to amirs who had only recently been awarded the rank of amir of ten. Jaraktamur Manjak was appointed *amīr majlis*, Uzdamur Abū Daqn *amīr silāḥ*, and Alṭunbughā al-Yalbughāwī became *ra's nawba kabīr*. Bayram al-ʿIzzī, 'one of the rank-and-file (*aḥad al-ajnād*)', was awarded the rank of commander of one thousand.[41]

The conduct of the Yalbughāwiyya Mamluks after their rebellion against their master introduced the next phase where the Mamluks demanded that they themselves appoint their own representatives to the key positions of government and even decide on who would become sultan. Barely one year after their rebellion, on 6 Ṣafar 769/2 October 1367, they demanded from Amir Asandamur al-Nāṣirī, who in effect held control at the time, that he hand over their leaders, Bayram al-ʿIzzī, Uzdamur Abū Daqn and others, to which he agreed. This was apparently not enough: 'They decided to murder Amir Asandamur and the sultan and replace him with another sultan (*wa-iqāmat sulṭān ghayrihi*)'.[42] The rank-and-file Mamluks were unsuccessful in their attempt, but the episode reveals again that they now had their own political power base upon which to rest their claim to rule.

While the rank-and-file Mamluks no longer needed the amirs' leadership in forming pressure groups for their own interests, the amirs, disunited by their personal ambitions, remained indecisive *vis-à-vis* the Mamluks' growing power and, by turning a blind eye to their mutinous deeds, tacitly relinquished their part in government.

This is clearly shown by the 778/1376 rebellion in Cairo against al-Ashraf Shaʿbān while he was away on the *ḥajj*. This rebellion was a mutiny of the rank-and-file Mamluks: 'And in this case there was no great or exalted personage who planned it, with the Mamluks following him (*lam yakun fī hādhihi al-waqʿa rajul ʿaẓīm lahu sha'n qāma bi-amr wa-tabiʿathu al-nās*)'.[43] When news of the mutiny reached the ears of the amirs left behind in Cairo to preserve order, those who put up resistance were imprisoned, while others 'ignored it, for fear of their lives (*fa-taghāfalū ʿanhum khawfan ʿalā anfusihim*)'.[44] After the rebellion had proved successful, these same amirs became mere rubber stamps for Mamluk decisions and only held purely honorary offices.[45]

Acting as the victorious faction in a Mamluk struggle over power, the rank-and-file Mamluks placed al-Ashraf Shaʿbān's son, al-Manṣūr ʿAlī, on the throne and divided the senior amirates among themselves. As they had no established hierarchy, each Mamluk was deemed worthy of holding any of these offices. Thus Ṭashtamur al-Laffāf, an amir of ten, took the *atābakiyya*

[41] *Sulūk*, vol. III, 116, 117, 118, 144; *Nujūm*, vol. XI, 41, 42, 44–5; *al-Jawhar al-thamīn*, vol. I, 230–1.
[42] *Sulūk*, vol. III, 150, see also 117, 164, 168; *Durar*, vol. I, 413; *Nujūm*, vol. XI, 47.
[43] *Nujūm*, vol. XI, 160. [44] *Sulūk*, vol. III, 277.
[45] *Nujūm*, vol. XI, 65; *Sulūk*, vol. III, 277, 292.

and the rank of commander of one thousand. Qarāṭāy al-Ṭāzī, who prior to the rebellion had been one of the *mufārada* (simple) Mamluks, became *ra's nawba kabīr* with the rank of commander of one thousand. Asandamur al-Ṣarghitmishī, again one of the *mufārada,* was also promoted to the rank of commander of one thousand and the post of *amīr silāḥ*. Damurdāsh al-Yūsufī, Balāṭ al-Ṣaghīr, Alṭunbughā al-Niẓāmī, and Yalbughā al-Niẓāmī were *mufārada* Mamluks but in the wake of the rebellion were all awarded the rank of commander of one thousand.[46]

Ibn Taghrībirdī has given us the following keen observation of the prevailing atmosphere in the Mamluk army following this rebellion:

> From the day of the murder of al-Ashraf Shaʿbān, Ṭashtamur al-Laffāf rose from the rank of simple soldier to [the office of] *atābak al-ʿasākir*. He was followed by Qaraṭāy al-Ṭāzī, Aynabak al-Badrī, Quṭluqṭamur, and the *atābak* Barqūq and Baraka. All of them were simple soldiers or amirs of ten and rose to their new ranks through aggression or fomenting civil war [and therefore] all the Mamluks desired to be like them and do what they had done (*ṭamaʿa kull aḥad an yakūna mithlahum wa-yafʿala mā faʿalūhu*).[47]

The abolition of the traditional Mamluk hierarchy, together with the fact that the power of decision regarding rule was now concentrated in the hands of the rank-and-file Mamluks, quite naturally encouraged the latter to demand the right to place one of their number in power. This explains the meteoric rise of Barqūq to power in 784/1382. Barqūq and Baraka were originally simple Yalbughāwiyya Mamluks in the service of the *asyād*. They were awarded the rank of amir of forty for helping Aynabak get rid of his governing partner, Qarāṭāy. Both Aynabak and Qarāṭāy made it to their high positions from the lowest ranks in the army. Later, Barqūq and Baraka had no difficulty in plotting with Yalbughā al-Nāṣirī against Aynabak. About a month after they were awarded the rank of amir of forty, they were both rewarded for their part in the removal of Aynabak with the rank of commander of one thousand, and became Yalbughā al-Nāṣirī's partners in government.[48] The rise of Barqūq and Baraka from the lowly rank of simple soldiers to their position as active rulers took a mere four months (Muḥarram–Rabīʿ al-Ākhir 779/May–August 1377).[49]

Obviously, the extreme ease with which Mamluks could rise through the ranks precluded the existence of a stratum of senior amirs. Amirs whose rise to the upper echelons of government had been extremely rapid were less likely to be as committed to social institutions as the senior amirs had been. Moreover, these new amirs had reached their senior status by shaking the foundations of the traditional Mamluk establishment. After Barqūq managed to rid himself of Baraka and gain sole power (783/1381), there were no senior

[46] *Sulūk*, vol. III, 287–9; *Nujūm*, vol. XI, 149–51.
[47] *Nujūm*, vol. XI, 214, see also 159–60, 191; *Sulūk*, vol. III, 316, 330.
[48] *Sulūk*, vol. III, 305, 313, 315; *Nujūm*, vol. XI, 158, 223. [49] *Nujūm*, vol. XI, 159.

amirs to be found in the military–political arena. With the exception of two (Aqtamur ʿAbd al-Ghanī and Aydamur al-Shamsī who held purely honorary posts), all amirs had achieved their senior status only quite recently as a result of their participation in one rebellion or another. After the death of these two amirs, Barqūq had little difficulty in persuading his colleagues to accept his sultanate.[50] Once they had given their consent, the new political reality of the Mamluks' power became unassailable.

The political power accumulated by the simple Mamluks and the recognition it was accorded quite naturally changed the Mamluk army's foci of power. After Barqūq's reign, the rank-and-file Mamluks held the power of legitimizing the sultan's rule within the Mamluk elite. Thus, for example, Jaqmaq's rise to rule in 842/1438 is shown in the sources as coming in response to the Mamluks' demands. The Mamluks decided to murder their leader, Īnāl al-Abū Bakrī, who held the strings behind the government of al-ʿAzīz, son of al-Ashraf Barsbāy. After Īnāl had escaped from the Citadel, they approached Jaqmaq and urged him to take sole power. When he seemed to hesitate, they exerted pressure upon him, saying: 'If the Grand Amir does not accede to our wishes, we will take another master in his place'.[51] Clearly the Mamluks held the power of legitimizing the sultan's rule.

The political influence the rank-and-file Mamluks had achieved enabled them to decide not only on who should rule, but also on matters of government management. They now had a say in appointments, especially those directly connected with the management of their own affairs. Thus, for example, in 854/1450 mass riots made Sultan Jaqmaq dismiss Jawhar al-Nawrūzī, *the muqaddam al-mamālīk*, and Abū 'l-Khayr al-Naḥḥās, the *wakīl bayt al-māl*.[52] The Mamluks also dictated to the sultan the allocation of *iqṭāʿāt*[53] and determined their own rate of pay and the size of the grants due to them.[54] In 855/1451 the Sulṭānī Mamluks united and demanded an increase in their annual clothing allowance. When news reached Sultan Jaqmaq, he hurried to the *īwān* to inspect in person the payment process. His presence, however, did not prevent the Mamluks from showing harsh persistence in their

50 Ibid., vol. XI, 208, 214–15, For another example of the Mamluks' demand to put on the throne a rank-and-file Mamluk see: *Sulūk*, vol. III, 1044–5, 1060–3, 1065; *Nujūm*, vol. XII, 236; XIII 27, 158; Muḥammad ibn Aḥmad ibn Iyās, *Badāʾiʿ al-zuhūr fī waqāʾiʿ al-duhūr*, (Bulāq, Cairo, 1898) (hereafter Ibn Iyās), vols. I–III, vol. I, 330, 335–7.

51 *Nujūm*, vol. XV, 236–7; ʿAlī ibn Dāwūd al-Ṣayrafī, *Nuzhat al-Nufūs wa-l-abdān fī tawārīkh al-zamān* (Cairo, 1970–1994) (hereafter al-Ṣayrafī), vols. I–IV, vol. III, 437.

52 Jamāl al-dīn Yūsuf ibn Taghrībirdī, *Ḥawādith al-duhūr fī madā al-ayyām wa-l-shuhūr*, ed. Muḥammad Kamāl al-dīn ʿIzz al-dīn (Beirut, 1990) vols. I–II (hereafter *Ḥawādith*), vol. I, 266–7; *Nujūm*, vol. XV, 411–14, 417. For other examples see *Nujūm*, vol. XVI, 40, 114, 136–7, 147–8, 175; *Ḥawādith*, vol. II, 533; Ibn Iyās, vol. II, 239, 240.

53 *Ḥawādith*, vol. II, 410, 431; *Nujūm*, vol. XIV, 190; vol. XVI, 142–3; Ibn Iyās, vol. II, 277.

54 *Nujūm*, vol. XIV, 213, 330, 371; vol. XV, 227, 279–80; vol. XVI, 94, 98, 100–2, 112, 132, 139, 362; *Ḥawādith*, vol. II, 426, 431–2, 434, 449, 504, 516, 529, 547; *Sulūk*, vol. IV, 480, 594–5, 804, 930, 1091, 1103; al-Ṣayrafī, vol. III, 160, 178; Shams al-dīn Muḥammad ibn ʿAbd al-Raḥīm al-Sakhāwī, *al-Ḍawʾ al-lāmiʿ li-ahl al-qarn al-tāsiʿ* (Beirut, n.d.), vols. I–X (hereafter *Ḍawʾ*) vol. II, 106; Shams al-dīn Muḥammad ibn ʿAbd al-Raḥīm as-Sakhāwī, *al-Tibr al-masbūk fī dhayl al-sulūk*, (Cairo, n.d.) (hereafter *Tibr*), 352.

demands. Although Jaqmaq left the place in anger, cursing the Mamluks, he nevertheless raised their clothing allowance.[55]

The process of the growing power of the rank-and-file Mamluks reached its peak with their control over the army's foci of power and the change wrought in the social stratification of the Mamluk elite. That is, rank-and-file Mamluks succeeded in bringing down the amir class from their elevated status whereas the sultan was made dependent on their will to such extent that soon his authority was reduced beyond recognition. In the fifteenth century we then find sultans who start maintaining a clear separation between rank-and-file Mamluks and the army's stratum of command: even with the tremendous power they had come to wield in matters of government, rank-and-file Mamluks were seldom advanced to high military ranks, which instead went to veteran Mamluks, but these of course had little say in government. A number of examples may illustrate this vulnerability of sultans and amirs *vis-à-vis* rank-and-file Mamluks.

For example, on 11 Jumādā al-Ūlā 854/2 July 1450, Amir Tanam min ʿAbd al-Rāziq, who was *amīr majlis*, complained to the sultan about his Mamluks' insolence and Jaqmaq imprisoned ten of them for their misconduct. The following day, while he was on his way from the Citadel together with Īnāl, the *atābak al-ʿasākir*, the sultan's Mamluks (the *julbān*) surrounded Tanam and took him to task for complaining to the sultan about his Mamluks. Īnāl succeeded in pacifying them, promising that the imprisoned Mamluks would be released. The Mamluks allowed them to proceed, but returning in the direction of the Citadel, they caught hold of Zayn al-dīn Yaḥyā, the *ustādār*, and beat him with their cudgels till he threw himself from his horse and fled on foot. Next day, the Mamluks' demands were met and their colleagues released.[56]

Another salient example of Mamluk independence and growing insolence occurred in 873/1468 when Uzbak, who was *atābak al-ʿasākir* at the time, refused to go into battle against the bedouin in al-Buḥayra province, afraid he would be unable to control the sultan's Mamluks, *al-ajlāb*, who had been placed under his command.[57]

Further proof of how the once great status of the amirs had declined in comparison to that of the rank-and-file Mamluks we find *inter alia* in the change that occurred in the fifteenth century in the position of the office of *amīr jāndār* (one of whose tasks was to notify the amirs of the sultan's decisions in matters of appointments, dismissals, and punishments). Ibn Taghrībirdī reports that 'this office was since filled by rank-and-file soldiers, but previously had been the most prestigious office'.[58]

With Mamluk military hierarchy now done away with, there was no need to maintain any correlation between the military ranks and the administrative

[55] *Nujūm*, vol XV, 435; *Ḥawādith*, vol. II, 332–3.

[56] *Nujūm*, vol XV, 410, 414.

[57] Ibn Iyās, vol. II, 106. For many other examples of the Mamluks' lack of discipline see: Ibid., vol. II, 218–19, 229, 230, 239–41, 247, 296, 322, 323, 330, 339; vol. III, 84; *Nujūm*, vol XV, 90, 352, 410, 414; vol XVI, 95–6, 100–2, 138–9, 159; *Ḥawādith*, vol. II, 528–31, 532; *Tibr*, 41.

[58] *Nujūm*, vol. XVI, 287; *Khiṭaṭ* vol. II, 222. See also *Ḥawādith*, vol. II, 431; *Khiṭaṭ*, vol. II, 223.

positions the Mamluks filled. Minor amirs and simple soldiers filled positions which in the past had been filled by amirs of one hundred and commanders of one thousand. Ibn Taghrībirdī bears testimony to this when, enumerating the amirs of ten and amirs of forty who held office in the sultan's court in 841/1437, he adds: 'And these, even though they were only amirs of forty and amirs of ten, their status was that of commander of one thousand, because, in previous generations, these positions had been filled by commanders of one thousand'.[59]

During the rule of al-Ẓāhir Khushqadam, government matters were for a long period in the hands of two amirs of ten, Jānibak al-Maḥmūdī al-Mu'ayyadī and ʿAlī Bey al-ʿAjamī al-Mu'ayyadī, who jointly held the post of *ra's nawba*.[60] Amir Khā'ir Bāk ruled in much the same manner behind Sultan al-Ẓāhir Yalbāy (872/1467), with the support of the younger Mamluks. He was *dawādār thānī* and held the rank of amir of twenty.[61]

The allocation of grants and salaries indicates a preferential treatment of the rank-and-file Mamluk class, constituting another encroachment on the amirs' status. Thus, for example, the size of the *nafaqa* (the payment which the soldiers received on the eve of a campaign or on the accession of a new sultan) to the rank-and-file Mamluks increased in the second half of the fourteenth century and remained high during the fifteenth century while the amirs' payments remained unchanged.[62] The adverse economic situation during the last hundred and fifty years of the Mamluks' autonomous rule compelled sultans at times to award grants first to influential pressure groups, and only then, if at all, to others. The Mamluks now constituted such a pressure group, while the amirs fell into the second category. Thus, in 865/1461, after his rise to power, Khushqadam first awarded the *nafaqa* to the Sulṭānī Mamluks and, against the norm, held those for the amirs in abeyance. The latter were given their grants only after their own Mamluks had staged demonstrations on their masters' behalf.[63] In 872/1467, with the rise to power of al-Ẓāhir Yalbāy, only the Sulṭānī Mamluks were awarded grants.[64]

Finally, a clear indication of the rank-and-file Mamluks' powerful position, not only within the Mamluk elite but also among the civilian population, is the rise in their function as arbitrators at the expense of the judicial system. While in 753/1352 it was the *sharʿī* judges, *al-quḍāt*, who lost their authority to the *ḥujjāb*, whose military judicial authority extended over civilians as well,[65] the importance and prestige of both of them were now eroded by the incursion of simple Mamluks into their domain. Paradoxically, while it was the Mamluks themselves who had broken the law and terrorized sultans, amirs

[59] *Nujūm*, vol. XV, 223. See also ibid., vol. XVI, 74–5. [60] Ibid., vol. XV, 286–7, 351.
[61] Ibid., vol. XVI, 361, 372. See also 75, 306.
[62] D. Ayalon, 'The system of payment in the Mamluk military society', *Journal of Economic and Social History of the Orient*, 1/1 (1958), 50. [63] *Nujūm*, vol. XVI, 259.
[64] Ibid., vol. XVI, 363. See also 382; *Sulūk*, vol. IV, 28.
[65] *Khiṭaṭ*, vol. II, 222; *Sulūk*, vol. II, 863–4.

and civilians,[66] in the anarchy that ensued, they proved to be the only ones capable of enforcing order through the power they now wielded. For purely practical reasons, the civilian population avoided the *sharʿī* and military courts and increasingly turned to the Mamluks with legal issues. The rank-and-file Mamluks' leaders amassed such immense power that some of them maintained an administrative apparatus which resembled that of an amir.[67]

In conclusion, to illustrate how the changes wrought in the Mamluk training system in the first half of the fourteenth century propelled rank-and-file Mamluks into the dominant position they occupied in the Mamluk elite in the fifteenth century, there is perhaps no better way than to quote Ibn Taghrībirdī's striking comparison between the Mamluks of his own age and those of Sultan Baybars' days:

> And most surprising of all was that they [the early Mamluks] were well endowed with courtesy, humility, and obedience towards their superiors, and good manners and courtesy towards their inferiors. [But] they [his contemporary Mamluks] . . . do not try to hold the reins of the horse and when they speak, they speak arrogantly. They have no profession other than robbery. They are mighty at the expense of the weak and greedy for even a loaf of bread. Deriding the leader is their *jihād* and their raids are for straw and dried clover.[68]

[66] Ibn Iyās, vol. II, 103, 141, 148, 149, 151, 153, 183, 195, 214, 215, 218–19, 220, 226, 228, 230, 239, 240, 241, 245, 248, 257, 287, 330, 339, 342–3, 346, 347, 351; vol. III, 5, 6, 33–4, 43, 54–5, 80; *Ḥawādith*, vol. I, 180–1, 266, 269, 271, 273; vol. II, 333, 338, 448, 481, 486, 505, 517, 527, 529, 538, 568–9, 570, 586, 592–3, 595; *Nujūm*, vol. XII, 271–2, 280, 289, 297, 300, 327; vol. XIV, 212–13, 220, 222–3, 321, 327–8, 330, 332, 340, 356, 371; vol. XV, 50–1, 83, 90, 228, 230, 232, 233, 263, 270, 279, 365, 397–400, 410–11, 418, 423, 433, 434, 435; vol. XVI, 84, 87–9, 94, 95, 96, 98, 100–2, 112, 117, 118, 123, 125, 130, 131, 132, 133, 134, 136–7, 138, 141, 158, 261–2, 276, 288, 290, 291, 297, 300, 361; *Sulūk*, vol. IV, 100, 105, 480, 551, 749, 784, 800, 804, 805, 818, 864, 930, 931, 1009, 1026, 1027, 1056, 1058, 1177; *Tibr*, 313–15, 322–3; al-Ṣayrafī, vol. III, 147, 157, 178, 279, 304–5, 340, 400, 401, 406, 425, 426, 433, 435–6; *Ḍaw'*, vol. II, 329.

[67] *Nujūm*, vol. XVI, 114, 130.

[68] Ibid., vol. VII, 329. See also 332; *Khiṭaṭ*, vol. II, 214.

CHAPTER 3

Mamluk amirs and their families and households

DONALD S. RICHARDS

In various publications of recent date one still finds traces of the proposition which in earlier writings was bluntly stated like this, that Mamluk society was inherently hostile to heredity. Recent publications may not put the proposition quite so starkly, but nevertheless the impression is left that the prospects of the descendants of *mamlūks* were inevitably and necessarily restricted and 'second class'. Ayalon's notion of a 'one-generation aristocracy' is still very persuasive.[1]

No absurd contrary notion will be advanced, that, for instance, first- or second-generation offspring of *mamlūks* inevitably had brilliant careers and were overwhelmingly important in the conduct of affairs of state. That would be nonsense, but the aim is to advance a further corrective to a view apparently still widely held. Haarmann has studied what share of Egypt's agricultural wealth the *awlād al-nās* as a whole, descendants of sultans and descendants of amirs, enjoyed as holders of *iqṭāʿs* according to cadastral survey information available at three moments of Mamluk history, 777/1376, 800/1397 and 885/1480.[2] Despite the acknowledged difficulties in interpreting the data available and what must be admitted to be a large margin of error due to terminological imprecision, one may accept that at the first date this group had a minor but not insignificant share, which dwindled considerably by the last of the three dates. While Haarmann highlights such economic and social influence as the *awlād al-nās* possessed from late in the fourteenth century to early in the fifteenth, one is left with the impression that any influence at all was the result of the breaking of some 'basic law'.

The *mamlūk* system was essentially a method of importing the manpower

For an explanation of my use of 'Mamluk' and '*mamlūk*', see the last paragraph of this chapter, p. 40.

1 See for example Robert Irwin, *The Middle East in the Middle Ages* (Champaign, 1986), chap. 1; P. M. Holt, *The Age of the Crusades* (London, 1986), 140; Jonathan Berkey, *The Transmission of Knowledge in Medieval Cairo* (Princeton, 1992), intro., 11.

2 Ulrich Haarmann, 'The sons of Mamluks as fief-holders in late medieval Egypt', in T. Khalidi (ed.), *Land Tenure and Social Transformation in the Middle East* (Beirut 1984), 141–68. The data from the surveys is derived from Heinz Halm, *Ägypten nach den mamlukischen Lehensregistern* (Wiesbaden, 1979 and 1982), vols. I and II.

that was considered suitable for certain functions, primarily the military. It persisted because of a lack of any sense of oneness between the rulers and the indigenous ruled, the lack of any trust and sense of common aims, and through habit and inertia. *Mamlūks* entered no charmed circle, no special caste, although individuals through fortunate placement, good luck and their own merits and efforts found opportunities for career advancement, at times, of course, to the highest positions. Yet it is as absurd to think that any *mamlūk*, merely by virtue of that legal status, had a real expectation of power, wealth and influence as it is to maintain that his descendants would, indeed should, have none. If it is true that *awlād al-nās* in general had a dwindling share in wealth, political influence and social status in the fifteenth century, it is dubious practice to make that the norm for preceding periods of the Mamluk state, even to elevate it to a principle. To assume that Mamluk society was willing to accept such a law of a one-generation aristocracy flies in the face of all human experience. Indeed, one must admit that attempts to pass on power and status continued throughout the fifteenth century, that in the same period the training and the collective ethos of *mamlūks* are understood to have declined and the recognition of kinship ties, through, for example, the ingathering of family members of *mamlūks*, intensified. That the *awlād al-nās* generally failed to maintain their position must be due to particular developments in the polity as a whole, which remain to be identified, rather than to any *a priori* rejection of the hereditary principle. Exactly where the idea that this group was doomed to accept a lesser status came from is a historiographical enquiry that will not be pursued now. It certainly has a long pedigree, however, because we find that Pietro Casola commented after his pilgrimage in 1494 that

> Jerusalem is ruled by these renegade dogs, because no one can rule over the Moors who is not a renegade Christian. And if one of these renegades should take a wife and have sons, these cannot succeed the father in any dignity. Such sons as these are called sons of the people [fioli de la gente], even though they be the sons of the Sultan.[3]

A reading of the sources for the fourteenth century gives, to my mind, an immediate and strong impression of a not insignificant role for the non-*mamlūk* elements in the governing circles, and inevitably the sons and further descendants of amirs played a major part. Family continuity is often a striking feature. There is, of course, a social and cultural reality which we call Mamluk, which is far from being dependent on the input of those who were in the strict sense *mamlūks*. The families of *mamlūks* made their contribution to this Mamluk whole. One can easily imagine that they were proud of their Turkish (and later their Circassian) descent. Many members of these families continued, as the sources put it, 'to wear the garb of the military'. Early in the

[3] In the translation of M. Newell (Manchester 1907), 729. The 'even though' seems to suggest that Casola may have misunderstood the phrase *awlād al-nās*, as though *al-nās* had the sense of 'the population at large', rather than 'the people that matter'.

fourteenth century we read of one *ḥalqa* command (*taqdima*) in which served 'all the sons of the leading Emirs'. Whatever its actual military value, the unit obviously had social caché and was rather conspicuously well equipped.[4] In 737 after the loss of forty or more members of the *ḥalqa* in an expedition to Sīs, 'the Sultan sought out their sons and gave them their fiefs (*akhbāz*)'.[5] The fact that the *awlād al-nās* were the offspring of a ruling class, whose privileges they wished to maintain and whose language they were proud to keep, separates them sharply from, and means that they may never be equated with, an exploited immigrant class that might have been tempted to seek wholesale integration with the indigenous population. In modern times too one has known families that through marriage remained 'foreign', particularly Turkish, while being firmly Egyptian in residence and economic involvement. The role of the *awlād al-nās* in intellectual pursuits, not least in the Islamic sciences, has been investigated, again by Haarmann.[6] I doubt whether this phenomenon can be interpreted as a rejection of their roots, as, after all, first-generation *mamlūks* could also be notable scholars. It demonstrates the attraction of an intellectual tradition, but is not a denial of Turkishness.

Clearly we should not be surprised at efforts to create continuity and to transmit position and power. In the Mamluk state there was a commonly accepted role for family connections in both the religious and the administrative spheres. Functions and privileges were frequently passed on to family members. With the example of these elites before them, apart from any perfectly natural human concern, it would be quite incredible if members of the *mamlūk* elite had not tried to ensure continuity of social and economic standing for their sons. However, the *mamlūk* system itself, predicated on the regular influx of fresh manpower, produced an inevitable tension between the aspirations and interests of the different generations of *mamlūks*, between those who had attained important positions in the state and amassed wealth and those who had aspirations in that direction.

However, it would be a false opposition to assert that only blood relations counted and that the *mamlūks* of an amir had no share in his concern. Certain especially favoured *mamlūks* of an amir could often be treated as quasi-kin, in that they were brought up in all respects as part of the family. That was true of the future historian, Baybars al-Manṣūrī, who was raised in the bosom of the family of Qalāwūn, when the latter was an amir. However, such a *mamlūk* could never inherit in regular fashion from his master. Provision would be made in other ways. One's *mamlūks* could benefit from *waqf* arrangements

4 Ibn al-Dawādārī, *Kanz al-durar wa-jāmiʿ al-ghurar*, ed. Hans Robert Roemer (Cairo, 1960), vol. IX, 154.

5 al-Yūsufī, *Nuzhat al-nāẓir fī sīrat al-Malik al-Nāṣir*, ed. Aḥmad Ḥuṭayṭ (Beirut, 1406/1986), (hereafter *Nuzha*), 416.

6 Ulrich Haarmann, 'Arabic in speech, Turkish in lineage: Mamluks and their sons in the intellectual life of fourteenth-century Egypt and Syria', *Journal of Semitic Studies*, 33 (1988), 103–14.

made on their behalf.[7] Their interests could remain linked to the children of their master, as, for instance, we read of Sayf al-dīn Bughā (d. 724/1324), a *mamlūk* of Mankūtamur al-Ḥusāmī, who served as agent (*wakīl*) for Mankūtamur's children and became wealthy in the process.[8] We may also infer that the *mamlūks* of an amir could face difficult times after the death of their master. When Baktamur al-Sāqī was dying, he appealed to the Sultan al-Nāṣir Muḥammad, on behalf of his *mamlūks*, not to 'leave them standing at the doors of the emirs'. In the event the sultan gave them *iqṭāʿs* in the *ḥalqa*, some of them with officer rank (*muqaddam*) and took several into his own service.[9] *Mamlūks* were also taken into families by marriage ties. The amir Baktamur al-Ḥājib held his treasurer Sayf al-dīn Bakhshī especially dear and gave him his daughter in marriage – although that ended badly with Bakhshī's involvement in a plot to steal the amir's fortune.[10] The daughter of the amir Bahādur al-Muʿizzī was given in marriage to his own *mamlūk*, Aqtamur.[11]

It must surely be true that if a great amir had *mamlūks* in any considerable number, then his relationship to the mass of them must have been of a more contractual nature, based on the satisfaction of maintenance expectations on the one hand, and the performance of their duties on the other.[12] It differed not greatly from the relationship of an amir with the troops he enlisted, his *mustakhdamīn*, who could be non-*mamlūk* or unattached *mamlūks*. This was likely to have been so with the *mamlūks* that an amir obtained through redistribution, as, for example, when the amir Baysarī al-Shamsī acquired sixty former *mamlūks* of Sultan Kitbughā.[13] When the charity of the amir Jamāl al-dīn Āqūsh al-Ashrafī was noted, the order of recipients, if at all corresponding to precedence, is interesting. He distributed first to 'his neighbours . . ., then to his troops [his *jund*], then to his *mamlūks*, then to his servants (*ghilmān*)'.[14] Here one might also mention, in passing, a group term which occurs from time to time. I refer to the *alzām* (presumably the plural of *lāzim*). On the battlefield facing the Mongols in 680/1281–2, Sultan Qalāwūn was surrounded by 'his *mamlūks*, his *alzām* and the *silāḥdāriyya,* etc'.[15] In the house-

[7] A tangential example is provided by the daughter of the amir Manjak who bought a house in the Barjawān district of al-Qāhira in 795/1392–3 and made it a *waqf* for her freedmen (*ʿutaqāʾ*), which 'remains in their hands until today' (al-Maqrīzī, *al-Khiṭaṭ al-Mawāʿiẓ wa-'l-iʿtibār fī dhikr al-khiṭaṭ wa-'l-āthār* (hereafter *Khiṭaṭ*), vol. II, (Cairo, 1853–4), 53).

[8] Ibn al-Ṣuqāʿī, *Tālī wafayāt al-aʿyān*, ed. and trans. Jacqueline Sublet (Damascus, 1974), (hereafter *Tālī*), no. 348. [9] *Nuzha*, 146, 155. [10] *Khiṭaṭ*, vol. II, 64. [11] Ibid., vol. II, 76.

[12] The amir Qawṣūn claimed, admittedly in a boasting context, that he had 700 *mamlūks* (Ibn Ḥajar al-ʿAsqalānī, *al-Durar al-kāmina fī aʿyān al-mi'a al-thāmina*, ed. M. S. Jādd al-Ḥaqq (Cairo, 1385/1965–6) (hereafter *Durar*), vol. III, p. 343). Amir Taghrībirdī, the historian's father, owned about 1,000 *mamlūks*, in two categories: his own purchases (*al-mushtarawāt*) and the *mamālīk al-khidma*, enrolled from other sources (Ibn Taghrībirdī, *al-Nujūm al-zāhira fī mulūk Miṣr wa-'l-Qāhira*, ed. William Popper (Berkeley and Los Angeles, 1915), vol. VI, 264 ff.) [13] *Khiṭaṭ*, vol. II, p. 69. [14] *Nuzha*, 327.

[15] Baybars al-Manṣūrī, *Zubdat al-fikra fī tārīkh al-hijra*, MS British Museum, fol. 114b (cf. al-Maqrīzī, *al- Sulūk li-maʿrifat duwal al-mulūk*, ed. M. Ziyāda and S. ʿĀshūr (Cairo, 1934–73), (hereafter *Sulūk*), vol. I, 693).

hold of the amir Baktamur al-Ḥājib there was a 'group of his resident *alzām*' (who were literally 'within his gate'),[16] and in 703/1303–4 the amir Jankalī b. Muḥammad came to Syria, and then to Cairo, with 'his immediate family, his relatives and his *alzām*', several of whom were assigned *iqṭāʿs*.[17] Baybars II in 709/1309–10 created twenty-seven new amirs from 'his *mamlūks* . . . and his *alzām*', but a rather puzzling phrase refers to 'the remainder of his *alzām* amongst the Burjiyya'.[18] When Qawṣūn heard of Quṭlūbughā al-Fakhrī's successes in Syria in 742/1341–2, he arrested some of the latter's *alzām* in Cairo, amongst whom was an individual called Qarā al-Muqaddam and his brother, the intendant of the buttery.[19] On the fall of the amir Baraka in 782/1380–1 all his comrades (*aṣḥāb*) were arrested 'and his *alzām* and his *mamlūks*'.[20] This word may or may not have had any technical sense. However, I do not rule out the possibility that it referred to individuals who had bound themselves to a master under some (perhaps lengthy) contract of service, as opposed to their having been purchased. As for the phrase quoted above, 'his *alzām* among the Burjiyya', it could be explained as follows: members of that group, *mamlūks* of Qalāwūn, had lost employment in the changing politics of the late thirteenth century, later to be 'bound' in service to Baybars II. There is amongst the Ḥaram documents in Jerusalem a suggestive item[21] which records a contract of bonded service drawn up in 722/1322, probably in Anatolia. The nature of the *khidma* involved is not specified, although the individual named hires himself (*ajāra nafsahū .. ijāratan ..*) to an amir, Timurbughā b. Nikūtāy (?), for forty years. The text contains the phrase *li-yakhdimahu wa-yulāzim khidmatahu safaran wa-ḥaḍaran* ('to serve him and be constant in his service abroad and at home'). Such a bound man could have been called a *lāzim*.

The importation of relatives of first-generation *mamlūks* is a phenomenon associated with the Circassian period. Examples can be found, however, for the fourteenth century. The brothers and relatives of the amir Qawṣūn were brought to Cairo by Sultan al-Nāṣir Muḥammad and all were made amirs,[22] and he had also sent abroad for the brothers of Baktamur al-Sāqī.[23] In 737/1336–7 al-Nāṣir sent to 'the land of Uzbak' for *mamlūks* and slave-girls and also for the relatives of the amir Bashtāk. The latter and two brothers, both by then amirs of forty, were arrested in 742/1341–2.[24] Yalbughā al-Yaḥyāwī's father along with two other sons of his came to Egypt, 'when he

[16] *Khiṭaṭ*, vol. II, p. 64. [17] *Durar*, vol. II, 76–7. [18] *Sulūk*, vol. II, 69–70, 71.

[19] al-Shujāʿī, *Tārīkh al-Malik al-Nāṣir Muḥammad b. Qalāwūn al-Ṣāliḥī wa-awlādihi*, ed. Barbara Schäfer (Wiesbaden/Cairo, 1398/1978), (hereafter *Tārīkh al-Malik*), 64. A civilian administrator could also have 'his *alzām* and his *ḥāshiya*' (*Tālī*, no. 273), as did Ibn Hilāl al-dawla (*Nuzha*, 243–4). In 680/1281–82 Qalāwūn faced the Mongols in battle, accompanied by his *khāṣṣa*, his *alzām*, the office holders and his *ḥalqa* of 4,000 *fāris* (*Sulūk*, vol. I, 693).

[20] *Tārīkh Ibn Qāḍī Shubha*, ed. ʿAdnān Darwīsh (hereafter *Tārikh Ibn Qāḍī Shubha*), (Damascus, 1977), vol. I, 26.

[21] Ḥaram document no. 41 (see D. P. Little, *A Catalogue of the Islamic Documents from al-Ḥaram aš-Šarīf in Jerusalem,* Beiruter Texte und Studien vol. 29, (Beirut, 1984), 192). I hope to publish this document. [22] *Nuzha*, 212; *Tārīkh al-Malik*, 39–40. [23] *Nuzha*, 150.

[24] *Nuzha*, 379; *Tārīkh al-Malik*, 7.

heard how his son flourished in the service of al-Nāṣir'. The father was given an amirate, and later held a *ṭablkhāna* amirate in Aleppo until his death in 750/1349.[25] In similar fashion the father and brothers of the amir Ṭāz came to Egypt in 752/1351–2. One of his brothers, Jāntamur, was an intimate of al-Ṣāliḥ, son of al-Nāṣir, until his execution in 793/1391.[26] In another case the amir Jaraktamur and his sister, respectively the favourite and the wife of al-Ashraf Shaʿbān, persuaded him to send for their father, Qarābughā, who was purchased, freed and made amir of twenty. He died in 797/1394–5.[27] I suspect that the fact that he was purchased has nothing to do with having to pass through some sort of 'refining fire' of mamlukdom, which was in any case of an extremely perfunctory nature in this instance, but rather reflects the mechanism of bringing the individual to Egypt through existing merchant networks.

There is a difficulty about the instance when a 'brother' relationship between two *mamlūks* is referred to, because *ukhuwwa*, sometimes linked with 'long friendship' (*al-ṣuḥba al-qadīma*), was undoubtedly used to denote a comradely 'brotherhood' relationship established between two *mamlūks* rather than a biological one. That seems to have been the case with the two amirs Aytamish al-Muḥammadī and Aruqṭāy al-Jamdār, because al-Yūsufī explicitly tells us that their brotherhood was an acquired relationship, although it was close enough for the sultan to prevent one of them from going to Syria when the other was viceroy of Ṣafad, a security measure presumably.[28] On the other hand, Bahādur, a *mamlūk* of the viceregent al-Afram, inherited from an amir of Damascus, Bahādur Samīr al-Manṣūrī (d. 704/1304–5), because he had previously been recognised as his full brother (*shaqīq*).[29] When the amir Quṭlūbughā al-Kūkā'ī died in 785/1383, his nephew (*ibn akhīhi*), Yallū, who had sought out his uncle when he rose to prominence and himself became amir of one hundred and *nā'ib* of Ḥamā, inherited his large fortune. There was no surprise that he resigned soon afterwards and built himself a fine residence in Damascus. He was also a relative (*qarīb*) of the *ḥājib* in Damascus, Amir Ṭurunṭāy.[30] These consanguineal ties affecting first generation *mamlūks* and the many affinitive ones, established by the network of marriages which it would be most interesting to document, cut across the other group and client relationships of the Mamluk elite, and I mention them here to provide a context for the more significant continuities created by the descendants of *mamlūk* amirs.

I would like to draw attention to the surprising stability of certain families established by *mamlūk* amirs. It is 'surprising', perhaps, because one's first

25 *Durar*, vol. II, 314.
26 See R. Burgoyne and D. S. Richards, *Mamluk Jerusalem. An Architectural Study* (London, 1987), 401 and refs. there cited.
27 *Tārīkh Ibn Qāḍī Shuhba*, vol. I, 565.
28 *Nuzha*, 287–8, 329. Aytamish left no issue, and al-Nāṣir Muḥammad allowed Aruqṭāy to inherit from him (ibid., 333).
29 *Durar*, vol. II, 31.
30 *Tārīkh Ibn Qāḍī Shuhba*, vol. I, 154.

thought is of the instability, both political and social, that colours one's picture of the Mamluk state. One should note, as somewhat comparable cases, the continuing firm social position of certain members of the Ayyubid house. Ghiyāth al-dīn Muḥammad of the Baalbak branch, who died in 693/1294, 'had enough to satisfy him from his *waqf*', and al-Muʿaẓẓam ʿĪsā of the Ḥimṣ branch (d. 719/1319) 'possessed properties which supported him'.[31] Other members of the Homs branch of the Ayyubids are recorded as still holding amiral rank into the fourteenth century. There was al-Awḥad Shādī b. Dāwūd b. Shīrkūh (d. 705/1305–6), who had been made an amir by Kitbughā and who ran affairs for the *nā'ib* of Damascus, Āqūsh al-Afram, and al-Awḥad's son, Ṣalāḥ al-dīn Yūsuf, an amir of forty, who died in 741/1340–1 and had been 'an overseer of many *waqfs*', and ʿAlī b. Yūsuf b. al-Awḥad, an amir of ten who died young in 757/1356.[32]

The great amirs gained large fortunes from the *iqṭāʿs* which were theirs by virtue of their position and function. In addition it is clear that many added to their wealth by investing in urban development, apart from the fine palaces that they built or extended for their own use. If they were fortunate, this property, amortized as charitable trusts (*waqfs*), continued to benefit their descendants. This was especially the case in the reign of al-Nāṣir Muḥammad when there was much building and development activity. The amirs grew rich on the rents of the blocks of housing, the shops and the markets that were created. Maqrīzī records much development on land towards the Nile, to the west and south-west of al-Qāhira, which was extensively built upon, although André Raymond – in his contribution to this volume – has cast doubt on the extent of these developments, basing his argument on the lack of any significant settlement there by the ruling elite. Early on, in the sultanate of al-Muʿizz Aybak, his brother-in-law, the amir Ildūd al-Jashnikīrī, had constructed a bath-house outside Bāb Zuwayla, which remained a *waqf* for his descendants, in this case via his daughters, until the time of Maqrīzī.[33] Another bath, known as Ḥammām Quṭlugh, passed to the heirs of amir Quṭlūbughā, *ḥājib* in the reign of al-Ashraf Shaʿbān, but fell into ruin after 790/1388.[34] The Cairo residence of the amir Mankūtamur was, according to Maqrīzī, 'a *waqf*, lived in until today by some of his descendants'.[35] The amir Baktamur al-Ḥājib developed land in the Arḍ al-Ṭabbāla, which his son, Muḥammad, and then his grandchildren, ʿAbd al-Raḥmān and ʿAlī, continued to own until the time when Maqrīzī was writing. As the latter says, 'This "house" still possessed its emiral rank and its wealth'.[36] Another example of long enjoyment of a property, expressly through the provisions of a *waqf*, involves the Qayṣariyyat al-ʿUṣfūr, which the amir ʿAlam al-dīn Sanjar al-Manṣūrī built in 692/1293. His heirs

[31] *Tālī*, nos. 247 and 326. See other cases of persons living off *waqfs*: 'From the *waqfs* of his father he had enough to satisfy him' (no. 294); 'He had properties and *waqfs* from his ancestors, the income from which contented him' (no. 343); and 'Content with what he along with his brothers had from the *waqf*' (no. 352).

[32] *Durar*, vol. III, 216; vol. II, 281; vol. V, 332–3; *Tālī*, no. 134.

[33] *Khiṭaṭ*, vol. II, 85.

[34] Ibid., vol. II, 83.

[35] Ibid., vol. II, 52.

[36] Ibid., vol. II, 64.

continued to benefit from it until the early years of the fifteenth century.[37] The amir Baybars al-Aḥmadī (d. 746/1345–6) had a fine house in the Bahā' al-dīn district of al-Qāhira in which his descendants still resided in Maqrīzī's time,[38] and Aḥmad b. Ālmalik al-Jūkandār, himself an amir, 'lived off the income of his father's *waqfs*'.[39] There is one remarkable case of family continuity, which started in the reign of al-Nāṣir Muḥammad. This is the family of the amir Manjak (d. 776/1374–5), whose descendants, centred in Damascus, continued to hold the rank of amir and to enjoy their extensive *waqfs* well into the Ottoman period, until late in the seventeenth century.[40] Much of this lengthy enjoyment of family wealth, but obviously not all, was interrupted early in the fifteenth century by the great upheavals of that time, external and internal, by the decay of much property and by the seizure and dissolution of many *waqfs*. This, at least, is the picture painted by Maqrīzī, who does not cease to lament the 'disasters' and 'trials' of his times.

Often one finds in the sources the provision of *iqṭā*ʿ*s* and amirates for senior amirs' sons when they are still very young. For example, when Barqūq was *amīr kabīr* in 782/1380, the amirate of one hundred, taken from Baraka after his arrest, was given to Barqūq's son with a full complement of *mamlūks* and a staff of clerks, and this when the child was only one month old.[41] This is to some extent a simple abuse of power, and it is comparable with the steps taken for the benefit of brothers and other family members. Such attempts to look after one's own were not infrequently of short duration and without great effect. But the failures, when they occurred, were the result of factional and personal differences, the ups and downs of politics, to which the careers of all, *mamlūks* and non-*mamlūks* alike, were subject. They can in no way be said to have been automatic, for a good number of them did succeed and a certain continuity was established.

It would be wrong to overstate the case. The *mamlūk* amirs generally held the highest positions because of the advantages of their closeness to the sultan, but they did not have the monopoly of high rank and the associated *iqṭā*ʿ resources. In an appendix to this chapter there are listed 193 individuals who may be identified as *awlād al-nās*. Of these, thirty-four held amirates of one hundred, the highest military rank; three held amirates of fifty, and there are fifty-one amirs of forty, five amirs of twenty and forty-five amirs of ten. That leaves fifty-five whose rank and status remain unclear. Incidentally, there were also a number of persons who had no base of descent from any *mamlūk* amiral family, yet who rose to office and amiral rank, sometimes from the most humble origins. These instances of social mobility are also important to note.

A 'snapshot' taken at one moment gives some interesting data. In 791/1389, soon after the victory of Yalbughā and the restoration of al-Manṣūr Ḥājjī, that is, after the first reign of Barqūq, a number of amirs were arrested in Cairo. Of

37 Ibid., vol. II, 89. 38 Ibid., vol. II, 52.
39 *Tārīkh Ibn Qāḍī Shuhba*, vol. I, 392.
40 See Burgoyne and Richards, *Mamluk Jerusalem*, 387.
41 *Tārīkh Ibn Qāḍī Shuhba*, vol. I, 26 and 567.

the amirs of a hundred (nine altogether), six were *mamlūks* and three were not. Of thirty-five amirs of forty, a high proportion (twenty-seven) appear to have been *mamlūks*[42] and only eight non-*mamlūks*. However, of the thirty-seven amirs of ten, seventeen were *mamlūks* and twenty non-*mamlūks*. For what the statistics are worth, that makes a total of eighty-one, of whom fifty were *mamlūks*. Roughly 38 per cent of the whole were non-*mamlūks*.[43]

From the details in the appendix it will be seen that several held an office of *nā'ib* in Egypt, in, for example, Alexandria, Damietta, Gaza, and in the North and South Districts (al-Wajh al-Baḥrī and al-Wajh al-Qiblī). In Syria, more than one held the office in each of the important centres, Damascus, Aleppo, Homs, Ḥamā, Baalbak, and also in lesser towns, Karak, Ṣafad, Jerusalem, Nablus and Raḥba. Others held local governorships throughout Egypt – in, for example, Aswān, Fayyūm, the Delta provinces – and the posts of prefect in al-Qāhira and Fusṭāṭ. These *wilāyāt* were at the base of the pyramid of Mamluk administration, but none the less significant for all that. All this hardly suggests that the *awlād al-nās* 'were excluded from important positions in the state'.

Perhaps at times there is a tendency to confuse the *mamlūk* element with the Mamluk state as a whole. Here a distinction has just been made that is totally lost when speaking. Throughout this piece I have used *mamlūk* to denote an individual who has that legal and social status and distinguished it from the adjective Mamluk (with a capital 'M' and without italics), which is used to describe the totality of the state, society and culture etc. This distinction is frequently not observed, and its reality not borne in mind. The sons, and further descendants, of amirs, non-*mamlūks*, were most certainly part of Mamluk society and played significant roles in it, even in the military and governmental spheres. It is highly possible that this is especially true of Syria, although the knowledge of what went on in the various provincial centres there is less than one would desire.

APPENDIX

Here is an illustrative list, with no pretensions to completeness, of amirs from the *awlād al-nās*, largely from the fourteenth century.

Amirs of one hundred

ʿAbdallāh Jamāl al-dīn b. Baktimur Sayf al-dīn *al-Ḥājib* (d. 786/1384) *ḥājib (thālith)* (*Khiṭaṭ*, vol. II, pp. 64, 77, 125–6; *Sulūk*, vol. II, 563; *Tārīkh Ibn Qāḍī Shuhba*, vol. I, pp. 29, 144 – *tarjama*). See Halm, *Ägypten*, 127, 511. In 742/1341–2 he was given the *iqṭāʿ* of his brother Muḥammad (q.v.) when latter arrested. Continued to hold father's

[42] Unless clear evidence is available, one should always say 'appear to be' since it is far from true that all bearing Turkish names were necessarily first-generation *mamlūks*. Conversely some persons with 'Islamic' names are expressly described as *mamlūks*.

[43] *Sulūk*, vol. III, 624 ff.

property (see *Khiṭaṭ*). Appointed *ḥājib thālith* in 782/1380. See son, Muḥammad. When Aynabak was *atabak*, he was appointed amir of one hundred and *ḥājib thānī*, then lost those positions. At end of career was *kāshif* of al-Gharbiyya, became ill there, was brought to Cairo in a litter, died, and was buried in his father's *turba*.

Abū Bakr b. Arghūn al-nāʾib (*Tārīkh al-Malik*, pp. 56, 99). Took the amirate of one hundred of Burlughī, the amīr silāḥ, in 742/1341–2. One of three amirs of one hundred to lead troops in tax collecting in provinces.

Abū Bakr Sayf al-dīn (Ibn al-Mushrif) b. Sunqur al-Jamālī (d. 803/1400–1) (Ibn al-Furāt, *Tārīkh*, eds. C. K. Zurayk and N. Izzeddin (Beirut, 1936 and 1938), vol. IX (parts I and II), index; al-Ṣayrafi, *Nuzhat al-nufūs wa-ʾl-abdān fī tawārīkh al-zamān*, ed. Ḥasan Ḥabashi, (Cairo, 1970) (hereafter *Nuzhat al-nufūs*), vol. I, 105, 131 – *tarjama;* al-Sakhāwī, *al-Ḍawʾ al-lāmiʿ* (Cairo, 1355/1936–7) (hereafter *al-Dawʾ*) vol. IX, 36; *Tārīkh Ibn Qāḍī Shuhba*, vol. I, 138 (see index); Halm, *Ägypten*, 124, 337). Given *taqdima* of his uncle (*ʿamm*) Bahādūr al-Jamālī in 786/1384, and made *amīr al-ḥājj*. Created *ḥājib* and amır of one hundred in 790/1388, and *amīr al-maḥmal* in 794/1391–2. Still *ḥājib* in 799/1396–7.

Aḥmad b. Baktimur al-Sāqī (b. 713/1313–14, d. 733/1332–3) (*Durar*, vol. I, 123; *Sulūk*, vol. II, 289, 364–5; Shāfiʿ ibn ʿAlī al-Ṣafadī, *al-Wāfī bi ʾl wafayāt*, ed. Wadād al-Qāḍī (Beirut/Stuttgart, 1982), 29 vols. (hereafter *al-Wāfī*), vol. VI, 26–7.) He was close to al-Nāṣir Muḥammad when young. Married Qutlūmalik bint Tankiz in 727/1327. Died on return from *ḥajj* with al-Nāṣir in 733/1332. Father's *tarjama* in *Durar*, vol. II, 19–20.

Aḥmad Shihāb al-dīn b. Yalbughā al-ʿUmarī al-Khāṣṣakī (d. 802/1400) *amīr majlis* (Ibn Taghrībirdī, *al-Nujūm al-zāhira fī mulūk Miṣr wa-ʾl-Qāhira*, 16 vols., (Cairo, [1963] – 1972), vol. XIII, 14; Ibn al-Furāt, *Tārīkh*, vol. IX, index; *al-Dawʾ*, vol. II, 246; *Nuzhat al-nufūs*, vol. II, 65–6; *Tārīkh Ibn Qāḍī Shuhba*, vol. I, 616; Halm, *Ägypten*, 83, 108, 143, 161). Banished to Syria, *baṭṭāl* in Tripoli, and executed. Age at death 'gone 40'.

Aḥmad Shihāb al-dīn (Abū'l-ʿAbbās) b. Āl-Malik al-Jūkāndār al-Ḥājj (d. 793/1391) *wālī, nāʾib, ḥājib* (*Durar*, vol. I, 116; Ibn al-Furāt, *Tārikh*, vol. IX, 275–6 – *tarjama; Tārīkh Ibn Qāḍī Shuhba*, vol. I, 392. Halm, *Ägypten*, 70, 401, 607(?), 760). Made amir of forty by al-Nāṣir Muḥammad, amir of one hundred by al-Nāṣir Ḥasan. In 775/1373–4 Shaʿbān appointed him *nāʾib* of Gaza. Later he was amir of forty in Egypt, and *ḥājib*. Resigned in 779/1377–8, became wandering *ʿālim*, and *mujāwir* in Mecca. 'He lived from the income of his father's waqfs'. He was an associate of Ibn al-Furāt.

Albakī *ibn akhī* Āl-Malik (d. 756/1355), *nā'ib* of Gaza (*Durar*, vol. I, 432).

ʿAlī ʿAlāʾ al-dīn b. Qarāsunqur (d. 748/1347–8) (*Durar*, vol. III, 169; *Tārīkh al-Malik*, 44, 47; *Sulūk*, vol. II, 109, 305). Late 711/1311–12 was in Egypt with his brother Faraj (q.v.). His father died in Mongol lands in 728/1327–8. He left Cairo for Damascus (received *ṭablkhāna* there) in 729/1329, and was advanced by Tankiz. Joined Quṭlūbughā al-Fakhrī against Qawṣūn in 742/1341–2.

ʿAlī ʿAlāʾ al-dīn (known as al-Wazīr) b. Qashtamur Sayf al-dīn al-Nāṣiri al-Turkī (d. 783/1381–2) (*Durar*, vol. III, 169; *Tārīkh Ibn Qāḍī Shuhba*, vol. I, 74–*tarjama*). His father was amir of one hundred, *ḥājib* and *nāʾib* in various places, including Aleppo and Damascus. He himself was *nāʾib* in al-Karak, then Alexandria. Appointed amir of one hundred in Egypt and *ḥājib thānī*. He was also learned in several branches of knowledge. See son Ḥasan.

Amīr ʿAlī ʿAlāʾ al-dīn b. Tughril al-Abghāʾī [or al-ghānī] (d. 749/1348–9) *ḥājib* in Damascus, then moved to Egypt as amir (*Durar*, vol. III, 127; *Tārīkh al-Malik*, 48; *Sulūk*, vol. II, 498, 738–9, 795). In 740/1339–40 and 742/1341–2 he was amir of forty in Cairo. He was involved in Yalbughā's politics. In 748/1347–8 replaced as *ḥājib* in Damascus and returned to Cairo.

Amīr Ḥājj Zayn al-dīn b. Mughulṭāy ('Alā' al-dīn) (d. 801/1398–9) *nā'ib, ḥājib thānī, ustādār* (*al-Ḍaw'*, vol. II, 322; Ibn al-Furāt, *Tārīkh*, vol. IX, 21, 140, 143, 160, 259; *Nuzhat al-nufūs*, vol. I, index, vol. II, 30; *Tārīkh Ibn Qāḍī Shuhba*, vol. I, 328, 378; Halm, *Ägypten*, 134, 351, 597, 701, 775). Born 'with a silver spoon'. Appointed *nā'ib* of Alexandria in 789/1387–8. Transferred to Cairo as amir of one hundred in 791/1388, and made *ḥājib (thānī)* later same year, then *ustādār*. Arrested by Minṭāsh 792/1390. Banished to Qūṣ in 793/1391, but sent to Damietta instead, where he died.

Asanbughā b. Baktimur al-Abūbakrī (d. 777/1375–6) *nā'ib* of Aleppo, *amīr kabīr* (*Durar*, vol. I, 412 (for his father see *Durar*, vol. II, p. 15); *Tārīkh al-Malik*, 50; *Sulūk*, vol. II, 603). Arrested after death of al-Nāṣir Muḥammad, but released under al-Ṣāliḥ Ismā'īl. According to al-Shujā'ī (*Tārīkh al-Malik*, 59) he was an amir in Alṭunbughā's army in 742/1341–2. He built al-Būbakriyya near the slave market in al-Wazīriyya. Aged over seventy at death. See brother 'Alī.

Asandamur Sayf al-dīn b. Ya'qūb Shāh al-Sharafī (d. 793/1390) *amīr majlis* (Ibn al-Furāt, *Tārīkh*, vol. IX, index; *Nuzhat al-nufūs*, vol. I, 326). He rebelled with Minṭāsh in late 789/1387, was made amir of one hundred in Egypt 791/1389, and later that year appointed *amīr majlis*, and sent on expedition to Upper Egypt by Minṭāsh. Defeated rebels against Minṭāsh. (Cf. 'Umar b. Ya'qūb Shāh?). Blinded and executed in 793/1391.

Faraj Zayn al-dīn b. Aydamur 'Izz al-dīn al-Sayfī Bābaq (or Yāyiq) (d. 798/1395–6) (*Nuzhat al-nufūs*, vol. I, 105, 248; Ibn al-Furāt, *Tārīkh*, vol. IX, 136, 384; *Tārīkh Ibn Qāḍī Shuhba*, vol. I, 598 – *tarjama*). Replaced as *wālī al-Gharbiyya* in 786/1384 by Muḥammad b. Ṭājār, and replaced again in same office by 'Umar b. al-Khaṭṭāb in 791/1389, moved to *kāshif al-Wajh al-Baḥrī*. In 796/1393–4 *wālī al-Gharbiyya* once again. After other *wilāyāt* appointments he was *nā'ib al-wajh al-baḥrī*, then in 797/1394–95 moved to be *nā'ib al-Wajh al-Qiblī*, and became amir of one hundred.

Ḥusayn Sharaf al-dīn b. Abī Bakr b. Ismā'īl b. Jandar Bak al-Rūmī (d. 729) *amīr shikār, ra's al-maymana wa'l-maysara* (*Durar*, vol. II, 137–8; *Khiṭaṭ*, vol. II, 47, 147; *Sulūk*, vol. II, 313–14. Intimate portrait in al-Wāfī, vol. XII, no. 326). His father was Seljuq amir (came in 675/1276–7). He was made amir by Lājīn, and joined al-Nāṣir after his second spell in al-Karak. Chequered career with Tankiz. Spent two-and-a-half years *baṭṭāl* in Ṣafad. Built *jāmi'* and *qanṭara* on canal in Cairo. Repaired the White Mosque and minaret at Ramla. *Iqṭā's* in *ḥalqa* given by al-Nāṣir to his *mamlūks* and *rawātib* to his mother and two daughters. He had a brother called Muẓaffar al-dīn (al-Wāfī, vol. XII, 349).

Khalīl Ṣalāḥ al-dīn b. Muḥammad b. 'Ārrām (d. 782/1380–1), *shādd, nā'ib* in Alexandria, *wazīr* (Ibn al-Furāt; *Tārīkh*, vol. IX, 140. Halm, *Ägypten*, 161, 399, 404, 610, 772).

Khalīl Ṣalāḥ al-dīn b. Sanjar (d. 791/1389) (Ibn al-Furāt, *Tārīkh*, vol. IX, 54; *Tārīkh Ibn Qāḍī Shuhba*, vol. I, 264). Killed in 791/1389 along with *nā'ib* of Tripoli by rebels against Barqūq. His son (amir of forty in Tripoli) was also killed.

Maḥmūd Najm al-dīn b. 'Alī b. Sharwān (or Sharwīn) (*Tārīkh al-Malik*, 9; *Sulūk*, vol. II, 563). Known as *wazīr Baghdād*. Appointed *wazīr* in 742/1341–2.

Malik or Amīr Malik b. Ṭāz (d. 793/1391) *nā'ib* of Raḥba (Ibn al-Furāt, *Tārīkh*, vol. IX, 115, 278; *Nuzhat al-nufūs*, 327. *Tārīkh Ibn Qāḍī Shuhba*, vol. I, 329–30, 397–8). *Ibn ukht* or *ibn akhī* of Jantimur Sayf al-dīn, his uncle (*nā'ib al-Shām* for Minṭāsh), called

Jardamur, but known commonly as Jantimur. He himself was appointed *nā'ib* of Raḥba in 791/1389 with an amirate of one hundred. Arrested by Minṭāsh in 792/1390 along with his uncle and cousin (Jarbughā). Executed at Cairo.

Muḥammad b. Minṭāsh (*Tārīkh Ibn Qāḍī Shuhba*, vol. I, pp. 288, 301). He was made amir of one hundred by his father in 791/1389. His father in preparation for an expedition the same year 'gave *nafaqa* to his *mamlūks* and to the *mamlūks* of his son Muḥammad'.

Muḥammad Nāṣir al-dīn b. al-Mihmāndār al-Ḥalabī (d. 793/1391) (Ibn al-Furāt, *Tārīkh*, vol. IX, p. 292).

Muḥammad Nāṣir al-dīn b. ʿAlī b. Uljaybughā al-ʿĀdilī (d. 781/1379–80) *ḥājib, nā'ib* of Gaza (*Tārīkh Ibn Qāḍī Shuhba*, vol. I, 19 – (*tarjama*). He was expert in *furūsiyya* and polo. Held amirate of forty 'for long time'. Became *ḥājib* in 776/1374. In 777/1375 became amir of one hundred, then "*nā'ib* of Emir Barqūq'. In same year he became *nā'ib* of Gaza (unwillingly) – fell ill, retired and died. Buried in grandfather's *turba* outside Jābiya gate (Damascus).

Muḥammad Nāṣir al-dīn b. Baktāsh (Badr al-dīn) al-Fakhrī (*amīr ṣilāḥ*) (d. 724/1324) (*Durar*, vol. II, 14–15; *Sulūk*, vol. II, 258). During illness of father requested al-Nāṣir Muḥammad for succession to emirate – allowed.

Muḥammad Nāṣir al-dīn b. Balabān al-Mihmāndār (d. 792/1390), *nā'ib* of Aleppo citadel (Ibn al-Furāt, *Tārīkh*, vol. IX, 211, & 236, *Tārīkh Ibn Qāḍī Shuhba*; vol. I, 363; *Durar*, vol. IV, 17). Rebelled with Yalbughā al-Nāṣiri. Dismissed from Aleppo post by Barqūq. Executed in Damascus by Minṭāsh. His sons, Muḥammad and Aḥmad, arrested with others by Yalbughā in Aleppo in 791/1389 (Ibn al-Furāt, *Tārīkh*, vol. IX, 53). Very rich. Brother of Ḥusām al-dīn?

Muḥammad Nāṣir al-dīn b. Mubārak, *nā'ib* of al-Karak (Ibn al-Furāt, *Tārīkh*, vol. IX, 433, 462). *Mamlūk* of his brought gift to sultan in 798/1396. Described as *ḥafīd* of Ibn al-Mihmāndār. He had trouble with inhabitants of al-Karak, and was transferred to Gaza as *baṭṭāl*.

Muḥammad Nāṣir al-dīn b. Ṭashtimur al-Badrī al-Nāṣiri (Ḥummuṣ Akhḍar) (*Tārīkh al-Malik*, 90, 93, 95; *Sulūk*, vol. II, 606). In 742/1342 given amirate of 100 and fief of Baybars al-Aḥmadī. His young brother given amirate of fifty and fief of Arghūn Shāh. Soon arrested with father in same year.

Muḥammad Nāṣir al-dīn b. Timurbughā Minṭāsh (Ibn al-Furāt, *Tārīkh*, vol. IX, 134, 165), made amir of one hundred in 791/1389.

Muḥammad Nāṣir al-dīn b. Ṭurunṭāy Ḥusām al-dīn al-Manṣūrī (d. 731/1330–1) (*Sulūk*, vol. II, 338; *Tālī*, no. 139; *Durar*, vol. IV, 79). One of two sons of the *nā'ib* of Egypt (d. 689/1290). He was blind and appeared before al-Ashraf Khalīl after his father's death and pleaded poverty. The sultan had pity and ordered release of their property (see brother ʿAlī).

Mūsā Muẓaffar al-dīn b. Ruqṭāy al-Ḥājj (d. 762/1360–1), *nā'ib* of Ṣafad (*Durar*, vol. V, 146: 'grew up in the lap of fortune').

Taliktimur Sayf al-dīn (or Maliktimur) b. Barka b. ʿAbdallāh al-Turkī (d. 794/1391–92), *ra's nawba kabīr*, *amīr majlis, ustādār*, *nā'ib* of Ṣafad, *ḥājib* (Ibn al-Furāt, *Tārīkh*, vol. IX, 319). Career between about 769 and 775/1367 and 1374. Ill, retired *baṭṭāl* in Cairo. Given a village in Daqahliyya by Barqūq – held until his death.

ʿUmar Rukn al-dīn b. Manjak (d. 800/1397–8) (*Tārīkh Ibn Qāḍī Shuhba*, vol. I, 132, 680). Given amirate of forty in Syria, and then his brother Ibrāhīm's amirate of one hundred after latter's death (in 793/1391). (A *mamlūk* of ʿUmar's given amirate of ten

which had been his half-brother Faraj's.) His sister (Fāṭima?) was wife of Sultan Barqūq.
ʿUmar Zayn al-dīn b. Arghūn *al-nāʾib* (d. 773/1371–2), *nāʾib* of al-Karak and Ṣafad (*Durar*, vol. III, 229; *Nuzha*, 235–6; *Sulūk*, vol. II, 338, 378). His father was *nāʾib al-salṭana*. Made amir of forty in 731/1330–1. Student of *ḥadīth*. He held the Cairo Citadel in the Yalbughā affair.
ʿUmar [Rukn al-dīn] b. Qilij al-Turkī, *kāshif al-wajh al-qiblī*, *wālī* and *kāshif* of Fayyūm, *nāʾib al-Wajh al-Qiblī* (Ibn al-Furāt, *Tārīkh*, vol. IX, 42). His son and successor in post, Aḥmad, died in 790/1388. See his brother Abū Bakr.

Amirs of fifty

Ibn Ṭashtimur al-Badrī al-Nāṣirī (Ḥummuṣ Akhḍar) (*Tārīkh al-Malik*, 90, 95).
In 742/1342 he was given an amirate of fifty and the *iqṭāʿ* of Arghūn Shāh, but was arrested with his father later that year. Father (d. 743/1342–43) (*Durar*, vol. II, 320) fled to Rūm. See his brother Muḥammad.
Muḥammad Nāṣir al-dīn b. Sunqur al-Bajkarī (al-Bakjarī) (d. 809/1406) (*Tārīkh Ibn Qāḍī Shuhba*, vol. I, 665; Ibn Taghrībirdī, *Nujūm*, (Cairo), vol. XII, 305, vol. XIII, 165; *Sulūk*, vol. III, 908, vol. IV, 49). He was *ustādār* of Amir Qalmaṭāy. In 800/1397–8 he was made *ustādār* of the sultan and given an amirate of fifty. Died in Aleppo. See *Nujūm,* ibid.: *'bayt Ibn Sunqur bayt maʿrūf bi'l-riyāsa wa'l-taḥashshum'*.
Ṭāmghāz b. Sunqur al-Ashqar (d. 731/1330–1) (*Durar*, vol. II, 316). Born in Mongol lands, he came to Cairo and was given an amirate. His brother Ibrāhīm came as envoy of Abū Saʿīd a little before death of Ṭāmghāz.

Amirs of forty

Ibn Aslam Shihāb al-dīn or Bahā' al-dīn (*Tārīkh al-Malik*, 23, 44). In 742/1341 made amir of forty. His father was *nāʾib* of Ṣafad.
Ibn Khalīl b. Sanjar (d. 791/1389) (Ibn al-Furāt, *Tārīkh*, vol. IX, 54; *Tārīkh Ibn Qāḍī Shuhba*, vol. I, 264). Killed by rebels along with his father.
Nāṣir al-dīn b. Bahādur (d. 791/1389) (*Tārīkh Ibn Qāḍī Shuhba*, vol. I, 9, 310), *wālī al-wulāt* 'several times' and *nāʾib* of Jerusalem . In 781/1379–80 dismissed as *wālī al-wulāt*, and imprisoned. Killed in 791/1389 in battle against Barqūq at Shaqḥab.
ʿAbd al-Raḥīm Zayn al-dīn b. Manklī Bughā al-Shamsī, *amīr al-maḥmal* (Ibn al-Furāt, *Tārīkh*, vol. IX, 97, 100, 115, 134, 234, 238; *Tārīkh Ibn Qāḍī Shuhba*, vol. I, 347; Halm, *Ägypten*, 81). Arrested in 791/1389 and sent to Alexandria, then *baṭṭāl* in Cairo; given amirate of forty late in 791/1389. In 792/1389–90 he was *amīr al-rakb al-Miṣrī* (with others in charge of *kiswa* prepared by ʿĀ'isha, sister of Barqūq). He was *sibṭ* of Sultan al-Nāṣir Muḥammad b. Qalāwūn. See brother ʿAbd al-Raḥmān.
ʿAbdallāh Jamāl al-dīn b. Baktimur Sayf al-dīn al-Ḥājib (d. 786/1384), *ḥājib thālith* (*Khiṭaṭ*, vol. II, 64, 77, 125–6; *Sulūk*, vol. II, 563; *Tārīkh Ibn Qāḍī Shuhba*, vol. I, 29, 144 *tarjama*. See Halm, *Ägypten*, 27, 511). In 742/1341–2 he was given *iqṭāʿ* of his brother Muḥammad (q.v.) when latter arrested. Continued to hold father's property (see *Khiṭaṭ*). Appointed *ḥājib thālith* in 782/1380. According to Ibn Qāḍī Shuhba he became amir of forty and *amīr shikār*, and several times *ḥājib*. When Aynabak was *atabak*, he was appointed Amir of one hundred and *ḥājib thānī*, but then lost those positions. At end of career he was *kāshif al-Gharbiyya*, became ill there,

was brought to Cairo in litter and died, buried in father's *turba*. See son, Muḥammad.
Aḥmad b. Āqtimur ʿAbd al-Ghanī (Ibn Taghrībirdī, *Nujūm* (Cairo), vol. XI, 54; Halm, *Ägypten*, 86, 127, 348). Given *ṭablkhāna* amirate in 764/1362–3. See brother ʿAlī.
Aḥmad (Amīr Aḥmad) b. Aydughmish (ʿAlāʾ al-dīn) (*Tārīkh al-Malik*, 20, 37, 77, 84, 96; Ibn al-Furāt, *Tārīkh*, vol. IX, 279, n.1). He was the last amir created by al-Nāṣir Muḥammad (amir of forty in 741/1340). He served as *amīr al-ḥājj*. Aydughmish (*Durar*, vol. I, 455–7) was *amīr ākhūr* and *nāʾib* of Aleppo at the end of 742/1341. His four sons were amirs.
ʿAlī b. Aydamur ʿIzz al-dīn al-Khaṭīrī (d. 762/1360–1) (*Durar*, vol. III, 98). His father was *amīr jāndār*. He himself was brought up in Cairo and came to Damascus as amir in 760/1359. Note his additions to his father's *waqf* (*Nuzha*, 385).
ʿAlī b. Kitbughā (*Tārīkh al-Malik*, 27). One of five amirs of forty created in Rabīʿ II 742/September 1341.
ʿAlī b. Aqtimur ʿAbd al-Ghanī (Ibn al-Furāt: *Tārīkh*, vol. IX, 100). Arrested and released in 791/1389. See brother Aḥmad.
ʿAlī ʿAlāʾ al-dīn b. Aruqṭāy al-Nāṣiri (d. 750/1349–50) (*Durar*, vol. III, 91; *Tārīkh al-Malik*, 73). Made amir while young by Tankiz. His father was *nāʾib* in Ṣafad, Tripoli, Homs, Aleppo and Cairo (*Durar*, vol. I, 376). Arrested by Aydughmish with father as follower of Qawṣūn in 742/1341–42.
ʿAlī ʿAlāʾ al-dīn b. Manjak al-Yūsufī (d. 788/1386) (*Tārīkh Ibn Qāḍī Shuhba*, vol. I, 210 – *tarjama*; Ibn Taghrībirdī, *Nujūm*, (Cairo), vol. XI, 71; Halm, *Ägypten*, 710). He went on *ḥajj* with al-Ashraf, and held an amirate of forty from 778/1376–7 until his death.
ʿAlī ʿAlāʾ al-dīn b. Qarāsunqur (d. 748/1347–8) (*Durar,* vol. III, 169; *Tārīkh al-Malik*, 44, 47; *Sulūk*, vol. II, 109, 305). In 711/1311–12 was in Egypt with brother Faraj (q.v.). Father died in Mongol lands in 728/1327–8. He left Cairo for Damascus (holding *ṭablkhāna* there) in 729/1329. Promoted by Tankiz, he later joined Quṭlūbughā al-Fakhrī to oppose Qawṣūn in 742/1342–2.
ʿAlī ʿAlāʾ al-dīn b. Ughurlū al-ʿĀdilī (d. 749/1348) (*Durar*, vol. III, 98). His father was *nāʾib al-Shām* under Kitbughā.
Faraj b. Qarāsunqur Shams al-dīn al-Manṣūrī (d. 734/1333–4) (*Durar*, vol. III, 312; *Sulūk*, vol. II, 109, 287, 305). When his father left Aleppo, Faraj was sent to Egypt with money (711/1312), and made amir of ten. Sent from Egypt to Damascus as amir of ten after father's death in 728/1327–8. Imprisoned in 727/1326–7. See brother ʿAlī.
Ibrāhīm Ṣārim al-dīn b. Quṭlū Aqtimur al-ʿAlāʾī (or b. Quṭluqtimur) (d. 791/1389) (*Sulūk*, vol. III, index; *Tārīkh Ibn Qāḍī Shuhba*, vol. I, 304 – *tarjama*. In 778/1376–7 made amir of forty; 785/1383–4 in plot to kill Barqūq – blinded(?). Same year released (intercession of his father, the amir Jandar) and promised *rizq*. In 791/1389 made amir of one hundred and *amīr majlis* by Minṭāsh, but arrested. Same year killed by *nāʾib* of Aleppo.
Ibrāhīm Ṣārim al-dīn b. Ṭashtimur Sayf al-dīn al-ʿAlāʾī, *dawādār* (d. 795/1392–3) (Ibn al-Furāt, *Tārīkh*, vol. IX, (index), 352; *Tārīkh Ibn Qāḍī Shuhba*, vol. I, 480; *Nuzhat al-nufūs*, vol. I, 368; *Sulūk*, vol. III, 601, 625, 653, 792). His father (see *Durar*, vol. II, 321) died 784/1382–3 (according to *Sulūk*. vol. III, 528–9; in 786/1384), and he had been *atabak al-ʿasākir* and *nāʾib al-Shām*. While father was alive he held an amirate, afterwards amir of ten. Made and remade amir of forty in 791/1389. Same year arrested with others by Yalbughā, soon released.
Jaraktimur Nāṣir al-dīn b. Bahādūr (*raʾs nawba*) (d. 742/1341–4) (*Durar*, vol. II, 70–1; *Tārīkh al-Malik*, 27, 73; *Sulūk*, vol. II, 499). He joined Baybars II after his father was

killed. Made amir in 708/1309. A son of his died after expedition to Sīs in 737/1336–7 (*Nuzha*, 416). He was one of the amirs sent to arrest Tankiz in 740/1340. Sent to Qūṣ in 742/1341–2. After fall of Qawṣūn that year he was arrested. Both his sons were amirs of forty. He was son-in-law of Qarāsunqur (*Durar*, vol. II, 70). A son of his aged twelve arrested 'to please mother of al-Manṣūr Abū Bakr' (*Sulūk*, vol. II, 598).

Khalīl b. ʿAlī b. Salār (d. 770/1368–9), *nāẓir* of Salār's *awqāf* (*Durar*, vol. II, 179; *Tārīkh al-Malik*, p. 36). See father, Amīr ʿAlī, whose amirate was given to this son.

Khalīl b. Aribughā (Ibn al-Furāt, *Tārīkh*, vol. IX, 164). Imprisoned in Citadel in 791/1389.

Khalīl b. Tankizbughā (Ibn al-Furāt, *Tārīkh*, vol. IX, 97; Ibn Taghrībirdī, *Nujūm* (Cairo), vol. XI, 321; Halm, *Ägypten*, 78, 105, 124, 181, 263, 267, 623). Given *ṭablkhāna* in 790/1388. In list of amirs arrested 791/1389 and later released. (Cf. Khalīl b. Dankiz, amir of ten, d. 803/1400–1 (*al-Ḍawʾ*. vol. II, 194.)

Khalīl Ṣalāḥ al-dīn b. Qawṣūn (d. 778/1376–7) (*Sulūk*, vol. II, 767, vol. III, 150–3, 296). Given amirate of forty in 749/1348–9. In 769/1367–8 took leading part in defence of sultan against *al-ajlāb al-Yalbughāwiyya* – suborned by Asandamur by promise of sultanate, imprisoned in Alexandria with other amirs. His mother was daughter of al-Nāṣir Muḥammad.

Mughulṭāy b. Sawsūn, *amīr shikār* (*Tārīkh al-Malik*, 27). One of five amirs of forty created in Rabīʿ II 742/September 1341.

Muḥammad b. Īnāl al-Yūsufī (Ibn al-Furāt, *Tārīkh*, vol. IX, 188, 212; *Nuzhat al-nufūs* vol. I, 483). Captured by Minṭāsh in battle in Muḥarram 792/December 1389 and later released by disaffected troops. Arrested with his uncle Amir Azdamur (brother of Īnāl) in 801/1398–9, and banished to Damascus as *baṭṭāl*.

Muḥammad b. Laqūsh al-Jūkandārī (d. 762/1360–1), *nāʾib* in Homs, Baalbak, Damascus (*Durar*, vol. V, 50.). Built a *khān* at ʿAqabat al-Rummān, and a mosque, *khān* and bath in Baalbak. See brother Kujkūn.

Muḥammad b. Āqush (d. 762/1360–1), *nāʾib* in Baalbak, Homs (*Durar*, vol. IV, 13). Firstly amir of ten in Aleppo, later amir of forty in Damascus, where he died.

Muḥammad (Shāh) Nāṣir al-dīn b. Muḥammad Nāṣir al-dīn b. Āqbughā Ās Sayf al-dīn (d. 795/1393) (Ibn al-Furāt, *Tārīkh*, vol. IX, 197–9, 201, 237, 260–1, 335, 356 – *tarjama*; *Tārīkh Ibn Qāḍī Shuhba*, vol. I, 379 etc.) Through father he was made amir of forty by al-Ashraf. After banishment of his father, his *iqṭāʿ* taken. Amir of ten in 791/1389. Made *shādd al-dawāwīn* in 792/1390, then *ustādār ṣaghīr*. Arrested (in Raydaniyya), mulcted 793/1391 (complaints from Shawbak etc.). In 795/1393, when *kāshif* of Giza, again arrested. Buried in father's *turba* near Qawṣūn's mosque.

Muḥammad Jamaq b. Aytamish (Sayf al-dīn) b. ʿAbdallāh al-Bajāsī al-Ẓāhirī (d. 798/1395–6) (Ibn al-Furāt, *Tārīkh*, vol. IX, 16, 23, 38, 97, 101, 137, 413, 448–9; see *Nuzhat al-nufūs*, vol. I, 218, 413, where called Muḥammad b. Jamaq). His father was *raʾs nawba and atābak al-ʿasākir*. As amir of forty, he himself was arrested 791/1389, sent to Alexandria. Supporter of Yalbughā al-Nāṣirī. Acted as *amīr al-maḥmal* in 797/1395. Buried in father's *madrasa* built near mosque of Āqsunqur.

Muḥammad Nāṣir al-dīn b. al-Dawādārī (Ibn al-Furāt, *Tārīkh*, vol. IX, 80, 98, 100, 461).

Muḥammad Nāṣir al-dīn b. Alṭunbughā al-Jūbānī (Ibn al-Furāt, *Tārīkh*, vol. IX, 31), created amir of 40 in 790/1388.

Muḥammad Nāṣir al-dīn b. Arghūn (d. 727/1326–7) (*Durar*, vol. III, 469; *Sulūk*, vol. II, 291, 339). Moved to Aleppo when father was *nāʾib* there. Died before his father. See brother Abū Bakr.

Muḥammad Nāṣir al-dīn b. Asandamur al-ʿAlāʾī, *nāʾib* of Alexandria (Ibn al-Furāt, *Tārīkh*, vol. IX, 140; *Nuzhat al-nufūs*, vol. I, 251; *Tārīkh Ibn Qāḍī Shuhba*, vol. I, 289). Appointed by Sultan Ḥājjī in 791/1389.

Muḥammad Nāṣir al-dīn b. Baktimur al-Sāqī (*Sulūk*, vol. II, 563; Halm, *Ägypten*, 119, 121, 165). Promoted from amir of ten to *ṭablkhāna* rank in 742/1341.

Muḥammad Nāṣir al-dīn b. Ibrāhīm b. Manjak (*Tārīkh Ibn Qāḍī Shuhba*, vol. I, 572). A *ṭablkhāna* amirate taken from his uncle Faraj b. Manjak, and given to him in 798/1395. Married daughter of Muḥammad Shāh b. Baydamur in 791/1389.

Muḥammad Nāṣir al-dīn b. Iyāz Fakhr al-dīn al-Dawādārī (d. 799/1396–97) (Ibn al-Furāt, *Tārīkh*, vol. IX, 475).

Muḥammad Nāṣir al-dīn b. Jamaq b. Aytamish (d. 798/1395–6) (*Nuzhat al-nufūs*, vol. I, 435). See father (Muḥammad) Jamaq.

Muḥammad Nāṣir al-dīn b. Janklī (Badr al-dīn) b. Albābā (d. 741/1340–41) (*Sulūk*, vol. II, 358, 498, 552–3). Made amir of forty in 733/1332–3. His brother made amir of ten. Sent on expedition to Syria against Tankiz (with father as one of the commanders).

Muḥammad Nāṣir al-dīn b. Jarkas Sayf al-dīn b. ʿAbdallāh al-Khalīlī al-Ẓāhirī (d. 798/1395–6) (Ibn al-Furāt, *Tārīkh*, vol. IX, 449). His father was *amīr ākhūr*.

Muḥammad Nāṣir al-dīn b. Julbān al-ʿAlāʾī (Ibn al-Furāt, *Tārīkh*, vol. IX, 11, 401). Mentioned as amir of forty amongst amirs ordered on expedition to Syria in 789/1387. In 797/1395 given amirate of twenty by Barqūq, to replace Qarābughā, the father of Jaraktimur, deceased.

Muḥammad Nāṣir al-dīn b. Kujlī (d. 755/1354), *amīr shikār* (Damascus), *nāʾib* in Homs (*Durar*, vol. IV, 268).

Muḥammad Nāṣir al-dīn b. Qifjaq (d. 792/1390) (*Tārīkh Ibn Qāḍī Shuhba*, vol. I, 363–4 – *tarjama*). Became amir of ten, and attached to Muḥammad b. Muḥammad b. Āqbughā Āṣ (q.v.). When latter was *ustādār*, Muḥammad became his *nāʾib* in Damascus, and powerful. The viceregent Amir Baydamur respected him, appointed him *nāẓir al-Jāmiʿ*. In 776/1374–5 amir of forty. Muḥarram 777/June 1375 made fourth *ḥājib*, later that year second *ḥājib*. Arrested 778/1376–7, with his master. Restored following year, but soon dismissed. 784/1382–3 *ḥājib* again. 788/1386 *mubāshir al-aghwār*, then recalled. By al-Jūbānī appointed *nāẓir al-māristān wa-khān Lājīn*. Supporter of Minṭāsh, but tortured. Died in his sixties.

Muḥammad Nāṣir al-dīn b. Ṭaynāl *al-nāʾib* (d. 750/1349–50) (*Durar*, vol. IV, 81). Notably handsome – a *qumāsh* named after him. He inherited much wealth from his father and lived in luxury. Died young.

Muḥammad Nāṣir al-dīn b. Talik (d. 799/1396–7), *Ḥājib* (Damascus) (*Tārīkh Ibn Qāḍī Shuhba*, vol. I, 639 – *tarjama*). Served as *ustādār* for Amir Īnāl (*nāʾib* in Damascus), then as administrator of the Manṣūrī waqf (when his *ustādh* held it). In 795/1392–3 became amir of forty, and *ḥājib* 'for a while'. Administrator in Ghawr in region of al-Quṣayr and Baysān, where he died.

Muḥammad Nāṣir al-dīn (Ibn al-Ḥusām) b. Lājīn Ḥusām al-dīn b. ʿAbdallāh al-Saqrī al-Manjakī (d. 794/1391–2) (Ibn al-Furāt, *Tārīkh*, vol. IX, 327–8 – *tarjama* and index; *Durar*, vol. V, 50; *Dhayl* of Ṭāhir b. Ḥabīb, Bodleian MS Marsh 319, fol. 280; *Nuzhat al-nufūs*, vol. I, 355; *Tārīkh Ibn Qāḍī Shuhba*, vol. I, 453–4 – *tarjama*). Served Manjak in Syria with his father, then passed to service of Amir Bahādūr al-Manjakī. *Dawādār* for Saʿd al-dīn b. al-Baqrī and Amir Sūdūn Bāq. *Shādd al-dawāwīn* in 790/1388 as amir of ten. Made amir of forty later that year, then *wazīr* for Barqūq. Arrested twice, but in 792/1390 *wazīr* again. Died in his house, known as Bahādūr al-Manjakī's house, near

al-Ḥusaynī *mashhad*. Buried in father's *turba* outside Bab al-Maḥrūq. (See his son (?) Aḥmad, see his nephew Muḥammad b. Rajab).
Muḥammad Ṣalāḥ al-dīn/Nāṣir al-dīn b. Muḥammad (Nāṣir al-dīn) b. Tankiz (Ibn al-Furāt, *Tārīkh*, vol. IX, 48, 73, 98, 101, 135, 400, 406, 407, 464–5;*Nuzhat al-nufūs*, vol. I, 69–71 (warns Barqūq of plot 785/1383–4); *Tārīkh Ibn Qāḍī Shuhba*, vol. I, 616 etc.). Husband of mother (d. 790/1388) of al-Ṣāliḥ Ḥājjī b. Shaʿbān. 791/1399 made amir of forty, arrested soon afterwards, later freed and made amir of ten. In 797/1395 amir of forty. That year appointed *ustādh al-amlāk al-sulṭāniyya*. In 799/1397 his *ṭablkhāna* rescinded, became *baṭṭāl* in Alexandria and lost his *ustādh* position. Mother of al-Ruknī Baybars, sister of al-Ẓāhir, interceded for him, to superintend Baybars' properties and *waqfs* in Syria.
Mūsā Sharaf al-dīn b. ʿAlī b. Mankūtimur (d. 757/1356) (*Durar*, vol. V, 149).
Quṭlījā b. Balabān al-Jūkandār (d. 720/1320) (*Durar*, vol. III, 340).
Quṭlūbak b. Qarāsunqur (d. 729/1328–9) (*Durar*, vol. III, 338–9). Built a *qanāt* at Jerusalem and planned one for al-Nāṣir Muḥammad in Egypt.
Samghār (or Sam'ān) Shihāb al-dīn b. Sunqur al-Ashqar (d. 731/1330–1) (*Durar*, vol. II, 307; *Khiṭaṭ*, vol. II, p. 191; *Sulūk*, vol. II, 337). His father was claimant to independence as al-Malik al-Kāmil in Syria. He himself, as an amir, was sent in a force to Barqa in Muḥarram 719/February–March 1319.
ʿUmar Rukn al-dīn b. Bahādur Āṣ Sayf al-dīn al-Manṣūrī (d. 731/1330–1) (*Sulūk*, vol. II, 326, 341; *Durar*, vol. II, 30–1). His father was amir of one hundred, who died in Damascus 730/1329. He had four sons, two of whom were amirs of forty.
Yūnus Sharaf al-dīn al-Qushtimurī al-Karakī (d. 795/1392–3), *nāʾib* of al-Karak (Ibn al-Furāt, *Tārīkh*, vol. IX, 249, 349, 359). Appointed *nāʾib* in 793/1391, still in post in 795/1393. He was killed in a fracas with local bedouin.

Amirs of twenty

Aḥmad b. Yāqūt (Bātūt ?) (Ibn al-Furāt, *Tārīkh*, vol. IX, 158, 164). Imprisoned in 791/1389.
Jaraktimur (Juraktamur) al-Khāṣṣakī al-Ashrafī b. Qarābughā Sayf al-dīn al-Turkī al-Ashrafī (*Tārīkh Ibn Qāḍī Shuhba*, vol. I, p.565 (*tarjama* of father)). He was favourite of al-Ashraf (Shaʿbān), and his sister was wife of al-Ashraf, and mother of Qāsim b. al-Ashraf.
Muḥammad b. Mughulṭāy al-Masʿūdī, *wālī Miṣr* (Ibn al-Furat, *Tārīkh*, vol. IX, 135, 214). Made amir of twenty in 791/1389. Dismissed as *wālī Miṣr* in 792/1390.
Muḥammad Nāṣir al-dīn b. Jaraktimur al-Manjakī (d. 788/1386), *wālī Nāblus* (*Tārīkh Ibn Qāḍī Shuhba*, vol. I, 205 – *tarjama*). His father, who served as *nāʾib* of Alexandria and of Qalʿat al-Rūm, was known as Ibn Manjak because Manjak purchased him and brought him up like an adopted son, before he had his own sons. After his father's death, Muḥammad joined the service of Manjak (then *nāʾib* of Egypt). After Manjak's death, he went with his sons to Damascus as amir of ten (aged less than twenty). In 784/1382–3 made amir of twenty. In 787/1385 made *wālī* of Nablus (bought office). Dismissed, then restored but died in Nablus (not yet thirty years old).
Mūsā Sharaf al-dīn b. Qumārī (d. 800/1397–8), *amīr shikār* and *shādd al-aḥwāsh al-sulṭāniyya al-mawḍūʿa li'l-ṭuyūr* (Ibn al-Furāt: *Tārīkh*, vol. IX, 334; *Nuzhat al-nufūs*, vol. I, 477 – *tarjama*; *Sulūk*, vol. III, 784, 913). Given *iqṭāʿ* of ten (previously that of Timrāz), in addition to the 'ten' he already had, in 795/1393. (See son Muḥammad).

Amirs of ten

Ibn Yūnus al-Dawādār (Ibn al-Furāt, *Tārīkh*, vol. IX, 99–100). Arrested in 791/1389 – released because of youth.
ʿAbd al-Raḥmān Zayn al-dīn b. Manklī Bughā al-Shamsī (d. 796/1393–4) (Ibn al-Furāt, *Tārīkh*, vol. IX, 99–100, 391; *Nuzhat al-nufūs*, vol. I, 105, 315 (correct ʿAbd al-Raḥīm); *Tārīkh Ibn Qāḍī Shuhba*, vol. I, 530 – *tarjama*). His father was *nāʾib al-Shām*. In 786/1384 he took over *imrat al-ḥājj* on death of the amir en route. Arrested and soon released in 791/1389. In 792/1390 he was again *amīr al-ḥājj*. Buried in father's *turba*. His mother was sister of al-Malik al-Ẓāhir (in Ibn Qāḍī Shuhba: 'sister of al-Malik al-Ashraf'). See brother ʿAbd al-Raḥīm .
Abū Bakr b. Aybak al-Ḥusāmī (d. 756/1355), *shādd al-awqāf* (*Durar*, vol. I, 71). He was close to Tankiz, and a friend of *ʿulamāʾ* and *Sufis*.
Abū Bakr b. Balabān (d. 751/1350–1) (*Durar*, vol. I, 472).
Abū Bakr Sayf al-dīn b. Burāq Sayf al-dīn al-Tatarī b. Baldaʾī (?) (See *Tārīkh Ibn Qāḍī Shuhba*, vol. I, 314 – *tarjama* of brother, Muḥammad Nāṣir al-dīn, with whom he shared his father's amirate of ten after latter's death).
ʿAlī b. Bahādur (*Tārīkh al-Malik*, 55). One of the short-lived appointments made by Qawṣūn in 742/1341–2.
ʿAlī b. Balāṭ al-Sayfī Aljāy (Ibn al-Furāt, *Tārīkh*, vol. IX, 99). Arrested in 791/1389.
ʿAlī b. Lājīn al-Ṭarabulsī (*amīr silāḥ*) (*Tārīkh al-Malik*, 55). A short-lived appointment made by Qawṣūn in 742/1341–2.
ʿAlī b. Salār (d. 742/1341–2) (*Sulūk*, vol. II, 75; *Tārīkh al-Malik*, p.36).
When Salār left the *niyāba* of Egypt and went to Shawbak (709/1309–10), ʿAlī stayed in Cairo with an amirate of ten. After his death his amirate given to his son, Khalīl.
ʿAlī b. Taydamur Kukuz (d. 749/1348–9) (*Durar*, vol. III, 128).
ʿAlī b. Ṭuruntāy al-Manṣūrī (d. 766/1364–5) (*Durar*, vol. III, 126).
ʿAlī b. Amīr Ḥājib (d. 739/1338–9), *wālī al-Qāhira* (*Durar*, vol. III, 98–9). His father was one of Ẓāhiriyya amirs. ʿAlī was made *wālī* and amir by al-Nāṣir Muḥammad. He collected panegyrics of the Prophet in ninety-five volumes.
ʿAlī (al-Shaykh) b. Dilanjī al-Qāzānī (*Tārīkh al-Malik*, 60; *Sulūk*, vol. II, p. 583). Served in Quṭlūbughā al-Fakhrī's expeditionary force in Syria in 742/1341–2. See his son Ibrāhīm.
ʿAlī ʿAlāʾ al-dīn b. Sūdūn Sayf al-dīn al-Fakhrī al-Shaykhūnī (d. 790/1388) (Ibn al-Furāt, *Tārīkh*, vol. IX, 44–5). His father (d. 798/1395–6) was *nāʾib* in Egypt. He died before his father, and the sultan gave his amirate to his father in addition to an *iqṭāʿ* he already had.
ʿAlī Rukn al-dīn b. Taydamur (d. 756/1355) (*Durar*, vol. III, 244).
Amīr Ḥājj b. Aydughmish (Ibn al-Furāt, *Tārīkh*, vol. IX, 99). In list of amirs arrested in 791/1389, but soon released. See his brother Aḥmad.
Amīr Ḥājj b. Ṭuquzdamur (*Sulūk*, vol. II, 337). In 731/1330 took over *iqṭāʿ* of Amīr ʿAlī, brother of Quṭlūbak.
Ḥasan Ḥusām al-dīn b. ʿAlī b. Qushtimur Sayf al-dīn (d. 791/1389) (Ibn al-Furāt, *Tārīkh*, vol. IX, 173; *Tārīkh Ibn Qāḍī Shuhba*, vol. I, 308 – *tarjama*). See his father (amir).
Ibrāhīm b. ʿAlī b. (Qarā) Dilanjī (Ibn al-Furāt, *Tārīkh*, vol. IX, 98; *Sulūk*, vol. III, 626). See father ʿAlī. (Ibn al-Furāt's text gives "Dilatjī"). In list of amirs arrested by Yalbughā in 791/1389.

Ibrāhīm b. Ṣarghitmish al-Nāṣirī (d. 770/1368–9) (*Durar*, vol. I, 29; *Sulūk*, vol. III, 177). Made amir of ten in 765/1363. According to *Durar*, died in 771. Buried in his father's *madrasa*.

Ibrāhīm Ṣārim al-dīn b. Yūsuf b. Burlughī, *wālī bāb al-qulla* etc. (Ibn al-Furāt, *Tārīkh*, vol. IX, index; *Sulūk*, vol. III, 652, 654, 701; Ibn Taghribirdī, *Nujūm* (Cairo), vol. XI, 346; Halm, *Ägypten*, 83, 155). He was *wālī al-Qalʿa* in 791/1389; 'restored' to *wilāya* of Citadel in 792/1390. Amir of five in 791/1389, then amir of ten , then *wālī bāb al-Qarāfa*.

Khalīl b. Qirṭāy al-Karakī, *shādd al-ʿamāʾir al-sulṭāniyya* (Ibn al-Furāt, *Tārīkh*, vol. IX, 99–100; Ibn Taghrībirdī, *Nujūm*, Cairo, vol. XI, 322; Halm, *Ägypten*, 260, 454, 578). Arrested with others in 791/1389, and released after special intercession. See brother Muḥammad.

Khiḍr Jamāl al-dīn b. ʿUmar Rukn al-dīn b. Aḥmad Shihāb al-dīn b. Baktimur *al-Sāqī* (Ibn Taghrībirdī, *Nujūm* (Cairo), vol. XI, 71, 345, vol. XII, 185, 192; Ibn al-Furāt, *Tārīkh*, vol. IX, 55, 135, 461; *Sulūk*, vol. III, index. Halm, *Ägypten*, 244). In 764/1363 he was an amir of ten, held this rank until 802/1399, then arrested.

Muḥammad b. Āqtimur al-Ḥanbalī/al-Ṣāḥibī (?) (Ibn al-Furāt, *Tārīkh*, vol. IX, 99, 100). Arrested and released in 791/1389.

Muḥammad b. Arghūn Shāh al-Aḥmadī (*Nuzhat al-nufūs*, vol. I, 219). One of the amirs arrested in 791/1389.

Muḥammad b. Asandamur al-Jūkāndār (d. 755/1354) (*Durar*, vol. IV, 12). See brother (?) Amīr ʿAlī.

Muḥammad b. Baktimur al-Shamsī (Ibn al-Furāt, *Tārīkh*, vol. IX, 99). One of the amirs arrested in 791/1389.

Muḥammad b. Mankūtimur ʿAbd al-Ghanī (Ibn al-Furāt, *Tārīkh*, vol. IX, 135). Made amir of ten in 791/1389.

Muḥammad b. Ṭughaytimur (Ibn al-Furāt, *Tārīkh*, vol. IX, 99). Mentioned among the amirs arrested in 791/1389.

Muḥammad b. Ṭughāy Timur al-Niẓāmī (*Nuzhat al-nufūs*, vol. I, 219). One of the amirs arrested in 791/1389.

Muḥammad b. Yūnus al-Nawrūzī (Ibn al-Furāt, *Tārīkh*, vol. IX, 135). Made amir of ten in 791/1389.

Muḥammad b. Sunqur al-Muḥammadī (Ibn al-Furāt, *Tārīkh*, vol. IX, 99; *Sulūk*, vol. III, 275, 626). As amir of ten, one of the many amirs who accompanied Sultan Shaʿbān when he went on *ḥajj* in 778/1377. Arrested in 791/1389. Served as *ustādār al-dhakhīra waʾl-amlāk* (see Halm, *Ägypten*, 661).

Muḥammad Badr al-dīn b. Aydamur ʿIzz al-dīn al-Khaṭīrī (d. 761/1359–60) (*Durar*, vol. IV, 13). Listed as amir of ten in 732/1331–2 (Ibn al-Dawādārī, *Kanz al-durar*, vol. IX, 367).

Muḥammad Nāṣir al-dīn b. ʿAbdallāh Jamāl al-dīn b. Baktimur Sayf al-dīn al-Ḥājib (d. 802/1400) (*Khiṭaṭ*, vol. II, 65/8, 64/7 ff, Ibn al-Furāt: *Tārīkh*, vol. IX, 298; *Nuzhat al-nufūs*, vol. I, 343, vol. II, 67; Halm, *Ägypten*, 678). See his father, and sons, ʿAlī and ʿAbd al-Raḥmān. The family remained 'a wealthy emiral house' (*Khiṭaṭ*).

Muḥammad Nāṣir al-dīn b. Baktimur Sayf al-dīn al-Ḥājib (*Sulūk*, vol. II, 314 (*tarjama* of Baktimur), 563). His father (very rich) died in 729/1328–9. Muḥammad (then aged thirteen) was granted an amirate of ten. His father's *iqṭāʿ* was distributed amongst several persons. He himself was arrested in 742/1341–2 and his *iqṭāʿ* given to brother ʿAbdallāh (q.v.).

Muḥammad Nāṣir al-dīn b. Burāq Sayf al-dīn al-Tatarī b. Baldaʾī (?) (d. 791/1389),

amīr ākhūr al-Sulṭān in Damascus (*Tārīkh Ibn Qāḍī Shuhba*, vol. I, p. 314 – *tarjama*). His father, Tatar in origin, had *nisba* al-Jamālī al-Aframī. After death of his father he held the *amīr ākhūr* post for fifteen years, and divided his amirate of ten with his brother, Sayf al-dīn Abū Bakr (q.v.).
Muḥammad Nāṣir al-dīn b. Būzlār Sayf al-dīn al-Turkī (d. 791/1389) (Ibn al-Furāt, *Tārīkh*, vol. IX, 177). His father was amir of one hundred in Egypt.
Muḥammad Nāṣir al-dīn b. Mūsā (Sharaf al-dīn) b. Yūsuf (Sayf al-dīn) al-Nāṣirī (d. 796/1393–94) (Ibn al-Furāt: *Tārīkh*, vol. IX, 393). His father and grandfather were both amirs of one hundred. He himself had '*ʿālim* tendencies'.
Muḥammad Nāṣir al-dīn b. Mūsā b. Aruqṭāy (Sharaf al-dīn b. Sayf al-dīn) (d. 796/1393–4) (*Tārīkh Ibn Qāḍī Shuhba*, vol. I, 535 – *tarjama*). 'Loved to attend *mawāʿid* and loved Sufis.' Father and grandfather both amirs.
Muḥammad Nāṣir al-dīn b. Qirṭāy al-Karakī, *naqīb al-juyūsh* (Ibn al-Furāt, *Tārīkh*, vol. IX, 99–100, 155). Arrested in 791/1389, then released after special intercession. Mentioned as *naqīb* late that year. See brother Khalīl.
Muḥammad Nāṣir al-dīn (Qishqalduq) b. Quṭlūbughā al-Muḥammadī (d. 790/1388) (Ibn al-Furāt, *Tārīkh*, vol. IX, 45). His father was brother of Manklī Bughā al-Shamsī, *nāʾib* of Aleppo etc. Came to Egypt with his uncle, and made amir of ten by al-Ashraf Shaʿbān.
Mūsā Sharaf al-dīn b. Abī Bakr Sayf al-dīn b. Salār (d. 797/1394–5), *amīr ṭabar* (Ibn al-Furāt, *Tārīkh*, vol. IX, 99–100, 426; *Nuzhat al-nufūs*, vol. I, 219, 420). Made *amīr ṭabar* after Amir Damurkhān b. Qarāmān after 780/1379–80. Arrested and soon released in 791/1389.
Nāṣir b. Salār al-Bīrī al-Manṣūrī (*Durar*, vol. II, 278). After return of al-Nāṣir and Salār's departure for Shawbak, this son was left in Cairo with an amirate.
Taghrībirdī b. Qarādamurdāsh Sayf al-dīn (Ibn al-Furāt, *Tārīkh*, vol. IX, 68). Made amir of ten in 791/1389.
ʿUmar b. Yaʿqūb Shāh (Ibn al-Furāt: *Tārīkh*, vol. IX, 99). In list of amirs, Barqūq's men, arrested by Yalbughā in Egypt in 791/1389. (Cf. Asandamur b. Yaʿqūb Shāh?)

Amirs of unspecified rank

Ibn Aruqṭāy Sayf al-dīn (*Sulūk*, vol. II, 332; Ibn al-Furāt, *Tārīkh*, vol. IX, 62). In 731/1330–1 one son was made amir of forty, and another amir of ten.
Nāṣir al-dīn b. *ukht* Shaykhū, *nāẓir al-Jāmiʿ* (Damascus) (*Tārīkh Ibn Qāḍī Shuhba*, vol. I, 22). Appointed in 782/1380–1.
ʿAbd al-Raḥmān b. Ayid (Halm, *Ägypten*, 530).
ʿAbd al-Raḥmān b. Baktāsh al-Mankuwarsā al-Manṣūrī (*Durar*, vol. II, p. 15). His father was *shādd al-awqāf* in Damascus in 722/1322, later *nāʾib* of Baalbak.
ʿAbd al-Raḥmān b. Muḥammad b.ʿAbdallāh b. Baktimur al-Ḥājib (*Khiṭaṭ*, 64, 129) See his father and grandfather, and brother,ʿAlī.
Abū Bakr b. Buluktimur (Halm, *Ägypten*, 147, cf. 430?).
Abū Bakr b. Sayf al-Jamālī (Halm, *Ägypten*, 109).
Abū Bakr b. Sharaf al-Jamālī (Halm, *Ägypten*, 68).
Abū Bakr Sayf al-dīn b. Isbāsalār (d. 679/1280–1), *wālī Miṣr* (*Nuzha*, 273; *Tālī*, 21; *Sulūk*, vol. II, 684–5).
Aḥmad b. Āqūsh al-ʿAzīzī (d. 719/1319), *naqīb al-juyūsh; mihmandār* (*Durar*, vol. I, 85).
Aḥmad b. Baktimur al-ʿAlāʾī (Halm, *Ägypten*, 70).

Aḥmad b. Bīlīk *al-Sāqī* al-Turkumānī (d. 754/1353), *shādd al-sharābkhānah, nā'ib* in Ṣafad, Ḥamāh etc. (*Durar*, vol. I, 122; *Sulūk*, vol. II, 837). Came from East with three brothers (Shādī, Ḥājjī,ʿUmar). Important political career – involved with Shaykhū in deposing al-Muẓaffar (name of sultan).
Aḥmad b. Yūsuf b. Manklī Bughā (Halm, *Ägypten*, 169).
Aydi (Aydamur ?) b. Qaraṭāy b. Sūdūn (Halm, *Ägypten*, 719).
al-Ṣārim al-Shihābī, *wālī Aswān* (Ibn al-Furāt, *Tārīkh*, vol. IX, 257). Dismissed from post in 793/1391.
ʿAlī b. Baybars (b. 700/1300–1, d. 756/1355), *ḥājib* in Damascus and Aleppo (*Durar*, vol. III, 101).
ʿAlī b. Balabān al-Badrī (d. 751/1350–1), *nāʾib* in Nablus etc. (*Durar*, vol. III, 101).
ʿAlī (Amīr ʿAlī) b. Baktimur al-Kīkī, *barīdī* (*Tārīkh al-Malik*, 10).
ʿAlī ʿAlāʾ al-dīn b. Ṭashtimur *al-Ustādār* (d. 799/1396–7) (Ibn al-Furāt, *Tārīkh*, vol. IX, 474).
ʿAlī ʿAlāʾ al-dīn b. al-Kūrānī, *wālī al-Gharbiyya*; *kāshif al-wajh al-baḥrī* (*Tārīkh al-Malik*, p.36).
Amīr ʿAlī b. Asandamur al-Zaynī (Ibn al-Furāt, *Tārīkh*, vol. IX, 153). Among others he submitted to Barqūq at Damascus in 791/1389.
Amīr ʿAlī b. ʿUmar Shāh, *wālī al-wulāt* (*Tārīkh Ibn Qāḍī Shuhba*, vol. I, 12). Resigned from post in 781/1380.
Āqbars b. Ṭaybars ʿAlāʾ al-dīn (*Sulūk*, vol. II, 312). In 729/1328–9 given *iqṭāʿ* (in Damascus) of ʿAlāʾ al-dīn Aydughdī al-Khwārizmī. (Is this the Amir Qalbars b. Ṭaybars al-Wazīrī who died in Damascus in 730/1329–30 (*Sulūk*, vol. II, 326; in *Durar*, vol. III, p.340: Qalbūs)?)
Āqbughā b. ʿAbd al-Wāḥid al-Nāṣirī (d. 744/1343–4), *nāʾib* in Ḥamāh etc., under Kuchuk (*Durar*, vol. I, 418–19). A *jāmdār* and *ustādār* under al-Nāṣir Muḥammad, then *shādd al-ʿamāʾir, muqaddam al-mamālīk* etc. Sultan married his sister Tughāy. He built a *madrasa* near the Azhar. His sons Aḥmad and Muḥammad made amirs by al-Nāṣir.
Arghūn b. Qīrān al-Salārī (d. 772/1370–1), *naqīb al-mamālīk, naqīb al-jaysh* (*Durar*, vol. I, 373). Succeeded his father as *naqīb al-mamālīk* under al-Nāṣir Ḥasan.
Asandamur b. Yaʿqūb Shāh (*Tārīkh Ibn Qāḍī Shuhba*, vol. I, 333). He was *nāẓir al-Jāmiʿ* in 792/1390 (acting with his son, Yūsuf Shāh, q.v.).
Bahādur Sayf al-dīn b. Banjār Ḥusām al-dīn al-Bālbīrī al-Awwī al-Rūmī (d. 680/1281–2) (*Tālī*, 54–5). Father was a great amir of Rūm – held Kharpūt. Marriage connection with Baygu Noyan, Mongol conqueror of Rūm. In 675/1276–7 came with son and others to Baybars. Father and son given *iqṭāʿs* in Egypt. Father died 681/1282–3 (aged 120!).
Faraj or Amīr Faraj b. ʿUmar Shāh, *wālī al-wulāt* (*Tārīkh Ibn Qāḍī Shuhba*, vol. I, 108, 138, 163, 338). In 785/1383 he was *mujarrad* in Sidon – exhibited a not very energetic or successful reaction to Frankish raid on town. In 786/1384 he was *amīr al-Rakb (al-Shāmī)*. Appointed to office unwillingly in 787/1385. In 792/1390 freed from Citadel along with other prisoners.
Ḥamza b. Sunqur al-Muḥammadī (Halm, *Ägypten*, 455).
Ḥamza al-Turkumānī (d. 725/1325) (*Durar*, vol. II, p. 166). He was Tankizʾ factotum – later quarrelled.
Ibrāhīm al-Ṣārim al-Bāshqirdī, *wālī Aswān* (Ibn al-Furāt, *Tārīkh*, vol. IX, 257). Appointed in 793/1391.

Ibrāhīm Shihāb al-dīn b. Baydamur (*Tārīkh Ibn Qāḍī Shuhba*, vol. I, 391 – *tarjama* – and index). See his brother Muḥammad Shāh. His son Aḥmad Shihāb al-dīn killed 793/1391.
Khalīl b. Aydamur Qarā (Halm, *Ägypten,* 183, 368, 545, 594).
Khalīl b. Khāṣṣ Turk (*Durar*, vol. II, 178).
Khalīl b. Timurbughā (Halm, *Ägypten,* 679).
Khalīl al-Dusharī (?), *wālī* in Damietta (Ibn al-Furāt, *Tārīkh*, vol. IX, 361). Appointed 796/1393.
Khalīl Ghars al-dīn b. al-Ḥusām, *wālī al-ṣināʿa* and *shādd al-ahrā'* (Ibn al-Furāt, *Tārīkh*, vol. IX, 10). Mentioned in 798/1395–6. See cousin (*ibn ukht*), the amir Ḥusām al-dīn Ḥusayn al-Gharsī.
Maḥmūd b. Arshā (Halm, *Ägypten,* 266).
Maḥmūd Jamāl al-dīn b. ʿAlī b. Asfar al-Sūdūnī (d. 799/1396–7), *ustādār* (*Durar*, vol. V, 97). Came to Cairo from Aleppo. *Ustādār* for Barqūq. He built a *madrasa* outside Bāb Zuwayla and endowed it with Ibn Jamāʿa's library which he had purchased.
Masʿūd b. Qarāsunqur b. al-Jāshnakīr (d. 719/1319), *ḥājib* (Damascus), *nā'ib al-Quds* (*Durar*, vol. V, 120).
Muḥammad b. Baktāsh (d. 749/1348–49), *wālī* of Damascus (*Durar*, vol. IV, 15).
Muḥammad b. Mūsā b. Qumārī (*Nuzhat al-nufūs*, vol. I, 477). See his father Mūsā. At his father's death in 800/1397–8 Muḥammad, in a general change-round of *iqṭāʿs*, took what had been his cousin's (Sayf al-dīn Timrāz).
Muḥammad Badr al-dīn b. Kaydughdī (Ibn al-Wazīrī) (d. 716/1316) (*Sulūk*, vol. II, 20, 111, 126, 139, 144, 169). In 705/1305–6 he was in sultan's service. In 711/1311 he shared charge of digging al-Khalīj. 713 he was appointed *nā'ib Dār al-ʿAdl* and *shādd al-awqāf*. In 714/1314 in expedition from Cairo to raid Sīs. Released from prison in 715/1315 to reside at Damascus.
Muḥammad Nāṣir al-dīn b. al-Muqtamīr (?) al-Barīdī (Ibn al-Furāt, *Tārīkh*, vol. IX, 154).
Muḥammad Nāṣir al-dīn b. Mu'min al-Shamsī, *wālī Qalyūb* (Ibn al-Furāt, *Tārīkh*, vol. IX, 308, 370.). Appointed in 794/1392 (although Ibn al-Furāt has Nāṣir al-dīn Mu'min!). Dismissed in 796/1394.
Muḥammad Nāṣir al-dīn b. Muqbil al-Jundī (d. 796/1394), *dawādār* of Ibn al-Kayyāl(?) (Ibn al-Furāt, *Tārīkh*, vol. IX, p. 393).
Mūsā b. ʿAbdallāh al-Nāṣirī (d. 756/1355), *nā'ib al-Bīra* (*Durar*, vol. V, 147).
Nāṣir Nāṣir al-dīn al-Budayrī (?) or al-Badrī (Ibn al-Furāt, *Tārīkh*, vol. IX, 184, 360). *Ustādār* of Yalbughā al-Nāṣirī and Minṭāsh in 792/1390. Arrested 796/1394.
Qurmushī b. Uqṭuwān (d. 747/1346–7), *ḥājib* (Cairo), *nā'ib* in Ṣafad (*Durar*, vol. III, 332–3). Raised in Ṣafad – he was a follower of Ibn Taymiyya. Favoured by Tankiz. *Nā'ib* in Ṣafad under al-Ṣāliḥ Ṣāliḥ.
ʿUmar b. Qādūs (?), *wālī Ashmūn al-Rummān* (*Sulūk*, vol. III, 659). Held post in 791/1389.
ʿUmar b. Qurt al-Turkumānī (*al-amīr*), *wālī Aswān* (*Tārīkh Ibn Qāḍī Shuhba*, vol. I, 293, also 123 (*tarjama* of father)). In 791/1389 plotted with incumbent *wālī Aswān* (Abū Durqa) to depose Minṭāsh. (NB Ibn Durqa = Quṭlūbughā Sayf al-dīn al-Asanqajawī (d. 795/1392–3) (*Tārīkh Ibn Qāḍī Shuhba*, vol. I, 491)). Qurt (father) was *nā'ib al-Buḥayra wa'l-wajh al-baḥrī* in 782/1380, and amir of one hundred, executed in 785/1383–4.
ʿUmar Rukn al-dīn b. Ilyās (*qarīb* of Qurt) [al-Turkumānī] (d. 800/1397–8), *wālī* of

al-Sharqiyya, Damietta; *kāshif* (Ibn al-Furāt, *Tārīkh*, vol. IX, 17, 146; *Nuzhat al-nufūs*, vol. I, 152, 193, 477 – *tarjama*). Appointed to al-Sharqiyya in 789/1387, made *kāshif al-wajh al-baḥrī*; moved to Damietta in 791/1389. Dismissed by Minṭāsh as *wālī Aswān* later that year (but then called 'Ibn Qurt al-Turkomān').

ʿUthmān b. Ismāʿīl b. ʿUthmān (b. 657/1259, d. 715/1315), *ḥājib* (Ibn Ḥajar: *Durar*, vol. III, 51). His *jadd* was one of the *mamlūks* of al-Dawādār al-Rūmī. His brother was *shādd al-awqāf* in Damascus and *nāẓir* of Jerusalem and al-Khalīl.

Yalbughā b. Tabūta *al-Sāqī* al-Yaḥyāwī al-Nāṣirī (b. 720/1320, d. 748/1347–8), *nāʾib* in Ḥamāh, Aleppo, Damascus (*Durar*, vol. V, 212–13). His father was in service of al-Nāṣir Muḥammad, of whom Yalbughā became a favourite. His *nāʾib* posts began under al-Ṣāliḥ Ismāʿīl. He built a mosque in Damascus. See Aḥmad b. Yalbughā al-Yaḥyāwī – son?

Yūsuf Jamāl al-dīn b. Quṭlūbak [b. al-Mazūq ?] (d. 802/1399–1400), *wālī al-Gharbiyya* (and *kāshif al-jusūr*)*Nuzhat al-nufūs*, vol. I, 449, 482; vol. II, 32–3; *al-Ḍawʾ*, vol. X, 328). He took over the *wilāya* after death of his uncle (*khāl*), Nāṣir al-dīn Muḥammad ibn Aydamur (d. 799/1396–7). Replaced in 801/1398–9, reappointed 802/1399. In *al-Ḍawʾ* called '*ṣihr* Ibn al-Mazūq'.

CHAPTER 4

Joseph's law – the careers and activities of Mamluk descendants before the Ottoman conquest of Egypt

ULRICH HAARMANN

The perceptive outsider

When Arnold von Harff,[1] a knight from Cologne, visited Cairo in the autumn of 1496 on his way to Jerusalem, two German Mamluks – one a certain

[1] I have used the English translation of the German original by Malcolm Letts: *The Pilgrimage of Arnold von Harff, Knight from Cologne, through Italy, Syria, Egypt, Arabia, Ethiopia, Nubia, Palestine, Turkey, France and Spain, which he accomplished in the years 1496 to 1499*. The Hakluyt Society. second series, vol. XVIV (Nendeln/Liechtenstein, 1967) (hereafter *The Pilgrimage of Arnold von Harff*). Alternatively one may also consult the French translation of the German text by Paul Bleser: 'Le pèlerinage du Chevalier Arnold von Harff', in Erich Hornung (ed.), *Zum Bild Ägyptens im Mittelalter und in der Renaissance/Comment se représente-t-on l'Egypte au moyen âge et à la renaissance* (Freiburg i.Ue. and Göttingen 1990), 59–141. Bleser copies Letts's notes and translates them into French without further ado. In order to find a first orientation in the copious literature on late medieval Western pilgrimage reports in general and on Arnold von Harff's famous travelogue in particular, one should start one's search with the general bibliography compiled by Christian Halm, *Europäische Reiseberichte des späten Mittelalters. Eine analytische Bibliographie. Teil I: Deutsche Reiseberichte,* Kieler Werkstücke, Reihe D, Beiträge zur europäischen Geschichte des späten Mittelalters (Frankfurt, 1994) vol. V, 273–81, no. 111. Modern studies on the literary structure and the intellectual discourse of late medieval pilgrims' reports are evaluated in Peter J. Brenner, *Der Reisebericht in der deutschen Literatur. Ein Forschungsüberblick als Vorstudie zu einer Gattungsgeschichte,* Zweites Sonderheft, Internationales Archiv für Sozialgeschichte der deutschen Literatur (Tübingen, 1990) (on Arnold von Harff's travelogue see 67f. and n. 165). Furthermore there are two useful repertories on late fifteenth-century Western travelogues to the East: Claudia Zrenner, *Die Berichte der europäischen Jerusalempilger (1475–1500). Ein literarischer Vergleich im historischen Kontext.* Europäische Hochschulschriften. Series I: Deutsche Sprache und Literatur, vol. CCCLXXXII (Frankfurt, 1981) (see 97 on Arnold von Harff); Aleya Khattab, *Das Ägyptenbild in den deutschsprachigen Reisebeschreibungen der Zeit von 1285–1500,* Europäische Hochschulschriften, Series I: Deutsche Sprache und Literatur, vol. DXVII (Frankfurt, 1982), (37f., 223f. and throughout on Arnold von Harff). For the historical and historiographical yield of this genre, also in comparison with Muslim travelogues, see Jean Richard, *Les récits de voyages et de pèlerinages,* Typologie des sources du moyen âge occidental, vol. XXXVIII (Turnhout/Belgium, 1981) (no explicit reference to von Harff). Two articles deserve to be singled out for their methodological concerns: Arnold Esch, 'Gemeinsames Erlebnis – individueller Bericht. Vier Parallelberichte aus einer Reisegruppe von Jerusalempilgern 1480', *Zeitschrift für historische Forschung,* 11 (1984), S. 385–416 (Arnold von Harff was bound not to be included in this study); Hannes Kästner, 'Nilfahrt mit Pyramidenblick. Altvertraute Wunder und fremde Lebenswelt in abendländischen Reiseberichten an der Wende zur Neuzeit', in Eijiro Iwasaki (ed.), *Begegnung mit dem 'Fremden'. Grenzen – Traditionen – Vergleiche. Akten des VIII. Internationalen Germanisten-Kongresses Tokyo 1990* (Munich, 1991), 307–16 (three German – Hans Tucher, Felix Fabri and Arnold von Harff – and two Jewish Italian travellers – Meshullam of Volterra and Obadiah of Bertinoro – are compared).

Conrad of Basle,[2] the other a citizen of the Baltic port of Danzig – took exemplary care of him. They opened many doors to him, as high as the private chambers of the sultan on the Cairo Citadel. In particular, they both seem to have enjoyed the opportunity to expound to their fellow countryman the exotic Mamluk ruling system which they had joined (voluntarily or involuntarily), and which they now represented themselves.

Externally, the Mamluk empire presented itself as a powerful monarchy, a bulwark of orthodox Islam. To the Westerner, the Mamluks were familiar as crucial partners in the Indian trade, as potential allies of and against the Ottomans, and especially as successors to the crusaders as rulers of Palestine and as guardians of the Holy Places in Jerusalem. Conrad of Basle, the cicerone and boon companion of our knight from the Rhineland, goes so far as to extol his Mamluk sovereign as the mightiest ruler in the world. For Jerusalem, so he argues, is under his sway, and Jerusalem is the coveted prize of the three faiths of the world, of Jews, Christians and Muslims, irrespective of all their internal sectarian strife.[3]

Much less was known in the West about the internal structure of the Mamluk state and about the meaning of the term Mamluk. Also here Arnold von Harff proves an interesting witness, who – as it turned out – selected for his visit on the Nile, in this respect, an exceptionally propitious historical moment.

In early August 1496, the eighty-year-old Sultan Qāytbāy, an energetic, pious and cultured ruler, had died after a rule of almost thirty years (1468–96).[4] A few months earlier, following the example of Sultan Jaqmaq (1438–53),[5] he had formally abdicated from the throne in favour of his son Muḥammad, who was strong-minded, ruthless and profligate, even at 14 years old. We may regard the dynastic succession as the normal mode of changing rulers in medieval monarchies. The attitude of the Mamluks, however, was cer-

2 *The Pilgrimage of Arnold von Harff*, 102–3, 106, 108, 111, 128. – As early as thirteen years before, another famous German pilgrim, the Dominican humanist Felix Fabri (Schmidt), had apparently met this same Conrad of Basle in Cairo; cf. *Voyage en Egypte de Félix Fabri 1483*, Collection des voyageurs occidentaux en Egypte, vol. XIV, part III, French translation of the German *Ejgentliche Beschreibung der hin unnd wider farth zu dem Heyligen Lanndt gen Jerusalem und furter durch die grosse Wüsteney zu dem Heiligen Bergk Horeb Sinay* (Cairo, 1975), 913, 915. I consulted the French translation of Fabri's two pilgrim's reports, both of the Latin *Evagatorium* (volumes I and II of the French translation), and of the short (and less learned) German *Ejgentliche Beschreibung* (volume III of the French translation). The pertinent studies on Felix Fabri's sophisticated and lengthy work are collected in: Halm, *Europäische Reiseberichte*, no. 83, 195 (year 1480) and no. 88, 210–20 (years 1483–4); Brenner, *Reisebericht*, 64–6; Zrenner, *Berichte*, 41–51; Khattab, *Ägyptenbild*, 32–4, 192; Esch, 'Gemeinsames Erlebnis'; and Kästner, 'Nilfahrt'.

3 *The Pilgrimage of Arnold von Harff*, 128f.

4 On his reign see Carl Petry's two recent monographs: *Twilight of Majesty. The Reigns of the Mamlūk Sultans al-Ashraf Qāytbāy and Qānṣūh al-Ghawrī in Egypt* (Seattle and London, 1993), 15–118, and *Protectors or Praetorians? The Last Mamlūk Sultans and Egypt's Waning as a Great Power* (Albany, 1994), 13–20 and generally.

5 Cf. Peter M. Holt, *The Age of the Crusades in the Near East from the Eleventh Century to 1517*, A History of the Near East (London and New York, 1986), 190.

tainly different, at least in the fifteenth century. As we learn from a Western source, a letter written by the Venetian consul stationed in Alexandria to Marino Sanuto in May 1496, for the Mamluks Qāytbāy's abdication was a coup, a flagrant breach of the law; for in their view, only a Mamluk could become sultan, i.e. 'a slave who had been bought and sold as it had always been'.[6] This young man, however, who was only a '*son* of the people' ('people' meaning the country's Mamluk ruling elite[7]), would not grow old on the throne, another authority sceptically wrote to Sanuto a few weeks later from Damascus.[8] Here we touch upon the basic idea of the Mamluk system. To quote Arnold von Harff's summary:[9] 'Item no heathen [by "heathen" he, as a Christian, of course means "no Muslim"] born in the Sultan's country can be a ruler; only the captured renegade Christians,[10] there called Mamelukes, rule the Sultan's country.'[11] Looking back on the golden days of the sultanate, the Franciscan André Thevet, when visiting Ottoman Cairo around 1550, finds similar words in his *Cosmographie universelle* to formulate this code: 'les enfants d'un Mamelu ne pouvoient estre honorez du tiltre d'hommes d'armes; qui estoit cause que le Soldan ne pouvoit faire que ses enfants lui succedassent.'[12]

And this principle of Mamluk exclusivity was by no means restricted to the sultan, the chief of state: 'One assumes that there are more than thirty thousand Mamluks in Cairo in the service of the Sultan who is their sole heir, because it is not permissible for a Mamluk to inherit his father's estate,' Felix Fabri, a German Dominican who visited Cairo in 1483, succinctly remarks.[13] And Arnold von Harff refers to the same principle: 'When a Mameluke dies, the Sultan takes his goods and all that he has left behind, and if he has ten children they inherit nothing for they are heathen [i.e. again, Muslim]) born . . . These children can never come to rule.'[14] Fabri's and von Harff's opinion is

[6] On this letter, in Sanuto's *Diarii*, see Mary Margaret Newett, *Canon Pietro Casola's Pilgrimage to Jerusalem in the Year 1494* (Manchester, 1907), 382–3, n. 88.

[7] I will return to this pivotal Italian term, *fiol di la zente*, and its Arabic equivalent.

[8] This second letter (*Diarii*, vol. I, 288) was dated 22 July, i.e. two weeks before Qāytbāy's death on 8 August; cf. Petry, *Twilight*, 117. We find it quoted in Newett, *Canon Pietro*, 392, as well as in Malcolm Letts's notes accompanying his translation of von Harff's pilgrimage report (*The Pilgrimage of Arnold von Harff*, 103f., n. 4) where Letts also refers to the first letter. Letts fails to give credit to Newett as his source for the two quotations from Sanuto's diaries.

[9] *The Pilgrimage of Arnold von Harff*, 121.

[10] On the alleged Christian background of *all* Mamluks, according to numerous Western travellers, I am preparing a separate study.

[11] Bleser's French translation of von Harff's crucial remark reads (at 99): 'Dans le pays du Sultan aucun paien de naissance n'a le droit de régner.'

[12] Jean Chesneau/Andé Thevet, *Voyages en Egypte des années 1549–1552,* Ed. Frank Lestringant, Collection des voyageurs occidentaux en Egypte, vol. XXIV (Cairo, 1984), 178.

[13] *Voyage en Egypte*, 553 (Latin text), 915 (German text). See also Jean Claude Garcin, 'Aux sources d'une idéologie: la force empruntée de l'Islam', in *Le miroir égyptien. Rencontres méditerranéennes.* Actes publiés par Robert Ilbert and Philippe Joutard, (Marseille, 1984), 167–8; reprinted in: J. C. Garcin, *Espaces, pouvoirs et idéologies de l'Egypte médiévale,* Collected Studies Series 251 (London, 1987), contribution no. 11.

[14] *The Pilgrimage of Arnold von Harff*, 122.

thus in full accord with the prevalent view among the historians that (in glaring contrast e.g. to the Janissary system) someone could only become a Mamluk, with all the concomitant political, military and economic privileges and, exceptionally, advance to the sultanate, if he fulfilled the following conditions: he had to be born a 'Turk' (i.e. with a white skin) outside the realms of Islam as a non-Muslim (at the Ottoman court someone arrogantly referred to them, at some time, wholesale as *awlād al-kafara*[15]). Then he had to be enslaved, brought to Egypt in bondage, sold, converted to Islam, educated in the chivalrous arts, and finally manumitted.[16] Felix Fabri's conception that the sons of Mamluks wilfully converted to Christianity in order to be able to reconvert to Islam and thus to qualify for the prestigious regular Mamluk status their fathers had once held, is not without an intrinsic logic, ludicrous as it is.[17]

Sanuto's Syrian correspondent of summer 1496 proved right. A high Mamluk general, Qānṣūh Khamsmi'a, who coveted the sultanate for himself, revolted during the weeks Arnold von Harff spent in Cairo. He spread the word that Qāytbāy's son al-Malik al-Nāṣir Muḥammad, by virtue of his free, Muslim, and Egyptian birth, was not qualified for the throne,[18] because 'no heathen born should be Sultan'. Heavy fighting ensued between the rebels and the young sultan, during which our pilgrim from the Rhine lost his abode and his chattels, yet – so to speak, in return, and largely thanks to his German-speaking Mamluk companions – gained a deeper insight into the strange view the Mamluks held of themselves as a ruling caste.

Arnold von Harff sought and found an answer to this apparently absurd principle of permanent renewal and rejuvenation of a political and military

[15] See *Nafā'is majālis al-sulṭāniyya fī ḥaqā'iq asrār qur'āniyya*, ed. 'Abd al-Wahhāb 'Azzām (Cairo, 1360/1941), 133–4: Jānibak, the Mamluk emissary to the Ottoman court, is asked why he and his like, sons of unbelievers, rule over the sanctuary of Mecca, while this privilege should rather go to the (Ottoman) sultan, the son of a sultan, son of a sultan. Jānibak's answer was a rhetorical question in return: who, after all, was Abraham's, who was Muḥammad's father . . .?

[16] That the term 'slavery', as it is used here, carries unusually positive connotations, such as career opportunities, promotion, social security, as well as freedom from poverty, need not be underscored.

[17] Cf. Fabri, *Voyage en Egypte*, 553 (Latin text), 915 (German text): 'Denn kein Heide [i.e. Muslim!] kann Mameluck werden, und darum so lassen die Mamelucken ihre Soehne taufen und Christenglauben lernen, wenn sie zu ihren Tagen kommen, daß sie auch verleugnen und Mamelucken werden und der Väter Vermögen erben, das alles nicht koennte sein, wenn sie nit waeren Christen vorher gewesen.' Jean Claude Garcin, who has commented upon this passage ('Aux sources', 168), attributes this legend of the temporary conversion of Mamluk offspring to Christianity to the enormous prestige the Mamluks enjoyed in the West at that time. By positing a Christian interval in their vitae, Fabri, so to speak, claims the Mamluks – with all their military and political prestige – for Christianity and thus helps assuage the collective feelings of inferiority cherished by the Christians of the time *vis-à-vis* the Muslim lords of Egypt and Palestine. See also U. Haarmann, 'Mit dem Pfeil, dem Bogen. Fremde und einheimische Stimmen zur Kriegskunst der Mamluken', in Harry Kühnel (ed.), *Kommunikation zwischen Orient und Okzident. Alltag und Sachkultur. Internationaler Kongress Krems and der Donau 6. bis 9. Oktober 1992,* Sitzungsberichete der Österreichischen Akademie der Wissenschaften, Philosophisch-historische Klasse, vol. DCXIX; Veröffentlichungen des Instituts für Realienkunde des Mittelalters und der frühen Neuzeit, vol. XVI (Vienna, 1994), 232 with further textual references.

[18] *The Pilgrimage of Arnold von Harff*, 104–6.

elite from the outside in the precedent of the biblical Joseph. He, too, came to Egypt in bondage; and he, too, rose to become the chief minister of the country. And so, Arnold von Harff muses, this odd custom is continued in our days.[19] But is this very exotic picture (exotic definitely also in universal terms) at all correct in its comprehensiveness and cogency? Was the Mamluk caste really so monolithic and at the same time so exclusive and so consistently aloof from the rest of the population during the Mamluk sultanate, from the crusade of St Louis in 1250 to the Ottoman conquest of Cairo in 1517, as is presented in this simple and highly suggestive model? When searching for answers to this question, I believe one may legitimately leave aside the complex and controversial issues regarding the origins of Mamluk military slavery in early Islam[20] and look primarily at the developments after the demise of the Ayyubids. Is Arnold von Harff's rigorous 'one-generation' principle, his model of the summary exclusion of non-Mamluks from power, a correct reflection of social reality all through Mamluk history from 1250 to 1517? Or is it at least partially valid, e.g. for Cairo during the closing years of the fifteenth century, when von Harff visited the city?

We will also have to ask about the legal nature of the Mamluk 'one-generation' phenomenon. We read of the maxim 'Kingship is childless' (*al-mulk ʿaqīm*), which stood in such glaring contrast to the 'genealogical' mentality of the surrounding Arab–Muslim domains. Was it a quasi-constitutional ruling, as has been argued in previous research? This is highly doubtful, for not one single Arabic text informs us of the existence of such a basic law, whether written or transmitted orally. I rather think we can adopt Felix Fabri's judicious contemporary interpretation of the Mamluk monopoly on power instead. He was the critical outsider, after all, who not only saw, but also contrived to summarize, the essentials of the strange ruling system of his host country, which to the denizens of Egypt was more or less naturally given, not worthy of comment or even explicit mentioning.

According to Fabri, a historical process had led to the situation he encountered in 1483. In his discourse on the Mamluks as born Christians he says:

> All Mamluks are renegade Christians. They have become so many that they wrested the rule over Egypt and Syria from the Saracens [i.e. the local Muslims]. . . . The situation has reached the point that, owing to the increasing number of Christian renegades and apostates, nobody is appointed sultan or king of Egypt who is not a Christian renegade. This procedure is not very old and it is no law for them. It is rather

[19] *The Pilgrimage of Arnold von Harff*, 103: 'For it was never questioned since the time of Joseph, who was sold by his brothers into Egypt, that a sultan should be a heathen born.' In his reference to Joseph, Arnold von Harff was most probably inspired by the learned Felix Fabri, who had visited Cairo thirteen years earlier and who, in the key passage of his *Evagatorium* dealing with the Mamluks, had drawn parallels to the story of Joseph as related in Genesis 37 and 39.

[20] I am thinking mainly of the following question, virulent ever since the publication of the work by Daniel Pipes, *Slave Soldiers and Islam. The Genesis of a Military System* (New Haven/London, 1981): was it the conviction that only uprooted slaves provided unadulterated loyalty to their masters that induced the Abbasid rulers to canvass Central Asian praetorians in large numbers?

the immense number of renegades that has brought about this state of affairs which is the greatest imaginable humiliation for the Saracens and an enormous abomination for the Christians and is disastrously ruinous to our belief.'[21]

In a paraphrase one could say: it is the continuing, more or less automated influx of Mamluks into Egypt and Syria, i.e. a material factor, that provides the basis for the preservation of the Mamluk system. There are no legal provisions whatsoever involved to support and legitimize it. It functions on its own. As long as Mamluks continue to be imported from the outside in large numbers, the 'system of Joseph' will prevail in a self-perpetuating, informal fashion.[22]

Taking Fabri's remarks as guidelines not only for the closing days of the sultanate after 1480, but tentatively also for the first two centuries of Mamluk history, one now wonders how this alleged rigid apartheid between a foreign ruling nobility and the native subjects should have operated in historical reality. The issue defies easy answers. One avenue, however, seems to me to be particularly promising, and this is an investigation of the following question: how did the *sons* of Mamluks fare and accommodate themselves in the different spheres of social life, when the privileges of their fathers were, according to Joseph's rather inhuman and unrealistic law, allegedly withheld from them? Their careers and other aspects of their biographies should help us effectively in gaining a better grasp of the true functioning and of the limits of the Mamluk system and may bring us closer to a deeper understanding of the dynamics of late medieval Egyptian society at large.

As a group squeezed between two firmly consolidated classes – the Mamluks and the local cultured elite – and furthermore as one that lacked exactly defined functions, the descendants of Mamluks found it difficult (and perhaps unattractive) to establish themselves as an independent social element both in their own esteem and in the consciousness of their environment. In the differentiated social models drawn up at the time,[23] the sons of Mamluks are never mentioned. But they must have had a distinct group identity, because

21 *Voyage en Egypte,* 551f.

22 Fabri's assessment reminds us of the question raised by Robert Irwin in his splendidly written survey of the *dawlat al-Turk*, *The Middle East in the Middle Ages. The Early Mamluk Sultanate 1250–1382* (London, 1986), 9–10, 17–18: what was the historical importance of the – more or less unlimited – *availability* of Turkish warriors on the fringes of the *dār al-islām*?

23 Systematic research on social models and taxonomies devised by late medieval Egyptian and Syrian authors has barely begun. Important sources for the perception of social hierarchies, classes and groups in the Mamluk period are – besides (pseudo-)Ibn al-Fuwaṭī al-Baghdādī who wrote in Mongol Baghdad (see his *al-Ḥawādith al-jāmiʿa fī ʾl-miʾa al-sābiʿa* (Beirut, 1407/1987), 165, lines 20ff.): Tāj al-dīn al-Subkī (d. 1370), *Muʿīd al-niʿam wa-mubīd al-niqam*, ed. David W. Myhrman (London, 1908) (German partial translation by Oskar Rescher, *Tâg eddîn Es Subki's Muʿîd en-niʿam wa mubîd an-niqam. Über die moralischen Pflichten der verschiedenen islamischen Bevölkerungsklassen*, (Istanbul, 1925) (Osnabrück, 1980 as vol. II, part 2 of his *Gesammelte Werke*)); al-Maqrīzī (d. 1442), *Ighāthat al-umma bi-kashf al-ghumma* (Beirut, 1980), 111–14 (English translation by Adel Allouche, *Mamluk economics. A Study and translation of al-Maqrīzī's* Ighāthah, (Salt Lake City, 1994), 73–6); and Abū Ḥāmid al-Qudsī (d. 1483): *Badhl al-naṣāʾiḥ al-sharʿiyya fī-mā ʿalā ʾl-sulṭān wa-wulāt al-umūr wa-sāʾir al-raʿiyya*, Arab manuscript Berlin, Ahlwardt catalogue no. 5618 (largely following Tāj al-dīn al-Subkī's arrangement of social groups). Maqrīzī draws a clear line between the alien ruling elite, the *ahl al-dawla,* on the one hand, and six native groups (rich merchants, retailers and small shopkeep-

down to the fourth[24] generation they bore a specific, unambiguous and precise designation, namely 'sons of the nobles, the gentry' (i.e. of the Mamluks) – in Arabic, *awlād al-nās*; in the singular, *ibn al-nās* (a term which even in modern Egypt denotes a citizen of high social status).

This Arabic term with its constituent *nās*, meaning 'people of high standing, elite, aristocracy, nobility', must have been very common in Egypt, at least in the late fifteenth century. Its consistent use is proven by its surprisingly frequent occurrence in its literal Italian translation, *fiol di la zente,* by contemporary European sources. One of these authors is Canon Pietro Casola, who visited Mamluk Jerusalem in 1494. As a good Christian he was angry at the domination of the Mamluks over the Holy City and attributed this tragedy to the internal strife and discord among his fellow believers. Then he goes on to claim (as did others before and after him) that only renegade Christians could become Mamluks and thus reign over the local Muslims (the 'Moors'). 'And if one of the renegades should take a wife and have sons, these sons cannot succeed the father in any dignity. Such sons as these are called sons of the people [the Italian original reads: *fioli de la gente*], even though they be the sons of the Sultan.'[25] As we can see, Casola misunderstood the word *nās* as denoting '(lowly) people', instead of 'elite'. The other source for the Italian rendering of *ibn al-nās* is Marino Sanuto's diary with its passages that were quoted above in connection with the 'illegitimate' succession of al-Malik al-Nāṣir Muḥammad to his father Qāytbāy in 1496. This expression also occurs in numerous other passages of Sanuto's *Diarii.*[26]

When exactly this designation *awlād al-nās* began to be used and how it was delineated in the course of the decades after 1250 has not yet been systematically investigated. In the final period of Mamluk history, preceding the Ottoman conquest, it coalesces quite poignantly with the phrase *banū 'l-atrāk*, 'sons of Turks'.[27]

There were not, nor could there be, any binding modes of socialization for the *awlād al-nās* as they existed for the Mamluks and also for the members of

ers, peasants, recipients of a stipend such as scholars and *ajnād al-ḥalqa*, artisans, salaried workers as well as the amorphous group of the needy and paupers), on the other. Subkī and his follower Abū Ḥāmid al-Qudsī at first sight give an incoherent tableau of dozens of offices and professions – from sultan to dog trainer, bedouin amir to story-teller, judge to janitor – and still classify them under three major headings: the military nobility; the *ʿulamāʾ*; and the craftsmen in the widest sense.

24 See Mohamed Mostafa, 'Beiträge zur Geschichte Ägyptens zur Zeit der türkischen Eroberung', *Zeitschrift der Deutschen Morgenländischen Gesellschaft,* 89 (1935), 217; he refers to the chronicler Ibn Iyās.

25 Newett, *Canon Pietro,* 279. This important quotation figures prominently also in Donald Richards' contribution to this volume (chap. 3). See also Haarmann, 'Mit dem Pfe:l, dem Bogen', 244, n. 121.

26 Newett, *Canon Pietro,* 392, note 88. The phrase *fioli de la gente* was used also by Canon Pietro Casola himself, who travelled to Jerusalem in 1494, i.e. two years before Arnold von Harff, cf. ibid., 279, and *The Pilgrimage of Arnold von Harff,* 103f., note 4.

27 A. N. Poliak, *Feudalism in Egypt, Syria, Palestine, and the Lebanon 1250–1900* (London, 1939), 14, n. 6; U. Haarmann, 'The sons of Mamluks as fief-holders in late medieval Egypt', in Tarif Khalidi (ed.), *Land Tenure and Social Transformation in the Middle East* (Beirut, 1984), 141–68, here at 141.

the Cairene civilian elite in the fourteenth and fifteenth centuries. The different components of their identity connected them to the poles of the society into which they had been born. Their Turkish descent, often also on the mother's side, tied them to the ruling elite. Their place of birth, their Arabic language and – last but not least – their non-Mamluk status tied them to the local Egyptians, even more so for one whose mother was Egyptian. As a shibboleth the *awlād al-nās* were customarily[28] given Arabic names[29] (often patterned after the Companions of the Prophet[30]), whereas their fathers kept, as a token of their nobility, their pagan Turkish names. As a corollary, the options chosen and the answers found by individuals of Mamluk parentage in the dilemma between Turkish and Arabic identity, between barracks and college, and between the Citadel and downtown Cairo, were bound to be complex and variegated.

I will try to give a first[31] (and certainly anything but final) survey of the scope of action such *awlād al-nās* enjoyed in late medieval Egyptian society. My conclusions are based on readings in chronicles, biographical dictionaries and, to a lesser degree, on archival material from the period. Three realms suggest themselves to such an inquiry: military and administrative careers; economic life; and cultural and religious activities in the period. In contrast to what Arnold von Harff suggests,[32] we will find ourselves well advised to draw a clear line between those *awlād al-nās* who were born into the family of the ruler (and were correspondingly privileged), i.e. the so-called *sīdīs* or *asyād,*[33] and those who were born into the households of non-Royal Mamluk generals, officers and privates.[34]

Second-class warriors

Besides the Royal Mamluks who enjoyed special prerogatives and formed the military backbone of the Mamluk system in Cairo and the amirs' soldiers of dis-

28 Exceptions to the rule are listed in U. Haarmann, 'Arabic in speech, Turkish in lineage: Mamluks and their sons in the intellectual life of fourteenth-century Egypt and Syria', *Journal of Semitic Studies,* 33 (1988), 81–114, at 103, n. 109; the individuals recorded there bore Turkish names. See also the list appended to Donald Richards' contribution to this volume (chap. 3).

29 A first précis on this subject is given by David Ayalon in 'Names, titles and 'nisbas' of the Mamluks', *Israel Oriental Studies,* 5 (1975) (reprinted in David Ayalon, *The Mamluk Military Society,* Collected Studies Series 104 (London, 1979), article 4), 189–232, here at 229–31.

30 Cf. Huda Lutfi, *Al-Quds al-mamlûkiyya. A History of Mamlûk Jerusalem Based on the Ḥaram Documents,* Islamkundliche Untersuchungen, vol. CXIII (Berlin, 1985), 178 and 210 n. 116.

31 I am working on a comprehensive monograph, in German, on the *awlād al-nās.*

32 *The Pilgrimage of Arnold von Harff,* 121.

33 On these royal scions and their status in Mamluk society see David Ayalon, 'Studies on the structure of the Mamluk army II', *Bulletin of the School of Oriental and African Studies,* 15 (1953), 448–76 (reprinted in David Ayalon: *Studies on the Mamlūks of Egypt (1250–1517),* Collected Studies Series, 62, (London, 1977), article no. 1), here at 458f. Abū Ḥāmid al-Qudsī, in his *Kitāb Duwal al-islām al-sharīfa al-bahiyya fī dhikr mā ẓahara lī min ḥikam Allāh al-khafiyya fī jalb ṭā'ifat al-atrāk ilā 'l-diyār al-miṣriyya,* ed. Ṣubḥī Labīb and Ulrich Haarmann, Bibliotheca Islamica 37 (Beirut and Stuttgart, 1997), 128, line 4, presents us with the novel term *faqīh al-asyād,* 'legal instructor for the sons of sultans'. See also the German introduction to this text, at 21, 36.

tinctly lower standing who remained under the command of their Mamluk overlords and were thus spread over the whole empire, there existed as a third corps the so-called *ḥalqa.*[35] This regiment probably goes back to the personal guard of Sultan Saladin (1171–93). In the early Mamluk period it still enjoyed high prestige,[36] although its financial status had always been inferior to the other two branches of the Mamluk army. In the *ḥalqa* of the early sultanate, free-born cavalry soldiers of the most diverse provenance served under Mamluk commanders (at least in Egypt[37]). Kurdish, Turkoman and Mongol tribal warriors who had joined the Mamluks in the turmoil accompanying the Mongol advance to the Middle East constituted the most valuable units of the *ḥalqa.*

Two interacting factors accelerated the decay of this non-Mamluk regiment from the late thirteenth century onwards. There was, on the one hand, the decreasing military attractiveness of this part of the army. Free-born professional soldiers of high military calibre no longer joined this army unit. And there was also, on the other hand, the beginning of inappropriate use of the military grants reserved for the *ḥalqa* for non-military dignitaries, e.g. for ousted Ayyubid princes, for bedouin chiefs in the Syrian desert whose benevolence had to be purchased in the showdown with the Mongol Ilkhans, or even for civilians to whom the Mamluks owed special gratitude.[38] Even Sultan Qalāwūn, generally regarded as a staunch and uncompromising guardian of Mamluk principles,[39] was ready to admit the impoverished sons of fallen fellow Baḥriyya officers into the *ḥalqa* and thus grant them a sinecure without any military obligations.[40] In 1315, in al-Malik al-Nāṣir Muḥammad's famous

[34] See Haarmann, 'Sons of Mamluks', 152–63 on the importance of keeping these two categories apart.

[35] On the institution of the *ḥalqa* one still has to start one's inquiries with Ayalon's standard description, 'Studies on the structure II', 448–59, as well as with his contribution, 'Ḥalḳa', in the *Encyclopaedia of Islam* (New Edition), vol. III, 99a–b.

[36] There is disagreement between R. Stephen Humphreys 'The emergence of the Mamluk army', *Studia Islamica,* 45 (1977), 67–99 and 46 (1977), 147–82, and D. Ayalon, 'From Ayyūbids to Mamlūks', *Revue des études islamiques,* 49/1 (1981), 43–57 (reprinted in D. Ayalon, *Islam and the Abode of War,* Collected Studies Series 456 (London, 1994), article no. 3) as to the time when the *ḥalqa* was degraded. Did this happen during the change of dynasties around 1250 (Humphreys) or only considerably later (Ayalon)? This discussion is neatly summarized by Amalia Levanoni, *A Turning Point in Mamluk History: The Third Reign of al-Nāṣir Muḥammad Ibn Qalāwūn (1310–1341).* Islamic History and Civilization, Studies and Texts 10 (Leiden, 1995), 8, n. 14. [37] Cf. Irwin, *The Middle East,* 51.

[38] It may suffice here to refer to the documentation given in Haarmann, 'Sons of Mamluks', 142–3, 164.

[39] He denied the sons of two of his most influential generals, the vice-sultan Ṭurunṭāy and the future sultan Kitbughā, the privilege of an *iqṭāʿ* in the *ḥalqa*, even though each had married a daughter of the other and were thus tied to the Mamluk establishment with double strength. See Levanoni, *A Turning Point*, 43. Her source is al-Maqrīzī, *Al-Mawāʿiẓ wa-ʾl-iʿtibār fī dhikr al-khiṭaṭ wa-ʾl-āthār* (Cairo, 1853–4), vol. II, 216.

[40] A special unit, also called Baḥriyya, was established within the *ḥalqa* for these *awlād al-nās*. See D. Ayalon, 'Baḥrī Mamlūks, Burjī Mamlūks – inadequate names for the two reigns of the Mamlūk sultanate', in: *Tārīḫ* (Philadelphia), 1 (1990), 3–53 (reprinted in Ayalon, *Islam and the Abode of War*, article no. 4), here at 28–31; Ayalon quotes Ibn al-Dawādārī, *Kanz al-durar wa-jāmiʿ al-ghurar*, ed. U. Haarmann (Cairo, 1971), vol. VIII, 303, lines 7–11. Qalāwūn's generosity towards these *awlād al-nās* met with the harsh disapproval of his deputy, the amir Ṭurunṭāy. See also Irwin, *The Middle East* 71; Levanoni, *A Turning Point,* 9, n. 14; 43.

land and army reform (*al-rawk al-nāṣirī*), the fiefs of the *ḥalqa* were drastically reduced to the benefit of the Royal fisc and the Royal Mamluks.[41] All efforts to reform the venerable *ḥalqa* notwithstanding,[42] it lost more and more of its military strength. *Ḥalqa*-fiefs became venal and many of them passed, often with the explicit approval of the fiscal authorities who profited from such transactions, into the hands of artisans[43] and small entrepreneurs in the Mamluk capital. To the chroniclers of the fifteenth century the *ḥalqa*-troopers had become, for the most part, miserable figures of low standing.[44] Only a few of them were fit for pitched battle, as the humiliating tests with the crossbow before a campaign[45] showed. Apart from that, the enlisted *ḥalqa*-soldiers[46] evidently tended to buy themselves out of dangerous undertakings. In the end they had degenerated to little more than a group of infantry guardsmen. When the Mamluk army fought in Syria during the Circassian period, it was their modest duty to protect the gates of the city, and especially the citadel, against potential aggressors. And in the final days of the sultanate, they were exonerated from even this duty.[47]

The *ḥalqa* must be discussed in such detail because the descendants of Mamluks, the *awlād al-nās*, formed an elite element within it. This unit, quite sensibly, was commanded by the sons of sultans, the *sīdīs*, *sayyidīs* or *asyād,* who were mentioned above.[48] These *asyād* were, at least in the early and formative period of the sultanate, qualified for such a military *taqdima* because they were exposed to the real Mamluk world, in particular if their fathers exercised pressure in this direction.[49] Al-Malik al-Nāṣir Muḥammad, Qalāwūn's

[41] On the Egyptian *rawk* of al-Nāṣir Muḥammad (which was preceded by a similar cadastral survey in southern Syria) see Hassanein Rabie, *The Financial System of Egypt AH 564–741/AD 1169–1341*, London Oriental Series 25 (London, 1972), 53–6; Heinz Halm, *Ägypten nach den mamlukischen Lehensregistern,* vol. I: *Oberägypten und das Fayyūm* (Wiesbaden, 1979), 24–30; Irwin, *The Middle East,* pp.109–12. A lively description of this event, including the ceremony of handing the new – and for the most part reduced – feudal warrants to the amirs is given in Holt, *The Age of the Crusades,* 116–17.

[42] These short-lived and, in the end, abortive attempts at reform are connected with the rule of al-Mu'ayyad Shaykh (1412–21): cf. Ayalon, 'Studies on the structure – II', 455.

[43] On artisans as members of the Mamluk army – i.e. its *ḥalqa* unit – see André Raymond, *Artisans et commerçants au Caire au XVIIIe siècle* (Damascus, 1973–4), vol. II, 661, n. 1 (quoting from Ibn Iyās).

[44] The beginnings of this decline in the fourteenth century are highlighted by Ibn Ḥajar al-ʿAsqalānī in his *vita* of Manjak al-Yūsufī: see his *al-Durar al-kāmina fī aʿyān al-miʾa al-thāmina*, ed. Jādd al-Ḥaqq, (Cairo, 1385/1966), vol. V, no. 4846, 130f: 'The riff-raff entered the high ranks; low class people and small vendors settled in the *jundiyya* and the status (*amr*) of the *ḥalqa*-troopers was ruined because of this.'

[45] Cf. Ayalon, 'Studies on the structure – II', 457.

[46] The make-up of a regional *ḥalqa* – in this case Ghazza and Jerusalem – is documented in Lutfi, *al-Quds al-mamlûkiyya*, 312.

[47] Cf. Ayalon, 'Studies on the structure – II', 454, note 8 (with references to contemporary chronicles); Haarmann, 'Sons of Mamluks', 142–3.

[48] Cf. Ayalon, 'Studies on the structure – II', 458.

[49] At times select Royal Mamluks were transferred from the barracks to the palace. Thus the *asyād*, when they were still young, met Mamluks who had come from abroad and thus had the typical Mamluk experience. In isolated cases we also hear of the reverse. In an act of humilia-

Egyptian-born son, for example, is known to have tried to be even more rigid in his Mamluk lifestyle[50] and ethics than his peers of genuine, i.e. first-generation, Mamluk status.[51]

The fates of the *ḥalqa* and the *awlād al-nās* were closely intertwined through all of Mamluk history. Of course the *awlād al-nās* could not fully escape the general demise of the *ḥalqa*, yet within the *ḥalqa* they drifted more and more apart from the inept and incapacitated rest of the regiment until, towards the end of the Mamluk history, the term *ḥalqa* quite significantly seems to have vanished altogether and was replaced *pars pro toto* by *awlād al-nās.*[52]

What were the career opportunities open to a Mamluk descendant, both within and outside the *ḥalqa*, in the course of the history of the Mamluk sultanate? If, in the early Mamluk period under Sultan Qalāwūn (1279–90), the son of an amir wanted to take up a military career, he was granted the necessary basic provisions, i.e. money (*danānīr*), food (*khubz wa-laḥm*) and fodder (*ʿalīq*).[53] Then he had to exercise patience until – if ever – he was granted an *iqṭāʿ* reserved for the *ḥalqa*, or was even commissioned as a commander within its special *awlād al-nās* unit. The *ḥalqa* assignments were considerably less valuable than those reserved for the Royal Mamluks. The half-pay rank of amir of five, the lowest rank of officer, was predominantly filled with sons of deceased Mamluks.[54]

In the early and 'classical' period of the Mamluk sultanate under Baybars and Qalāwūn, the high command in battle, as well as the concomitant lucrative *iqṭāʿ*-benefices, remained barred to *awlād al-nās.* In the tumultuous era following the assassination of al-Ashraf Khalīl b. Qalāwūn in 1293, however, several sons of leading generals advanced into high military echelons. This process continued and even accelerated during al-Malik al-Nāṣir

tion, the son of one of the late Circassian sultans was sent to the barracks to be castigated under the strict command of the responsible *aghā* like the ordinary military slaves. Cf. D. Ayalon,*L'Esclavage du Mamelouk*, Oriental Notes and Studies 1 (Jerusalem, 1951) (reprinted in Ayalon, *The Mamlūk Military Society*, article no. 1), 22–4. On the function and different ranks of the supervisors, *aghawāt,* of the barracks, see Ayalon, *Esclavage,* 31–4; see also Haarmann, *Einleitung* to the edition of Abū Ḥāmid's treatise on God's blessing of having sent the Turks to Egypt: *Kitāb Duwal al-islām*, German text, 39 and n. 6.

50 Al-Malik al-Nāṣir's famous hippomania, so sympathetically and elegantly described in Irwin, *The Middle East,* pp.114–16, may conceivably be seen also in this context.

51 This takes us back to the more general question why, in all likelihood, real Mamluks were usually granted priority over *awlād al-nās* in military matters. D. Ayalon, in his 'Mamlūkiyyāt', *Jerusalem Studies in Arabic and Islam,* 2 (1980), pp.321–39 (reprinted in D. Ayalon, *Outsiders in the Land of Islam. Mamluks, Mongols and Eunuchs*, Collected Studies Series 269 (London, 1988), article no. 1), here at 329–30, offers a three-pronged explanation: 'Even the most sturdy sons of the Mamlūks were usually inferior as military stuff to those who were born in the steppe . . . In their [i.e. the Mamluks'] case no clash could take place between the real family and the slave family . . . Only the very best [i.e. Mamluks] were picked – the toughest among those tough ones who managed to survive.'

52 Ayalon, 'Studies on the structure – II', 457.

53 Cf. al-Qalqashandī: *Ṣubḥ al-aʿshā fī ṣināʿat al-inshāʾ*, (Cairo, 1331/1913–1338/1919), vol. IV, 51, lines 10–12 (he quotes from ʿUmarī's *Masālik al-abṣār*); see also al-Maqrīzī's *Khiṭaṭ*, vol. II, 216. This famous passage was commented upon by Poliak, *Feudalism,* 28; Ayalon, 'Studies on the structure – II', 456; Levanoni, *A Turning Point*, 43.

54 Holt, *The Age of the Crusades,* 148.

Muḥammad's long and peaceful third sultanate (1310–41). We now know that as early as this period, *awlād al-nās* were promoted even to the highest military rank available in the hierarchy of the Mamluk army, the amirate of a hundred.[55] One of these felicitous Egyptian-born generals, Aḥmad b. Baktamur al-Sāqī, the son of one of al-Nāṣir's key aides, was only thirteen years old (and physically handicapped at that) when this high dignity was conferred upon him in 1325.[56] The five sons of Bahādur Āṣ, a highly respected Mamluk general of the old school ('the last Syrian dignitary to kiss the soil and the hand of the sultan') who died around 730/1330, were all appointed amirs by al-Malik al-Nāṣir.[57] Unfortunately, the lack of comprehensive figures makes it difficult to place such spectacular promotions in the right historical perspective.

Later in the fourteenth century, the sons of Mamluk grandees gradually even seem to have developed into some kind of a subsidiary, yet well consolidated, military aristocracy. Typical examples are Muḥammad b. Ṭashtamur (Ibn Ḥummuṣ Akhḍar), who began his career rather spectacularly as a *muqaddam alf* in Cairo and was then demoted to serve in Ṣafad as *amīr ṭablkhāna* (amir of forty),[58] or Rankāl b. Ashbughā (died 749/1349–50), the offspring of a noble Mongol family, who, in the rank of *amīr ṭablkhāna,* helped ward off potential Frankish invaders in Beirut.[59] For the period between al-Malik al-Nāṣir's death in 1341 and the inception of the Circassian dynasty under Sultan Barqūq in 1382, A. Levanoni has counted more than 250 amirs of Mamluk descent.[60] Their political and military influence was enormous and was evidently mirrored also in the increase of their *iqṭāʿ* assignments. Al-Malik al-Nāṣir's ingenious marriage policy, reminiscent of the dynastic manoeuverings of the house of Habsburg in fifteenth-century *Felix Austria*, created a network of dependencies and loyalties between the sultan and his sons and daughters, on the one hand, and the senior amirs and their offspring, on the other.[61] Through their mothers, al-Malik al-Nāṣir's daughters, several sons of powerful generals were direct descendants of the sultan, with the concomitant enhancement of their status. Khalīl b. Qawṣūn, al-Nāṣir Muḥammad's grand-

[55] Levanoni, *A Turning Point*, 42–52.

[56] He was married to a daughter of the Syrian viceroy Tankiz and died after his return from the pilgrimage to Mecca, only twenty years old, in 733/1332. Sultan al-Malik al-Nāṣir himself married his widow. Cf. al-Ṣafadī, *al-Wāfī bi-'l-wafayāt*, vol. VI, ed. Sven Dedering (Wiesbaden, 1972), 266, no. 1258; Ibn Ḥajar, *al-Durar al-kāmina*, vol. I, 123, no. 318. See also Levanoni, *A Turning Point*, 47f.

[57] Al-Ṣafadī, *al-Wāfī bi-'l-wafayāt*, vol. X, ed. Jacqueline Sublet and Ali Amara (Beirut and Wiesbaden, 1980), 297, no. 4810.

[58] Al-Ṣafadī, *al-Wāfī bi-'l-wafayāt*, vol. III, ed. Sven Dedering (Beirut and Wiesbaden, 1974), 170f., no. 1140.

[59] Al-Ṣafadī, *al-Wāfī bi-'l-wafayāt*, vol. XIV, ed. Sven Dedering (Beirut and Wiesbaden, 1402/1982), 147, no. 196.

[60] See Levanoni, *A Turning Point*, 49 and the impressive list of references (though not of names) in note 98.

[61] Biljik, the son of Qawṣūn's sister, for example, was named amir, cf. al-Ṣafadī, *al-Wāfī bi-'l-wafayāt*, vol. X, 285–6, no. 4793.

son through his mother, and Aḥmad b. Yalbughā, another scion of the house of Qalāwūn (albeit with a contested genealogy), were at some time even considered candidates for the sultanate.[62]

This ascendancy of the *awlād al-nās* in the mid-fourteenth century[63] is inseparably connected with the rule of the third-generation *sīdī* al-Malik al-Nāṣir Ḥasan, the son of al-Malik al-Nāṣir Muḥammad and grandson of Qalāwūn (ruled twice, 1347–51, 1354–61). Ten among the twenty-four generals holding the supreme rank of amir of a hundred were *awlād al-nās* during Ḥasan's second rule.[64] *Awlād al-nās* (together with – equally 'non-Mamluk' – eunuchs)[65] were in charge of some of the highest command posts in the empire. Among these assignments were the important governorships of the fortresses in the ever seditious and troublesome Syrian part of the empire. Thus Ḥasan created a counterpoise to the Mamluk grandees from whose tutelage he unmistakably tried to free himself. Compared with his predecessors – this may be added in parenthesis – Sultan Ḥasan was a cultured ruler.[66] One of the most spectacular mosques of medieval Cairo was erected by him. Revoking his original Turkish proper name Qumārī[67] and replacing it with the Arabic 'Ḥasan' must be seen as a symbolic act. It demonstrated his intention to dissociate himself from the Mamluk system which he, as sultan, himself epitomized.

62 Levanoni, *A Turning Point*, 51–2. On Khalīl b. Qawṣūn see also the important study by Werner Krebs, 'Innen- und Außenpolitik Ägyptens 741–784/1341–1382' (Ph.D. dissertation, University of Hamburg, 1980), 104–5 and note 2.

63 When the amir ʿAlam al-dīn Sanjar al-Ḥimṣī, one-time governor of Raḥba on the Euphrates, resigned from his responsibilities (some time before 743/1343), his *iqṭāʿ* was given to an *ibn al-nās*, the son of the amir ʿAlāʾ al-dīn Aydughmish; see al-Ṣafadī, *al-Wāfī biʾl-wafayāt*, vol. XV, ed. Bernd Radtke, (Wiesbaden, 1979), 484, no. 646.

64 They are enumerated by al-Maqrīzī in *al-Sulūk*, ed. S. ʿĀshūr, (Cairo, 1970–1), vol. III, 63, lines 1–4; the first two were his own sons. Many others held the lesser ranks of *amīr ṭablkhāna* and *amīr ʿashara*. Cf. also the remarks in Holt, *The Age of the Crusades*, 124.

65 On this development see the detailed work of D. Ayalon in 'The eunuchs in the Mamluk sultanate', in M. Rosen-Ayalon (ed.), *Studies in Memory of Gaston Wiet* (Jerusalem, 1977), 267–95 (reprinted in Ayalon, *The Mamlūk Military Society*, article no. 3), here at 291–4. Cf. also Irwin, *The Middle East*, 143.

66 'He was one of the best kings of the Turks,' al-Maqrīzī wrote nostalgically (*Sulūk*, vol. III, 62, line 16). Ḥasan had spent years in confinement, a time of leisure during which he had studied theology, notably al-Bayhaqī's (d. 1066) famous work *Dalāʾil al-nubuwwa*. Also, Ḥasan's Arabic was said to be exceptionally good. Not surprisingly, such a sultan was a favourite of contemporary Arab writers (although, as an individual, he must have been quite repellent: see Irwin, *The Middle East*, 142–4). The Tlemcen-born author Ibn Abī Ḥajala (d. 1375), for instance, who was in the charge of a Ṣūfī convent outside the gates of Cairo, in 757/1356 dedicated a treatise to Ḥasan in which he eulogizes his sovereign as 'the lord of the seven', the noblest figure. This text, the *Kitāb Sukkardān al-sulṭān* (cf. Carl Brockelmann, *Geschichte der arabischen Litteratur* (Leiden, 1949) (hereafter GAL),vol. II, II, 13 (13–14), *Supplementband* II (Leiden, 1938), 6), should be added to the table of 'accession offerings' which is presented by Peter M. Holt in this volume (chap. 1). The list of the 'cabbalistic' ties connecting the sacred seven and al-Nāṣir Ḥasan is given by Otfried Weintritt in his work *Formen spätmittelalterlicher islamischer Geschichtsdarstellung. Untersuchungen zu an-Nuwairī al-Iskandarānīs Kitāb al-Ilmām und verwandten zeitgenössischen Texten,* Beiruter Texte und Studien 45 (Stuttgart, 1992), 192–200, here at 193.

67 See the data in Haarmann: 'Arabic in speech, Turkish in lineage', 104 and note 112.

Sultan Ḥasan's assassination by one of his own Mamluks and the ensuing abolition of most of his anti-Mamluk policies in no way impeded the further strengthening of the position of *awlād al-nās* in the military and in the administration. We continue hearing of *awlād al-nās* in responsible positions. The popular Aḥmad b. Baydamur of Damascus, who met such a tragic end because he had sided with Minṭāsh against Barqūq, is one of the better-known examples.[68] Certain high offices with limited strategic and military influence seem to have remained something of a preserve of the *awlād al-nās* even after Sultan Ḥasan's intermezzo. I am thinking, among other offices, of the vizierate, the administration of the exchequer, the governorship of the cities of Cairo and Alexandria, the office of chamberlain in the Syrian provinces, the inspection of the royal hippodrome, down to the night security in a small centre such as Jerusalem.[69]

For the years 1377 and 1388–9, we have data to compare. They indicate the steadily increasing participation of *awlād al-nās* also in those top offices that, in the 'golden' early days of the sultanate, had been reserved for Mamluks proper. Among the nine officers of the highest rank who accompanied Sultan al-Ashraf Shaʿbān on his last trip, from Cairo to ʿAqaba, in 1377, there was no *ibn al-nās*. In the second rank – the so-called amirs of forty – where one had always found scions of Mamluks, there were seven *awlād al-nās* in a total of twenty-four. And in the third rank, the amirs of ten, the ratio was even five out of fourteen.[70] Eleven years later, seventy-four generals accompanied Sultan Barqūq to the dungeon. Among nine amirs of the highest rank there were now two sons of Mamluks; in the rank of amir of forty, the ratio was eight out of thirty-one; and in the third rank we now even encounter a majority of *awlād al-nās* (nineteen out of thirty-four). The lowest rank of amir of five had practically become a domain for Mamluk descendants in that year.[71] It seems as if these generals recruited from the ranks of *awlād al-nās* were fully integrated into the Mamluk army structure, i.e. they no longer counted as members of the *ḥalqa*.

This ascendancy of the *awlād al-nās* did not survive the change of dynasties from the *dawla turkiyya* to the *dawlat al-jarākisa* under Sultan Barqūq for long. Perhaps the establishment of the *dīwān al-mufrad* by Barqūq in 1395

[68] See Ibn Ṣaṣrā *al-Durra al-muḍīʾa fī al-dawla al-ẓāhiriyya*, ed. and trans. William M. Brinner as *A Chronicle of Damascus 1389–1397* (Berkeley and Los Angeles, 1963), vol. I, 139–42; 139, note 823.

[69] Cf. Lutfi *al-Quds al-mamlûkiyya*, 313, on ʿAlāʾ al-dīn ʿAlī b. Qīrān, from among the *ḥalqa* of Tripoli, who was *mutawallī al-layl* of Jerusalem. Another *ibn al-nās*, Ghars al-dīn Khalīl b. Sayf al-dīn Ṭ-ṭ-mur, for example, served in Jerusalem as assistant of the local *nāʾib* (cf. ibid., 179; 264–5 on non-Mamluks serving as officials in Jerusalem). Under al-Nāṣir Ḥasan *awlād al-nās* (Ibn al-Qushtamurī and a certain Ibn Ṣubḥ) held the *niyāba* of Aleppo and Ṣafad.

[70] al-Maqrīzī, *Sulūk*, vol. III, 274, line 8–275, line 11. See also Haarmann, 'Sons of Mamluks', 163, n. 5, and U. Haarmann, 'Der arabische Osten im späten Mittelalter 1250–1517', in U. Haarmann (ed.), *Geschichte der arabischen Welt*, Munich (3rd edn, 1994), 227–8.

[71] al-Maqrīzī, *Sulūk*, vol. III, 624, line 13–626, line 11.

(which has tentatively been connected with the demise of the Qalāwūnid *sīdīs*[72]) also impaired – in some way or another – the status of the non-royal *awlād al-nās*. A comparison between the tax districts held by Mamluk descendants in 777/1376 during the sultanate of al-Malik al-Ashraf Shaʿbān and the corresponding listings for the year 885/1480 suggests the large-scale disappearance of *awlād al-nās* as fief-holders in Egypt,[73] even though exceptions to this decline cannot have been all too infrequent in the fifteenth century, as we shall see in the next chapter. The *ḥalqa* (including its comparatively prestigious *awlād al-nās* unit) degenerated, yet did not vanish, in the course of the fifteenth and early sixteenth centuries. The gradual and, in the end, irreversible triumph of the rank-and-file Mamluks from the time of Sultan Barsbāy's rule (1422–38) – a process vividly described by Abū Ḥāmid al-Qudsī in the colourful epilogue to his work on the Turks[74] – may also have had an effect on the chances (and the visibility) of the *awlād al-nās* in the competition for power, riches and privileges in a polity whose public[75] resources became increasingly scarce. We do not know enough about these issues for the time being. Certainly one gains the impression that the non-Mamluk *awlād al-nās* found it increasingly hard to play a crucial and prominent role in the central institutions of the Mamluk state and army.[76] And this impression was evidently shared by our two German travellers who visited Cairo during the final two decades of the century.

This does not mean that we no longer hear of sons of Mamluks as holders of public office and as members of the *ḥalqa* even in this late period (one typical example will be introduced in the next chapter). One may refer to Aḥmad b. Nawrūz (d. 852/1448), who is explicitly cited as *ibn al-nās* by contemporary historians.[77] He rose to become amir of twenty in Syria as well as

[72] Haarmann, 'Sons of Mamluks', 162.

[73] Whereas the tax yield granted to sons of officers (i.e. the *sīdīs* are excluded) in 1376 amounted to 573,676 *dīnār jayshī* in the whole of Egypt, distributed over twenty-one tax districts (*jihāt*), we have only 9,175 *dīnār jayshī* (1.6 percent of the former figure) and four tax districts in 1480, allotted to members of this class. These data have been compiled and compared by Haarmann, 'Sons of Mamluks', esp. 158–62. The unique source for this statistical material for both years is Ibn al-Jīʿān's (d. 1480) *al-Tuḥfa al-saniyya bi-asmāʾ al-bilād al-miṣriyya*, ed. B. Moritz (Cairo, 1898), cf. also Halm, *Ägypten*, vol. I, 30–1; Haarmann, 'Sons of Mamluks', 146–7. Such selective statistical material, of course, has its intrinsic weaknesses. On the pitfalls, limitations and contradictions inherent in the data taken from the Egyptian *jarīda iqṭāʿiyya* of Ibn al-Jīʿān's days, see Haarmann, 'Sons of Mamluks', 147–52.

[74] *Duwal al-islām*, 130. On this development see also Amalia Levanoni's contribution to this volume (chap. 2).

[75] This qualification is important, if we keep in mind Carl Petry's rich findings on the rise of a 'shadow economy' in late fifteenth-century Egypt which was closely tied to the institution of *awqāf*; see his key article 'A Paradox of patronage during the later Mamluk period', *Muslim World*, 73 (1983), 183–207, and the chapter on 'Fiscal innovations' in his recent monograph *Protectors or Praetorians?*, pp.196–219.

[76] This opinion is supported by the texts read by Carl Petry for his work *Protectors or Praetorians?*, 86, 99.

[77] Cf. al-Sakhāwī: *al-Ḍawʾ al-lāmiʿ fī aʿyān al-qarn al-tāsiʿ*, (Cairo, n.d.), vol. II, 240.

amir of ten in Cairo. Like other Mamluk descendants in the fifteenth century – another example is Aḥmad b. al-Atābakī Tānī Bak (d. 877/1472–3)[78] – he also officiated for the sultan in the annual pilgrimage to the Ḥijāz (*amīr [al-rakb] al-awwal*). The administration of pious foundations seems to have been another favourite assignment for Mamluk descendants;[79] we will return to this subject. But these were no longer any pivotal appointments. The heyday of the *awlād al-nās* was definitely over by then.

Endowments and real estate

Mamluk officers, members of the *ḥalqa* and selected civilians were remunerated for their services by corresponding *iqṭā*ʿs, i.e. the allocation of the yield of a tax district consistent with the rank and duty of the beneficiary. In accordance with the Mamluk principle of the permanent renewal of the ruling elite from the outside, these grants could not be passed on to heirs. Exceptions[80] did occur (especially at times when the supply of Mamluks could not meet demand, as during the devastating epidemics of the plague,[81] and also in the formative period of the Mamluk polity under the first sultans[82]), yet were always highlighted as an anomaly by contemporary observers. Grants for deserving retired (or disabled) Mamluks as well as their widows and orphans were available in the institution of *rizaq mabrūra,*[83] yet only for a limited time and without any legal claim.

[78] Ibid., vol. I, 265. He held an *iqṭā*ʿ, a quarter of the village Minyat Mirajjā in the delta province of Daqahliyya (see Muḥammad Ramzī, *al-Qāmūs al-jughrāfī li-ʾl-bilād al-miṣriyya* (Cairo, 1953–4), vol. I, 447; Halm: *Ägypten*, vol. II, 739), which was passed on, after his death, to his successor as *amīr al-ḥājj.*

[79] One example is Aḥmad b. Arghūnshāh al-Ashrafī Shaʿbān (d. 833/1429–30), who was both *amīr ʿashara* and in charge of the *awqāf*, see Sakhāwī, *Ḍawʾ*, vol. I, 226.

[80] See Rabie, *Financial System*, 59–60; Haarmann, 'Sons of Mamluks', 145–6 (the case of Ḥusayn b. Jandar Bag whose Mamluks, widow and daughters – at the explicit orders of al-Malik al-Nāṣir Muḥammad – kept the proceeds of his fief after his death in 1327–8; for the contemporaries this ruling was sensational).

[81] As al-Ṣafadī remarks (see *al-Wāfī bi-ʾl-wafayāt*, vol. X, 356, lines 5 and 11–12; I took the reference from Irwin, *The Middle East*, 138), Baybughā al-Ārūs, who was vice-sultan during the first wave of the plague in 1348/9, allowed the sons of *muqta*ʿs to inherit their fathers' fiefs, much to the joy of the people 'who loved him very much for this'. Even so, not all free benefices could be reassigned during the bleak days of the Black Death.

[82] Irwin, *The Middle East*, 50.

[83] These funds accrue from the army *diwan* and are made available to retired officers as well as to their widows and orphans, to *awlād al-nās*, including the descendants of sultans, to scholars and turban-bearers; cf. Muḥammad Muḥammad Amīn, *Al-Awqāf wa-ʾl-ḥayāt al-ijtimāʿiyya fī Miṣr 648–923h./1250–1517 A.D. Dirāsa tārīkhiyya wathāʾiqiyya*, (Cairo, 1980), 109–10; and Muḥammad Muḥammad Amīn, *Catalogue de documents d'archives du Caire de 239/853 à 922/1516 (depuis le IIIᵉ/IXᵉ siècle jusqu'à la fin de l'époque mamlouke) suivi de l'édition critique de neuf documents,* Textes arabes et islamiques, vol. XVI, (Cairo, 1981), 370, n. 1 (see also 356, note 8). The term *rizqa mabrūra* (also *ṣadaqa mabrūra*, *aḥbās mabrūra*) is explained by Qalqashandī, *Ṣubḥ al-aʿshā*, vol. VI, 185, lines 16–20. But once more one should also turn to Arnold von Harff, *The Pilgrimage of Arnold von Harff*, 122: 'But if the Sultan is pleased, out of his grace, to give them something, that they may keep. But these children can never come to rule.'

This philosophy of limiting Mamluk benefits strictly to the first generation, however, collided again and again with the powerful and all-too-human urge of an individual Mamluk dignitary to gather possessions that were safe against collection by the fisc and could be disposed of freely to provide appropriate upkeep for his own progeny. Legal stratagems were elaborated that helped to circumvent this prohibition of alienating state land[84] and provided the all-too-often venal judiciary with lucrative sources of income. One popular device seems to have been returning one's fief voluntarily to the army office, then purchasing it back as private property (*milk*)[85] that could now be sold, passed on to heirs, and turned into an endowment (*waqf*) in full consistency with the Sacred Law of Islam. Exchanging valuable for mediocre *awqāf*[86] with a high profit margin for the *mustabdil* was also common practice in Mamluk times, especially in the Circassian period.[87] Whereas private property was, for all practical purposes, not safe against claims and confiscation[88] by the state, the immunity of an endowment promised at least a certain guarantee against infringements on the part of those in power.

A further word on pious foundations in this period is appropriate. Agricultural yields and proceeds could be endowed not only for the establishment and the upkeep of mosques, colleges and other public charities, but also as so-called family *awqāf* for feeding the donor of a grant and his family. It is not without irony that contemporary observers such as Ibn Khaldūn and Abū Ḥāmid al-Qudsī comment upon the eagerness of Mamluk generals to invest

84 Cf. Poliak, *Feudalism*, 36–7; Halm, *Ägypten*, 54; Haarmann, 'Sons of Mamluks', 165, n. 39, 40.

85 Poliak, *Feudalism*, 36–7 (with an analogy from Muslim Central Asia, the home territory of the Mamluks).

86 This procedure implied three inseparable steps: the alienation of the endowed object by its sale; the purchase of an alternative property from the proceeds of this sale; the endowment of the (inferior) new *milk* in lieu of the original *waqf*. See Amīn, *Catalogue*, 465, n. 1. Both the documents no. 8 (at 463–79) and no. 9 (at 481–508), which are appended to Amīn's *Catalogue* in critical edition, are exchange deeds. See also the remarks in Halm, *Ägypten*, vol. I, 51.

87 This coercive procedure (with all its patently negative aspects) could also have the advantage of uniting small lots owned by different individuals or institutions into sizeable territories on which city planning became possible again; see Haarmann, 'Der arabische Osten', 251. In Amīn's catalogue of Mamluk documents (nos. 819–28, 830, see *Catalogue*, 307–11) we read of the civilian Aḥmad b. Barakāt b. Ḥasan, known as al-Najāniqī, who acquired, through *istibdāl*, a total of eleven objects, half of them state property of one or the other category, which were then summarily sold (*bayʿ*) or transferred (*intiqāl*) to Sultan Qānṣūh al-Ghawrī who, in turn, made them *waqf*. Aḥmad b. Barakāt evidently served as a broker or agent for his ruler. It would be interesting to see whether the lots listed in these eleven entries form a geographical whole; for this purpose the presently inaccessible documents themselves would have to be consulted. On the ease with which the illegal exchange of *awqāf* was carried out in the days of Sultan Qānṣūh al-Ghawrī, see Annemarie Schimmel (trans.), *Ibn Iyās. Alltagsnotizen eines ägyptischen Bürgers*, Bibliothek arabischer Klassiker, vol. XIII (Stuttgart, 1985), 26.

88 Qānṣūh al-Ghawrī, 'otherwise the best Circassian, if not Egyptian ruler', was especially notorious for his confiscations; see Schimmel, *Ibn Iyās*, 7. Petry, *Protectors or Praetorians?* also castigates Sultan Qāytbāy for his excessive indulgence in random confiscations. In both cases the reasons for this policy were clear: the treasury was empty and other ways had to be found to fill the coffers of the state. Even *awqāf* were seized by Qāytbāy in 1491, see Elizabeth M. Sartain, *Jalāl al-dīn al-Suyūṭī*, (Cambridge, 1975), vol. I, 97.

in pious foundations.[89] Enhancing their status in this and in the other world, as well as making provisions for their families for the time after their own death or demotion, were, they maintain, the real motives behind this liberality. Very much to the wrath of incorruptible legists, it became a dubious custom to appoint one's own descendants as administrators of such pious endowments – a practice that fitted perfectly the needs of Mamluk fathers and of their sons who were given control over all the revenue and expenditure of the foundation.[90] Hundreds of charitable and learned institutions thus came into being in late medieval Cairo and proved an important link between the Mamluks and the learned civilians who were the spokesmen of the local population.[91]

One very negative effect of this policy was the unavoidable rapid shrinking of the state land that was needed for the military grants. In large quantities, *iqṭāʿ*s were transformed into *rizaq mabrūra* or into private property. The Mamluk army was deprived of much of its material basis and correspondingly weakened. By his own days, the chronicler Ibn Taghrībirdī (d. 1467) laments, the Egyptian forces had shrunk to one-third of their former strength.[92] Ibn Taghrībirdī, himself a Mamluk scion (and, through his mother, a great-great-great-grandson of Qalāwūn[93]), incidentally did not forget to endow a sizeable *waqf* for himself one year before his death, through which the erection and appropriate equipment of his personal funerary mosque 'in the Desert' (the City of the Dead to the north of the Cairo Citadel) was supposed to be financed.[94] Many villages which, at the end of fourteenth century, were still recorded as feudal (*iqṭāʿ*) territory had, two generations later, reverted to allodial or *waqf* land.[95]

Of course there were among the successful *awlād al-nās* not only those who had inherited real estate or acquired a current income from a pious foundation, thanks to the farsightedness and flexibility of their fathers, but also – as we have seen in the passages on the military – those Mamluk scions who had qualified as full-fledged members of the Mamluk hierarchy thanks to their

[89] On Ibn Khaldūn see D. Ayalon, 'The Muslim city and the Mamluk military aristocracy', *Proceedings of the Israel Academy of Sciences and Humanities,* 2 (1968) (reprinted in Ayalon, *Studies on the Mamlūks of Egypt,* article 7), 311–29, here at 327. For Abū Ḥāmid see his *Badhl al-naṣā'iḥ*, fol. 11a.

[90] Taqī al-dīn al-Subkī (d. 1355) wrote on this sensitive issue his (unpublished) tract *al-Qawl al mūʿib fī 'l-qaḍā' al-mūjib*: see *GAL*, vol. II, 87 [107].

[91] Ira M. Lapidus, *Muslim Cities in the Later Middle Ages* (Cambridge, Mass). 1967, 74 also mentions the *awlād al-nās* in this context.

[92] Ibn Taghrībirdī's pertinent text, a passage in his chronicle *al-Nujūm al-zāhira*, is translated by Ayalon: 'Studies on the structure of the Mamluk army – I', 26. See also Halm, *Ägypten*, vol. I, 54. [93] Holt, *The Age of the Crusades*, 125.

[94] This document of 870/1466 is registered in Muḥammad Muḥammad Amīn, *Catalogue*, no. 159, at 35. The content of this *waqfiyya,* the begining of which is not preserved, is summarized – with some verbatim quotations from the text – by: ʿAbd al-Laṭīf Ibrāhīm 'Alī: 'Al-Muḥāḍara al-tāsiʿa: Waqfiyyat Ibn Taghrī Birdī', in *al-Mu'arrikh Ibn Taghrī Birdī. Majmūʿat abḥāth* (Cairo, 1974), 181–222. [95] Halm, *Ägypten*.

personal achievement and who were assigned a land grant commensurate with their rank and duty in their own right. As has been said before, their number seems to have been much larger than has hitherto been the accepted opinion – at least up to Barqūq's time when their dramatic demise seems to have begun. In the year 1377, as much as 6 per cent (or even 14 per cent, if we include the sons and brothers of ruling sultans, who naturally formed a category with special privileges) of all the cultivated land of Egypt was granted to sons of Mamluks as military fiefs.[96]

Among the almost 900 private documents from Cairo, which were made available by Muḥammad Muḥammad Amīn in brief descriptions (which include the date of issue, the names of the persons involved in the act as well as its legal category, but unfortunately no geographical data), there are specimens testifying to at least 200 transactions in which sons, grandsons, and, last but not least, daughters of Mamluks play a part.[97] The vast majority of these documents involving the progeny of Mamluks are sales, exchange and endowment deeds. The most variegated groups within Mamluk society participated in these dealings.[98] In one case, for example, a *sīdī* (the short-term sultan Aḥmad b. Īnāl) establishes a foundation together with his former slave.[99] Property is passed on from *awlād al-nās* to Mamluks and vice versa.[100] We find female descendants of Mamluks doing business not only with Mamluks,[101]

96 Haarmann, 'Sons of Mamluks', 158–62.

97 Amīn's *Catalogue* offers itself for this type of statistical enquiry. In the following documents of this work, *awlād al-nās* (including grandsons and female relatives of Mamluks) are recorded as subjects of deeds which contain up to fourteen (see nos. 322, 389, 514) individual transactions (marked by letters): nos. 41, 42, 43, 45, 46, 48, 58, 86, 98, 107, 112b, 120, 129, 132, 143, 144, 145, 149, 150b, 153, 155, 158, 159, 171b, 178b, 185c, 189, 190, 192, 213c, 224, 247, 254, 262, 264, 272a–c, 274, 282, 292, 308b, 309b, 310a, 311b, 314b, 314c, 322g,k, 327b, 333a–c, 339a,d, 349a, 350b, 357b, 361d, 362a, 366d,e, 374a, 375d,f, 379a, 381a,b, 382, 389, 390b, 404, 406a,d, 407, 409, 410, 418, 428 (see below), 430a,b,d, 438, 439, 441, (442), 445, 447, 449b,c, 453b, 457a, 458c,d, 459a,b, 463a, 464, 469a,b, 478a, 480a, 482a, 485, 489c, 493a, 497a, 501, 506, 523, 525a–d, 526a–c, 527c, 529a, 532b, 541d,e, 557, 559a,b, 561, 565, 575a, 584, 585(?), 586a–b,e–f, 593a,b, 594a, 595a, 611a, 620b,c, 629a,c,d, 630a, 654a, 661a, 679, 680a, 681a, 686a, 689a, 692a, 693, 694c,d, 696a,b,d, 697c, 712a,c, 713a,c, 717a,b, 731, 732a,b, 741d,e, 742c,d, 743b,c, 744a,b, 753a,b, 754a–c, 756a–c, 759a–c, 761a,b, 769, 784, 799, 800, 803a, 806a, 811a–b, 814, 815, 832, 838, 845c, 847, 848a,b, 849, 850a,b.

98 See my review of Amīn's catalogue in *Welt des Islams,* 27 (1987), 127–30. An example of such social permeability is no. 231.

99 Amīn, *Catalogue*, no. 247. The manumitter Aḥmad, the son of Sultan Īnāl, ruled as sultan for a brief period in the year 865/1461; his regnal title was al-Malik al-Mu'ayyad. His freedwoman was a certain Dilbār bt ʿAbdallāh. The establishment of the common *waqf* occurred decades after Aḥmad had been dethroned. In document no. 129, a freedman (eunuch) of a daughter of Sultan Faraj makes an endowment.

100 In document no. 389, Mamluks and the *ibn al-nās* Yaḥyā b.Ṭūghān succeed each other several times as owners of the given object. In the end, Yaḥyā b.Ṭūghān turns it into an endowment. On Yaḥyā b. Ṭūghān see the detailed remarks at the end of this chapter.

101 Documents nos. 308 (Fāṭima, presumably an old lady, gives away in exchange her great-great-grandfather Alāqūsh's *waqf* to the Mamluk chief treasurer and superintendent of the *ḥisba* in the year 908/1502, see also documents no. 565 and 655) and 310 (Shīrīn bt Quṭlūbughā al-Silaḥdār al-Manṣūrī sells property to a Mamluk general in 743/1344).

but also among themselves.[102] Religious boundaries are easily crossed in these dealings.[103] We encounter *awlād al-nās* and eunuchs together in a document of the mid-eighth/fourteenth century, when both groups were close partners not only in the ranks of the *ḥalqa* and in the special favour of Sultan Ḥasan, but obviously in Mamluk society at large.[104]

I have selected one particularly interesting endowment deed of the year 861/1457[105] that contains the type of information to be gained from the Cairo documents on *awlād al-nās*. The grantor of the *waqf*, a certain Yaḥyā b. Ṭūghān al-Ḥasanī,[106] was – as can be seen from his name – an *ibn al-nās*. He also quite appropriately served in the *ḥalqa*, whose reputation, however, as has been discussed, had deteriorated by the middle of the fifteenth century. Yaḥyā b. Ṭūghān, who is mentioned also in several other documents of the Cairo collection,[107] owned rural property in the Nile delta that he could afford to endow as a family *waqf*. His relative affluence stands for the material opportunities that were open for a member of the Mamluk second generation under felicitous circumstances even in this period. It also stands for the necessity to try to salvage part of that wealth for one's progeny and relatives through the institution of the pious endowment.

Yaḥyā's private holdings consisted of the whole village of Barshans on the right branch of the Nile in the province of al-Manūfiyya[108] and of one-fifth of another village, Shinrāqā in the northern province of al-Gharbiyya.[109] The latter was divided into two shares (*ḥiṣṣa*). For 1376, the year for which we have

102 See no. 379a: Tatar, the daughter of ʿAlī b. Bahādur, sells to Mughul, the daughter of al-Sayfī Dimurdāsh, in 854/1450, who two years later sells the property to a civilian. See also no. 137. In no. 361, the Mamluk al-Sayfī Taghrībirdī makes his daughter owner of the property; later on (after a brief 'male' interlude) it seems to have been transferred to another woman, Güzel, the daughter as well as wife of a Mamluk, who then endows it as *waqf*.

103 Excellent examples are the documents nos. 390 and 511a-d. In no. 580, a Christian lady buys property from a Muslim.

104 See document no. 311. Shaun Marmon (Princeton) has studied the careers of eunuchs in Mamluk Egypt, also on the basis of the Cairo documents. Reference should also be made to Ayalon, 'The eunuchs in the Mamluk sultanate', and Petry, *Protectors or Praetorians?*, 202f.

105 Amīn, *Catalogue*, no. 428, at 133–4. I gratefully acknowledge Shaun Marmon's kindness in procuring me a photocopy of this important document, which is preserved in the Ministry of Pious Foundations in Cairo (registration no. 571 jīm).

106 His father (if this ascription is right) was the *dawādār* Ṭūghān al-Ḥasanī 'al-Majnūn'; see Michael Meinecke, 'Zur mamlukischen Heraldik', *Mitteilungen des Deutschen Archäologischen Instituts Abteilung Kairo* 28 (1972), 213–87, here at 282. The respectable social status of Ṭūghān al-Ḥasanī is reflected in the fact that he had Mamluks of his own; one of them, a certain Shāhīn al-Ṭūghānī, is mentioned by Sakhāwī in: *Ḍaw'*, vol. III, no. 1138, at 295f. Both al-Sakhāwī and Ibn Taghrībirdī (*al-Manhal al-ṣāfī*) fail to mention Yaḥyā in their biographical dictionaries. The blazon of Ṭūghān of the year 815/1412–13 is mentioned in Meinecke, 'Zur mamlukischen Heraldik', 282.

107 See also nos. 389, 525; possibly also in 561. It would be desirable to consult these texts also before a final word is said on our *wāqif*. Should the Mamluk al-Sayfī Ṭūghān, mentioned in document no. 166, have been his father, the chronology notwithstanding (he made an endowment in the year 872/1467–8, i.e. ten years later)?

108 Halm, *Ägypten*, vol II, 361 (map no. 23, north of Cairo).

109 Ibid., 577 (map no. 35, south of Samannūd).

Ibn al-Jīʿān's cadastral survey, the first object is recorded as the *iqṭāʿ* of a *sīdī*, Amīr Ḥājj, the son of al-Ashraf Shaʿbān and future sultan. At that time the second village was under the control of unnamed *muqṭaʿ*s. By 1400 (the time for which we have Ibn Duqmāq's statistical data[110]), Shinrāqā had become a fief of *ḥalqa* troopers. After that time, the information on these two tax districts breaks off, until they re-emerge in the document as *milk* or partial *milk* of our *ibn al-nās*.

The dispositions of the *wāqif,* as they are fixed in his deed, are telling for the historian. The yield of his endowment is to be made available, in shares (one-eighth, one-sixteenth etc.), first for his children, his sister and his half-sister, then for his mother (possibly a relative of the historian Ibn Taghrībirdī), then for his maternal grandmother, a Turkish lady with the beautiful name Jijik (Çiçek) 'blossom', and finally for his wives and for his stepmother. Particular care was to be given to his tomb. Every Friday the Koran was to be read there on his behalf. During the week, sessions in the house of his son should suffice – if my reading is correct. Should his lineage and the lineage of his freed slaves (the customary beneficiaries of a will if no immediate relatives are left[111]) die out, the proceeds of his endowment were to be made available for charitable purposes in the Holy Cities of Mecca and Medina.[112]

The control over his trust and its provisions was conferred on a sequence of obviously highly respected Mamluk dignitaries (beginning with a certain Kumushbughā[113] b. ʿAbdallāh al-Timrāzī). If they all should prove inept or unavailable, the holder of the office of chief eunuch in the royal palace (*zimām al-ādur al-sharīfa*), an experienced administrator by virtue of his function, was to step in. He would not embezzle funds for the benefit of descendants of his own.

Incidentally, his services were not needed. Almost thirty years after the *waqfiyya* had been drawn up, i.e. presumably after the death of the grantor, his son Muḥammad al-Sibāʿī, in connivance with Kumushbughā, the first controller named in the deed, disposed of two parts of the endowed property in two instalments (890/1485 and 891/1486) through *istibdāl*, selling it to two civil-

110 Halm has also collated the (fragmentary) information contained in Ibn Duqmāq's *Kitāb al-Intiṣār* on the Egyptian tax districts and integrated it into his catalogue.

111 We find similar dispositions, for example, in the *waqfiyya* of the eunuch Jawhar, a resident of Jerusalem in that time; see Donald Richards in Michael Burgoyne and Donald Richards, *Mamluk Jerusalem: An Architectural Study* (London, 1987), no. 58, at 557b and 567a note 20, but also in Ottoman times. See Daniel Crecelius, 'The waqf of Muhammad Bey Abu al-Dhahab in historical perspective', *International Journal of Middle East Studies,* 23 (1991), 57–81, here at 67.

112 This final provision is also customary in Egyptian *waqfiyya*s up to the nineteenth century. Donald Richards points out the essential logic of such decreasing lists of beneficiaries (Burgoyne and Richards, *Mamluk Jerusalem*, 66b), saying that no charitable trust was allowed to fail for want of an object and that the series of benficiaries enumerated in the *waqfiyya* always ended 'with some permanent category'. Among those we can also count the eunuchs of Mecca: see Petry, *Protectors or Praetorians?*, 202–3.

113 See line 51 of the document. Kumushbughā/Gümüshboghā means 'silver bull'. Amīn, *Catalogue*, 133, falsely reads K-m-t-bughā.

ians. Alienating *waqf* property through this stratagem had by then become a common practice. The first portion of the sale went, as early as 890/1485, to the daughter of a Mamluk in the name and probably also at the order of her father.[114] The other half was purchased by a son of a Mamluk, Ibrāhīm b. Khushqadam[115] in 891/1486, who again sold it to a Mamluk, al-Sayfī Timrāz al-Khāṣṣakī of the royal guard, in 894/1489. Four years later, in 898/1493, this officer, together with his wife, finally turned the estate into a pious foundation, as it had originally been.

These changing patterns of proprietorship illuminate the permanent availability of such fortunes, even if they should legally have remained inalienable forever. More important still, we observe a highly permeable society in which by no means all real estate transactions ended in the hands and to the benefit of the mighty Mamluk ruling caste. One rather gains the impression that Mamluk descendants were important mediators, brokers, and often also proxies in such transactions. We know of one *ibn al-nās*, al-Nāṣirī Muḥammad b. Taghrībirmish b. ʿAbdallāh al-Muḥibbī, who is credited with owning (or holding) as many as twenty-three units of real estate (or other comparable property),[116] which Sultan Qānṣūh al-Ghawrī then took over[117] and invested in his numerous pious endowments.[118] That *awlād al-nās* were clever businessmen is attested in sources as early as the late thirteenth century.[119] The general

114 Ibn al-Jīʿān (reporting on the state of affairs some time between 872/1468 and 885/1480, see Halm, *Ägypten*, vol. I, 32) names the Mamluk Uzbak al-Atābakī as *muqṭaʿ* of the village of Barshans in his time. This Uzbak is not mentioned in the document. Obviously the two shares, sold in 890 or 891 respectively, refer only to the one-fifth of the village of Shinrāqā.

115 We find him figuring prominently in numerous documents; see Amīn, *Catalogue*, nos. 389, 428, 525, 526, 527 and 529.

116 See Amīn, *Catalogue*, nos. 274, 314, 366, 458, 585, 620, 629, 717, 731, 732, 741, 742, 743, 753, 754, 756, 759, 769, 784, 799, 811, 814 and 815. Eight transactions (nos. 458, 742, 753, 754, 756, 759, 769, 784) in which Ibn Taghrībirmish acquired holdings took place in the second half of the year 914 (September 1508 to March 1509) alone; the others are distributed more or less evenly from 910/1505 to 919/1513. The (incomplete) list given in my review of Amīn's catalogue (*Welt des Islams* 27 (1987), 129) also includes two entries (nos. 680 and 681) that refer to Muḥammad b. al-Sayfī Taghrībirmish al-Ḥalabī, known as Ibn Q-j-q, whose father had served as *nāʾib al-qalʿa* in 872/1467 as we learn from document no. 168. In the end, both holdings of this second Ibn Taghrībirmish also became part of Ghawrī's *waqf*; in the second case (no. 681, year 911/1505), Maḥmūd b. Ajā al-Ḥanafī (the son of the well-known historian? see *GAL Supplementband* III, 1250) served as agent for the sultan. Only in no. 532 is Ibn Taghrībirmish al-Muḥibbī mentioned in a transaction that did *not* end up in Ghawrī's hands. The names of all the individuals through whose mediation Ghawrī acquired *milk* (which could then be changed into *waqf*) are listed in the comprehensive study by Petry, *Protectors or Praetorians?*, 215–16.

117 Petry, *Protectors or Praetorians?*, 204–8 makes clear that these transferrals were, for the most part, anything but voluntary. The notion of 'purchasing', if applied to Ghawrī's huge acquisitions of former state land, appears as a mere euphemism.

118 In one case indirectly, see no. 732. On Ghawrī's (and Qāytbāy's) *waqf* policies, see the long (and lavishly documented) discourse in Petry, *Protectors or Praetorians?*, chap. 7, part 2: 'Fiscal innovations: waqf manipulation as investment strategy', 196–210.

119 One example is the amir Nāṣir al-dīn Muḥammad b. Khaṭlubā, d. 763/1362. see al-Ṣafadī, *al-Wāfī bi-ʾl-wafayāt*, vol. III, 41f; Haarmann, 'Arabic in speech, Turkish in lineage', 106, note 121. Another case is Dāwūd b. Asad al-Qaymarī, d. 763/1362, provided he qualifies as an *ibn al-nās*, see Ibn Ḥajar, *al-Durar al-kāmina*, vol. II, no. 1679, at 186.

picture of the economic activities of Mamluk scions in the late Middle Ages, however, remains very incomplete and uneven for the time being. Research has hardly begun and will largely depend on the full availablility of the archival documents.

The Haven of Culture

The *awlād al-nās*, as a corporate body, enjoyed specific social advantages. They constituted a bridge between the alien Turks and the native Egyptians and Syrians. It was their collective privilege to have unencumbered access to, and membership rights in, both the military and the civil worlds which were otherwise so rigidly kept apart from each other. They were thoroughly familiar with the Turkish–Mamluk cosmos of their fathers and with the world of culture that was articulated in Arabic by the local civilian elite. This twofold competence is visible in their manifold contributions to contemporary writing and scholarship. They enjoyed the freedom of choice as to where to direct their loyalties. Should they be Mamluks first, or rather opt for a full integration into the local population? Or was it not sensible to try to keep the best of both worlds?

In the *vitae* of fourteenth-century *awlād al-nās,* we find in roughly half the sample the coalescence of a military career (up to the rank of *amīr ṭablkhāna*, 'amir of forty', and even beyond) with an involvement in religious and cultural matters.[120] One person may have sought academic honours, whereas his brother was employed in the military administration.[121] Offices which were not clearly defined as military or civil – like the vizierate[122] – seem to have been

120 See for example al-Amīr Aḥmad b. Kushtughdī (d. 744/1343); al-Ṣafadī received an *ijāza* from him in Cairo in 728/1327–8. See *al-Wāfī bi'-l-wafayāt*, vol. VII, ed. Ihsan Abbas (Wiesbaden, 1969), no. 3285, at 298; Ibn Ḥajar, *al-Durar al-kāmina*, vol. I, no. 608, at 253; or, one military degree below, the *jundī* Abū Bakr b. Aydughdī, also of the fourteenth century, who was a sedulous scholar with a special penchant for Arabic: cf. Ibn Hajar, *al-Durar al-kāmina*, vol. I, no. 1170, at 471f. A third name is al-Amīr Aḥmad b. Bīlīk al-Muḥsinī (died 1353), *muqṭaʿ* in Damascus and sometime governor of Dimyāṭ; see al-Ṣafadī, *al-Wāfī bi-ʾl-wafayāt*, vol. VI, no. 2773, at 280; Ibn Ḥajar, *al-Durar al-kāmina*, vol. I, no. 322, at 124. He was a long-time companion of the famous Syrian governor Tankiz, had studied Shāfiʿite law and wrote prose and poetry, including an anthology with the title *Rawḍ al-nāẓir wa-nuzhat al-khāṭir,* see *GAL Supplementband* II, 54 (7a). One of his poems was also greeted with great applause by critical contemporaries. On the general topic see also Haarmann, 'Arabic in speech, Turkish in lineage', 108f. In most cases it must have been the civil and not the military qualification that brought these individuals into the scope of the authors of biographical works.

121 This seems to have been the case – at least in tendency – with the two sons of Bīlīk al-Muḥsinī, Shihāb al-dīn Aḥmad (see preceding note) and Nāṣir al-dīn Muḥammad; see al-Ṣafadī, *al-Wāfī bi-ʾl-wafayāt*, vol. VI, no. 2773, at 280. Unlike his brother Aḥmad, Nāṣir al-dīn Muḥammad was no scholar. He was governor of Cairo (Ibn Ḥajar, *al-Durar al-kāmina*, vol. IV, no. 3610, at 31) and, among other public duties, administered the polo field at Bāb al-Lūq. But he too maintained at least some contacts to contemporary intellectuals, such as the chronicler Ibn al-Dawādārī: see Haarmann, 'Quellen zur Geschichte des islamischen Ägyptens', *Mitteilungen des Deutschen Archäologischen Instituts Abteilung Kairo* 38 (1982), 201–10, here at 204 (sub anno 676).

122 This office passed into Mamluk hands only under Sultan Qalāwūn: see Ibn al-Dawādārī, *Kanz al-durar*, vol. VIII, 281, line 16.

particularly attractive for *awlād al-nās*. In writing, military topics, not surprisingly, were among their favourites; Ibn Aranbughā al-Zardakāsh of the fifteenth century, for example, compiled the standard work on siege engines.[123] The coexistence of Arabic and Turkish as means of communication in contemporary society was another topic tailored to their specific needs and strengths.[124]

The heraldic emblem of the pen-box, which both the *dawādār*, the Mamluk secretary of state, and many *awlād al-nās* were entitled to wear,[125] also symbolizes the placement of Mamluk descendants at the fulcrum between the powerful military ruling caste and the learned classes. Normally only Mamluks were entitled to have a blazon. And it is telling to find the military technical term *taqdima*, 'command (in the *ḥalqa*)', also used metaphorically for academic excellence in the civilian career of an *ibn al-nās*.[126]

As trustees of important endowed institutions of higher learning of Sunni Islam, *awlād al-nās* represented the interests both of the Mamluks – the patrons of these colleges, and of the academic establishment itself. If they knew Arabic, the main vehicle of culture, well enough,[127] they could not be labelled barbarians like their Mamluk forebears with their ignorance of, or their heavy accents in, the language of the Koran and of the Prophet.

Admittedly, not all *awlād al-nās* were ready or able to function as mediators. Some opted unambiguously for one side or the other. Many – preferably the sons of Turkish mothers, one must surmise – remained attached to the court and contented themselves with the limited military careers open to them and with the culture that was cultivated in the palaces and barracks of the Mamluk amirs. We hear of Anas b. Kitbughā, the son of a sultan, who made himself a name through his prowess in archery.[128] Mamluk noble birth was not so easily forgotten[129].

Other *awlād al-nās* turned their backs disdainfully (and with a feeling of disappointment, frustration and resentment) on the realm of their soldier fathers, a world smelling of horses, sweat and weaponry. At times they even rejected the Ḥanafī, 'Turkish', *madhhab* inherited from their fathers. These 'renegades' seem to have been particularly numerous in Syria with its strong *'ulamā'* body and tradition. The dull sessions with his apathetic comrades-in-arms proved

[123] *Al-Anīq fī 'l-manājanīq*, ed. Nabīl Muḥammad 'Abd al-'Azīz. Maṣādir wa-dirāsāt fī tārīkh al-tiknūlūjiyā al-'arabiyya, vol. IV (Aleppo, 1405/1985).

[124] See my remarks on al-Ṣafadī and Ibn Taghrībirdī in 'Arabic in speech, Turkish in lineage', 112–13, n. 158, 162.

[125] Meinecke 'Zur mamlukischen Heraldik', 281–5. His findings are partially based on the prior research by Leo A. Mayer; see especially his article 'A propos du blason sous les Mamluks circassiens', *Syria*, 8 (1937), 389–93.

[126] Sakhāwī: *Ḍaw'*, vol. II, no. 1044, at 322 (*taqdima fī 'l-'ilm* of Amīr Ḥājj b. (Al)Ṭunbughā).

[127] Having an Egyptian mother was helpful – although not necessarily sufficient – in this regard, keeping the Arabic diglossia in mind.

[128] On him, see my other contribution to this volume (chap. 11).

[129] See the pertinent remarks in the biogram of Amīr Ḥājj b. Mughulṭāy in Sakhāwī, *Ḍaw'*. vol. II, no. 1047, at 322. The *ism* Amīr Ḥājj, incidentally, seems to have been especially popular among *awlād al-nās*. See the numerous entries in Sakhāwī's *al-Ḍaw'*.

too much for the amir Muḥammad b. Jankalī b. al-Bābā[130] (d. 1340). He turned to pious and learned men and acquired remarkable skills in disciplines which were of particular prestige to local academicians, such as *ḥadīth* and Arabic grammar. A contemporary chronicler lauds him[131] as 'a member of the *awlād al-nās* who had an excellent command of Arabic'. One of the most important theoreticians in the science of tradition, the Shāfiʿī Khalīl b. Kaykaldī al-ʿAlāʾī (d. 1359), was an *ibn al-nās* who at some time no longer found satisfaction in the Mamluk professions and exchanged the 'garment of the *ḥalqa* soldier' for 'the garment of jurisprudence'.[132] Badr al-dīn Muḥammad b. Bahādur al-Zarkashī, named 'the Turk' because of his ethnic background (d. 1391), was a highly respected authority in the lofty sciences of *uṣūl* and logic;[133] he had studied both with 'civilian' and Mamluk teachers. Idrīs b. Baydakīn al-Turkumānī of the fourteenth century excelled as a preacher against the perils of popular religious practices.[134]

Sons of Mamluk soldiers and officers who were attracted to the Sufi path also played their part in mysticism. One may want to single out the well-known Aḥmad b. Ālmalik al-Jūkandār (d. 1391), who had been one of the ten highest generals whom Sultan Ḥasan had nominated from the ranks of *awlād al-nās.* He had already been promoted to an officer's rank in his father's lifetime. Among his assignments we find the governorship of Gaza province. He had acquired considerable wealth from his rich fiefs stretching from the Nile delta to the southern tip of Upper Egypt.[135] One day in the year 779/1377–8 he took off the 'garment of war', was seen riding on a donkey, learned to live from the proceeds from the foundations his father had established, and devoted the rest of his life to *dhikr*, the remembrance of God, in the Holy City of Mecca.[136]

The disciplines in which Mamluk descendants opting for a non-military

130 See Ṣafadī, *al-Wāfī bi-ʾl-wafayāt,* vol. II, ed. Sven Dedering 2nd edn, (Wiesbaden, 1974), no. 755, at 310–13, as well as Mufaḍḍal b. abī ʾl-Faḍāʾil, *al-Nahj al-sadīd*, ed. Samira Kortantamer, in *Ägypten und Syrien zwischen 1317 und 1341 in der Chronik des Mufaḍḍal b. Abī ʾl-Faḍāʾil* (Freiburg, 1973), 266f. See also Haarmann, 'Arabic in speech, Turkish in lineage', 109. Muḥammad b. Jankalī was thc son of a *wāfidī*, a non-slave Mamluk. On the reading 'al-Bābā' instead of 'Albābā' see Ṣafadī, *al-Wāfī bi-ʾl-wafayāt* vol. X, no. 4502, at 61 (the name is classified under the letter bāʾ).

131 *Wa-kāna min fuṣaḥāʾ awlād al-nās.* See Shams al-dīn al-Shujāʿī, *Tārīkh al-Malik al-Nāṣir Muḥammad b. Qalāwūn al-Ṣāliḥī wa-awlādihi*, ed. Barbara Schäfer, Quellen zur Geschichte des Islamischen Ägyptens, vol. IIa (Cairo, 1398/1978), p.121, line 5; German translation (vol. IIb) (Wiesbaden, 1985), at 157.

132 Ṣafadī, *al-Wāfī bi-ʾl-wafayāt,* vol. XIII, ed. Muḥammad al-Ḥujayrī (Wiesbaden, 1404/1984), 410–16; Ibn Ḥajar, *al-Durar al-kāmina*, vol. II, no. 1666, at 179–82. Al-Ṣafadī corresponded with him in prose and verse.

133 *GAL* vol. II, 91; *Supplementband* II, 108. One of his works bears the title *Luqṭat al-ʿajlān fī uṣūl al-fiqh wa-ʾl-manṭiq.*

134 See his *Kitāb al-Lumaʿ fī ʾl-ḥawādith wa-ʾl-bidaʿ*, ed. Subhi Labib, Quellen zur Geschichte des Islamischen Ägyptens, vol. III, (Wiesbaden, 1986). Another Turkoman, the *ibn al-nās* Dāniyāl b. Manklī (d. 696/1296–7), who served as qāḍī in Shawbak in Transjordan, was another faithful member of the scholarly community of the time. Among his students we find luminaries such as al-Mizzī and al-Birzālī.

135 See Haarmann, 'Sons of Mamluks', 143.

136 Ibn Ḥajar, *al-Durar al-kāmina*, vol. I, no. 298, at 115f.

career tried to excel are correspondingly varied. Certainly they did not shun those arts and sciences held to be particularly prestigious and at the same time demanding, especially as far as the command of Arabic was concerned. So we find them active in legal hermeneutics and *ḥadīth,*[137] in grammar,[138] poetry[139] and calligraphy.[140] Some of them were prolific in numerous of these difficult subjects at the same time.[141] The mathematical discipline of time-keeping, an essential craft for proper everyday religious practice, was also pursued by members of their class (as well as by genuine Mamluks).[142] One wonders whether the *awlād al-nās* did not, at times, approach the religious sciences and the fields of literature and language with so much zeal because they wanted to make visible to everybody which social choice they had taken. This effort did not necessarily remain unappreciated; al-Sakhāwī presents an individual, who proved more knowledgeable than expected, as a typical *ibn al-nās.*[143]

The historian Khalīl b. Aybak al-Ṣafadī (d. 1363), the author of the largest medieval prosopography in both Islam and the West, the *Kitāb al-Wāfī bi-'l-wafayāt*, may well be the foremost representative of those *awlād al-nās* who were committed to assimilating into their environment without cutting their ties to their Turkish background. He left us important and precise information on his Mamluk acquaintances in Galilee and elsewhere, his book was unmistakably held in high esteem in Mamluk circles,[144] and he even pondered over the riddles of Turkish. Nevertheless, his predilection for the world of the *kuttāb* and *ʿulamāʾ* is obvious, as if he wanted to draw a line between himself and the world of his father. If this hypothesis is correct, it would no longer be surprising that Arabic literary theory and rhetoric, the queens among the

[137] Two examples are Aḥmad b. Quṭlū al-ʿAlāʾī (d. 1391), who had his own group of students: see Ibn Ḥajar, *al-Durar al-kāmina*, vol. I, no. 607, at 252f, and Aḥmad b. Aybak al-Ḥusāmī al-Dimyāṭī (Ibn Aybak) (d. 749/1348–9 of the plague), a specialist in tradition, who wrote a supplement to ʿAbd al-ʿAẓīm al-Mundhirī's well-known thirteenth-century dictionary of *muḥaddithīn:* see Ibn Ḥajar, *al-Durar al-kāmina*, vol. I, no. 299, at 116.

[138] See, e.g., Abū Bakr b. Mughulṭāy of the fourteenth century; Ibn Ḥajar, *al-Durar al-kāmina*, vol. I, no. 1252, at 499.

[139] Their flirtations with Arabic poetry and prosody were not always successful – the above-mentioned Muḥammad b. Jankalī b. al-Bābā is an example if one follows his biographers – others, however, became respected *udabāʾ*. We already mentioned the Shafiʿite jurist Aḥmad b. Bīlīk al-Muḥsinī (d. 1353) as a successful author of verse.

[140] For example, Muḥammad b. Baktūt al-Ẓāhirī, better known as al-Qarandalī (d. 1334); he excelled in the seven calligraphic scripts (*al-aqlām al-sabʿa*) and was appointed royal calligrapher at the Ayyubid court of Ḥamāh. See al-Ṣafadī, *al-Wāfī bi-ʾl-wafayāt*, vol. II, no. 670, at 256f.

[141] One may want to name – *pars pro toto* – Burhān al-dīn Ibrāhīm b. Lājīn (d. 749/1349–50 of the plague). Grammar, logic, *uṣūl al-fiqh*, the seven readings, the law of inheritance, arithmetic and medicine were all his specialty. See Ṣafadī, *al-Wāfī bi-ʾl-wafayāt*, vol. VI, no. 2614, at 164f; Ibn Ḥajar: *al-Durar al-kāmina*, vol. I, no. 201, at 77f.

[142] See David King's contribution to this volume (chap. 9) with his list of Mamluk and non-Mamluk *muwaqqitūn*.

[143] *Ḍawʾ*, vol. III, no. 45, at 10 (biography of Barsbughā al-Julbānī).

[144] The key manuscript of *al-Wāfī bi-ʾl-wafayāt* (it also serves as the basis of the critical edition appearing in *Bibliotheca Islamica*) was in the property of the famous fifteenth-century general and chief *dawādār* Yashbak al-Ẓāhirī.

Arabic sciences, became his favourite disciplines. His brother Ibrāhīm (d. 742/1341) followed a similar career. After a dubious, albeit highly successful, first career in gambling, he became an expert in profoundly 'civilian' sciences, such as legal procedure and mathematics (together with its sister discipline of the shares of inheritance), grammar and medicine.[145]

The rejection of his martial and Turkish parentage can sometimes be traced to the youth of the Mamluk descendant. Balabān ('the falcon'), the Mamluk father of one future expert in tradition and linguistics, Aḥmad b. Balabān al-Baʿlabakkī (d. 1363), had shown the way to his son when – following the example of Sultan Ḥasan – he ceremonially discarded his (and his father's) Turkish names.[146]

A few historians from *awlād al-nās* circles made an effort to bring the exotic world from which the Mamluks had sprung closer to contemporary Egyptians. One of them, Abū Bakr b. ʿAbdallāh b. Aybak al-Dawādārī (d. after 1337), interspersed precious specimens of Turkish folk tradition from Central and even East Asia into his universal chronicle in Arabic, and angrily repudiated the contention that the Turks were more susceptible to Shamanistic superstitions than their Arab co-religionists.[147] His enthusiasm is all the more surprising as he was only the grandson, not the son, of a Mamluk. Mamluk nobility was not forgotten in one generation. Another prolific chronicler, this time even of fourth generation Mamluk descent, was very conscious of his Turkish–Ḥanafī heritage, 'knew everything about the affairs of the Turkish dynasty' (*al-dawla al-turkiyya*) and for some time even 'put on the garment of war' (*tazayyā bi-ziyy al-jund*): Ibrāhīm b. Muḥammad b. Aydamur, better known (after his great-grandfather) as Ibn Duqmāq (d. 809/1406).[148]

Another chronicler, Abū 'l-Maḥāsin ibn Taghrībirdī (d. 1467) – himself the son of one of the leading generals and ministers of the time – eagerly tried to bridge the gap between the alien rulers and their Arab subjects. Like Ibn al-Dawādārī,[149] he was a passionate archer; he is said to have studied Mamluk *furūsiyya* with the best teachers of the time.[150] He demonstrated his ties to the world of the Mamluks in various ways. Thus he composed a treatise on the

145 al-Ṣafadī, *al-Wāfī bi-'l-wafayāt*, vol. V, ed. Sven Dedering (Wiesbaden, 1970), no. 2403, at 330–7.

146 Changing them to ʿAbd al-Raḥmān and ʿAbd al-Raḥīm respectively, because 'all men are servants of the Lord of the worlds': see Ibn Ḥajar, *al-Durar al-kāmina*, vol. I, no. 320, at 123f.

147 See U. Haarmann, 'Alṭun Ḫān und Čingiz Ḫān bei den ägyptischen Mamluken', *Der Islam,* 51 (1974), 1–36, esp. 32.

148 See his long biography in Sakhāwī's *Ḍaw'* vol. I, 145–6 (see also at 50); his Mamluk background is visible in his strong anti-Shāfiʿī bias. Ibn Duqmāq's *fuṣḥā* Arabic was pitifully weak, not because Turkish took its place, but rather because he spoke the *ʿāmmiyya*. Interestingly enough he used the handwritten original of Ibn al-Dawādārī's universal chronicle *Kanz al-durar* for his own historical works, as one can see from his signature on the last page of several of Ibn al-Dawādārī's volumes: see *Kanz al-durar*, vol. VIII, 400, note.

149 Ibn al-Dawādārī, *Kanz al-durar* vol. IX, ed. H. R. Roemer (Cairo, 1379/1960), 122.

150 See the references given in D. Ayalon, 'Notes on the *furūsiyya* exercises and games in the Mamluk sultanate', *Scripta Hierosolymitana,* 9 (1961) (reprinted in Ayalon, *The Mamluk Military Society*, article no. 2), 31–62, here at 32f.

phonetic value of Turkish sounds, arguing that contemporaries should at least be able to pronounce the names of their foreign lords properly.[151] But such lessons were anything but welcome. 'What else can be expected from a Turk,' sniffed one of his own Arab disciples,[152] reminding us that the mediating potential of the *awlād al-nās* and their susceptibility to attack from either elite, the Mamluks and the *ʿulamāʾ*, were two sides of the same coin.

For the Egyptian religious scholars of the time, it was not always easy to accept the supremacy of the Mamluks, i.e. of a class that recruited itself – as they liked to see it – from uncouth barbarians. 'Unless we had taught them the two phrases (*al-kalimatayn*) of the confession [i.e. 'there is no god but God and Muḥammad is God's messenger'], these amirs could never have risen to such rank and prominence', a typical voice[153] justified their xenophobic *superbia.* Behind this haughtiness hid a feeling of helplessness and perhaps, here and there, even the wise insight that the culture they themselves stood for was not unimpeachable. One development was particularly painful for them to accept: the Mamluks challenged the monopoly of the *ʿulamāʾ* on the adjudication of legal strife by submitting inter-Mamluk litigation to a separate class of army judges.[154]

It would stand to reason that here and there sons of Mamluks, who so eagerly sought admittance to the world of learning, and also to local trade and artisanry, were not granted a roaring welcome. They may rather have tasted the anti-Mamluk bias rampant among the local civilian elites. In such a case, the *awlād al-nās* would have had to pay a price for the humiliations their own tempestuous fathers had continuously inflicted upon the autochthonous Egyptians. Members of the second generation no longer had the supreme power and the means of sanction their fathers had commanded. They were rather left unprotected by their fathers – just as these same Mamluk fathers could not count on their sons to avenge whatever brutality they had to experience from their fellow Mamluks.[155] Many natives – although far from all – hated the Mamluks for their arrogance and despotism.[156] They despised them for their uncivilized behaviour. Worst of all was the special gratitude owed to

[151] See Barbara Flemming, 'Šerīf, Sultan Ġaurī und die 'Perser'', *Der Islam*, 45 (1969), 81–93, here at 88, note 71; Josef van Ess, 'Ṣafadī-Splitter. I', *Der Islam,* 53 (1976), 249, note 17.

[152] Sakhāwī, *Ḍaw'*, vol. X, 306; William Popper, 'Sakhāwī's criticism of Ibn Taghrī Birdī', in: *Studi Orientalistici in onore di Giorgio Levi della Vida* (Rome, 1956), vol. II, 388.

[153] Abū Ḥāmid al-Qudsī, *Badhl al-naṣāʾiḥ*, fol. 10b; U. Haarmann, '*Rather the Injustice of the Turks than the Righteousness of the Arabs* – Changing *ʿulamāʾ* attitudes towards Mamluk rule in the late fifteenth century', *Studia Islamica* 68 (1988), 61–77, here at 67.

[154] Abū Ḥāmid al-Qudsī: *Badhl al-naṣāʾiḥ* (paraphrasing a passage from Tāj al-dīn al-Subkī's *Muʿīd al-niʿam wa-mubīd al-niqam*), fol. 15b; Haarmann, '*Rather the Injustice*', 68–9.

[155] This has been suggested as an important reason for the grisly atrocities common within the Mamluk ruling caste: see Irwin, *The Middle East*, 86f.

[156] Felix Fabri's report on Gaza strongly supports this point: see his *Voyage en Egypte*, 32f. Local 'Saracens' (i.e. Muslim Arabs) bitterly complained to the German pilgrims about the haughtiness of the Mamluks 'in whose presence they themselves hardly dare raise their heads'. They take the Christians to task for their dealings and common meals with the Mamluks 'who, after all, are indubitably damned forever because they have renounced your faith'.

them, because it had been the Mamluk barbarians from the northern steppes who had turned the tide of the Mongol advance. As if sent by divine Providence, they had rescued – voluntarily and without any effective help from the local population – the lands and culture of orthodox Islam in its Arabic garb from destruction at the hands of the infidels. And such feelings of debt are known to have particularly devastating effects on those who owe gratitude.[157]

Conclusion

To sum up, one can make a few general statements on the status of the sons of Mamluks in late medieval Egyptian society, though for the time being the basis for definitive judgement remains incomplete and fragmentary, if only because we are, once more, limited to information about the winners – and not the losers – from among their ranks in the fight for success.

The *awlād al-nās* constituted an extremely volatile, mobile and not easily visible group between two classes that were firmly established in contemporary Egyptian and Syrian society: the Turkish ruling caste and the local economically active and learned civilians. As stated at the beginning of this chapter, this informal status between two powerful poles impeded the formation of a tangible collective identity and of the resulting group solidarity. Instead, the *awlād al-nās* were forced to seek an identity beyond their own ranks. And many of them seem to have made the best of this freedom. They often married Egyptian women of noble descent, as well as sisters and daughters (sometimes even widows) of first-generation Mamluks. They do not give the impression of having been caught helplessly between the millstones of two powerful antagonistic camps. On the contrary, they seem to have recognized their potential of surviving and indeed thriving as *born* (in the true sense of the word) mediators and interpreters. And there must have been a strong need for such go-betweens in the highly polarized Mamluk society. In this function they are clearly reminiscent of their fellow 'half Turkish' cousins, the *qulogh-li*s, of Barbary North Africa before 1830.[158]

The general idea that the Mamluk caste was impenetrable should also be questioned. Although the Turco-Circassian rulers were aloof from the rest of society, they were by no means totally segregated. There was no rigorous apartheid, either between the various social groups – Mamluks and non-Mamluks – or between generations. Much of what has been said on the *awlād al-nās* as active participants in the contemporary civilian world is valid also for individual Mamluk privates and amirs. We find Mamluks also creative

[157] I have discussed this subject in my article 'Ideology and history, identity and alterity: the Arab image of the Turk from the ʿAbbasids to modern Egypt', *International Journal of Middle East Studies,* 20 (1988), pp.175–96, here at 182f.,188.

[158] See the succinct analysis of their social role in: Peter von Sivers, 'Nordafrika in der Neuzeit', in: U. Haarmann (ed.), *Geschichte der arabischen Welt* (3rd edn., Munich, 1994), 522–3.

outside the military and political realms as artisans and entrepreneurs as early as the late thirteenth century. Not only *awlād al-nās*, but also 'real' Mamluks discovered *ʿilm* and *adab* as rewarding pastimes for themselves.[159] Mamluk society could not have functioned without viable contacts and alliances between the military strongmen and the urban and rural populace. Non-Mamluks, and especially non-Mamluks of Mamluk extraction, certainly did have a chance to partake in the wealth of the country and even, under propitious circumstances, in the highest echelons of the political and military system. In short: there was no rigorous and clearly defined one-generation nobility; it would have been a social *absurdum*.

If outside observers such as Felix Fabri or Arnold von Harff, relying on Mamluk informants, however, present the picture of such a monolithic, all-Mamluk ruling caste, they certainly also reproduce the ideological bias and perhaps the wishful thinking of their informants. The Mamluks must have been tempted to talk themselves (as well as those surrounding them) into believing that only by ever-recurrent recruitment of warlike youngsters from the northern steppes could they stand up to the hallowed duty of defending the *umma* – even after the last Mongol and crusader had long since been driven out of Syria. Arnold von Harff's two companions from southern and northern Germany are not likely to have pointed out the intrinsic weaknesses and the inconsistencies of the system they themselves represented and constituted – even if they were at all detached and sagacious enough to recognize them.

[159] See Haarmann, 'Arabic in speech, Turkish in lineage', 86–103; Jonathan Berkey, ' 'Silver Threads among the Coal': a well-educated Mamluk of the ninth/fifteenth century', *Studia Islamica,* 73 (1991), 109–25 (on Sayf al-dīn Taghrībirmish al-Mu'ayyadī); Jonathan Berkey, *The Transmission of knowledge in medieval Cairo. A Social History of Islamic Education* (Princeton, 1992), chap. 5, pp.146–55; Jonathan Berkey, 'Mamluks and the world of higher Islamic education in medieval Cairo, 1250–1517', in *Modes de transmission de la culture religieuse en Islam* (Cairo, 1993), 93–116.

PART II

Mamluk households: coherence and disintegration

CHAPTER 5

The re-emergence of the Mamluks following the Ottoman conquest

MICHAEL WINTER

Posing the question: how did the Mamluks survive the Ottoman conquest?

In August 1516, in the battle of Marj Dābiq, north of Aleppo, the Ottoman Sultan Yavuz Selim defeated the Mamluk army led by Sultan Qānṣūh al-Ghawrī. After pacifying and organizing the Syrian part of the Mamluk empire, Selim proceeded to overthrow the Mamluk sultanate, inflicting the final blows on the Mamluk army led by Ṭūmānbāy, the newly elected sultan, in January 1517. While the two-and-a-half-centuries-old sultanate was thus finished, the Mamluks survived under Ottoman sovereignty.[1]

As Professor Holt showed in a basic study written in 1961, the beylicate, which became the leading political and military force in seventeenth-century Egypt, was in many respects a continuation (or revival) of the high amirate of the Mamluk sultanate.[2] The institution of the beylicate saw ups and downs, but through it Mamluk traditions were preserved. By the eighteenth century, the Mamluk beys were virtually in control of Egyptian politics, although they recognized the Ottoman sultan in Istanbul as their supreme sovereign – the revolt of ʿAlī Bey 'Bulūṭ Ḳapan' al-Kabīr, who in the years 1760–72 rose in rebellion against the Ottoman state, attempting to sever Egypt's ties with Istanbul and to restore the Mamluk sultanate, being the one exception. As Professor Ayalon demonstrated in his study based mainly on the great chronicle of ʿAbd al-Raḥmān al-Jabartī, the military society in Ottoman Egypt, particularly in the eighteenth century, showed the characteristics of a fully fledged Mamluk organization and culture, strikingly similar to that of the late medieval Mamluk sultanate, despite some very important differences which Ayalon describes in detail.[3] As the title of Ayalon's study indicates, the

[1] For an account of the overthrow of the Mamluk sultanate, see P. M. Holt, *Egypt and the Fertile Crescent, 1516–1922; A Political History* (Ithaca, N.Y., 1966), 33–45.

[2] P. M. Holt, 'The beylicate in Ottoman Egypt during the seventeenth century', in P. M. Holt (ed.), *Studies in the History of the Near East* (London, 1973), 177–219.

[3] D. Ayalon, 'Studies in al-Jabarti I: notes on the transformation of Mamluk society in Egypt under the Ottomans', *Journal of the Economic and Social History of the Orient*. 3/2 and 3/3 (1960), 148–74, 275–325.

Mamluk military society underwent a deep transformation during the Ottoman rule of Egypt. That is hardly surprising, given the length of time which had passed since the conquest and the relegation of Egypt from a centre of an empire to a province of the Ottoman state. What is more significant is the resilience of Mamluk traditions and mentality despite that transformation.

The present chapter is limited to the sixteenth and the early seventeenth centuries, and attempts to investigate how the Mamluks survived the Ottoman conquest and its aftermath and what the conditions which preserved the Mamluk traditions were. It is well known that the re-emergence of the Mamluks in the seventeenth century and their dominance in the eighteenth century were made possible by the decline of the Ottoman empire, which was no longer able to rule Egypt and other provinces nearly as firmly as was the case during the peak of Ottoman power and greatness, particularly during the long reign of Sulaymān Qānūnī, 'the Magnificent' (1520–66). Yet in that glorious era the Ottomans did control Egypt effectively, and still the Mamluks survived, or else their re-emergence into political power in the seventeenth century would not have been possible. This situation poses many intriguing questions that are especially hard to answer because of the dearth of historical source materials precisely in this crucial period of transition from Mamluk to Ottoman rule.

The sources

The Ottoman conquest itself and the following years are superbly chronicled by Ibn Iyās, a native of Cairo of Mamluk descent, who was the last representative of the great tradition of Egyptian Arabic historiography.[4] ʿAbd al-Ṣamad al-Diyārbakrī, an Ottoman *qāḍī*, who came to Egypt with Selim's army and stayed to serve as a judge, translated Ibn Iyās's work (with considerable changes of the text) and continued it in detail for two-and-a-half more years. The chronicle goes down to the year 947/1540, but beyond Shawwāl 931/August 1525 there is no really detailed account or substance.[5]

Two Arabic contemporary sources have their shortcomings, although they provide some important information. Quṭb al-dīn al-Nahrawālī al-Makkī, the author of a book describing mainly the Ottoman exploits in Yemen, writes also about Egyptian matters, since Egypt was the strategic and logistic base for operations in the Red Sea region. Yet al-Nahrawālī was not so familiar with Egyptian affairs as, say, Ibn Iyās.[6] A book by ʿAbd al-Qādir al-Jazīrī, who served for many years as the secretary of the annual Egyptian *ḥajj* caravan to

[4] Muḥammad Ibn Iyās, *Badāʾiʿ al-zuhūr fī waqāʾiʿ al-duhūr*, ed. M. Muṣṭafā (Cairo, 1961), Vol. V (hereafter Ibn Iyās).

[5] ʿAbd al-Ṣamad al-Diyārbakrī, *Dhikr al-khulafāʾ wa-ʾl-mulūk al-miṣriyya,* British Library, MS Add. 7846 (hereafter Diyārbakrī). Benjamin Lellouch of Paris, in a yet unpublished paper, read at the CIEPO conference in Amsterdam (June 1994), argues convincingly that two-and-a-half years of the detailed continuation of Ibn Iyās's chronicle, believed to have been written by Diyārbakrī, is only the latter's translation into Turkish of a lost part of Ibn Iyās's work.

[6] Quṭb al-dīn Muḥammad al-Nahrawālī al-Makkī, *al-Barq al-Yamānī fī 'l-fatḥ al-ʿUthmānī*, ed. Ḥāmid al-Jāsir (Riyad, 1967).

Mecca (he succeeded his father in that office), is an excellent source for the *ḥajj*, yet the information he provides concerning political and social matters is very limited. Nevertheless, this work is of much value to the present study, since it lists all the *umarā' al-ḥājj*, commanders of the *ḥajj* caravan, down to the year 957/1550, and adds illuminating details about them, which cannot be found elsewhere.[7]

The writings of ʿAbd al-Wahhāb al-Shaʿrānī (d. 1565), the Sufi writer and social commentator, throw a light on the social and religious life of the Egyptians, but have nothing important to say about the ruling class. There are also copious Hebrew sources, mainly the rabbinical responsa, which teach us a great deal about Jewish life and the economy in general, but again, these are only marginally concerned with our subject.[8] Even the Ottoman archival documents start to be abundant only towards the end of Sulaymān Qānūnī's reign, leaving a gap of the crucial first four decades following the Ottoman conquest of 1517, although several documents, mostly imperial decrees, sometimes provide interesting information about earlier events. The best and richest corpus of documents for our period are the imperial decrees, *Mühimme Defteri*, located in the central Turkish archives of the prime minister's office in Istanbul. One kind of important archival source, available for many other Ottoman provinces, is missing. The Ottomans did not apply in Egypt the *timar* system, the typical fiscal and military organization of their territories. For the purpose of the *timar* system, the Ottoman administration carried out detailed surveys of the province; these registers are gold mines of information for Ottoman historians. The government's decision not to turn Egypt into *timar* land, in order to avoid disrupting its ancient administrative traditions, deprives us of an extremely useful research tool.

Towards the end of the sixteenth century, the quality and quantity of the available sources improve considerably. The archival materials are abundant and orderly. There are also local chronicles in Arabic and Turkish. We have also a unique and fascinating description of Cairo of 1599 by Muṣṭafā ʿĀlī, an Ottoman writer, intellectual and traveller, whose account is too literary to be a straightforward dependable description, but it does include many insightful and vivid observations on Egyptian society, including many interesting facts and assessments concerning the army and the ruling class.[9]

Shaping Ottoman policy towards the Mamluks: 1517–1522

It is obvious from Ibn Iyās's account that Ottoman attitudes towards the Mamluks during the conquest and the first few years that followed it oscillated

[7] ʿAbd al-Qādir ibn Muḥammad al-Jazīrī, *Durar al-fawāʾid al-munaẓẓama fī akhbār al-ḥajj wa-ṭarīq Makka al-muʿaẓẓama* (Cairo, 1384/1964), (hereafter al-Jazīrī).

[8] See M. Winter, *Society and Religion in Early Ottoman Egypt: Studies in the Writings of ʿAbd al-Wahhāb al-Shaʿrānī* (New Brunswick, N.J., 1982); I. M. Goldman, *The Life and Times of Rabbi David ibn Abi Zimra* (New York, 1970).

[9] *Muṣṭafā ʿĀlī's Description of Cairo of 1599*, ed. and trans. A. Tietze (Vienna, 1976), (hereafter *Muṣṭafā ʿĀlī*).

between persecution and accommodation. At first, the Ottomans put to death any Mamluk they caught, often despite promises of safe conduct.[10] Later, the executions stopped, and gradually the Mamluks were pardoned, and finally they were integrated into the Ottoman army, although the division between them and the regular Ottoman units was always carefully maintained.[11] Ayalon suggests that the Ottomans came to the conclusion that it was a waste to kill the Mamluks, who were superb horsemen and fighters, Turkish speaking, and Sunni Muslims.[12]

It is certain that the man who influenced Sultan Selim to stop the killings was Khā'ir Bey, the Mamluk amir who had been the governor of the Aleppo province under Sultan Qānṣūh al-Ghawrī. Khā'ir Bey betrayed his sultan during the battle of Marj Dābiq, and was rewarded by Selim by being made the first Ottoman governor of Egypt. He administered the country until his death in October 1522. His loyalty to the Ottomans was total; he refused to join the rebellion raised in 1520 by Jānbardī al-Ghazālī, the Ottoman governor of Syria, who like himself had crossed the lines to the Ottoman side, but changed his mind again. Ibn Iyās thinks that the Mamluks were sympathetic to al-Ghazālī. That is hardly surprising, but only a few actually joined the rebellion, which was crushed very quickly anyway. Those Mamluks were put to death by Khā'ir Bey's order.[13] Generally, Khā'ir Bey was an obedient tool of the Ottomans. Yet he successfully interceded with Selim for the Mamluks. They started to emerge from their hiding places, and were allowed to carry arms and ride horses again.[14] The Mamluks were paid their salaries; sometimes these were not paid in full or were in arrears, but this was nothing new, and had happened frequently under the Mamluk sultans as well. Ibn Iyās attributed these delays to Khā'ir Bey's hatred of the Mamluks, but this judgement is not justified: when Khā'ir Bey told the angry Mamluks that had it not been for his intervention, Selim would have put all of them to death, he was probably stating a fact.[15] Ibn Iyās himself writes that the treasury of Egypt was overburdened by having to pay the salaries of many army units, Ottoman as well as Mamluk.[16]

For their part, the Ottoman soldiers were envious of the Mamluks' salaries and rations, and repeatedly pressured Khā'ir Bey to increase their own pay or else allow them to go home to Istanbul (after Selim's departure from Egypt in September 1517).[17] Skirmishes in the streets of Cairo between Mamluk and Ottoman troops, the Janissaries in particular, became frequent and often ended with casualties.[18] The Janissaries, the sultan's elite corps, were arrogant

10 Ibn Iyās, 149, 150, 169. 11 Ibid., 205, 208, 212, 213.

12 D. Ayalon, 'The end of the Mamluk sultanate (Why did the Ottomans spare the Mamluks of Egypt and wipe out the Mamluks of Syria?)', *Studia Islamica*, 65 (1987), 125–48.

13 Ibn Iyās, 383, 387, 388. 14 Ibid., 212, 215. 15 Ibid., 323, 485. 16 Ibid., 429.

17 Ibid., 283, 303, 306, 308.

18 Ibid., 283, 388. It should be pointed out, however, that quarrels among the Ottoman units themselves, in particular between the Janissaries and the Sipahis, also occurred frequently. See ibid., 298, 319, 396.

and aggressive, and often attacked the governor with harsh words and physically assailed his adjutant (*dawādār*), a Mamluk high-ranking amir.[19] The antagonism between the Mamluks and the Ottoman soldiers grew out of envy and group solidarity, but was deepened by differences of mentality and outlook, as well as by negative stereoptypes. Ibn Iyās describes the Ottoman soldiers as unruly men and as bad Muslims. He says that they failed to fast during Ramadan, were drinkers, hashish addicts, and pederasts. They often stole from the civilian population and molested women and young boys. Ibn Iyās describes them as riffraff, among whom it is impossible to tell an amir from a common soldier.[20] Ibn Iyās reports many crimes committed by the Ottoman soldiers against the Egyptian population in Cairo and the villages. Their behaviour is described as worse than that of the Mamluks, whose own conduct was far from exemplary.[21] The contrast between the irreligious Ottoman Turks and the more devout Mamluks is a constant theme in the annals of Ottoman Egypt and other provinces. Several episodes from the early days of Ottoman rule in Egypt seem to support Ibn Iyās's view. One example is the opposite attitudes of these two groups to a Christian who was condemned to death and declared a last-minute conversion to Islam. Unlike the Mamluks, the Ottomans were unmoved.[22] Conversely, Ottoman soldiers tried to prevent the execution of a seller of wine and drugs; some were his customers.[23]

These stereotypes would not vanish in later periods. Ibn Iyās regards the Ottoman regime as un-Islamic, accusing it of contravening the *sharīʿa* sacred law in various ways.[24] Yet even Ibn Iyās, whose bitterness at the Ottomans is evident from every page of his chronicle, mellows somewhat after the death of the harsh Selim and the advent to the throne of Sulaymān, who was regarded as more benign than his father.[25] The Mamluks were relieved at Selim's departure from Egypt, and even more so when his death in 1520 was announced.[26] The attitude towards the Mamluks clearly changed for the better both in Cairo and Istanbul. A *qāḍī*, who had called the Mamluk amirs 'old shoes' (*zarābīl*), now addressed them politely as 'masters' (*aghāwāt*).[27] Khā'ir Bey sent Mamluks to chase and arrest Ottoman soldiers who disobeyed the sultan's order to return to Istanbul; these hid in the countryside and were caught by the Mamluks and were forced to comply with the order. The soldiers had already discovered what would become a well-known fact in the empire, that service in Egypt was safer and more pleasant than elsewhere. In addition, many Ottoman soldiers had married Egyptian women (in spite of official prohibition).[28] According to Ibn Iyās, when Sultan Sulaymān saw the excellent performance of the Mamluk contingent that had been sent to take part in the

[19] Ibid., 213, 308, 333, 446. [20] Ibid., 150, 153–5, 162, 170, 207–8.
[21] Ibid., 233, 234, 294, 309, 327. [22] Ibid., 445. [23] Ibid., 313–14.
[24] See M. Winter, *Egyptian Society under Ottoman Rule, 1517–1798* (London and New York, 1992), 9–12. [25] Ibn Iyās, 397, 403, 435, 475. [26] Ibid., 208, 366. [27] Ibid., 367.
[28] Ibid., 238, 239, 256–7.

conquest of the island of Rhodes alongside regular Ottoman troops stationed in Egypt, he was strongly impressed by their performance in battle, and expressed his amazement at his father's bad judgement in killing such magnificent Mamluks.[29]

Although the Mamluks were now integrated into the Ottoman garrison of Egypt, the principle of separating them from the regular Ottoman troops was upheld. This policy was necessary primarily for security reasons, the Mamluks and the Ottoman units being constantly on the verge of fighting. Even when the two groups were assigned a common task, each went separately under its own commanders.[30] There was no consistent policy regarding uniforms and appearance. Sometimes the Mamluks were ordered to wear customary *zamṭ* and *mallūṭa*, but at other times they were prohibited from doing so.[31] The confusion was caused at least in part by considerations of public safety. Ibn Iyās reports instances of Ottoman soldiers disguised as Mamluks going out at night and committing crimes; and a reverse case is also recorded.[32] An outstanding difference in appearance was the fact thaṭ the Ottomans were clean-shaven and the Mamluks were bearded. At one point, Khā'ir Bey himself, during a military review, cut several amirs' beards and told them to shave their beards and narrow their sleeves, the Ottoman way. Also, the manner in which amirs used to walk or ride in the streets accompanied by their own Mamluks had to change to accord with the Ottoman regulations.[33] Eventually, the Mamluks seem to have had their own distinctive dress, which consisted of red trousers called *shalvār*.[34]

Finally, it is important to notice that the Ottomans did not need the Mamluk amirs merely as military commanders, but also as administrators. The pragmatic and thrifty Ottoman government realized that the immense economic potential of Egypt could best be guaranteed by the continuity of the time-tested administration of agricultural production. That required above all good management of the complicated and sensitive irrigation system, which was the responsibility of the provincial governors, the *kushshāf* (sing. *kāshif*). The term *kāshif*, which survived in Ottoman Egypt and was unknown in other Ottoman provinces, is the shortened form of *kāshif al-jusūr al-sulṭāniyya*, 'the supervisor of the imperial dams,'[35] who was in charge of the proper functioning of the system; he had also to maintain law and order and to protect the region against marauding Arab tribesmen. Selim appointed at least one Ottoman officer as a *kāshif*,[36] but soon Mamluk amirs were being reappointed to *kushūfiyya* positions;[37] apparently the Ottomans found out that their experience made them indispensable. Eventually, the office of *kāshif* was one of the niches that preserved the Mamluks under Ottoman rule.

[29] Ibid., 475. [30] Ibid., 246, 321, 466. [31] Ibid., 150, 186–7, 213, 220, 263, 407.

[32] Ibid., 213, 434.

[33] Ibid., 407–8, 429. On the *jündis'* habit of letting their servants walk behind them carrying their swords from them, see also *Muṣṭafā ʿĀlī*, 54.

[34] Winter, *Egyptian Society under Ottoman Rule*, 72–3.

[35] Al-Jazīrī, 365, 374. [36] Ibn Iyās, 160. [37] Ibid., 295, 378, 488.

While Cairo was protected and policed by 'organic' Ottoman troops, the Janissaries in particular, who resided in the Citadel, Mamluk amirs controlled much of the countryside in their capacity as *kāshifs*. It is remarkable that Muṣṭafā ʿĀlī, who describes Egypt in 1599, speaking of what he regards as the oppressive rule of the *kāshifs* and the *multazims* (tax farmers), says that this is done 'according to the Circassian law' *(Çerkes qānūnu üzere)*.[38] It does not mean that every *kāshif* was necessarily Circassian (that is, a Mamluk), although many certainly were, but it does mean that the provincial administrative system was still based on Mamluk methods and traditions.

Selim left in Egypt a garrison of Ottoman infantry and cavalry, but it was evident that their service in Egypt was temporary. The sultan's troops, especially the Janissaries, were the 'Slaves of the Porte', *Qapu Qulları*, and were ordered to return to the core lands of the empire, namely Anatolia and Rumeli. On the other hand, the Mamluks were the permanent element in Egypt. They were sometimes sent to perform duties or to participate in campaigns outside Egypt, but it was taken for granted that they would return to Egypt eventually.

Mamluk Rebellions against the Ottomans

Khāʾir Bey died in October 1522, and the new governor (*beylerbeyi* or *vālī*) was Muṣṭafā Pasha, a member of the Ottoman establishment; Khā'ir was the first and the last Mamluk amir who was appointed governor of Egypt. In May 1523, Jānim al-Sayfī and Īnāl, two provincial governors of Middle Egypt, led the first Mamluk revolt, attempting to restore the Mamluk sultanate. They were supported by a number of Mamluks and bedouin Arabs. The revolt was suppressed quickly, but it further strained the relations between the Mamluks and the Ottoman soldiers. Many Mamluks joined the rebels and were killed (Diyārbakrī says their number reached 500); those who remained loyal to the Ottomans marched against their comrades with little enthusiasm.[39]

It is noteworthy that Ottoman policy towards the Mamluks even during this revolt and afterwards was to appease them. An imperial decree ordered that their salaries be paid without delay.[40] It was inevitable, however, that the pasha would be wary of them. He scattered them in the provinces, keeping in Cairo only a handful of Mamluks, to be on the safe side (*iḥtiyāṭan*).[41] The revolt instigated in 1524 by Aḥmad Pasha, later known as *al-Khāʾin*, 'the traitor', was a more serious challenge to the Ottomans, since he was the governor of Egypt. Soon after his arrival, he confiscated the Janissaries' muskets, because he rightly concluded that of all the units in Egypt they would be the most loyal to the sultan. Aḥmad Pasha wooed the Mamluks and even pardoned some of them who had been proscribed for taking the side of the previous rebels. Aḥmad Pasha declared that he was a Circassian, like the majority of the Mamluks, and then assumed the title of sultan, and brought back some of the

[38] *Muṣṭafā ʿĀlī*, 56. [39] Diyārbakrī, fols. 306a, 306b. [40] Ibid., fol. 310a. [41] Ibid., fol. 311b.

ceremonies associated with the Mamluk regime. In February 1524, he rose in armed rebellion, his force occupied the Citadel and massacred the Janissaries who were stationed there. Aḥmad Pasha's rule lasted only a few months; then he was surprised by a loyalist group of amirs. He was caught and put to death.[42]

The story of Aḥmad Pasha's revolt does not have to be told here in detail. Yet it is important to emphasize that despite, or perhaps because of, this 'Mamluk' revolt, the Ottoman policy was unchanged – namely, continuous efforts to court the Mamluks and win their goodwill. The Ottoman authorities announced several times: 'Let us not call one another Turkoman or Circassian. We are all the sultan's servants and brothers in Islam'.[43] After the suppression of the revolt, a decree arrived from Istanbul ordering that the Circassians (i. e. Mamluks) should be handled kindly.[44]

A year after the suppression of the revolt, Ibrāhīm Pasha, Sultan Sulaymān's grand vizier, arrived to reorganize Egypt's administration. He promulgated the edicts codifying the administrative practice of the country. The document was called *Qānūn-nāme-i Mıṣır*[45] and speaks extensively about the army, among other things. One of the code's outstanding features is the principle of continuity from Mamluk times, even though the Ottomans had to suppress two serious Mamluk rebellions. The *Qānūn-nāme* expressly states that laws dealing with taxes, customs duties and other fiscal and administrative matters promulgated by Qāytbay, the Mamluk sultan from 1468 to 1496, who fought the Ottomans in Anatolia, were to remain in force. The code gave the Mamluks official recognition and organized them into a regiment. Pensions and titles from Mamluk times were recognized. Yet it is obvious that the Mamluks were not completely trusted. The regimental command – the *agha* (commander), the *kâhya* (or *katkhudā*, deputy commander) and the *kātib* (clerk) – had to be Turkish (*Rumlu*). The need to maintain discipline in their ranks is expressed in very strong terms. By contrast with the other regiments discussed in the *Qānūn-nāme*, vacant positions were not to be manned, but reverted to the Treasury. Vacancies occurring in the *Chavush* regiment – the pasha's envoys and pursuivants, aides and messengers – were to be filled only from the ranks of the cavalry regiments of the *Gönüllüyān* and *Tüfenkjiyān* (and not the Circassians, who were also cavalrymen). It is expressly stated that no soldier's salary (*ʿulūfe*) was to be paid in any of the regiments to Circassians sons, *fallāḥīn* (i. e. native Egyptians, not necessarily peasants), or bedouins.[46]

The policy of excluding from the army anyone not of Turkish origin was not unique to Egypt; it reflected a deep-rooted and ancient conviction in the mil-

42 On the revolt, see Holt, *Egypt and the Fertile Crescent*, 48–51.

43 Diyārbakrī, fols. 341a, 344b, 355b.

44 Ibid., 345b.

45 See Winter, *Egyptian Society under Ottoman Rule*, 17, 37–9. The text of the *Qānūn-nāme* was published by Ö. L. Barkan, *XV ve XVI ncı asırlarda Osmanlı Imparatorluğunda ziraî, ekonominin hukûkî ve mâli esasları* (Istanbul, 1943), vol. I, 355–87.

46 Ibid.

itary superiority of the Turkish race. The Circassians were believed to belong to a kindred stock and to be endowed with similar warlike qualities and spirit. (Note that the Circassians are consistently called 'Turks,' *Atrāk*, by the Arab chroniclers during the Mamluk sultanate.) Two revealing documents, dated 994/1586, order that able soldiers from among the Turks and the Circassians (*yarar qul Rumlu ve Çerkes qulundan*) be sent to Yemen.[47] The ethnic emphasis is unmistakable: Turks and Circassians are the two races that supplied the kind of manpower the Ottoman high command sought. However, the frequency of official references to the Turks is far greater than to the Circassians, itself highly significant.

In sum, the qualities and usefulness of the Mamluks were appreciated by the Ottoman government, which feeling strong and confident at that time, admitted them to the army of Egypt, with a measure of caution, of course. The resilience of the Mamluks is impressive, having survived the conquest and the suppression of two rebellions, but it is obvious that the Mamluk–Circassian presence in the sixteenth century was kept alive by importation of fresh recruits, although information about this is lacking.

Aḥmad Pasha's revolt was the last Mamluk uprising until ʿAlī Bey's rebellion in the second half of the eighteenth century. The soldiers' riots at the end of the sixteenth and the beginning of the seventeenth centuries were motivated by economic reasons alone and must be seen in the wider Ottoman context of rising inflation which affected the fixed salaries of the soldiers.[48] In Egypt, the soldiers serving in the countryside extorted special payment, called *ṭulba*, from the *fallāḥın*, although the practice was illegal. This is the background to the riots which culminated in the killing of Ibrāhīm Pasha (later known as *al-Maqtūl*, 'the Slain') by the soldiers (September 1604). Order was not fully restored until the rule of Muḥammad Pasha (1607–11), whose resolute suppression of the unruly soldiers won him the epithet *Qul Qıran*, 'the breaker of the (rebellious) soldiers'. The *ṭulba* was duly abolished. Muḥammad b. Abī 'l-Surūr al-Bakrī al-Ṣiddīqī, the chronicler who describes the events, calls the suppression of the revolt 'the second conquest of Egypt'. Some modern historians have tried to explain the revolt as yet another Mamluk uprising against the Ottoman sultan. While there is no doubt that there were Mamluks among the rebels, there is no convincing evidence that there was any 'Mamluk' ideology behind the revolt. The chronicler emphasizes the Turkish (*Rūmī*) character of the rebels. It is significant that it was a Turkish *ʿālim*, known as Shaykh Altı Parmak Efendi, rather than an Egyptian one, who was sent by the Pasha to try to talk sense to the rebels.[49]

47 *Mühimme Defteri* (hereafter *MD*), vol. 60, nos. 595, 596, at 254, 8 Jumādā I 994 (27 April 1586).

48 Ö. L. Barkan, 'The price revolution of the sixteenth century: a turning point in the economic history of the Near East', *International Journal of Middle East Studies*, 6 (1975), 3–28.

49 Muḥammad ibn Abī 'l-Surūr al-Bakrī al-Ṣiddīqī. *Kashf al-kurba fī rafʿ al-ṭulba*, ed. ʿAbd al-Raḥīm ʿAbd al-Raḥmān ʿAbd al-Raḥīm, in *al-Majalla al-taʾrīkhiyya al-Miṣriyya*, 23 (1976), 291–384.

Mamluks in the army in early Ottoman Egypt

In the Mamluk sultanate it was easy to tell Mamluks from non-Mamluks. The ruling class was exclusively composed of freed Muslim military slaves, born to non-Muslim parents outside the abode of Islam. Turkishness was their distinguishing mark: they alone in Egypt and Syria had Turkish names, and they spoke Turkish (although the administrative work of the empire was conducted in Arabic). Even the Circassians, the dominant element in the sultanate since the late fourteenth century, were considered Turks by the Arabic-speaking population. The Circassians who, of course, had a language of their own, learned Turkish in Egypt as the language of the ruling caste.[50]

The Ottoman conquest of Egypt caused a profound change in this social and cultural situation. As Ayalon argued, in a Turkish empire whose Turkish-speaking leaders and administrators mostly (though not exclusively) had Arabic names (naturally pronounced in the Turkish way), the Mamluks could not be called by Turkish names.[51] The Mamluks were no longer the only military and political elite, and thus the dividing line between Mamluks and other soldiers and officers became blurred. Nevertheless, as has already been mentioned above, the Mamluk element kept coming with Ottoman approval, or at least acquiescence.

The sources provide clear evidence about Mamluks in the army. Firstly, there was the Circassian regiment, *Çerākise Ocağı*, but not much information exists about this unit, which was established to absorb the Mamluks. There is some evidence about Mamluks serving in other corps as well.[52] Mamluks are mentioned in the service of high-ranking officers and dignitaries from the *beylerbeyi* down, and they served within the regular units, and also as Mamluks and retainers of military grandees outside the army's payroll.

The following are some references to Mamluks, although the term itself does not appear in the official documents.

Writing about the various assistants of the *amīr al-ḥājj*, al-Jazīrī discusses the *shādds*, the commander's aides-de-camps. He says that they are usually Turks (meaning non-Arabs, Turks or Circassians) and are either the Mamluks of *amīr al-ḥājj* which is preferable, or soldiers (*ʿaskar*, of the Ottoman regiments) of whom he approves.[53] Likewise, the officer responsible for the pantry, *shādd al-sanīḥ*, or *kilerji* in Turkish, was one of the amir's Mamluks, or again, one of the regular soldiers, if the amir trusted him.[54] Al-Jazīrī speaks of the Mamluks of *amīr al-ḥājj*, as distinct from soldiers belonging to 'the various regiments'.[55] It is mentioned that Murād Pasha, who was governor of Yemen, had his own military slaves, *qullar*, whom he had purchased.[56]

[50] The information about this fascinating subject is scarce. Yet Sanuto, the Venetian compiler of the *Diaries*, tells of a young Circassian sultan who could hardly speak Arabic or Turkish because he had arrived in the country (Egypt) only recently. Marino Sanuto, *I Diarii* (Venice, 1879–1902; repr. Bologna, 1969), vol. II, 311, 397.

[51] Ayalon, 'Studies in al-Jabarti', *JESHO*, 3/2, 148–74.

[52] *MD*, vol. 90, no. 114, at 35, 20 Muḥarram 1054 (29 March 1644). [53] Al-Jazīrī, 413.

[54] Ibid, 134. [55] Ibid., 96. [56] *MD* vol. 28, no. 334, at 140, 25 Rajab 984 (7 October 1576).

In striking contrast to the practice during the Mamluk sultanate, some Mamluks in Ottoman Egypt were in the possession of civilians, native Egyptians, *awlād ʿArab*, probably bureaucrats or rich merchants. When the soldiers revolted for the first time against the governor, during the term of Üveys Pasha, in 1589, they proclaimed in the streets that *awlād al-ʿArab* were forbidden to keep white slaves (one source says 'Turkish slaves', meaning Mamluks).[57] This prohibition was motivated by the wish of the soldiers, all of them Turkish speaking and including Mamluks or Sipahis (Ottoman Cavalrymen), to preserve their privileges.

A military term which could have a Mamluk referent is *jündi*, cavalryman (in the Turkish, not Arabic, usage). This is evident from the way Diyārbakrī translates the term *awlād al-nās* (Mamluk's sons) as *jündi oghulları*.[58] Muṣṭafā ʿĀlī devotes long and detailed passages to the Egyptian *jündis*, and it seems that he speaks about Mamluks, at least in part.[59] *Jündī* may sometimes be used as the Egyptian equivalent of the Ottoman *Sipahi*, horseman. Muṣṭafā ʿĀlī complains that men rose to become officers in the army without the necessary Ottoman background and training. Many were men of the bazaars or Mamluks in the service of well-to-do *Tats* (a pejorative term for non-Turks; here, Arabic-speaking Egyptians), instead of serving high-ranking amirs.[60] A decree dated 975/1567 gives the numerical breakdown of the Egyptian army by units and corps. Out of overall 8,811 soldiers, 200 are listed under the category of 'men (in the service) of beys and aghas' (*beyler ve aghalar adamları*).[61] These must have included Mamluks, but perhaps also retainers who were not Mamluks. It is impossible for this period to mark with certainty the limits of either the *jündi* or the Mamluk entities, since both were not official, clearly defined terms like the seven regiments.

As the 'classical' Ottoman system of recruitment and training weakened and then collapsed, emancipated Mamluks were allowed to serve in the regular regiments. An interesting edict from 1056/1646 tells about a freed Mamluk of Top Atan Muṣṭafā Bey who arranged for him an appointment in the Janissary corps of Egypt. After the bey's death, the *kâhya* (deputy commander) of the regiment took away the soldier's title deed (*temessük*), obviously taking advantage of the fact that the man was left without his patron's protection. The central government in Istanbul ordered him to be given his rights back.[62]

The Egyptian–Ottoman divide within the army

After the Ottoman conquest, the military was divided between 'Ottomans' and 'Egyptians', although that split assumed with time different names and shapes. The tensions and clashes between the Ottoman regiments and the

[57] Winter, *Egyptian Society under Ottoman Rule*, 46, 55, 56.
[58] Diyārbakrī, fols. 116b, 241a. [59] *Muṣṭafā ʿĀlī*, 51–6. [60] Ibid., 57ff.
[61] *MD*, vol. 7, no. 1335, at 462–3, 1 Dhū 'l-Qaʿda 975 (17 April 1568).
[62] *MD*, vol. 90, no. 114, at 35, 20 Muḥarram 1054 (29 March 1644).

Mamluks after the conquest have been discussed above. Yet during the following decades, an Egyptian territorial army with an *esprit de corps* and interests of its own began to emerge.[63] The term *Mıṣır qulları,* 'the soldiers of Egypt' appears as early as 975/1568 in an official document dealing with clashes between them and the *Qapu qulları.*[64] A seventeenth century chronicle describes the envy on the part of the *Qapu qulları* at what they considered to be the better salaries paid to the *Mıṣır qulları.*[65] The language of the official imperial decrees makes a distinction between stationary or permanent (*muqīm*) military units and units that are on the move (*müsāfir*).[66] It was the strategy of the Ottoman high command in Istanbul to move military units around throughout the vast empire. For example, when troops from Egypt were ordered to go to Yemen to fight local rebels, soldiers from Syria were sent to replace them in Egypt, or conversely, Egyptian troops were sent to maintain the sultan's rule in Syria to replace soldiers stationed in Syria who were sent to the Persian front. Now it is remarkable that even in the sixteenth century, Egyptian soldiers serving in Palestine were under the command of their own officers, and were responsible not to the *beylerbeyi* of Damascus under whose jurisdiction their sancaḳ lay, but to the *beylerbeyi* of Egypt. As soon as their term in Palestine was over, they were ordered to return to Egypt.[67]

Ethnic and racial stereotypes were central to the social concepts of the people at that time, and this includes, of course, the Ottoman Empire. All sources, literary and official alike, emphasize the distinctions between Circassians and Turks, Arabs and Turks, etc. The infiltrations of *awlād ʿArab* into the army, despite repeated prohibitions, was a widespread phenomenon in Egypt and other provinces.[68]

Sharīf Muḥammad Pasha, governor of Egypt from 1004/1596 to 1006/1598, expressed the ethnic bias of the Ottoman establishment bluntly: 'I will not give salaries to *fallāḥīn* [i.e., to Egyptians, not necessarily peasants, here clearly used in a derogatory sense]. Salaries are for the Turks (*Rum oghlanı*).' He also stated that there must be a distinction between the sultan's slaves (*padishah qulı*) and grandees' slaves (*akābir qulı*), many of whom must have been Mamluks.[69]

The tensions between the 'Egyptian' and the 'Ottoman' troops find an elo-

[63] Holt, *Egypt and the Fertile Crescent*, 77. This process of creating an Egyptian army with identity and interests of its own had already started in the sixteenth century.

[64] *MD,* vol. 7, no. 1329, *awāʾil* Dhū ʾl-Qaʿda, 975 (28 April–7 May 1568).

[65] ʿAlī Efendi (?), *A Chronicle of the Pashas of Egypt*, MS. 1050, Muzaffer Ocak collection, Ankara University, fol. 19b.

[66] *MD*, vol. 79, at 64, 15 Muḥarram 1018 (20 April 1609); *MD*, vol. 85, at 602, 5 Muḥarram 1041 (3 August 1631).

[67] M. Winter, 'Military connections between Egypt and Syria (including Palestine) in the early Ottoman period', in A. Cohen and G. Baer (eds.), *Egypt and Palestine: A Millennium of Association (868–1948).* (Jerusalem, 1984), 139–49.

[68] See, for example, U. Heyd, *Ottoman Documents on Palestine, 1552–1615* (Oxford, 1960), 68–9.

[69] ʿAlī Efendi (?), *Chronicle of the Pashas*, fol. 20a.

quent expression in a treatise written in the middle of the seventeenth century by ʿAlī Efendi, an obscure scribe in the Egyptian military bureaucracy. He describes a high-ranking official of the Ottoman court, who stops off in Egypt during a pilgrimage to Mecca. He repays the hospitality extended to him by the chief army officers with a diatribe about the soft life of the Egyptian soldiers in contrast with the harsh conditions of their Ottoman comrades, who have to go to war every year. ʿAlī Efendi defends the Egyptian army for the various services it renders to the empire. More importantly, although the Egyptians are not worse or less dedicated fighters than the *Qapu qulları*, they far exceed them in their religious and ethical behaviour.[70]

The treatise may be a work of fiction, but the issues and sentiments were real enough. The author did not have on his mind primarily the ethnic divisions; the antagonism is between the Egyptian army and Ottoman outsiders. It is not a plea for *awlād ʿArab*; the treatise is written in Turkish. Nevertheless, the predominance of the Circassian beys in the Egyptian army is noticeable. ʿAlī Efendi's hero is Ṣāliḥ Bey, a Circassian bey whom ʿAlī served as a secretary. Also, resentment toward the Turks from Anatolia (*Rum oghlanı*) is expressed at the end of the treatise.[71]

While the merits of the Egypt-based Circassian beys are only implied by ʿAlī Efendi behind a wider 'Egyptian' identity, there is another literary work from about the same period that makes an explicit case for the privileges and historical rights of the Circasssian Mamluks. Holt studied a genealogy written for Riḍwān Bey al-Faqārī, *amīr al-ḥājj* for almost a quarter of a century. The author of Riḍwān's spurious pedigree claims that the great *amīr al-ḥājj* was descended both from the Circassian Mamluk sultans and from Quraysh, the Prophet's tribe, thus making him of a nobler origin than the Ottoman dynasty itself.[72]

It must be emphasized that both the 'Egyptians' and the 'Ottomans' in the army were loyal subjects to the sultan in Istanbul. Even ʿAlī Efendi's defence of the Egyptians praises the service rendered by them to the Ottoman Empire. The tensions and antipathies were of social, economic and mental nature. The Mamluks, whatever their exact definition, were certainly on the 'Egyptian' side of the divide.

Defender beys (*Muḥāfaẓa beyleri*) and Circassian beys (*Çerākise beyleri*)

The chief keepers of Mamluk identity and traditions were not the Mamluk soldiers serving in the *Çerākise Ocağı* or in other units or places, but the ranking Circassian beys (*Çerākise beyleri*). They appear in the sixteenth- and

70 M. Winter, "ʿAlī Efendi's 'Anatolian Campaign Book': a defence of the Egyptian army in the seventeenth century', *Turcica*, 15 (1983), 267–309.

71 Ibid., 280, 293.

72 P. M. Holt, 'The exalted lineage of Riḍwān Bey: some observations on a seventeenth century Mamluk genealogy', in Holt (ed.), *Studies in the History of the Near East*, 220–30.

seventeenth- century sources – archival materials and chronicles alike – as a identifiable group, distinct from both the common Circassians and the beys, who are referred to as *sancaḳ (or ṣanjaq) beyleri* or *muḥāfaẓa beyleri* (defender beys). This distinction beween the two categories of beys gives us a clue about the Mamluk phenomenon in Ottoman Egypt, since here alone we have a tangible, clearly recognizable group that is the carrier of Mamluk values and traditions. The Circassian beys were, of course, army commanders, who were occasionally specifically mentioned in imperial decrees calling upon the army of Egypt to send a contingent to the sultan's campaigns.[73] In festive processions, the *Çerākise beyleri* marched under their own flags, separately.[74]

It is necessary in this connection to discuss the *sancaḳ beyi*s, also called *muḥāfaẓa beyleri.* In his study of the beylicate, Holt rightly concludes that unlike the situation in other Ottoman provinces, where *ṣanjaq* (lit. a standard, flag) meant a district under the jurisdiction of a *sancaḳ beyi*, in Egypt the term did not have a territorial connotation[75] (since the *timar* system was not applied here). The term used was *muḥāfaẓa ṣancağı*, a defender's standard.[76] Holt's suggestion about the strong similarity of the functions of the beys in the seventeenth century to those of the defunct Mamluk sultanate is convincing. Yet there is no evidence that the beylicate in the sixteenth century had anything to do with Mamluk institutions or traditions. The beys were members of the high command of the army which assisted the governor. There is also information about beys in charge of specific tasks, such as guarding the seaports of Alexandria or Damietta, or acting as *amīr al-ḥājj.*[77] Muṣṭafā ʿĀlī lists the thirty *sancaḳ beyi*s he knew in Egypt at the end of the sixteenth century. He complains that only a small number of them have served in the imperial palace in Istanbul or in the residence of military dignitaries. The majority, he claims, rose in the service of rich Arabs or as a result of their service in Yemen. Even from his flowery style one learns about the beys' assignments and tasks.[78] It is remarkable that none of them was a Mamluk. A bey's commission, or *sancaḳ*, was sometimes given to a pasha's son, a Meccan *sharīf*, or even to former members of the ʿ*ulamā*ʾ class.[79]

It was the intention of the government that the number of beys in Egypt should not exceed twelve, yet it is obvious from numerous decrees that the number reached at least thirty towards the end of the sixteenth century and about forty by the mid seventeenth century. Thc Portc's insistence in the sixteenth century that there be no more than twelve beys, and that no one be made bey before there was a vacant post, obviously went unheeded. When Qul Qıran Muḥammad Pasha reorganized the army after crushing the Sipahi

[73] For example, *MD*, vol. 27, no. 282, at 118, 25 Shawwāl 983 (25 January 1576); vol. 59, no. 34, at 10, 5 Rabīʿ I 993 (7 March 1585).
[74] Evliya Çelebi, *Seyahatname* (Istanbul, 1938), vol. X, pp.131, 143, 328, 401.
[75] Holt, 'The beylicate in Ottoman Egypt', 181 ff.
[76] *MD*, vol. 46, no. 261, at 131, 10 Ramaḍān 989 (8 October 1581).
[77] A letter from ʿAlī Pasha to the sultan, dated 957 (1550), MS E 2283, Topkapı Sarayı Archives, Istanbul. [78] *Muṣṭafā ʿĀlī*, 57ff. [79] Ibid., 60.

revolt in 1609, he dismissed all but twelve of the ablest beys, the other seventeenth were banished to Istanbul. But like some of his other reforms, this measure was soon abandoned.[80] It is important to note that there was no similar limitation on the number of the *Çerākise beyleri*, whose rank was clearly of a lower echelon than the *ṣanjaq beyi*s, as the following evidence will demonstrate:

As already indicated, there was a policy of restricting the number of the *ṣanjaq beyleri* to twelve – the copy of the document of appointment had to be sent to Istanbul to be filed among those of the high Ottoman personnel.[81] The order of addressees in the imperial edicts (reflecting the hierarchy) is: *muḥāfaẓa beyleri, ümarā-i Çerākise, Müteferriqa;* and Çāvūs.[82] The beys had authority to impose death sentences, which the Circassian beys did not have.[83]

A decree of 1013/1605 ordered the Egyptian military chiefs to send to Istanbul, 'according to an old custom', fine, trained horses. The *ṣanjaq beyi*s and the *kāshif*s had to give two horses each; the Circassian beys and the Arab chiefs (*shaykh ʿArab*) – clearly less rich – were required to give only one horse each.[84]

The Circassian beys, then, were among the elite cavalry groups, above the Müteferriqa and the Çāvūs corps, and well beneath the *sanjaḳ* (or *muḥāfaẓa*) *beyleri*. Another edict, dated 984/1576, clearly demonstrates the rank of the Circassian soldiers and the Circassian beys in the military hierarchy. This document discusses the problem of soldiers getting control of villages as tax-farmers (*multazims*) or salaried tax-collectors (*ümenā*), by way of buying their revenues from *kāshif*s and Arab shaykhs in their capacity as provincial governors. The edict orders that only the higher-ranking officers, namely the Circassian beys, the Müteferriqa and the Çāvūs be given villages to administer for the treasury, but not members of the (lower ranking cavalry corps) Gönülliyān, Süvāri (i. e. Sipahis) and the Çerākise (the latter were the Circassian Mamluks who had not reached the rank of bey).[85]

The role of Circassian beys as commanders of the pilgrimage caravan

The office of *amīr al-ḥājj* was an extremely important one, which conferred on its incumbent political influence and religious prestige, and required considerable military and logistical talents. This office was one of the positions through which the Mamluk amirs succeeded in holding their own under

80 Winter, *Egyptian Society under Ottoman Rule*, 48. According to Holt ('The beylicate in Ottoman Egypt', 185) there were traditionally twenty-four beys, just as there had been twenty-four amirs of the first class (*amīr miʾa)*. Yet both the Turkish chronicle by ʿAlī Efendi, and, more importantly, several edicts in the *Mühimme Defteri* collection, state that the number of beys allowed by the government was limited to twelve. See, for example, the next note.

81 *MD,* vol. 75, no. 193, at 109, Shaʿbān 1013 (January 1605).

82 See, for example, MD, vol. 39, no. 418, at 203, 10 Muḥarram 988 (26 February 1580).

83 *MD,* vol. 24, no. 616, at 232–3, 26 Muḥarram 982 (18 May 1547).

84 *MD*, vol. 75, no. 172, 16 Shawwāl 1013, (6 March 1605).

85 *MD*, vol. 29, no. 9, at 5, 1 Ramaḍān 984 22 (November 1576).

Ottoman sovereignty, although, as will be presently shown, the office had not yet become their monopoly as it would be in the future. An *amīr al-ḥājj* had to be able to protect the huge caravan against bedouins, who often attacked and pillaged it.

Under the Mamluk sultans, the post was invariably held by one of the highest-ranking amirs, *amīr mi'a muqaddam alf*. In 923/1517, soon after the conquest, the Ottomans appointed a bureaucrat, the director of the sultan's domain (*nāẓir al-khawāṣṣ al-sharīfa*).[86] The following year the office was conferred upon Barakāt b. Mūsā, the market inspector (*muḥtasib*) of Cairo, to the consternation of Ibn Iyās, who considered this appointment as yet another proof of Ottoman insensitivity and bad judgement.[87] In 925/1519, however, the *amīr al-ḥājj* was Barsbāy, the adjutant (*dawādār*) of Khā'ir Bey. Al-Jazīrī, our principal source on the subject of *umarā' al-ḥājj* in the sixteenth century, says: 'He was the first Turk [i. e. Mamluk, non-Arab, most certainly a Circassian; the Ottomans were called Turkomans, *Tarākima*, or Anatolians, *Rūmī* or *Arwām*] appointed to this office by the Ottoman state. Since that year, the routine (*niẓām*) of this amirate became established after [the fall of] the Circassian state'.[88]

In the year 926/1520, the appointee was another Mamluk amir and *kāshif*, the above-mentioned Jānim ibn Dawlatbāy, the future rebel. He held the post for three years, until 929/1523, followed by Fāris ibn Özdemir, another Circassian amir, the *kāshif* of Buḥayra province.[89] In 930/1524 and 931/1525 the office was given to Jānim al-Ḥamzāwī, who was also a Mamluk, socially if not legally, and was a powerful political figure at that time with a rank of *amīr ṣanjaq*.[90]

In 932/1526, the line of Circassian *umarā' al-ḥājj* was broken by the appointment of a certain Sinān, an old Turkish (Rūmī) amir. Qanīm ibn Maʿalbāy, once again a Circassian amir, was the incumbent in the years 933/1527–936/1530. He was the supervisor of the important Dashīsha (lit. porridge) *waqf* endowment for the support of the inhabitants of Mecca and Medina. In 937/1531 and 938/1532 the incumbent was Yūsuf, Jānim al-Ḥamzāwī's son.[91]

The amir who held the office for the longest period in the sixteenth century was Muṣṭafā b. ʿAbdallāh[92] al-Rūmī. He started his unusually successful career from total obscurity and poverty. As a youngster, he was a saddler working for the army and became rich by looting the treasury of Aḥmad Pasha al-Khā'in. After serving as a *kāshif* in increasingly important regions, he was named to the amirate of the *ḥajj* in 938/1532 for the first time. He served ten times (not consecutively) as *amīr al-ḥājj*, five years as *kāshif* of the important Gharbiyya Province, then after being promoted to *ṣanjaq beyi*, he was appointed as governor of Yemen, and later served three more years as *amīr al-*

[86] Al-Jazīrī, 364. [87] Ibid., 364; Ibn Iyās, 246. [88] Al-Jazīrī, 365. [89] Ibid., 368.
[90] Ibid., 368–9. [91] Ibid., 371–2.
[92] The name Ibn ʿAbdallāh often indicates either a man whose father was unknown or a convert. Of course, Mamluks belonged to that category.

ḥājj. Finally, he was raised to the rank of pasha and served as governor of Egypt (1561–4).[93]

Other *umarāʾ al-ḥājj* were Sulaymān, a pasha's son (940/1534), and Yūsuf al-Ḥamzāwī again in 941/1535. It is interesting that for six consecutive years (946/1539 – 951/1545) the office was held by Jānim ibn Qāṣrah, who had been a Mamluk of Sultan Qānṣūh al-Ghawrī, and had held high office in the Mamluk sultanate. Al-Jazīrī praises his personality and notes that he insisted on being called 'amir', alluding to his high position during the former regime.[94]

The incumbent in 952/1546 was another Ibn ʿAbdallāh al-Rūmī, Aydın by name, probably a convert to Islam, but not a Mamluk, who started out as a hawker in the Khān al-Khalīlī bazaar of Cairo. He became an officer (*kâhya*) in the Circassian regiment, then served as the commander of the garrison at Azlam, a meeting point on the *ḥajj* route. Finally, he was appointed as the *kāshif* of al-Gharbiyya province. Although he was not a Mamluk, his background in the Circassian corps, his service on the *ḥajj* route and his experience as *kāshif* prepared him for the job.[95]

In 953/1547, another Circassian amir, Ḥusayn Abāẓa by name (note the Arabic name, the first for a Circassian *amīr al-ḥājj*), was given the office. He too was a *kāshif*. He was embroiled in a bitter quarrel with the above-mentioned Muṣṭafā Pasha, who led the *ḥajj* himself for three years until 957/1550.[96] Then Muṣṭafā was ordered to leave the *ḥajj* and go to Yemen to fight against the Zaydī Imam. He was replaced as *amīr al-ḥājj* by Muḥammad Katkhudā, of the elite Müteferriqa corps. He won this appointment as a favour from ʿAlī Pasha the Fat, the *beylerbeyi* of Egypt at that time, and was the only incumbent of such relatively low rank.[97] We learn from a letter sent by ʿAlī Pasha to the sultan, and now in the Topkapı Sarayı archive, that indeed the governor felt he had to justify this unusual appointment. ʿAlī Pasha writes that three other candidates had been considered, all of them with the rank of bey, but all three had other vital assignments – one was a captain of the navy and the others were in charge of guarding the seaports of Alexandria and Damietta. Therefore, Muḥammad Katkhudā, a Müteferriqa officer with a daily salary of 40 aqçe was appointed.[98]

After 957/1550, where al-Jazīrī's book stops, there is only sporadic information about *umarā' al-ḥājj* for the rest of the century. For the year 992/1584 the post was held by a civilian, Khawāja Muḥammad, refered to as *malik al-tujjār*, the head of the merchants. Unfortunately, nothing more is known about this surprising appointment.[99] A decree dated 23 Rajab 999 (17 May 1591) mentions as *amīr al-ḥājj* Amir ʿUmar b. ʿĪsā, an Arab chief who acted as the governor of the Buḥayra province.[100] He must have been a man of unusually high standing for an Arab chief. He is mentioned in imperial decrees as the

93 Ibid., 374–6, 398–9. 94 Ibid., 381. 95 Ibid., 384–5. 96 Ibid., 393–5.
97 Ibid., 399. 98 The letter cited in note 77 above.
99 *MD*, vol. 52, no. 793, at 297, 8 Rabīʿ I 992 (20 March 1584).
100 *MD*, vol. 67, no. 331, at 123, 23 Rajab 999 (17 May 1591).

commander of an Egyptian contingent sent to join the Ottoman army that was going towards Tabriz to fight the Safavids. He is ordered to enlist in this force Arab shaykhs, *kāshif*s, Circassian beys and 'whoever wants to join'. It is obvious that this contingent, led by an apparent outsider to the Egyptian military establishment, was not composed of soldiers of the regular 'seven corps', but of 'substandard' troops, mainly, it seems, bedouins, Mamluks, and even Circassian beys.[101]

Two decrees of 993/1585 mention Muṣṭafā, 'one of the Circassian amirs, an able and a very wealthy man', as *amīr al-ḥājj*. The same documents speak about a certain Muḥammad, an Egyptian bey (not a Circassian bey) who held the office previously.[102] Muṣṭafā ʿĀlī mentions Piri Bey, a Bosnian, who also served as *amīr al-ḥājj* in the last years of the sixteenth century.[103]

This brief survey of the office of *amīr al-ḥājj* shows that as early as the sixteenth century Circassian (therefore Mamluk) amirs were natural and even favoured candidates for that post. The total monopoly the beys established on the office belongs to later times, but even in early Ottoman Egypt we have clear evidence of the continuous influence and power of the Mamluk amirs. Their experience in dealing with bedouins, which, as has been already indicated, made them also preferred candidates to become *kāshif*s, was an important asset in their functioning as commanders of the *ḥajj* caravan. Background and experience as *kāshif*s also seems to have been vital, as well as revenues accruing from the management of a *kāshif*'s province; there is evidence that a part of these revenues was used to help finance the *ḥajj*.[104]

Conclusion

It is important to note that by the eighteenth century the term 'Circassian bey' disappears. The distinction which has been discussed in the present chapter between Circassian beys and the higher-ranking *ṣanjaq bey*is, or just beys, becomes gradually blurred. With the shrinking presence of 'organic' Ottoman beys from the heartland of the empire, which became increasingly decentralized, the two groups merged into what has been aptly called neo-Mamluk culture, which was shared by all the military grandees, Circassians, Bosnians, or others. Also, the Circassian racial element was not as dominant in later Mamluk society, which now included also Georgians, Abaza, Turks and others.

101 *MD*, vol. 59, nos. 34, 161, 162, 172, at 10, 36, 12 Rabīʿ II 993 (13 April 1585).

102 *MD*, vol. 58, nos. 690, 691, at 271, 17 Ramaḍān 993 (12 September 1585).

103 *Muṣṭafā* ʿĀlī, 58. Holt, 'The beylicate in Ottoman Egypt', 184. As has been shown above, there were other beys who were appointed as *umarāʾ al-ḥājj* before him.

104 *MD*, vol. 61, no. 74, at 26, 10 Rajab 994 (27 June 27, 1586). In this interesting document ʿUmar ibn ʿĪsā says that if he is granted the province of Manṣūra as *iltizām* for five years, and if he is appointed *amīr al-ḥājj* for that period, he promises to cover out of his own money the sum of 10,000 gold pieces, which Egypt's treasury pays annually for the expenses of the *ḥajj*. The government recommends that his wish be granted, but it is not known whether in fact he was appointed again. See also *MD*, vol. 30, no. 536, at 230, 13 Rabīʿ I, 985 (31 May 1577).

The characteristics of the (neo-) Mamluk political culture have been described by Ayalon and Holt and need not be repeated in detail here; this subject is also outside the scope of the present chapter. Suffice it to say that culture consisted mainly of a strong Egyptian identity as contrasted with a more general Ottoman or Turkish one. This consciousness had at least a latent hostility toward the Ottomans,[105] although it very rarely translated into an armed rebellion or even a declaration of disloyalty towards the sultan. One central component of the general Mamluk outlook was the devotion to orthodox Islam, which was also markedly Egyptian, having for example a positive attitude to the al-Azhar and its *ʿulamāʾ* and to the orthodox Sufism of the Egyptian variety.[106] Yet, the strongest cohesive motive must have been to group solidarity as Mamluk amirs in general and as members of Mamluk factions or houses. As I have tried to show elsewhere, they became, despite their many shortcomings and misrule, a genuine Egyptian aristocracy.[107]

The re-emergence of Mamluk power must be understood in the wider context of the 'localization' of the elites in Egypt as in other provinces. The late period in Ottoman Egypt witnessed the emergence of *Shaykh al-Azhar*, the passing of the office of *Naqīb al-ashrāf* from Ottoman to Egyptian dignitaries, and the flourishing of Sufism and popular Islam peculiar to Egypt.[108]

In conclusion, it was Ottoman policy immediately after the conquest that laid the foundations for the preservation and eventual re-emergence of the Mamluks. The Ottomans decided to use Mamluk military manpower to their advantage. They also needed the Mamluk amirs to administer the country to avoid jeopardizing the flow of revenues into the empire's treasury. Ultimately, this policy proved successful and safeguarded Istanbul's basic interests, even when the Mamluk amirs were the effective rulers of Egypt, and the Ottoman governor a mere figurehead.

An attempt has been made to explain the difficulty of finding evidence of the Mamluks' presence in the historical sources. It is in part due to the scarcity of sources for certain decades and also to the changed social and political conditions as a result of Egypt's integration into the Ottoman Empire. The difficulty of identifying the Mamluks, who were now called by Arabic names, adds to the confusion. Nevertheless, as I have tried to show, there is evidence of Mamluks and Mamluk amirs, usually referred to as Circassians, the predominant race. Mamluk amirs, although inferior to the Ottoman pasha and the *ṣanjaq beyleri*, were already fulfilling vital functions as *kāshif*s, *umarāʾ al-ḥājj* and army commanders. The Ottoman–Egyptian divide within the army was a well-known social phenomenon in the sixteenth century and later periods. The Mamluks, who did not have any permanent contacts or ties outside Egypt, were a natural part of the 'Egyptian' side.

As the empire declined and its hold on the provinces weakened, local forces,

105 See, for example, Winter, *Egyptian Society under Ottoman Rule* (54), about the hostility of Mamluk amirs to the memory of Khāʾir Bey and the veneration of the tombs of the Mamluk amirs who had resisted the Ottomans. 106 Ibid., 159. 107 Ibid., 76f.

108 Ibid., chaps. 5 and 6.

in Egypt and elsewhere, were coming to the fore. This trend took different forms in the various provinces. It was natural that the local forces that seized power in Egypt were the Mamluks, who had a long political and military experience and a long collective memory of the great days of the Mamluk sultanate, with whom the neo-Mamluk military society had racial, social and ideological affinity.

CHAPTER 6

'Mamluk households' and 'Mamluk factions' in Ottoman Egypt: a reconsideration

JANE HATHAWAY

It is well known that after conquering Egypt from the Mamluk sultanate in 1517, the Ottomans retained key Mamluk usages, above all in subprovincial administration, and that a number of the defeated Mamluks who were willing to co-operate with the new regime were allowed to join the Ottoman administration. In consequence, a number of practices of the Mamluk sultanate survived the Ottoman conquest. In particular, the custom of recruiting boys and young men from the Caucasus as military slaves, or Mamluks, and training them as soldiers in households geared to that purpose appears not only to have survived but to have flourished in Ottoman Egypt. By the time of the 1798 French invasion, in fact, Egypt's military elite was dominated by Caucasian, and notably Georgian, Mamluks.[1] In the face of such apparent similarities with the Mamluk sultanate, it is tempting to define the military society of Ottoman Egypt as a continuation or revival of the sultanate. In fact, the historiography of Ottoman Egypt before the nineteenth century has typically defined the military regime in just such terms; it is quite common in the field today to describe Ottoman Egypt's military society as Mamluk or neo-Mamluk.[2]

This is not to imply, however, that historians do not acknowledge key administrative innovations under the Ottomans. The Ottomans rejected the Mamluk system of cavalry-supporting assignments of usufruct, or *iqṭāʿ*s,

[1] Ahmad Pasha al-Jazzār, *Ottoman Egypt in the Eighteenth Century: The Nizâmnâme of Cezzâr Ahmed Pasha*, ed. and trans. Stanford J. Shaw (Cambridge, Mass., 1962), 33.

[2] See, for example, P. M. Holt, 'The beylicate in Ottoman Egypt during the seventeenth century', *Bulletin of the School of Oriental and African Studies*, 3 (1961), 218, 223, 225; P. M. Holt, *Egypt and the Fertile Crescent, 1516–1922* (Ithaca and London, 1966), 73, 85, 90–2; Stanford J. Shaw, *The Financial and Administrative Organization and Development of Ottoman Egypt, 1517–1798* (Princeton, 1962), 33, 37, 63, 186, 194; David Ayalon, 'Studies in al-Jabarti I: notes on the transformation of Mamluk society in Egypt under the Ottomans', parts 1–2, *Journal of the Economic and Social History of the Orient*, 3 (1960), Daniel Crecelius, *The Roots of Modern Egypt: A Study of the Regimes of ʿAlī Bey al-Kabīr and Muḥammad Bey Abū ʾl-Dhahab, 1760–1775* (Minneapolis and Chicago, 1981), 30–1; Michael Winter: 'Turks, Arabs, and Mamluks in the army of Ottoman Egypt', *Wiener Zeitschrift für die Kunde des Morgenlandes*, 72 (1980), 100, 120–2; Gabriel Piterberg, 'The formation of an Ottoman Egyptian elite in the eighteenth century', *International Journal of Middle East Studies*, 22 (1990), 280.

which itself resembled the *timar* system in force in the Ottoman Empire's central lands at the time of the conquest of Egypt. Instead, the Ottomans installed a regime of tax collectors known as *amīns*, who were appointed from Istanbul and delivered the revenues they collected directly to the governor's treasury. During the seventeenth century, the system of *amīns* gradually gave way to tax farms, or *iltizāms*, which were sold at auction to the highest bidders.[3] The tax farmers were predominantly military grandees, many of whom were manumitted Mamluks. There is no question, however, that these Mamluk tax farmers served different administrative functions from the amirs of the Mamluk sultanate. Moreover, their ranks had been joined by large numbers of non-Mamluk military personnel: free-born Anatolian mercenaries; Ottoman soldiers recruited through the *devşirme*, the classical Ottoman system of collecting non-Muslim boys from conquered territories; Kurdish, Turkoman, and bedouin tribal levies; and various sorts of enterprising locals. Yet the method of recruitment and training, these historians hold, survived from the Mamluk sultanate; slaves and mercenaries alike were recruited into and trained within households inspired by the households of the sultanate. Thus, not only are individual households termed Mamluk households; Mamluk households are regarded as a fundamental characteristic of Ottoman Egypt's military establishment as a whole.

While there were certainly households in Ottoman Egypt, we cannot prove that they took their inspiration directly or entirely from comparable structures in the Mamluk sultanate. On the other hand, households were a key feature of Ottoman society at large in the years following the reign of Sultan Sulaymān I (1520–66). The prototype of the Ottoman elite household was, naturally, the household of the sultan himself, which reached its full development during Sulaymān's reign.[4] After the sixteenth century, imperial power became dispersed among an ever-widening network of interest groups in the palace and capital. As a result, tension developed among competing loci of power, such as the coterie of the sultan's mother (*valide sultan*) and those of the various government ministers, or viziers. This same sort of tension existed in the Ottoman provinces, where the governors' households imitated the sultan's palace on a smaller scale. But any governor's household was itself liable to face competition from the households of local elites.

[3] On land tenure in the Mamluk sultanate, see Hassanein Rabie, *The Financial System of Egypt, AH 564–741/AD 1169–1341* (London, 1972), chap. 2; Hassanein Rabie, 'The size and value of the *iqṭā*ʿ in Egypt, 564–741 AH/1169–1341 AD', in M. A. Cook (ed.), *Studies in the Economic History of the Middle East* (Oxford 1970), 129–38; A. N. Poliak; 'Some notes on the feudal system of the Mamluks', *Journal of the Royal Asiatic Society* (1937), 97–107. On the Ottoman *timar*, see Halil Inalcik, *The Ottoman Empire: The Classical Age, 1300–1600*, trans. Norman Itzkowitz and Colin Imber (London, 1973), 104–18. On developments in Ottoman Egypt, see Shaw, *Financial and Administrative Organization*, 28ff., 65ff.

[4] Leslie Peirce, *The Imperial Harem: Women and Sovereignty in the Ottoman Empire* (New York and Oxford, 1993); Gülru Necipoğlu-Kafadar, 'The formation of an Ottoman imperial tradition: The Topkapı Palace in the fifteenth and sixteenth centuries', facsimile of a Ph.D. diss. (Harvard, 1986), 588–97.

Egypt's local elite consisted primarily of officers of the seven Ottoman regiments stationed in the province[5] and the group of grandees known as beys, who held subprovincial governorships and such posts as pilgrimage commander (*amīr al-ḥājj*) and treasurer (*daftardār*). Localized Ottoman officials, such as long-time administrators or exiled palace eunuchs, could also join this elite. A grandee typically built up an entourage of slaves, domestic servants, bodyguards, and assorted clients who collected at his place of residence. He might provide for the Mamluks and mercenaries among his clients by placing them on the regimental payrolls, an increasingly frequent practice after the sixteenth century. The governor's entourage, naturally, coalesced in Cairo's Citadel, while the entourages of beys and officers typically gathered in the palatial houses that many of them owned in various neighbourhoods of the city.[6] Chronicles of the period typically refer to such a residence-based conglomerate as *bayt*.[7] Such a structure is what most historians have in mind when they speak of the Mamluk household, taking into account that not all the members of a grandee's entourage need be slaves.

Yet groups of clients could also form within the barracks where the Ottoman troops were garrisoned, much as they did in the Janissary barracks in Istanbul. In this process, an officer cultivated clients among the soldiery in the subdivision of the corps that he led. Histories of Ottoman Egypt give ample evidence of such groups, typically led by lower officers who did not have the money or status to build lavish houses outside the barracks. The seventeenth and eighteenth centuries saw the rise of two particularly aggressive Janissary bosses, Küçük Muḥammad and Ifranj Aḥmad. Both held the rank of *başodabaşı*, or chief commander of a barracks (*oda*), the smallest subdivision of the Janissary corps.[8] The hierarchical structure and routine of barracks life no doubt facilitated their attempts to attract clients among those under their command. Such followings within a regiment are usually called *ṭaraf*,

[5] These were the Mutafarriqa, Çavuşān, Janissaries (Mustaḥfiẓān), ʿAzabān, Gönüllüyān, Tüfenkçiyān and Çerakise.

[6] In the course of the seventeenth and eighteenth centuries, the hub of elite residence shifted from Birkat al-Fīl in southern Cairo to Birkat al-Azbakiyya in the western part of the city. See André Raymond, 'Essai de géographie des quartiers de résidence aristocratique au Caire au XVIIIe siècle', *Journal of the Economic and Social History of the Orient*, 6 (1963), 58–103.

[7] Ahmad Çelebi and al-Jabartī refer to the large household of ʿUthmān Çavuş al-Qāzdughlī in this manner. See Aḥmad Çelebi b. ʿAbd al-Ghanī, *Awḍaḥ al-ishārāt fī man tawalla Miṣr al-Qāhira min al-wuzarāʾ wa'l-bāshāt*, ed. ʿAbd al-Raḥīm ʿAbd al-Raḥmān ʿAbd al-Raḥīm (Cairo, 1978), 608; and ʿAbd al-Raḥmān al-Jabartī, *ʿAjāʾib al-āthār fī 'l-tarājim wa'l-akhbār* (Cairo, 1958–67), 7 vols., vol. II, 12.

[8] On Küçük Muḥammad, see, for example, Aḥmad Katkhudā ʿAzabān al-Damūrdāshī, *Al-durra al-muṣāna fī akhbār al-kināna*, British Museum, MS or. 1073–1074, at 14, 26; Aḥmad Çelebi, *Awḍaḥ*, 190ff.; al-Jabartī, *ʿAjāʾib*, vol. I, 130ff.; P. M. Holt, 'The career of Küçük Muḥammad (1676–94)', *Bulletin of the School of Oriental and African Studies*, 26 (1963), 269–87. On Ifranj Aḥmad, see ʿAbd al-Karīm b. ʿAbd al-Rahmān, *Tārīh-i Mısır*, MS Hekimoğlu Ali Pasa 705, Süleymaniye Library, Istanbul, fols. 128r-146v; Aḥmad Çelebi, *Awḍaḥ*, 229ff.; al-Jabartī, *ʿAjāʾib*, vol. I, 107ff.; André Raymond, 'Une 'révolution' au Caire sous les Mamelouks: la crise de 1123/1711', *Annales islamologiques*, 6 (1966), 95–120.

ṭā'ifa, or *jamāʿa* in the chronicles, although these terms can denote a number of other sorts of social and military groups, as well.[9] They do not easily fit the rubric of the Mamluk household. Yet the chronicles suggest that such gangs were contiguous with residence-based households, for once a regimental officer had attained a high enough rank and income – typically those of *çavuş*[10] – he would normally leave the barracks and purchase, confiscate or build a house in one of Cairo's neighbourhoods. Here, he would build up a domestic-cum-military household of his own on the foundation of the followers he had cultivated in the barracks.[11]

In all, then, three types of household coexisted on the local scene: the households of the governor and other Ottoman officials and former officials; the households of local grandees; and groups within the barracks. These were all, however, interconnected: Ottoman functionaries who formed households on the spot became local grandees, as did barracks strongmen who left the barracks and formed sophisticated households. In the latter case, the household could serve as an instrument of social mobility within the military cadre, or at the least as an affirmation of having attained an influential status. In the former case, it served as a meeting ground for imperial and local interests by providing an opportunity for imperial functionaries to exercise local influence and to co-opt local luminaries.

Thus it appears that the term 'Mamluk household' confuses the reality of Ottoman Egypt's military society because it excludes the barracks groups and ignores precedents for and parallels to the Egyptian household in other parts of the Ottoman Empire. I believe that the concept of the household, allowing for a wide range of variation, from relatively informal barracks coalitions to highly articulated residence-based conglomerates, provides a more flexible and representative framework within which to place Ottoman Egypt's military society than the conventional notion of a neo-Mamluk military regime. Focusing on the household as a unit of social organization in its own right, rather than as an inherently Mamluk phenomenon, also allows us to accommodate the disparate elements who participated in household-building: officers and beys, Caucasian slaves and free-born Anatolian Muslims, merchants and artisans, *ʿulamā'* and *ashrāf*. Emphasizing the household also enables us to link Egypt to the pattern followed by the Ottoman Empire as a whole during the period after Sulaymān I's death. A hallmark of the diffusion of imperial power was the efflorescence of households removed from the political centre: those of provincial governors and of high palace officials. Such

[9] For example, the entourages of the early Qāzdughlī leaders Muṣṭafa Katkhudā and Ḥasan Çavuş are called variously *ṭaraf* and *ṭā'ifa*. See al-Jabartī, *ʿAjā'ib*, vol. I, 107, 238; ʿAbd al-Karīm, *Tārīh-i Mısır*, fol. 135v.

[10] A *çavuş* was the third-highest-ranking officer in most regiments, behind the *agha* and the *katkhudā*.

[11] On ʿUthmān Çavuş al-Qāzdughlī's house, see al-Jabartī, *ʿAjā'ib*, vol. II, 48; Doris Behrens-Abouseif, *Azbakiyya and its Environs: From Azbak to Ismail, 1476–1879* (Cairo, 1985), 55–62; Raymond, 'Essai de géographie', 74.

households were the prototypes for the households of local notables (*aʿyān*) that came to dominate provincial society during the eighteenth and nineteenth centuries.[12] Egypt's prospective *aʿyān* consisted in part of military grandees. These grandees had numerous examples of the residence-based elite household before them in the households of the high Ottoman functionaries dispatched to administer the province. Foremost, of course, was the Ottoman governor's household, but a number of other imperial figures established households, as well: for example, the chief judge (*qāḍī ʿaskar*); the head of the descendants of the Prophet (*naqīb al-ashrāf*);[13] and above all, the exiled Chief Black Eunuchs of the imperial harem.[14] The habit of patronage through the household created common ground between imperial officials, both on the spot and in Istanbul, and local grandees. Ambitious local figures sought favour with the imperial centre by joining the households of imperial functionaries in Cairo; imperial figures in turn injected their clients into the households of local grandees. In this respect, the household served as a nexus between centre and province.

Emphasizing the household allows us to rethink the notion of a revival of Mamluk society following the Ottoman conquest of Egypt. It would, however, be too simplistic to assert that Egypt's households and the offices and institutions associated with them were Ottoman as opposed to Mamluk. Rather, the political culture of elite households provided a point of continuity between the Mamluk and Ottoman regimes and enabled the localized military elite that arose in Egypt to be absorbed into Ottoman elite politics. Under the new order, a wide range of elements joined Egypt's military society and began to build households that drew on both Ottoman and Mamluk examples. The recruits who entered these households were a similarly diverse group of Mamluks and non-Mamluks. Under the varied influences that came to bear on Egypt following its incorporation into the Ottoman Empire, the province's military society changed significantly, whatever continuities may have existed with the Mamluk sultanate.

The Faqārī and Qāsimī factions

Acknowledging this change obliges us to reassess key features of Ottoman Egyptian military society for which purely Mamluk antecedents have been assumed. A case in point is the two factions that permeated that society during the seventeenth and early eighteenth centuries. Under the Mamluk sultanate,

[12] Metin I. Kunt, *The Sultan's Servants: The Transformation of Ottoman Provincial Government, 1550–1650* (New York, 1983), esp. chap. 5 and conclusion. See also Rifaat Abou-el-Haj, 'The Ottoman vezir and paşa households, 1683–1703: a preliminary report', *Journal of the American Oriental Society,* 94 (1974), 446, n. 37.

[13] The *naqīb al-ashrāf* was appointed from Istanbul until the eighteenth century, when the Bakrī family, a prominent Cairene clan of descendants of the Prophet, came to monopolize the post.

[14] See Jane Hathaway, 'The role of the Kızlar Ağası in seventeenth-eighteenth century Ottoman Egypt', *Studia Islamica,* 75 (1992), 41–58.

factionalism was a concomitant of a new sultan's accession. Particularly under the Circassian Mamluks, each new sultan was himself a manumitted Mamluk who on taking power installed his own Mamluks in the posts closest to the throne, meanwhile divesting the Mamluks of his predecessor. Hence we encounter Mamluk factions associated with individual rulers and their houses: Ẓāhirīs, Ashrāfīs, and so on.[15] In Ottoman Egypt, the households of individual grandees, along with those of their clients and allies, can be construed as factions of this sort. But transcending these household alliances were two pervasive political blocs, the Faqārīs and Qāsimīs, which virtually divided Egyptian society between themselves from roughly 1640 to 1730. These blocs have been treated as a fairly typical instance of Mamluk factionalism,[16] implying that they differ little from the factions of the Mamluk sultanate, despite their magnitude and longevity.

The origin myths of the Faqārīs and Qāsimīs that the Arabic chronicles report, however, ascribe the emergence of these two blocs to the Ottoman conquest of Egypt. Thorough analysis of the origin myths of the Faqārī and Qāsimī factions and the probable reality behind them lies beyond the scope of this chapter.[17] Nonetheless, it appears that the two blocs schematically represent Ottoman and non-Ottoman elements within Egypt's military population, as symbolized by specific Ottoman and Mamluk heraldic devices. At the end of his account of the origin myth, the chronicler al-Jabartī notes: 'The way one faction (*farīq*) was distinguished from the other was that when they rode in processions, the Faqārīs' flag was white, and their lances had a knob, while the Qāsimīs' flag was red, and their lances had a disc'.[18] The processional paraphernalia are key. The Faqārīs carry the knob-headed *ṭuġ* of the Ottoman armies while the Qāsimīs carry the Mamluk *ʿalam*, topped not by a knob but normally by an inscription worked in metal in the shape of a spade or disc. In fact, it is conceivable that the epithet Faqārī derives from the caliph ʿAlī's sword Dhū'l-Faqār, whose image was commonly emblazoned on Ottoman battle standards, above all those of the Janissaries.[19]

We might speculate that the Faqārī and Qāsimī factions sprang to the fore in the seventeenth century as a result of jockeying for position between Ottoman and non-Ottoman elements in Egypt's military population. During the sixteenth century, the central Ottoman government had made a concerted effort to Ottomanize the rank of bey in Egypt by limiting it to garrison commanders appointed from Istanbul.[20] Meanwhile, the various non-Ottoman

[15] David Ayalon, 'Studies on the structure of the Mamluk army', part 1, *Bulletin of the School of Oriental and African Studies,* 15 (1953), 206–8.

[16] See, for example, *Encyclopaedia of Islam*, 2nd edn, s.v. 'Mamluks', by P. M. Holt.

[17] I am currently conducting research for such a study.

[18] Al-Jabartī, *ʿAjāʾib*, vol. I, 71 (my translation).

[19] Zdzislaw Zygulski, Jr., *Ottoman Art in the Service of the Empire* (New York, 1992), 45–51, 69ff.; Fevzi Kurtoğlu, *Türk Bayrağı ve Ay Yıldız* (Ankara, 1938), 74–7; Riza Nour, 'L'histoire du croissant', *Revue de turcologie,* 1 (February 1933), 117/346.

[20] *Mühimme Defteri* vol. 6, Başbakanlık Osmanlı Arşivi, Istanbul, no. 487, Jumāda I 972 (January 1565); 29, no. 9, Ramadān 984 (December 1576).

elements noted earlier continued to enter the military echelons. Mamluk amirs who had joined the Ottoman administration continued to purchase Mamluks from the Caucasus as, no doubt, did many of the Ottoman beys themselves. Gradually, it appears, these non-Ottoman elements began to assert themselves. Thus, for example, the seventeenth-century Qāsimī chieftain Riḍwān Bey Abū 'l-Shawārib named two of his sons Özbek and Khushqadam, evoking the Mamluks of old and flouting Selim I's desire that amirs take only Arab Muslim names.[21]

To this brand of Circassian self-assertion belongs the spurious genealogy of one Riḍwān Bey, whom P. M. Holt has identified as the Faqārī chieftain who monopolized the post of pilgrimage commander during the 1630s and 1640s.[22] The genealogy traces Riḍwān's lineage to the Mamluk sultan Barqūq (1382–99) and thence to the Quraysh. Holt construes the genealogy as Riḍwān Bey's attempt to forge a more legitimate pedigree than that of the Ottoman sultan and perhaps to justify a bid for autonomy. I suspect, however, that the political reality behind this genealogical work was more complex. The work is obsessed with the Bayt al-Ḥarām in Mecca and, if anything, seems to create a case for Riḍwān Bey's appointment as pilgrimage commander.[23] Since the sultan would have made this appointment, it would seem unwise for Riḍwān Bey to attempt a rebellion. Descent from the Quraysh would give him a cachet of religious legitimacy, but the claim of Qurayshi descent did not originate with Riḍwān Bey. Rather, it belonged to indigenous Circassian lore and was documented by the seventeenth-century Ottoman traveller Evliya Çelebi during his travels in Circassia.[24]

The novel element in this genealogy is the purported link to the Mamluk sultan Barqūq, the first of the Circassian Mamluk sultans. In the context of Egyptian society alone, it would seem that Riḍwān Bey was attempting to portray himself as heir to the Mamluk sultanate and therefore as an alternative to the Ottomans. Viewed in a broader context, however, Riḍwān Bey's strategy gains greater subtlety. The tactic of invoking a past power was not uncommon among Ottoman provincial elites. In early seventeenth-century Basra, for a notable example, the local Afrāsiyāb dynasty claimed descent from the Seljuqs.[25] In the principalities of Moldavia and Wallachia, the

[21] On Özbek, see ʿAbd al-Karīm, *Tārīh-i Mısır*, fol. 78v; on Khushqadam, see ibid., fol. 91v.

[22] P. M. Holt, 'The exalted lineage of Riḍwān Bey: some observations on a seventeenth-century Mamluk genealogy', *Bulletin of the School of Oriental and African Studies,* 12 (1959), 224–7.

[23] Anonymous, *Nisba sharīfa wa-risāla munīfa tashtamil ʿalā dhikr nasab al-Jarākisa min Quraysh* (Princeton University Library, Garrett Manuscript Collection 186H). Holt examined manuscripts in the John Rylands Library, Manchester, England, and the British Museum. The Princeton manuscript gives Riḍwān Bey's title not as *amīr al-ḥājj* but as *khādim al-maḥmil al-Muḥammadī*, thus leaving open the possibility that the Riḍwān in question is not Riḍwān Bey al-Faqārī but the Qāsimī Riḍwān Bey Abū 'l-Shawārib. The manuscript also notes that Riḍwān Bey has two sons named Özbek and Khushqadam, as did Abū 'l-Shawārib.

[24] Evliya Çelebi, *Evliya Çelebi Seyahatnamesi*, ed. Ahmed Cevdet (Istanbul, 1314 A.H.), vol. VII, 718ff. See also Schora Bekmursin-Nogmow, *Die Sagen und Lieder des Tscherkessen-Volks* (Leipzig, 1866), 63ff.

[25] Holt, *Egypt and the Fertile Crescent*, 134. Holt notes the similarity to Riḍwān Bey.

Phanariot Greeks whom the Ottomans appointed governors, or *hospodars*, posed as neo-Byzantines to the extent of replicating Byzantine court ritual.[26] Yet no serious historian would claim that these regimes represented genuine revivals of the Seljuq or Byzantine Empire. Nor, on the other hand, did either of them use claims to a more ancient legitimacy to undermine Ottoman authority. Afrāsiyāb and his descendants recognized the Ottoman sultan; the Phanariots were installed by the Ottomans as a reliable alternative to the volatile indigenous suzerains known as *voyvodas*.

The tactic that the Afrāsiyābs and the Phanariot *hospodars* were employing was a calculated and highly selective nostalgia whose effect was subtle. By evoking the pre-Ottoman rulers of the regions where they held sway, they probably achieved the impression of having strong local roots that did not depend on the Ottoman authority. Nonetheless, this perceived local authority complemented, rather than rivalled, the authority vested in them by their allegiance to the Ottoman sultan.

Seen in this light, Riḍwān Bey's evocation of Barqūq and, indeed, the very notion of a resurgence of Mamluk culture in Egypt becomes more comprehensible. Riḍwān may have harked back to the founder of the Circassian phase of the Mamluk sultanate to give himself leverage against the beys and other officials who had been installed from Istanbul. The fictive bond to the Quraysh, meanwhile, bolstered his claim to command of the pilgrimage. Yet he never overtly rebelled against the sultan, although he did on occasion ignore imperial orders and withhold revenues from the imperial treasury. In Riḍwān Bey's case, as in the cases of the Afrāsiyāb dynasty and the Phanariots, selective nostalgia of this type was a concomitant of loyalist but localized authority. In short, Riḍwān Bey's genealogy and the factionalism of which it was a symptom resulted not from a revival of Mamluk political culture but from a distinctive amalgam of Ottoman and Mamluk usages adapted to the priorities of the diverse groups that now belonged to Egypt's military elite.

The late eighteenth-century beylicate

The case of the Faqārī and Qāsimī factions offers an object lesson in the interpretation of Ottoman Egypt's military elite: namely, that outward similarities to the customs of the Mamluk sultanate do not necessarily bespeak a revival of Mamluk usages but often overlie a multifaceted political culture unique to the Ottoman period. This lesson could profitably be applied to analysis of late eighteenth-century Egyptian military society.

Towards the end of the eighteenth century, Egypt fell under the sway of a group of beys of predominantly Georgian Mamluk origin, the most famous of whom was no doubt ʿAlī Bey al-Kabīr, who rebelled against the Ottoman

[26] William H. McNeill, *Europe's Steppe Frontier, 1500–1800* (Chicago and London, 1964), 107–10, 140–1, 173–6.

sultan in 1768. In light of ʿAlī Bey's career, it is tempting to see in this upper echelon of Caucasian beys a throwback to the Circassian regime of the late Mamluk sultanate. However, this beylicate stemmed from the unprecedented practice, beginning in the late 1720s, of regimental officers promoting their clients to the rank of bey.[27] Foremost among these officers was ʿAlī Bey's patron, Ibrāhīm al-Qāzdughlī, the *katkhudā* of the Janissary corps,[28] who exercised *de facto* control over Egypt from 1748 to 1754. He established a Qāzdughlī hegemony in Egypt; most of the Georgian beys of the late eighteenth century belonged to the Qāzdughlī household.

Yet from all appearances, Ibrāhīm Katkhudā, who appears to have been a Georgian Mamluk himself, did not seek to create a purely Mamluk household for its own sake. The clients whom he raised to the beylicate during his lifetime, as well as those who were promoted just after their patron's death, present an array of defectors and hand-me-downs from other households. ʿAlī Bey al-Qird, later known as al-Ghazzāwī, and his brothers had been Mamluks of the Chief Black Eunuch in Istanbul, while Ḥusayn Bey al-Ṣābūnjī had served as treasurer (*khaznadār*) to Muḥammad Çorbacı al-Ṣābūnjī of the ʿAzabān corps. Ḥamza Bey Abāẓa, meanwhile, defected to Ibrāhīm Katkhudā's household from the household of Muḥammad Bey Abāẓa. Most of these beys were Georgian or Abkhazian; however, they were acquired not solely because of their ethnicity but to ensure Ibrāhīm Katkhudā's and his heirs' control of the pilgrimage route to Mecca and Medina and of the tax farms of the grain-rich districts of Upper Egypt. All these beys, like ʿAlī Bey and others of Ibrāhīm's clients, served at various times as protectors of the pilgrimage caravan and as governors of grain-producing villages and subprovinces.[29]

In general, the acquisition of Mamluks was for the Qāzdughlīs and other ambitious grandees of the eighteenth century not so much a programme of ethnic consolidation or the implementation of a slave ethos as a strategy for expeditious household building. For those with the requisite rank and income, Mamluks were by the mid-eighteenth century a means towards a strong, self-sustaining household. Indeed, Georgian Mamluks represent not a reversion to the practices of the Mamluk sultanate but a practical new trend in the Ottoman provinces during the eighteenth century. The disintegration in 1722 of the rival Safavid Empire in Iran, which had employed Georgian Mamluks on a large scale, freed up a source of eastern Georgian slaves for the Safavids' Ottoman neighbours. (Western Georgia had been an Ottoman sphere of

[27] Aḥmad Çelebi (*Awḍaḥ*, 514) records what is to my knowledge the first instance of a garrison officer raising a client to the beylicate in 1727, when the Janissary *katkhudā* Ḥusayn al-Dimyāṭī made his client Muṣṭafa Agha al-Wālī *sancaḳ bey* of Jirjā and Minya in Upper Egypt.

[28] The *katkhudā*, also rendered *kâhya* or *kethüda*, was nominally second in command to the *agha*; by the eighteenth century, however, the *katkhudās* of the Janissary and ʿAzābān corps exercised *de facto* control over their respective regiments.

[29] On al-Qird, see al-Jabartī, *ʿAjāʾib*, vol. III, 158; on al-Ṣābūnjī, see al-Damurdāshī, *Durra*, 491, 546, 549–52, and al-Jabartī, *ʿAjāʾib*, vol. III, 116–18; on Ḥamza Bey and the Abāẓa household generally, al-Damurdāshī, *Durra*, 533, 542, 543, 559.

influence and an important source of slaves since the late fifteenth century.) In 1724, furthermore, the Ottoman Empire and Russia signed a treaty giving the Ottomans suzerainty over all of Georgia, which they retained until 1735.[30] Egypt's grandees, like local elites in other Ottoman provinces,[31] took aggressive advantage of this new supply of manpower.

ʿAlī Bey stands out among the clients of Ibrāhīm Katkhudā al-Qāzdughlī for revolting against the sultan, although his patron had himself achieved what the Ottoman chancery termed 'independence' (*istiqlāl*) in his actions.[32] ʿAlī Bey's exact motives remain somewhat unclear. Nonetheless, according to al-Jabartī, the rebellious bey drew inspiration from histories of the Mamluk sultans.[33] These accounts would have had little to do with ʿAlī Bey's own circumstances. He was, after all, the Georgian or Abkhazian Mamluk of a regimental commander. If the Ottoman authorities associated ʿAlī Bey with any stereotype, it was rather that of the untrustworthy, ignorant Georgian or Abkhazian.[34] Thus the chronicler Şemdānizade Fındıklılı Sulaymān Efendi has ʿAlī Bey plotting Abkhazian supremacy, exclaiming at one point, 'There cannot be a more favorable time for Abkhazian assumption of power (*tasalluṭ*) than this!'[35] If ʿAlī Bey did, indeed, invoke the Mamluk sultans in staging his revolt, he was repeating the pattern of selective nostalgia employed by the Afrāsiyābs in Basra and by the Phanariots in Moldavia and Wallachia, as well as by his predecessor Riḍwān Bey. He was, however, taking this strategy a step further by using it not only to cement his local authority but also to challenge the central authority. ʿAlī Bey's rebellion was by no means a nationalist revolution, but one cannot help speculating on whether his brand of selective nostalgia does not bear some resemblance to the nineteenth-century Greek rebels' evocation of their Hellenic heritage and the Romanian nationalists' evocation of ancient Dacia.

Conclusion

The military society that had evolved in Ottoman Egypt by the seventeenth century was a provincial variation on a household-based elite culture that spanned the entire empire. The political culture that this society cultivated was

30 David M. Lang, *The Last Years of the Georgian Monarchy, 1658–1832* (New York, 1957), 11–22, 57–8, 69, 74, 105, 114–15, 139–42. Lang notes (at 105) that the slave trade with western Georgia also intensified early in the eighteenth century.

31 The autonomous governors of Ottoman Baghdad stand out for cultivating an entourage of Georgian mamluks, but Georgian mamluks also appear in Damascus. See Holt, *Egypt and the Fertile Crescent*, 146; and Abdul-Karim Rafeq, *The Province of Damascus, 1723–1783* (Beirut, 1966; 2nd edn 1970), 234.

32 *Mühimme-i Mısır*, Başbakanlık Osmanlı Arşivi, Istanbul, vol. VII, no. 237, Ṣafar 1169 (November 1755).

33 Al-Jabartī, *ʿAjāʾib*, (Beirut, 1983), vol. I, 432–3.

34 Metin I. Kunt, 'Ethnic–Regional (*Cins*) solidarity in the seventeenth-century Ottoman establishment', *International Journal of Middle East Studies,* 5 (1974), 233–9.

35 *Semdānizade Fındıklılı Süleyman Efendi Târîhi*, ed. M. Münir Aktepe (Istanbul, 1976), vol. III, 99.

richly evocative, drawing on a number of traditions – Ottoman, Mamluk, Arab, and others. If we insist on interpreting this culture and those who participated in it predominantly according to the usages of the Mamluk sultanate, we shortchange and even misrepresent a complex array of customs that evolved from heterogeneous influences. The households and factions that we encounter in Egyptian military (and even non-military) society during the Ottoman period were neither wholly Ottoman nor wholly Mamluk. To comprehend their true nature and significance, however, we must not discount the Ottoman context in which they emerged. Egypt from the sixteenth to the nineteenth centuries was the largest province of an enormous and diverse empire. The provincial grandees communicated with other provinces and with the capital and drew on trends in these locations. Their political culture had thus evolved beyond that of the Mamluk sultanate even if they periodically evoked the sultanate in order to achieve legitimacy. This, after all, was the nature of selective nostalgia.

CHAPTER 7

Personal loyalty and political power of the Mamluks in the eighteenth century

THOMAS PHILIPP

In a political system in which the institutional organization – especially at the centre – is weak, or has been decisively weakened, informal aspects of patron–client relationships or loyalty among the members of specific groups play an important role in the maintenance and stabilization of the political system. The general consensus seems to be that in the Mamluk system, personal loyalty of two kinds played at all times an important role: in a vertical link the loyalty of the Mamluk to his master, even after the latter had set him free; and in a horizontal link the loyalty of the Mamluk to his comrades, his *khushdāshiyya*. The aim of this chapter is to see what role such loyalty played in the Mamluk system in the eighteenth century and whether we can detect any patterns of change which might help to explain the demise of that system. Or, more modestly but more precisely, it will be mainly an attempt to reconstruct how al-Jabartī viewed this question and tried to provide an explanation for the downfall of the Mamluks, since this chapter will largely rely on the information he provides.

My own interest in the issue of loyalty and its betrayal was first aroused when studying the person of Aḥmad Pasha al-Jazzār. A product of the Egyptian Mamluk system, he was the last Mamluk to wield real power, though not in Egypt but in Acre, where he carved out his own realm of power during the last quarter of the eighteenth century. Ever since Volney reported an Aḥmad Pasha al-Jazzār in his *Voyages*, the latter had received a bad press in Europe. Participating intensely in the political debates raging in France on the eve of the French Revolution, Volney decided to use Aḥmad Pasha al-Jazzār as the archetype of the despotic tyrant. Since then, no literary vilification of al-Jazzār could be bad enough. Increasingly, he was depicted as a murderous, paranoid, treacherous and cruel despot. His epithet al-Jazzār, 'the Butcher', seemed ample proof of his character and actions.[1] But while

[1] Interestingly, there existed in the early eighteenth century another Mamluk named al-Jazzār: Yūsuf Bey al-Jazzār, a Mamluk of Īwāẓ Bey. In both cases al-Jabartī explains the epithet by the fact that its bearer had carried out a considerable slaughter among bedouins: al-Jabartī, *ʿAjāʾib al-āthār fī ʾl-tarājim waʾl-akhbār* (Būlāq, 1879–80), (hereafter al-Jabartī), vol. I, 110; vol. III, 321. It is remarkable that in a time when assassinations and violent conflicts seemed the rule, the epithet 'Butcher' is only used in connection with the killing of bedouins.

European descriptions would outdo each other in reciting the crimes of Aḥmad Pasha al-Jazzār, al-Jabartī provides us with a much more sober account of al-Jazzār's life which is also corroborated by another Arabic source.[2] True,d al-Jazzār must have been a highly unpleasant ruler and probably did suffer towards the end of his life from paranoia, but there were also very different sides to his personality. Both Arabic sources agree that hew came originally from Bosnia and arrived in Istanbul around 1755 at the age of approximately twenty. Either as a soldier or as a barber he reached Egypt in 1756 in the entourage of ʿAlī Bey Agha, who had been appointed pasha of Egypt. Upon the recommendation of the pasha he joined the pilgrimage to Mecca under the *amīr al-ḥājj* Ṣāliḥ Bey al-Qāsimī. The two seem to have become close friends. Having returned from the *ḥajj*, 'Aḥmad al-Busnāwī' took service with ʿAbdallāh Bey, a retainer of ʿAlī Bey Bulūṭ Ḳapan. He began to wear Mamluk clothes, learned Arabic, and acquired the skills and knowledge of the Mamluks. When his master ʿAbdallāh Bey was killed by bedouins, Aḥmad wreaked bloody revenge on them, ambushing and killing some seventy of them. This gained him the full respect of the Mamluks who gave him the epynom 'al-Jazzār' and who began to consider him one of their own. ʿAlī Bey Bulūṭ Ḳapan was duly impressed by him, put him into his service, and made him a *sancaḳ* bey. ʿAlī Bey charged him with maintaining law and order and occasionally entrusted him, sometimes together with Muḥammad Bey Abū ʾl-Dhahab, with the discreet liquidation of enemies. In the words of the chronicler, Aḥmad Pasha al-Jazzār had finally 'exchanged the blade of the razor for that of the sword'. His career in Egypt, however, found an abrupt end in September 1768. ʿAlī Bey, who had been a close ally of Ṣāliḥ Bey, felt threatened by the power of the latter and ordered his two henchmen to kill Ṣāliḥ Bey. Aḥmad Pasha al-Jazzār thought of their old friendship and could not bring himself to kill his friend. On the contrary, he went to him in order to warn him of the impending danger. But Ṣāliḥ Bey could not conceive of such betrayal on the part of his friend and ally ʿAlī Bey and dismissed the warning. When later he was actually assassinated, Aḥmad Pasha al-Jazzār was present but did not draw his sword. Well knowing that with this act of disobedience he had lost the trust of ʿAlī Bey Bulūṭ Ḳapan and was in mortal danger, he left Egypt immediately.

The point I want to make is that al-Jazzār, a man on the way up, was willing to risk his career, and indeed his life, for the sake of an old friendship and a sense of loyalty. Equally remarkable is the fact that Ṣāliḥ Bey overestimated the value of loyalty built on a solid political alliance and had to pay with his life for this mistake. By the time ʿAlī Bey Bulūṭ Ḳapan ruled, the meaning of loyalty and the obligations that arose from it were no longer self-evident.

At first sight, the political scene in Egypt during the eighteenth century

[2] Ḥaydar Aḥmad Shihāb, *Tārīkh Aḥmad Pasha al-Jazzār* (Beirut, 1955), 37–41. Shihāb, a contemporary of Aḥmad Pasha al-Jazzār and an eyewitness to many of the events in Syria and Lebanon, does not indicate his sources. We have no reason to believe that he was in touch with al-Jabartī.

seems to be a never-ending sequence of random intrigues, violence and assassinations. Political organization is characterized by a high degree of instability and decentralization. In early 1710, the Mamluk amirs deposed for the first time the Ottoman pasha and replaced him with a *qāʾim maqām* from their own people. This step spelled out a situation that had already existed for some time: the government in Istanbul could no longer effectively exert its central control in Egypt. But it also signified the unease with which the Mamluks stepped into this power vacuum. After having taken the initiative in deposing the Ottoman governor they felt neither strong enough militarily nor sufficiently legitimized politically to establish a rule of their own. Instead, they provided a temporary stop-gap by appointing a *qāʾim maqām* until the next Ottoman governor, politically weaker than ever, had arrived. The deposition of the governor which the Mamluks initiated without, however, attempting to abolish the institution of governorship became a regular feature in Egyptian politics in the eighteenth century. The Ottoman governor had become one power factor among others in the politics of Egypt. He, too, needed to conspire in secrecy and to ally himself with other factions in order to carry out the government's intention or his own designs. When in 1743 the governor accepted an invitation by one of the Mamluk amirs to a banquet at the latter's residence,[3] Jabartī rightly points out the deviation from traditional habits. The invitation to the house of a Mamluk grandee demonstrated publicly that the governor had become one among equals. Similarly, Mamluk amirs no longer necessarily felt obliged to attend the *dīwān* held by the governor in the Citadel.[4]

Power devolved on various amirs and their households and the leaders of the military corps though often it is almost impossible to determine whether the power base of a particular military leader was in his corps or his Mamluk household which he built up outside the corps. How fluid the situation had become can be learned from al-Jabartī's list of claimants to power after Ibrāhīm Katkhudā al-Qāzdughlī and his partner Riḍwān Katkhudā al-Jalfī had died in mid-century: ʿAbd al-Raḥmān Katkhudā al-Qāzdughlī wanted power just as

> each of Ibrāhīm Katkhudā's amirs was also aspiring to the position of *raʾıs*. And there were others in the city – notables, *ikhtiyāriyya*, and prominent men such as: [here follow a dozen prominent names and al-Jabartī continues:] the household of Hayātim, Ibrāhīm Agha ibn al-Sāʿī, the household of Darb al-Shamsī, ʿUmar Jāwīsh al-Dāwūdiyya, Muṣṭafā Efendī al-Sharīf Ikhtiyār Mutafarriqa, the household of Balfiyya, the household of Ḥasan Bey Qaṣabat Riḍwān, and the household of al-Fallāḥ, who were numerous and included *ikhtiyāriyya* and *odabaşıs*. Among them were Aḥmad Katkhudā, Ismāʿīl Katkhudā, Dhū ʾl-Faqār Jāwīsh, Ismāʿīl Jāwīsh and others.[5]

Physically the centres of power were to be found in the Citadel, the ʿAzab barracks, the Janissary barracks and the various residences of the amirs; all

[3] Al-Jabartī, vol. I, 151. [4] Ibid., vol. I, 127. [5] Ibid., vol. I, 202.

located in the web of alleys, streets and markets of the city where frequently only the faster draw determined who was in control. When a certain al-Ṣayfī had orders to assassinate two individuals he initiated a quarrel with his own servant in their presence so as to draw his pistol without arousing their suspicion. Once he and his servant had both drawn, they turned around and killed the two bystanders. A very similar ruse was tried later on ʿAlī Bey al-Hindī.[6] Frequently, assassinations were carried out from an ambush. Even when the Ottoman governor in 1715 had an imperial firman to kill Qīṭās Bey, he executed the order only after having lured Qīṭās Bey into an ambush.[7]

The unlimited use of individual assassination, however, was inhibited by the awareness that the faction of the victim, his master, or his *khushdāshiyya* would avenge his murder. Loyalty to a particular household could be assumed and was expected. During the great rebellion of 1711 the lines were drawn fairly clearly: a Qāsimī-ʿAzab alliance under the leadership of Īwāẓ Bey faced a Faqārī-Janissary alliance under Ayyūb Bey and others. This division did not hold down to the last man. A small group from the Faqāriyya under Qīṭās Bey had sought the protection of the Qāsimiyya faction. The same group, however, later turned against its benefactors. Damurdāshī gives a detailed list of the complaints the other six military corps had against the Janissaries. Their privileges and sources of wealth are given as the cause of the rift. But when discussing the accompanying split among the Mamluks Damurdāshī points only to the membership in various Mamluk households – for him reason enough to rally to the one side or the other.[8]

During the rebellion Īwāẓ Bey was killed, Ayyūb Bey, his opponent, far from being cheered by this turn of events, lamented it and foresaw the doom of the Faqāriyya in Egypt. He assumed, quite correctly, that the Qāsimiyya would now make an all-out effort to take revenge.[9] Swiftly Yūsuf Bey al-Jazzār, a Mamluk of Īwāẓ Bey, rallied the Mamluks of Īwāẓ Bey around himself and the son of his master, Ismāʿīl ibn Īwāẓ. Within three years they had vanquished the Faqāriyya faction. The examples showing how political positions and behaviour were determined by the respective membership in a Mamluk household abound. During the duumvirate of Ibrāhīm Katkhudā al-Qāzdughlī and

[6] Ibid., vol. I, 132.

[7] Ibid., vol. I, 99; D. Crecelius and ʿAbd al-Wahhab Bakr, *Ahmad Katkhuda ʿAzaban Damurdashi's Chronicle of Egypt* (Leiden, 1991) (hereafter Damurdāshī), 192.

[8] Damurdāshī, 139.

[9] Noteworthy is the dialogue between Ayyūb Bey and Muḥammad Bey al-Ṣaʿīdī which Damurdāshī reproduces. Muḥammad Bey seemed to believe that with the death of Īwāẓ Bey, the Faqāriyya had won. But Ayyūb Bey berated him: 'You have grown up in the Ṣaʿīd. You don't understand [the politics of] Cairo. The Qāsimīs have nothing to do with this dispute. It is a dispute between conflicting factions of the Faqāriyya. ʿAwad Bey left a fortune which [his faction] will spend to seek revenge' (Damurdāshī, 158). In al-Jabartī's text the question is rephrased: 'Where were you raised? Don't you know that Īwāẓ Bey left behind men, children and wealth? . . . Now that blood has been spilled [they] will demand their revenge' (al-Jabartī, vol. I, 43). Muḥammad Bey was the son of another Mamluk amir, Ismāʿīl Bey al-Faqārī al-Kabīr. Are we to assume that in Upper Egypt the loyalty to the Mamluk houses was not as strong or rather that Muḥammad Bey was just not familiar with the importance and power of individual houses in Cairo?

Riḍwān Katkhudā al-Jalfī in the mid-century, both sides took great care that a proportionate number from each household was made *sancaḳ bey*, thus maintaining the balance of power. Loyalty within one's own Mamluk household was expected and determined, among other things, political behaviour. There existed also a loyalty beyond one's own household in cases where a personal friendship was established, a particular favour granted, or even protection of life and possessions offered. Such was the relationship between Aḥmad Pasha al-Jazzār and Ṣāliḥ Bey, which prevented the former from participating in the assassination of the latter. But the bond forged by an obligation, a favour, or a personal friendship was not necessarily that strong: when Muḥammad Bey Qīṭās al-Faqārī suggested to Dhū 'l-Faqār Bey al-Faqārī that they have ʿAlī Bey al-Hindī killed, Dhū 'l-Faqār hesitated because ʿAlī Bey al-Hindī had hidden him some time earlier from the murderous designs of Muḥammad Bey Çerkes. Dhū 'l-Faqār told Muḥammad Bey Qīṭās: 'I will not help you shed his blood, because he has done me a favor, but if you must do it . . . you must also kill Muḥammad Bey al-Jazzār.' Muḥammad Bey Qīṭās: 'Ibn al-Jazzār did me a favor by protecting my house and harem in my absence.' Dhū 'l-Faqār: 'In the same way I remained hidden in ʿAlī Bey [al-Hindī's] house.' In the end they overcame their *crise de conscience* and proceeded with their plot. They were, after all, Faqārīs while the other two were Qāsimīs.[10]

Mamluk society was a segmented society where each household was self-contained and independent. The basic pattern of the household could be reproduced an indefinite number of times without changing the overall structure. Coherence within each household was, of course, also susceptible to great instability as every freed Mamluk could begin to build up his own household. The question arose very quickly as to what loyalty was still owed to the house of origin. The Qāsimīs all came from the same household but within their ranks there developed an Īwāẓī faction and an Abū Shanabī faction, which engaged in murderous intrigues against each other.[11] It seems to me that here the decisive factor was generational: the Mamluks and sons of one master maintained an almost unshakeable loyalty towards their common master and towards each other. Their own respective Mamluks and sons did not all feel the same amount of loyalty to each other but, again, only to those with whom they shared a common master. Loyalty to all those who shared a common master one generation removed could or could not determine their own political behaviour. Perhaps we should limit the concept of a household to the first generation. Only the *khushdāshiyya* of one immediate master seems to value a loyalty so strong that it becomes a predictable factor in their political behaviour. The Qāsimīs may serve as an example. Īwāẓ Bey, a Circassian by origin, and Ibrāhīm Bey Abū Shanab, probably of Bosnian origin, were both Mamluks of Murād Bey al-Daftardār al-Qāsimī, both were elevated to the rank of amir and *sancaḳ bey*, and both were appointed *amīr al-ḥājj* in short

[10] Damurdāshī, 271 gives the same conversation but with a different nuance: they will have to kill *all* Qāsimīs in order to be safe from their revenge.

[11] Al-Jabartī, vol. I, 126 ff.

succession. During the rebellion of 1710–11 they, together with other Mamluks of Murād Bey such as Qānṣūḥ Bey and Muṣṭafā Bey Ḳizlār, collaborated to defeat their opponents. After the death of Īwāẓ Bey in 1711, it was his Mamluk Yūsuf Bey al-Jazzār who, in close co-operation with the son of Īwāẓ Bey, Ismāʿīl Bey, rallied the Mamluks of his master's household, and claimed the leadership of the Qāsimī faction for himself and Ismāʿīl Bey. This development was fully supported by the *khushdāsh* of Īwāẓ Bey, Ibrāhīm Abū Shanab, who was present at the decisive meeting.[12] But after the death of the latter in 1718, his own son Muḥammad Bey ibn Abī Shanab came to resent the predominance of Ismāʿīl Bey, the son of his father's *khushdāsh*. Over the next few years he continued, together with Muḥammad Bey Çerkes, a Mamluk of his father, to plot murderous intrigues against the Īwāẓī faction.[13] In the process of this struggle against the Īwāẓī section of his own Qāsimī faction, Muḥammad Bey Çerkes did not hesitate to seek the support of Faqārī elements.[14] It would be going too far to claim that the wider Qāsimī bond had lost all meaning. Ismāʿīl Bey ibn Īwāẓ repeatedly refused to liquidate Muḥammad Bey Çerkes when he had the occasion, though he had ample proof of the latter's animosity towards him,[15] Al-Jabartī himself seems highly critical of Muḥammad Bey Çerkes' behaviour and puts the blame for the downfall of the Qāsimīs squarely on him.[16] In the Faqārī faction we can observe very similar patterns: during the rebellion of 1710–11 Ayyūb Bey al-Faqārī, a retainer of Darwīsh Bey and of Circassian origin, sided with Ifranj Aḥmad of the Janissaries, while Qīṭās Bey al-Faqārī, a retainer of Ibrāhīm Bey Dhū 'l-Faqār and of Kurdish origin, sought the support of the Qāsimiyya against Ayyūb Bey. Ibrāhīm Bey Dhū 'l-Faqār was the son, and Darwīsh Bey apparently was the Mamluk, of Dhū 'l-Faqār Bey.[17] In another incident ʿUmar Bey al-Qaṭāmish, son of ʿAlī Bey al-Qaṭāmish, was incited by the Egyptian governor in 1740, Sulaymān al-ʿAẓm, to assassinate among others Ibrāhīm Bey al-Qaṭāmish, a *khushdāsh* of his father, both having been retainers of Muḥammad Bey al-Qaṭāmish. At the decisive moment, however, Ibrāhīm Bey talked ʿUmar Bey out of killing him and they became allies.[18] At the best, it seems that the wider bond to a household one generation removed remained of ambivalent meaning.

The bond between sons and Mamluks of a master seems to have been remarkably strong. The two above-mentioned cases of the Qāsimiyya give the impression that the Mamluk took the political initiative while the respective sons provided rather the legitimization for the political ambitions.[19] In the case

[12] Ibid., vol. I, 115. [13] Ibid., vol. I, 119, 134. [14] Ibid., vol. I, 54.
[15] Ibid., vol. I, 126, 127. [16] Ibid., vol. I, 130. [17] Ibid., vol. I, 24.
[18] Ibid., vol. I, 150, 151; Damurdāshī, 331.
[19] Damurdāshī, 52 explains that Ayyūb Bey was made *sancak*, when his master Darwīsh Bey died, because the latter's son was too young to succeed him. A similar situation seems to have existed when Ḥasan Jāwīsh al-Qāzdughlī died. His Mamluk ʿUthmān succeed him, but when he died his own retainer, Sulaymān Jāwīsh, cheated ʿAbd al-Raḥmān al-Qāzdughlī, son of Ḥasan Jāwīsh al-Qāzdughlī 'who was the heir' out of his inheritance and successorship: al-Jabartī, vol. I, 168, 173; vol. II, 5.

of Ibrāhīm Bey Dhū ʾl-Faqār, the son, and Darwīsh Bey, the Mamluk, we know too little about their relationship and perhaps it is too early to generalize from these examples. It is certain that the bonds of loyalty formed by Mamluks and sons of one common, immediate master were the truly decisive ones, which the *khushdāshiyya* could not count on and their foes had to fear.

It would appear that by the second half of the eighteenth century these patterns of loyalty began to shift. By mid-century the frenzy of political conspiracy and assassinations reached new heights. The Qāsimiyya had been liquidated, the Faqāriyya was being reduced and the governors sent from Istanbul, rather than staying above the fray, engaged in every plot and stratagem, creating alliances and conspiracies with some Mamluks against others. In return, shifting alliances of Mamluks would depose the governor and appoint *qāʾim maqāms* of their own choosing. Perhaps the life and deeds of Ḥusayn Bey al-Khashshāb can exemplify the new style of intrigue and infighting. Interestingly neither Damurdāshī nor al-Jabartī give any information on his origins or on any master in whose service he might have been. In 1727 he was *sirdār* of Rosetta and in this function apprehended and executed Muḥammad Bey al-Jazzār. Thereupon Dhū ʾl-Faqār made him *sancaḳ bey* and *kāshif* of Buḥayra. Two years later he had a hostile encounter with Muḥammad Bey Çerkes, who was returning from Europe. Obviously Ḥusayn Bey al-Khashshāb was taking an anti-Qāsimī stand. But whether he himself was a Faqārī is not evident. In 1735 he was governor of Jirjā, and later participated actively in the politics of Cairo. When Muḥammad Pasha Rāghib came to Egypt as governor in 1746 he conspired with Ḥusayn Bey to have the households of the Qaṭāmish and the Dimyāṭī liquidated. For this purpose, Ḥusayn Bey sought the assistance of Ibrāhīm al-Qāzdughlī. The governor then approached him to liquidate Ibrāhīm Bey Jāwīsh al-Qāzdughlī and Riḍwān Bey al-Jalfī, promising him leadership of Egypt thereafter. This, however, backfired and Ḥusayn Bey al-Khashshāb had to flee to Upper Egypt. Later he ingratiated himself again with the powers that be and in 1755 was even appointed *amīr al-ḥājj*.[20] He was a man with no particular power base who was determined to make a career for himself. Shifting alliances, conspiracies and individual assassinations were his means.

ʿAbd al-Raḥmān al-Jabartī was aware of the change in Cairo politics but, typically, he personalized the causes and wrapped them in a dream interpretation:

It is related concerning [Ibrāhīm Katkhudā al-Qāzdughlī] that he dreamt that his hands were full of scorpions. He told this dream to Shaykh al-Shubrāwī, who said: 'These are mamluks who will be like scorpions, whose evil will spread, and whose corruption will touch all the people. For scorpions once stung the Prophet – may God bless and preserve them – and he said "God curse the scorpion, for it leaves neither prophet nor ordinary man until it has stung him." Thus shall your mamluks be,' And so it was.[21]

[20] Damurdāshī, 365 ff; al-Jabartī, vol. I, 134, 151–3, 348. [21] Al-Jabartī, vol. I, 192.

I am inclined to agree with al-Jabartī that the rise of the Qāzdughlī household brought with it a further deterioration of the already weak political structure. The metaphor of the scorpion is not so far fetched, because we are again dealing with questions of loyalty.

The Qāzdughlī household was founded by Muṣṭafā Katkhudā al-Qāzdughlī, who became *katkhudā* of the Mustaḥfiẓān at the end of the seventeenth century. In 1732 four out of ten amirs in Egypt were Qāzdughlīs. But the decisive step towards the predominance of the Qāzdughlī house on the Egyptian political scene was taken in 1748, when Ibrāhīm Katkhudā al-Qāzdughlī and Riḍwān Katkhudā al-Jalfī established a duumvirate over Egypt. The latter was 'the sleeping partner in this duumvirate: he had no interests in the affairs of state'.[22] Thus political power actually devolved on the Qāzdughlīs alone.

When Ibrāhim Kathudā died, the Qāzdughliyya tried to liquidate Riḍwān Kathudā and induced one of his Mamluks to kill him. It is the first time al-Jabartī mentions such a case of 'patricide': a Mamluk killing his master. Even the instigators of this assassination were shocked by this event. They refused the promised reward to the would-be assassin, whose shot had wounded but not killed his master. In fact, he escaped execution only very narrowly and was exiled, because 'he is a traitor in whom there is no good' – this the comment by those who had suborned him in the first place![23] The house of al-Jalfī, in general, must have generated only a very weak sense of loyalty. Though we hear of quite a number of al-Jalfī Mamluks and direct offspring of Riḍwān Bey, they never rallied to avenge their master and did not, as the phrase goes, 'keep the household of their master open'.

The struggle for power became the exclusive affair of the Qāzdughlī Mamluks. The first of Ibrāhīm Katkhudā's Mamluks to wield power was ʿUthmān Bey al-Jirjāwī, the senior *sancaḳ bey*. He was, however, soon removed by his *khushdāshes* because of his arrogance towards his comrades and master's widow. They named Ḥusayn Bey al-Ṣābūnjī as *shaykh al-balad*; he promptly proceeded to neutralize his own *khushdāshes* by exiling them. Jabartī claims he isolated them in order to kill them. This threat must have been a real possibility and was taken seriously by the other Mamluks who, under the initiative of Ḥusayn Bey Kishkish, conspired and killed Ḥusayn Bey al-Ṣābūnjī in 1759. It seems that with this deed – *khushdāshes* killing one of their own – a new threshold was crossed, a new level of violence and betrayal reached. Clearly, al-Jabartī sensed the extraordinary gravity of the event, marking it with quotations from two poems.[24] The new *shaykh al-balad*, ʿAlī Bey al-Kabīr al-Ghazzāwī, soon planned to have ʿAbd al-Raḥmān Bey al-Qāzdughlī ibn Ḥasan Jāwīsh, who was not a Mamluk of Ibrāhīm Katkhudā, liquidated. ʿAlī Bey Bulūṭ Ḳapan, though an immediate *khushdāsh of* ʿAlī Bey

[22] P. M. Holt, *Egypt and the Fertile Crescent, 1516–1922: A Political History* (Ithaca, N.Y., 1967), 92. [23] Al-Jabartī, vol. I, 202. [24] Ibid., vol. I, 206–8.

al-Ghazzāwī, allied himself with ʿAbd al-Raḥmān to counter this plot. In the end ʿAlī Bey al-Ghazzāwī was apparently poisoned by some of his *khushdāshes*. Thereafter ʿAlī Bey Bulūṭ Ḳapan widened his power base. After having tried to kill Ḥusayn Bey Kishkish with poison he was exiled by his *khushdāshes*. In fact, he only narrowly escaped execution, as his comrades still showed more of a sense of loyalty than he was ever capable of. It was argued: 'It is not right [to kill him]. He is our brother and has been a guest in our homes.'[25] ʿAlī Bey, however, soon re-established his power base in Cairo. As one of his first acts he had Ḥasan Bey al-Jūjā, another of his *khushdāshes*, liquidated after the latter had helped him to regain power. In the next year or two ʿAlī Bey assassinated, amongst others Ḥusayn Bey Kishkish, Khalīl Bey al-Kabīr and Ismāʿīl Bey Abū Madfaʿ – all, like himself, Mamluks of Ibrāhīm Katkhudā al-Qāzdughlī. He also did not hesitate to plot the murder of his own Mamluk, Muḥammad Bey Abū ʾl-Dhahab. Assassination of most of his own *khushdāshes* guaranteed him a monopoly of power, heretofore unknown among the neo-Mamluks. The conclusion, however, that 'ʿAlī Bey al-Kabīr [i.e. Bulūṭ Ḳapan] had succeeded, temporarily in stemming the decay in Egypt's political institutions'[26] is completely erroneous. ʿAlī Bey al-Kabīr had actually changed the rules of the game in the process. Assassination among *khushdāshes* became an acceptable political ploy. Even the assassination of one's own master had become thinkable as the case of Riḍwān Bey shows. ʿAlī Bey experienced the same fate when his Mamluk Muḥammad Bey Abū ʾl-Dhahab rebelled against him and, most likely, was the one to have him killed. Ironically, by reaching for absolute power, ʿAlī Bey undermined his very base of power and, in fact, destroyed the Mamluk political system. By crossing the threshold of 'fratricide' and 'patricide' and tearing the bonds of loyalty between master and Mamluks and between *khushdāshiyya* themselves, a very essential part of the structure of the Mamluk system was put into question. That is not to say that from this point on mayhem and murder prevailed and all loyalty had disappeared. But this loyalty, which had given to Mamluk politics a minimum amount of stability and predictability, could not be taken for granted anymore.

After ʿAlī Bey Bulūṭ Ḳapan and Muḥammad Abū ʾl-Dhahab, Mamluk rule in Egypt lingered on until it collapsed at the first challenge from outside. In 1786 Ḥasan Ḳapūdān Pasha, commander of the Ottoman fleet, invaded Egypt with the Mamluks offering no resistance worth mentioning. His invasion and the disarray into which it threw the Mamluks appear in retrospect almost as a rehearsal for the French invasion in 1798. Already in 1786 it seemed that Mamluk rule had come to its end. Not only did the Ottomans denigrate and berate the Mamluks for having abandoned their own traditions and rules,[27] but also al-Shaykh al-Bakrī, of the local ʿ*ulamā*ʾ, was, for instance, willing to

[25] Ibid., vol. I, 256.

[26] D. Kimche, 'The political superstructure of Egypt in the late eighteenth century', *Middle East Journal*, 22 (1968), 462.

[27] Ibid., vol. II, 145.

surrender financial deposits of fleeing Mamluks to Ḥasan Ḳapūdān Pasha, because he 'and most other people were convinced that the Egyptian amirs [i.e. the Mamluks] would die out and soon be forgotten among the vicissitudes of time'.[28] This impression of Mamluk irrelevance is reinforced by the following scene; at the height of the second Turkish–Russian war in 1789, when the Ottoman army tried desperately to stem the Russian advance, the sultan invited Egyptian Mamluks to the court to demonstrate their horsemanship and spear-throwing art.[29] A touch of folkloric entertainment, while the real army was struggling in a disastrous war.

The short-lived invasion of the Ottomans 1786 had exposed the decay of the Mamluks' system, but the latter were unable or unwilling to draw the right conclusions from their defeat and rebuild a system which had been destroyed by their own doing. Once more, Mamluk rule in Egypt lingered on, not because of any inherent resilience and strength of its own, but because of the Ottomans' attention to more urgent matters. The second invasion, this time by the French, brought the final collapse of Mamluk rule in Egypt.

[28] Ibid., vol. IV, 189. [29] Ibid., vol. II, 182.

CHAPTER 8

The Mamluk beylicate of Egypt in the last decades before its destruction by Muḥammad ʿAlī Pasha in 1811

DANIEL CRECELIUS

The Mamluk system, so firmly embedded in the political, social and economic life of Ottoman Egypt, was not immune to the wrenching changes that battered and at least partially transformed this key province during the course of the eighteenth century. So weakened were the Mamluk military households by the opening of the nineteenth century that the vigorous governor Muḥammad ʿAlī Pasha was able to destroy finally the remnants of the system that had provided the dominant class for Egypt for almost seven centuries. He was then able to create a modern army, drawn from different social and ethnic origins, on the basis of a new method of recruitment and training.[1] The factors leading to the rapid decline of the Mamluk military system in the second half of the eighteenth century are many, but intertwined.

Throughout its turbulent history the neo-Mamluk system was weakened by factionalism and incessant internal war as one faction sought to gain complete victory over its rivals. These struggles became particularly intense in the eighteenth century, which saw but few periods of respite between long and debilitating civil wars that left the greater part of both the urban and rural segments of Egyptian society cowed and battered. Ultimately, both the administration and the economy of the province were to suffer noticeable decline, just as Cairo, where many of the pitched battles took place, was to sustain considerable physical damage to its palaces, *khāns*, mosques and dwellings.

[1] While destroying the Mamluk military system, Muḥammad ʿAlī did not totally abolish the recruitment of slaves (Mamluks) into his own and the households of leading members of his family. While these new recruits in the nineteenth century no longer formed a coherent military elite, they did continue, upon their manumission, to enter the social elite as holders of significant portions of agricultural lands given to them by their former masters. As late as the reign of Khedive Ismāʿīl Mamluks were being manumitted, married to chosen partners by their masters, and established among the social elite by grants of significant portions (500–1,000 feddans) of agricultural lands. Numerous *waqfiyyat* preserved in the Ministry of Awqāf in Cairo attest to the survival of such a modified system of slavery and to the continued intrusion of this foreign-born element into Egyptian society. For an interesting excursion into this world of Circassian slaves, see Ehud R. Toledano, 'Shemsigul: a Circassian slave in mid-nineteenth-century Cairo', in Edmund Burke, III (ed.), *Struggle and Survival in the Modern Middle East* (Berkeley, 1993), 59–74.

Factionalism and civil war, two endemic features of the neo-Mamluk system, coalesced with other factors, both internal and external to Mamluk Egypt, to transform the system significantly between the drive for autonomy by ʿAlī Bey al-Kabīr[2] in the 1760s and the destruction of the neo-Mamluk households by Muḥammad ʿAlī Pasha in 1811.

The decline of the beylicate in the period after ʿAlī Bey al-Kabīr

The famous Mamluk amir ʿAlī Bey al-Kabīr (1760–7; 1768–72) succeeded in overwhelming his Mamluk and Ottoman rivals and created an autonomous Qāzdughlī regime in Egypt. But ʿAlī Bey had initiated significant forces that would adversely affect the neo-Mamluk system. First of all, for the first time since Mamluk armies had fought a losing battle against the Ottoman forces under Sultan Selim at Marj Dābiq in Syria in 1516, ʿAlī Bey sent his armies on expeditions of conquest outside Egypt, first along the Arabian coast of the Red Sea in 1770, then to Palestine and Syria in 1771. These efforts were an unusual burden on the manpower and economy of the neo-Mamluk state, for ʿAlī Bey assembled the largest armies (up to 25,000 men) an Egyptian regime had raised in centuries. Because the Mamluk system could not support his expansionist plans from its own limited human resource pool, ʿAlī Bey assembled bedouins, hired mercenaries, deployed the forces of allies such as Shaykh Ḍāhir al-ʿUmar in Palestine, and sought economic, political and military aid from the infidel states of Europe. In his struggle with the Ottoman Empire and in his campaign into Syria, for instance, he allied with the Russian state, which was then at war with the Ottoman Empire and maintained a marauding fleet in the eastern Mediterranean Sea, hired a handful of European military advisers, and on the advice of a coterie of Christian economic advisers that included the Cypriot S. Lusignan, the Venetian Carlo Rosetti, the Copt Muʿallim Rizq and the Greek Catholic customs agent Anṭūn Qassīs Firʿawn, opened Egypt's ports, particularly Suez, to the ships of Europe. Although his career and conquests were cut short by the conflict that was to erupt with his own Mamluk Muḥammad Bey Abū ʾl-Dhahab, the trends that ʿAlī Bey had set in motion continued, causing significant disruption to the neo-Mamluk state.

ʿAlī Bey had overwhelmed his enemies by his ferocious attack upon their positions and persons. Some, such as Aḥmad al-Jazzār, were driven from Egypt and had illustrious careers elsewhere; others were forced to relinquish their positions, whether within the neo-Mamluk hierarchy or within the Ottoman military corps, and accepted banishment in return for their lives. Most were attacked and killed. ʿAlī Bey, we are told, purchased many Mamluks. It is estimated that he himself had 1,000 Mamluks and that the total

[2] On the period of ʿAlī Bey and his Mamluk Muḥammad Bey Abū ʾl-Dhahab, see Daniel Crecelius, *The Roots of Modern Egypt: A Study of the Regimes of ʿAli Bey al-Kabir and Muhammad Bey Abu al-Dhahab, 1760–1775* (Minneapolis and Chicago, 1981).

of Mamluks in his day numbered between 10,000 and 12,000.[3] Yet one of the characteristics of the Mamluk beylicate between the death of ʿAlī Bey in 1773 and the rise of Muḥammad ʿAlī Pasha in 1805 is the noticeable decline in the numbers of Mamluks. Weakened by constant factional fighting, by their wars against the forces of Ghāzī Ḥasan Pasha (1786–7), Napoleon Bonaparte (1798–1801), and the troops of Ottoman governors (1801–7), decimated by the pandemic plagues which struck Lower Egypt, particularly the capital city, in the 1780s and 1790s, cut off from their traditional recruiting grounds by the advance of the Russian Empire into the Caucasus region, and destabilized by the chaos that preceded the rise of Muḥammad ʿAlī Pasha in 1805, the Mamluk households were on the verge of internal collapse some years before Muḥammad ʿAlī Pasha dealt them their death blow in 1811.

Estimates of the number of Mamluks

Reliable estimates of Mamluk numbers are not available at present, so we must content ourselves with the rough figures provided by a handful of European and native sources. The French traveller Volney, whose work was criticized heavily by his contemporaries, claims that there were at the time of Ghāzī Ḥasan Pasha's expedition in 1786 about 8,500 Mamluks.[4] George Baldwin, a colourful and long term resident in Egypt at different times from the 1770s to the 1790s, mentions the supposed 10,000 Mamluks during the period of ʿAlī Bey al-Kabīr, but remarks that their numbers had declined to 4,000 in 1788 following the expedition of Ghāzī Ḥasan Pasha. This he attributes to the wars ʿAlī Bey fought, to the incessant internal strife among the Mamluk factions in the period since ʿAlī Bey's death, and to the deprivation of their normal recruiting grounds by the Russian advance into the Caucasus region.[5] The

[3] George Baldwin, 'Memorial relating to the slave trade in Egypt', in George Baldwin, *Political Recollections Relative to Egypt* (London, 1802), 223. The pioneering study by David Ayalon, 'Studies in al-Jabarti: I. Notes on the transformation of Mamluk society in Egypt under the Ottomans', *Journal of the Economic and Social History of the Orient,* vol. 3 (1960), 148–74; 275–325, maintains most of its validity even today. Pages 162–5 speculate on the number of Egyptian Mamluks in the late eighteenth century.

[4] Constantin-François Chasseboeuf Volney, *Voyage en Egypte et en Syrie,* ed. Jean Gaulmier (Paris, 1959), 101. Mure, the French consul-general in Egypt, estimated that in the period before Ghāzī Ḥasan Pasha's expedition of 1786–7 the number of Mamluks was still 10,000. See *Memoire politique sur l'Egypte,* Archives Nationales (Paris), Marine, B7, vol. 449 (1784–5), 3. The Ottoman Empire apparently made an attempt at this time to stop the flow of new Mamluks to Egypt, for a British report remarks that a number of Georgian slaves destined for Egypt were returned to the slave merchants by order of the government. See Public Record Office (London), Foreign Office 261, vol. 2 (1785–7), 9 September 1786. Gabriel Guémard, *Aventuriers Mameluks d'Egypte* (Alexandria, 1929), 15, claims that Ghāzī Ḥasan Pasha himself closed the Istanbul slave market to the beys, so that they had to purchase Greeks and blacks.

[5] See Baldwin, 'Memorial Relating to the Slave Trade in Egypt', 223. Baldwin also notes that since Russia gained control of their recruiting grounds, only about 100 Mamluks a year were being brought for service in Egypt. The French vice-consul, seconding Baldwin, remarked in 1788 that the Mamluks' inability to replenish their losses and the appearance of the plague

decades of the 1780s and 1790s brought a succession of severe plagues that hit the Mamluk factions anchored in Egypt's urban areas particularly hard. The faction of Ismāʿīl Bey, which Ghāzī Ḥasan Pasha had built up in Cairo on his departure in 1787, was virtually wiped out by the great plague of 1791, so that Murād Bey and Ibrāhīm Bey, in banishment in Upper Egypt since the arrival of Ghāzī Ḥasan Pasha in 1786, could re-enter Cairo and take control of the regime without a fight. Towards the end of the decade, and through the few remaining years of their tenuous existence, the Mamluk factions, with diminished human resources, suffered heavy losses in their struggles against the French, the Ottomans and Muḥammad ʿAlī's forces. The contemporary historian al-Jabartī estimates that they numbered only 2,000 plus before Muḥammad ʿAlī was appointed governor of Egypt in 1805.[6] Estimates by Englishmen associated with the two military campaigns into Lower Egypt in 1801 and 1807 mention between 1,500 and 8,000 Mamluks, but the latter estimate, I suspect, does not correctly differentiate between true Mamluks and non-Mamluk forces.[7] Working backwards from the estimates of Mamluks killed by Muḥammad ʿAlī, Prince Omar Toussoun concludes there were approximately 3,000 Mamluks on the eve of the famous massacre in the Citadel of Cairo in March 1811.[8]

If the total number of Mamluks in Egypt was declining seriously in the period between ʿAlī Bey's death in 1773 and Muḥammad ʿAlī's appointment as governor in 1805, it is logical to assume that the size of individual Mamluk households was also declining. Evidence of such a downsizing can be found scattered in the available material. S. Lusignan, one of the trusted confidants of ʿAlī Bey, exaggeratedly states that ʿAlī Bey personally had about 6,000

among them promised to destroy them. See Archives Nationales (Paris), Affaires Etrangères, B1, vol. 114 (Alexandrie, 1788–1891), fols. 55–6, 25 June 1788. On the other hand, G. A. Olivier, *Voyage dans l'Empire Othoman, l'Egypte et la Perse* (Paris, 1804), vol. II, 112, estimates that there were between 7,000 and 8,000 Mamluks in the early 1790s. William G. Browne, *Travels in Africa, Egypt, and Syria, from the year 1792 to 1798* (London, 1799), 70, also gives a seemingly high estimate of about 8,000 Mamluks in the year after the great plague of 1791. He adds that 'I was assured that during the last eleven years, no fewer than sixteenth thousand white slaves of both sexes, have been imported into Egypt'. A brief discussion on the number of Mamluks in Egypt can be found in Ayalon, 'Studies in al-Jabarti', 162–5.

6 Cited in Ayalon, 'Studies in al-Jabarti', 163–4.

7 The British consul-general, Major Missett, estimated the number of Mamluks in 1804 at not more than 3,000, including such forces as the Greeks under Ḥusayn Bey the Zantiote. See Georges Douin, *L'Angleterre et l'Egypte: La Politique Mameluke (1803–1807)* (Cairo, 1930), 110. In a long report on Egypt addressed to Lord Elgin, William Hamilton states that, 'the Mamluke force if united is certainly not above 4,000 men'. See G. Douin and E. C. Fawtier-Jones, *L'Angleterre et l'Egypte: La Politique Mameluke (1801–1803)* (Cairo, 1929), vol. I, 430. In a letter dated 4 May 1803 addressed to the English merchant Edward Lee, the writer mentions the strength of the Mamluks at 8,000 men. See Douin, *L'Angleterre et l'Egypte, 1803–1807*, 16. By 1806 the English consul-general Missett remarked that 'all the Mamlouks in arms against the Viceroy may be computed at fifteen hundred, divided into three distinct parties.' He added, however, that with allies and mercenaries they could raise a force of 25,000. See 252–3.

8 Prince Omar Toussoun, 'La fin des Mamlouks', *Bulletin de l'Institut d'Egypte,* 25 (1933), 188.

Mamluks, sixteen of whom he raised to the beylicate.[9] Other estimates are much more realistic. Agostini, a long term Italian resident in Alexandria who acted as agent for various foreign courts, offers an unusually low figure. He estimated in 1787 that there were only about 400 Mamluks remaining from Muḥammad Bey Abū 'l-Dhahab's faction.[10] Volney, on the other hand, says that Ibrāhīm Bey had 600 Mamluks and Murād Bey had 400 in that period.[11] In a report of 21 May 1789, when Ismāʿīl Bey and his ally Ḥasan Bey al-Jiddāwī were in control of Cairo, a British observer reported that the *shaykh al-balad* Ismāʿīl Bey had 150 Mamluks, ʿAlī Bey al-Daftardār had 400, Ḥasan Bey al-Jiddāwī had 200, and Murād Bey and Ibrāhīm Bey, who remained in Upper Egypt, had a combined total of approximately 1,000 Mamluks.[12] A French source estimated that Murād Bey, back in power in Cairo after the death of Ismāʿīl Bey and most of his faction in the plague of 1791, had 400 Mamluks and Ibrāhīm Bey only 200.[13] The English traveller William G. Browne, whose figures appear inflated, claims that Ibrāhīm had about 1,000 Mamluks and Murād about 1700.[14]

The noticeable weakening in Mamluk numerical strength, the difficulty of replenishing their numbers from their traditional recruiting grounds in the Caucasus region and the intensity of their continuing struggles, both internal and against the Ottomans and the French, led the Mamluk leaders to accept a number of fundamental changes to their system which can be summarized as follows. They broadened the areas from which they sought new manpower, obtaining recruits, in fact, from Europe or from wherever they could find them, and increasingly used entire ethnic contingents, whether Muslim or Christian, Albanian or Greek, to strengthen their factions. The beys advanced their Mamluks more quickly than normal, took shortcuts in their training, especially their traditional religious training, and used mercenaries, both Muslim and Christian, to a greater extent than in previous decades. We shall deal with each of these aspects of the changing Mamluk system in the pages that follow.

Changes to the recruitment and training of new Mamluks

Ayalon has shown that the neo-Mamluks continued to receive religious training well into the eighteenth century.[15] But evidence of the need to either

[9] S. Lusignan, *A History of the Revolt of Aly Bey against the Ottoman Porte* (London, 1783), 81. Lusignan's work was written from a fading memory ten years after he had been forced to flee Egypt in his patron's dispute with Muḥammad Bey Abū 'l-Dhahab. It must be used with caution.

[10] Haus-, Hof- und Staatsarchiv (Vienna), Türkei II, 96, Agostini to Internuncio, 10 December 1787.

[11] Volney, *Voyage en Egypte et en Syrie,* 102.

[12] India Office Archives (London), G/17/5A – Egypt and the Red Sea (1786–99), fol. 181.

[13] Archives du Ministère des Affaires Etrangères (AMAE), Quai d'Orsay (Paris), Correspondance Consulaire et Commerciale, Alexandrie, vol. 16 (1792–1804), 27 Prairial, Year III.

[14] Browne, *Travels in Africa, Egypt, and Syria,* 91.

[15] Ayalon, 'Studies in al-Jabarti', 158–61.

shorten this training or advance young Mamluks into the beylicate appears with more frequency from the period of ʿAlī Bey al-Kabīr. ʿAlī Bey, for instance, advanced his favourite Mamluk, Muḥammad Bey Abū ʾl-Dhahab, to the beylicate after the youth spent only a short time in his master's *khazna*.[16] Muḥammad Bey, in turn, acquired Murād and Muṣṭafā on the same day and promoted both of them to the beylicate in a very short time.[17] Mortality rates among the beys became so high in the final three decades of the century that young Mamluks were appointed to the beylicate five or six at a time. In early 1772, ʿAlī Bey appointed seven Mamluks to the beylicate who were so young that the people of Cairo derisively referred to them as 'the seven girls'.[18] At the end of the eighteenth century, for instance, a French observer noted that it was not rare to see a youth of twenty become one of the chief beys.[19] For his part, Ibrāhīm Bey made a bey of his son Marzūq when he was still a baby.[20] It is perhaps because the amirs of the Qāzdughlī *bayt* were not receiving sufficient religious education that al-Jabartī castigates the Mamluks of Muḥammad Bey Abū ʾl-Dhahab so vehemently. He remarks that Muḥammad Bey was the last of the Mamluk beys who conformed to the traditional manners and values of the past and who heeded the advice of the *ʿulamāʾ*. His own Mamluks, however, did not live by the same rules of equity and justice, but had acquired in their youth the habits of injustice which led the country into ruin.[21]

The *mashyakha* of Ismāʿīl Bey following the occupation of Lower Egypt by Ghāzī Ḥasan Pasha in 1786–7 gives us an insight into several of the practices that had opened Mamluk society to new elements and traditions. Christian and Muslim troops from the Balkans, whites from the Christian countries of central and western Europe, and blacks from Africa came to replace the Georgians, Circassians and others from the Caucasus region who no longer were available in sufficient numbers for service in Egypt. Jabartī, for instance, notes that Ismāʿīl Bey recruited many non-Mamluks from the Balkans and Albania, many of whom must have been attached to the Mamluk houses as

16 Newly purchased Mamluks were assigned to their masters' *khaznas*, a term usually rendered as treasury. The Mamluk chosen as *khāzindār*, or treasurer, of his master stood ready for promotion to a higher rank in the Mamluk hierarchy, either to the position of *kāshif* of a province or directly to the rank of *sancak bey*. Numerous references to the young Mamluks of the *khazna* 'going out' with their masters or fighting as a unit suggest that *khazna* ought to be thought of as more than just the treasury; it was also the unit to which young Mamluks were attached and in which they received their military instruction.

17 See Crecelius, *The Roots of Modern Egypt*, 45.

18 P. M. Holt, *Egypt and the Fertile Crescent: 1516–1922* (Ithaca, 1966), 98, citing al-Jabartī for the year AH 1185.

19 AMAE, Quai d'Orsay (Paris), Correspondance Consulaire et Commerciale, Alexandrie, vol. 16 (1792–1804), 11 Vendemiare, IV.

20 Cited in Ayalon, 'Studies in al-Jabarti', 156. In this section Ayalon remarks on the growing custom of the sons of *sancak beys* acquiring these positions upon the death of their fathers, a practice unknown in the Mamluk sultanate.

21 Shaykh ʿAbd al-Raḥmān ibn Ḥasan al-Jabartī, *ʿAjāʾib al-āthār fī ʾl-tarājim wa-ʾl-ākhbār* (Būlāg, 1297 AH) vol. I, 420. See the English translation edited by Thomas Philipp and Moshe Perlman, *ʿAbd al-Raḥmān al-Jabartī's History of Egypt* (Stuttgart, 1994) where the pagination of the Būlāg edition is given.

sarrājūn (see below) or mercenaries. He also purchased a great number of Mamluks. Jabartī complains that most of these troops were of bad character, were moustached and belonged to unfamiliar races. He adds that Ismāʿīl Bey gave them only military training and neglected to teach them any manners; nor did he give them religious instruction.[22] Despite the example of Ismāʿīl Bey, Ayalon concludes that until their final destruction by Muḥammad ʿAlī, Mamluks continued to receive religious instruction and before their executions said their Muslim prayers and undertook their Muslim rituals.[23] Ayalon's conclusion on their faithfulness to Islamic belief and ritual, even in the final hours before their death, may be accurate, but it obscures somewhat the Mamluk's close ties to his natural family and to his country of origin, and his willingness to switch allegiances.

The Mamluk's attachment to his homeland

It appears that earlier in the eighteenth century Mamluk amirs still introduced pre-pubescent youths into their households, for in writing of the destruction of the Qāsimī faction by Muḥammad Bey Qaṭāmish in 1731, the contemporary historian Aḥmad Katkhudā ʿAzabān al-Damurdāshī says that Muḥammad Bey even killed the young Mamluks who had not yet reached puberty.[24] Such youths continued to be purchased and given military and religious training, but evidence would suggest that in the second half of the eighteenth century, a large percentage of these 'youths' introduced into the Mamluk households in Egypt were in their early to middle teens, meaning that they knew fully from whence they had come, had some possible lasting attachment to the land and religion of their birth and early youth, and remembered who their fathers, mothers, siblings and relatives were. Many Mamluk beys, for instance, maintained a correspondence with their Christian families, invited their parents, brothers and sisters to join them in their good fortune in Egypt, and even appointed brothers or other male relatives to positions of importance within the Mamluk structure.

ʿAlī Bey al-Kabīr was taken at about the age of thirteen, while his favourite Mamluk, Muḥammad Bey Abū ʾl-Dhahab, was given to ʿAlī Bey at about the age of sixteen. ʿAlī Bey is supposed to have brought his father, said to be a Greek orthodox priest, and his sister to Cairo and to have appointed his nephew, named Riḍwān, the son of his sister, to the beylicate.[25] Qāsim Bey the Muscovite, the Mamluk of Ibrāhīm Bey, was taken at the age of sixteen or

22 Ibid., vol. II, 180; also cited by Ayalon, 'Studies in al-Jabarti', 163–5.

23 Ayalon, 'Studies in al-Jabarti', 168.

24 Ahmad Katkhuda ʿAzaban al-Damurdashi, *Al-Damurdashi's Chronicle of Egypt: 1688–1755*, trans. and annotated by Daniel Crecelius and ʿAbd al-Wahhab Bakr (Leiden, 1991), 296 (fol. 390).

25 Jabartī at least verifies that ʿAlī Bey appointed his nephew to the beylicate. Riḍwān Bey died in the great plague year of 1791. See *ʿAjāʾib al-āthār*, vol. II, 220.

seventeen by Tartars.[26] Ibrāhīm Bey, one of the favourite Mamluks of Muḥammad Bey Abū 'l-Dhahab, retained memories of the land of his origin and maintained close contacts with his family. He mentioned, for instance, that he remembered having served the mass (his father, too, was said to be a Greek orthodox priest). His brother, of whom he was cognizant, died in the service of Russia and left a son, a lieutenant of artillery, who joined Ibrāhīm Bey in Cairo.[27] As we shall see, towards the end of the eighteenth century, when the Mamluks were having difficulty replenishing their ranks, adults captured in war were used in the stead of the youths who earlier had been routinely introduced into the system, given both military and religious training, and manumitted in their proper time. In their haste to leave Cairo in advance of Napoleon's entry into the city, many of the beys left behind their young Mamluks. These Napoleon entered among his own forces; it was an adjustment easily made by these adolescents.[28] Of note here is that these 'youths' were adolescents, that they apparently attached themselves easily to the service of a new, and Christian, master, and were ready to engage in combat.

European visitors to Egypt have remarked on the ties that the Mamluks maintained with their parents; once they achieved a position of importance in Egypt, Mamluks sent for their families to join them.[29] The Georgians and Circassians in particular frequently remained in correspondence with their families.[30] The French consul in Egypt claimed that these Mamluks used the intermediary of both the Russian consul in Egypt and the Russian ambassador in Istanbul for this correspondence. Not only did these Mamluks send money to their families, but they received frequent letters from them. Many Georgian parents, the French consul noted, came to Egypt to visit their sons.[31] When Ismāʿīl Bey became *shaykh al-balad* in 1775 it was rumoured that his Georgian father arrived in company with the parents of several other beys.[32] If youths were taken in their teens, and later adult prisoners of war were introduced into the Mamluk system, it is not difficult to imagine that they would maintain contact with their families, even after their required conversion to Islam. The fact that they sent them money, that they received visits from their families, and that their Christian parents were received with honours in their houses in Cairo suggests that the conversion of these youths and the introduction towards the end of the eighteenth century of adult prisoners of war

26 AMAE, Quai d'Orsay (Paris), Correspondance Politique-Turquie, vol. 174 (1786), fol. 72, 15 March 1786. 27 Ibid.

28 See Gabriel Guémard, 'Les auxiliares de l'armée de Bonaparte en Egypte (1798–1801)', *Bulletin de l'Institut d'Egypte*, 9 (1926–7), 4.

29 See Haus-, Hof- und Staatsarchiv (Vienna), Türkei II, 106, fol. 248–53.

30 Paul Masson, *Histoire du Commerce Français dans le Levant au XVIIIe Siècle* (Paris, 1911), 579, says that this correspondence was carried on through the intermediary of the Russian consul in Egypt and the Mamluks sent by this channel considerable sums of money to their families.

31 Archives Nationales (Paris), Affaires Etrangères, B1, vol. 113 (Alexandrie), 1783–7, fols. 213–15, 15 July 1786.

32 AMAE, Quai d'Orsay (Paris), Correspondance Consulaire et Commerciale, Rosette, vol. 4 (1774–1807), fol. 110, 9 August 1777.

meant as much an embrace of a new career as a deeply felt religious conversion. Although the Mamluk beys defended Islamic territory, undertook their religious obligations, maintained close social contacts with the *ʿulamāʾ* and continued to endow religious institutions, many seem to have kept some of their Christian habits or sentiments. On a visit to Middle Egypt in 1738, for instance, Richard Pococke wrote of the amir of Akhmīm: 'The prince appeared in a Turkish habit, and received me with great civility. He is much beloved by his subjects, and the Christians are particularly favoured here. The father of the present sovereign was suspected of being a Christian, having married a Christian slave'.[33] And John Antes, a German–American missionary who departed in 1784 after living in Egypt for twelve years, remarked that he had found some disguised Christians among the Mamluks.[34] ʿAlī Bey, who fought his way to the top of the Mamluk system and who is certainly thought of as a Muslim leader of a powerful Muslim province, apparently had no qualms about surrounding himself with Christian advisers and entering into alliance with the Russian Empire in his struggle against his Ottoman sovereign. Native Christian and Jewish subjects had frequently occupied positions of some importance in the central Ottoman administration and had acted as customs agents for previous Mamluk beys, but foreign non-Muslims had never achieved such influential positions within the ruling bey's inner circle of advisers as Rosetti and Lusignan had with ʿAlī Bey.

The situation was entirely different among the lower ranks of the Mamluk household and those, such as the *sarrājūn*, attached to it. For these members of the *bayt*, religious identification or performance of religious duties does not seem as important; among them were Christians or disguised Muslims. (See below.)

Ethnic origins of the Mamluks

The beylicate was dominated, as mentioned above, by Mamluks drawn from Georgia and Circassia but on occasion, members of the non-Muslim minorities indigenous to the Ottoman Empire were accepted into the Mamluk system once they made the conversation to Islam. Of the small number of individual Jews and Armenians of whom we are certain, most made it into the upper ranks of the *ocaks* or even into the beylicate itself, which probably explains why we have been able to identify them. How many more have remained unknown in the lower ranks of the system we cannot say. Ibrāhīm Agha al-Muslimānī (where Muslimānī is a name frequently given to converts) was given responsibility for the *bayt al-māl,* while another Jewish convert by the name of Ḥusayn

[33] 'Travels of Richard Pococke', in *A General Collection of Voyages and Travels* (London, 1810), vol. XV, 350. Lusignan, ʿAlī Bey's friend and biographer, remarked that ʿAlī's favourite wife was named Mary and refused to give up Christianity. Not always a reliable source, Lusignan claims that ʿAlī Bey told her she could keep her religon if she kept her beliefs private. See Lusignan, *A History of the Revolt of Aly Bey,* 82–3.

[34] John Antes, *Observations on the Manners and Customs of the Egyptians* (Dublin, 1803), 167.

attained the rank of *kāshif.*[35] Sulaymān Agha al-Mustaḥfiẓān had a Mamluk of Jewish origin named Sulaymān, while one of the five *sancaḳ beys* created by Murād Bey on 29 Rajab 1197 (30 June 1783) was named Ḥusayn Kāshif al-Yahūdī, presumably the same Mamluk referred to in the previous note.[36] In al-Damurdāshī's chronicle of Egypt, which covers the period 1688–1755, one finds references to Aḥmad Efendī Ashkināzī, who became Aḥmad Bey al-Muslimānī, Yūsuf Bey al-Muslimānī al-Faqārī, and to Ibrāhīm al-Yahūdī who, facing death, converted, took the name Ismāʿīl Agha, and was assigned the customs of Alexandria.[37] The only Armenian known to me to have become a *sancaḳ bey* is ʿAlī Bey Abū ʾl-ʿAdab al-Armanī,[38] but several Armenians became prominent commanders during the French occupation. At the end of the eighteenth century we find references to Muḥammad Katkhudā al-Muslimānī, a Mamluk of Armenian extraction who had converted to Islam and was appointed *agha* of the Janissaries (chief of police) by the French,[39] and to Papazoghlu, another Armenian, known as Niqūlā Re'īs. (See below.)

Throughout Mamluk history a steady stream of black slaves was introduced annually into the Ottoman–Islamic worlds through Egypt and other trade routes linking the sub-Saharan region with the Mediterranean basin. In his *Memorial Relating to the Trade in Slaves* George Baldwin estimated that fewer than 5,000 blacks were imported annually, while the Frenchman Truguet claimed that the slave merchants brought only 500–600 blacks a year into the country.[40] This group had provided military recruits for the Fatimid rulers and Mamluk sultans; they continued to appear among the neo-Mamluks, and ultimately formed whole units under Muḥammad ʿAlī Pasha. Only seldom did they rise to the top ranks of the beylicate. Ḥasan Bey al-Dakrūrī, a Mamluk of ʿUthmān Bey, is mentioned by al-Damurdāshī in the period 1741–3.[41] Damurdāshī mentions that most of the young Mamluks of Khalīl Bey Qaṭāmish in 1747 were black slaves from Jirjā, meaning that they had been purchased there.[42] Because the supply of Circassian and Georgian recruits had been disrupted by Russian advances in the Caucasus region, we find a number of black Mamluks of importance in the service of the beys near the end of the eighteenth century. The French author of the *State of the Beys in Egypt* prepared on 25 February, 1778 cites ʿAlī Bey al-Ḥabashī, a newly created bey, and

[35] Jabartī, *ʿAjāʾib al-āthār,* vol. II, 73, 103–105.
[36] Bibliotheque Nationale (Paris), Fonds Arabe 1856, Anonymous, Fī Ta'rīkh ʿĀm 1191, fols. 1 and 25.
[37] Crecelius and Bakr (trans.), *al-Damurdashi's Chronicle of Egypt,* 236, 244–5, 70–1, 104–5, 115.
[38] Ibid., 204, 206.
[39] Nicolas Turc, *Chronique d'Egypte: 1798–1804,* ed. and trans. Gaston Wiet (Cairo, 1950), 25, 38. Muḥammad Katkhudā al-Muslimānī eventually fled to Palestine where he was hanged by Aḥmad Jazzār Pasha. See also *Al-Jabarti's Chronicle of the First Seven Months of the French Occupation of Egypt*, ed and trans. S. Moreh (Leiden, 1975), 56, 92.
[40] Public Record Office (London), Foreign Office 24, vol. 1 (1786–96), Memorial Relating to the Trade in Slaves Carried on in Egypt, fol. 161; Archives de la Guerre (Vincennes), MR 1677, Reconnaissance de Egypte jusqu'a en 1830, *Memoire sur l'Egypte* by Truguet, 166.
[41] Crecelius and Bakr (trans.), *al-Damurdashi's Chronicle of Egypt*, 342–4, 347.
[42] Ibid: 360, fol. 525.

lists among the principal *ocak* officers ʿAbdallāh al-Jarf, the *kāshif* of Manūfiyya. Apparently ʿAlī al-Ḥabashī had crossed a significant colour barrier, for a note beside the name of ʿAbdallāh al-Jarf remarks that this black slave would have been a bey had he been white.[43] Murād Bey also had a famous black *katkhudā* named Ibrāhīm al-Sinnārī who acquired enormous power as the representative of his master in Cairo.[44]

The ethnic origins of the Mamluks of the late eighteenth century were very broad, and colour, while perhaps being a barrier to advancement to the top of the Mamluk military hierarchy, formed no obstacle to induction into the lower or middle ranks of Mamluk society.[45] In the famous incident of 1779, when Ibrāhīm Bey and Murād Bey seized the English ships from India which dropped anchor in the harbour of Suez, it was reported that many of the young Indians were forced to become Muslims and were circumcised.[46] The implication is that they were taken into the households of the beys, who were at that time desperate for recruits and who were not concerned about colour or racial origin. In 1801–2 the Ottoman governor Muḥammad Khusraw Pasha purchased a group of blacks from Takrūr as well as twenty-four French deserters who acted as instructors for the Takrūrīs and for the white Mamluks who formed the household of the governor.[47] The infantry unit serving under Ḥusayn Bey the Zantiote at the end of the century (see below) was said to consist of blacks and Greeks.[48]

Near the end of the eighteenth century the beylicate was dominated by beys drawn from the Circassian and Georgian pool, but one finds a broad array of Mamluks from among blacks, Jews, Russians and Western Europeans. Clearly, the ethnic composition of the beylicate had broadened as a result of the decreasing number of youths from the traditional recruiting grounds in the Caucasus region. Among the common Mamluks of the beys near the end of the eighteenth century we find large numbers of Greeks, Croats, Hungarians, Austrians, Italians, Frenchmen and Englishmen. (See below.)

Russian Mamluks

As early as the time of ʿAlī Bey, one finds references to Russians in large numbers in the households of the leading beys.[49] When Muḥammad Bey Abū ʾl-Dhahab died on campaign in Syria in 1775, it was reported by the English cannoneer

[43] AMAE, Quai d'Orsay (Paris), Correspondance Consulaire, Damiette (sans numéro), 1777–1818, fols. 55–6. Ethiopians (*ḥabashīs*) were distinguished from blacks (*zanjis*) and were more highly prized as slaves, whether male or female, which might explain why ʿAlī al-Ḥabashī became a bey and ʿAbdallāh al-Jarf did not. [44] Jabarti, *ʿAjāʾib al-āthār*, vol. III, 219.

[45] The black aghas of the imperial harem, for instance, played a significant political role in Mamluk politics of the eighteenth century. See Jane Hathaway, 'The role of the Kizlār Agāsī in 17–18th century Ottoman Egypt', *Studia Islamica,* vol. 65 (1992), 141–58.

[46] Archives Nationales (Paris), Affaires Etrangères, B1, Correspondance Consulaire, vol. 112 (Alexandrie) 1779–82, Letter of the Consul Taitbout, 3 August 1779.

[47] Turc, *Chronique d'Egypte*, 151–2. [48] Douin, *L'Angleterre et l'Egypte, 1803–1807,* 175.

[49] It might be suggested that the term 'Russian' applied to Circassians and particularly Georgians, but French sources specifically speak of 'pure' or 'true' Russians, and Jabartī identifies some beys as 'Muscovites'.

(Robinson) in Muḥammad Bey's employ that 250 Mamluks of Russian birth entered his tent with drawn swords, took some of his treasure, and left the camp.[50] Apparently a large number of Russians captured by the Ottomans during the Russo-Ottoman War of 1768–73 and after were introduced into Egypt. The French merchant Magallon, a long-term resident in Egypt, reported in 1789 that 'the household of Muḥammad Bey, with Ibrāhīm as its head, is entirely Russian (*est tout Russe*)'.[51] Earlier, it had been reported that one fourth of the new Mamluk households were 'true Russians', the others being Georgian and Circassian.[52] Ibrāhīm Bey's household in particular had a high percentage of Russians. His *khāzindār* carried on a correspondence with the Russian consul, the Baron de Thonus, in Russian, and one of his favourite Mamluks, a Russian, was dispatched as governor of Upper Egypt.[53] Ismāʿīl Bey, the *khushdāsh* of ʿAlī Bey and chief rival of Ibrāhīm and Murād, the Mamluks of Muḥammad Bey Abū ʾl-Dhahab, apparently had no Russians in his household, for it is reported that a letter in Russian which the Russian consul Baron de Thonus wrote to Ismāʿīl Bey was translated only with difficulty.[54]

Jabartī does not have as much evidence on the Russians as is contained in the European consular reports, but he nevertheless does mention Qāsim Bey 'the Muscovite' and remarks that when the Russians came to Damiette they were of the same race as the ruling beys in Cairo.[55] A number of Russians were captured by the French during their campaigns against the Mamluks at the end of the century, for in an undated letter from General Dugua's papers is a list of fourteen captured Mamluks, among whom were Ṣāliḥ the Muscovite, Joseph the Muscovite, and Rustum the Muscovite. Muṣṭafā, Ibrāhīm, ʿUthmān and Mūsā were Circassians; Shāhīn, Salīm, Ṣāliḥ and Ḥusayn were Georgians; Qāsim was Abazan; and Ḥusayn was German.[56] It appears, therefore, that a growing number of Russians, differentiated from Circassians and Georgians, had been introduced into the Mamluk system in the last decades of the eighteenth century. These joined the Georgians and Circassians as the dominant ethnic groups in the Mamluk households.

Sarrājūn

There is still much debate over the origin and functions of *sarrājūn* and their relationship to the beys in whose households they served. A late eighteenth-

[50] AMAE, Quai d'Orsay (Paris), Archives des Postes – Ambassade Turquie, Correspondance avec les Echelles, Alexandrie-Le Caire, 1771–77; bulletin of 17 June 1775.
[51] AMAE, Quai d'Orsay (Paris), Archives des Postes – Ambassade Turquie, Correspondance avec les Echelles – Egypte, 1788–III, 18 March 1789.
[52] AMAE, Quai d'Orsay (Paris) Correspondance Politique-Turquie, vol. 174 (1786), fol. 72, 15 March 1786.
[53] Archives Nationales (Paris), Affaires Etrangères, B1, Correspondance Politique, vol. 113 (Alexandrie), fols. 213–15, 15 July 1786.
[54] Archives Nationales (Paris), Affaires Etrangères, B1, Correspondance Consulaire, vol. 114 (Alexandrie), 1788–91, fols. 81–2, 19 September 1788.
[55] Jabarti, *ʿAjāʾib al-āthār*, vol. II, 164; on Qāsim Bey al-Musqū; vol. III, 174.
[56] Archives de la Guerre (Vincennes), B6–15, Armée d'Orient-Pièces en Arabe et Pièces diverses.

century Turkish description of Egypt's administration, the *Niẓāmnāme-i Mıṣır*, notes that every amir maintained a group of forty to fifty *sarrājūn* who were apparently free-born Muslims from the Balkan and Asiatic provinces of the Ottoman Empire who originally desired to serve in the army of the *amīr al-ḥājj* as a means of completing the pilgrimage to Mecca. After several years of satisfactory military service the amir would secure for these troops positions within the *ocaks*, permit them to grow beards, and make them partners of merchants doing business with Jidda. On the basis of this testimony, P. M. Holt suggested the existence of a clear career line between a *sarrāj* and a Mamluk. The former, a freeborn Muslim, could only hope to be enrolled in one of the seven Ottoman corps as an ordinary soldier and be established in business with a prosperous merchant. But the Mamluk, upon manumission, could hope to become part of the military aristocracy, entering either the beylicate or the officer ranks of one of the seven corps.[57] Stanford J. Shaw has argued that the *sarrājūn*, who have been described as the armed retainers of an amir who accompanied and defended him wherever he went, were newly enrolled Mamluks or simply private troops who received their pay from the leaders they served.[58] In his translation of Nicolas Turc, Gaston Wiet calls them simply Mamluks.[59] In following Holt, André Raymond calls them free-born individuals serving as guards in the corps of their masters.[60] David Ayalon calls them merely 'mounted servants'.[61]

There does seem to have existed a career line separating the *sarrājūn* from the Mamluks. In the late seventeenth century Muṣṭafā al-Qāzdughlī crossed some form of barrier when he became the *çirak*[62] of Ḥasan Agha Balfīyā. Muṣṭafā, who is credited with founding the Qāzdughlī *bayt*, the Mamluk faction that controlled Egypt in the second half of the eighteenth century, dominated Cairo politics around the turn of the eighteenth century as an ally of his patron and his patron's son-in-law, Ismāʿīl Bey al-Daftardār. Although some *sarrājūn* were given broad powers by their patrons and were as close to their patrons as some of their patrons' personal Mamluks, we have no examples of *sarrājūn* becoming Mamluks in the eighteenth century excepting, perhaps, Aḥmad al-Jazzār. The chronicle by Aḥmad Katkhudā ʿAzabān al-Damurdāshī gives us a good deal of information on the hated and feared *sarrāj*

57 P. M. Holt, 'The career of Küçük Muḥammad', in P. M. Holt (ed.), *Studies in the History of the Near East* (London, 1973), 236–7.

58 See Stanford J. Shaw (ed. and trans.), *Ottoman Egypt in the Eighteenth Century: The Niẓāmnāme-i Mıṣır of Cezzar Aḥmed Pasha* (Cambridge, Mass., 1962), 24n.

59 Turc, *Chronique d'Egypte*, 20n.

60 André Raymond, *Artisans et Commerçants au Caire au XVIIIe Siècle* (Damascus, 1974), vol. II, 698n.

61 Ayalon, 'Studies in al-Jabarti', 304–6.

62 Even the term *çirak* causes some controversy. Of Persian origin, it was accepted into Turkish and meant retainer or servant, but also identified an apprentice, such as a young boy, under the supervision of a guild member. It is clear from its usage in Damurdāshī's history that it usually refers to a dependent Mamluk, even a *sancak bey*, serving under the protection or auspices of an important person, such as a pasha or the sultan, who is not his original master, but who appointed him to his position. See also Ayalon, 'Studies in al-Jabarti', 321–2.

of Muḥammad Bey Çerkes named al-Sayfī, a Balkan Armenian whom Çerkes brought to Egypt from the battle of Belgrade and who undertook the worst deeds for his patron, and of the chief *sarrāj* of Zayn al-Faqār Bey, who was named al-Shitwī,[63] but these clearly could not claim the prerogatives of Mamluk amirs.

The short *Mémoire sur le Gouvernement de l'Égypte* written by Colonel Pretot during the French occupation identifies the *sarrājūn* as troops, either on foot or horseback; they were neither Mamluks nor freed Mamluks, but were youths (gens) from Turkey whom circumstance had forced to take up residence in Egypt. Because they had no money they were hired as armed retainers by the beys.[64] Although they were not Mamluks, the *sarrājūn* were well integrated into the households of their patrons. When a bey rode in procession, such as on a festival day or on those days when he went up to the Citadel for a meeting of the divan, he was preceded by a band of *sarrājūn* acting as bodyguards to clear his path and followed by a group of his personal Mamluks. The *sarrājūn* were often considered undisciplined, or roughnecks, and were called the hired killers of their Mamluk patron.

Free-born Muslims from the Balkans and Anatolia formed an important element in the military expeditions the Ottomans sent to various provinces of their empire, and Jane Hathaway has shown that large numbers of such troops were to be found in the households of both the *ocak* officers and Mamluk beys in Egypt in the last decades of the seventeenth century and the first decades of the eighteenth century. Muṣṭafā Qāzdughlī, a *sarrāj* from the Kāzdāgh (from whence the corrupted Arabic Qāzdughlī) in western Anatolia is but one example of this phenomenon.[65] Free-born Muslim *sarrājūn* thus formed the same recruiting ground for induction into the *ocaks* and the Mamluk households, but they remained, with few exceptions, distant from the beys and of less significance than the beys' personal Mamluks.

The line between Muslims and non-Muslims in the lower ranks of the *ocaks* and Mamluk households was somewhat blurred due to the chaos that characterized the last years of the eighteenth century. It is logical to suspect that as normal recruitment from their traditional recruiting grounds had been seriously reduced in this period, the Mamluk beys would seek to maintain the military strength of their households by increasing the number of *sarrājūn* in their

63 Crecelius and Bakr (trans.), *al-Damurdashi's Chronicle of Egypt*, 207–9, 222–3, 246–51, 289, 291.

64 Archives de la Guerre (Vincennes), Mémoires Historiques, MR 571 a 577, fols. 3–4. An anonymous French report emphasizes the lawless nature of the *sarrājūn*, stating that the *sarrājūn* were guards of a Mamluk bey on foot and horseback who were Turks of the Ottoman Empire and brigands who had been obliged to leave their homelands for breaking the law. See Archives de la Guerre (Vincennes), MR 1677, Reconnaissance de l'Egypte jusqu'a en 1830, *Questions sur l'Egypte*, at 134–5.

65 See Jane Hathaway, 'Years of ocak power: the rise of the Qazdagli household and the transformation of Ottoman Egypt's military society, 1670–1750' (unpublished Ph.D. dissertation, Princeton University, 1992), 100–4, 120–38.

ranks. Moreover, at that time, a growing number of recruits from the Balkans were becoming available as the Ottoman Empire renewed its wars with the Habsburg Empire.

The ethnic and religious background of these troops was quite broad. So undisciplined, so unruly, and so necessary had they become that many were disguised Christians. Ayalon has cited the famous conversation between ʿAbd al-Raḥmān al-Qāzdughlī, the *agha* of the Janissaries, and Ḥusayn Bey al-Maqtūl, who complained to ʿAbd al-Raḥmān that the *agha* was too harsh with the *sarrājūn*. ʿAbd al-Raḥmān replied that 'these are the worst of God's creation and the most harmful to the Muslims. Most of them are Christians who make the outward appearance of Muslims. The reason for their serving you is their desire to be in a position from which they can harm the Muslims. If you doubt my words, please let me examine them in order to distinguish between the circumcised and the uncircumcised amongst them'. The next day, al-Jabartī reported, most of the *sarrājūn* of Ḥusayn Bey fled and only a few, who were Muslims and circumcised, remained.[66]

It is true that a large number of Balkan Muslims, particularly Albanians, and European Christians, had been introduced into the households of the Mamluk beys in a variety of ways in the last decades of the eighteenth century. Some were acquired as Mamluks, many were introduced as *sarrājūn,* others were hired as mercenaries for their particular skills. Albanian units were introduced at the time of Ghāzī Ḥasan Pasha's expedition of 1786–7 and remained a distinct military force in Egypt that rivalled Mamluk or Ottoman power until Muḥammad ʿAlī finally eliminated them after 1815. Most, but not all, of these troops at least outwardly embraced Islam and performed the Muslim rites. As the military situation became more chaotic and desperate for the remaining beys near the end of the eighteenth century, entire units of Christians were hired as mercenary forces. We turn now to the newest ethnic element in the Mamluk household, the European recruit.

Europeans in the Mamluk households

The renewal of war with the Russian and Habsburg Empires had brought large numbers of prisoners into the Ottoman Empire, some of whom were introduced into the households of leading Ottoman officials.[67] As an act of

66 Ayalon, 'Studies in al-Jabarti', 305–6, citing al-Jabartī.

67 The Austrian ambassador's reports to the Habsburg capital are full of concern for the release of prisoners of war and the presence of Europeans in the households of Ottoman officials. The Habsburg ambassador, Baron Herbert Rathkeal, mentions that the Venetian *bailo* was trying to repatriate 400 Venetians, that there were about 200 Habsburg slaves held in the Bursa area, and that thirty-eight slaves had been freed via Varna and another thirty at Janina. Carlo Rosetti, then the Austrian representative in Egypt, had also secured the release of ten to fifteen youths. See Haus-, Hof- und Staatsarchiv (Vienna), Türkei II, 89, letters from Rathkeal of 10 February, 1786, 25 August 1792, 25 May 1793, 10 July 1793. A letter of 8 February 1786 (fol. 171) from Vienna notes that among the North African prisoners taken were twelve Flemish captives.

goodwill in 1802, the grand admiral of the Ottoman fleet, Ḥusayn Pasha, for instance, freed 160 Maltese whom he had employed in the arsenal and in his own ships. Most of these had been slaves for six to eight years, but one, aged eighty-three, had been a slave for forty-eight years.[68] Imperial officials obviously had first choice of purchasing the prisoners of war, but some prisoners were sent to Egypt to serve in the households of the Mamluk amirs. Gabriel Guémard mentions that Ibrāhīm Bey and Murād Bey counted Russians, Germans and Frenchmen among their cavaliers, that after Ghāzī Ḥasan Pasha closed the Istanbul slave-market to the beys they used Greeks and blacks, and that many Austrians, Hungarians and Croats in the service of Murād Bey surrendered to General Desaix.[69]

Prior to the French invasion of 1798 a small number of Europeans of Christian origin, whether renegades who sought a change of fortune in the Ottoman world or prisoners of war forcibly placed in the service of Muslim amirs, are to be found in the records. Eyles Irwin found a number of Christian renegades residing in Mocha (Yemen) and two Europeans dressed as natives among the inhabitants of Egypt's Red Sea port of Quṣayr. In Cairo he met the Englishman Robinson who had originally taken service as Muḥammad Bey Abū 'l-Dhahab's cannoneer.[70] Niebuhr found on his trip to Arabia in 1761 that the pasha of Jidda had in his service three French and Italian renegades who spoke Turkish.[71] It was, of course, quite useful for these Ottoman or Mamluk grandees to have as broad a spectrum of ethnic diversity in their households as possible, for Europeans in particular brought not only a range of languages not ordinarily spoken in the East, but a knowledge of military weaponry or techniques that were deficient in the Ottoman Empire at the time. The Englishman Robinson, who commanded Muḥammad Bey Abū 'l-Dhahab's artillery corps, performed the same functions for his successors because the Mamluks were so maladroit in using cannons to good effect. Robinson introduces us to another type of household asset, the free Christian mercenary acting in the service of the bey, perhaps alongside other Christian renegades or prisoners who were the bey's Mamluks.[72]

It is only infrequently that we know the names of Europeans serving in the Mamluk armies. ʿAlī Bey al-Kabīr's *wakīl* was his Mamluk Vicenzo Taberna,

[68] Douin and Fawtier-Jones, *L'Angleterre et l'Egypte, 1801–1803*, 407.

[69] Guémard, *Aventuriers Mameluks d'Egypte*, 12–16.

[70] Eyles Irwin, *A Series of Adventures in the Course of a Voyage up the Red Sea, on the coasts of Arabia and Egypt . . . in the Year 1777* (London, 1787), vol. I, 13, 165; vol. II, 67–8. Irwin also mentions that the empress of Morocco was an Englishwoman: vol. II, 131.

[71] C. Niebuhr, *Travels through Arabia and other Countries in the East* (Edinburgh, 1792, rep. Beirut), vol. I, 229.

[72] ʿAlī Bey al-Kabīr had hired a handful of European artillery experts to train his forces, among whom were a Frenchman by the name of Moisson, a Florentine, and others. We find European military officers in the service of the Qāzdughlī successors of ʿAlī Bey. Muḥammad Bey took seven European artillery officers on his second Syrian campaign in 1775, among whom were the Englishmen Robinson and Harvey, two Ragusans, one Dane, and two of unspecified nationality. See Crecelius, *The Roots of Modern Egypt*, 76–8.

a Piedmontese who, because of his knowledge of Arabic and Turkish, later served as secretary and interpreter for the English mission to Egypt in the early nineteenth century, and one of Murād Bey's chief officers was Colonel Altamare, who became an instructor in Muḥammad ʿAlī's army from 1810 to 1812.[73] Murād Bey recruited mainly Greeks from the archipelago to man the Nile fleet he created for himself. Jabartī reprovingly remarked that a Christian named Niqūlā, who commanded this group, rode through Cairo on horseback, preceded by many Greek soldiers, implying that these Greek troops behaved like the Mamluk beys and their entourages.[74] The historian Niqūlā al-Turk provides much more information on this Armenian, named Papazoghlu, and the unit of 300 soldiers he commanded for Murād Bey.[75] He was known to the Egyptians as Niqūlā Re'īs because he built and commanded Murād Bey's Nile fleet, but the French knew him as Barthelemy.[76] He is frequently confused, therefore, with Barthelemy Serra, a Greek from the island of Chios who had served in the household of Muḥammad Bey Alfī. Both Niqūlā Re'īs (Barthelemy) and Barthelemy Serra became commanders of special corps which the French created from indigenous forces.

Barthelemy Serra was a magnificent horseman, knew Greek, Italian, Arabic and Turkish, and was called Pomegranate (*fart al-rummān,* a pun on Bartulumī al-Rūmī), by the Egyptians. He had been chief of artillery for Alfī Bey, then was made police chief under the French. He gained a particularly unsavoury reputation, among both the Egyptians and the French, for his tendency to cut off the heads of those he apprehended.[77] He was ultimately made commander of the cavalry corps that was created from among the captured Mamluks.[78]

Murād also had a physician named Dimitri who took the name Sulaymān,[79] but perhaps the most famous European adventurers in the service of Murād

[73] L. A. Balboni, *Gl'Italiani nella Civilta' Egiziana del Secolo XIX* (Alexandria, 1906), vol. I, 213, 215. For more on Vicenzo Taberna, see Douin and Fawtier-Jones, *L'Angleterre et l'Egypte, 1801–1803*, 108n.

[74] al-Jabartī, *ʿAjāʾib al-āthār*, vol. III, 168, vol. III, 56 identifies him as an Armenian. Browne, *Travels in Africa, Egypt and Syria*, 82, also mentions Murād Bey's small Nile fleet commanded by Niqūlā Re'īs and manned by Greeks of the archipelago.

[75] Turc, *Chronique d'Egypte,* 112–13, reveals that Nicolas had been a guard at a castle near Istanbul in which some of the hostages Murād Bey had given to Ghāzī Ḥasan Pasha to ensure his good conduct had been imprisoned. In return for helping them escape and seeing them safely back to Cairo, Murād took Nicolas into his service and gave him command of a unit of 300 Greeks and Cretans who were barracked in Giza. He constructed a large Nile ship which Murād kept outside his palace. Nicolas fought against the French, but when the battle was lost he swam across the Nile and presented himself to Bonaparte, who made him a commander of a locally recruited unit.

[76] Gabriel Guémard, 'Les auxiliaires de l'armée de Bonaparte', 3; Henry Laurens, Charles C. Gillispie, Jean-Claude Golvin and Claude Traunecker, *l'Expéditon d'Egypte, 1798–1801: Bonaparte et l'Islam, Le Choc des Cultures* (Paris, 1989), 72, 86, 268.

[77] al-Jabartī, *ʿAjāʾib al-āthār*, vol. III, 11–12, 27–29; Stanford J. Shaw (trans.), *Ottoman Egypt in the Age of the French Revolution* (Cambridge, MA., 1964), 84. Turc, *Chronique d'Egypte*, 113–14; Guémard, 'Les auxiliaires de l'armée de Bonaparte', 10–15.

[78] Turc, *Chronique d'Egypte*, 113–14.

[79] Auriant, *Aventuriers et Originaux* (Paris, 1933).

Bey were the three Gaeta brothers from Zanta, who willingly came to Egypt around 1790, became Muslims, and were appointed *kāshifs* with the title of *agha*. The brothers made artillery pieces for Murād Bey and had known careers in Egypt. Ibrāhīm Agha, one of the brothers, commanded a unit of Greeks. Giovanni took the name Aḥmad Agha and in 1796 accompanied a Mamluk expedition to Darfur, where he was cruelly executed by the sultan of Darfur in 1799.[80] The third brother, by the name of Ḥusayn Agha, who commanded a unit of 800, including Greeks, Copts, blacks from Takrūr, and Frenchmen, submitted to General Desaix during the years of the French occupation (1798–1801), but resumed his command in the chaotic period that followed the departure of the French from Egypt.[81]

Germans or Austrians are also found among the Mamluks. On his journey from Cairo to the Niger in 1797–8, the German adventurer Friedrich Hornemann took along a fellow German by the name of Joseph Frendenburgh who had been a Mamluk ten to twelve years and had made three pilgrimages to Mecca.[82] An unnamed Austrian who had been captured by the Ottomans at the siege of Belgrade had been brought as a slave to Egypt. Two months after the death of his master in Manṣūra he presented himself to the French.[83] Ḥusayn the German, who was captured by the French, was mentioned above, as was the group of Austrians freed by Carlo Rosetti.

The occupation of Egypt by the French from 1798 to 1801 and the landing of British forces there in 1801 and again in 1807 provided opportunities for the capture of prisoners by all parties. The appearance of French and English armies in Egypt was the occasion for the submission of many European Mamluks to the invaders, but there are numerous recorded incidents of French and English troops crossing the lines into Mamluk armies, or later into the service of Muḥammad ʿAlī Pasha.[84]

General Damas reported that seven Mamluks taken captive in an attack upon the camp of ʿUthmān Bey al-Tamburjī were French deserters.[85] This was

[80] See Auriant, 'Histoire d'Ahmed Aga le Zantiote, un projet de conquete du Darfour', *Revue d'Histoire des Colonies Françaises* (1926), 181–234.

[81] Guémard, *Aventuriers Mameluks d'Egypte*, 18–19; Auriant, *Aventuriers et Originaux*, 10–78. Turc, *Chronique d'Egypte*, 226–7, states that Ḥusayn Agha was called Ḥusayn Bey the Jew because he was supposedly born a Jew, converted to Christianity in Zante, then embraced Islam in Egypt. He is frequently mentioned as being in command of Greeks and blacks in the records of the British campaigns. See Douin, *l'Angleterre et l'Egypte, 1803–1807*, 28, 32, 49, 57, 102–3, 110, 132, 151, 175.

[82] Friedrich Hornemann, *Missions to the Niger: The Journal of Friedrich Hornemann's Travels from Cairo to Murzuk in the years 1797–98*, ed. E. W. Bovill (Cambridge, 1964), vol. I, 25, 56.

[83] Archives de la Guerre (Vincennes), B6–26, Armée d'Orient 1799, letter of Poussielgue, 19 July 1799.

[84] There is evidence that in earlier decades, at least in Alexandria, French sailors from the ships visiting the harbour were taken into the Janissary corps, for on one occasion fifty French sailors forcibly retrieved some of their compatriots from that corps in the city. Archives Nationales (Paris), Affaires Etrangères, B1, Correspondance Consulaire, vol. 114 (Alexandrie), 1788–1791, fols. 55–6, 25 June 1788.

[85] Archives de la Guerre (Vincennes), B6–38, Armée d'Orient, Correspondance 20–31 December 1799. Letter from Damas to General Dugua, 31 December 1799.

not an isolated incident, and in October 1800, the French command issued a pardon for French deserters serving with the Mamluks.[86] The British, in fact, were not only cognizant of large numbers of French serving with the Mamluks, but contended that these troops had been purposely planted in unit strength among the Mamluks so they could maintain French control of Upper Egypt and act as the ready force when the French reinvaded Egypt at some future date.[87] Some of the French who remained behind had distinguished careers in Egypt. The pharmacist Royer was driven out of the French army because, on Napoleon's orders, he had administered poison to thirty French soldiers suffering from the plague in Jaffa. He remained in Cairo after his dismissal and became the doctor for Bardīsī Bey, then served Muḥammad ʿAlī before moving to Istanbul, where he spent fifteen years. He died in 1818 in a fall from a horse.[88] Philippe-Joseph Machereau, who for the love of a woman converted to Islam and took the name Muḥammad Efendī, became professor of art for Muḥammad ʿAlī and in 1860 was named director of Muḥammad Saʿīd Pasha's theatre.[89]

Two young Scottish soldiers captured in the campaign of 1807 chose to become Mamluks rather than be decapitated. Both had distinguished careers in Egypt. Thomas Keith, who was purchased by Aḥmad Agha (Giovanni Gaeti), became Ibrāhīm Agha and served with Muḥammad ʿAlī's son Ṭūsūn in Arabia. In April 1815 he was named governor of Medina, but died in that area the same year. William Thompson became ʿUthmān Efendī after he was purchased by Qādir Agha. He was the English-speaking Mamluk whom Thomas Legh met at Minya in 1812. His freedom was won in 1816 by Shaykh Ibrāhīm (the traveller Burckhardt), whom he had accompanied on his famous trip to Mecca and who passed on to him his inheritance (and his wife) when he died in Cairo. Thompson/ʿUthmān Efendī, who refused to renounce Islam, became rich from urban real estate in Cairo, was assimilated into

[86] Archives de la Guerre (Vincennes), B6–54, Armée d'Orient 1800, 4 October 1800.

[87] The British consul-general Missett wrote to Lord Camden on 10 October 1804 that

> the Beys and the Viceroy have in their respective armies many Frenchmen who are generally believed to be deserters; but I can assure Your Lordship that they were designedly left in the country, together with the Greeks and Cophts, who had enlisted in the troops of the Republic. This measure is a small branch of an extensive plan, by the success of which the French would have retained possession of Egypt, when they pretended to evacuate it. It was intended to abandon in Upper Egypt whole demi-brigades, generals, engineers, and civil officers, whom the world would have been told to consider as rebels. After the signature of the Treaty of El-Arich, the French troops were ordered to move toward the coast for the purpose of being embarked. But General Donzelot, with the 22nd and 85th demi-Brigades and a complete military establishment, remained in the Said, where he was instructed to form alliances with the Mamlouks and the Bedouins, and to expect a regular supply of recruits, as both the Cophtic and Greek Clergy had promised to exert, to that effect, their influence among their countrymen'. Douin, *L'Angleterre et l'Egypte, 1803–1807,* 197–198.

As early as 1801 the British noted that 300 Frenchmen had become Mamluks. See Douin and Fawtier-Jones, *L'Angleterre et l'Egypte, 1801–1803*, 150.

[88] Auriant, *Aventuriers et Originaux*, 105–30; Turc, *Chronique d'Egypte,* 287.

[89] Auriant, *Aventuriers et Originaux*, 175–89.

Egyptian–Turkish society and was well situated to act as an intermediary between English visitors and Egyptian society. He was buried in the Bāb al-Naṣr cemetery in Cairo in the same tomb as his friend Burckhardt following his death in 1835.[90]

When the British signed the agreement with Muḥammad ʿAlī for their evacuation of Egypt in late 1807, they retrieved most, but not all, of their prisoners of war. Four hundred and sixty-six prisoners were returned to them, but there were still about forty to fifty unaccounted for; it was suspected that they had been dispersed into households in Upper Egypt.[91] By this time the Mamluk system was in disarray and the lines between Christians and Muslims, Ottomans and Europeans, at least in military matters, were frequently blurred. The traditions and dominance of the Mamluk households were overwhelmed by the influx of thousands of Christian and Muslim troops from the Balkans or such areas as Malta and Syria. Napoleon, for instance, created special corps of Maltese, Greeks, Copts, Syrians, North Africans and Mamluks/Janissaries.[92]

It appears, therefore, that in the last years of the eighteenth century the beys, desperate to replenish their ranks, opened their households to recruits from new territories and new ethnic backgrounds. These came to outnumber the dominant ethnic composition of Georgians and Circassians. Although the Georgian and Circassian remnants of the Qāzdughlī households belonging to Murād Bey and Ibrāhīm Bey still dominated these households, they found it increasingly necessary to recruit Russians, Europeans and blacks to fill the places of their fallen comrades; they also increased the number of mercenaries in their ranks. By the end of the century we are able to identify a wide range of Europeans, such as Croats, Hungarians, Austrians, Italians, Greeks, French and English, enrolled in the factions of the Mamluk beys.[93] Greeks were particularly noticeable in large numbers. General Kléber assembled a corps of 1,500 Greeks drawn from local sources and stationed one company each in Cairo, Damiette and Rosette.[94] These Europeans almost never, it seems, reached the rank of bey themselves, but took their places in the households on the basis of special skills they might have had. The most obvious examples are those, whether English, French or Italian, who commanded artillery units for the beys, but others, especially Greeks, built and manned Murād's Nile fleet or commanded special units. At the same time, the Mamluks were recruiting free-born Muslims from Asia Minor and the Balkans. One finds references partic-

[90] Jason Thompson, 'Osman Effendi: a Scottish convert to Islam in early nineteenth century Egypt', *Journal of World History*, vol. 5 (Spring 1994), 99–123. See also Auriant, *Aventuriers et Originaux*, 152–64.

[91] G. Douin and E. C. Fawtier-Jones, *L'Angleterre et l'Egypte: La Campagne de 1807* (Cairo, 1928), 169.

[92] See Guémard, 'Les auxiliares de l'armée de Bonaparte'; Jabartī, *ʿAjāʾib al-āthār*, vol. III, 49.

[93] Toussoun, 'La fin des Mamlouks', 189, mentions Hungarians, Vlachs, Serbs, Bulgarians, Germans, Catalans, Sicilians and Italians among the Mamluks.

[94] Guémard, 'Les auxiliaires de l'armée de Bonaparte', 4–5.

ularly to Albanians, who in the first years of the nineteenth century were said to number 9,000, or two to three times the number of Mamluks.[95] These undisciplined Albanian troops who had been brought to Egypt by the Ottomans fought for pay, not principle, and, when not in conflict with the Mamluk factions and Ottoman governors, or even their own unit commanders such as Muḥammad ʿAlī, served as mercenaries. The English consul-general, Colonel Missett, reported in September 1803, for instance, that the better part of the remaining force of ʿUthmān Bardīsī Bey was Albanian.[96] In the chaos following the withdrawal of the French some Albanians were able to claim the title of bey. ʿUmar Bey, who was Albanian, joined Khurshīd Pasha against Muḥammad ʿAlī, while Ḥasan Bey, another Albanian, was the brother of ʿĀbidīn Bey and the nephew of Ṭāhir Pasha, an Albanian leader.[97]

Another indication of the breakdown of the Mamluk system at that time was the loss of command by the older generation of *sancaḳ beys.* It was reported that Ibrāhīm Bey had become so old that he had lost his influence in the councils of the Mamluks and even subordinate *kāshifs* could with impunity dispute and oppose the orders of the *shaykh al-balad.*[98] Another revealing incident involves the troops under the command of Niqūlā Re'īs who killed several inhabitants of old Cairo. Murād Bey ordered his arrest, but had to back off when Niqūlā Re'īs aimed the cannons of his Nile ships at Murād's palace in Giza.[99] Clearly, the Mamluk leaders did not have the same authority they had enjoyed only a decade earlier.

Conclusion

The political system long dominated by Mamluk beys of the Caucasus region was under heavy pressure in the last four decades before its destruction by Muḥammad ʿAlī Pasha in 1811. Constant factional fighting and the appearance of two virulent plagues in the period before the arrival of the French in 1798 had destroyed the equilibrium of the Mamluk beylicate and seriously depleted the number of Mamluks in Egypt. Factors beyond the control of the Mamluk beys, such as the loss of their traditional recruiting grounds to the Russian Empire and the arrival of three foreign armies bent on their destruction in the period between 1786 and 1801, had reduced their numbers to approximately 20–25 per cent of what they had been in the period of ʿAlī Bey al-Kabīr. Without the ability to replace these massive losses from the Caucasus region, the remaining Mamluk leaders sought to recruit Mamluks and mercenaries from the new flow of prisoners and renegades from the border regions of the Ottoman Empire and from ethnic minorities from the Balkans. Russians in particular were recruited by Ibrāhīm Bey, but we also find blacks, Indians,

[95] Douin, *L'Angleterre et l'Egypte, 1803–1807*, 131. [96] Ibid., 34.
[97] Turc, *Chronique d'Egypte*, 208, 268. [98] Douin, *L'Angleterre et l'Egypte, 1803–1807,* 33.
[99] Guémard, 'Les auxiliaires de l'armée de Bonaparte', 3n.

Hungarians, Croats and Austrians mentioned among Mamluk ranks. Near the end of the eighteenth century the number of mercenaries in the Mamluk households seems to be greater than the number of personal Mamluks belonging to the beys. Most were enrolled as *sarrājūn*, but we find also renegades or mercenaries from Europe who did not seem to have been required to convert to Islam. Italians, Frenchmen and Englishmen served in the households of the Qāzdughlī amirs even before the arrival of the French in 1798. Murād Bey, for instance, had hundreds of Greeks serving on the small Nile fleet that was constructed for him and in special units commanded by Greek officers. Mamluk ranks were also strengthened with the purchase of prisoners of war from the Austrian front and with the capture or desertion of French and English troops from the French and English armies that fought in Egypt between 1798 and 1807. Finally, the Ottomans introduced into Egypt thousands of Muslim troops, notably Albanian, from the Balkans and Anatolia. At the time Muḥammad ʿAlī was named governor of Egypt in 1805, Albanian troops, undisciplined and unruly, significantly outnumbered the remaining households of approximately 2,000 Mamluks who fought on in divided households. It was from this pool of Albanian troops that Muḥammad ʿAlī arose, and it was this leader who dealt the final blow to the Mamluk system.

PART III

Mamluk culture, science and education

CHAPTER 9

Mamluk astronomy and the institution of the *muwaqqit*

DAVID A. KING

Dedicated to the memory of my friend Salah Abdel-Khalek

Introduction

The contents of this chapter are not in the main new to the literature. I have already written preliminary surveys of Mamluk astronomy[1] and of the institutions of the muezzin and of the *muwaqqit*, the latter being a professional astronomer associated with mosques and *madrasas*.[2] In addition I have shown how various Mamluk treatises on astronomy can be of interest to a far greater audience than historians of science: Mamluk treatises on the *qibla* and on the ventilators that graced both the religious and secular architecture of Mamluk Cairo provide the answer to the questions surrounding not only the different orientations attested in Cairene religious architecture but also the orientations of the various parts of the medieval city.[3] In this brief overview I shall try to suppress technical details and to concentrate on mainstream developments and on issues that might be of interest to colleagues outside the history of science.

In the 1970s a distinguished historian of Islamic art, whose name need not be mentioned here, wrote that the Mamluks made no contributions whatsoever to science. This would be the opinion of most Islamists (as well as of most Egyptians and Syrians).[4] That scholar was, however, unaware that in the

[1] D. A. King, 'The astronomy of the Mamluks', *Isis*, 74 (1983), 531–55 (hereafter 'Mamluk astronomy'; reprinted in D. A. King, *Islamic Mathematical Astronomy* (London, 1986; 2nd edn 1993) (hereafter *Studies*, A), III. See also D. A. King, *Islamic Astronomical Instruments* (London, 1987) (hereafter *Studies*, B) and D. A. King, *Astronomy in the Service of Islam* (Aldershot, 1993) (hereafter *Studies* C). These books contain several articles on aspects of Mamluk astronomy, including, in addition to A–III, the overview of Mamluk astronomy, A-IX–XII, descriptions of the corpora of tables used for time-keeping in Mamluk Cairo, Damascus and Jerusalem, B-VIII–X, XII, and XVI–XVII, descriptions of various Mamluk astrolabes, quadrants, sundials and compendia, and C-VI–VII, universal solutions to problems of spherical astronomy.

[2] D. A. King, 'On the role of the muezzin and the muwaqqit in medieval Islamic society', in: F.J. and S. Raqeb (eds.), *Tradition, Transmission, Transformation* (Leiden, 1996), 285–346.

[3] D. A. King, 'Architecture and astronomy: the ventilators of medieval Cairo and their secrets', *Journal of the American Oriental Society*, 104 (1984), 97–133.

[4] The exception to the latter would be those who have seen the chapter 'L 'astronomie en Syrie à l'époque islamique', in *Paris IMA Catalogue,* 386–95.

1950s E. S. Kennedy had discovered that the solar, lunar and planetary models proposed by a scholar of fourteenth-century Damascus were mathematically identical to those of Copernicus 150 years later. He can perhaps be forgiven for not knowing that a young historian of Islamic science had just prepared the first description of some thirteenth- and fourteenth- century Egyptian and Syrian tables for time-keeping and had labelled one of these 'the most sophisticated trigonometric tables known to me from the entire Middle Ages'. And in 1979 when I first described a spectacular astrolabe from early fourteenth-century Aleppo I labelled it 'the most sophisticated astrolabe ever made'.

I was soon to reap the rewards of having catalogued the 2,500 scientific manuscripts in the Egyptian National Library[5] as well as having studied Mamluk manuscripts in libraries elsewhere (notably in the Chester Beatty Library), and having catalogued all available Mamluk astronomical instruments.[6] This was the activity that provided enough momentum to produce the first overview history of Mamluk astronomy and a preliminary study of the institution of the *muwaqqit*. We can now say with confidence that Mamluk contributions to astronomy were among the most remarkable of their time, and that they were certainly as impressive as, and even more colourful than, those of the better-known regional schools in Iran and Central Asia (contemporaneous activity in the Islamic West and in Islamic India were simply not on a comparable level).[7]

Who were the Mamluk astronomers? Were the astronomers of Mamluk Egypt and Syria themselves Mamluks or did they simply work for the Mamluks? Or were they regular Egyptians and Syrians who were active during the Mamluk period? My earlier survey, and perhaps also the present chapter, would in fact be better entitled 'Astronomy under the Mamluks'. Nevertheless, a small minority of the astronomers were indeed *mamlūks*, if not (as was the

[5] See D. A. King, *A Survey of Scientific Manuscripts in the Egyptian National Library* American Research Center in Egypt, catalogs, vol. V (Winona Lake, Ind., 1986) (hereafter Cairo Survey; (see especially section C: Egyptian and Syrian authors from c. 1100 to c. 1600). This is based on the 2–volume Arabic catalogue published by the General Egyptian Book Organization in 1980–86.

[6] See D. A. King, *A Catalogue of Medieval Astronomical Instruments* (forthcoming: sections will deal with Mamluk astrolabes, quadrants and sundials – see also D. A. King, 'Medieval astronomical instruments: a catalogue in preparation', *Bulletin of the Scientific Instrument Society*, 31 (Dec. 1991), 3–7; and D. A. King, '1992 – a good year for medieval astronomical instruments', *Bulletin of the Scientific Instrument Society*, 36 (March 1993), 17–18), and the Mamluk Syrian examples in S. Cluzan, E. Delpont and J. Mouliérac (eds.), *Syrie, mémoire et civilisation* (Paris, 1993), 434–41.

[7] 'Better-known' is used advisedly. The *Zīj*es of al-Ṭūsī and Ulugh Beg are still available only in manuscript form and no editor (or researcher) is in sight; at least the influential *Tadhkira* of al-Ṭūsī is available in a masterly study by F. J. Ragep (1993). There is no survey of astronomy in Iran and Central Asia beyond E. S. Kennedy's chapters on the exact sciences under the Seljuqs and Mongols and then the Timurids in *The Cambridge History of Iran* (Cambridge, 1968 to present), 6 vols. to date (vol. V, 659–79, and vol. VI, 568–80), which are restricted to general trends. Some of the literature published in 1994 to celebrate the 600th anniversary of Ulugh Beg is indicative of the poor understanding of his achievements.

case in Rasulid Yemen) the sultans themselves.[8] On the other hand, the institution of the *muwaqqit* seems very much to have been inaugurated during the Mamluk period, encouraged by the same rulers who founded and endowed the splendid mosques and *madrasas* of Mamluk Cairo. It is not surprising that this institution appeared for the first time in Mamluk times, because much of astronomy under the Mamluks was 'astronomy in the service of Islam', dedicated to the three areas of concern relating to the very pillars of Islam: the lunar calendar, the times of prayer and the sacred direction.[9] This having been said, it should be added that a great deal of energy was also expended by astronomers in Mamluk times on planetary astronomy, theoretical and practical, the most obvious application being mathematical astrology. When the sultan al-Nāṣir Muḥammad ibn Qalāwūn became ill with diarrhoea, astrologers and geomancers were consulted as well as his doctors.[10] But this anecdote, recorded by Ibn Abī ʾl-Faḍāʾil, is the only one of its kind known to me. There is in fact remarkably little astrology in the known Mamluk scientific treatises known to me. Perhaps colleagues can help by drawing my attention to other references in historical works.

An overview of Mamluk astronomy

First a general overview:[11] Let us, for the sake of convenience, begin in mid-thirteenth-century Syria. There we find an intensive programme of astronomy being pursued by various scholars (mentioned by Ibn Abī Uṣaybiʿa and Ibn al-Qifṭī), but these appear to have been mainly involved in teaching and few of them compiled treatises. At least three astronomers, on the other hand, produced zījes, that is, astronomical handbooks with tables, the emphasis being very much on planetary astronomy. For example, Muḥyī ʾl-dīn al-Maghribī, an immigrant, compiled a couple of zījes in Damascus before moving on to participate in the observation programme of Naṣīr al-dīn al-Ṭūsī in Marāgha.[12]

[8] See D. A. King, *Mathematical Astronomy in Medieval Yemen – A Biobibliographical Survey*, American Research Center in Egypt, Catalogs, vol. IV, (Malibu, Ca., 1983), especially at 9, and 23–6, 27–9, 33, 34, 37 and 38 on individual sultans.

[9] For a survey see the study reprinted in *Studies*, C-I.

[10] 'Mamluk astronomy', 535.

[11] For details the reader is referred to my articles cited in notes 1 and 2 above, as well as to E. S. Kennedy and I. Ghanem (eds.), *The Life and Work of Ibn al-Shāṭir, an Arab Astronomer of the Fourteenth Century* (Aleppo, 1976) and G. Saliba, *A History of Arabic Astronomy* [sic] – *Planetary Theories during the Golden Age of Islam* (New York, 1994). (This deals only with non-Ptolemaic planetary theory, including that of Ibn al-Shāṭir; hereafter Saliba, *Studies.*). The major figures mentioned here, such as Ibn Yūnus, al-Ṭūsī, Ibn al-Shāṭir, al-Khalīlī and Ulugh Beg, are treated in *The Dictionary of Scientific Biography* (New York, 1970–80), 16 vols. (See generally articles 'Ibn al-Shāṭir', 'al-Khalīlī and 'Ulugh Beg'.) See also the article on al-Marrākushī in *The Encyclopaedia of Islam* (Leiden, 1960 to present), 8 vols. to date. (See generally articles 'Mīḳāt' (astronomical time-keeping); 'Ru'yat al-hilāl' (lunar crescent visibility); and (forthcoming) 'Taḳwīm' (ephemerides) and 'Zīdj' (astronomical tables).

[12] A. Sayılı, *The Observatory in Islam* (Ankara, 1960; repr. New York, 1981), 187–223.

We continue with late thirteenth-century Egypt, where the emphasis was very much more on spherical astronomy and astronomical time-keeping. The most popular *zīj* in use in Egypt at that time was the anonymous *Muṣṭalaḥ Zīj*, compiled from various sources, not least from the monumental *Ḥākimī Zīj* of the illustrious Fatimid astronomer Ibn Yūnus (*c*. 990).[13] The most important astronomers were Shihāb al-dīn al-Maqsī, Najm al-dīn al-Miṣrī and Abū ʿAlī al-Marrākushī. Al-Maqsī compiled a corpus of tables for time-keeping for the latitude of Cairo, with some 30,000 entries. For each degree of solar longitude, corresponding roughly to each day of the year, the main set of tables gives the time since sunrise, the time till midday and the azimuth (direction on the horizon) of the sun. Smaller tables enable the user to find the time of the *ʿaṣr* prayer and the time when the sun is in the direction of Mecca. Others display the duration of morning and evening twilight to facilitate the determination of the *fajr* and *ʿishā'* prayers.[14] This corpus, which inspired the later ones for Damascus and Jerusalem (see below), was used in Cairo in one form or another until the nineteenth century. Najm al-dīn compiled a set of tables for time-keeping by the sun and stars that would work for all latitudes, with a grand total of 440,000 entries. This monumental table exists in a single copy, doubtless in the hand of Najm al-dīn himself, for it was not calculated to attract many copyists. The table was in a tradition much favoured by Mamluk astronomers, namely the compilation of tables and the development of instruments for solving the problems of spherical astronomy and time-keeping for all latitudes. They achieved some rather spectacular solutions.[15]

In 1280 Abū ʿAlī al-Marrākushī, another immigrant, compiled in Cairo a monumental compendium of spherical astronomy and instrumentation in several hundred folios. This was to form the basis of all later developments in the subject in Mamluk and Ottoman times (it remained unknown in the Maghrib and in the Islamic East).[16] At the same time we find the first mention of a family of *muwaqqit*s at the Mosque of ʿAmr in Fusṭāṭ, who served there from the middle of the thirteenth century to the first decades of the fourteenth. Their contributions are mentioned in a treatise on spherical astronomy which appears to be written by a later member of the family, Naṣīr al-dīn ibn Simʿūn (d. 1337).[17] If the office of the *muwaqqit* was introduced first in Egypt it did not take long to spread to Palestine and Syria: a manuscript of a treatise by Naṣīr al-dīn was copied in 1306/7 by Ibrāhīm ibn Aḥmad, *muwaqqit* at the Sacred Mosque in Hebron.[18] We should mention that before this time, in both Egypt and Syria, various muezzins had produced sophisticated astronomical instruments. As we know, however, from such works as the treatise on law

[13] On the *Muṣṭalaḥ Zīj* see *Studies*, A-III, 535–36. On Ibn Yūnus see the article in *DSB*.
[14] See the analysis in *Studies*, A-IX. [15] Surveyed in *Studies*, C-VI–VII.
[16] The first part of this work was translated by Sédillot-*père* in 1834–5, and the second part was summarized by Sédillot-*fils* in 1844. For references see the article on al-Marrākushī in *EI*².
[17] King, 'Muwaqqit', section 6, quoting MS Leiden Or. 468.
[18] *Cairo Survey*, Pl. CIIIb at 323, with caption at 215.

enforcement (*iḥtisāb*) by Ibn al-Ukhuwwa (Cairo, *c.* 1300), the astronomical knowledge expected of muezzins was restricted to the basics of folk astronomy (simple schemes involving shadows and the lunar mansions for time-keeping by day and night, respectively).[19]

Moving back to Syria we find in about 1325 a lone astronomer, Ibn al-Sarrāj, in Aleppo. Not only did he devise and make instruments, he also wrote treatises on their construction and use. Ibn al-Sarrāj developed a universal astrolabe that could be used for all latitudes, apparently independently of eleventh-century Andalusian instruments of the same kind. He then devised an astrolabe that was universal in five different ways, an example of which happily survives in the Benaki Museum in Athens.[20] In one of his treatises, yet to be studied properly, Ibn al- Sarrāj describes all of the different kinds of instruments known to him and all those invented by himself. The instruments and writings of Ibn al-Sarrāj represent the culmination of astronomical instrumentation in the Islamic world.

A slightly later contemporary was al-Mizzī of Damascus who, in addition to making instruments, compiled a set of tables for time-keeping for the latitude of his home city. Al-Mizzī had studied astronomy in Alexandria under Ibn al-Akfānī, celebrated author of the bibliographical work *Irshād al-qāṣid.* So had Ibn al-Shāṭir, who was to become the chief *muwaqqit* at the Umayyad Mosque in Damascus. He wrote two *zīj*es and a treatise on theoretical astronomy in which he refined the non-Ptolemaic planetary models developed by the Marāgha school and produced geocentric models mathematically identical to those of Copernicus. Ibn al-Shāṭir's writings represent the culmination of the Islamic tradition of planetary astronomy.[21] He also made instruments, portable ones like the astrolabe and the compendium known as the *ṣandūq al-yawāqīt*, and fixed ones like an astronomical clock and a sundial 2 × 1 metres, which is the most spectacular sundial made between late Antiquity and the late Renaissance.[22] A colleague of Ibn al-Shāṭir in Damascus was Shams al-dīn al-Khalīlī, *muwaqqit* first at the Yalbughā Mosque and then at the Umayyad mosque. He compiled a new set of tables for time-keeping for Damascus (based on Ibn al-Shāṭir's new parameters), as well as a universal table for finding the *qibla* for any locality, and a set of tables for solving any problem of spherical astronomy for any latitude[23]. His works represent the culmination of the Islamic science of astronomical time-keeping (*ʿilm al-mīqāt*).

In the fifteenth century the main activity is in Egypt again, with

[19] King, 'Muwaqqit', section 4. On folk astronomy see ibid., section 3 and also D. A. King, 'A survey of medieval Islamic shadow schemes for simple time-reckoning', *Oriens*, 32 (1990), 199–249, esp. 192–6. [20] *Studies*, B-IX, and *Paris IMA Catalogue*, 434–5.

[21] See the article in *DSB* and Saliba, *Studies.*

[22] On the compendium see *Studies*, B-XII (with L. Janin). On an astrolabe by him see *Paris IMA Catalogue*, 435. On his sundial see a study by L. Janin in *Centaurus* 16 (1972) reprinted in Kennedy and Ghanem (eds.), *Ibn al-Shāṭir*, 107–21, and *Paris IMA Catalogue*, 439.

[23] See the article in *DSB*, supp., and the various analyses in *Studies*, A-XI and XIII. A complete analysis of his tables has been prepared but is not yet published.

astronomers such as Ibn al-Majdī, not known to have been associated with any mosque, interested in planetary astronomy and time-keeping, and Sibṭ al-Māridīnī, *muwaqqit* at the Azhar Mosque, interested mainly in time-keeping and small instrumentation. Ibn Abī ʾl-Fatḥ al-Ṣūfī, also not known to have been associated with any mosque, prepared a recension for Cairo of the *Zīj* of Ulugh Beg (Samarqand, *c.* 1430).

In addition there are a host of minor figures, all competent astronomers, who were active as *muwaqqit*s in various mosques in Syria and Egypt. Of these we may mention Aḥmad al-Kawm al-Rīshī, *muwaqqit* at the Mosque of al-Muʾayyad in Cairo, who in about 1410 compiled a recension for Cairo of the *Zīj* of Ibn al-Shāṭir; ʿIzz al-dīn al-Wafāʾī, *muwaqqit* at the same mosque around 1450, who wrote on small instrumentation and made sundials and compendia; and ʿAbd al-Raḥmān al-Ṣāliḥī, *muwaqqit* at the Umayyad Mosque in Damascus, who in about 1500 prepared a recension of the *Zīj* of Ulugh Beg, modifying the planetary tables for the longitude of his own city.

Although astrological topics are not featured in most known Mamluk astronomical treatises we can be sure that there was an active interest in astrology in Mamluk society. A magnificent copy of a *malḥama* or handbook of prognostications for each month of the Syrian year written for the treasury of the Sultan Qāytbāy (1468–96) survives as a witness to this interest.[24] What one can expect if a solar or lunar eclipse, a shooting star, a halo around the sun or moon, or various meteorological phenomena, occur during a given month is clearly outlined.

It was Sibṭ al-Māridīnī who, unwittingly and in total innocence, contributed most to the decline of astronomy in Egypt, and by extension in Syria, after 1500. He wrote several short handbooks on the basics of time-keeping and the use of the instruments (mainly on the quadrant, which had come to replace the astrolabe as the most popular instrument). Likewise Ibn al-Hāʾim (Jerusalem, *c.* 1400) wrote several works on the algebra of inheritance.[25] Commentaries and supercommentaries on these works clutter the shelves of manuscript libraries to this day. About the year 1800, as we know from the titles mentioned by ʿAbd al-Raḥmān al-Jabartī in his *History of Egypt*, it was the works of Ibn al-Hāʾim and Sibṭ al-Māridīnī which predominated in Egyptian scientific circles,[26] and writings such as those of al-Marrākushī, let alone Ibn al-Sarrāj, Ibn al-Shāṭir and al-Khalīlī, had been virtually, if not

[24] MS Dublin Chester Beatty 4041.

[25] H. Suter, 'Die Mathematiker und Astronomen der Araber und ihre Werke', *Abhandlungen zur Geschichte der mathematischen Wissenschaften,* 10 (1900); and 'Nachträge und Berichtigungen', *Abhandlungen zur Geschichte der mathematischen Wissenschaften,* 14 (1902), 157–85, repr. Amsterdam, 1982, and again in H. Suter, *Beiträge zur Geschichte der Mathematik und Astronomie im Islam* (Frankfurt am Main, 1986), 2 vols., no. 423, and *Cairo Survey*, no. C58.

[26] J. Heyworth-Dunne, *An Introduction to the History of Education in Modern Egypt* (London, 1940), 62–64, and King, 'Mamluk astronomy', 552. The only work on theoretical planetary astronomy mentioned by al-Jabartī was the very elementary treatise of al-Jaghmīnī (Central Asia, *c.* 1220: see Suter, *MAA,* no. 403, and *Cairo Survey,* no. G17). See also note 36 below.

completely, forgotten. At the same time the centre of astronomical activity had moved from Cairo and Damascus (and from Samarqand) to Istanbul.[27] It is not surprising that the director of the short-lived observatory in Istanbul around 1577 was a Syrian who had worked both in Cairo and Nablus.

On *muwaqqits* and their role in Mamluk society

The function of the *muwaqqits* in their mosques and *madrasas* was to provide reliable information not only about the astronomically determined times of prayer, but also about the regulation of the lunar calendar and the determination of the sacred direction towards Mecca. Some of these men made instruments, such as sundials or quadrants; many of them wrote treatises on the use of this instrument or that, or on time-keeping in general. In Cairo by the thirteenth century, as mentioned above, there was a corpus of tables available for time-keeping by the sun (if not by the stars). Similar corpora followed in the fourteenth century for Damascus and Jerusalem. Some *muwaqqit*s compiled new tables of this function or that, or 'published' new arrangements of existing tables. The *muwaqqit*s do not seem to have been involved in the compilation of annual ephemerides giving the positions of the sun, moon and stars for each day of the year. (No Mamluk examples of such ephemerides exist, but we do have fragments of various Fatimid examples, two complete Rasulid Yemeni examples[28] and numerous Ottoman examples.[29]) Likewise they do not seem to have been involved in astrology.

On the organization of the activities of the *muwaqqits* in the mosques we have no information beyond the lists of numbers of such individuals and their salaries as found in the *waqf* documents of various Cairene *madrasas*.[30] As noted above, the earliest references to *muwaqqits* are from the second half of the thirteenth century and it seems that we are dealing with a very small group of individuals at the Mosque of ʿAmr in Fustat. I know of no references to this occupation at that time or indeed from the entire fourteenth century from Cairo itself. Nevertheless in the mid-fourteenth century we are confronted with an apparently well-organized team of *muwaqqit*s at the Umayyad Mosque in Damascus, headed by Ibn al- Shāṭir. (The activity there lasted until the nineteenth century.) In fifteenth-century Egypt we have a series of *muwaqqits* employed at different mosques and *madrasas* in Cairo. (This activity likewise lasted through the Ottoman period.)

The *muwaqqits* of Mamluk Egypt and Syria were known already by name

[27] On Ottoman astronomy see *Studies*, A-XII (on astronomical time-keeping), and a forthcoming bio-bibliographical survey edited by E. İhsanoğlu (to be published by IRCICA, Istanbul).

[28] *Cairo Survey*, no. E11, and King, *Yemen*, 33 (no. 11) and 39 (no. 22). These ephemerides are currently being investigated by Michael Hofelich, Frankfurt.

[29] About 140 examples are listed in *Cairo Survey*, no. H78.

[30] King, 'Muwaqqit', section 7, based mainly on E. Strauss, 'Prix et salaires à l'epoque mamlouke: une étude sur l'état économique de l'Égypte et de la Syrie à la fin du moyen âge', *Revue des Études Islamiques*, 17 (1949), 49–94. Unfortunately no information on the salaries of *muwaqqit*s is contained in E. Ashtor's survey of prices and salaries in the medieval Islamic world (1969).

and by the titles of their works to H. Suter in about 1900,[31] but the writings of Ibn al-Shāṭir were not investigated before the 1950s, and the writings of the others not before the 1970s and 1980s. Now that we have an overview of them and can appreciate their scientific merit it is time to investigate the backgrounds of these men and their role in society. This is the difficult part. We have as yet no information on the rise and development of the institution of the *muwaqqit* other than the scraps that can be gathered from the biographies of these men (no doctoral student ready to undertake such a task is available yet), from their libraries, as far as these can be reconstructed (only one has been investigated but with surprising results), and from the *waqfiyyas* of the buildings in which they were employed (information is available for Egypt, that is, Cairo, but not, as far as I am aware, for Damascus or elsewhere). Thus, for example, the *waqfiyya* of the Mosque of the amir Qānim (dated 1446) mentions 900 dirhams per month for the imam, 500 for the preacher, 200 for the muezzin, 200 for the *muwaqqit* and 300 for the servant (!). On the other hand, the *waqfiyya* of the Mosque of al-Muʾayyad (dated 1420) mentions 650 for the Ḥanafī shaykh, 150 for the Shāfiʿī shaykh, . . . and 15 for the muezzin; no *muwaqqit*s are mentioned, which is curious because two well-known astronomers (al-Kawm al-Rīshī, *c.* 1410 and al-Wafāʾī, *c.* 1450) were *muwaqqits* in that mosque.

It has been possible – using marks of ownership in various manuscripts – to reconstruct part of the private library of ʿAbd al-Raḥmān al-Ṭūlūnī, who was imam and *muwaqqit* at the Mosque of Ibn Ṭūlūn in about 1650.[32] Al-Ṭūlūnī compiled a few treatises himself, which are fairly unimpressive, but his library contained, in addition to many of the more recent sophisticated works on time-keeping and instrumentation, a set of highly impressive treatises by various major scientists from earlier centuries, including al-Farghānī, al-Khujandī, al-Bīrūnī and Sharaf al-dīn al-Ṭūsī. But if al-Ṭūlūnī had read any of these there is no evidence of that in his own writings.

The fate of the instruments of the *muwaqqits* is rather sad. A sundial constructed in 1296/7 for the Mosque of Ibn Ṭūlūn was broken into pieces and used to fill a column in the mosque. It was recovered by Marcel, one of the scholars of Napoleon, put back together and copied in ink. One of the workers noticed the French scholars' interest in the pieces and liberated them. Marcel's copy was published in the *Description de l'Egypte*.[33] Al-Ṭanṭāwī, the last *muwaqqit* of any consequence at the Umayyad Mosque in Damascus, who was active around 1875, tried to realign the magnificent sundial of Ibn al-Shāṭir, made in 1371, and broke it. He was able to make a new copy which is still *in situ* on the main minaret of the mosque, and the pieces of the original sundial were used to line various water-conduits under the main courtyard of the

[31] Suter, *MMA*, still the main source for late Islamic astronomy, but to be supplemented by *Cairo Survey* for the late ('post-Sezgin') period. See King, 'Mamluk astronomy', 553–5, for a list of Mamluk astronomers with bibliographical references.

[32] *Cairo Survey*, no. D16. On his library, see King, 'Muwaqqit', section 10.

[33] *Studies*, B-XVI.

mosque. During excavations in 1958 some of the pieces were recovered and they have been set up in the garden of the Archaeological Museum in Damascus.[34] Most of the sundials still found in mosques in Cairo, Damascus and Jerusalem are non-functional, having lost their gnomons. I have seen one in Damascus covered by a drain-pipe.

Tasks accomplished and tasks for the future

There are so few researchers in the field that it is the duty of institutions with the necessary endowments (there are only two at present: the Institut für Geschichte der Arabisch–Islamischen Wissenschaften in Frankfurt and the Furqan Foundation in London) to produce facsimile editions of the best available manuscripts of works of major importance.[35] The treatise of al-Marrākushī was partly translated and partly summarized by the Sédillots *père et fils* in the mid-nineteenth century. With the exception of C. Schoy, who investigated the sundial theory, and myself, no one has worked on it since. G. Saliba is preparing an edition and translation of, and a commentary on the treatise on planetary astronomy by Ibn al-Shāṭir. The one extant *zīj* of the latter should be published in facsimile; no one is working on it at present. I have published a description and analysis of the corpus of tables for timekeeping used in Mamluk Cairo. Together with E. S. Kennedy I have published an analysis of the unusual planetary tables of Ibn al-Majdī. I have also written a detailed analysis of al-Khalīlī's corpus of tables for Damascus. Numerous treatises on instruments are available and merit study; foremost amongst these is the treatise by Ibn al-Sarrāj. The few available astrological writings have yet to be studied. And finally, the biographical dictionaries and chronicles have yet to be exploited for the background information that they could provide relating to Mamluk astronomy.

Interest in astronomy continued apace during the Ottoman period, and materials, both scientific texts and biographical information, are not lacking to continue a survey of Egyptian astronomy down to, say, 1900.[36]

Conclusion

In brief, there is a lot still to be done. If I have been able to convince colleagues that there is such a subject as Mamluk astronomy, that it is perhaps the most colourful chapter in the history of Islamic astronomy, and that historians as

34 Kennedy and Ghanem (eds.), *Ibn al-Shāṭir*, 69–71, and *Paris IMA Catalogue*, 439.

35 D. A. King, 'Some remarks on Islamic scientific manuscripts and instruments and past, present and future research', in J. Cooper (ed.), *The Significance of Islamic Manuscripts* (London, 1992), 115–44, esp. 128–30 and 134.

36 al-Jabartī 's monumental *History of Egypt*, now available in translation with commentary (3 vols., Stuttgart, 1994), provides a remarkable amount of information on several of the astronomers whose works are so well represented in the manuscripts of the Egyptian National Library. These materials merit a separate study in the light of our recently acquired knowledge of the works themselves (see note 5 above).

well as historians of science can contribute to this topic, my present goal will have been achieved. We now know what the *muwaqqit*s wrote, if not how precisely they used their tables and instruments. How they received their training, how they were regarded in the society, what their attitude was to astrology, we do not know. Only when more research has been done will it be possible to say more on the relations of the astronomers, both the *muwaqqit*s and the independent scholars, to the ruling class and on the interest of that class in astronomy and astrology.

CHAPTER 10

The Mamluks as Muslims: the military elite and the construction of Islam in medieval Egypt

JONATHAN P. BERKEY

In recent years, historical scholarship on the Mamluks has significantly revised our view of their role in the intellectual and religious life of the Middle Ages.[1] The Mamluks may still appear on the surface as culturally alien – Turkish rather than Arabic in speech, in some cases only superficially Islamicized, participants in a culture which had its roots in the nomadic, even shamanistic world of Central Asia. Certainly many medieval chroniclers and biographers perceived them to be not only culturally alien but racially unfit for sophisticated intellectual pursuits, and as Ulrich Haarmann has noted, their prejudice has infected our own historical understanding of the Mamluks' place in the culture of medieval Egypt.[2] But we can now be more precise about the contributions they made to the world of religion and scholarship in Cairo and the other cities of the empire.

First and foremost, of course, the Mamluks were responsible for constructing and endowing the lion's share of those mosques and schools in which Muslims worshipped and pupils studied. This was, perhaps, only natural: since the Mamluks controlled the major sources of wealth and revenue, they alone among the various social groups were in a position to make the necessary investment. And in political terms, their investment paid off, since it formed one end of a complex web of patronage through which the ruling elite secured the acceptance and even the support of the *ʿulamāʾ*, the educated class which represented the only other major locus of social power.[3] But the Mamluks' expenditures on the institutional framework of religion and education was not simply a cynical ploy to co-opt potential rivals for political power.

1 See, for example, Barbara Flemming, 'Literary activities in Mamluk halls and barracks', in Myriam Rosen-Ayalon (ed.), *Studies in Memory of Gaston Wiet* (Jerusalem, 1977), 249–60; Donald Little, 'Religion Under the Mamluks', *The Muslim World,* 73 (1983), 165–81; Ulrich Haarmann, 'Arabic in speech, Turkish in lineage: Mamluks and their sons in the intellectual life of fourteenth-century Egypt and Syria', *Journal of Semitic Studies,* 33 (1988), 81–114; Leonor Fernandes, 'Mamluk politics and education: the evidence from two fourteenth century waqfiyya[s]', *Annales Islamologiques,* 23 (1987), 87–98; Jonathan Berkey, *The Transmission of Knowledge in Medieval Cairo: A Social History of Islamic Education* (Princeton, 1992); and Jonathan Berkey, 'Silver threads among the coal': a well-educated Mamlūk of the ninth/fifteenth century', *Studia Islamica,* 73 (1991), 109–25.

2 Haarmann, 'Arabic in speech, Turkish in lineage', 81–3.

3 Ira Lapidus, *Muslim Cities in the Later Middle Ages* (Cambridge, Mass., 1967).

As I have argued elsewhere, many of those individual soldiers and statesmen who made the decision to endow an institution of worship or learning did so out of a genuine interest in the religious and educational activities that took place within them.

That said, it comes as no surprise to find numerous members of the military elite participating actively in the transmission of religious texts and knowledge. We know, after all, that basic instruction in Arabic and in the religious sciences formed an important part of the training to which all young Mamluks were subjected, a part of their acculturation into the society over which they would rule. Many Mamluks, who were, after all, selected primarily for their physical vigour and martial potential, no doubt displayed little aptitude or interest in such bookish pursuits, but others could be found engaged in reading, studying, and even reciting and transmitting some of the fundamental works of Islamic religion and law, especially various collections of *ḥadīth*.

There is at least one aspect of this interest on the part of the Mamluks in education and the transmission of religious texts which has not yet received all the attention it deserves. The chronicles and biographical dictionaries of the period are full of accounts of Mamluks, in particular sultans, intervening directly in debates and disputes among leading members of the scholarly establishment. One of the more famous such episodes, and one which has received extensive treatment in a recent monograph, was that which erupted during the reign of Qāytbāy over the orthodoxy of the Ṣūfī poet Ibn al-Fāriḍ, a dispute in which the sultan and other ranking members of the military elite took an active and, perhaps, decisive role.[4] The construction of a dome over the tomb of Ibn al-Fāriḍ by a prominent Mamluk amir in the late fifteenth century, a physical marker of the saint's popularity and respectability, was only one of the more concrete and visible means by which a Mamluk could affect the outcome of religious debate.

The picture of the Mamluks' role in intellectual and religious life which I have been describing is fundamentally a revisionist one. It seeks to present the Mamluks as something other than two-dimensional characters, riotous boors unconcerned with and unconnected to the more refined and sophisticated cultural patterns of those over whom they ruled. I am increasingly concerned, however, that this picture is in itself not complete, that the question of the Mamluks' place in the cultural life of the Middle East is even yet more complex and multi-dimensional. What I would like to do in this chapter is to sketch the outlines – the barest outlines, I should stress – of another level on which this subject could be tackled.

The question of the role played by the Mamluks in the intellectual and religious life of Egypt and Syria in the Middle Ages is all the more critical because

[4] T. Emil Homerin, *From Arab Poet to Muslim Saint: Ibn al-Fāriḍ, his Verse, and his Shrine* (Columbia, S.C., 1994), esp. 55–75. Cf. Michael Winter: *Society and Religion in Early Ottoman Egypt: Studies in the Writings of ʿAbd al-Wahhāb al-Shaʿrānī* (New Brunswick, N.J., 1982), 160–5.

of what I perceive to be a certain instability in the very definition of 'Islam' in this period. I suspect that no serious historian would overtly claim that Islam represents a monolithic and unchanging entity, fixed for all time in a form which those who claim to be Muslims may or may not fully approximate. After the polemical debates of recent decades, to do so would be to expose oneself to the charge of being an 'Orientalist'. More seriously, it would also suggest a failure to take into account the scholarship of the last twenty or thirty years which has painted an ever more detailed and nuanced picture of Muslim life in all times and places. Some historians have gone so far as to raise the question whether 'Islam' itself can be coherently discussed, or at least whether 'Islamic civilization' is a meaningful unit of analysis.[5]

Nonetheless, we still suffer, I think, from a residual and perhaps unconscious tendency to treat Islam as a clearly defined object, one with which marginal groups such as the Mamluks might interact, but one whose identity they played no positive role in shaping. Naturally we could cite plenty of excuses for treating both Islam and the Mamluks in this way. Muslims themselves, of course, glorify and idealize the first generations of Islamic history, an attitude which found graphic expression in a *ḥadīth* attributed to the Prophet (and one quoted by the Mamluk-period jurist Ibn al-Ḥājj). The best of generations, Muḥammad is reported to have said, is my own, followed by that which comes next, followed in turn by that which follows. But as for those that come after . . . the Prophet indicated with a wave of his hand that they would amount to nothing.[6] With the articulation of the doctrine of the 'closing of the gates of independent reasoning (*ijtihād*)' and its corollary, the requirement of *taqlīd* ('imitation'), a picture formed of an Islam which had, by at least the twelfth century, been authoritatively defined: Islam had been set in concrete, and the Mamluks (as well as other later Muslims) could only aspire to follow the path laid down before them.[7] Moreover, the Mamluks themselves by their behaviour lent credence to the notion that, whatever their formal profession of faith,

[5] Compare the remarks of Edmund Burke III in his conclusion, 'Islamic history as world history: Marshall G. S. Hodgson and *The Venture of Islam*', in Marshall G. S. Hodgson, *Rethinking World History: Essays on Europe, Islam, and World History*, ed. Edmund Burke III (Cambridge, 1993), 314–19, 327–8.

[6] Cited in Ibn al-Ḥājj, *Madkhal al-shar' al-sharīf* (Cairo, 1929), 4 vols., vol. I, 73.

[7] It is worth noting, however, that the impossibility of some scholar or scholars exercising *ijtihād* at some level was not universally accepted, and that this issue was particularly fierce at the end of the fifteenth century. Jalāl al-dīn al-Suyūṭī (d. 1505), the great scholar noted for his exalted opinion of himself, insisted upon his right as a *mujtahid* to exercise independent reasoning. To be sure, he carefully distinguished his claim from the more sweeping assertion that the entire system of law needed to be reformulated, a position he apparently rejected; his claim was simply to exercise independent reasoning in matters left untreated or unclear by earlier legal authorities. Elizabeth Sartain, *Jalāl al-dīn al-Suyūṭī*, vol. I: *Biography and Background*, (Cambridge, 1975), 61–71. Nonetheless, al-Suyūṭī's claims, and in particular the fact that they generated such hostility, and also that they were understood by some to be more categorical than he himself indicated, seem to me to suggest both the breadth and depth of the ideological commitment to *taqlīd* ('imitation') on the part of the community, and also the persistence of notions of change or movement among at least certain sectors of the educated class.

a vast cultural if not religious gap separated them from their Muslim subjects and from Islam. Mamluk-period chronicles are, as we all know, full of anecdotes describing antics and activities on the part of the Mamluk amirs which patently contravene Islamic guidelines and values; even after discounting such stories to counteract the hostility of writers such as al-Maqrīzī, it is easy to conclude that many Mamluks lived in a state of confrontation with Islam, rather than one of symbiosis. Many Mamluks may have sought to participate in 'Islamic' activities such as the transmission of the religious sciences, as I described earlier, but we may wonder how well the majority of them succeeded: the famous scholar Ibn Ḥajar al-ʿAsqalānī, for example, scorned the intellectual efforts of his own Mamluk son-in-law, dismissing his efforts to copy a famous collection of *ḥadīth* as 'worth less than the paper [on which it was written]'.[8]

But we may wish to rethink the schema that casts Islam and the Islamic establishment, on the one hand, and the Mamluks (as well as other social groups) on the other, in interacting but thoroughly independent roles. The problem, as I see it, lies not so much in our understanding of the Mamluks as in our conceptualization of that 'Islam' which the Mamluks and their contemporaries inherited. The model that differentiates sharply between, say, the *ʿulamāʾ* and the Mamluks perhaps inevitably risks making ontological distinctions between 'high' culture and 'low' culture, distinctions which historians in other fields have, of late, largely rejected. Recently several Islamists have begun to challenge this dichotomy in our own field of study.[9] Marilyn Waldman, for example, has noted that the different cultural strata seem, in most Islamic societies, 'to be present in varying proportions simultaneously in most specific cultural settings'.[10]

These issues – and behind them, the struggle over the identity and character of Islam – became more heated during the Mamluk period. This development may perhaps be reflected most clearly in one particular aspect of the cultural history of Mamluk Egypt and Syria: namely, the flurry of treatises produced condemning innovations in the beliefs and customs and especially the religious practices of the people of the time. Not, of course, that treatises against innovations were new: there was a long tradition of such works, an inevitable by-product of an intellectual framework which made normative the idealized 'golden age' of Islam's first decades, and which traced to the Prophet himself the dictum that 'every new thing is an innovation, and every innova-

[8] Cited in Berkey, *Transmission of Knowledge*, 151.

[9] See, for example, Marilyn Waldman: 'Primitive mind/modern mind: new approaches to an old problem applied to Islam', in Richard C. Martin (ed.), *Approaches to Islam in Religious Studies* (Tucson, 1985), 91–105. On the medieval period, see Boaz Shoshan, 'High culture and popular culture in medieval Islam', *Studia Islamica,* 73 (1991), 67–109, and Boaz Shoshan, *Popular Culture in Medieval Cairo (*Cambridge, 1993). See also the present writer's 'Tradition, innovation and the social construction of knowledge in the medieval Islamic Near East', *Past & Present*, vol. 146 (1995), pp. 38–65, from which much of the following argument is derived.

[10] Waldman, 'Primitive mind/modern mind', 94.

tion is an error, and every error leads to Hell'.[11] But the Mamluk period did see something of a boom in the production of such works. Ibn al-Ḥājj's long treatise is of course well known, and the passion with which it is written suggests the level of concern and interest generated by the topic, but it has plenty of company, including tracts by Abū Shāma, Ibn Baydakīn al-Turkumānī, an early sixteenth century Sufi named ʿAlī b. Maymūn al-Idrīsī, and of course the irrepressible Ibn Taymiyya.[12]

The significance of the controversy over innovations may become clear if we step outside the texts themselves, and try to understand the Mamluk regime and its impact on the society and culture of Egypt and Syria as part of a broader pattern of disturbance and challenge in the medieval Islamic Near East. The centuries between, say, the arrival of the Crusaders and the conquest of Egypt and the Levant by the Ottomans were ones of enormous upheaval in the social, political and cultural fabric of the Islamic societies of the Near East. The European Crusaders were in some ways the least of the problems faced by contemporary Muslims: more threatening to the social and political order were the repeated waves of Turkic and Mongol invasion and settlement, culminating in the continual stream of immigrating Mamluks themselves. The challenge posed by these immigrants and conquerors, I suspect, lay at the roots of the feeling of vulnerability and decay which fuelled the frustrations of men such as Ibn al-Ḥājj and Ibn Taymiyya, and of their articulation of a rigorously traditional ideology. This was especially true of those Turkish and other Central Asian immigrants who, in states such as that of the Mamluks, dominated the area politically and militarily, since they, unlike the Europeans, for the most part converted to Islam, and therefore had an opportunity to influence Muslim society from within. One of the major desiderata of Mamluk studies must be an investigation of the ways in which alternative patterns of thought and practice, those associated with the new Turkish elite, may have challenged older Islamic patterns and influenced them.

Islamic social and cultural practice was under pressure not only from external sources during the later Middle Ages. Internal forces, too, threatened changes which could only undermine, subvert or at least modify established normative practice. This was certainly true with regard to politics. Egypt, like Syria and other lands at the eastern end of the Mediterranean, was subjected over the centuries to the rule of self-consciously Shīʿī and militantly Sunnī

[11] Cited in Ibn al-Ḥājj: *Madkhal al-sharʿ al-sharīf*, vol. I, 79. For an invaluable analytical catalogue of this genre, see Maribel Fierro, 'The treatises against innovations (*kutub al-bidaʿ*)', *Der Islam*, 69 (1992), 204–46.

[12] Abū Shāma (d. 1267), *al-Bāʿith ʿalā inkār al-bidaʿ wa-'l-ḥawādith* (Cairo, 1955); Ibn Taymiyya (d. 1328), *Iqtiḍāʾ al-ṣirāṭ al-mustaqīm mukhālafat aṣḥāb al-jaḥīm* (Cairo, 1950), trans. Muhammad Umar Memon as *Ibn Taymīya's Struggle against Popular Religion* (Paris, 1976); Ibn Baydakīn al-Turkumānī (fl. late fourteenth century), *al-Lumaʿ fī 'l-ḥawādith wa-'l-bidaʿ*, ed. Subhi Labib (Wiesbaden, 1986), in 2 vols.; ʿAlī b. Maymūn al-Idrīsī, '*Bayān ghurbat al-islām bi-wāsiṭat ṣinfay al-mutafaqqiha wa-'l-mutafaqqira min ahl Miṣr wa-'l-Shām wa-mā yalīhimā min bilād al-aʿjām*', Princeton Garret MS 828H.

regimes, regimes which often identified themselves in opposition to their rivals and competed with them for the religious allegiance of the Muslim population. The Black Death, which swept through the Middle East repeatedly during the fourteenth and fifteenth centuries, had an enormous impact on Egyptian society which has been measured in an oustanding monograph by Michael Dols. Its effects were tremendous but by no means uniform: on the one hand, the omnipresence of death left Muslims with a renewed commitment to Islam and to formal expressions of piety and morality, and on the other it carved a deeper niche for mysticism, magic, and other expressions of popular religion.[13] A recurring fear of the opponents of innovation was the influence that indigenous non-Muslims, or recent converts to Islam, might have on believers. The process of Islamization was not complete in the thirteenth, fourteenth and fifteenth centuries, and Egypt in particular may well have seen large-scale conversions of Copts to Islam in this period.[14] Proselytes, of course, often carried with them much psychological and ritual baggage, and must have, in various ways, enriched their new community of faith with customs and beliefs that an Ibn al-Ḥājj might well consider 'innovations'. Indeed, Ibn Baydakīn al-Turkumānī specifically alleges that the popularity among Muslims of certain festivals of Coptic Christian origin was a consequence of their practice by Christian converts to Islam.[15]

The point is that what Marshall Hodgson referred to as the 'Islamic Middle Period' was one in which social, political, cultural and even religious institutions and practices were all in a state of flux. That being so, might we not see the polemics of men such as Ibn al-Ḥājj and Ibn Taymiyya, not so much as rearguard actions to defend an Islam they had inherited intact from earlier generations, but rather as an attempt to assert control, to define authoritatively a cultural complex which had always been fluid and dynamic, but which, through a variety of external and internal pressures, looked to their eyes to be on the verge of spiralling out of control? If so, what may be of interest to the present audience is considering the possibility that the Mamluks may have had a positive role, albeit a limited one, in the emergence and acceptance of practices or convictions, or simply emphases as to what was important, which became, at least in the eyes of some, characteristic of 'Islam', broadly defined. Ibn al-Ḥājj, for example, condemns the practice of the melodic singing of the call to prayer, as a result of which, he says, no one can understand the muezzin's words. Interestingly, although he acknowledges that the custom was by his day widespread, he traces this 'innovation' specifically to certain Mamluk amirs who had, he claimed, instituted the practice at the *madrasas*

[13] Michael Dols, *The Black Death in the Middle East* (Princeton, 1977).

[14] See, for example, Donald Little, 'Coptic conversion to Islam under the Baḥrī Mamlūks, 692–755/1293–1354', *Bulletin of the School of Oriental and African Studies*, 39 (1976), 552–69.

[15] Subhi Labib, 'The problem of the *bida*' in the light of an Arabic manuscript of the 14th century', in A. K. Ghosh et al (eds.) *Proceedings of the 26th International Congress of Orientalists, 1964*, (New Delhi, 1970), 4 vols., vol. IV, 277.

they had constructed.[16] Similarly, he blames the Mamluks – literally, 'those who hold the reins of political power' (*man lahu riyāsa fi 'l-dawla*) – for the custom of having muezzins walk at the front of funeral processions, leading the mourners in chanting '*allāhu akbar*'. This, too, he says, began among certain members of the ruling elite, from which it soon spread among the people more generally, until it became one of the most commonly recognized features of funeral rituals.[17]

The writers of treatises against innovations mourned the loss of a world in which the scholars of religion stood out in the crowd, in which they were easily identifiable by their learning and their reverence, and in which the rest of the population held them in awe and respect. We may wonder whether that world ever existed outside their imaginations; certainly in the Mamluk period it represented little more than a wistful memory. Ibn al-Ḥājj, again, complained bitterly that the scholars now flocked to the doors of those who held political and social power, seeking their approval, and currying their favour through praise and flattery[18] – the sincerest form of which, of course, is imitation. If a Mamluk was immediately identifiable through his ethnicity, his language, his monopoly on political or military power, the same could not exactly be said of the *ʿulamāʾ*. As I have argued elsewhere, one of the most salient and admirable features of medieval Islam was the openness of its system of transmitting knowledge.[19] That system was always personal, oral and accessible, and in the absence of any formal institutional system of control, the *ʿulamāʾ* remained an inherently open and permeable body, and included not only professional teachers, but a host of educated or semi-educated individuals active on the margins of intellectual life. Moreover, the openness of the scholarly class inevitably rendered the category of religious knowledge itself somewhat porous, as men such as Ibn al-Ḥājj accurately perceived. Consequently, much of his treatise focuses on attempting to define the parameters of *ʿilm* and *ʿibādāt* which, from his perspective, were undermined by innovation and popular customs, innovations and customs which might be absorbed from every stratum of the society, including its ruling elite.

It would be easy to overstress my point. I am not trying to suggest that, in a religious atmosphere in which human models were the points of reference by which individual Muslims guided their lives, by the later Middle Ages the Mamluks had become lodestars for religious thought and behaviour. I am trying to suggest, however, that the question of the place of the Mamluks in the religious and cultural life of the society they ruled should not be reduced to one of asking how thoroughly the Mamluks participated in already established intellectual and cultural patterns and practices. The controversy over Ibn al-Fāriḍ, involving Qāytbāy and other leading Mamluks as well as ranking scholars and the popular crowds, may point to the potential of dif-

[16] Ibn al-Ḥājj: *Madkhal al-sharʿ al-sharīf*, vol. II, 244. [17] Ibid., vol. II, 263.
[18] Ibid., vol. II, 111–12. [19] Berkey, *Transmission of Knowledge*.

ferent social strata to influence the setting of standards for acceptable religious practice and behaviour, at least in certain areas. And such opportunities were more common than we might, at first, suspect. Ulrich Haarmann, in an important article, drew our attention to a Mamluk named Alṭunbughā al-Jāwulī (d. 1343), a scholar in his own right who was a partisan of the strict teachings of Ibn Taymiyya, and who thus was indubitably Muslim. Yet this same Mamluk was criticized by Ibn Ḥajar al-ʿAsqalānī for his addiction to alchemy, which reminds us of the complex of magic, alchemy, and divination that saturated the Mamluk elite, and which grew out of their shamanistic Central Asian background.[20] Yet magic, alchemy and divination were of course also staples of folk practice and even religious belief in Egypt and throughout the Near East. Might such customs have provided yet another point of contact between Mamluks and locals, a field of religio-cultural practice to which the Mamluks were especially poised to contribute?

Bearing in mind that Islam as a cultural complex was in a dynamic rather than a static state, we should be open to the possibility that the Mamluks (and, indeed, all social groups) participated actively and positively in the construction of 'Islam', as it was known and understood at the time. Given the state of the research, I am not prepared at this point to offer any definitive answers. Let me simply conclude by making some suggestions and observations drawn from two underutilized sources from the tail end of the Mamluk period.

Two separate accounts have survived of the meetings of a reading and discussion circle held in the presence of the sultan Qanṣūh al-Ghawrī, one by a court poet, the other of unknown authorship. These texts were first brought to our attention by an Egyptian scholar at the Twentieth International Congress of Orientalists, held in 1938; were published in Cairo in 1941; were treated briefly by Barbara Flemming in several important articles; and have been mentioned occasionally by other historians.[21] Despite certain difficulties with their use, they are fascinating documents, and well repay re-reading.

The scope of issues and topics dealt with by these royal *majālis* was truly prodigious. Many of them were dominated by discussions of a superficial nature, in which the participants exchanged jokes, riddles and amusing stories. Some of these exchanges had no moral or didactic character whatsoever, as for example that in which one participant posed the question: what bird is it which is found the world over, which can be eaten baked or fried, and which has no

[20] Haarmann, 'Arabic in speech, Turkish in lineage', 96–7.

[21] The texts themselves are: Ḥusayn b. Muḥammad al-Ḥusaynī: *Nafāʾis al-majālis al-sulṭāniyya fī ḥaqāʾiq asrār al-qurʾāniyya*, and Anonymous, *al-Kawkab al-durrī fī masāʾil al-Ghūrī*, ed. ʿAbd al-Wahhāb ʿAzzām, *Majālis al-sulṭān al-Ghawrī* (Cairo, 1941). See also Mohammad Awad, 'Sultan al-Ghawri. His place in literature and learning (three books written under his patronage)', in *Actes du XXe congrès international des orientalistes* (Louvain, 1940), 321–2; Flemming, 'Literary activities in Mamluk halls and barracks;' Barbara Flemming, 'Aus den Nachtgesprächen Sultan Ġaurīs', *Folia rara Wolfgang Voigt . . . dedicata* (Wiesbaden, 1976), 22–8.

hands or mouth, neither legs nor tail, brains nor blood, bones nor down? Sultan al-Ghawrī himself is credited with the answer to this easy riddle: an egg.[22] More often, however, even the jokes and riddles had a pronounced religious content, such as that concerning the bedouin who was found eating a piece of fruit during the daytime in Ramaḍān. When asked why he had deliberately broken his fast, he replied that he had read in the Koran the injunction 'Eat the fruit of [the trees]' (6:141), and had feared that if he did not eat the fruit right away, he might die before sunset, and thereby end his life in a state of sin.[23] On a separate occasion, the gathering discussed whether there was an act which it was *ḥarām* both to do and not to do (the answer being prayer performed by a drunkard), and whether, according to the different schools of law, swallowing a gold coin invalidated one's fast.[24]

More often, however, the discussions took a more serious turn. They debated, for example, whether or not the game of chess was permitted, an issue that seems to have had a peculiar fascination for the medieval *fuqahā*ʾ, given the number of treatises produced on the subject.[25] A question posed by al-Ghawrī – 'Why is the colour of the heavens green?' – may seem an idle one to our jaded, modern ears, but it was hardly trivial to medieval minds which found an answer in a koranic text.[26] Those present told stories about the Hebrew prophets and Muslim heroes, in particular about Sultan Maḥmūd of Ghazna, who represented a sort of model of righteousness and strength for medieval Islamic rulers.[27] Pre-Islamic figures such as Alexander the Great, Khusrau Anūshirvān, and even Plato were mentioned and, at least ostensibly, quoted.[28] One evening al-Ghawrī and the scholars assembled with him discussed the meaning of a few verses of the poetry of Ibn al-Fāriḍ, and thereby, like Qāytbāy and his entourage, showed themselves attuned to one of the most compelling and persistent intellectual controversies of the Mamluk period.[29]

Many of the discussions centred on various points of law, including prayer, the Islamic law of inheritance, and other matters. If these documents can be trusted, al-Ghawrī took a keen personal interest in matters which directly or potentially touched on his position and authority as sultan. Was it legitimate, he asked, according to the Ḥanafī school of law, for the Friday prayers to be said in the mosque in the Citadel? No doubt he was relieved that the scholars present found ample authority for them in the famous textbook *al-Hidāya* and other works of Ḥanafī law.[30] Perhaps the sultan was less sanguine about the equivocal response of the *ʿulamā*ʾ to another of his questions: namely, whether or not an individual who had established charitable endowments on behalf of the poor could himself benefit from those endowments if his circumstances were transformed, and he were to find himself among the *fuqarā' wa-'l-*

[22] Al-Ḥusaynī, *Nafā'is al-majālis,* 22. [23] Ibid., 9. [24] Ibid., 9, 11.
[25] Ibid., 57–8; *al-Kawkab al-durrī*, 34. [26] *al-Kawkab al-durrī*, 88.
[27] Al-Ḥusaynī, *Nafā'is al-majālis*, 59–60, 82–3. [28] Ibid., 34. [29] *al-Kawkab al-durrī*, 46.
[30] Ibid., 80–1. The textbook *al-Hidāya* was written by Burhān al-dīn ʿAlī b. Abī Bakr al-Marghīnānī (d. 1197).

masākīn.[31] As Carl Petry has shown us, al-Ghawrī was a prodigious endower of *awqāf*, and in the tumultuous conditions of late Mamluk politics, he may, in asking this question, have had someone very close in mind.

Among the most interesting discussions are those in which the participants debated the meanings of various koranic verses. Those discussions took a familiar form: one participant, often the sultan himself, posed a question about some ambiguous statement in the Koran, to which one or more answers might be given. One evening, for example, they debated the meaning of the verse 'He [who] takes the living from the dead, and the dead from the living' (*[man] yukhriju al-ḥayy min al-mayyit wa-yukhriju 'al-mayyit min al-ḥayy*) (10:31). One scholar present, identified only as Sharīf Nūr Allāh, explained that the expression referred to the appearance of a chicken from an egg, and of an egg from a chicken. Al-Ghawrī apparently found this explanation amusing, since he said to the *sharīf*, with evident sarcasm: 'Truly, you have enlightened us [concerning] this verse. May God whiten your face in this world and the next' – punning, of course, on the word 'egg' (*bayḍa*) and the verb 'to whiten' (*yubayyiḍu*). Nūr Allāh was startled by this response, and he tried to justify his view by claiming that he had read it in *tafsīr*. The hapless scholar was embarrassed, however, when numerous works of exegesis were brought, and nothing comparable to his explanation could be found. At that, according to the document, the sultan laughed, and gave his own explication of the verse: that a virtuous boy can be produced by an ignorant father, and an ignorant son by a virtuous man.[32]

It is worth pausing at this point to look more closely at certain features of this episode, as recounted by one of the two texts under discussion. That al-Ghawrī emerged from the occasion as the hero is no accident: both of the two texts were written in some manner for the sultan, and a high degree of flattery is present in each. On another occasion, the texts claim that a scholar of as high standing as Jalāl al-dīn al-Suyūṭī praised the acumen of al-Ghawrī in explicating the Koran.[33] On a different night, someone identified only as the '*shaykh al-islām*' complimented al-Ghawrī for his exegesis, saying with some hyperbole: 'There is nothing in the world to match the sultan's intellect, his preparation, and his understanding'. The shaykh then prostrated himself before the ruler and exclaimed: 'Were it not for the wonder of the sultanate and the sacredness of the kingdom, I would dance for joy in this *majlis* for hearing such a subtle answer, and such marvellous words!'[34] Such fulsome praise should probably put us on our guard, although whether the report is accurate or not, it certainly confirms Ibn al-Ḥājj's complaint that the '*ulamā*' – whether al-Suyūṭī, the *shaykh al-islām*, or the court scholars who produced these works – eagerly sought the approbation of 'those who hold the reigns of political power'. But we need not accept uncritically their generous appraisal

[31] *al-Kawkab al-durrī*, 34–5. [32] Ibid., 86. [33] al-Ḥusaynī, *Nafā'is al-majālis*, 5–6.
[34] *al-Kawkab al-durri*, 34.

of al-Ghawrī's intellectual abilities to note certain things about these sessions. They indicate, in the first place, a relatively vigorous exchange of ideas. That exchange was not perhaps altogether a free one – on one occasion, the sultan took aside the author of one of the texts to demand that he bring to the next meeting '*fatwās*' from reputable scholars proving that the brothers of the prophet Joseph were not in fact prophets themselves, threatening, if he failed to do so, to cut off his beard.[35] But they were vigorous, nonetheless: the debate which might have been ended by the scissors of a barber in fact turned on the acceptability of the famous work of *tafsīr*, *al-Kashshāf*, by al-Zamakhsharī, in light of its author's reputed Muʿtazilī sympathies. The accounts may exaggerate the sultan's wit, but he consistently emerges from them as one who took an active and aggressive role in the discussions.

Accounts such as these, read sympathetically, may begin to point to a refined understanding of the place of the Mamluks in the intellectual and religious life of medieval Egyptian society. To be sure, even a charitable reading of them would not suggest that we need to place al-Ghawrī in the leading ranks of the intelligentsia of his day. Once the question was raised: what should be done with a man who heaped verbal abuse upon the Prophet? Should one seek to reason with him, or should he be bound and flogged until he died? The sultan perhaps betrayed his instincts and his training by preferring unreservedly the latter course.[36] But it would be wrong to assume that one must have been an intellectual in order to have a profound influence on the common understanding of what it meant to be a Muslim. Accounts such as those of the assemblies in the sultan's presence in fact bear a close resemblance to the records of study circles and preaching sessions held among the people at large, and even among certain groups of 'scholars'.[37] The kinds of issues and questions they faced – stories of the prophets; tales of the heroes of early Islamic and even pre-Islamic history; various points of law and worship; ambiguities in the meaning of the Koran – these are the kinds of issues and questions which, for most Muslims, went a good part of the way toward defining 'Islam' as they understood and experienced it. As jurists such as Ibn al-Ḥājj were painfully aware, religious belief and practice were, in a way, redefined by each succeeding generation. There was nothing to prevent the Mamluks, as well as any other social group, from participating in the dynamic process of constructing and reconstructing Islam.

[35] Al-Ḥusaynī: *Nafāʾis al-majālis*, 140. [36] Ibid., 18.
[37] I am currently preparing a study of one such record, dating from the sixteenth century.

CHAPTER 11

The late triumph of the Persian bow: critical voices on the Mamluk monopoly on weaponry

ULRICH HAARMANN

The exclusive Mamluk entitlement to carry arms and to ride on horseback has provoked numerous surprised comments by European travellers of the fourteenth, fifteenth and early sixteenth centuries. When coming to Palestine or Egypt they saw, with their own eyes, that the native, Arabic-speaking, Muslim population – the Saracens or Moors of the Western travelogues – was excluded from this privilege.[1] Whoever trespassed this law was – at least in principle – subject to severe punishment, even though the Castilian Pero Tafur, who visited Egypt under Sultan al-Ashraf Barsbāy (r. 1421–35), certainly exaggerated when he claimed that 'Moors' riding a horse were doomed to be executed.[2] For some foreign observers, horseman and Mamluk even were, for all practical purposes, synonymous terms. The contemporary Arabic sources corroborate the role of the horse as the most cherished symbol of rank and prestige.[3] Emmanuel Piloti of Crete[4] who saw the country in the 1440s declares the

The research towards this chaper was carried out during a one-term visitorship at the School of Historical Studies at the Institute for Advanced Study in Princeton in spring/summer 1992. My stay in Princeton was generously supported by a grant of the Breuninger-Stiftung, Stuttgart, which is herewith gratefully acknowledged.

1 On this subject see my article, 'Mit dem Pfeil, dem Bogen – Fremde und einheimische Stimmen zu der Kriegskunst der Mamluken', in Harry Kühnel (ed.), *Kommunikation zwischen Orient und Okzident. Alltag und Sachkultur. Internationaler Kongress Krems an der Donau 6. bis 9. Oktober 1992*. Sitzungsberichte der Österreichischen Akademie der Wissenschaften. Philosophisch-historische Klasse, vol. DCXIX, Veröffentlichungen des Instituts für Realienkunde des Mittelalters und der frühen Neuzeit, vol. XVI, (Vienna, 1994), 223–49. Much of the material used for the present article is contained in this earlier publication.

2 Pero Tafur, *Travels and Adventures 1435 – 1439*, trans. and ed. with an introduction by Malcolm Letts (The Broadway Travellers, London, 1926), 74.

3 Cf. al-Sakhāwī, *al-Ḍaw' al-lāmi' li-ahl al-qarn al-tāsi'*, 2nd edn, Beirut, n.d. vol. III, 201, no. 761: Barqūq's grandson and Faraj's son Khalīl has to fight for the privilege to ride his own horse. In the beginning he is only granted the right to use the governor's horse to attend the Friday prayer, then receives his own horse, loses it again, and in the end is given his own steed (even with a golden cover) permanently. Another interesting biography in this context can be mentioned here, Sūdūn al-Balaṭī 'on horseback', see *Ḍaw'*, vol. III, 277f., no. 1055.

4 Emmanuel Piloti, *L'Egypte au commencement du quinzième siècle d'après le traité d'Emmanuel Piloti de Crète*, (ed.) P. H. Dopp (Cairo, 1950), 11.

sword the distinctive feature of the Mamluk elite. Only the Mamluks, not the two other 'nations' of Egypt – i.e. the bedouins (Arabs) and Saracens – may bear it. The German dominican Felix Fabri,[5] one of the most informative European sources on the Mamluk sultanate during the last quarter of the fifteenth century, appears to be the sole Western traveller to hint at both privileges simultaneously: 'They [i.e. the Mamluks] do not allow the Saracens to serve as soldiers nor do they permit them the carrying of arms.' In his opinion, wherever these wondrous ideas originated, the sons of Mamluks (who by virtue of their Muslim birth were not eligible for full membership in the ruling caste of their fathers) converted in large flocks to Christianity. Only so could they hope to be counted as full-fledged Mamluks and thus find the gate open towards 'mounting a horse and bearing weapons', he continues. When visiting Egypt in 1384, Leonardo Frescobaldi of Florence states, full of surprise, that although 'the men of Egypt are the vilest' one can possibly imagine, they nevertheless always remain unarmed.[6]

How did these Moors or Saracens, i.e. the non-Mamluk Muslims of the country, see this discrimination directed against their own group? The precarious and tenuous relationship between the two dominant layers of late medieval Egyptian and Syrian society, the civilian and military elites, is also reflected in the contemporary literature on *furūsiyya*: literally, the crafts to be mastered by a *fāris*, a mounted archer. *Furūsiyya* encompassed the whole realm of warfare and weaponry,[7] i.e. subjects which everybody knew to be a Mamluk *chasse gardée*. The Mamluks and their non-military partisans were liable to see (and, if deemed necessary, to present) the Mamluk monopoly on arms and horses as a lawful and necessary social given. After all, it had been they who had saved the Muslim polity west of the Syrian desert from perdition in the crucial battles against the Mongol and Christian infidels in the thirteenth century. From this historical achievement they derived their ongoing claim for political domination and for the exploitation of the economic resources of the country.

The members of the autochthonous civilian elite, however, had a more difficult stance. All begrudging gratitude for the Mamluk contribution towards the survival of Islam notwithstanding, they were bound to see the

[5] Felix Fabri, *Evagatorium*, quoted from the French translation, *Voyage en Egypte de Felix Fabri 1483,* Collection des voyageurs occidentaux en Egypte, vol. XIV, (Cairo, 1975), 553.

[6] Leonardo Frescobaldi, Giorgio Gucci and Simone Sigoli, *Visit to the Holy Places of Egypt, Sinai, Palestine and Syria in 1384*, trans. from the Italian by Fr Theophilus Bellorini and Eugene Hoade, Publications of the Studium Biblicum Franciscanum, 6 (Jerusalem, 1948), 48.

[7] See also the division of Arabic – one should rather say, Islamic – military literature into (a) horsemanship, (b) archery, and (c) military tactics and organization, given by G. Rex Smith in his, *Medieval Muslim Horsemanship A Fourteenth-Century Arabic Cavalry Manual (*London, 1979), p.8.

military and social privileges reserved for the alien Mamluks as a problematic infringement upon the lawful Islamic order and as a serious psychological impediment. To them, these prerogatives, at least potentially, constituted a reprehensible innovation (*bidʿa*). And they were also, and foremost, a blatant violation of the pride of Egyptian men. Unless one was prepared to rationalize: Abū Ḥāmid al-Qudsī (d. 1483) – an *ʿālim*, to be true, yet one who was profoundly estraged from his own class and who ingratiated himself with the Mamluks instead – saw the reason for the local Egyptians' abstention from the acquisition of arms in their innate laziness and in their conviction that only the Mamluks were strong enough to defend them successfully.[8]

Let us now briefly turn to the first group of *furūsiyya* authors, i.e. to the professional military writers with a Mamluk background or, if they were non-Mamluks, with close ties to the Mamluk institution. Their treatises[9] often quote pre-Mamluk military works yet basically seem to describe the situation from the mid-thirteenth century onwards when the Ayyubid sultan al-Ṣāliḥ Ayyūb began to recruit Mamluk military slaves in huge numbers and established the practice of training them towards a military career. Both Arabic and – less frequently – Qipchaq or Old Anatolian Turkish are used as languages in these manuals.[10]

These *furūsiyya* works primarily served practical grounds. The Mamluk trainees were to be informed on the exigencies of their job. Undoubtedly for didactic reasons, some of these books were versified. The Mamluk cadets could thus easily, and in their proper sequence, memorize the numerous steps, grips and postures to be mastered in riding, in charging with the lance and in shooting with the crossbow. In the late Mamluk period a certain Minqār al-Ḥalabī wrote a four-hundred-verse *urjūza* on the art of shooting with arrows.[11] Ḥasan 'the Greek' – of uncertain dates – wrote an ode on the Mamluk cross-

8 Abū Ḥāmid al-Qudsī, *Duwal al-islām al-sharīfa al-bahiyya*, ed. Subhi Labib and Ulrich Haarmann, Bibliotheca Islamica, 37 (Beirut/Stuttgart, 1997), 119, lines 11–15.

9 Also in this field the master in Mamluk studies, David Ayalon (Jerusalem), has written an authoritative contribution, 'Notes on the *Furūsiyya* exercises and games in the Mamluk sultanate', *Scripta Hierosolymitana* (Jerusalem), 9 (1961), 31–62, especially 34. The article was reprinted in David Ayalon *The Mamluk Military Society*, Collected Studies Series CS 104 (London, 1979), article 2. A recent panorama of the *furūsiyya* literature, including its literarary sources, can be found in Maya Shatzmiller, 'The Crusades and Islamic warfare – a re-evaluation', *Der Islam*, 69 (1992), 247–88.

10 On the works on horsemanship, arms and warfare as well as hippiatrics written in Turkish see the research done by Kurtuluş Öztopçu, University of California at Los Angeles. On the 1985 MESA conference in New Orleans he presented a paper on 'Early military literature of the Turks and a contribution to the military lexicon of the Middle Turkic' which contained the gist of his Ph.D. project on Mamluk–Qipchaq military treatises. The horse and its place in Mamluk exercices is the topic of Nabīl Muḥammad ʿAbd al-ʿAzīz, *al-Khayl wa-riyāḍatuhā fī ʿaṣr salāṭīn al-mamālīk* (Cairo, 1976).

11 *al-Urjūza al-Ḥalabiyya fī ramy al-sihām ʿan al-qusiyy al-ʿarabiyya*, Carl Brockelmann, *Geschichte der arabischen Litteratur* (Leiden, 1949) (hereafter GAL), vol. II, 136 (170). On his son Jamāl al-dīn Yūsuf, who held various administrative posts in Aleppo in 1490, see *Ḍaw'*, vol. X, 339, no.1284.

bow.[12] The best-known author of such versified *furūsiyya* was the Mamluk Ṭaybughā al-Baklamishī, another 'Greek' *(yūnānī)*. He wrote, at the behest of Sultan al-Ashraf Shaʿbān (r. 1363–77) his famous poem on archery *Ghunyat al-ṭullāb fī maʿrifat ramy al-nushshāb.*[13]

The catalogue of subjects covered by these conventional *furūsiyya* treatises is more or less uniform, although the individual authors tended to emphasize particular issues. The Mamluk Baktūt al-Rammāḥ 'the lancer' (d. 1311), for example, stressed the close ties between the military and the veterinary aspect of *furūsiyya*, a term which in this context should be rendered as 'horsemanship'.[14] Only he who knew how to tend to his sick horse could become a seasoned *fāris*. He carefully studied the question which riding beasts were suitable for the *mujāhid* lancer and which were not.

Other authors placed the *maydān*, the hippodrome, at the centre of their writings. Here the equestrian games and tournaments were held which baffled European visitors to Cairo. Machiavelli (who, in his *Il Principe*, adroitly compares the succession to the papacy and to the Mamluk sultanate, the college of the cardinals and the assembly of the mighty Mamluk amirs[15]) praises their perpetual military exercices.[16] Sophisticated lance-games[17] with special targets, which were either placed on the ground to be lifted by the horse-borne *fāris* or on wooden poles the height of a horse, formed the core of these exercises. The titles of two works, *Tuḥfat al-mujāhidīn fī ʾl-ʿamal bi-ʾl-mayādīn*[18] and *Bughyat al-qāṣidīn bi-ʾl-ʿamal bi-ʾl-mayādīn*[19], 'Gift for God's warriors on the hippodrome' and 'Design for those who wish to excel in the hippodrome', are telling. Their authors were Lājīn al-Ḥusāmī al-Ṭarābulusī (d. 1337–8) and his son Muḥammad. Perhaps the best known *furūsiyya* work produced in Mamluk times is Muḥammad b. ʿĪsā b. Ismāʿīl al-Ḥanafī al-Aqṣarāʾī's *Nihāyat*

[12] Brockelmann, *GAL*, vol. II, 136 (170).

[13] J. D. Latham and W. F. Paterson, *Saracen Archery. An English Version and Exposition of a Mameluke Work on Archery (ca. A.D. 1368) with Introduction, Glossary, and Illustrations* (London, 1970). This work is preserved in numerous manuscripts and with different titles. Cf. Hellmut Ritter, '*La Parure des Cavaliers* und die Literatur über die ritterlichen Künste', *Der Islam*, 18 (1929), 116–54, here 135–9.

[14] See, *GAL, vol.* II, 135 (168); Hassanein Rabie, 'The training of the Mamluk faris', in V. J. Parry and M. E. Yapp (eds.), *War, Technology and Society in the Middle East* (London, 1975), 153–63, here at 155 and note 5.

[15] See the German translation of *Il Principe*, *Der Fürst*, trans. Rudolf Zorn (6th edn Stuttgart, 1978), chap. 19, at 86. I owe this reference to my student Nader Pournaqcheband (Kiel).

[16] *Discorsi. Gedanken über Politik und Staatsführung*, trans. R. Zorn (2nd edn Stuttgart 1977), book 1, chap. 1, at 10.

[17] One of the famous fifteenth-century lance masters was the chamberlain Baydamur al-Ḥājib al-Ṣaghīr, see *Ḍawʾ*, vol. III, 22, no. 107. How dangerous these tournaments were is reported with awe and consternation both in the Arabic sources (see e.g. the vita of the Syrian viceroy Āqbughā al-ʿAlāʾ al-Timrāzī, (d. 1439), who died of an accident in the hippodrome, in *Ḍawʾ*, vol. II, 316f., no. 1012) and in the European travelogues (Fabri, *Voyage*, 554; see also Haarmann, 'Mit dem Pfeil, dem Bogen', 230).

[18] *GAL* II, vol. 135 (168); Ritter, '*La Parure*', 125, 128–30.

[19] *GAL* II, vol. 136 (169); Ritter, '*La Parure*', 131.

al-su'l wa-'l-umniyya fī 'ilm al-furūsiyya written in the middle of the fourteenth century. It is preserved in numerous manuscripts.[20] Its supposed author was not a Mamluk. He rather belonged to those numerous immigrants from Anatolia, Azerbayjan and Iran to Egypt who, as Hanafites and Turks, enjoyed the special favour of the Mamluks who themselves had originally come from those regions. The local *'ulamā'*, quite understandably, tended to view these newcomers from the inclement north with palpable reserve. If one wishes to divide the *furūsiyya* authors into two distinct groups according to their social loyalties, these latter writers should certainly be counted with the Mamluks, and not with the local Egyptian jurists.

Such an attribution to clearly delineated ideological camps is more difficult with those men mentioned here and there in the Arabic biographical works of the fourteenth and fifteenth centuries who, as civilians, acquired expertise in *furūsiyya*. Only a few names should be presented for the time being: the well-known historians Ibn Aybak al-Dawādārī (d. after 1336) and Ibn Taghrībirdī (d. 1467) were proud of their prowess in archery.[21] According to his biographer, Ibn Taghrībirdī had mastered all the different disciplines of *furūsiyya*, including polo.[22] 'Imād al-dīn 'Abd al-Salām b. Abī 'Abdallāh al-Dimashqī (d. 1297–8), evidently of Syrian background, was another champion in the discipline of *al-ramy*.[23] Aḥmad al-Bījūnī, a learned man of fifteenth-century Cairo, studied archery and the handling of heavier weapons with one of the masters (*usṭā*) of the time.[24] Another native, Arabic-speaking Egyptian of this period, Aḥmad b. Muḥammad, known as Ibn al-'Aṭṭār, is credited with having

[20] This work has been edited twice on the basis of different manuscripts, by Lutful Haqq (Ph.D. dissertation, University of London, 1955), and by Nabīl 'Abd al-'Azīz (Ph.D. dissertation, University of Cairo, 1972). see also Ritter, *'La Parure'*, 132, 135; Mohamed Mostafa, 'An illustrated manuscript on chivalry from the late Circassian Mamluk period', *Bulletin de l'Institut d'Égypte* 51 (1969–70), 1–13 (English text), 1–14 (Arabic text), here at 4 (English). On the – contested – authorship of Aqṣarā'ī see also Rabie, *'Mamluk faris'*, 154, n. 6, and Rudolf Sellheim, *Materialien zur arabischen Literaturgeschichte.* Verzeichnis der orientalischen Handschriften in Deutschland. XVII, Reihe A, vol. I (Stuttgart, 1976), 273–5 (no. 72); vol. II (Stuttgart, 1987), 117–18. The particularly famous London manuscript (British Library, Oriental Manuscripts, Add. 18866) has been made the subject of a brief (and most intriguingly illustrated) study by G. Rex Smith, *Medieval Muslim Horsemanship* (London, 1979). See furthermore Geoffrey Tantum, 'Muslim warfare, a study of a medieval Muslim treatise on the art of war', in Robert Elgood (ed.), *Islamic Arms and Armour* (London, 1979), 188; David James, 'Mamluke painting at the time of the 'Lusignan Crusade', 1365–70', *Humaniora Islamica,* 2 (1974), 74, and Boaz Shoshan, *Popular Culture in Medieval Cairo* (Cambridge, 1993), 84, n. 16 and 17.

[21] *Kanz al-durar wa-jāmi' al-ghurar,* vol. IX, ed. Hans Robert Roemer, Quellen zur Geschichte des islamischen Ägyptens, vol. Ii, (Cairo 1960), 122; Ulrich Haarmann, 'Arabic in speech, Turkish in lineage; Mamluks and their sons in the intellectual life of fourteenth-century Egypt and Syria', *Journal of Semitic Studies,* 33 (1988), 81–114, here at 111.

[22] See the references in Ayalon, "*Furūsiyya* exercises', 32, 60.

[23] Sakhāwī, *Kitāb al-Qawl al-tāmm fī faḍl al-ramy bi-'l-sihām,* autograph MS Princeton no. 4759, (herafter *Qawl*) at 114, on the margin. On this precious manuscript, which I consulted during my stay in Princeton in 1987 and 1992, see Rudolf Mach, *Catalogue of Arabic Manuscripts (Yahuda Section) in the Garrett Collection, Princeton University Library (*Princeton, 1977), 410.

[24] *Ḍaw',* vol. II, 66, lines 15–16.

mastered *furūsiyya* in its various branches both 'in theory and practice' (*ʿilman wa-ʿamalan)*[25] in a fashion unmatched among the members of his race in his days, as his biographer Sakhāwī states with unmistakable respect.[26] Ibn al-ʿAṭṭār, an amateur of poetry and history, was *dawādār* 'inkwell-holder, secretary' of various ranks and with different Mamluk employers (including Sultan Jaqmaq). He was thus in a position ideally suited to build bridges between the Mamluk and local, civilian, worlds. Another civilian excelling in the craft of *al-ramy bi-ʾl-nushshāb* (the list is far from complete) was the fifteenth-century Damascene scholar Khaṭṭāb b. ʿUmar al-ʿAjlūnī, who, incidentally, was also a passionate chess player.[27]

As has been mentioned before, the legists of the time had a much more reserved and critical attitude towards Mamluk lore in general and towards the Mamluk monopoly on horsemanship and weaponry in particular. They faced a serious dilemma: they despised the barbarian Mamluks on cultural grounds, yet they knew all too well that it was their Turkish and Circassian overlords who alone had the means to guarantee security and tranquillity in the cities and villages of Egypt. And – more important yet – the Mamluks were the sole active defenders of Sunnī Islam against infidel and sectarian foes. An author like Abū Ḥāmid al-Qudsī (d. 1483) is one of the few to break the silence that was customary among the *ʿulamāʾ* concerning these painful truths.[28]

It is interesting to see how different religious scholars of the time, in their respective books on *furūsiyya*, tried to cope with this dilemma. It was not easy to justify for themselves the reality of the Turco-Circassian monopoly on arms. The systematic study of this question has barely begun. In this research it is helpful to make a clear distinction between the tracts on *furūsiyya* written by representatives of the military (see above), and those composed by jurists.[29] It is the latter group to which we shall now turn.

My analysis is based on three works, written by noted scholars, one of the fourteenth, the other two of the fifteenth century. The first is Ibn Qayyim al-Jawziyya (Ibn al-Qayyim) (d. 1350), the great Ḥanbalī theologian and disciple

[25] This pair of linguistically 'related' notions is to be found also in Suyūṭī's (d. 1505) short tract on archery: see *Ghars al-anshāb fī ʾl-ramy bi-ʾl-nushshāb*, MS Berlin Wetzstein II, 1858, part II, fols. 6b–21a (hereafter *Ghars*), here at fol. 12a. We often encounter it in biograms of Sakhāwī's *Ḍawʾ* in which *furūsiyya* qualities are extolled.

[26] *Ḍawʾ*, vol. II, 82–3, no. 243. See also Sakhāwī's special treatise on archery, *Qawl,* 114 (on the margin). [27] *Ḍawʾ*, vol. III, 181f., no. 709, here at 182, line 18.

[28] On the biographical motives for his voluntary desertion from the *ʿulamāʾ* camp see Ulrich Haarmann, '*Rather the Injustice of the Turks than the Righteousness of the Arabs* – changing *ʿulamaʾ* attitudes towards Mamluk rule in the late fifteenth century', *Studia Islamica,* 68 (1988), 61–77. A critical edition of Abū Ḥāmid al-Qudsī's tract on the 'blessings' accruing to the lands of Egypt from the arrival of the Turks (Mamluks), *Duwal al-islām al-sharīfa al-bahiyya fī mā ẓahara lī min ḥikam Allāh al-khafiyya fī jalb ṭāʾifat al-Atrāk ilā ʾl-diyār al-miṣriyya,* is in the press as vol. XXXVII of *Bibliotheca Islamica*, ed. Subhi Labib and Ulrich Haarmann (Beirut/Stuttgart, 1997).

[29] This salient distinction has not been heeded in Rabie's otherwise masterful article on the chivalrous crafts in Mamluk times.

of Ibn Taymiyya. His book bears the brief title *Kitab al-Furūsiyya*[30] or respectively, as we read in the text itself, the longer variant: *Kitāb al-Furūsiyya al-sharʿiyya al-nabawiyya.* A third rendering is *Kitāb al-furūsiyya al-muḥammadiyya.*[31] The second author is the Shāfiʿī polymath al-Sakhāwī (d. 1497). His work on *furūsiyya* is focused on archery and is named *al-Qawl al-tāmm fī faḍl al-ramy bi-ʾl-sihām*[32]. These two works are related to each other. Sakhāwī has used (and quoted) Ibn al-Qayyim's treatise, although not uncritically of course, since the two authors belonged to different *madhāhib.* Finally, the third writer is the famous, extremely prolific Jalāl al-dīn al-Suyūṭī (d. 1505). He composed a brief epistle on our subject which, however, turns out to be devoid of any major original material: *Ghars al-anshāb fī ʾl-ramy bi-ʾl-nushshāb.*[33]

All three works are explicitly concerned *not* with the practical aspects of fighting and of sports, but rather with the religious foundations of *furūsiyya.* There is enough literature available on the technical aspects of warfare and horsemanship, Sakhāwī[34] justifies his concentration on early Islam, and thus takes conscious notice of the existing copious military literature written by the professional warriors and their intimate associates. As we have seen, Ibn Qayyim al-Jawziyya's work even carries this intrinsic limitation in its title: *On the Prophetic, legally binding* furūsiyya. Quoting the famous Seljuq vizier Niẓām al-Mulk, Sakhāwī[35] emphatically praises the superiority of the weapons of the imams and scholars, through which the legal foundations of the Muslim community were laid, over the weapons of the soldiers.

In consistency with these priorities, the three treatises abound in information on the use of arms in the age of the Prophet and the Companions and on the practice of sports such as racing, swimming and shooting in early Islam. The names quoted are primarily those of the Prophet, ʿUmar, ʿAlī, Khālid b. al-Walīd, as well as those of the founders of the legal schools. With what attitude – support, disdain, or indifference – did the Prophet follow the competitions and athletic activities of his surroundings? How did he himself – the epitome of bravery (*ashjaʿ al-nās*)[36] – use arrows, thus establishing an unimpeachable *sunna*? At Uḥud Muḥammad himself fought with the bow. He is reported to have had three different types of bows (*al-rawḥāʾ, al-bayḍāʾ, al-ṣafrāʾ*) at his disposal.[37] Sakhāwī[38] carefully lists the *ṣaḥāba* known by him to have shot with the crossbow (*al-rumāt min al-ṣaḥāba*). The Companions, 'the warriors of Islam and knights of religion' (*ghuzāt al-islām wa-fawāris al-dīn*),[39] were the perfect and unmatched *furūsiyya* masters. Among the three favourite

[30] Ed. ʿIzzat al-ʿAṭṭār al-Ḥusaynī (Cairo, 1942; second edn Beirut, n.d) (hereafter *Furūsiyya*).
[31] See *Qawl,* 13. [32] See preceding note and n. 23.
[33] See n. 25; see also *GAL,* vol. II, 154 (198), no. 233. Both Ritter, '*La parure*', 143, and Rabie, 'Mamluk faris', 159, n. 4, used the Istanbul MS Ahmet III, no. 2425. In the Berlin MS the text is followed by an equally brief treatise on wrestling (*al-Musāraʿa ilā ʾl-muṣāraʿa*).
[34] *Qawl,* 11. [35] Ibid., 19. [36] *Furūsiyya,* 19, line 14. [37] *Furūsiyya,* 104, lines 14–16.
[38] *Qawl,* 103ff. [39] *Furūsiyya,* 107, line 27.

pastimes of men, riding, women and archery, clearly the latter deserves the highest rank.[40] (The stern ʿUmar replaces the pleasures of love with those of swimming in cold water.[41]) Archery, Sakhāwī emphasizes, can bring as many as three people into Paradise: the producer of the arrow, he who draws – and keeps ready – the bow, and the bowman himself.[42]

Apart from legally binding information about the Prophetic precedent, these books are plentiful in general instruction and edification. We read, for example, about the modalities of fighting, practising, and riding, the psychology of competitive sports,[43] the mistakes the archer as well as the *ṣāniʿ* of the crossbow may make, and (ensuing) injuries and their treatment (*ṭibb al-ramy wa-ʿilāj ʿilalihī wa-āfātihī*).[44] Sakhāwī and Suyūṭī add interesting subchapters on the *awāʾil* ('who was the first to do what and when') in archery[45] and on the Arabic technical vocabulary in this particular domain.[46]

Yet there are also salient differences in these works. They refer to the varying importance the three authors grant to problems of the present. Unlike Ibn al-Qayyim a century earlier, Sakhāwī and Suyūṭī almost totally neglect the issues of their own time, at least explicitly. In Sakhāwī's *Qawl* there is only one direct reference to the Mamluk period, in a marginal note[47] which the author adds to his own autograph. The context is a list of the eminent bowmen of history. Beginning with Gog and Magog, he ends this table with a few representatives of the *mutaʾakhkhirūn* including the two civilians Ibn al-ʿAṭṭār and al-ʿImād (ʿImād al-dīn) ʿAbd al-Salām mentioned above. Most prominent is Anas b. Kitbughā al-Mujāhid: this Anas, the son of the Oyrat-born Mamluk sultan Kitbughā (r. 1294–96), was of a truly legendary strength (*ṣāra awḥad ʿaṣrihī*). Despite his half-blindness he is said to have been able to shoot with a bow weighing 180 Egyptian *raṭl* (roughly 90 kilograms).[48]

Yet there also seem to exist quite a few scattered implicit references to contemporary problems and affairs (possibly including the crucial Mamluk

40 *Qawl*, 32. 41 Ibid., 27. 42 Ibid., 33; *Ghars*, fol. 7a, lines 18–19.

43 *Qawl*, 92, it serves to strengthen the hearts of those competing. Chapter IV in Sakhāwī's book deals with the dictum '*man taʿallama ʾl-ramy thumma tarakahā fa-qad ʿaṣānī*' (who has mastered archery and then neglects it, disobeys me), see 75.

44 *Furūsiyya*, 114, lines 20ff.

45 *Qawl*, chap. VII, 105–15. *Furūsiyya*, 104, lines 13–14, cites Ṭabarī's history according to which Gabriel handed the bow to Adam and made him the first archer of all times. And it is, so Ibn al-Qayyim continues, uncontested that also Ismāʿīl, the son of Abraham, was an archer. Suyūṭī, in *Ghars*, fol. 6b ult. ff., relates – on the authority of Ibn Abī ʾl-Dunyā – that Abraham taught his two sons Isḥāq and Ismāʿīl how to use the bow.

46 *Ghars*, fol. 9b–11a, *Dhikr fawāʾid lughawiyya tataʿallaq bi-ʾl-qaws wa-ʾl-nushshāb wa-ʾl-ramy.* Suyūṭī, a seasoned philologist himself, begins with a quote from Thaʿālibī's *Fiqh al-lugha*. On fol. 11a there follows a separate chapter on the occurrence of these – and of related – terms in Arabic proverbs. See also *Qawl*, chap. VIII, 115–31. The lexicographer will find comparatively little of importance in these lists of Arabic and *muʿarrab* words related to archery; the difference between *sahm*, pl. *sihām*, and *nushshāb*, pl. *nashāshīb*, is a favourite subject.

47 *Qawl*, 114.

48 On Anas and his reputation see also Ayalon, '*Furūsiyya* exercises', 58. Ayalon's source is Ibn Ḥajar al-ʿAsqalānī's biographical dictionary *al-Durar al-kāmina* vol. I, 445–6.

monopoly on *furūsiyya*?) at least in Sakhāwī's *Qawl.* To give only two examples for the time being: in his table of the subcategories of *furūsiyya* – riding, archery, and fighting with lances[49] (Ibn al-Qayyim in one place adds swordcraft as a fourth discipline[50]) – Sakhāwī judiciously reproduces Mamluk tournament and battle activities. In another passage[51] he raises the question whether certain sports – such as polo (*al-laʿib bi-ʾl-kura wa-ʾl-ṣawlajān)*, chess and shooting with the crossbow (*bunduq*)[52], which turn out to be the favourite (and privileged) pastimes of the Mamluks – are permissible or not. The great jurists of early Islam are cited as legal authorities on these activities, although some of them were introduced to the Middle East only *after* the formative period of the *sharīʿa*. Yet this anachronism does not seem to have disturbed the author any further. Legitimizing controversial practices of his own time with proper reference to the old masters seems to have been Sakhāwī's main design in this instance.

Unlike the Shāfiʿī Sakhāwī, the Ḥanbalī[53] Ibn al-Qayyim one century earlier is much more candid and explicit – and at the same time pragmatic – about the problems of his time. Certainly he, too, does not highlight Mamluk topics in his work. Therefore one also has to search for the military themes in his treatise which, according to its title, as has been said, is supposed to deal more or less exclusively with the Prohetic norms. The yield of such a search is, however, surprisingly rich.

Thus Ibn al-Qayyim, like the 'real' military authors, goes into detail about the materials the (hand-)bows are made of, i.e. wood (maple or *shawḥaṭ* wood[54]), sinew (*ʿaqab*), horn, and glue (*gharan, ghirāʾ).*[55] In this constellation our author, a cultured *adīb*, recognizes superior wisdom, for it reminds one of the constituents of man: wood corresponds to bones, horn to flesh, sinews to muscles, and glue to blood.[56] Like Ṭaybughā, the great expert on the practical aspects of archery,[57] Ibn al-Qayyim discusses the 'fundamentals of archery' (*uṣūl al-ramy*) as they are said to have been instituted by Muḥammad.[58] He quotes a current verse by an anonymous poet on the five elementary qualifications the bowman must master: grasping (*qabḍ*), locking (*ʿaqd*), drawing

49 *Qawl,* 30, *al-rukūb wa-ʾl-ramy wa-ʾl-laʿib bi-ʾl-rumḥ.* See also 118 (glossary of pertinent terms) where he speaks of *furūsiyya* only in the limited sense of 'horsemanship', *al-furūsiyya hiya rukūb al-khayl wa-rakḍuhā*, before he switches over to defining *firāsa,* 'physiognomy'.

50 *Furūsiyya*, 107, lines 25–6.

51 *Qawl*, 85.

52 On the permissibility of using the powerful crossbow in hunting see also Idrīs b. Baydakīn al-Turkumānī's anti-*bidʿa* work *al-Lumaʿ fī ʾl-Ḥawādith wa-ʾl-bidaʿ*, ed. Subhi Labib, Deutsches Archäologisches Institut. Quellen zur Geschichte des Islamischen Ägyptens, vol. IIIa, (Cairo and Wiesbaden, 1986), 125–33.

53 Does his membership in the Ḥanbalī *madhhab* at least partially explain his fortitude *vis-à-vis* political authorities?

54 See also *Ghars,* fol. 9b, lines 5ff.

55 *Furūsiyya*, 103, lines 4–5, and 104, line 6. On these constituents of the Mamluk reflexed bow see also Ernst Petrasch et al., *Die Karlsruher Türkenbeute* (Munich, 1991), 217–18.

56 *Furūsiyya*, 104, lines 6–12.

57 Latham and Paterson, *Saracen Archery*, 37ff. (chap. VII).

58 Suyūṭī, in *Ghars*, fol. 12b, lines 8ff., names – in a special subchapter (*qāʿida*) – alternatively four, six, seven or ten *uṣūl al-ramy*.

(*madd*), releasing (*iṭlāq*) and sighting (*naẓar*)[59]. Others, so he goes on – again in consistency with Ṭaybughā's didactic poem *Ghunyat al-ṭullāb* - only count four such *uṣūl*, leaving aside the drawing of the bow. He scrupulously appends nine ancillary qualifications – such as the proper posture of the sitting or standing archer – and states the different physical requirements, including a taxonomy of the parts of the body that move or, respectively, remain stable, during the act of shooting.[60] Ibn al-Qayyim's – main? sole? – source for this excursion into the technicalities of archery is the *Kitāb al-Wāḍiḥ fī (ʿilm) al-ramy wa-ʾl-nushshāb (fī ʾl-rimāya)* written by the contemporary *ustādh* Abū Muḥammad ʿAbd al-Raḥmān b. Aḥmad al-Ṭabarī[61] or (in Suyūṭī's rendering) al-Ṭabaristānī.[62]

Ibn al-Qayyim also mentions the *bunūd*, the 'lance exercises', an intricate subject on which military experts such as Baktūt al-Rammāḥ have concentrated their works.[63] Various manoeuvres are presented here, too: parrying (*tabṭīl*), change of location (*naql*), disenganging from battle (*tasrīḥ*), extricating oneself from difficulties (*nashl*), thrusting (*ṭaʿn*), joining (*dukhūl*) and leaving battle (*khurūj*). Thrusting and parrying are the two essentials (*aṣlān*) in lance games and real battle, Ibn al-Qayyim continues; an experienced lancer has to learn how to perform these two actions in their proper place without confusing them. The metaphors and similes Ibn al-Qayyim employs in this brief technical memorandum for the *rammāḥ* betray his intellectual background. Fighting with the sword and spear is like fighting with proofs and arguments, hitting the target in tournament or battle is like scoring points in a dispute, he continues in carefully composed rhymed prose.[64] There are two *furūsiyyas*, the *furūsiyya* of knowledge and elucidation, and the *furūsiyya* of shooting and thrusting; both have been practised perfectly by the Companions, the paragons of proper manly conduct.[65] So Ibn al-Qayyim elegantly contrives to proffer military prowess and scholarly acumen as equally exemplary modes of behaviour, appropriate for those jointly in charge of society, namely the Mamluk *umarāʾ*, and his own group, the *ʿulamāʾ*.

Certainly the most important passage for our purposes is the discussion of the question whether or not the Persian bows (*qusiyy/qisiyy fārisiyya*)[66] may be employed by righteous Muslims in the time of the author.

59 *Furūsiyya*, 108, lines 5ff. 'on the number of fundamentals of archery'.

60 Ibid., 108, line 24 to 109, line 5.

61 We find him quoted in Ibn al-Qayyim's *Kitāb al-Furūsiyya* in several places (e.g. 110, lines 20ff.; 111, lines 12 and 21; 112, line 6; 113, lines 6 and 8). On Ṭabarī/Ṭabaristānī (cf. following note) see Ritter, '*La Parure*', 136. Ritter refers to the research done by Joachim Hein ('Bogenhandwerk und Bogensport bei den Osmanen nach dem 'Auszug der Abhandlungen der Bogenschützen' . . . des Muṣṭafā Kānī. Ein Beitrag zur Kenntnis des türkischen Handwerks und Vereinswesens', *Der Islam,* 14 (1925), 289–360, here at 299–301). According to Rabie, 'Mamluk faris', 154, n. 2, the author is identical with Aḥmad b. ʿAbdallāh Muḥibb al-dīn al-Ṭabarī, who died in 694/1295.

62 *Ghars*, fols. 12b, line 3; 13a, line 18; 14b, lines 8 and 18.

63 *Furūsiyya*, 18, line 17. On the relevant passages in Baktūt's work and in the *Nihāyat al-suʾl* – as well as in yet other *furūsiyya* treatises – see Rabie, 'Mamluk faris', 156–7 (with notes).

64 *Furūsiyya*, 18, lines 25–8.

65 Ibid., 19, lines 1–6. The connotation of *muruwwa* is evident.

66 Suyūṭī mentions the Persian bow only in one brief phrase (*Ghars,* fol. 9b, line 16) in his paragraph on the nomenclature of bows (*fī tafṣīl asmāʾ al-qusiyy wa-awṣāfihā*).

The context of this excursus is a brief discussion of the rules that are to be observed when judging the individual accomplishment in a competition, whether in racing or archery. If a bow breaks by accident in a contest, can it be replaced only by one of the same type or can bows of a totally different make be substituted? Only the first option – i.e. remaining in one and the same *jins* – guarantees the comparability of the achievement of the two (or more) archers' achievement and is therefore acceptable.[67] One may trade a crossbow of olive wood *(qaws al-zaytūn)* for a crossbow fitted with a 'wheel' (stirrup: *qaws al-jarkh*)[68] – customary in the Maghrib[69] – since both are drawn by foot (*qaws al-rijl*) and are therefore compatible, yet one must not substitute a cross(foot)bow for an ordinary hand bow, just as it is illogical to have a horse and a donkey run against each other.

There are two basic types of crossbows, the *qaws al-jarkh* and the Turkish bows,[70] as well as of hand bows, the Arab and Persian bow.[71] The Arab bow exists in a bedouin (Ḥijāzī) and a regular variant (which again is subdivided). The latter is called *munfaṣila* 'disjoined' (it consists of clearly separate pieces) or *wāsiṭiyya* (not because of the city of Wāsiṭ in Mesopotamia but by virtue of its middle – *wāsiṭī* – position between the traditional nomadic type and the Persian bow[72]). The Turkish bow, on the other hand, resembles the Persian bow, yet is much heavier and has, in the overwhelming majority of cases, a stirrup-type drawing device added to it,[73] so that it must be counted among the foot bows. Whereas crossbows and mangonels are the right weapons in siege warfare,[74] the hand bow is the bow proper, as our author emphasizes. Its users are the real archers (*ahluhā humu ʾl-rumāt bi-ʾl-ḥaqīqa*).[75]

In his day, muses Ibn al-Qayyim, the military uses only the Persian and Turkish bows.[76] The (Persian) handbow has the advantages of superb pliability and light weight; furthermore it grants the possibility of changing arrows in battle at high speed.[77] The (Turkish) crossbow, by contrast, is much more powerful. In a lengthy *mufākhara* Ibn al-Qayyim, indulging in his ubiquitous predilection for literary digressions, lets the foot and hand bows present their respective assets and advantages over each other.[78] The author adds that the Turkish bow enjoys particular prestige in his day because of its enormous speed and impact, although the Persian bow – which the Turks had come to

[67] *Furūsiyya*, 100, lines 22ff.

[68] On this type of 'wheeled' crossbow see Latham and Paterson, *Saracen Archery*, 184, s.v. *jarkh* (Persian, *charkh*). [69] *Furūsiyya*, 103, line 13. [70] Ibid., 103, line 12.

[71] Ibid., 102, lines 25ff. Here we find added, as a third *ṣinf*, the 'Turkish' bow; later in the text it is made clear that it is counted as foot-bow. In his *urjūza* on archery, mentioned above, Abū Bakr Minqār speaks of the Arab bow; does he also mean what Ibn Qayyim labels the Persian hand-bow? [72] *Furūsiyya*, 103, lines 4–7.

[73] Ibid., 103, lines 8–12. On the stirrup crossbow and the difficulties of shooting with it from horseback, see Latham and Paterson, *Saracen archery*, 85–89.

[74] *Furūsiyya*, 103, lines 22ff.; 101, lines 21ff. [75] Ibid., 103, line 25. [76] Ibid., 101, line 17.

[77] Ibid., 103, lines 13–16.

[78] Ibid., 104, lines 21ff. Suyūṭī is susceptible to similar digressions. The second half of his epistle on archery is an anthology of poetry and *sajʿ* on archers, including (*Ghars*, fol. 15b ff.) a *maqāmat al-qaws* by a certain Ismāʿīl b. ʿAbd al-Rāziq al-Iṣbahānī.

know, and then adopted, in their century-long proximity to the Persians – actually fits the military exigencies of his day much more.[79]

The predominant problem in this argument for the Ḥanbalī Ibn al-Qayyim is the legality of the Persian bow, the standard weapon of the contemporary Muslim – i.e. Mamluk – army in Egypt and Syria.[80] In Ḥanbalī scholarly circles of the time there was evident disagreement on this point. To be true, Ibn al-Qayyim concedes, there is the Prophetic saying in which the user of a Persian bow is called upon by Muḥammad to throw it away 'because it is cursed and because you must use the Arab bows and the spears; for it is through them that God supports the religion and grants you power on earth' (*alqihā fa-innahā malʿūna wa-lākin ʿalaykum bi-ʾl-qisiyy al-ʿarabiyya wa-bi-rimāḥ al-qanā fa-bihā yuʾayyidu ʾllāh al-dīn wa-yumakkinu ʾllāh lakum fī ʾl-arḍ*).[81] But not only the authenticity of this tradition can be contested, as Ibn al-Qayyim makes clear. Even if it should be *ṣaḥīḥ*, one must judge and value the historical context in which this alleged interdiction was promulgated, our author muses in a refreshingly historical, almost modernist way. In Muḥammad's time, being Arab meant being Muslim, and being Persian meant being hostile to Islam. The Muslim army was all Arab. But in his time – he continues arguing – the situation is virtually reversed: Persians and Turks – and no longer Arabs – carry the burden of the *jihād* for Islam. 'Nowadays the bows of the army of Islam are of the Persian and Turkish type', even if the language, the equipment and the spirit (*furūsiyya*) of the fighters continue to be Arabic and Arab. If one were to prevent the Mamluks from using their proper arms, 'the world would deteriorate, the market of the Holy War would be shut down and the unbelievers would triumph over the Muslims'.[82] Change and innovation in military technology must be accepted and applied if it is to the benefit of the Muslim community. This holds true for the powerful *qaws al-jarkh*, but also for the *manjanīq* siege engine[83] which is far superior to conventional arrows in conquering the fortresses of the enemy. This is the prime objective: subduing the foes of Islam, whatever means are needed and available. 'If today's Muslim [i.e. Mamluk] army were to fight successfully with its Persian bows for God and His Prophet in the presence of the Prophet, we could be sure that he would praise and commend these [weapons] and not prohibit their use', Ibn Qayyim al-Jawziyya closes this important, highly political passage. It helps to demonstrate, once more, how flexible and pliable Muslim legal doctrine was *vis-à-vis* the necessity to cope with the challenges of the day.[84]

[79] *Furūsiyya*, 104, lines 16–19. Originally the Persian bow was alien to them, yet then they adopted it together with the language, clothes and habits of the Persians.

[80] Ibid., 103, line 9; 104, line 17. [81] Ibid., 101, lines 5–6. [82] Ibid., 101, lines 14–18.

[83] We now have the beautifully illustrated, ninth/fifteenth-century treatise on the mangonels by the *ibn al-nās* Ibn Aranbughā: see Ibn Aranbughā al-Zardakāsh, *al-Anīq fī ʾl-manājanīq*, ed. Iḥsān Hindī. (Maṣādir wa-dirāsāt fī tārīkh al-tiknulūjiyā al-ʿarabiyya, vol. IV) (Aleppo, 1405/1985).

[84] On this general topic see the stimulating article by Baber Johansen, 'Legal literature and the problem of change: the case of the land rent', in Chibli Mallat (ed.), *Islam and Public Law. Classical and Contemporary Studies* (London, 1993), 33–47.

Our three texts help us in gaining a better understanding of the attitude of educated contemporary civilians towards the Turkish monopoly on riding and fighting. Divergent feelings and convictions had to be harmonized – the obligation towards the Mamluks without whom Islam would be imperilled, yet also the irritation at being excluded from activities and privileges which, in the past, had been intrinsically Arab.

A very comprehensive concept of *furūsiyya* seems to have served as a device for harmonizing these contradictory attitudes, at least on the surface. In our texts *furūsiyya* essentially denotes the *sunna* of the Prophet and his Companions in battle, on the race track and on tournament grounds. This 'archetypal' *furūsiyya* lives on in two distinct manifestations. One is *furūsiyya* in the strictly technical and down-to-earth sense of 'horsemanship and military proficiency'. In this meaning it has passed, according to our authors, into the hands of aliens – at least for the time being. The Persian bow epitomizes this exclusive, Mamluk, *furūsiyya* to which non-Mamluks (quite to the chagrin of Arab contemporaries and to the surprise of European travellers) were rigorously denied access. This foreign weapon, much as one may regret it, guarantees the integrity of the *umma*.

Furūsiyya, however, also seems to have retained a more basic and more elusive second meaning. It is the continuing ethos of manly endeavour of early Islam, the persistent – one is almost tempted to say 'eternal' – Arab *furūsiyya* hallowed by the Prophet himself. Distinctly unsoldierly qualities such as generosity[85] or mental awareness and vigilance (*yaqẓa*)[86] are associated with this meaning of *furūsiyya*. Not even the most despotic and rapacious Mamluk overlord would ever be able to take this prestigious attribute away from the Arabs and to arrogate it for himself and his group. It consists of many small *sunan*, which, for the most part, were to form the basis of the new, Turkish-Mamluk, *furūsiyya*, in a historical process. Its pivotal characteristic is the spirit of sacrifice and *jihād*, which takes us unexpectedly close to the meaning of Western chivalry.[87]

Unlike Suyūṭī and Sakhāwī, Ibn al-Qayyim addresses these issues unequivocally. He does not hesitate to concede to the Mamluks their uncontested and most noteworthy merits for Islam – as well as their corollary title for social predominance. This is the main message of his discourse on the Persian bow. Also, in another work, he shows manifest fairness towards the Mamluk lords of the country. He defends them against unfounded and vicious accusations con-

[85] See *Ḍaw'*, vol. III, 280–1, no. 1049, Sūdūn Ṭāz. [86] Ibid., vol. III, 37, line 27.

[87] The exclusive Mamluk pride in horsemanship carried in itself the germ of self-destruction, as has been known since David Ayalon wrote his famous work on the battle of Marj Dābiq. Machiavelli (*Discorsi*, vol. II/17, German translation, 219: see above note 16) keenly noted this causality: Ottoman field artillery brought victory to Sultan Selim over the Mamluk cavalry army, not because of the effect the cannons had upon the intrepid Mamluk soldiers, but because their horrible noise frightened and paralysed horses and horsemen alike.

nected with their slave origin.[88] Sakhāwī and Suyūṭī are far less outspoken. They remain totally silent on the exigencies of a genuinely Mamluk *furūsiyya* and give their readers the impression that all the answers for the problems of his time could be gained from the *salaf*. (Does this not sound very 'fundamentalist' and modern?) One reason for Sakhāwī and Suyūṭī's remarkable reticence could, of course, have been their deep irritation with these Mamluk special rights. In the fifteenth century, in the *dawlat al-Jarākisa*, Mamluk rule had become more authoritarian and, owing to political and economic constraints, less predictable than in the times of the *dawla turkiyya*. Apart from this, Suyūṭī and Sakhāwī[89] were in close personal contact with representatives of the Mamluk ruling class, and therefore – so one may assume – they were especially taciturn with regard to the perpetual Mamluk violations of the established rights and traditions of the civilian population. These were highly sensitive issues. We know of at least two leading Mamluk amirs, the learned Qānim al-Maḥmūdī (d. 1485) and Yashbak al-Faqīh (d. 1473), who studied Sakhāwī's treatise on archery with the author himself.[90] And Sakhāwī gave a copy of this work as a gift to his ruler, Sultan Qāytbāy.[91]

But this structural deficit of information is offset by the detached and unprejudiced, yet at the same time lively and detailed, reports provided by Western visitors to Egypt. They do not withhold their impressions. From them we learn that the local population, the *ʿulamāʾ* included, suffered badly from Mamluk autocracy and elitism. An itinerant foreign visitor could risk describing these social tensions without subterfuge because he did not face the wrath of those who held the reins of power. Yet it was only in the most recent past that their colourful, often pensive, and always informative travelogues, written in Latin, German, Catalan, Polish etc., reached the banks of the Nile as an indispensable counterpoise to local historiography with its – as I would like to posit – voluntary (or involuntary?) self-censorship.

88 *al-Manār al-munīf fī ʾl-ṣaḥīḥ wa-ʾl-ḍaʿīf*, ed. Aḥmad ʿAbd al-Shāfī (Beirut, 1408/1988), chap. 21, at 93–4, nos. 189–91. I owe this valuable reference to Professor Maher Jarrar (American University of Beirut).

89 The two hated each other, cf. Suyūṭī's venomous *maqāma contra* Sakhāwī, *al-Kāwī fī tārīkh al-Sakhāwī*, ed. Muḥammad Muḥammad Amīn, in Ḥasanayn Muḥammad Rabīʿ, (ed.), *Saʿīd ʿĀshūr ilayhi fī ʿīd mīlādihī al-sabʿīn* (Cairo University Press, 1992), 71–86.

90 *Ḍawʾ*, vol. VI, 200, line 16 and vol. X, 271, line 27. See also Jonathan Berkey, 'Mamluks and the world of higher education', in H. Elboudrari (ed.), *Modes de transmission de la culture réligieuse en Islam,* Institut français d'archéologie orientale (Cairo, 1993), 93–116, here at 109, n. 58. Sakhāwī names this text in the list of his own writings among the *miscellanea*; see *Ḍawʾ* vol. VIII, 18, lines 19–20.

91 *Ḍawʾ* vol. VI, 211, line 4.

CHAPTER 12

Concepts of history as reflected in Arabic historiographical writing in Ottoman Syria and Egypt (1517–1700)

OTFRIED WEINTRITT

The decades following the Ottoman conquest of Egypt in 1517 did not favour the writing of history. After a period of intellectual recovery, historiographical works became more numerous again at the end of the sixteenth century, and in the first half of the seventeenth century a new kind of historiography came into existence. Mamluk historical writing with the sultan as its natural focal point had looked from the centre of an Egyptian empire outwards to the periphery. This was obviously no longer possible after Egypt had become a province at the periphery of the Ottoman Empire. But the now provincial historiographers were not prepared to write purely provincial Egyptian historiography devoid of all imperial claims either. Relating both provincial and imperial affairs, they set out to devise a history of the Ottomans that could be termed Localized Imperial Historiography.

We should like to analyse this concept through the works of a single historian writing in this period, Muḥammad ibn Abī ʾl-Surūr al-Bakrī (d. 998/1589–90?).[1] This seems appropriate because his works are numerous as well as exemplary of different historiographical genres. There are specimens of dynastic chronicles, local histories and universal chronicles – although, as will become clear in the course of the following considerations, unambiguous classifications are impossible. What can be determined is their historical outlook as shaped by both historiographical traditions and the new context of Ottoman rule. Future research will have to show to what extent his use of genres and the concept of history implied are representative for the writing of history in the early period of Ottoman domination.

Four of al-Bakrī's writings shall be investigated in particular. There is, above all, his universal history: *ʿUyūn al-akhbār wa-nuzhat al-abṣār*;[2] (2) a local history in the tradition of the *Khiṭaṭ*-works: *al-Kawākib al-sāʾira fī akhbār*

[1] See Abdul-Karim Rafeq, 'Ibn Abī ʾl-Surūr and his works', *Bulletin of the School of Oriental and African Studies*, 38 (1975), 24–31. He has ascertained in this article that there is just one historian called al-Bakrī contrary to the assumption in the *Encyclopaedia of Islam* (new edition), q.v. 'al-Bakrī'.

[2] MS 9474 (We II 380), Staatsbibliothek zu Berlin – Preußischer Kulturbesitz, 172 fols.

Miṣr wa-'l-Qāhirai[3] and a panegyrical work: *Durar al-athmān fī dawlat āl ʿUthmān.*[4] The last work is *al-Minaḥ al-raḥmāniyya fī 'l-dawla al-ʿuthmāniyya,* a history of Ottoman rule in general and in Egypt with a continuation in identical form: *al-Laṭāʾif al-rabbāniyya ʿalā 'l-minaḥ al-raḥmāniyya.*[5]

Al-Bakrī's account of his own books is less than reliable. In *al-Laṭāʾif al-rabbāniyya* he says that the preceding *al-Minaḥ al-raḥmāniyya* contains the history of the Ottoman governors in Egypt whereas in *al-Minaḥ* he says he will portray both the governors and their sultans, and so he does. There are, in fact, lengthy biographies of the sultans which the statement in *al-Laṭāʾif* passes over in silence. Even more misleading is an explicit reference to these biographies in *al-Kawākib al-sāʾira* that places them in *ʿUyūn al-akhbār* instead of *al-Minaḥ al-raḥmāniyya.*

Al-Bakrī's main subject concerns the transition of power from the Circassians to the Ottomans. For that reason the events of Marj Dābiq and al-Raydāniyya, crucial for the Ottoman conquest of Egypt, are narrated at length in all his works except in *ʿUyūn al-akhbār*. This is representative of the historical perspective that had developed by the middle of the seventeenth century: Egyptian history written in Ottoman times had to begin with these events, until the middle of the eighteenth century, when they eventually lost much of their historiographical significance. Thus the principal themes of Egyptian historiography were moulded and varied over and over again starting from Ibn Iyās's description of the Circassians' end in *Badāiʿ al-zuhūr* to al-Bakrī's narrations in different genres. The force of this pattern can be gleaned from the fact that his panegyric *Durar al-athmān*, supposedly a description of the Āl ʿUthmān and Sultan Sulaymān in particular, is little more than a circumstantial description of the Ottoman conquest.

Mamluk historiography was predominantly annalistic in form. Al-Bakrī on the contrary does not apply this form in any of his works. Instead, the biographies of sultans – which makes for a dynastic approach – and, less prominently, those of the Ottoman governors in Egypt structure *al-Minaḥ al-raḥmāniyya* and its continuation *al-Laṭāʾif al-rabbāniyya*. On closer inspection, the *tarjama* of, for example, Sultan Murād III in *al-Minaḥ* contains a lengthy biography of the author's grandfather (d. 994/1587) which consists mainly of an extract of his grandfather's autobiography (*wa-qad tarjama nafsahu*).[6] The inclusion of his life in an Ottoman context is all the more surprising in veiw of the fact that al-Bakrī does not mention his grandfather at all in his *al-Kawākib al-sāʾira* in the tradition of the *Khiṭaṭ*-works. In *al-Laṭāʾif*, on the other hand, there is even space for the long-winded praise of the fourteen-year-old Muḥammad al-Bakrī[7] – probably the author's son – who died a victim of the plague in the year 1028/1617. He is characterized as an extraor-

[3] MS Arab. 398, Staatsbibliothek München, 210 fols.
[4] MS orient. A 1614, Forschungs- und Landesbibliothek Gotha, 201 fols.
[5] M 782/94, Österreichische Nationalbibliothek, 106 fols.
[6] *al-Minaḥ al-raḥmāniyya*, fol. 51b.
[7] al-Laṭāʾif al-rabbāniyya, fol. 104a.

dinary scholar and is praised in poems.[8] In this instance the 'structuring' reign of Sultan ʿUthmān and the governorship of Jaʿfar Pasha must be judged mere decorations.[9] These two examples serve to show that the narrative can stray from political history if necessary. The sultan–pasha scheme is only formally maintained while the historiographical material filling the period of a governor and a sultan is, to a large degree, made up of local events. In the case of al-Bakrī's grandfather, for instance, there are twenty pages on his life as compared to two pages on the reigning sultan,[10] as well as several pages on his father.[11] The author is obviously trying to reconcile the local and the imperial dimension of historiography. But why does he abandon the annalistic scheme in favour of sequences of biographies? Here another tradition of Mamluk historiography comes in: the sultan or imperial ruler functions as focal point or centre of a government-minded historical narrative. Now that events of local interests can no longer be directly connected to the distant ruler as their true centre of gravity, the narrative hiatus resulting from the displacement of power can best be bridged by making the sequence of rulers, instead of years, the principal structuring device. Thus, the extensive reporting of local or even private events under the heading of the biographies of successive Ottoman sultans and their governors exactly mirrors the supreme ruler's metamorphosis from the real to the nominal centre of Egyptian local events. The result could be called the realization of a provincial variant of Ottoman history that integrates imperial and local interests by reinterpreting the ruler-focus of Mamluk historiography. Whether similar problems and solutions characterize the historiographical writings of other provinces in this period remains to be seen.

The writing of history has to be justified. However, in *al-Minaḥ* and *al-Laṭāʾif* – chronicles in the proper sense – no theoretical explanations of *ʿilm al-taʾrīkh*, as they often appear in Mamluk chronicles, are provided. This is done only in al-Bakrīs universal history.[12] Chronicles are justified differently. It shows a different historical understanding when the author cites his grandfather, who explained the high position of the Ottomans by saying that Ottoman rule guaranteed the proper application of the *sharīʿa*. Perhaps al-Bakrī also wants to say that far-sighted persons did recognize Ottoman greatness[13] very early on and that, furthermore, the Bakrī family was equipped with a particular ability to appreciate their greatness. The author's grandfather is supposed to have perceived the importance of the conquest of Rhodes while staying in Cairo at the same time.[14] Al-Bakrī tries to build a firm connection between Egypt and the Ottomans by writings of this kind.

A moral aspect of al-Bakrīs attitude towards the duties of the historiographer should not be overlooked. He prefers, several times, not to mention the awful details of historical events. In the case of Çerkes Aḥmad Pasha, for

[8] Ibid., fols. 99a–104b. [9] Ibid., fols. 95b–98b.
[10] *al-Minaḥ al-raḥmāniyya*, fols. 51a–60a, 50a–51a. [11] Ibid., fols. 69b–72b.
[12] *ʿUyūn al-akhbār*, fols. 2a–b. [13] *al-Minaḥ al-raḥmāniyya*, fol. 2a. [14] Ibid., fol. 30a.

instance, al-Bakrī just mentions his tyranny in general and expresses his intention not to inform readers about the events around his person.[15] The same is said with regard to Tīmūr for whose atrocities the reader is told to consult Ibn ʿArabshāh's work.[16] The struggles among the sons of Bāyazīd during the twelve year interregnum following his death are not mentioned either.[17]

Al-Minaḥ al-raḥmāniyya, a history of the Ottomans starting with ʿUthmān Khān, originally formed part of ʾ*Uyūn al-akhbār* but was later separated. In their independent form both texts show that this was not a case of arbitrary re-editing: Ottoman history with events in Egypt was not supposed to be just the last part of Islamic history, but was considered important enough to constitute a volume of its own. ʿ*Uyūn al-akhbār* is a universal history that follows the principle of dynastic periodization.

There are parallels between the first chapter about the value of history (*ʿilm al-taʾrīkh*) and the introductory passages of al-Sakhāwī's *Iʿlān*.[18] The second chapter about the extension of time quotes al-Ṭabarī.[19] Chapters 18 and 19 treat the Turks and the Circassians in as short and superficial a manner as the representatives of all the other Islamic dynasties, reporting for the most part only the dates of their reigns. The reasons al-Bakrī gives in *al-Minaḥ al-raḥmāniyya* for having separated the twentieth chapter of his universal history appear to consist of standard literary *topoi* only. He says that somebody (*baʿḍ al-fuḍalāʾ al-aʾimma al-nubalāʾ*[20]) requested him to separate the history of the Ottomans. In fact, the principle of dynastic periodization in the ʿ*Uyūn* could not have allowed for the chapter on the Ottomans to deal with their provincial governors in Egypt. Following the requirements of universal history, he would have had to report about the successive Ottoman sultans as representatives of the dynasty that upholds the unity of Islam. In that concept it would not have been justified to insert particulars of Egyptian history. As a universal historian al-Bakrī writes from a dynastic point of view (in contrast to al-Isḥāqī's *Akhbār al-uwal* containing the history of the Ottomans[21]).

There is at any given time only one dynasty which is paramount in the Islamic realm. This is Ibn Khaldūn's concept as well. He explains in *Kitāb al-ʿIbar* that, by God's grace, the weak Abbasids were followed by strong rulers coming from the Turks.[22] It is not astonishing that ʿ*Uyūn al-akhbār* does not contain the full description of the Mamluks' end as is the case in *al-Minaḥ al-raḥmāniyya*[23] and *Durar al-athmān*.[24] They were an Islamic dynasty in Egypt which guaranteed and defended the unity of Islam.

The ʿ*Uyūn* are meant to contain lists of rulers and nothing else. The book is written with the objective of demonstrating the continuity of Islamic history.

15 Ibid., fol. 49a. 16 Ibid., 5a. 17 Ibid., fol. 6a.
18 Franz Rosenthal, *A History of Muslim Historiography* (Leiden, 1968), 269ff.
19 al-Ṭabarī, *Tārīkh al-rusul wa-ʾl-mulūk*, ed. Muḥammad Abū ʾl-Faḍl Ibrāhīm (Cairo, 1960), vol. I, 10. 20 Fols. 1b–2a.
21 Muḥammad b. ʿAbd al-Muʿṭī al-Isḥāqī, *Akhbār al-uwal* (Cairo, 1887).
22 Ibn Khaldūn, *Kitāb al-ʿIbar* (Būlāq, 1867–68), vol. V, 371.
23 Fols. 17b–27a (ch. 9, 'Salṭanat Salīm Fātiḥ Miṣr'). 24 Fols. 112a–179b.

The Ottoman dynasty is in al-Bakrīs view the visible proof of continuity and for that reason separated from the *ʿUyūn*. The concept of universal history that takes dynasties as its organizing principle would have required the history of the Ottoman dynasty to commence after the decline of the Mamluks, with Sultan Selim I, and not with the beginning of the Ottoman dynasty. However, this would not have been compatible with the panegyrical aims of the author.

It is characteristic for this period of Islamic historical thought that universal history still functions as a confirmation of the continuity of Islam despite the changes of dynasties. This genre is not concerned with the contemporary dynasty but in those which are gone. Since examples for this genre are few in Mamluk times, it is all the more remarkable that al-Jannābī,[25] al-Isḥāqī and al-Bakrī adhered to them in early Ottoman times. It seems to me that universal history gradually lost its significance in the course of the seventeenth century.

Durar al-athmān belongs to the literary tradition of the *sīras* written for several sultans in Mamluk times. These *sīras* extol the sultan as an individual, but not the whole dynasty. In this text, however, the Ottoman dynasty in general and Sultan Sulaymān in particular are praised. The central theme is the circumstances that made it possible for Egypt and Syria to fall under Ottoman rule. Al-Bakrī has an Ottoman outlook but the contents have an Egyptian focus. He cannot maintain the emphasis on the central government as was the case in Mamluk historiography. Because of this, the panegyric parts on the Ottoman family and Sultan Sulaymān comprise only about 15 per cent of 400 pages.[26] Praising the Ottomans means narrating the conquest of Egypt, in this case using exceedingly florid language.

Al-Bakrī's intention was to write a *sīra* of Sultan Sulaymān. It is a remarkable modification of the *sīra* genre which in Mamluk times was often used for reigning sultans. In this case, however, it was written posthumously. According to the end of the text it was finished in 1048/1638; Sultan Sulaymān died in 974/1566. It is a result of al-Bakrī's historical outlook that Sulaymān represents the highest rank among the Ottoman sultans up to this time. He was even qualified for the caliphate (*mimman tarashshaḥa li-ʾl-khilāfa*).[27] In the introductory chapter on Ottoman history the author wants to show the origin of Sulaymān. ʿUthmān I is called a renewer of Islam (*istamarra yujaddidu ʿuhūd al-islām*),[28] whereas Sulaymān is called renewer of the faith of the Islamic community in the tenth century (*mujaddid dīn hādhihi ʾl-umma al-muḥammadiyya fī hādhā ʾl-qarn al-ʿāshir*) in *al-Minaḥ al-raḥmāniyya*.[29]

The Ottomans are extolled since they overcame three remarkable enemies of whose fierceness (*sawra*) al-Bakrī speaks persistently: the Mamluk sultans, the shahs of Persia and the Frankish unbelievers.[30] The defeat of the unbelievers is the success of Sultan Sulaymān.[31] Moreover the Ottomans are character-

[25] *Taʾrīkh al-Jannābī*: see Carl Brockelmann, *Geschichte der arabischen Litteratur* (Leiden, 1949), vol. II, 387. [26] From fol. 28 the subject is Sultan Salīm.

[27] *Durar al-athmān*, fol. 13a. [28] Ibid., fol. 20a. [29] Fol. 27b.

[30] *Durar al-athmān*, e.g., fols. 61a–b–112a. [31] Ibid., fol. 3a.

ized as successful in general in their fight against the unbelievers. They threw out the Portuguese from Islamic territory (*al-firanj al-burtuqāl*)[32] and ejected the Franks from Tunis.[33]

Ottoman history before Selim is brief and consists of biographies of the Ottoman rulers. When Selim's turn comes, the conquest of Syria and Egypt is narrated. Al-Bakrī says that his original intention was to write about the events between the Ottomans, the shahs of Persia and the 'kings of this our Egypt'.[34] These are the most remarkable events, from his point of view, in the sixteenth century and even until the lifetime of the author. The rise of the Shīʿa at the beginning of the tenth century is compared with the outbreak of a fire. It has to be kept in mind that *Durar al-athmān* was completed in 1048/1638 with the main theme being the conquest of Egypt and Syria.

Al-Bakrī's references are few and represent only the tradition of Arabic historiography. He refers to Ibn Ḥajar al-ʿAsqalānī concerning the origin of the Āl Uthmān and to al-Maqrīzī.[35] There is no indication that he used Ottoman works or that he had access to oral information. There is a lengthy analytical description in which al-Bakrī tries to explain the behaviour of the Egyptians under the rule of Ṭūmānbāy, the last Circassian sultan[36] – explanations of little importance in the context of a eulogy but important to al-Bakrī all the same. The Circassians established a system of loyalty by marriages and commercial connections which protected them from criticism and attacks and allowed them to live in luxury (*mā kānat fīhi ʾl-Jarākisa min al-rafāhiya*).[37] It was a peaceful coexistence that included all Egyptians (*ahl Miṣr*).[38] However, at the time of Ṭūmānbāy the majority of Egyptians saw that the Circassians' rule was coming to an end. Only a 'small group of deluded men'[39] deeply involved in Circassian rule continued to support Ṭūmānbāy (*munāṣarat Ṭūmānbāy*)[40] – a fact that, of course, has to be dealt with at length in order to exculpate the majority. In this respect it is also instructive to examine thoroughly the description of the Circassians' defeat and the Egyptians' delight about their expulsion from Egypt.[41] Islamic history is traditionally concerned with the 'conquest of countries and their liberation from usurpers, and changes of dynasties'.[42] This is al-Bakrī's theme as well insofar as he describes the transition from Mamluk to Ottoman rule exhaustively. However, in the context of a history of the Ottomans, one would expect a broader Ottoman outlook. The Circassians left their Egypt (*miṣrahum*).[43] When Selim passed through Cairo, the people knew that his time would last longer than that of his predecessor.

Historiographers disclose something about their own perspectives in writing about past times. Al-Bakrī frequently mentions the cannons and the gunpowder of the Ottomans, as if possession of these things presupposes authority and prudence – characteristics the Circassians were not endowed

32 Ibid., fol. 10b. 33 *al-Minaḥ al-raḥmāniyya*, fols. 47b–48b. 34 *Durar al-athmān*, fol. 14b.
35 Ibid., fols. 17b, 23a. 36 Ibid., fols. 168a–170a. 37 Ibid., fol. 168a.
38 Ibid., fol. 169a. 39 Ibid., fol. 169b. 40 Ibid. 41 *Durar al-athmān*, fols. 148b–150a.
42 al-Sakhāwī, *Iʿlān*: see Rosenthal, *History*, 273. 43 *Durar al-athmān*, fol. 149a.

with. The victory over them is justified for this reason.[44] Ottoman power is, in al-Bakrī's eyes, based on their cannons. The Mamluks believed in spears and swords whereas the Ottomans relied upon cannons and gunpowder – one may add that they continued to do so in the author's time. Nevertheless, it was also the Circassians' life of luxury that caused, in al-Bakrī's outlook, the end of their rule.[45] In the panegyrical context, it is the lofty position of the Ottoman dynasty that entitles it to conquer Egypt. Al-Bakrī's main concern is the description of Egypt's transition to Ottoman rule, which leaves little space for the history of the Ottomans, and Sulaymān's reign in particular, which al-Bakrī had intended to describe originally.

With *al-Kawākib al-sā'ira*, a different historical perspective is realized. Explicitly describing Egyptian affairs, it represents local history. Al-Bakrī does not focus on the Ottomans but on Egypt, especially Cairo. Half the text consists of the third chapter, which comprises the history of the rulers of Egypt starting with the time before the deluge up to the year 1055/1645. The ratio of the parts is interesting in this case. The political history from the beginning to the end covers 30 pages compared to 180 pages about the Ottoman period up to the year 1055/1645. The author says that in *al-Kawākib* he wants to report about the Ottoman governors in Egypt and not about the Ottoman sultans because this is done in *ʿUyūn al-akhbār*. We know that the Ottoman sultans appear in *al-Minaḥ al-raḥmāniyya*. This formula is used, for example, in the case of Sultan Murād III[46] and his successor Sultan Mehmet.[47] From his provincial point of view, the governors of Egypt represent the continuity of political history in Egypt but the Ottoman sultans do not. However, they are needed as the organizational principle of the text.

The introduction of *al-Kawākib* deserves further investigation. Al-Bakrī does not praise Egypt or start with references to Egypt in general but treats the big city as a general phenomenon. By citing sayings such as al-Shāfiʿī's 'I like to live at a place from which orders go out and not a place to which orders go in'[48] or Anūshirwān's 'Do not settle in a place where no strong sultan is present',[49] he lays stress on the great city as a compensating factor to the provincial reality. This would not be possible without Cairo's imperial past which is still alive in al-Bakrī's perception of the present situation. Egypt is an Ottoman province but Cairo, though lacking central power, is better than other towns. The genre of topographical descriptions such as al-Maqrīzī's *Khiṭaṭ* is still formative in al-Bakrīs *al-Kawākib al-sā'ira*. Information on the quarters of Cairo (mosques, gates, buildings) are collected with appropriate relevant historical details.[50] The question of literary sources cannot be answered for the moment. The architectural survey, however, does not include the post-Mamluk period up to the author's life. Instead, he begins with the city's foundation and describes structural changes up to Circassian rule. This

[44] Ibid., fols. 123a, 152b. [45] Ibid., fol. 168a. [46] *Al-Kawākib al-sā'ira*, fol. 31a.
[47] Ibid., fol. 34b. [48] Ibid., fol. 2b. [49] Ibid.
[50] *al-Kawākib al-sā'ira*, fols. 159b–166b (chap. 17).

kind of information, on the other hand, can be found in part on the governors of Egypt, as can the details of thier biographies.[51] For what reason does al-Bakrī not include Ottoman times in the topographical chapter? The omission reveals, and this holds true for the universal histories as well, that the proven genres cannot be fully applied anymore. They have been changed in their function and meaning by Ottoman reality.

Summing up our findings, we may say that al-Bakrī's work represents two strategies of coming to terms with the changed status of Egypt after the Ottoman conquest: as a rule, the imperial Mamluk concept of historiography was reinterpreted in order to combine both imperial Ottoman and provincial Egyptian affairs. Thus, in the final analysis, modification served to retain the formative characteristics of Mamluk historiography – the focus on Egyptian history and the imperial point of view. Alternatively – but less frequently so – the imperial outlook could be given up in order to write pure and unabashedly local history.

[51] E.g. *Masīḥ Bāshā al-Khādim*, ibid., fol. 31b.

CHAPTER 13

Cultural life in Mamluk households (late Ottoman period)

NELLY HANNA

Studies on the cultural life of the Ottoman period have tended to emphasize its negative sides, the fact that it did not produce great works of literature or of science, that learning had degenerated from the levels it had reached some centuries before, that its institutions of learning, the *madrasas*, so numerous in the fourteenth and fifteenth centuries, were reduced in number and the quality of teaching had deteriorated.[1] Implicit in this view of culture is its emphasis on the formal aspects of learning, education and culture, and on those aspects linked to institutions. A wider view of cultural life, one that includes those aspects that were not necessarily linked to institutions, notably the informal sides of education and learning, can reveal another set of realities. Also implicit in this approach is an emphasis on cultural production, whether this consists of literary, artistic or historical works. These are considered to be a sort of measure for the level of culture at any particular time. One could, however, argue that an awareness of, and a receptivity to, such works are also valuable indicators of cultural life at any particular moment in history.

These views on culture can be explored more concretely by analysing one specific form of cultural activity taking place in the private residences of the Mamluk amirs in Cairo, notably that of private libraries.[2] The analysis of these phenomena addresses both the question of informal culture and that of cultural production, within the framework of one particular social group, the Mamluk amirs.

The relationship between Mamluks and culture or education is still so far, by and large, an unexplored field. Much of what is written about the Mamluks and beys concerns their impressive and violent rise to political and economic power, a rise that allowed them to become virtual rulers of Egypt. Their struggles among themselves, in fact, took up so much of their time and effort that it is reasonable to ask whether they had any links to cultural life, both in the

[1] J. Heyworth-Dunne, *An Introduction to the History of Education in Modern Egypt* (London, 1938), 1–95, is still the most extensive work to cover the Ottoman period, in spite of its serious shortcomings.

[2] Jonathan Berkey, *The Transmission of Knowledge in Medieval Cairo. A Social History of Islamic Education* (Princeton, 1992), also remarks on the importance of various forms of informal education during the Mamluk sultanate.

more limited sense of a conscious and learned culture, and in the more global one encompassing the heritage and values of the population that they came to rule. By exploring their relationship to culture, a number of questions are addressed, about the nature of knowledge and culture, about the links that the Mamluks had with it and with society, and about their role in the transmission of knowledge.

What we know about the cultural life of Mamluk amirs is mainly derived from al-Jabartī's chronicle. He mentions two specific aspects, the first being their participation in the *majālis* or literary salons of Cairo, and the second their private libraries. Al-Jabartī narrates, for instance, that the amirs (and others as well) had cultural evenings in their houses. Every one is familiar with al-Jabartī's comments on Riḍwān Katkhudā al-Jalfī, who held one of the most notable literary salons of Cairo in his house. Poets, singers and literary figures came to recite poetry, improvise verses and sing, and the salon was known to have attracted the major literary figures of his time. Prizes were distributed for the best performances. Panegyrics, *maqāmas, qaṣīdas*, were composed in his honour by poets and scholars such as Shaykh Yūsuf al-Ḥifnī, Shaykh ʿAbdallāh al-ʿIkdawī, Shaykh ʿAlī Jibrīl, Sayyid Ḥammūda al-Sadīdī and many others. Artistic talent was doubtless encouraged by such patronage. The example of Riḍwān Katkhudā is significant because it was part of a trend on the part of Mamluk amirs and beys to play a leading role in the cultural life of Cairo. This is especially evident during the first part of the eighteenth century, before the acute economic crises and the severe rivalries among the amirs disrupted the scene in the latter part of the century. That is one facet of the kind of cultural activity held in Mamluk households. Al-Jabartī also uncovers the trend among amirs and Mamluks to own private libraries, a phenomenon which, according to this historian, also prevailed amongst other groups such as shaykhs, efendis and merchants. But the trend is significant enough among the military elite to deserve attention.

The books forming these libraries could be obtained from more than one source. Some, of course, were inherited. But for the very large libraries, there must have been quite a bit of purchasing involved. Cairo, in fact, had a book market, Sūq al-Kutubiyyīn, very close to al-Azhar. Al-Jabartī gives us an important insight when he deplores how the libraries of many of the *madrasas* of Cairo, which had been very well endowed with books and manuscripts, were dispersed, and their books stolen or sold in the markets. Many people must have purchased parts of these collections from the book market, and presumably some of these found their way to the houses of Mamluk beys and amirs, who were in possession of private libraries. Purchases included many works that could well have come from college libraries, but the market also included contemporary writers, al-Shaʿrānī being one of the most popular. *Tāj al-ʿArūs*, *Tārīkh al-Isḥāqī*, and the works of al-Kharashī, and Ibn Nujaym, another popular jurist, were bought and kept in these private libraries. There must also have been a certain amount of patronage for literary works, with Mamluks commissioning specific works from poets or writers.

The existence of this particular form of culture is confirmed by archival sources, and to an extent which actually goes way beyond what the historian al-Jabartī suggested, both in the number of persons involved and in the scope and breadth of their private libraries. The archives in question are the court records of Cairo, specifically in the inheritence registers in the court of *al-Qisma al-ʿAskariyya*, where the property of deceased persons was recorded and sometimes sold so that the proceeds might be divided among heirs: their property could include houses or commercial buildings, their clothing, jewellery, arms, household items (copperware, silverware, ceramics) and, most significant for our purposes here, their books.

These inheritance deeds show that the phenomenon of private libraries was more widespread than al-Jabartī's biographies indicate. Not only amirs, Mamluks, shaykhs or merchants had libraries, but also sometimes, on a smaller scale, a tradesman or artisan owned a few books which he kept in his house. Obviously, the scope of the libraries was a function of how much a person could afford. For some people the library consisted of a few books. Fifteen books priced at 340 *nisfs* adorned the library of Shunūda, a spice seller (*ʿaṭṭār)* in Sūq al-Faḥḥāmīn;[3] and six books were found in the inheritance of the *bawwāb* (doorkeeper) to one of the *wakālas* of Khaṭṭ al-Mūskī[4]. For some of the amirs, and shaykhs, however, the libraries were very important, going into several hundreds of volumes. As far as the Mamluks are concerned, it is particularly significant to consider not only the number of books they could have had in a library, but the portion of the inheritance that this library could constitute; one can do this by comparing the cost of their books to their total inheritance. ʿUthmān Katkhudā al-Qāzdughlī, for example, had a library in his house that was estimated at some 82,000 *nisfs*, out of an inheritance of 31,537,176.[5] Another very important Mamluk, the amir Aḥmad Bey Mīr Liwā, left books that were worth 37,783 *nisfs* while all his household items together were estimated at 101,188 *nisfs*, i.e. over a third of his household property, according to that deed.[6] This indicates that in some cases, the libraries in private households were very large.

The inheritance deeds provide detailed information about the books. Sometimes only the number of books is indicated, or their total value. Usually, however, the register has a list of all the books, one by one, and sometimes, the price of each one. Usually the titles are given in abbreviated form, with or without the author's name, which makes them sometimes difficult to identify. Sometimes the indications that are given are clear enough to identify a particular book without any doubt (*Khiṭaṭ al-Maqrīzī*, for instance, or *Rasāʾil Ibn Nujaym*). At other times, the indications are vague and insufficient to identify a particular work, for instance *kitāb fī ʾl-ṭibb*, a medical book, or simply *kitāb*

[3] *Qisma ʿArabiyya* 118, 515 dated 1175/1761, at 293.
[4] *Qisma ʿArabiyya* 120, 1025 dated 1180/1766, at 437.
[5] *Qisma ʿAskariyya* 147, 25 dated 1152/1739, at 17–34.
[6] *Qisma ʿAskariyya* 123, 532 dated 1137/1724, at 413 ff.

fī 'l-taṣawwuf, a book on Sufism. In either case, one will usually be able to know what subject the book is about.

Unlike what one might be led to expect from reading the biographies of al-Jabartī, the contents of the private libraries contained a wide variety of subjects. The impression these biographies give can be misleading because of the long listings of *fiqh, ḥadīth* and *sharḥ* works that imply that the only books that were read during that time were books of religious scholarship. The books available in private libraries, however, covered far more diverse subjects than one might expect, with books ranging from religious, literary, artistic and historical to scientific works.

As one would expect, the large majority of books are in Arabic. Nevertheless, it is significant that a certain number of books in some libraries were written in Persian and in Turkish.[7] Even though Turkish and Persian may have been excluded from the curriculum of al-Azhar, the presence of books in these languages in various private libraries in the city provided an opening to non-Arab Islamic culture, during a period when Egypt has often been described as being culturally isolated.

In other words, these libraries in the private collections of Mamluks had books and manuscripts that were available in the libraries of the various colleges in Cairo, but nevertheless the owners of the private collections were not under the same constraints as the libraries of formal teaching institutions. It would, of course, be very interesting to have a detailed comparison between the books contained in the Azhar catalogue and the books in these libraries to analyse the extent to which the privately owned libraries covered broader fields of knowledge.

Foremost among the subjects of the books were religious topics, *fiqh*, *tafsīr*, *ḥadīth* and a very large number of commentaries (*sharḥ*), the kind of reading one would have thought too specialized for the audience we are dealing with. Works of religious scholarship seem to have been common reading, books such as *al-Muwaṭṭa'*, *Tafsīr al-Bayḍāwī*; and the libraries had books about *waqfs* for instance, an institution the Mamluks made ample use of. There were numerous works on Sufism, including many lives of holy men (*manāqib al-ṣūfiyya, ṭabaqāt al-ṣūfiyya*); many books or short works containing *fatwās* (*fatāwī Qāḍīkhān, fatāwī al-Sakhāwī, fatāwī al-Ḥalabī, fatāwī al-Ashmūnī*); *risālas* or treatises which could cover a wide variety of subjects; philosophical works such as *Rasā'il Ikhwān al-Ṣafā'*.

Two other subjects of great interest, judging from the titles of books in private libraries, were history and literature. The libraries of eighteenth century Cairo contained such classic works as the basic histories of the Mamluk period like al-Nuwayrī, the *Khiṭaṭ* of Maqrīzī, *Tārīkh al-Khulafā'* of Suyūṭī, Ibn Khaldūn, *Kashf al-Ghumma*, and *al-Tibr al-Masbūk* of al-

[7] See for instance the inheritance of Amir Sulaymān Bāsh Jāwīsh Mustfaḥfiẓān and enfranchised Mamluk of Amir ʿUthmān Katkhudā Mustaḥfiẓān, *Qisma ʿAskariyya* 147, 108 dated 1152/1739, at 96–110.

Sakhāwī; in addition, al-Ṭabarī, Ibn Khallikān and Ibn al-Furāt, as well as works on the history of specific towns such as Jerusalem (*Tārīkh Bayt al-Maqdis*) and Mecca (*Tārīkh Makka*). The history books therefore cover chronicles, universal histories and regional histories. Historians of the Ottoman period such as al-Bakrī or al-Isḥāqī obviously interested the readers of the time as well. To this one must add a few history books in Turkish and in Persian with the titles of *Shāh nāmeh*, *Tīmūr nāmeh*, *Humāyūn nāmeh* and other books simply entitled *Tārīkh turkī*. The numerous books on history indicate that people had a vivid interest in this subject. This leads one to make a distinction between an interest in reading historical works which no doubt existed, and the actual writing of history, which was not as prolific as it had been in the fourteenth or fifteenth centuries, or a distinction between the interest in a subject, and the production in this subject, which apparently did not always coincide.

Books on literature include many works, in Turkish, Arabic and Persian, as well as classics such as *Kalīla wa-Dimna* and *Maqāmāt al-Ḥarīrī*, a very popular work – in poetry as well as in prose.

The libraries reflect a very vivid interest in certain scientific fields, notably medicine and astronomy. There are numerous works on medicine, general medical works, veterinary books especially on horses as well as medical works in Turkish. Occasionally titles of these books are mentioned (*al-Ṭibb al-Nūrī*, for instance, probably related to the Nūrī hospital of Damascus), but usually the persons making the inventories contented themselves with an indication such as *kitāb fī ʾl-ṭibb* or *risāla fī ʾl-ṭibb*. As a matter of fact, medical books were the most popular scientific works and could often be bought at ridiculously low prices, 20, 30 or 50 *niṣfs*, for instance. Any library of some scope had a medical book or two, not only the libraries of amirs and Mamluks, but also libraries belonging to shaykhs and merchants. We therefore have to ask what constituted specialized knowledge and what did not. The indications here are that medicine was not a specialized field for doctors only, an impression that al-Jabartī confirms when he talks of a poet, for instance, who knew a lot about medicine.[8]

People were apparently also interested in astronomy (*falak*). By the way, the Catalogue of Scientific Manuscripts in *Dār al-Kutub*[9] shows that an extraordinary number of works on astronomy and astrology were copied in the seventeenth and eighteenth centuries, works from different periods and different lands. This confirms the vivid interest people had in this subject, and it would certainly be worthwhile to try and find out the reasons for this interest. Again, as with history, the distinction should be made between the keen interest in reading these scientific works, and the level of scientific invention or exploration, which may have shown less originality than in earlier centuries.

8 Al-Jabartī, *ʿAjāʾib al-āthār* (Beirut, n.d., I) (hereafter al-Jabartī), vol. 427.

9 David King, *A Catalogue of the Scientific Manuscripts in the Egyptian National Library*, part I (Cairo, 1981).

In addition, the libraries had a few books on scientific subjects such as alchemy (*kīmiyā'*), and mathematics (*ḥisāb*). One should finally mention works on geography, such as *Iqlīm Miṣr*, *'Ajā'ib al-buldān* (Ibn Dulaf, tenth century) and various *mamālik* words (often with no further elaboration of the title), and an occasional *riḥla* or travel book. A minute comparison (with a database) of the contents of the libraries would be able to show the patterns of taste and how they evolved. Hopefully such work will be undertaken.

The analysis of the contents of some of the private libraries of these Mamluk amirs brings up a number of comments. On the one hand, the titles of the books in these libraries indicate a vivid interest amongst readers for subjects such as history, medicine and astronomy, at a period when these subjects are considered to have been in decline.[10] One could argue that at a time when production of new or innovative works was at a low point, readership trends were not necessarily following the same direction, but seem, on the contrary, to point to a wider readership. This is a matter of significance that deserves a more extensive exploration.

On the other hand, this analysis contradicts a widely held view that the only kind of knowledge available to society was religious knowledge and demonstrates that religious scholars were not the only people to be educated. The idea that the *'ulamā'* had a monopoly of knowledge can be somewhat modified, since one can see people dealing with other forms of scholarship recognized by society. According to al-Jabartī, one amir, Qāsim Abū Ṣayf, was very knowledgeable in *handasa* (geometry),[11] while another, Sulaymān Bey al-Armanī Bārim Dhaylah, was good at reciting poetry.[12] One often reads of a person who knew a lot about medicine, for instance. Al-Jabartī's comments, confirmed by the inheritance deeds, indicate a significant variety of interests among more than a single social stratum.

These collections and the books they contain tell us something about the Mamluk amirs who owned them, and about their relationship to the culture in which they lived. The fact that the Mamluk amirs associated themselves with this heritage implied some level of identification with it. In spite of the linguistic and ethnic differences between the ruling Mamluks and the rest of the population, as well as the great economic gap between the indigenous population and the military, the Mamluks were not completely ignorant of their cultural environment. If some Mamluks owned and read books in Arabic, both contemporary and classical works, then they were, at a certain level at least, 'speaking the same language' as many other members of society, both in the literal and the figurative sense. That many Mamluk amirs were familiar with Arabic, or fluent in it, is quite clear. Many of them were actually born in Egypt, so one would expect this kind of familiarity with the language. The cultural evenings (*majālis adab*) referred to earlier, such as those organized by Riḍwān

[10] A different approach to the histories and chronicles of the period is contained in D. Crecelius (ed.), *Eighteenth Century Egypt. The Arabic Manuscript Sources* (Los Angeles, 1990); see introduction by Jack Crabbs, at 18–19. [11] Al-Jabartī, vol. II, 523. [12] Ibid., I, vol. 149.

Katkhudā were likely to have been conducted in Arabic, since such gatherings would often include men of learning. We know from Jabartī, for instance, that the house of amir Ibrāhīm Katkhudā al-Birkāwī was a meeting place for scholars and men of learning, indigenous scholars most certainly communicating in Arabic. The concept of a clear-cut linguistic divide, with Turkish-speaking Mamluks on the one hand and an Arabic speaking population on the other, needs to be modified.[13]

One cannot realistically argue that the beys and amirs had no connection to the books they owned and that they only had libraries because of the prestige this gave them rather than because they read books. This attitude is not a sufficiently convincing explanation for the trend in the development of private libraries. Amir Sulaymān Bey al-Armanī Bārim Dhayluh, we are told, was fond of reading books;[14] Amir Ibrāhīm Katkhudā al-Birkāwī not only could read and write but also made sure that his own Mamluks were well trained in *belles-lettres*, in Koran recital and in calligraphy;[15] and Amir Ṣāliḥ Efendi, a Mamluk of Ibrāhīm Katkhudā al-Qāzdughlī, was also known for his love of reading.[16] One can moreover discern the tastes and predilection of the owner in the choice of books. Al-Jabartī tells us that Amir Ḥasan b. al-Sayyid, for instance, was fond of medical books[17] and that the amir Ḥasan Efendi Shaqbūn liked to collect books illuminated with gold, such as *Kalīla wa-Dimna* or the *Shāh nāmeh*.[18] A predilection for books of a particular *madhhab* is apparent in some of these private libraries: the library of Ibrāhīm Çorbaci b. ʿAlī Katkhudā, for instance, had an emphasis on the Ḥanafī school of law, with biographies of Hanafites *(Kitāb Ṭabaqāt al-Ḥanafiyya)*; and Ḥanafī *fiqh (Aḥkām al-Khaṣṣāf* and *al-Isʿāf* of al-Ṭarābulusī).[19] These are important indications of the links between the owners of libraries and their books.

One also needs to modify some generally held views about the period. For instance, the idea that the works of the classical tradition were lost or forgotten should be seriously revised. It is obvious that the transmission of this heritage worked on more than one level. Important works were physically preserved in libraries and passed on to later generations, including major works of the classical patrimony such as *Iḥyāʾ ʿulūm al-dīn*; Ibn al-ʿArabī, al-Bukhārī, al-Rāzī and many more. Works were also preserved thanks to the fact that they were recopied during this period, either for commercial use or for a patron. The role of the Mamluks in this process of transmission is self-evident.

Mamluk amirs' involvement in cultural transmission also took another form, namely that of opening their private libraries to the public. This was apparently a frequent occurrence, both in the houses of amirs and in other people's houses, those of merchants and shaykhs for instance. Al-Jabartī, talking about the library of Amir Ibrāhīm Katkhudā al-Birkāwī, who died in

[13] Gabriel Piterberg, 'The formation of an Ottoman Egyptian elite in the 18th century', *IJMES*, 22 (1990), 275–89. [14] Al-Jabartī, vol. I, 153. [15] Ibid., vol. I, 590.
[16] Ibid., vol. II, 90. [17] Ibid., vol. II, 171. [18] Ibid., vol. II, 130.
[19] *Qisma ʿAskariyya* 131, 796 dated 1143/1730, at 413–17.

1198/1784, says that it was very well furnished and that al-Birkāwī allowed people to use it. They could come to his house, sit, read, and copy what they wanted. This library, as a matter of fact, had the reputation of possessing books that could not be found anywhere else. Likewise, al-Jabartī narrates that Amir ʿAlī b. ʿAbdallāh *mawlā* of Bashīr Agha Dār al-Saʿāda, collected rare books and allowed people to borrow them;[20] and that Amir Ḥusayn al-Qādirī's books could also be borrowed.[21] This seems, in other words, to represent a trend to permit interested people, perhaps students or others, to make use of these libraries which were located within the private houses of these individuals, allowing people with whom there was no other connection to enter the house and read the books there.[22] This trend is very significant because it places the phenomenon of private libraries in a much wider social context. One can argue for a broader base of readers besides the individual amir who owned the books and his immediate circle, or of readers strictly associated with institutions of learning.

This trend is also very significant at the level of the transmission of knowledge. For students, it probably meant that they had access to books that were not likely to be available in formal educational institutions, and it allowed them the perusal of works that were not included in the curriculums of their institutions. If the formal educational institutions concentrated their teaching on religious subjects, these private libraries made available a broader range of readings.

One could conclude by asking why the Mamluk amirs made a special effort in linking themselves to the indigenous culture by, among other things, opening the doors of their houses to outsiders, or by concerning themselves with the transmission of learning, especially at a time when they were involved in rivalries with other Mamluk households, with all the violence this led to. In the eighteenth century, the Mamluks had put their hands on the major sources of wealth. By controlling the various tax farms, *iltizāms*, they were able to accumulate great riches and, consequently, significant political power. In fact, they had all the requirements for effective rule: economic power, political power, even their own small armies. The one thing they did not have was legitimacy. The legitimacy of the sultan of Istanbul was (except at the very end of the eighteenth century) unchallenged, even at times when his authority over the various provinces of the Ottoman state had become restricted. It was therefore in search of legitimacy that some of them involved themselves in activities such as these forms of transmission of learning that would make them look good, mainly to the ʿ*ulamā*', but also to the population in general.

[20] Al-Jabartī, vol. I, 329. [21] Ibid., vol. II, 171.

[22] The phenomenon of opening to the public libraries that were situated in private residences seems to have been widespread and was by no means limited to the Mamluks. Shaykhs and merchants were doing the same thing. Al-Jabartī, for instance, says that *khawājā* Aḥmad al-Sharāyibī, a prominent merchant, allowed people to come to his house to use the books in his library. They were even allowed to borrow them (al-Jabartī, vol. I, 289). He gives other examples in vol. I, at 415 and 526.

In conclusion, in the light of the archival sources that are now becoming accessible, we need to look again at many of the statements that were made about culture and learning in this period: the rigidity of the learning process, which emphasized memorization; the loss of touch with the medieval Islamic heritage apparent in the curriculum of al-Azhar, the major institution of learning; the fact that intellectual production offered nothing new but simply consisted of commentaries and annotations of older texts.[23] All these views have only taken into consideration what was happening in the formal educational institutions and have neglected the informal sides of the transmission of learning. The private libraries in the houses of Mamluks and amirs were one of these informal sides. The documents in the archives confirm that the number of books in private possession was considerable, not only in the libraries of Mamluks, but also in those of shaykhs and merchants as well. This observation qualifies our existing knowledge about the level of literacy and of general erudition among the inhabitants of Cairo.

[23] Gamal el-Din el-Shayyal, 'Some aspects of intellectual and social life in eighteenth century Egypt', in P. M. Holt (ed.), *Political and Social Change in Modern Egypt* (London, 1968), 118.

PART IV

Mamluk property, geography and urban society

CHAPTER 14

The residential districts of Cairo's elite in the Mamluk and Ottoman periods (fourteenth to eighteenth centuries)

ANDRÉ RAYMOND

Introduction

Some thirty years ago, I had the opportunity to write a paper on the residential quarters of Cairo's ruling elite in the Ottoman era,[1] a subject of interest to social and political as well as urban history. More recent work on the Mamluk period has brought me to resume this research and extend it to cover both periods, from the fourteenth to the eighteenth centuries. These two eras of Cairo's history would appear to be more closely linked, in this aspect, than one often imagines, which can lead us to some useful observations on the character of the Ottoman era and on the general development of the city.

In both cases, my research focused on what one may call the ruling elite; essentially the Mamluk amirs in the first case, and the military and beylical caste in the second, which excludes the civilian, indigenous elite. In this study, which can only count as partial and provisional, I have limited my investigation of the Mamluks to a few sources that allow us to cover the entire period, from 1293 (Sultan al-Nāṣir Muḥammad's accession) up to 1517: Maqrīzī's *Sulūk* and *Khiṭaṭ*, Ibn Taghrībirdī's *Nujūm* and *Ḥawādith*, and Ibn Iyās' *Badā'i' al-zuhūr*. I have added a text of secondary import, Ibn al-Rammāl's *Kitāb futūḥ Miṣr*, which nevertheless provides some very useful information for the years 1516–17.[2] As a reference date I have not always used the date of construction, which is unknown for many residential buildings, but have relied on the first mention of its occupants, each building being listed only once for each period under consideration. I have also included those houses that

Translated by Stefan Winter.

[1] 'Essai de géographie des quartiers de résidence aristocratique au Caire au XVIIIème siècle', *JESHO*, 6 (1963), 58–103.

[2] Aḥmad al-Maqrīzī, *Kitāb al-sulūk*, ed. M. Ziyāda and S. 'Āshūr (Cairo, 1941–73); Aḥmad al-Maqrīzī, *Kitāb al-Khiṭaṭ*, (Būlāq, 1270/1853); Yūsuf ibn Taghrībirdī, *an-Nujūm al-zāhira*, ed. W. Popper (Berkeley, 1926–29); Yūsuf ibn Taghrībirdī, *Ḥawādith*, ed. W. Popper (Berkeley, 1930–42). Muḥammad ibn Iyās, *Badā'i' al-zuhūr*, ed. M. Muṣṭafā (Wiesbaden, 1962–72); Aḥmad ibn al-Rammāl, *Kitāb futūḥ Miṣr*, Bibliothèque Nationale, Paris, fonds arabe, no. 1838.

constitute historical monuments and are registered in the Index to Mohammedan Monuments in Cairo.[3] A systematic investigation in the historical sources would admittedly give a more complete picture. Nonetheless, the data presented here seems consistent enough to permit some first conclusions to be drawn.

For the Ottoman period, the information supplied by the historical sources for the sixteenth and seventeenth centuries up until about 1660 is very sparse and does not provide a sample large enough for this sort of study. I have surveyed the documents relating to the estates of amirs found in Cairo's tribunal (*Maḥkama*) archives for the years 1679–1700, when the amir's residence was mentioned. I have also used those textual indications that can be found scattered in the principal chronicles of that period. This documentation complements in some ways my older *JESHO* article, its advantage being that it provides a larger quantity of information for a shorter period of time. This allows us to shed further light on the urban evolution that had remained unclear in the earlier study, both for its long time-frame (1650–1755) and because it straddled two distinct phases in the history of the elite residences. For the *terminus ad quem* (later eighteenth century) I made use of the same sources as in the earlier article, namely the *Description de l'Égypte* and the chronicles, primarily al-Jabartī.[4]

In order to bring out a possible evolution in the phenomenon we are studying, it is first necessary to establish a periodization that divides the Mamluk era into relatively homogeneous, and preferably balanced, periods. Rather than resorting to the traditional periodization (Baḥrī Turkish and Burjī Circassian 'dynasties', with the cut in 1382) which hardly seems purposeful,[5] it appeared more logical to divide the two-and-a-half centuries into four sub-periods:

- 1293 to 1341 – the reign of al-Nāṣir Muḥammad, covering a period of lively urban expansion and architectural activity;
- 1341 to 1412 – era of crises that reached its height with the reigns of al-Nāṣir Faraj (1399–1412);
- 1412 to 1496 – an age of recovery and urban renewal;
- 1496 to 1517 – the two last decades of Mamluk rule, which I thought it necessary to consider separately, so as to permit conclusions to be drawn on this aspect of Mamluk Cairo's urban history.

As regards the Ottomans, the choice of the period of the later seventeenth century will allow us to underline the continuity of features inherited from the Mamluk age. And lastly, the closing two decades of the eighteenth century

[3] When their founders are identified. See the archaeological map of Cairo and the *Index to Mohammedan Monuments in Cairo*, Survey of Egypt, 1951. These monuments are cited with their classification numbers.

[4] These documents are contained in the Cairo court (*Maḥkama*) registers; *qisma ʿaskariyya,* nos. 75 to 93. ʿAbd al-Raḥmān al-Jabartī, *ʿAjāʾib al-āthār* (Būlāq, 1297/1879), 4 vols.

[5] See A. Raymond, *Le Caire* (Paris, 1993), 120.

Table 14.1 *Localization of the ruling elite's residences by period and by area*

area	1293–134	134–1412	1412–1496	1496–1517	1679–1700
Ḥusayniyya	1	1	—	—	—
Qāhira	23 (54.8%)	19 (48.7%)	21 (38.2%)	9 (15.8%)	11 (12.5%)
(north)	20	15	9	5	8
Southern Suburb	16 (38.1%)	18 (46.1%)	31 (56.4%)	38 (66.7%)	65 (73.9%)
(Birkat al-Fīl)	6	2	9	10	34 (38.6%)
(Citadel)	6 (14.3%)	12 (30.8%)	12 (21.8%)	18 (31.6%)	12 (13.6%)
Western Suburb	2 (4.8%)	1 (2.6%)	3 (5.4%)	10 (17.5%)	12 (13.6%)
(north)	2	—	1	4	2
(south)	—	1	2	6	10
Total	42	39	55	57	88

make possible a conclusion upon the Ottoman era and on the significant changes that took place in the first half of that century. The fact that we can avail ourselves of the *Description de l'Égypte* for this final period, with its invaluable wealth of information and its plan of Cairo, ideally suited to locating urban structures, makes this choice obvious.

In order to express the phenomenon under consideration geographically, I have split Cairo into three main sectors, Ḥusayniyya constituting a northern suburb that hardly figures in the present study: (1) al-Qāhira, the Fatimids' creation, was the centre of power up until Saladin built the Citadel in 1176, which opened this area to an influx of a more civilian population. Its 'northern part' I define as that zone, demarcated by al-Azhar, where the two palaces had stood. (2) The 'southern suburb', outside al-Qāhira beyond Bāb Zuwayla and east of the canal (al-Khalīj), began to develop when the Citadel became the military and political centre of Cairo and remained so throughout the Mamluk and Ottoman eras.[6] (3) The 'western suburb' is that area located across the canal from al-Qāhira and the southern suburb. I have further taken the street leading to Bāb al-Lūq (M 15) to mark a northern and a southern section within it.[7]

All the data for the Mamluks and for the first two centuries of the Ottoman period can be summarized in table 14.1. The first general conclusions one may draw from the table are as follows:

[6] This delimitation is not without its problems, particularly where the geographical point of reference given is a bridge (*qanṭara*) across the Khalīj. In these cases, we have considered the residence to belong either to al-Qāhira or to the southern suburb. The Qanāṭir al-Sibāʿ (Lions' Bridges; 160 V 12 in the *Description*) are thus included in the southern region; perhaps they should further have been included in the sub-sector Birkat al-Fīl, to which they are quite close. In this instance we have taken their location to be a separate zone in the southern suburb.

[7] See Raymond, 'Essai de géographie'.

- the almost total absence of Ḥusayniyya, a poor quarter of no interest to the elite;
- the steady decline of al-Qāhira as a residential zone for the elite, which concentrated primarily in its northern part;
- the continuous rise of the southern suburb, becoming the region most favoured by the ruling class with Birkat al-Fīl and the Citadel as its main poles.
- the subsidiary importance of the western suburb, where only the southern part is increasingly chosen as a residential site by the elite (the northern part registering a peak at the end of the fifteenth century).

Generally speaking, the period 1679–1700 appears to be perfectly continuous with the Mamluk period, maintaining the same urban development pattern.

The Mamluk era (1293–1517)

The first century of Mamluk rule (1293–1412) was dominated by the personality of al-Nāṣir Muḥammad ibn Qalāwūn. In his time, and particularly during his third reign (1310–41), when he participated actively in the planning and execution of many monumental works, Cairo experienced a profound transformation of its urban structure.

First, it is worth noting that the Ḥusayniyya suburb is virtually never cited as the place of an amir's residence, despite Maqrīzī's portrayal of a region of great urban expansion, followed by rapid decline as Cairo falls into crisis in the latter half of the fourteenth century. This fact supports the hypothesis that Ḥusayniyya was relatively unimportant during this period.

The district of al-Qāhira, which was opened to civilian habitation by the fall of the Fatimids and where the Ayyubids are known to have promoted the settlement of amirs in the area previously occupied by the two palaces, long remained the primary residential area for Mamluks. Approximately half of our sample of amirs resided in al-Qāhira in both periods 1293–1341 and 1341–1412. The opening of al-Qāhira for commercial activity, whose vigour and intensity is recorded by Maqrīzī,[8] did not adversely influence the ruling elite, which continued to erect large and beautiful residences in that area. Primarily the northern half of al-Qāhira was home to the elite, doubtless because the amirs, just as in Ayyubid times, chose to settle in the expansive area where the eastern and western Fatimid palaces had stood originally. The two palaces were torn down progressively, opening up large plots for the construction of magnificent residences. The Bashtāk palace (registered as no. 34; constructed 1334–9) is a good example of this trend.[9]

The most significant changes took place in the southern suburb, outside the

[8] See especially the description of the markets and the caravansaries in A. Raymond and G. Wiet, *Les Marchés du Caire* (Cairo, 1979).

[9] Maqrīzī, *Sulūk*, vol. II-2, 501–2 ; Maqrīzī, *Khiṭaṭ*, vol. II, 69–70.

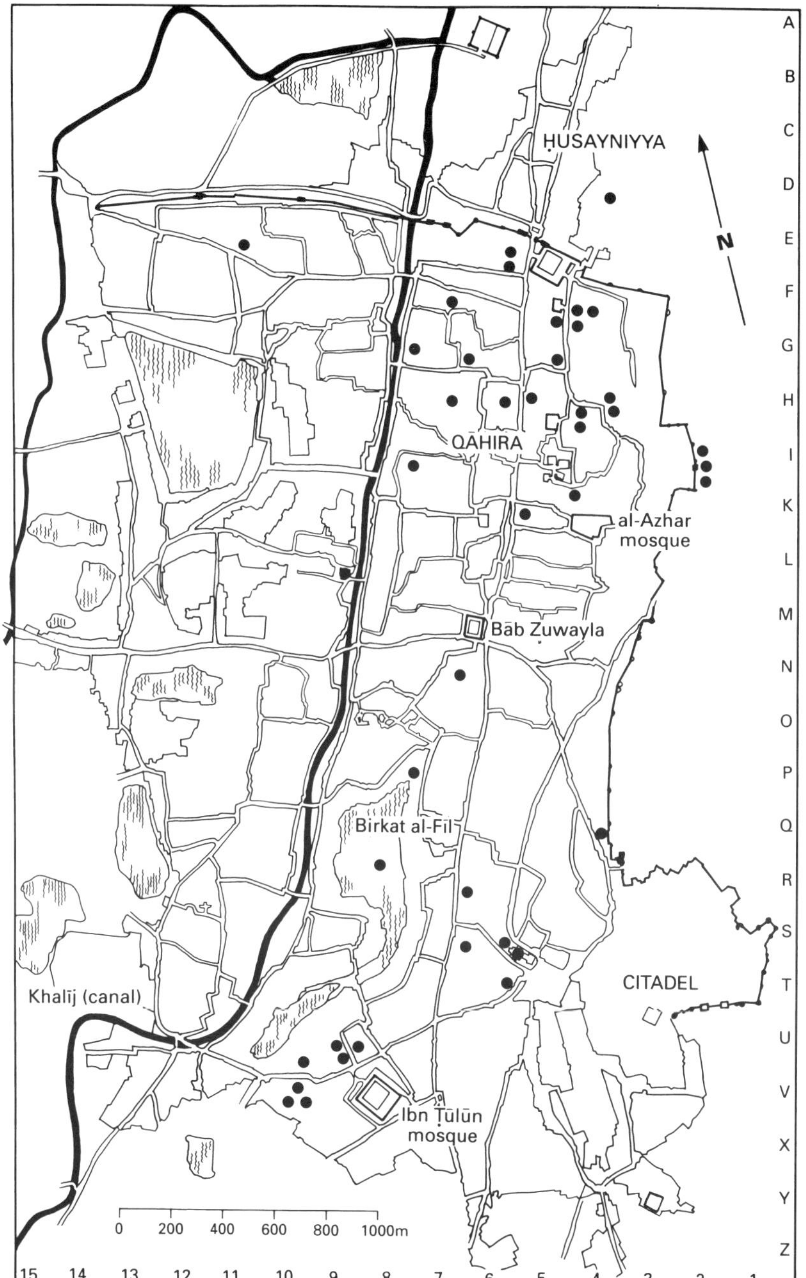

14.1 The ruling elite's residences, 1293–1341

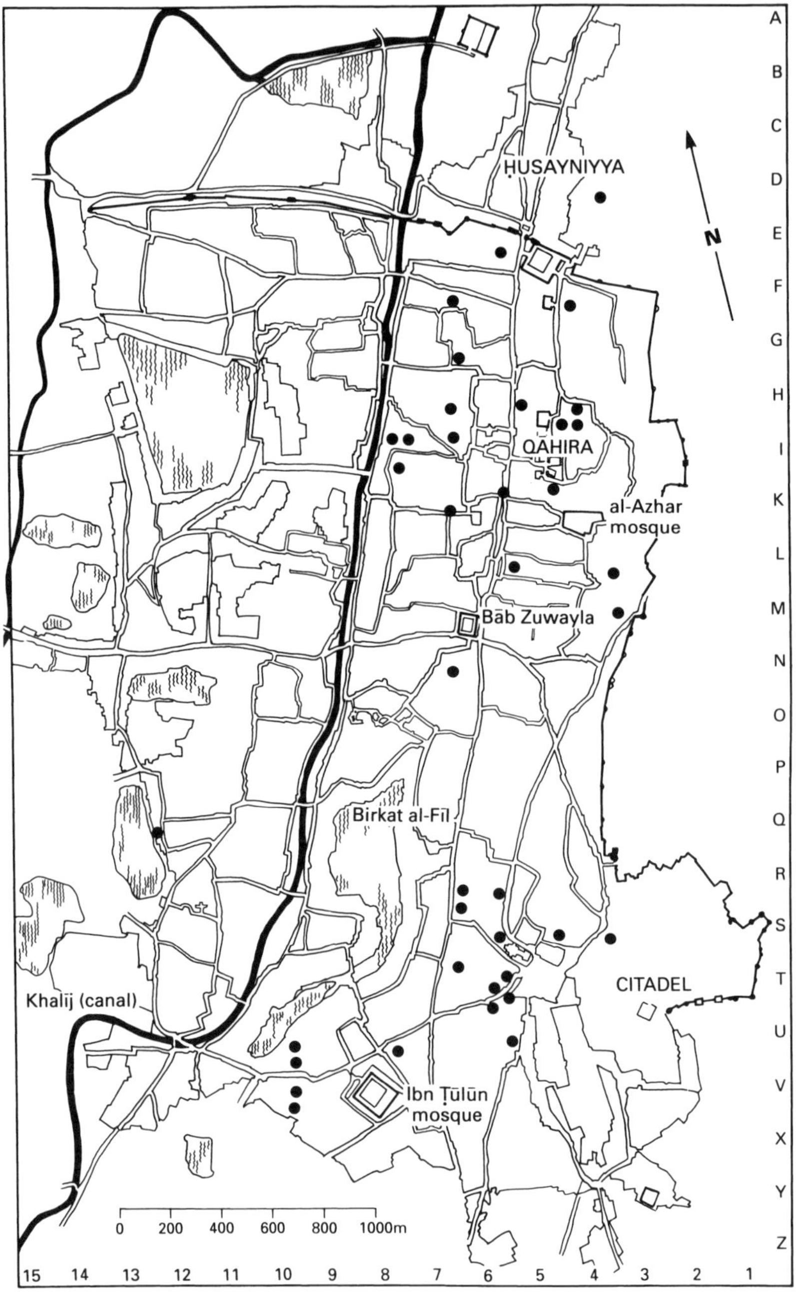

14.2 The ruling elite's residences, 1341–1412

walls of al-Qāhira. This region, located between the walled city which became the actual city centre, and the military/political centre situated in the Citadel throughout most of the millenium, was now the principal theatre of expansion for Cairo. Added to this 'natural' growth were the effects of an intentional policy on the part of al-Nāṣir Muḥammad, who encouraged the notables to erect monumen ts and residences in the south and led the way by his own example. He himself built several mansions for his favourite amirs: the palace of Baktamur al-Sāqī, near Birkat al-Fīl (near V 10), at a cost of 1,000,000 dirhams; the Ṭaqtamur palace at Ḥaḍrat al-Baqar (near S 7) for 1,000,000 dirhams; the palace of Alṭunbughā al-Māridānī at Rumayla (S 6); and the palace of Yalbughā al-Yaḥyāwī for 460,000 dirhams, the most beautiful of all according to Maqrīzī, on the site where the Sultan Ḥasan mosque would be built later (S 6).[10] Several of these imposing mansions are extant at least in part: the Alīn Aq palace (no. 249; Q 4, erected 1293); Qawṣūn palace (no. 266; S 7, 1337); Ṭāz palace (no. 267; T 7, 1352). This building trend lasted throughout the century. As could be expected, most of the amirs houses were built near the Citadel, the centre of power; this being the case for virtually all those cited above. Due to their great size, several of them – and in particular the Qawṣūn palace – would play a central role in the violent military incidents occasioned by struggles for power among the amirs. Birkat al-Fīl, the district of the 'Elephant Pond', stretched over a vast area that the Nile flood inundated each year. It began to attract, from the fourteenth century onwards, those amirs seeking residences with the comforts of water and vegetation as well as a less confined space compared with the urban centre of Qāhira and its economic activity.

Conversely, it is surprising how few amirs' residences were constructed in the western suburb, especially when one bears in mind al-Nāṣir Muḥammad's efforts to develop this part of the city by granting concessions of building land (*ḥikr*).[11] The figures in table 14.1 show clearly that the sultan's policy did not cause any substantial, sustained movement toward the west. In this respect the amirs' behaviour corroborates what we know already concerning the dearth of mosques in the western suburb and leads to the same conclusion: this vast region would not begin to become urbanized until much later, despite Maqrīzī's sanguine depiction which modern historians have often accepted too uncritically.

After the serious crisis in Faraj's reign, a period of renewal commenced in 1412 and lasted until the end of the century. The decline of the walled city (Qāhira) as a place of residence for the elite, however, is apparent from the table: 48.7 per cent of the surveyed mansions in the fourteenth century, compared with 38.2 per cent in the fifteenth. The final numbers for the Mamluk

[10] Maqrīzī, *Sulūk*, vol. II-2, 438, 540; Maqrīzī, *Khiṭaṭ*, vol. II, 68, 72.
[11] Raymond, *Le Caire*, 130–3.

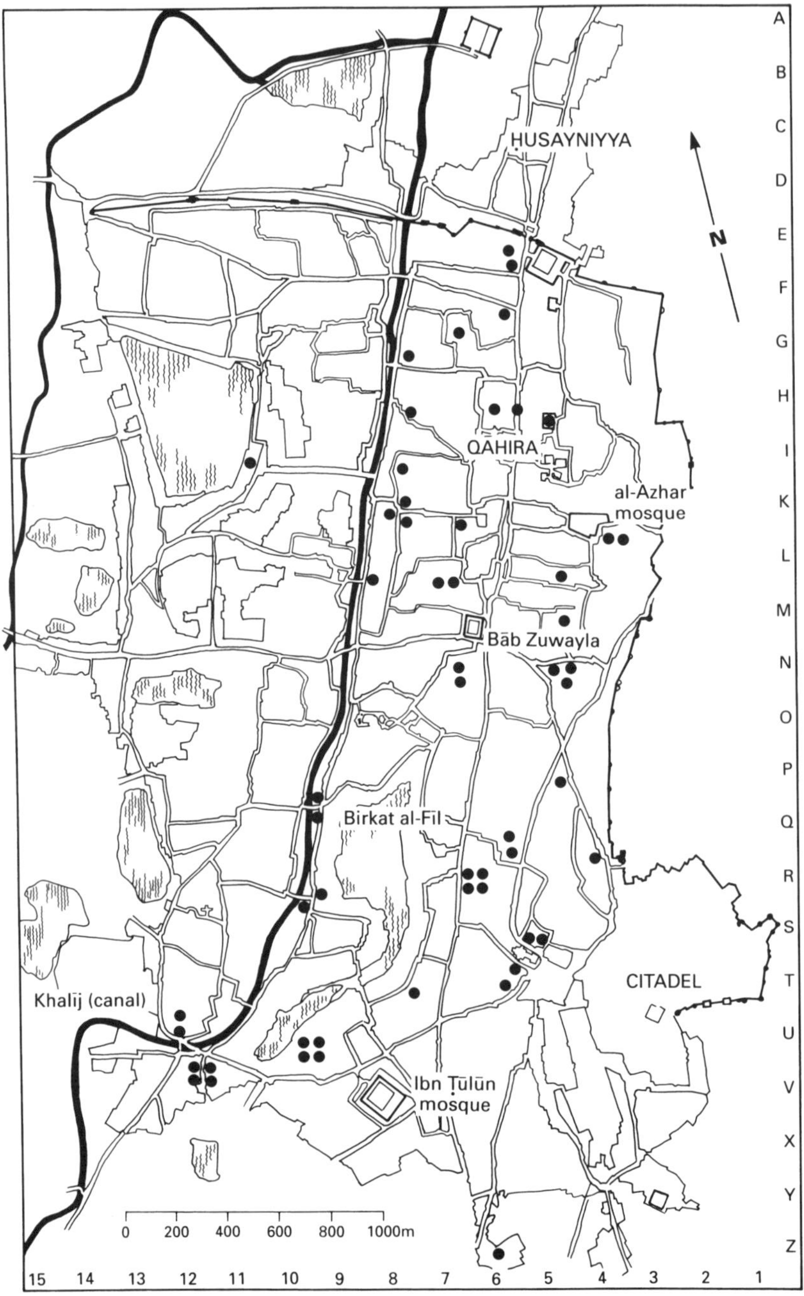

14.3 The ruling elite's residences, 1412–1496

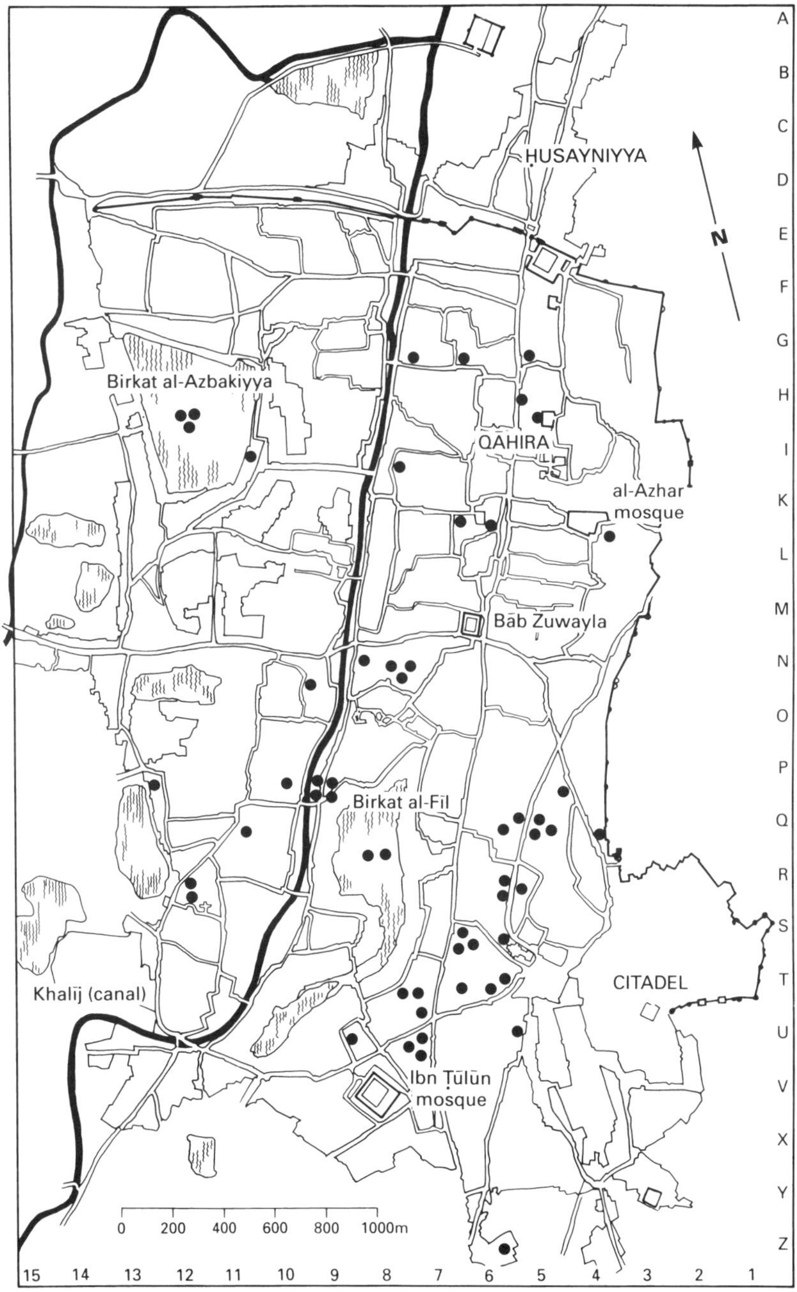

14.4 The ruling elite's residences, 1496–1517

period (1496–1517), a drop to 15.8 per cent, confirm the growing disaffection with al-Qāhira. This process continued in line with a trend which originated in the Ayyubid period, and can be explained by the rising prominence of economic activity in the historical city centre and the increasing settlement of native Egyptians, causing the members of the elite to seek more exclusive residential quarters. The Māmāy al-Sayfī palace (no. 51, H 5, built 1496), later converted into the *bayt al-qāḍī* and of which only the four-arcade *maqʿad* remains today, is one of the rare extant examples of a grand Mamluk mansion in al-Qāhira.

In consequence, the southern suburb was subject to a remarkably even rate of growth as a residential area for amirs: the relative number of mansions located in the south during the four periods of Mamluk rule (table 14.1) are 38.1 per cent; 46.1 per cent 56.4 per cent and 66.7 per cent. The greater part of the Mamluk elite – nearly 50 per cent at the end of the period – continued to concentrate in the two traditionally preferred zones, below the Citadel and around the pond of Birkat al-Fīl. Before becoming, very briefly, the last sultan of the dynasty, the amir Ṭūmānbāy himself had his residence on Ibn Bābā street (U 9). and his palace, giving onto the pond, would be used by Sultan Selim during his stay in Cairo following the Ottoman conquest.[12] The strenuous urbanization of the Birkat al-Fīl neighbourhood during the nineteenth century entailed razing what had remained of the old buildings. Despite later alterations, the Razzāz house near the Citadel (no. 235, P 5) retains something of the general architectural ordonnance of these great residences.

The western suburb, which had been ignored by the elite throughout almost the entire century, experienced a short-lived 'boom' during the reign of Qāytbāy (1468–96). The building venture undertaken by the amir Azbak in 1476, on a site 500 metres beyond the Khalīj on the pond that would bear his name, is well known: a palace, a public fountain and a commercial ensemble were to form the heart of a new urban development. Ibn Iyās asserts, rather optimistically, that 'the people started building magnificent palaces and splendid places on the lake . . . Everyone wanted to live at Azbakiyya, and it became a city of its own.' For the time being, a number of mansions were indeed built in Azbakiyya for members of the elite, which helps explain the size of the western suburb's share (17.5 per cent) in the total of amirs' residences during the final Mamluk period, including the four houses located in Azbakiyya (see Table 14.1). However, the building craze in the northern section of the suburb subsided rather quickly after the deaths of Sultan Qāytbāy and of the *atābak* Azbak. In the sixteenth and seventeenth centuries, Azbakiyya no longer figured among the elite's preferred residential areas. Of some significance is the fact that by the early eighteenth century, the site of the former Azbak palace had become the domicile of a very rich Cairene 'bourgeois', the *tājir*

[12] Ibn Iyās, *Badāʾiʿ*, vol. V, 104; ʿAlī Pasha Mubārak, *al-khiṭaṭ al-jadīda* (Būlāq, 1306/1888), 20 vols., vol. II, 58.

Table 14.2: Localization of the ruling elite's residences during the Ottoman period (beys and officers)[13]

area	1679–1700	end of eighteenth century
Ḥusayniyya	—	—
al-Qāhira	11 (12.5%)	22 (16.9%)
Southern Suburb	65 (73.9%)	46 (35.4%)
(Birkat al-Fīl)	34 (38.6%)	29 (22.3%)
(Citadel)	12 (13.6%)	8 (6.1%)
Western Suburb	12 (13.6%)	62 (47.7%)
(Azbakiyya)	1	20 (15.4%)
(southern part)	10	29
Total	88	130

Sharāyibī. The southern part of the suburb, on the other hand, underwent sustained development from the late fifteenth century onwards, particularly in the districts of Nāṣiriyya (S 13), ʿĀbidīn (P 11) and Ḥanafī (R 11).[14]

The first two centuries of Ottoman rule (sixteenth and seventeenth)

The Ottoman period, as far as the location of residential areas for the governing elite is concerned, was not in any way homogenous. Up to the start of the eighteenth century, the geographic evolvement follows the same pattern that we have sketched for the Mamluk period. The first decades of the eighteenth century are then marked by changes that signify a new era in the urban history of Cairo.

If we compare table 14.2 with table 14.1, it becomes clear that the trend we noted during the Mamluk period concerning the geography of the elite residential districts remained unchanged in the first two centuries of Ottoman rule. This impression of continuity also emerges in a more general manner from the study of Cairo's urban history.

Al-Qāhira was relegated to a position of minor importance according to table 14.2. The amirs by and large quit a district marked by constantly expanding commercial activity (57 markets and 228 caravansaries crowded on approximately 60 hectares of land), leaving it to the indigenous population and in particular to middle-class bourgeois habitation.[15] The amirs who still

[13] The figures for the eighteenth century are taken from the 'Essai de géographie', 83. Please note, however, that the borders of the Birkat al-Fīl quarter are defined somewhat differently.

[14] Ibn Iyās, *Badāʾiʿ*, vol. III, 117, 292: trans. G. Wiet as *Histoire des Mamelouks circassiens* (Cairo, 1945), 131–2, 389. Doris Behrens-Abouseif, *Azbakiyya and its Environs* (Cairo, 1985), 22–33. Raymond, *Le Caire*, 185–6.

[15] On this issue, see Nelly Hanna, *Habiter au Caire* (Cairo, 1991).

lived in al-Qāhira (in houses located on the periphery of the economic activity zone) were also the less affluent members of the ruling caste. An examination of the court documents for the estates of fifty *ocaq* officers who died between 1679 and 1700 shows that the average wealth of the six al-Qāhira residents mentioned, 169,000 paras, was well below the average of 432,000 paras for the entire sample.[16]

The process – under way since the early Mamluk period – by which members of the ruling elite were coming to live in the southern suburb of Cairo continued and was, in a sense, completed in this period: between 1679 and 1700, three quarters (73.9 per cent) of the amirs and beys were residing in the south. The average wealth of the officers (443,000 paras in a sample of thirty-eight individuals) is consistent with the overall group average. The tendency to concentrate around the Birkat al-Fīl was reinforced after 1517, with thirty-four of eighty-eight amirs, or 40 per cent of the elite, now settled there. Furthermore, these residents were wealthy: The officers whose fortune is recorded (twenty-two cases) left estates averaging 513,000 paras, somewhat above the group average. This concentration attests to a rather striking social exclusivism. The perimeter of the *birka* was in effect reserved for the ruling caste while the native populace was excluded. Meanwhile the Citadel zone suffered a perceptible decline as an elite residential area, which constituted a new phenomenon *vis-à-vis* the Mamluk era. This decline is underscored by the comparatively smaller wealth of the officers living in this quarter, with an average of only 96,000 paras each (sample of seven). Two factors may account for this region's loss of favour: the relative disorder around the Citadel, caused by military rebellions and civilian rioting; and also the development of lively commercial centres around Rumayla and Ibn Ṭūlūn. The presence of the rather numerous amirs mansions in the northern portion of the suburb, along the north shore of Birkat al-Fīl, can no doubt be explained by the relocation of the tanneries, around 1,600, from the south-west of Bāb Zuwayla to Bāb al-Lūq, which had opened the former zone to a more affluent style of living. This was the great period of Birkat al-Fīl. Ibn Abī 'l-Surūr al-Bakrī wrote, around the year 1650, that 'most of the *sancaḳs* of Egypt have magnificent constructions and superb buildings there', and the nights at Birkat al-Fīl moved travellers and poets to the most eloquent of descriptions.[17]

The situation in the western suburb around 1700 did not differ much from the one described for the Mamluk period. While amirs continued to settle in the southern part, in the quarters that had become urbanized before 1517 (ʿĀbidīn and Ḥanafī), the northern part was apparently less sought for. Only two palaces are recorded, and only one of these on the shore of the Azbakiyya pond, which had definitely gone out of fashion since the first decades of the Ottoman occupation. Instead of the amirs, the upper middle class of Cairo

[16] These averages are calculated in real terms (i.e. constant-price paras).
[17] Ibn Abī 'l-Surūr, *Kitāb al-kawākib*, Bibliothèque Nationale, Paris, fonds arabe, 1852, 163 ff.

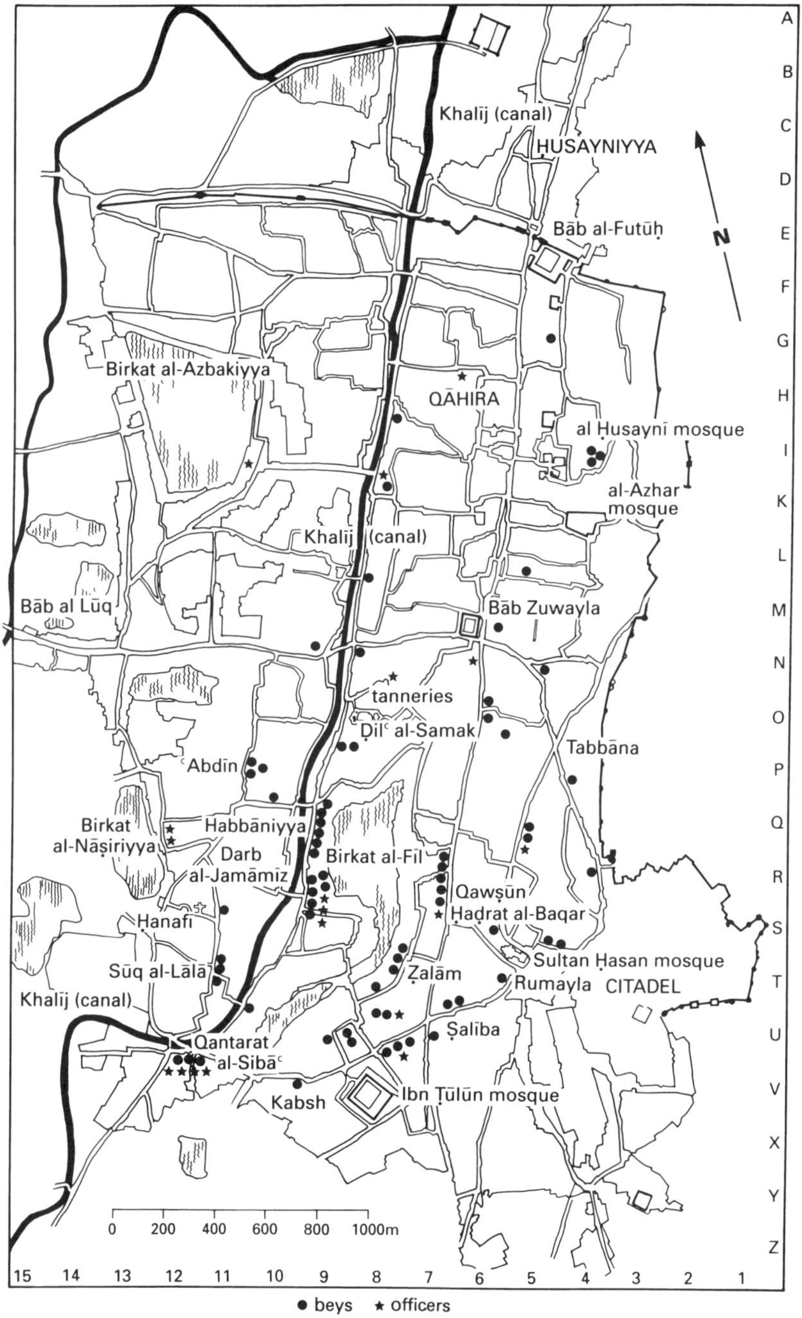

14.5 The ruling elite's residences, 1679–1700

had been moving into the vicinities since the early seventeenth century, putting up houses or summer residences. It is in fact telling that the house of Salīm Bey (I 11), the only amir known to have lived at Azbakiyya, was bought after his death in 1692 by the *qāḍī* Mawāhib Çorbacı, an *ʿaskar* but belonging to the group of *ʿulamāʾ* that freely lived in this neighbourhood.[18] We noted above how the site of the Azbak palace had been taken by an important merchant from the Sharāyibī family. The situation was reverting to what it had been before the amir Azbak launched his ambitious urbanization scheme in the west.

The eighteenth century

The first decades of the eighteenth century were marked by a significant change in Cairo's urban history. The city's expansion had been directed primarily towards the south for five centuries, but from then on the main population flow was oriented toward the west, picking up where the failed ventures of al-Nāṣir Muḥammad in the fourteenth century and of Azbak in the late fifteenth had left off. A period of economic prosperity, and most likely of population increase, in early eighteenth century Cairo may be at the root of a territorial expansion made necessary by the southern district having attained a certain saturation. Increasing crowdedness was surely a factor that impelled people of the elite to seek less populated tracts on which to build large, commodious houses, abounding with water and vegetation, well away from the brouhaha of the sizeable native population. The development of the Birkat al-Azbakiyya sector, which began to take shape around 1720, was punctuated by two important events: the erection of a mosque and fountain on the eastern shore of the *birka* by the prominent merchant Qāsim al-Sharāyibī, near his home (191 G 11, 1728); and especially the construction, by the famous amir ʿUthmān Katkhudā al-Qāzdughlī, of a large complex by the south-western corner of the pond, comprising a mosque (264 K 13, 1734), a fountain, a public bath and several commercial buildings.[19]

We need not go over the features of the elite residential geography again, which have been studied in the *JESHO* article, but we will comment on their novelty in relation to the situation at the close of the seventeenth century. Al-Qāhira would appear to have remained quite active (see table 14.2). However, many of the 'residences' mentioned were in effect only small dwellings, backup homes where amirs could take refuge or hide their possessions in times of crisis. The amirs' forsaking of al-Qāhira was becoming final.

A comparison of the figures for the later seventeenth and eighteenth centuries (Table 14.2) clearly shows the decline of the southern suburb as an elite residential area, its share falling from 73.9 per cent to 35.4 per cent. This decline was particularly marked in the Citadel neighbourhood, which the elite

[18] Al-Jabartī, *ʿAjāʾib*, vol. I, 90. [19] See Behrens-Abouseif, *Azbakiyya*, 55–8.

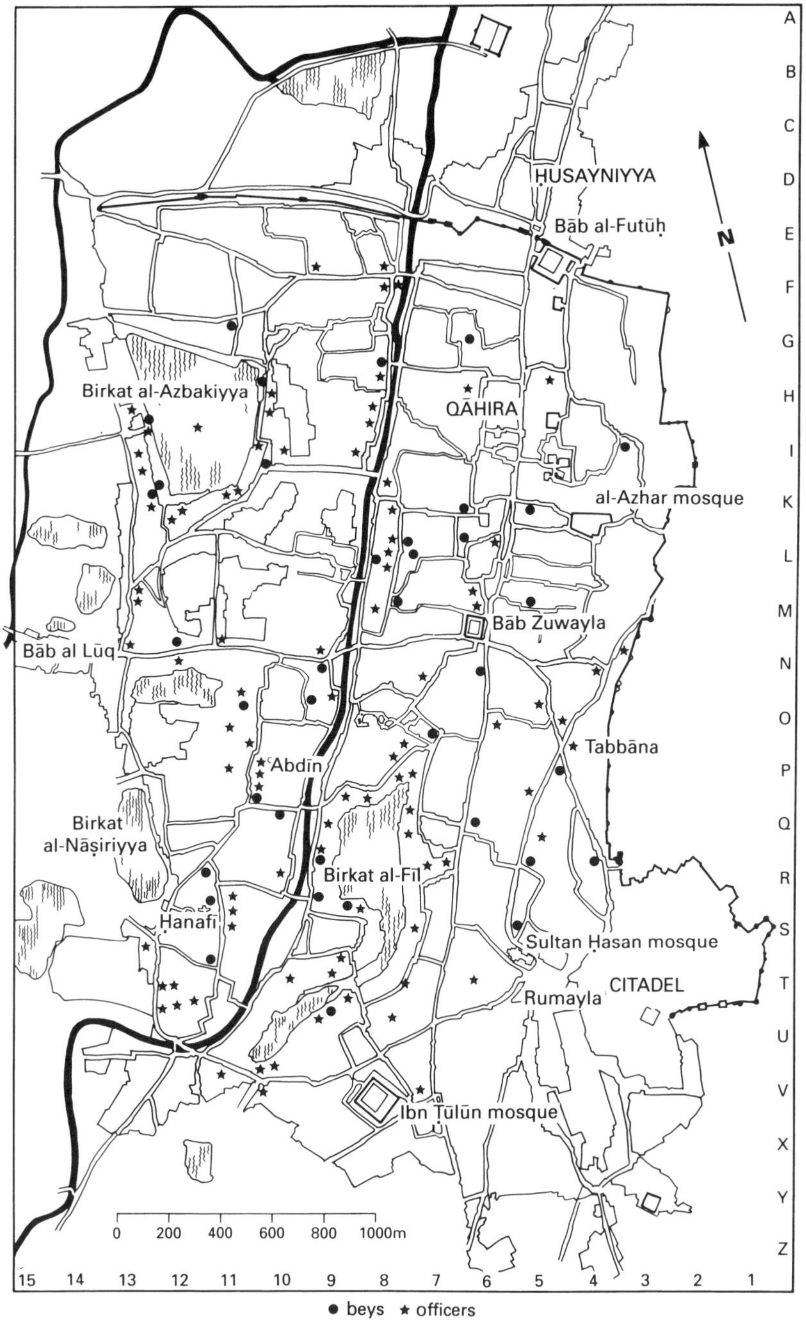

14.6 The ruling elite's residences at the end of the eighteenth century

all but abandoned. Birkat al-Fīl, even while still attracting a number of amirs, lost its primacy and plainly ceased to be the most fashionable quarter. In the course of their promotions, a number of amirs moved from this *birka* to the more 'chic' Azbakiyya. Such was the case of Muḥammad Bey al-Alfī, who in 1798, after having lived in Shaykh al-Ẓallām (S 8) and then Qawṣūn (Q 7), built himself a magnificent palace on the west side of Azbakiyya which would serve later as Napoleon Bonaparte's headquarters (310 H 13).

At that time the greater proportion of amirs, almost half (47.7 per cent) at the end of the century, lived on the west bank of the Khalīj. Led by the paramount amirs Ibrāhīm Katkhudā of the Janissaries and Riḍwān Katkhudā of the ʿAzab, the elite began to agglomerate around the Birkat al-Azbakiyya. The development of its eastern, southern and western edges gradually pushed out the bourgeoisie that had enjoyed living here since the seventeenth century. This *prise de possession* was heralded and epitomized by the sale of the famous Sharāyibī house (176 I 11), before 1744, to Riḍwān Katkhudā, who enlarged it and turned it into a palace that al-Jabartī extols for its sumptuousness.[20] From this time on, it was the 'Azbakiyya nights' that inspired poets, and that remained, after the cataclysm of 1798, as the symbol of the happy days of a world lost forever.

Conclusion

The history of the ruling elite's residential areas informs us about the social and communal behaviour of this group. Examining this evolution over a long period of time, in Cairo's case, reveals a striking continuity from the Mamluk period to the year 1700. To some degree, Cairo's urban fate had been programmed in 1176. In building the Citadel and making it the centre of political power, Saladin transformed the imperial city of the Fatimids, once reserved for the ruling class, into an 'ordinary' city, devoted to commercial activity and open to all native subjects. He also directed the further expansion of the capital towards the vast area located between Bāb Zuwayla and the Citadel. The relocation of the elite quarters from al-Qāhira into the southern suburb, which began in the thirteenth century, continued with remarkable consistency until the end of the seventeenth century. Only at the start of the eighteenth century did the shift toward the west set in.

However, the geography of elite residential areas and its evolution also tell us about the city's urban history, our limited knowledge in this field being otherwise derived from the history of monumental architecture, since the historical texts often yield very little (or mislead by way of excessive optimism or pessimism) on urban flux.[21] The long-term progress of the elite residential

[20] Al-Jabartī, *ʿAjāʾib*, vol. I, 192.

[21] See A. Raymond, 'L'activité architecturale au Caire à l'époque ottomane', *Annales Islamologiques*, 25 (1992); A Raymond, 'Architecture and urban development. Cairo during the Ottoman period', in J. Spagnolo (ed.), *Problems of the Modern Middle East* (Oxford, 1992).

areas would appear to confirm the growth of the southern suburb, which was in fact the essential aspect of Cairo's urban evolution over a period of five centuries. It also proves that, despite two successive tries in the Mamluk era, the city's western suburb was not the object of significant urban development, except in its southern part, until the great boom of the first half of the eighteenth century. In this shape then, Cairo was eternalized in the first scientific maps by Niebuhr (1762) and the *Description de l'Égypte* (1798).[22]

[22] For the development of Cairo during the first half of the eighteenth century, see A. Raymond, *Le Caire des Janissaires* (Paris, 1995).

CHAPTER 15

Patterns of urban patronage in Cairo: a comparison between the Mamluk and the Ottoman periods

DORIS BEHRENS-ABOUSEIF

Historians of Islamic urbanism distinguish between two types of urban genesis: the garrison town that gradually develops into a real city, and the princely city planned to celebrate a new dynasty and to demonstrate its authority. Princely urbanism is not only manifested in the creative phase of a city but can also determine its further development. My chapter aims to show the relationship between patterns of urban development and patterns of political power. I will try to demonstrate that Cairo throughout its history experienced two different trends of urban development, one spontaneous and decentralized and the other centralized and premeditated. Whenever the capital was the seat of a sovereign government and residence of a court, it was the object of premeditated or voluntary urbanism which implied global schemes and transformations involving the city as a whole. In times when the city's role was confined to that of a provincial capital, its development took place in a decentralized and spontaneous mode. The case of Cairo is particularly interesting in this respect because of its persistent continuity as the capital of Egypt since the Arab conquest. Within this continuity, however, various forms and rhythms of urban development took place according to the changes in the city's status. I intend to focus on a comparison between urbanism in the Mamluk and Ottoman periods.

As we all know, Cairo includes more than one capital founded consecutively between the seventh and the tenth centuries. The choice of the geographical location for the first capital, al-Fusṭāṭ, proved to be so adequate that there has never been any attempt to transfer the capital to another area. Consequently, subsequent urban foundations, al-ʿAskar and al-Qaṭāʾiʿ, were in close proximity to the original capital to enable a gradual and ultimate fusion, creating a greater al-Fusṭāṭ; the same phenomenon occurred once again, when al-Qāhira fused with Greater al-Fusṭāṭ.

The development of the first capital, al-Fusṭāṭ, originally a garrison city which became the provincial capital of Egypt, can be qualified as spontaneous without much interference from the political authorities. As we understand from Kubiak's study on the subject, once the site was chosen and the land allocated to the tribes and groups of Arab conquerors and settlers, the city was left to expand according to a decentralized tribal system that characterized the structure of the Arab settlers' society. In al-Fusṭāṭ's early history, the tribal *khiṭṭa* was the dominating element in the town's structure. No governmental agency interfered in urban administration, either on the level of the city as a whole, or on the level of the quarters.[1]

Unlike al-Fusṭāṭ, however, which was founded in circumstances related to the conquest, al-ʿAskar, al-Qaṭā'iʿ and al-Qāhira were palace-cities erected by the rulers as residences for themselves and their dynasties. Their plan and design was largely dictated by the rulers' concepts. We know little about al-ʿAskar, except that it was the residence of the Abbasid governors, but al-Qaṭā'iʿ and al-Qāhira were planned palace-cities, the first to be the residence of the autonomous Tulunid dynasty and the second to be the seat of the Fatimid caliphate.

While al-Qāhira was planned as an exclusive princely capital, and designed to serve the religious and political self-image of the Shīʿa dynasty, al-Fusṭāṭ continued to flourish under the Fatimids as a cosmopolitan, commercial and economic centre without fundamental interference from the rulers. Medieval descriptions emphasize the flourishing markets and the dwellings without referring to important monuments.

After the foundation of al-Qāhira in 969, there was no further initiative in Egypt to found a new capital city. However, the urban development of the double city al-Qāhira and al-Fusṭāṭ between the tenth and the sixteenth centuries was deeply marked by the presence of a powerful princely court. During this period, the fate of the Egyptian capital was to a great extent moulded by the initiatives of three energetic sultans, the Ayyubid Ṣalāḥ al-dīn Yūsuf (1169–93), and the Mamluks al-Nāṣir Muḥammad (1293–1341) and al-Ashraf Qāytbāy (1468–96).

Ṣalāḥ al-dīn's rule marked the opening of a new era in the history of Egypt, and this was manifested in the development of its capital. He planned the transformation of al-Fusṭāṭ and al-Qāhira into a great urban complex without the hierarchy established under the Fatimids. Al-Qāhira's character as exclusive caliphal residence and spiritual centre of the Ismāʿīlī Shīʿa imamate was radically obliterated. The Fatimid palaces, seat and symbol of the imamate, were dismantled and a number of Sunnī religious institutions were founded to confirm Egypt's return to Sunnism. The Citadel was built to replace the Fatimid palace-city as residence of the rulers and centre of political power. Moreover, Ṣalāḥ al-dīn projected the unification of al-Fusṭāṭ and al-Qāhira by enclosing them within one great wall.[2] The unification of the two cities was

[1] Wladyslaw B. Kubiak, *Al-Fustat. Its Foundation and Early Urban Development (*Cairo, 1987), 92.

[2] Paul Casanova, *Histoire et Description de la Citadelle du Caire* (Cairo, 1897); K. A. C. Creswell, *The Muslim Architecture of Egypt* (Oxford, 1959; repr. New York, 1978), 2 vols, vol. II, 1–63; M. Clerget, *Le Caire. Etude de Géographie Urbaine et d'Histoire Economique* (Cairo, 1934), 2 vols, vol. I, 144–80; Janet Abu-Lughod, *Cairo. 1001 Years of the City Victorious* (Princeton, 1971), 27ff.

supposed to bring about the urbanization of the deserted area between the two agglomerations. The intermediary location of the Citadel between them contributed to this scheme. Ṣalāḥ al-dīn assigned the execution of this tremendous task to his energetic chamberlain Bahāʾ al-dīn Qarāqūsh, who was also the *de facto* governor of Egypt during Ṣalāḥ al-dīn's long absences. His aggressive measures to realize such schemes earned Qarāqūsh his qualification in contemporary sources as a capable and energetic man as well as an absurd tyrant.[3]

Ṣalāḥ al-dīn's measures to transform the Egyptian capital were endorsed by subsequent generations. The Citadel continued to be the residence of the rulers until the time of Muḥammad ʿAlī in the nineteenth century. Cairo's urban development continued to take place within the frame of the unified two cities, with al-Qāhira as the main centre and al-Fusṭāṭ as its port and satellite.

Although it was originally Ṣalāḥ al-dīn's idea to unify the two cities, it was al-Nāṣir Muḥammad ibn Qalāwūn who contributed the most to achieving this goal. Among the great number of handsome monuments erected by al-Nāṣir Muḥammad and his amirs were religious foundations and palaces for the sultan and the amirs, as well as important civil and infrastructural works. As I have tried to demonstrate elsewhere, it would be unjust to evaluate these works merely in terms of individual foundations and monuments.[4] Their sheer number – the religious foundations alone amounted to more than forty, which exceeds by far the building average in any contemporary Muslim city – indicates that the sultan pursued a scheme more global and ambitious than a mere response to public requirements – the expansion and embellishment of an imperial capital.

Maqrīzī's *Khiṭaṭ* is the most convincing document for this interpretation as it not only describes the individual buildings, but the development of their urban environment. The historian emphasizes the fact that religious buildings were the nuclei around which new quarters were to expand. He often mentions that orders were given to urbanize an area or that people were encouraged to do so. He describes the morphology of the capital during the reign of al-Nāṣir, referring to entire areas and landscapes, as if he were talking while holding a map in his hands. Maqrīzī frequently uses the word *taʿmīr* and praises such initiatives as constructive and productive, as a factor of security and prosperity replacing chaos and lawlessness, thus putting an end to *kharāb* and desolation.[5]

Al-Nāṣir's reign was the most prosperous and longest of all the Mamluk sultans, amounting to approximately forty years. The threat of Crusaders and

[3] M. Sobernheim, 'Ḳarāḳūsh', in: *The Encyclopaedia of Islam* (Leiden, 1986; new edition); Ibn Khallikān, *Wafayāt al-aʿyān* (Cairo, 1310/1892), 2 vols, vol. I, 439f.; al-Maqrīzī, *Kitāb al-mawāʿiẓ wa-ʾl-iʿtibār fī dhikr al-khiṭaṭ wa-ʾl-āthār* (Būlāq, 1270/1853), 2 vols, vol. I, 364f.; vol. II, 201ff.

[4] Doris Behrens-Abouseif 'Egypt and Syria in the Fatimid and Ayyubid Eras' in: U. Vermealen, D. De Smet (eds.), *Orientalia Loveneasia Anelecta*, vol. 73 (1995), 267–284.

[5] al-Maqrīzī, *Khiṭaṭ*, vol. II, 132.

Mongols had been overcome and Cairo was for the first time the capital not only of Egypt, but of the whole of Syria as well. These circumstances allowed al-Nāṣir to achieve easily his ambitious goals. His and Ṣalāḥ al-dīn's initiatives were encouraged by two simultaneous natural factors, a demographic expansion and the withdrawal of the Nile bed to the west, offering new land to the city of Cairo.[6]

Al-Nāṣir and his amirs erected buildings, not only in locations of the double capital Fusṭāṭ–Qāhira, but far beyond, as if they were to mark the extension of the new metropolis. At a distance of 20 km to the north of Cairo, he founded the complex of Siryāqūs which combined religious and pleasance structures.[7] This remote site was on the road from Syria or the Ḥijāz to Cairo. To the south, his amirs began to erect residential quarters around Birkat al-Fīl.[8]

Whereas Ṣalāḥ al-dīn unified the two cities by encompassing them within a great wall, al-Nāṣir's method of unification was to build up the uninhabited area between them.[9] He therefore erected his most important mosque and a hippodrome in an area between al-Fusṭāṭ and al-Qāhira that had not yet been urbanized, and encouraged his amirs to follow suit. A mosque and a hippodrome were the nuclei of new agglomerations. As Ibn Khaldūn said, *'al-nās ʿalā dīn mulūkihā wa-ʿawāʾidihā'*;[10] he wrote these words referring to how people tend to follow the rulers in their taste for luxury and lavish lifestyle.

A further goal set by al-Nāṣir was the urbanization of the western zone of al-Qāhira and the exploitation of the new land. In order to encourage his amirs to urbanize the area, the sultan gave them the land at favourable conditions which gradually led to the settling of the Nile riverside from Būlāq in the north to al-Fusṭāṭ. During his reign, the cemeteries along the eastern fringe of the city were crammed with princely mausoleums, *khānqāhs* and *madrasas*. Al-Nāṣir personally built and planned additional elegant palaces for his amirs.

This building activity was systematic and accompanied by orders to the population to come and settle in the new quarters. Here it is also important to note the personal involvement of the sultan and his amirs in the construction works and planning of their monuments, which clearly indicates that urban expansion was a political matter.

6 Abu-Lughod, *Cairo*, 31–50.

7 John A. Williams, 'The khanqah of Siryaqus, a Mamluk royal religious foundation', in: A. H. Green (ed.), *In Quest of an Islamic Humanism, Arabic and Islamic Studies in Memory of Mohamed al-Nowaihi* (Cairo, 1983), 109–22.

8 Georges Salmon, *Etudes sur la Topographie du Caire – La Ḳalʿat al-Kabch et la Birkat al-Fîl* (Cairo, 1902).

9 Viktoria Meinecke-Berg, 'Quellen zur Topographie und Baugeschichte in Kairo unter Sultan an-Nāṣir Muḥammad b. Qalāʾūn', *Zeitschrift der Deutschen Morgenländischen Gesellschaft*, Suppl. 3.1 (1977), 538–50; John A. Williams, 'Urbanization and monument construction in Mamluk Cairo', *Muqarnas*, 2 (1984), 33–45; Gaston Wiet, *Cairo, City of Art and Commerce* (Oklahoma, 1964); David Ayalon, 'The expansion and decline of Cairo under the Mamlūks and its background', in: Raoul Curiel (ed.), 'Itinéraires d'Orient – Hommages à Claude Caben', *Res Oreintales*, vol. 6 (1994), 13–20.

10 Ibn Khaldūn, *Muqaddimat Ibn Khaldūn* (Cairo, 1957), 3 vols, vol. II, 696; see also 253, 451 where he writes, *'al-nās ʿalā dīn al-malik'*.

In the late fifteenth century another great builder, al-Ashraf Qāytbāy, directed his zeal to embellishing the Egyptian capital despite economic and political problems. As in the case of al-Nāṣir Muḥammad, Qāytbāy enjoyed a particularly long tenure, allowing him to leave a long-lasting impact on the capital, although his empire was exhausted and impoverished by several military campaigns in Asia Minor.

The area of the Egyptian capital had reached large dimensions and its architectural legacy was substantial. The sultan's urban policy was to consolidate this legacy and to rejuvenate the capital.[11] He undertook upgrading and restoration works all over the city, including the Citadel, and he erected a number of fountains in various quarters. The building activities of Qāytbāy were significantly influenced by religion, whereby his restoration works not only covered all shrines and important mosques of al-Qāhira and al-Fusṭāṭ, but also the holy cities of Jerusalem, Mecca and Medina. The sultan used to ride through the city and personally inspect the condition of the streets and buildings and give orders for clearing, upgrading or rebuilding. I believe that one can qualify the attitude of Qāytbāy towards the capital with historicism. Contrary to al-Nāṣir Muḥammad, he never endeavoured to replace the founder's name with his own in the course of his restoration activities.

This sense for restoration is also demonstrated by Yashbak al-Dawādār's clearing of Cairo's streets. He took the opportunity of the sultan's return from pilgrimage to eliminate all encroachments from the streets and restore their original width, and he ordered buildings to be painted.[12] Apparently this initiative was met with anger and protest by those who saw their shops and booths destroyed; in a recently published document, a kind of *fatwā*, the jurist Abū Ḥāmid al-Maqdisī, a Shāfiʿī, defended Yashbak's regulations with legal arguments based on the four schools of Islamic law.[13] Herein the author revises Cairo's history and enumerates all the open spaces that originally abounded in the city, arguing that it was necessary and legal to restore them in order to restore Cairo's original beauty and give it the appearance of an '*ʿarūs*'. This document is significant as it evokes an interest in bringing Cairo back to its past urban and architectural glory.

Qāytbāy himself was not directly involved in the creation of new quarters, but he allowed his two most powerful amirs, Yashbak al-Dawādār and Azbak (Uzbak) the *atābak*, to initiate ambitious projects that were far from merely philanthropic.[14] These projects transformed large areas in the suburbs.

[11] Shams al-dīn Muḥammad b. ʿAbd al-Raḥmān al-Sakhāwī, *al-Ḍaw' al-lāmiʿ li-ahl al-qarn al-tāsiʿ*, (Cairo, 1353/1934), 12 vols, vol. VI, 201ff; Ibn Iyās, *Badāʾiʿ al-zuhūr fī waqāʾiʿ al-duhūr*, ed. M. Muṣṭafā (Cairo, 1963), vol. III, 329ff. [12] Ibn Iyās, *Badāʾiʿ*, vol. III, 127.

[13] *al-Fawāʾid al-nafīsa al-bāhira fī bayān ḥukm shawāriʿ al-Qahīra fī madhāhib al-aʾimma al-arbaʿa al-zāhira,* ed. by A. al-ʿImārī (Cairo, 1988).

[14] Doris Behrens-Abouseif, *Azbakiyya and its Environs from Azbak to Ismāʿīl (1476–1879)* (Cairo, 1985); Doris Behrens-Abouseif, 'A Circassian Mamluk suburb north of Cairo', *Art and Archaeology Research Papers,* 14 (1978), 17–23; Doris Behrens-Abouseif, 'The north-eastern extension of Cairo under the Mamluks', *Annales Islamologiques,* 17 (1981), 157–90.

Yashbak in the north founded a pleasance quarter with religious and residential structures which he connected with the northern part of the city by a monumental elevated passage. As for Azbak, he transformed the western periphery of the city by digging the large pool of Azbakiyya and building a new quarter on its southern shore. Perhaps he had in mind the pond called Baṭn al-Baqara dug by the Fatimid caliph al-ʾĀmir on the same site centuries earlier to create a panorama for the caliph's belvederes.[15] In the meantime the area had fallen into decline. Ibn al-Jīʿān, a prominent bureaucrat, chose another suburb, that of al-Zāwiya al-Ḥamrā' in the north-west, for his residential religious complex.[16]

In all three cases, Ṣalāḥ al-dīn, al-Nāṣir Muḥammad and Qāytbāy, we are dealing with a programme to define the urban development of the city: Ṣalāḥ al-dīn designed the shape of post-Fatimid Cairo, al-Nāṣir built it up and Qāytbāy endeavoured to preserve it.

Al-Nāṣir Muḥammad and Qāytbāy did not envisage the city merely in the perspective of single monuments or quarters, but in its entirety. The capital as residence of the sultan was in fact the object of their vision. It may not be an exaggeration to see the profusion of religious buildings as a means of intensifying the urbanization and the embellishment of the capital. Although not always to the same degree, other Mamluk sultans and amirs continued to adorn the capital with monuments – even as late as Sultan al-Ghawrī, who knew that the Ottomans were on their way to Egypt.

The building activity of the Mamluk period on the whole and the urban development of Cairo do not directly reflect the extent of the depopulation that followed the Black Death in 1347–9. The excessive urbanization of al-Nāṣir's era could not be upheld, but later sultans and amirs went on erecting monuments. Michael Dols noticed that the epidemics did not cause a marked change in the economic and psychological attitudes of the Egyptians.[17] Amir Shaykhū built a religious complex of great importance during the years of the Black Death, and Sultan Ḥasan, only a decade later, erected the most monumental building of medieval Cairo. Travellers in the fifteenth and sixteenth centuries were impressed by Cairo's size and prosperity.[18] The Mamluks' enthusiasm for building could not be halted by the recessions. They did not build merely to respond to specific public needs, but also to enhance their imperial capital. It has been said that historiography and architecture were the arts that flourished most in the Mamluk period.

As in other cultures, absolutist regimes in Islamic society were able to undertake urban and architectural projects of gigantic proportions. In pre-modern Islamic society, moreover, the role of the ruler *per se* included municipal competence and religious sponsorship involving building activity. In his *Siyāsat-*

[15] al-Maqrīzī, *Khiṭaṭ*, vol. II, 162. [16] Ibn Iyās, *Badāʾiʿ*, vol. III, 280, 363.
[17] Michael Dols, *The Black Death in the Middle East* (Princeton, 1977), 264.
[18] André Raymond and Gaston Wiet, *Les Marchés du Caire* (Cairo, 1979), 65ff.

nāmeh Niẓām al-Mulk wrote that the ruler has the responsibility of carrying out all infrastructural and civil works, founding new cities and building fortifications and representative monuments.[19] In fact the greatest part of the Islamic architectural heritage was due to the patronage of the ruling establishment.

The Mamluk sultans and their amirs personally carried out many of the administrative functions in providing a water supply, sanitation and public works essential to city life, and endowed religious and educational institutions. They took their responsibility for the condition of the streets, the protection of public spaces and urban improvements for granted. Ambitious urban projects required energetic and absolutist rulers who could apply unorthodox methods such as the use of corvée, mobilization of prisoners and soldiers for labour, the recruitment of craftsmen, and the supply of spoils and other material, as well as confiscations, demolitions and *waqf* manipulations. In a highly centralized system where the economic resources were almost entirely administered by the ruling establishment and its clientele who dwelt in the great cities, the urban centres and especially the capital were the main beneficiaries of princely patronage. The Mamluk aristocracy's lack of involvement with the land, except as a source of revenue, led to the concentration of all energy and purchasing power in the capital. Their strong grip on the economic activities of the cities enabled the sultan and his amirs to penetrate all aspects of urban life. As noted by Lapidus, the Mamluk household was a means of transforming public into private powers and state authority into personal superiority.[20] This was the case with the extensive use of *waqf*, which channelled public funds into individual philanthropic endowments whereby public services took the image of princely patronage. In periods of political stability and strength such as during the reigns of Ṣalāḥ al-dīn, al-Nāṣir Muḥammad, and al-Ashraf Qāytbāy, princely patronage served an urban vision.

Cairo's Mamluk architecture confirms the supremacy of the urban environment in the builder's mind. The buildings were rarely monumental and their proportions tended to become reduced and asymmetrical with time. Architecture was subordinated to the urban environment. It was the street perspective that dictated the silhouette of the facade and the position of the various exterior elements. As the majority of Egypt's medieval monuments were concentrated in Cairo, the city and its architecture are closely linked. The architectural styles developed in Cairo were rarely transmitted elsewhere, not even to the Egyptian province. What we in fact know as Mamluk style is the imperial style of Cairo.

The Ottoman conquest of 1517 brought Cairo back to provincial status. The purpose of the Ottoman presence in Egypt was the exploitation of its revenues for the sultan in Istanbul. The Ottoman authorities, however, had obligations

[19] Niẓāmulmulk, *Das Buch der Staatskunst Siyāsatnāma* trans. K. E. Schabinger Frhr. von Schowingen (Zürich, 1987), 162.

[20] Ira Lapidus, *Muslim Cities in the Later Middle Ages* (Cambridge, 1984), 49f.

to fulfil in Egypt, such as public works, especially those concerning irrigation and water supply. Moreover, charitable endowments made by the Ottoman governors reveal an intelligent religious and social policy which aimed at strengthening religious ties with the Egyptian population.

The system of patronage elaborated in the Mamluk period could not survive. At the same time, the limited tenure of the Ottoman governors prevented them from identifying with the city and developing personal ties and ambitions. This does not at all imply that Cairo was abandoned to decline, but merely that it no longer enjoyed the luxury of visionary urban innovations. Although neither the Ottoman sultans nor the pashas sought their glory in the expansion of the Egyptian capital, they were eager to sponsor the religious sites, as an important number of charitable endowments made by the governors document.[21]

The pashas of Egypt erected mosques and restored old ones, but they did not plan the creation of new quarters or any kind of urban expansion or transformation. The quarters created in the late Mamluk period for prestige rather than necessity, such as Yashbak's and Azbak's quarters, could not be maintained, and declined in the period following the conquest. Būlāq, however, which had the vital function of a port connecting Egypt with Turkey, flourished.[22]

Unlike Istanbul, where the *waqfs* or pious foundations of the ruling establishment were designed to create new urban centres as *maḥallas* with charitable and commercial structures concentrated within the same area, the governors' *waqfs* in Cairo were rather scattered all over the city. For example, Sulaymān Pasha (1525–35, 1537–8) founded a mosque at the Citadel, another at Būlāq, a *madrasa* in the quarter of Qawṣūn and a *zāwiya* in the quarter of Sūq al-Silāḥ. He had a *khān* near al-Azhar and houses in the Jewish quarter. This pattern shows that the founder was not tied to a specific urban project, but rather that his *waqf* was flexible and conceived according to needs and to available estates.

The *waqf* of Muḥammad Pasha Qūl Qīrān (1607–11), one of the most important made by a governor in Egypt, endowed mosques, primary schools in various provincial cities such as Rosetta, Jirjā and Damanhūr, and furthermore contributed to the maintenance of the al-Aqṣā mosque in Jerusalem. The commercial buildings that financed the religious foundations were similarly located in various places all over the country.

Ottoman patronage was guided by religious motivations. They were particularly eager to sponsor the Egyptian shrines or sanctuaries venerated by all Muslims. The governors restored the mosque of ʿAmr ibn al-ʿĀṣ, the first mosque of Egypt, and sponsored al-Azhar, the first mosque in al-Qāhira.

21 Doris Behrens-Abouseif, *Egypt's Adjustment to Ottoman Rule. Institutions, Waqf and Architecture in Cairo (16th & 17th Centuries)* (Leiden, 1994). The following discussion of Ottoman urbanism relies on the research presented in this book.

22 Nelly Hanna, *An Urban History of Būlāq in the Mamluk and Ottoman Periods* (Cairo, 1983).

They promoted the shrine of Sayyida Zaynab and the shrine of ʿUqba ibn ʿĀmir in the cemetery (Muḥammad Pasha al-Silāḥdār, 1652–6), and rebuilt the shrine called Ribāṭ al-Āthār (Ibrāhīm Pasha, 1661–4), dedicated to the relics of the Prophet. A mausoleum was built for Shaykh al-Ṭaḥāwī who died in the ninth century (Ḥamza Pasha, 1683–87). Important *waqfs* provided water to all shrines of the southern cemetery as well as the transport of water with the pilgrimage caravan. Such endowments did not have an impact on the urban development of the city itself. The Ottomans also restored Mamluk buildings, giving them new functions, turning them for example into *tekkes* for Turkish Sufi orders, such as the Baktāshīs, the Mawlawīs and many others. As a result, the Mamluk institutions were gradually overshadowed.

It is also important to note that by a close examination of the *waqf* documents, as recent research has shown, it appears that many of the commercial buildings and dwellings included in the *waqfs* of the Ottoman governors were already in existence during Mamluk times and often even belonged to Mamluk *waqfs*, which implies that they must have been acquired by means that were not always legal. *Istibdāl* of *waqfs*, although theoretically refuted in the *Qānūnnāme* of Egypt, was widely applied by the governors.[23] For example, an important number of commercial structures included in the *waqf* of Iskandar Pasha (1556–9) were not newly erected by him but had belonged to the Mamluk amir Jānim al-Ḥamzāwī who was executed with his son by Sulaymān Pasha.[24] The *waqf* of Sulaymān Pasha included commercial structures founded by Mamluk predecessors. As Ḥusām al-dīn Ismāʿīl has demonstrated, many of the Ottoman residences mentioned in *waqf* documents were a Mamluk heritage.[25] This does not necessarily diminish the philanthropic effect of Ottoman endowments, but it shows that the foundations of this period did not mean urban expansion, though they might have served the revitalization of certain areas.

Although no urban programme was elaborated by the Ottoman authorities for Cairo, economic activity and the needs of an increasingly affluent military class did not abandon the Egyptian capital to stagnation.[26] Unlike the pashas, the local aristocracy did not set out before the seventeenth century to make large endowments; these were usually family trusts, i.e. the beneficiary was primarily the founder, his family and clan. The *waqfs* established by the members of the military aristocracy, as well as those of Ottoman residents in Cairo, consisted essentially of urban upgrading projects established in the area where the founder dwelt together with his clan. These projects were not part

[23] Muḥammad ʿAfīfī, 'Asālīb al-intifāʿ al-iqtiṣādī bi-ʾl-awqāf fī Miṣr fī ʾl-ʿaṣr al-ʿUthmānī', *Annales Islamologiques*, 24 (1988), 103–38.

[24] Gerd Winkelhane and Klaus Schwarz, *Der osmanische Statthalter Iskender Pascha (gest. 1571) und seine Stiftung in Ägypten und am Bosporus* (Bamberg, 1985), 79.

[25] Muḥammad Ḥusām al-dīn Ismāʿīl, 'Arbaʿ [sic!] buyūt mamlūkiyya min al-wathāʾiq al-ʿuthmāniyya', *Annales Islamologiques*, 24 (1988), 49–102.

[26] André Raymond, *Le Caire* (Paris, 1993), 194ff.; André Raymond, *Le Caire des Janissaires* (Paris, 1995).

of a governmental urbanization policy but due to private initiative serving the founder's needs. As in the cases of Riḍwān Bey (1660s) and Ibrāhīm Aghā Mustaḥfiẓān (1640's-50's), documented by André Raymond,[27] the founder would restore the buildings of his neighbourhood and build or rebuild a residence for himself, sometimes adding a small mosque and a *sabīl-maktab*. There were other similar cases such as the quarter of ʿĀbidīn Bey (1630s), that of Dāwūdiyya founded by Dāwūd Aghā (1600s) and ʿUthmān Katkhudā at Azbakiyya (1730s). These urban projects were not motivated by global ideas of urban expansion or landscape transformation. Their philanthropic aspect was also limited. Instead of the educational institutions of the Mamluk predecessors, neighbourhood mosques and *sabīl-maktabs* were preferably founded. The absence of prestige thinking in terms of architecture can also be recognized by the fact that the military aristocracy of Ottoman Egypt erected very few funerary monuments for themselves.

The large number of *sabīl-maktabs* established during the Ottoman period all over Cairo are a product of neighbourhood upgrading initiatives. The majority of the free-standing *sabīl-maktabs* were founded by the members of the military aristocracy, the religious establishment and merchants.

For more than two centuries, the aristocracy of the Ottoman regime in Egypt did not regard the foundation of monuments as a priority, but rather as the consolidation of their power through the purchase of Mamluks, as demonstrated by the often-cited allegory of Qāsim and Dhū ʾl-Faqār.[28] During the eighteenth century the affluence of the local notables is evident through the expansion of areas which had been left in stagnation for more than two centuries, such as the western suburbs. This urban expansion was also a spontaneous process.

Cairo's urban development in the Ottoman period was not dictated by a central policy or guided by an imperial vision. It was rather pragmatic and conservative. Thanks to this policy, the Mamluk heritage was maintained and preserved until modern times. However, to use Abu-Lughod's words, on the eve of Muḥammad ʿAlī's reign Cairo had become 'a senile provincial capital'.[29] The notables required a long period of time to channel the affluence produced by commerce into prestigious buildings and institutions. ʿAbd al-Raḥmān Katkhudā, in the mid-eighteenth century, was the first to have a vision of the city as a whole as demonstrated by his restoration and embellishment of religious monuments in various areas of the capital.[30] The first *madrasa* founded in Ottoman Cairo to teach the four rites of Islamic law was that of Muḥammad Bey Abū ʾl-Dhahab in the late eighteenth century.

I would like to conclude this characterization of urban development pat-

[27] 'Les grands waqfs et l'organisation de l'espace urbain à Alep et au Caire à l'époque Ottomane (XVIe-XVIIe siècles)', *Bulletin d'Etudes Orientales* 31 (1979), 113–28.

[28] Behrens-Abouseif, *Adjustment*, 116ff. [29] Abu-Lughod, *Cairo*, 85.

[30] Doris Behrens-Abouseif, 'The ʿAbd al-Raḥmān Katkhudā style in 18th century Cairo', *Annales Islamologiques*, 26 (1992), 117–26.

terns in Cairo with a short reference to Muḥammad ʿAlī. The ascendance of Muḥammad ʿAlī to a life tenure in Egypt marks the return of law and order after a period of disorder and French occupation. Abu-Lughod compares Muḥammad ʿAlī's initiatives in Cairo with those of Ṣalāḥ al-dīn, but one can also compare his urban projects with those of al-Nāṣir Muḥammad. He cannot be compared, however, with Qāytbāy whose programme was characterized by a desire for conservation. Under his reign Cairo was again to play the role of capital and residence to a dynasty. It is therefore not surprising that Muḥammad ʿAlī's building activity in Cairo commenced with his own personal palace in the northern outskirt together with a road leading to it, followed shortly thereafter by the foundation of a mausoleum for his family.[31] This was the second time only that an Ottoman governor in Egypt built a funerary structure for himself. Muḥammad ʿAlī founded his mosque in 1830, which also served as his own mausoleum, on the most visible spot of the capital. These monuments celebrated the founder's authority over Egypt and symbolized his identification with its capital.

It thus appears that pre-modern Cairo owed its heyday to princely urbanism. In its early history this was manifested in the foundation of new palace-cities, in later periods urban transformations were favoured. Nevertheless, the status of the city as capital and residence of a princely household was a prerequisite for the deployment of spectacular urban schemes. As for the spontaneous form of urbanism, it manifested itself in early medieval al-Fusṭāṭ and in Ottoman Cairo. We do not have enough information about al-Fusṭāṭ to draw a parallel between the mode of its development and that of Ottoman Cairo, but we may globally say that in the absence of princely patronage, but with the support of a sturdy economy, both cities were able to maintain themselves through the perspective of the neighbourhood, be it the tribal *khiṭṭa* or the quarter.

[31] Gaston Wiet, *Mohammed Ali et les Beaux-Arts* (Cairo, n.d.), 259.

CHAPTER 16

Notes on the early *naẓar al-khāṣṣ*

DONALD P. LITTLE

In the year 740/1339, after serving some eight years as *nāẓir al-khāṣṣ* under Sultan al-Malik al-Nāṣir Muḥammad ibn Qalāwūn, al-Qāḍī Sharaf al-dīn ʿAbd al-Wahhāb b. al-Tāj Faḍl Allāh, known as al-Nashw, died as a result of tortures designed to induce him to disclose the whereabouts of the vast wealth he was suspected of accumulating and concealing during his tenure of office. Now the death of financial officers of state under such conditions was certainly nothing new in Islamic medieval history, and al-Nashw himself was notorious for the use of prolonged and excruciating torture of his colleagues and rivals as an instrument of extortion. What was unusual and noteworthy was the public reaction to the arrest, ordeal and death of this villain. According to al-Maqrīzī, when the people of Cairo heard the news of the arrest of al-Nashw and his family, 'the people came out like a swarm of locusts', and this, according to al-ʿAynī, was the occasion for great celebration.[1] Furthermore, some months after the death of al-Nashw the confectioners of Cairo enjoyed a landslide business in selling candy dolls representing al-Nashw, his two brothers, his mother and his sister. These figures, realistically depicted down to the strips of cloth wrapped around al-Nashw's legs to the Baghdādī *izār* and *zarkhūfī* sandals adorning his sister, were paraded by dancers around the city, pantomiming the torture and suffering of the family. So great was the demand for these effigies that the confectioners continued to make them for twenty days, finding the greatest demand among Coptic clerks, who used them to decorate their homes.[2] These details are noteworthy not so much for their own sake, I believe, as for their indication of the wealth of data available in the sources for this personage, greater, I suspect, than for any other figure of al-Nāṣir's rule, with the possible exception of Ibn Taymiyya. This wealth of material and the historiographical opportunities and problems it poses provide one of the impulses for my own interest in al-Nashw as part of my preoccupation with Baḥrī Mamluk historiography in general and the reign of al-Malik al-Nāṣir in particular. But there are reasons other than historiographical for studying al-

[1] Aḥmad ibn ʿAlī al-Maqrīzī, *Kitāb al-Sulūk*, ed. M. M. Ziyāda, (Cairo, 1941–58), vol. II, 478.
[2] Badr al-dīn al-ʿAynī, *ʿIqd al-jumān*, Istanbul Topkapısaray Ahmet III MS 2911/c34, fol.154b.

Nashw, such as: his role in al-Nāṣir's rule and the light he sheds on the sultan himself and his sultanate; the nature of al-Nashw's office, the *naẓar al-khāṣṣ*; and his status as a Copt forced to convert to Islam. Needless to say, all these factors are interrelated.

Given the abundance of material available on al-Nashw, it is curious that most of it comes from only one or two contemporary sources. As I have argued elsewhere, the fullest, most detailed source for the last decade of al-Nāṣir's reign is *Nuzhat al-nāẓir fī sīrat al-Malik al-Nāṣir* by Mūsā ibn Muḥammad ibn Yaḥyā al-Yūsufī (d. 759/1358), preserved anonymously in a unique manuscript for the years 733–8/1332–8; in extensive, acknowleged quotations by the fifteenth-century historian al-ʿAynī (d. 855/1451); and by extensive, unacknowledged paraphrases by al-Shujāʿī (d. after 756/1355) and al-Maqrīzī (d. 845/1441–2), all three of whose annals for this period are based largely, almost exclusively, on al-Yūsufī's.[3] Syrian historians for obvious reasons were not very interested in the Egyptian financial bureaucracy unless it directly affected them; other, nearly contemporary historians who would have been interested in such matters did not live long enough, in the case of Baybars al-Manṣūrī (d. 725/1324–5) and al-Nuwayrī (d. 732/1331–2), or did not choose to write much about the events in question, as with Ibn al-Dawādārī (d. after 735/1335–6), Badr al-dīn Baktāsh al-Fākhirī (d. 745/1344–5), and Mufaḍḍal ibn Abī ʾl-Faḍāʾil (d. after 759/1358).[4] All these authors mention al-Nashw on only a few occasions, and then briefly, as compared to the page after page devoted to him by al-Yūsufī. Other than the latter, there is to my knowledge only one other important source for this figure: a biography in two forms by Khalīl b. Aybak al-Ṣafadī in his *Aʿyān al-ʿaṣr wa-aʿwān al-naṣr,* a biographical dictionary of his contemporaries, and in *al-Wāfī bi-ʾl-wafayāt*, a dictionary of great Muslims from all eras.[5] Each of these historians takes a different point of view towards al-Nashw. Since Ibn al-Dawādārī's work *al-Durr al-fākhir fī sīrat al-Malik al-Nāṣir*, as its title suggests, borders on encomium, this author, not surprisingly, takes a non-committal stance towards al-Nashw on the three occasions he mentions him. Accordingly, he uses the occasion of al-Nashw's appointment

[3] Donald P. Little, 'The recovery of a lost source for Baḥrī Mamlūk history', *Journal of the American Oriental Society,* 94 (1974); 43–6, Donald P. Little, 'An analysis of the relationship between four Mamluk chronicles for 737–45', *Journal of Semitic Studies*, 19 (1974), 252–68. Both articles are reprinted in Donald P. Little, *History and Historiography of the Mamlūks* (London, 1986), nos. III and IV.

[4] Ibn al-Dawādārī, *Kanz al-durar*, ed. H. R. Roemer (Cairo, 1960) (hereafter Ibn al-Dawādāri), vol. IX, 364, 376, 392; al-Fākhirī, untitled fragment in *Beiträge zur Geschichte der Mamlūkensultane*, ed. K. V. Zetterstéen (hereafter al-Fākhirī), (Leiden, 1919), 185, 194, 203, 204; Mufaḍḍal, *al-Nahj al-sadīd*, in *Ägypten und Syrien zwischen 1317 und 1341 in der Chronik des Mufaḍḍal b. Abī l-Faḍāʾil*, ed. and trans. Samira Korantamer (Freiburg im Breisgau, 1973) (hereafter Mufaḍḍal), 30, 113, 153, 157, 181, 197, 198, 200, 201, 205–7, 210–12, 216, 241, 255. For this article I have not consulted al-Muqrī's *Nathr al-jumān fī tarājim al-aʿyān.*

[5] *Aʿyān,* facsimile edn, ed. Fuat Sezgin and M. Amawi (Frankfurt, 1990), vol. II, 123–5; *Das biographische Lexicon des Ṣalāḥaddīn Ḫalīl ibn Aibak aṣ Ṣafadī*, ed. Riḍwān as-Sayyid (Stuttgart, 1993), vol. XIX, 324–7.

as a *mustawfī* (accountant) as yet another opportunity to praise the sultan: '*fa-laḥaẓathu al-sa'āda al-sulṭāniyya allatī law laḥaẓat al-ṣakhr la-ayna'a wa-azhara wa-athmara, aw al-layl al-dājī awākhir al-shahr al-aqmar* (the royal felicity perceived him, which if it perceived stone, it would mellow, bloom, and give forth fruit, or the gloomy night at the end of the month would become moon-bright).'[6] Not much, then, can be expected about al-Nashw from this quarter. Nor from the abbreviated annal by al-Fākhirī, who mentions al-Nashw briefly on four occasions; nevertheless, he makes his sentiments clear when he commemorates the death of al-Nashw and his family with '*Arāḥa Allāh al-'ālam min ẓulmihim, la'anahum Allāh* (May God rid the world of their iniquity, God curse them!)'[7] Mufaḍḍal also mentions al-Nashw only a few times, which is unfortunate, since Mufaḍḍal was a Copt. But, as I have just recently discovered, Mufaḍḍal's source, identified only as '*al-mu'arrikh*', after al-Jazarī dried up in 738/1338–9, was none other than al-Yūsufī! Although Mufaḍḍal was not as vituperative as his model, he acknowledges that 'al-Nashw's iniquity was known to all'.[8] Al-Ṣafadī, who alludes to his personal acquaintanceship with al-Nashw, makes an obvious effort to be fair to him. Thus, while acknowledging that 'when he became *nāẓir al-khāṣṣ*, through him the prosperity of the financial administration (*al-dawla*) became general and his fame and power spread',[9] al-Ṣafadī goes on to explain that al-Nashw was transformed by the exigencies of office, one of which was the necessity to convert to Islam:

> When he served as an accountant and was still a Christian, his morals were good; he was joyful, with a cheerful countenance, quick to fulfil the needs of the people, so that they loved him. But when he assumed the *khāṣṣ* and the sultan increased his demands upon him by proliferating boons and buildings, paying excessive prices for *mamlūks,* marrying off his daughters, making pilgrimage, and requiring great, unlimited outlays, al-Nashw's morals decayed and he showed himself as a tiger to the people, denying those who had known him. The gates of the sequestration of clerks and the wealthy opened; people rose and fell with him until he was cornered and evil was compounded. Many people were killed and some had their assets plundered.[10]

In contrast to al-Ṣafadī, al-Yūsufī's characterization of al-Nashw is unrelieved by any statement of extenuating circumstances; there is certainly no hint that his morals suffered after conversion to Islam or that pressure from the sultan corrupted him. Instead, al-Yūsufī speaks invariably of al-Nashw as an unprincipled, hypocritical schemer who manipulates the sultan for his own purposes, though these happen to coincide with the sultan's interests:

> Mention has already been made of al-Nashw's plan to ingratiate himself with the sultan and to bend him to his will. That is to say, al-Nashw would attain his purposes if the sultan attained his by taking the people's money, oppressing merchants, and

[6] Ibn al-Dawādārī, vol. IX, 344. [7] Al-Fākhirī, 204. [8] Mufaḍḍal, 283.
[9] Al-Ṣafadī, *A'yān*, II, 123. [10] Ibid.

plundering wealth wherever it was found . . . When al-Nashw realized that the sultan agreed with him in his goals, he began telling him that his circumstances were weak, that he had no money, and that the sultan had raised, established, and drawn him close, and that he [al-Nashw] wanted to fill the treasuries and storehouses with money, produce, etc . . . He reached agreement with the sultan to destroy inhabited dwellings, violate womenfolk, and to acquire money: that he [al-Nashw] would act in the financial administration (*al-dawla*) as he would choose and rule in all matters.[11]

From this paraphrase of a confidential conversation and many other such summaries and even verbatim quotations we are led to question al-Yūsufī's use of his informants. These we know to be numerous and privileged, and he usually names names, on at least one occasion he was presented to the sultan himself, and he was sometimes in company that included al-Nashw.[12] Nevertheless it is clear from vivid reconstructions of events that took place in the Citadel in Cairo when al-Yūsufī was actually campaigning in Little Armenia that his fertile imagination supplied him with much of the detail found in his annals.[13] Accordingly, any study of al-Nashw must be prefaced with the realization that other than al-Ṣafadī, al-Yūsufī is almost our only source of information on this figure and that al-Yūsufī, though apparently well informed, was manifestly biased and wrote a highly literarized version of events.

With this caveat in mind, let us look at al-Nashw's career pattern; it has much in common with that of other Coptic functionaries in the Baḥrī Mamluk financial bureaux. Like his most eminent predecessor as *nāẓir al-khāṣṣ*, Karīm al-dīn al-Kabīr, al-Nashw was born into a Coptic family of clerks and worked himself up the bureaucratic ladder, capitalizing on his family background and connections. Unlike Karīm al-dīn, however, al-Nashw was extremely poor and had to rely on other assets, including his good looks and luck. Insofar as I have been able to collate the data from al-Ṣafadī and the several transmissions on the authority of al-Yūsufī, al-Nashw began his career, while still a Christian, with his father and brothers in the service of the amir Baktamur al-Ḥājib as an accountant. Baktamur was not a leading amir of al-Nāṣir's reign but served him in various capacities, including the vizierate and the viceroyships of Gaza

[11] Al-Yūsufī, *Nuzhat al-nāẓir fī sīrat al-Malik Nāṣir*, ed. Aḥmad Ḥuṭayṭ (Beirut, 1986) (hereafter al-Yūsufī), 178–9. I have resisted the temptation to translate '*al-dawla*' with modern connotations of 'the state', or even 'the dynasty'. In the present context al-Nashw was clearly discussing financial measures with the sultan, and '*dawla*', I believe, is used in the technical sense defined by Aḥmad b. ʿAlī al-Qalqashandī, *Ṣubḥ al-aʿshā fī ṣināʿ at al-inshā'*, (Cairo, 1913–19) (hereafter al-Qalqashandī), vol. V, 465, as 'the term pertaining by custom to the affairs connected with the vizierate, so the *nāẓir al-dawāwīn* is spoken of as *nāẓir al-dawla*'. In fact, al-Qalqashandī speaks of assistants to viziers as *nāẓir al-dawla* and *mustawfī 'l-dawla.* Both Carl Petry, *The Civilian Elite of Cairo in the Later Middle Ages* (Princeton, 1981), 397–8, and Robert Irwin, *The Middle East in the Middle Ages* (London, 1986), 113, 131, translate these terms as financial officials, as do I below. Viziers obviously at times had duties other than their financial ones. But according to Hassanein Rabie, *The Financial System of Egypt* (Oxford, 1972), 139, 'the Mamluks entrusted the vizier only with the financial administration'.

[12] Al-Yūsufī, 184. Cf. Little, 'Lost Source', 49.

[13] Al-Yūsufī, 362–415.

and Ṣafad before dying in 728/1327–8, a few years before al-Nashw came to the sultan's attention.[14] After al-Nashw and his kin left Baktamur's service they were unemployed for a time, and so destitute that they had to sell all their belongings and were reduced to collecting and selling old sandals. Al-Nashw and his brother, al-Mukhliṣ, had to share a single chemise, which they took turns wearing when one or the other left the house. But the pathos of their plight is undermined by the fact that the family was able to retain the services of a black slave, Mufliḥ, who provided food for them, once in the form of 'a nice fat fish (*samaka malīḥa samīna*)'. True, they had no money to buy any sesame oil, so that Mufliḥ had to fry it in its own fat; nevertheless, they had food from time to time and a servant to prepare it.[15] Of such trivia is the material for al-Nashw's biography largely composed; nevertheless, these anecdotes have an obvious purpose behind entertaining the reader – namely, to contrast al-Nashw's early penury with his eventual acquisition of unimagined wealth and influence. *Al-Faraj baʿd al-shidda* was soon forthcoming, as his father, Faḍl Allāh, had predicted, when al-Nashw was unexpectedly summoned to the service of another amir, ʿAlāʾ al-dīn Aydughmish Amīr Ākhūr. Although al-Nashw served Aydughmish for only six months, he was able to benefit from this employment in at least two ways. First, he sold the robe of honor (*al-tashrīf*) bestowed upon him by his master in order to buy material for the chemises he and his brother so desperately needed. Second, and more importantly, this service helped bring him to the attention of the sultan: according to al-Maqrīzī al-Nashw appeared before the sultan on several occasions to testify in auditing procedures 'while he was in the service of amirs, and his words and audits pleased the sultan'.[16] Al-Maqrīzī also reports that al-Nashw became a protégé of Ibn Hilāl al-Dawla, al-Nāṣir's *shādd al-dawāwīn* (controller of financial bureaux), whom al-Nashw had cultivated until he commended him and his work to the sultan and was appointed as an accountant. Al-Yūsufī says that he used to observe al-Nashw fawning over Ibn Hilāl al-Dawla, kissing the ground before him when he entered his presence and his foot before he left, eventually winning his favour.[17] In any event al-Ṣafadī reports that the sultan once noticed al-Nashw standing at the back of a group of amirs' clerks that he had assembled, and, attracted by his youthful, tall bearing and handsome face, appointed him *mustawfī* of Giza (or, according to al-Shujāʿī, *mustawfī* of Lower Egypt) and later as *mustawfī al-dawla* (chief accountant of the (former) vizierate), in which capacity he would have controlled, according to Rabie, 'the accounts of the financial revenue and expenditure of the dīwāns'.[18] This position, in al-Ṣafadī's words, 'he filled for a time, serving the people and treating them well so that they loved him'![19] Then, in

[14] Ibn Ḥajar al-ʿAsqalānī, *al-Durar al-kāmina*, ed. M. S. Jādd al-Ḥaqq, (Cairo, 1966–67) (hereafter Ibn Ḥajar), 4 vols. vol. II, 17.
[15] al-Ṣafadī, *Lexicon*, vol. XIX, 326–7.
[16] Al-Maqrīzī, *al-Sulūk*, vol. II, 343.
[17] Ibid., al-Yūsufī, 184–5.
[18] Rabie, *The Financial System of Egypt*, 156.
[19] Al-Ṣafadī, *Aʿyān*, vol. II, 134; al-Ṣafadī, *Lexicon*, vol. XIX, 324.

another (or perhaps the same) assembly of functionaries, convoked as candidates for the stewardship of the estates of the sultan's son and heir Ānūk, Ibn Hilāl al-Dawla praised al-Nashw as 'a fine Christian and a good clerk'.[20] After chatting with al-Nashw long enough to perceive his perspicacity (*firāsa)*, al-Nāṣir appointed him to the *dīwān* of Ānūk.[21] Thus al-Nashw was given access to the sultan himself and was soon meeting privately with him. In these tête-à-têtes al-Nashw used to confide to the sultan 'many goals hidden in his mind, for which he could find no one who concurred with him'.[22] As was his custom al-Maqrīzī translated and elaborated al-Yūsufī's colloquialisms into a more formal version, in this case as 'al-Nashw began to meet alone with the sultan and speak to him about the condition of the financial administration (*al-dawla*) and impart much gossip about its functionaries, until he had made a deep impression on the sultan, who got the idea al-Nashw could obtain much money for him'.[23]

Up to this point information in the sources about al-Nashw's progress has been somewhat impressionistic, and there is the distinct possiblility that some incidents have been conflated with others. Nevertheless, it is clear that his story is the typical one of poor Coptic boy makes good in the Mamluk bureaucracy. Capitalizing on his family profession, in which he was apparently trained as an apprentice, using its connections, exploiting his good looks and fluent tongue, never losing an opportunity to ingratiate himself with his betters, al-Nashw quickly climbed the ladder to success. Finally, in 732/1332–3, the first date assigned to him, the sultan appointed him *nāẓir al-khāṣṣ* in a reshuffling of several offices.

What was the nature of *nāẓir al-khāṣṣ*? This is not easy to determine, partly because in this early stage of its development it was used in conjunction with several other titles conferred on al-Nashw. Al-Yūsufī says only that he 'took over the *khāṣṣ*,' without mentioning *naẓar*.[24] Ibn al-Dawādārī specifies '*nāẓir al-khāṣṣ*'.[25] Al-Ṣafadī and al-ʿAynī state that al-Nāṣir appointed him as *nāẓir al-khāṣṣ* along with the clerkship of Ānūk's *dīwān*, with the implication that he held the two posts simultaneously, for a while at least.[26] According to Baktāsh al-Fākhirī, when al-Nashw was arrested in 740/1339–40 he was *nāẓir al-khawāṣṣ al-sharīfa* and *nāẓir al-dawla* (supervisor of financial administration).[27] Al-ʿAynī says that he was called *mudabbir al-dawla*.[28] According to al-Shujāʿī, al-Nāṣir appointed him *nāẓir al-khāṣṣ wa-'l-wakāla*.[29] Part of the confusion in his titles and offices is related to the fact that al-Nāṣir abolished the vizierate in 729/1329 and, according to al-Qalqashandī and al-ʿUmarī, he

20 Al-Yūsufī, 185. 21 Ibid. Cf. al-ʿAynī, MS 2912/4, fol. 409a. 22 Al-Yūsufī, 185.
23 Al-Maqrīzī, *al-Sulūk*, vol. II, 348. 24 Al-Yūsufī, 185.
25 Ibn al-Dawādārī, vol. IX, 364.
26 Al-Ṣafadī, *Aʿyān*, vol. II, 134; al-Ṣafadī, *Lexicon*, vol. XIX, 325. 27 Al-Fākhirī, 203.
28 Al-ʿAynī, MS 2911/c34, fol. 144a.
29 Shams al-dīn al-Shujāʿī, *Tārīuh al-Malik al-Nāṣir Muḥammad b. Qalāwūn wa-Aulādihī*, ed. and trans. Barbara Schäfer (hereafter al-Shujāʿī), (Wiesbaden, 1985), vol. II, 86.

divided its jurisdiction and powers among three officials: *nāẓir al-māl/shādd al-dawāwīn, kātib al-sirr* and *nāẓir al-khāṣṣ*.[30] Perhaps some of the previous functions of the vizier were subsumed under the title(s) *nāẓir/mudabbir al-dawla*, which were passed on to al-Nashw.[31] The *wakāla* mentioned by al-Shujāʿī represents a vestige of the title *wakīl al-khāṣṣ*, which was held by Ibn ʿUbāda until 710/1310, when he was replaced by Karīm al-dīn, as we shall see. In any case, according to al-Qalaqashandī and al-ʿUmarī it was the function of 'the *shādd al-dawāwīn* to acquire funds and disburse stipends; the *nāẓir al-khāṣṣ* to administer the affairs of the common people and appoint functionaries; the *kātib al-sirr* to sign at Dār al-ʿAdl what the vizier had previously signed, either in consultation or independently'.[32] Al-Qalqashandī later amplifies this when he states that 'the *nāẓir al-khāṣṣ* had jurisdiction over the private property of the sultan and freedom to administer all affairs and to appoint functionaries, but without independent command, for he had to consult the sultan'.[33] Complementing this later, abstract formulation of the nature of the office is a statement based on practical experience from al-Wazīr Amīn al-Mulk, who served three times as vizier under al-Malik al-Nāṣir before the abolition of the office. On the last occasion, in 727/1326–7, he left his retirement in Jerusalem to take up the post but complained to al-Ṣafadī:

> 'Had I known there remained in the world an office called *nāẓir al-khāṣṣ* I would never have left Jerusalem!' 'Why?' [al-Ṣafadī asked.] He replied, 'The *nāẓir al-khāṣṣ* enters the sultan's presence every morning and speaks with him about everything the sultan wants to spend on his close retainers, his slave girls, and whomever else he chooses. Then the *nāẓir al-jaysh* enters and discusses increasing, reducing, and assigning the fiefs of the amirs and troops in Egypt and Syria. Then the *kātib al-sirr* enters to read the mail to him concerning appointment and dismissal of all those in Syria'. Then I enter and the sultan says, 'Go out and take this and that to the *nāẓir al-khāṣṣ*!' I am but a peasant to that master. I speak to the sultan only about the cheese depot, the apple house, and the processing of dates . . .![34]

Another indication of the interrelatedness of offices can be seen in the circumstances of al-Nashw's appointment to the *khāṣṣ*. He replaced Sharaf al-dīn Mūsā ibn al-Tāj Isḥāq, who had succeeded his father in the office. Mūsā, in turn, was now appointed *nāẓir al-jaysh*, replacing the deceased Fakhr al-dīn. Ironically, Mūsā was arrested and imprisoned along with his brothers a month later at the instigation of the new *nāẓir al-khāṣṣ*, al-Nashw.[35]

At this point it may be helpful to look at the development of the office under al-Nashw's predecessors. Although it is generally agreed that it was created by al-Malik al-Nāṣir, he does not seem to have acted with deliberation and foresight; instead, the office evolved from another post, which was expanded by its first occupant to the extent that al-Nāṣir decided to give it a new title.

[30] Al-Qalqashandī, vol. IV, 28–29.
[31] Rabie, *The Financial System of Egypt*, 138–44.
[32] Al-Qalqashandī, vol. IV, 28–9.
[33] Ibid., vol. XI, 316.
[34] Al-Ṣafadī, *Aʿyān*, vol. II, 37–8.
[35] Ibid., vol. II, 134; al-Ṣafadī, *Lexicon*, vol. XIX, 325.

Specifically, this person was originally regarded as the agent rather than the supervisor of the sultan's privy purse and accordingly was called *wakīl al-khāṣṣ al-sharīf*,[36] which I take to mean that the more or less private agent of the sultan came to be regarded as a public official who ranked high in the state financial bureaucracy. The sultan's *wakīl* was a clerk named al-Qāḍī al-Ra'īs Shihāb al-dīn Aḥmad b. ʿAlī b. ʿUbāda al-Anṣārī al-Ḥalabī, who had worked for the Mālikī *qāḍī* Ibn Makhlūf and as a legal witness in Qalāwūn's *khizāna*.[37] Upon the death of Qalāwūn he was involved in the settlement of his estate; in this capacity he came into contact with the boy Muḥammad, later to be al-Nāṣir, and was able to win his favour. He accompanied the sultan on his first campaign against the Mongols in 699/1299–1300 and in 707/1307–8 'was put in charge of Qalāwūn's tomb in Cairo and the royal endowments and properties'.[38] He accompanied al-Nāṣir to Karak during the sultan's self-imposed exile, and when they returned to Cairo in 709/1309 Ibn ʿUbāda was assigned the sultan's *wakāla*.[39] Although the sources give no information about his specific duties they agree that he had great personal power because of the sultan's favour.[40] Students of Mamluk historiography may be interested to know that when the great encyclopaediast Shihāb al-dīn al-Nuwayrī dared to criticize him to the sultan, Ibn ʿUbāda managed to have him flogged with impunity.[41] Curiously, Ibn ʿUbāda refused the sultan's offer of the vizierate, but al-Ṣafadī says that he did so out of deceit and hyprocrisy.[42] In any event he held on to his office until his death in 710/1310, the only lifelong Muslim to have held this position under al-Nāṣir.

His successor was the famous Akram/ʿAbd al-Karīm b. Hibat Allāh b. al-Sadīd al-Miṣrī, al-Qāḍī Karīm al-dīn al-Kabīr, whose accomplishment it was, according to al-Maqrīzī, to pre-empt the duties and prerogatives of the vizerate and the *naẓar al-khizāna al-sulṭāniyya* and add them to the office of *naẓar al-khāṣṣ*.[43] In many ways Karīm al-dīn's career is similar to al-Nashw's, as we shall see. First, however, it should be noted that in addition to al-Ṣafadī, al-Yūsufī, and Ibn al-Dawādārī, al-Nuwayrī and Ibn al-Ṣuqāʿī have much to say about Karīm al-dīn, so that there are five contemporary views towards him recorded.[44] In a long biography al-Ṣafadī, as was his custom, takes a balanced perspective but stresses Karīm al-dīn's merits and good deeds: *makārim*.[45] Ibn al-Dawādārī, though he mentions Karīm al-dīn on many pages, says very little about his policies and activities in office except to note that the great fortune and prosperity he enjoyed was not his own achievement but a bounty from the

[36] Ibn al-Dawādārī, vol. IX, 350; al-Maqrīzī, *al-Sulūk*, vol. II, 95.

[37] Ibn al-Ṣuqāʿī, *Tālī kitāb wafayāt al-aʿyān*, ed. and trans. Jacqueline Sublet (Damascus, 1974) (hereafter Ibn al-Ṣuqāʿī), no. 45; al-Ṣafadī, *Aʿyān*, vol. I, 88.

[38] Al-Ṣafadī, *Aʿyān*, vol. I, 88. [39] Ibn Ḥajar, vol. I, 223.

[40] Al-Maqrīzī, *al-Sulūk*, vol. II, 82. [41] Ibn Ḥajar, vol. I, 223.

[42] Al-Ṣafadī, *Aʿyān*, vol. I, 88.

[43] *Al-Khiṭaṭ wa-'l-āthār fī Miṣr wa-'l-Qāhira* (Cairo, 1853–4), vol. II, 227.

[44] Here I have not taken Mufaḍḍal's views into consideration, pending a study of his sources.

[45] Al-Safadī, *Aʿyān*, vol. II, 112–13, 115–16; al-Ṣafadī, *Lexicon*, vol. XIX, 101–2.

sultan.[46] Al-Nuwayrī, on the other hand, is quite critical of Karīm al-dīn, as he uniformly is of Coptic converts to Islam serving in the government.[47] Al-Nuwayrī singles him out for his violations of the *sharīʿa,* abuse of his office and influence against the interests of the people in general, the merchants in particular, and his arrogance in appropriating the appurtenances of the sultanate to himself. Curiously, contrary to the case of al-Nashw, the sultan is said by al-Nuwayrī to have disapproved of Karīm al-dīn's shady practices, though this disapproval was not manifested until he deposed him. Only then did the sultan abolish the commercial and agricultural innovations and enable the people to buy and sell freely, and only then, according to al-Nuwayrī, did the people realize that contrary to what they had believed, Karīm al-dīn had been operating without the approval of a just and benevolent sultan! As far as al-Nuwayrī is concerned, the sultan's only mistake was to disregard complaints against Karim al-dīn, believing that they were inspired by envy.[48] Al-Yūsufī, who knew Karīm al-dīn personally, stresses, like al-Ṣafadī, his good deeds and attributes his downfall to the amirs' jealousy of Karīm al-dīn's wealth, power and influence.[49] This sentiment is echoed by the Coptic biographer Ibn al-Ṣuqāʿī; while willing to give Karīm al-dīn credit for his achievements, he also accuses him of bringing great distress to the people of Egypt.[50]

Despite the historians' divergent verdicts with regard to Karīm al-dīn's policies, it is not difficult to compile a consistent sketch of his life from the same sources. Like al-Nashw, Karīm al-dīn received his training as a clerk from a family member, in this case his uncle, Tāj al-Riyāsa b. Saʿīd al-Dawla. A clerk of the military governor of Qūṣ, al-Amīr Bahāʾ al-dīn Qarāqūsh al-Ẓāhirī al-Barīdī, Tāj al-Riyāsa employed Karīm al-dīn as *kātib al-masṭaba* (clerk of the bench) and *kātib niyābat al-wilāya* (clerk of the provincial government). Still an apprentice to his uncle, Karīm al-dīn subsequently worked for at least two others amirs until in 695/1295 he was made *kātib* or *mustawfī al-buyūtāt al-sulṭāniyya* (clerk or accountant of royal storehouses).[51] In this capacity he came to the attention of Royal Mamluks in Cairo, and one of them, al-Amīr ʿAlam al-dīn Sanjar al-Jāwulī, recommended him to al-Amīr Rukn al-dīn Baybars al-Jāshnikīr, whose clerk had deserted him at the Battle of Shaqḥab in 702/1302–3.[52] While Baybars was *ustādār*, Karīm al-dīn became his *nāẓir dīwān*, and by spending a lot of money conspicuously he became well known, even among poets.[53] Karīm al-dīn flourished even more, of course, when Baybars became sultan in 708/1309, and in the following year he succeeded his uncle, Tāj al-Riyāsa, as *nāẓir al-dawla*.[54] But his good fortune was eclipsed

46 Ibn Dawādārī, vol. IX, 217.
47 See Donald P. Little, 'Coptic converts to Islam during the Baḥrī Mamlūk period', in Michael Gervers and Ramzi Jibran Bikhazi (eds.) *Conversion and Continuity* (Toronto, 1990), 263–4.
48 Shihāb al-dīn al-Nuwayrī, *Nihāyat al-arab*, Leiden OR MS 19b (hereafter al-Nuwayrī), fols. 24a–26b. 49 al-ʿAynī, MS 2912/4, fol. 356a. 50 Ibn al-Ṣuqāʿī, no. 350.
51 For references see Little, 'Coptic converts', 275. Thanks to P. M. Holt for the translation of this term. 52 al-ʿAynī, MS 2912/4, fol. 354b. 53 al-Nuwayrī, fol. 21a. 54 Ibid., fol. 21b.

when Baybars was deposed and Karīm al-dīn fled with him and the royal treasury. The new sultan, al-Nāṣir, arrested and sequestered Karīm al-dīn and then made him an accountant under still another amir, Jamāl al-dīn Āqūsh al-Ashrafī. At the urging of Āqūsh, al-Nāṣir agreed to appoint him as *nāẓir al-khāṣṣ* in Upper Egypt in order to retrieve the wealth of the deposed Sultan Baybars, whose apanage this had been. In this capacity Karīm al-dīn had the acumen to ask Ibn ʿUbāda, the sultan's *wakīl al-khāṣṣ*, to act as his own agent (*wakīl)* and again cultivated Royal Mamluks, such as al-Amīr Sayf al-dīn Ṭughāy al-Ḥusāmī and al-Amīr Sayf al-dīn Baktamur, at whose urging Karīm al-dīn was appointed *nāẓir dīwān* of the sultan's son and heir, al-Manṣūr ʿAlī.[55] It will be recalled that al-Nashw in his advance to power occupied the same position with another of al-Nāṣir's sons, Ānūk. Finally, when Ibn ʿUbāda died in 710/1310–11, some of the Royal Mamluks, especially Ṭughāy, seconded by the Muslimānī Fakhr al-dīn Muḥammad, Nāẓir al-Jaysh, persuaded al-Nāṣir to appoint Karīm al-dīn to replace him, first as *wakīl*, later as *nāẓir al-khāṣṣ* – the first person, according to al-Ṣafadī and others, to bear the latter title.[56] Mufaḍḍal, on the other hand, says he was appointed *nāẓir al-khāṣṣ al-sharīf wal-wakāla al-sulṭāniyya*.[57] Again this confusion in titulature may indicate that the *nāẓir al-khāṣṣ* evolved into a separate and distinct institution gradually. Indeed, initially Karīm al-dīn kept the royal treasuries in his own home, so that if the sultan needed something he had to send a Mamluk to fetch it; he also conducted sales of merchandise from his home, and, in a rare mark of royal favour, the sultan visited Karīm al-dīn and enjoyed his hospitality.[58] Even when the fire of 721/1321 threatened to burn his residence, he moved the royal stores (*al-ḥawāṣil al-sulṭāniyya*) to the home of his son, ʿAlam al-dīn, who seems to have been his assistant.[59] In this respect it should be pointed out that Karīm al-dīn continued the family tradition of nepotism, also followed by al-Nashw, by appointing his nephew, known as Karīm al-dīn al-Ṣaghīr, as *nāẓir al-dawla*, having succeeded in persuading the sultan to suspend the vizierate in 713/1313–14. Karīm al-dīn al-Ṣaghīr gained considerable notoriety as an innovator in techniques of torture.[60]

In the last analysis all sources agree that Karīm al-dīn al-Kabīr was able to gain unprecedented power in the state apparatus. According to al-Nuwayrī the sultan delegated to him 'complete disposal of property, appointments, buying and selling, marriage, manumission of slaves, etc., publicly delegating to Karīm al-dīn his jurisdiction over all these functions'.[61] Al-Maqrīzī adds that even 'the kings of neighboring lands addressed correspondence to him as they did to the sultan.[62] Further evidence that Karīm al-dīn's functions were not

[55] Ibid., fols. 21b–22a.
[56] Al-Ṣafadī, *Aʿyān* vol. II, 113; al-Ṣafadī, *Lexicon*, vol. XIX, 98; Ibn Ḥajar, vol. I, 430. Cf. Ibn al-Ṣuqāʿī, no. 350, for *wakīl.*
[57] Mufaḍḍal, 25.
[58] Al-Nuwayrī, fol. 24a; al-Ṣafadī, *Aʿyān*, vol. II, 112; al-Ṣafadī, *Lexicon*, vol. XIX, 98; Ibn al-Ṣuqāʿī, no. 350.
[59] Al-ʿAynī, MS 2912/4, fol. 336b; al-Maqrīzī, *al-Sulūk*, vol. II, 222.
[60] Al-Maqrīzī, *al-Sulūk,* vol. II, 125; Ibn Ḥajar, vol. I, 429, 430.
[61] Al-Nuwayrī, fol. 23a.
[62] Al-Maqrīzī, *al-Sulūk*, vol. II, 125.

limited to domestic or financial affairs comes from al-ʿAynī's claim that he was instrumental in establishing peace between the Mamluks and Īlkhāns in 722/1322, and he is known to have travelled extensively to Arabia on pilgrimage and to Syria and Palestine on state business.[63] Nevertheless, the titles assigned to him as listed by Ibn al-Dawādārī for 720/1320–1 reflect his domestic duties: *mudabbir al-dawla* (manager of the financial administration), *wakīl al-khāṣṣ al-sharīf* and *nāẓir khizānat al-khāṣṣ*; al-Ṣafadī refers to him as *wakīl al-sulṭān wa-nāẓir khāṣṣihi wa-mudabbir dawlatihi*.[64] He is known to have held two other financial positions, minor to be sure, but which certainly gave him additional influence and leverage. In 721/1321 he was appointed *nāẓir* of the Mosque of Ibn Ṭūlūn and at some point *nāzir* of the Qalāwūn complex.[65] In both posts he was charged with administering the endowments in order to provide the necessary income for these institutions. As far as we know al-Nashw was not offered such religiously sensitive duties.

Combining all these posts, Karīm al-dīn was eminently successful in providing and managing the sultan's funds. This success was apparently due to several factors, the first being the sultan's acquiescence in his suggestion that the *matjar* (office of commerce) should be placed under his – Karīm al-dīn's – authority and that his revenues, which had previously gone to the state treasury, should accrue directly to the sultan.[66] Karīm al-dīn began his efforts on the sultan's behalf with a capital grant of 40,000 dinars that he invested in such commodities as sugar, mastic and stuffs, setting up commercial enterprises to trade in them.[67] The profitability of these investments depended on his ability to manipulate the merchants and to persuade or coerce them to sell to him or buy from him at lucrative prices. He seems to have preferred to deal with the Frankish merchants who traded in Egypt through the network of local entrepreneurs, the Kārimīs, and on at least one occasion he was able to settle an embarrassing debt which the sultan had incurred to the Franks only because the Kārimīs were able to add it to their own.[68] In addition to providing loans, the Kārimīs also acted as Karīm al-dīn's suppliers. It was his custom to buy cargoes at a favourable price with the obvious purpose of creating a shortage on the market of particular commodities.[69] On the other hand he used to assemble merchants at his son's house, where he plied them with drink before showing them the goods he wanted them to purchase, at his price, so that 'they would buy from him with happy hearts, without malice or anger'.[70] The profits he earned were so great that the sultan's wealth became 'a bottomless pool', but in the process many merchants were ruined and had to close their shops;

[63] Al-ʿAynī, MS 2912/4, fol. 344a.
[64] Ibn al-Dawādārī, vol. IX, 303; cf. al-Ṣafadī, *Aʿyān*, vol. II, 112; al-Ṣafadī, *Lexicon*, vol. XIX, 97.
[65] Al-Nuwayrī, fols. 22b–23a; al-Maqrīzī, *al-Sulūk*, vol. II, 215; al-Ṣafadī, *Aʿyān*, vol. II, 114; Ibn Ḥajar, vol. I, 43.
[66] Rabie, *The Financial System of Egypt*, 94 (quoting al-ʿAynī).
[67] Al-ʿAynī, MS 2912/4, fol. 354b.
[68] Al-Maqrīzī, *al-Sulūk*, vol. II, 103–4; Ibn Ḥajar, vol. I, 430.
[69] Al-Nuwayrī, fol. 26a; al-ʿAynī, MS 2912/4, fol. 354b.
[70] Al-ʿAynī, MS 2912/4, fol. 354b.

his restrictions on the Frankish and Kārimī traders were so great that 'had they persisted, imports to Egypt would have been curtailed'.[71] In addition to his efforts to intervene in trade and commerce, Karīm al-dīn also had extensive agricultural holdings throughout Egypt in the form of sugar-cane processing equipment and cultivated lands.[72] One of the issues that led to his downfall, of course, was who was the ultimate owner of the lands and commodities under his control. This issue was settled when in 723/1323 the sultan ordered his arrest and the confiscation of all his property. It took about a year to seize his enormous resources, during which he lived first at the Qarāfa, then in exile in Shawbak and Jerusalem, and finally in Aswān, where he died under mysterious circumstances. According to al-Nuwayrī, on the authority of the *mutawallī* of Aswān, 'one of those who undertook the murder', Karīm al-dīn was strangled to death and then strung up to simulate suicide by hanging.[73] Al-Yūsufī corroborates the story on the authority of Karīm al-dīn's son, as does al-Ṣafadī, implicating one of the sultan's Mamlūks – al-Amīr Rukn al-dīn Baybars al-Fāriqānī.[74] Typically, Ibn al-Dawādārī has a different tale to tell which completely exonerates the sultan:

> On 20 Shawwāl 724/10 October 1324 news arrived that Karīm al-dīn al-Kabīr had hanged himself in Aswān. After his son ʿAbd Allāh was brought to Cairo as ordered, deposits, stores, and other moneys of Karīm al-dīn's came to light, much of which had come to him from Frankish merchants, for he used to deposit large sums with them. His intention was to flee to the lands of the Franks in that year in which he was arrested, without delay. Time after time he planned to enter al-Jazāʾir from the port of Alexandria, but security measures at the port prevented that. Therefore he recommended to the sultan that he go that year to rebuild Latakia and to make it a harbor like Alexandria's. But his intention was to set out from there for al-Jazāʾir. Our Lord the Sultan forestalled him and apprehended him by the strength of his good fortune, may God increase him with His grace! News of Karīm al-dīn ceased until it was as if he had never existed.[75]

The reasons assigned by historians to Karīm al-dīn's dismissal are virtually the same as those for al-Nashw's fall. In spite of Karīm al-dīn's campaign to buy the favour of the Royal Mamluks, his public display of pomp and power gradually increased their resentment and envy; nevertheless, al-ʿAynī claims that some of the amirs intervened on his behalf with the sultan in order to mitigate his punishment.[76] But by this time the sultan himself had succumbed to envy when he realized that he could not afford to maintain himself in the same style as his *nāẓir al-khāṣṣ*. Be that as it may, it is interesting that Karīm al-dīn was by no means as unpopular with the people as was al-Nashw. Although he was stoned by a mob during the 721 fires because of his Coptic connections, there was certainly no dancing in the streets after his death as there was to be for al-Nashw's demise. In fact, when Karīm al-dīn recovered from a period of illness

[71] Al-Nuwayrī, fol. 24a. [72] Ibid., fol. 25a. [73] Ibid.
[74] Al-ʿAynī, MS 2912/4, fol. 355a; al-Ṣafadī, *Aʿyān*, vol. II, 116.
[75] Ibn al-Dawādārī, vol. IX, 315. [76] Al-ʿAynī, MS 2912/4, fol. 354a.

during the same year, Cairo was decorated to celebrate his return to his duties.[77]

After Karīm al-dīn's conspicuous tenure as *nāẓir*, on his advice the sultan appointed a less flamboyant figure to succeed him as *nāẓir al-khawāṣṣ wal-wakāla*: al-Qāḍī Tāj al-dīn ʿAbd al-Wahhāb Isḥāq b. al-Qammāṭ.[78] But Tāj al-dīn Isḥāq was second choice, for Karīm al-dīn's nephew, al-Ṣaghīr, 'refused to take charge of the *khāṣṣ* and the *matjar* in order to manage all affairs'.[79] In this respect it is noteworthy that Tāj al-dīn Isḥāq's portfolio was initially restricted to the *khāṣṣ*, excluding the *matjar al-kḥāṣṣ*; nevertheless, later in the year this too was handed over to him.[80] Tāj al-dīn had also made his way up the ladder of the accounting bureaucracies, serving as a clerk in the *dīwān*, then as a *mustawfī*, until in 717/1317–18 he became *nāẓir al-dawla* (or, perhaps, *nāẓir al-dawāwīn*), an office also filled by Karīm al-dīn.[81] Nevertheless, once he became *nāẓir al-khāṣṣ*, he conspired with Fakhr al-dīn Nāẓir al-Jaysh to discredit Karīm al-dīn with the sultan in an effort to obtain possession of Karīm al-dīn's assets.[82] In contrast to Karīm al-dīn and al-Nashw, very little is recorded in the sources about Tāj al-dīn's tenure as *nāẓir al-khāṣṣ*, which, in fact, is characterized by al-Ṣafadī as one of 'extreme tranquillity'.[83] This judgement is borne out by the fact that he died peacefully in office. Perhaps this lull in high-profile financial activities can be explained in part by al-Nāṣir's decision in 728/1327–8 to oversee the accounts for receipts and disbursements himself, on a daily basis. Interestingly enough, a son of Tāj al-dīn, ʿAlam al-dīn Ibrāhīm, assumed responsibility for preparing and submitting these accounts when he was appointed *nāẓir al-dawla* in the following year. At the same time another son, Tāj al-dīn Mūsā, was made *nāẓir khizānat al-khāṣṣ* and sometimes served as deputy to his father. In any event al-Maqrīzī gives credit to the brothers, among others, for increasing state revenues.[84] When Tāj al-dīn Isḥāq died in 731/1330–1, he was succeeded briefly by Mūsā as *nāẓir al-khāṣṣ* and *wakīl al-sulṭān*, but was relieved of the latter title a few days later, and in the following year was replaced by al-Nashw. Al-Nashw soon had Mūsā and his brother arrested and subjected to intermittent torture for a number of years in an attempt to squeeze more money out of them or, by putting them to death, silence them.[85]

Under al-Nashw the *nāẓir al-khāṣṣ* did not change perceptibly as an institution, though al-Nashw seems to have increased its power by the ingenuity and ruthlessness he brought to it. It remained as the sultan's personal agency responsible for providing funds required for such things as construction (both his own and that of his amirs); the *ḥajj* (his own and his family's); celebrations

77 Al-Nuwayrī, fol. 23b; al-Ṣafadī, *Aʿyān*, vol. II, 116; al-Maqrīzī, *al-Sulūk*, vol. II, 241.
78 Al-Nuwayrī, fol. 26b; al-Ṣafadī, *Aʿyān*, vol. I, 156, al-Maqrīzī, *al-Sulūk,* vol. II, 277.
79 Ibn Ḥajar, vol. I, 427. 80 Al-Maqrīzī, *al-Sulūk,* vol. II, 249.
81 Al-Nuwayrī, fol. 26b; Ibn Ḥajar, vol. III, 45. 82 Al-ʿAynī, MS 2912/4, fol. 354a.
83 Al-Ṣafadī, *Aʿyān,* vol. I, 156; al-Maqrīzī, *al-Sulūk*, vol. II, 340.
84 Al-Maqrīzī, *al-Sulūk*, vol. II, 312. 85 Ibid., vol II, 330–31, 334.

(for the marriages of his children, for example, and the birth of children); gifts; hunting expeditions; robes of honour; uniforms for the Royal Mamluks; food for the court; slave-girls; horses; plus routine expenses of the sultan and his family. For all these expenditures we have little precise information except when the outlays were so lavish they caught historians' attention. Thus in 738/1337–8 even al-Nashw was appalled when the sultan presented 200,000 dinars in one day to four favourite amirs (Qawṣūn, Alṭunbughā, Malaktamur al-Ḥijāzī, and Bashtāk) and a landed estate worth 1,000,000 dirhams to an Arab amir.[86] In the same year 500,000 dinars had to be provided for a party celebrating the birth of a son, and the following year more than 300,000 dinars were spent for the birth of a daughter.[87] For the edification of feminists among us, on the latter occasion one of the grandfathers, the famous al-Amīr Tankiz, is said to have remarked, 'O Lord, I was hoping it would be a girl, for if my daughter had given birth to a boy, I would have been frightened by perfect bliss!'[88] After the celebrations had ended al-Nāṣir gave Tankiz 150,000 dinars worth of horses and supplies to ease his journey back to Damascus, in addition to 240,000 dirhams that he had received to cover his living expenses in Cairo.[89] It was al-Nashw's undeniable achievement that he was able to provide the funds for these and other extravagances through his own clever and cruel devices. In some respects he adopted the practices followed by Karīm al-dīn and others – forced sales, for example, of such commodities as wood, cloth, sugar, perfume, clothing, beans, clover, iron, wheat, spices, resin, linen, used uniforms, honey and confectionery, plus whatever might be found in Kārimī cargoes. On the other hand he paid only half price or less for property and food he needed.[90] In a time-honoured tradition he frequently resorted to sequestration and confiscation of the properties and possessions of the rich and influential, not sparing civilian and sometimes military state functionaries, and employing spies to ferret out likely candidates for such treatment. The roster of victims includes the *nāẓir dīwān al-jaysh*, *nāẓir al-dawla, mushidd al-dawālīb*, *shādd al-dawāwīn*, *nāʾib al-Karak*, *kātib sirr Dimashq*, *nāẓir Qalyūb*, *wālī Ashmūn*, *mutawallīs* of Maḥalla, Gharbiyya, Ashmūnayn, Saʿīd and Fayyūm, *mushidd* Sūq al-Ghanam, *shādd dawālīb al-khāṣṣ*, *muḥtasib* of Alexandria, *amīn al-ḥukm*, the Coptic patriarch, plus various merchants and rich private individuals.[91] Not even the assets of the dead were safe as al-Nashw required the *dīwān al-mawārīth al-ḥashriyya* (bureau of escheat estates) to turn over to him the estates of the deceased, including those with legal heirs.[92] *Waqf* money and funds for orphans were also seized.[93] Another of his tactics was to audit

86 Ibid., vol. II, 432. But cf. al-ʿAynī, MS 2911/c34, fol. 77b, who says 80,000 dinars, in this manuscript at least.

87 Al-Maqrīzī, *al-Sulūk*, vol. II, 433, 460. Also instructive is al-Ṣafadī's claim that al-Nashw showed him documents itemizing the purchase of *mamlūks* for 4,000,000 dinars between 732 and 737: *Aʿyān*, vol. II, 124.

88 Al-Maqrīzī, *al-Sulūk*, vol. II, 461–2.

89 Ibid., vol. II, 462.

90 Al-Yūsufī, 266, 346.

91 Ibid., 11, 119, 126, 127, 195, 253, 256, 262–3, 312, 342, 358–9, 369–70.

92 Ibid., 353, 357–8; al-ʿAynī, MS 2911/c34, fols. 84a, 95a–b; al-Maqrīzī, *al-Sulūk*, vol. II, 435–6.

93 Al-Yūsufī, 188, 292–3; al-Maqrīzī, *al-Sulūk*, vol. II, 443.

carefully the activities of government officials in order to confront them with alleged irregularities for which they would have to provide compensation. These included the governors and functionaries of Bahnasā, Manūfiyya and Gharbiyya, bureaucrats from Aleppo and Tripoli, numerous clerks in the *dīwāns* of amirs, and others.[94] Amirs were accused of such crimes as fostering homosexuality in order to discredit them, and such venerable personages as the shaykh of Khānqāh Bahā' al-dīn Arslān Amīn al-Ḥukm and even Ibn Sayyid al-Nās were defamed in order to discredit the *ʿulamāʾ*.[95] Al-Yūsufī would have us believe that al-Nashw was the evil genius behind all these illicit activities which he invariably characterizes as *maẓālim.* He also credits al-Nashw with recruiting a staff of rogues to assist him. In the process he divested himself of anyone whose loyalty and obedience to him were not absolute, beginning with his former patron, Ibn Hilāl al-Dawla, the *shādd al-dawāwīn*, an extremely powerful official, who, according to Rabie, 'assisted the vizier in collecting financial revenue', but in the absence of a vizier performed his functions.[96] Normally a Mamluk served as *shādd*, regardless of his 'lack of financial experience',[97] but Ibn Hilāl al-Dawla was an interesting exception. According to Ibn al-Dawādārī he was a peasant from Bahnasā, a Muslim, and reached high office after years of humble and degrading service to an uncle in the *dīwān al-mawārīth* and then to Ibn al-ʿUbāda in the *khāṣṣ*. By a stroke of good luck he managed to get possession of Karīm al-dīn's treasury upon his arrest and used it for bribes to further his own career until in 726/1326 he was made *amīr ṭablkhāna* and *shādd al-dawāwīn*, 'with jurisdiction over all positions in the financial administration *(dawla)*'.[98] Having become too powerful and independent, he was dismissed in 734/1333–4 at al-Nashw's instigation and replaced by one al-Amīr Ukuz al-Nāṣirī and Lu'lu' Ghulām Fandash. Both of these unsavoury characters became notorious, like Karīm al-dīn al-Ṣaghīr, for their innovative application of torture to their victims.[99] Be that as it may, they were useful to al-Nashw in ferreting out likely sources of money from government officials, both in Syria and Egypt, until they eventually fell out of al-Nashw's favour. Others of their ilk included al-Shams b. al-Azraq, *nāẓir al-jihāt* (supervisor of taxes), 'a despot and oppressor',[100] Amīn 'Alā' al-dīn Qarmūṭ al-Mustawfī, who advised the sultan on exactions;[101] and al-Amīr ʿAlāʾ al-dīn Aydakīn, *mutawallī* of Cairo, who, backed by al-Nashw, stooped so low as to harass public drunks and strip nocturnal revellers of their clothes and sell them the next morning.[102] In recruiting malleable and unscrupulous cohorts, al-Nashw benefited, like Karīm al-dīn, from his power to make appointments, with or without the sultan's review. Thus he was able to appoint

[94] Al-Yūsufī, 121, 177, 349.
[95] Al-Yūsufī, 222, 269, 271; al-Maqrīzī, *al-Sulūk*, vol. II, 432. For more details of his iniquities see al-Shujāʿī, 90–1.
[96] Rabie, *The Financial System of Egypt,* 151, citing al-Qalqashandī. Cf. Ibn al-Dawādārī, vol. IX, 350. [97] Rabie, *The Financial System of Egypt,* 152.
[98] Ibn al-Dawādārī, vol. IX, 310, 350. But cf. Ibn. Ḥajar, vol. III, 210–11, who gives a drastically different biography! [99] Al-Yūsufī, 128. [100] Ibid. [101] Ibid., 180–1. [102] Ibid., 211.

his two brothers and a brother-in-law to the *dīwāns* of prominent amirs; other cronies were appointed as *nāẓir* al-Gharbiyya and *nāẓir dīwān al-mawārīth*.[103]

But what really distinguished al-Nashw from his predecessors, apart from his remarkable power of persuasion with the sultan, was his resourcefulness and dedication as a planner. Relying on information provided by his cronies, contacts and spies, he used to meet every night with his brothers, brother-in-law and other confidants in order to devise innovative ways of obtaining money. Thus, in 739/1338–9, the year before his arrest, plans were made to obtain 500,000 dinars and 100,000 *irdabbs* of grain; for the following and final year we are fortunate to have preserved by al-Maqrīzī, al-Shujāʿī and al-ʿAynī copies or summaries of position papers prepared by al-Nashw and submitted to the sultan for approval designed to obtain 1,000,000 dinars in new revenue to be assigned to the *khāṣṣ*.[104] This sum was to be raised from the following hitherto unexploited sources:

1. *Al-taqāwī al-sulṭāniyya*, seed provided by the sultan to *muqṭaʿs* for distribution to the peasants, some 160,000 *irdabbs* besides the sultan's own:[105] al-Nashw claimed that the military, their financial agents, and the peasants were selling it rather than planting it. He recommended that this be prevented by collecting and bringing the seed to the *khāṣṣ* in Cairo.
2. *Waqf* proceeds from about 130,000 feddans suspected of being used to support defunct or idle mosques, *zāwiyas*, and other pious institutions: a new *dīwān* was to be created to survey these institutions and their endowed lands in order to divert unjustified income to the *khāṣṣ* at preferential rates.
3. Lands on Rawḍa Island previously used to pay stipends to the descendants of rulers (*awlād al-mulūk)* but subsequently sold at lower than market rates or rented by government functionaries: these lands were also to be diverted to the *khāṣṣ* at preferential rates.
4. Stipends paid to welfare recipients, many of whom were fictitious or undeserving: these were to be reviewed against the original letters of appointment; the stipends of those found to be unwarranted were to revert to the *khāṣṣ*.
5. Funds embezzled by high-ranking officials from construction projects, for example, and non-Muslim community taxes (*jawālī)*: these officials included prominent amirs, judges and notaries. All these funds were to be reviewed and as much as possible was to be deposited in *khizānat al-khāṣṣ*.

From these last-ditch efforts alone, quite apart from what has already been observed, it is clear that al-Nashw must have alienated many segments of Mamluk society – amirs, the judiciary, bureaucrats, landowners, welfare recipients, Sufis, and even peasants. Although one might argue on the basis of these

[103] Ibid., 179–80; al-ʿAynī, MS 2911/c34, fol. 84a.

[104] Al-Maqrīzī, *al-Sulūk*, vol. II, 460, 473–5; al-ʿAynī, MS 2911/c34, fols. 113a, 144b–47a; al-Shujāʿī, 83–5.

[105] See Rabie, *The Financial System of Egypt,* 55, 68.

same measures that al-Nashw was expert in detecting and rooting out corruption and diverting ill-gotten gains to the benefit of the sultanate, he had made too many enemies to survive the cumulative complaints and protests lodged by the sultan's highest-ranking amirs – Tankiz and Qawṣūn to mention only two – and even his wives.[106] It is true that al-Nāṣir seems to have been a partner in al-Nashw's policies and deeds, but he could not in the end tolerate them, when, steadily bombarded over the years by complaints from his top advisers, he finally realized that his chief supplier of funds had become a liability. In this connection it is interesting to note that although al-Yūsufī documents al-Nāṣir's complicity in al-Nashw's crimes and misdemeanours, on at least one occasion the sultan is given credit for acting decisively and independently for the welfare of his subjects and the state. This was in 736/1335–6 when the price of wheat jumped in Cairo from 15 dirhams to 50, resulting in shop closures and panic. Fearing the consequences of unchecked inflation, the sultan intervened to ensure that the vast amounts of wheat stored in depots belonging to amirs were not hoarded for speculative purposes but sold at an affordable rate until such time as supplies could be rushed from Syria, Palestine and Upper Egypt. During the crisis the sultan monitored the activities of the amirs and their financial agents carefully through a new *muḥtasib* he appointed for this purpose, with the power to punish those who tried to evade or circumvent the sultan's policy. As a result of these measures prices decreased substantially by the end of the year.[107] Curiously, al-Nashw is never mentioned throughout the whole episode. Whether this is because he played no role or because al-Yūsufī was reluctant to give him any credit is impossible to say.

Perhaps this is an appropriate point at which to raise the issue of the character of the sultan al-Malik al-Nāṣir Muḥammad and his reign in the light of the fact that most of the contemporary sources were biased in his favour, with the notable exception of al-Yūsufī, who, as we have seen, focused on al-Nashw during the last decade of al-Nāṣir's reign and portrayed him as a thoroughgoing villain. Probably al-Ṣafadī, as usual, had the most balanced view when he wrote that al-Nāṣir was 'a great and fortunate, obeyed and awesome king, both violent and cunning, sternly resolute, and extremely crafty'.[108] Along the same lines but less politely, Robert Irwin has recently characterized him as 'certainly one of the greatest Mamluk sultans; he was perhaps one of the nastiest'.[109] Peter Holt sees him as an autocrat who built 'his power by the force of his pertinacious, devious and ruthless personality'.[110] David Ayalon minces no words: al-Nāṣir was an 'irresponsible and vain' waster 'of the Sultanate's resources . . . who made up his mind to demonstrate, with much bitterness, cruelty and hatred, his superiority over all other sultans', in 'a megalomanic

106 Al-Yūsufī, 128, 241, 269, 305–6, 308, 350, 353. Cf. al-Shujāʿī, 86.
107 Al-Yūsufī, 294–30; al-Maqrīzī, *al-Sulūk*, vol. II, 394–6; al-ʿAynī, MS 2911/c34, fols. 9a–12a.
108 Al-Ṣafadī, *Aʿyān*, vol. III, 140; al-Ṣafadī, *Lexicon*, vol. IV, ed. Sven Dedering (Wiesbaden, 1959), 370. 109 Irwin, *The Middle East*, 121.
110 'Al-Nāṣir Muḥammad b. Ḳalāwūn', *Encyclopaedia of Islam* (new edition), vol. VII, 992.

project . . . which spoiled and corrupted the military aristocracy and the beduins and bled the people white by taxations and extortions'.[111] This harsh verdict might be mitigated by reference to the judgement of the great German scholar Gustav Weil, who wrote almost a century and half ago in his often neglected history of the caliphate in Egypt which, in tribute to our hosts, I quote in the original German:

> Er hatte viel Verstand und Einsicht, ein aussergewöhnliches Gedächtnis, einen durchdringenden Geist und war von einer unermüdlichen Tätigkeit. Diese Eigenschaften wurden aber durch eben so viele Untugenden verdunkelt. An die Stelle der Klugheit trat oft Schlauheit und Hinterlist, sein Argwohn erstreckte sich bis auf seine eigenen Kinder und verleitete ihn nicht weniger als seine Verschwendung und Genußsucht zu mancher Gewalttat und Grausamkeit. Wo diese beiden Leidenschaften nicht beteiligt waren, zeigte er sich gerecht, freundlich und gütig gegen jedermann, bis auf seinen letzten Diener.[112]

These divergent opinions draw attention, I believe, to the possibility of and need for writing a biography of this sultan in the light of the historiographical complexity of the sources. In such a biography al-Nashw would of necessity loom large.

The question of the religion of the *wakīl/nāẓir al-khāṣṣ* remains. As already mentioned, only one of the five covered in this survey – Ibn ʿUbāda – was a lifelong Muslim. All the rest were Musālima, Coptic converts to Islam. The circumstances of Karīm al-dīn's conversion are not altogether clear. Al-ʿAynī says that he was converted by a Mamluk amir, Sanjar al-Jāwulī, who kept at him until he had driven him from Christianity to Islam.[113] Al-Ṣafadī states merely that he converted in middle age during the reign of Baybars al-Jāshnikīr, 'whose clerk he was[/had been]'.[114] Tāj al-dīn Isḥāq was believed to have remained a Christian after his conversion, 'without changing anything'.[115] Al-Nashw and Mūsā b. al-Tāj Isḥāq were two among a group of Copts whom al-Nāṣir forced to convert in 732/1331–2 before he would approve their promotion – the former as *nāẓir al-khāṣṣ* and the latter as *nāẓir al-juyūsh*.[116] The sincerity of Karīm al-dīn's conversion was the subject of considerable doubt, in spite of the fact that he demonstrated his devotion to Islam by supporting the *ʿulamāʾ*, generously distributing alms to Muslims, and financing the construction of three mosques and a *khānqāh*.[117] In spite of all these public displays of his commitment to Islam, in times of communal strife his sincerity and his private loyalties were questioned.[118] Insofar as can be

[111] David Ayalon, 'The expansion and decline of Cairo under the Mamluks and its background', *XXIXe Congrès Internationale des Orientalistes résumés des communications*, Sections 1–5 (Paris, 1973), 64–5.
[112] Gustav Weil, *Geschichte des Abbasidenchalifats in Ägypten* (Stuttgart, 1860), vol. II, 410–11.
[113] Al-ʿAynī, MS 2912/4, fol. 354b.
[114] Al-Ṣafadī, *Aʿyān*, vol. II, 113, al-Ṣafadī, *Lexicon*, vol. XIX, 97.
[115] Al-ʿAynī, MS 2912/4, fol. 395b. [116] Little, 'Coptic converts', 278 (quoting al-ʿAynī).
[117] Ibid., 281–2. [118] Ibid., 282.

determined, no one ever took al-Nashw's conversion seriously except, perhaps, the sultan for reasons of expediency. After all, unlike Karīm al-dīn, al-Nashw never made the slightest effort to demonstrate the sincerity of his conversion by supporting Muslim pious institutions. Indeed, during his detention it was discovered that he had never been circumcised, and Christian sacred objects were found in his home, along with four thousand jars of wine and large quantities of pork. According to al-ʿAynī he 'was one of the worst Christians and most wicked of Copts. He entered Islam outwardly, with infidelity in his heart'.[119] 'The glory and rule of al-Nashw and his family came to an end', al-Shujāʿī exulted; 'May God never restore their likes over Islam! Never has such a sly dog smitten Islam!'[120] Nevertheless, as mentioned at the outset it was not only Muslims who rejoiced in al-Nashw's downfall; he had persistently hounded the Coptic clerks, and it was they who bought up all the candy dolls of al-Nashw and his family *in extremis* to adorn their homes. And despite Muslim distrust of Coptic converts to Islam, reinforced by the example of al-Nashw, the Mamluk sultans persisted in appointing them to high and influential offices.

[119] Ibid., 280. [120] al-Shujāʿī, 89.

CHAPTER 17

Coptic festivals of the Nile: aberrations of the past?

HUDA LUTFI

> On Tuesday, the 5th of Muḥarram, year 415 AH, it was the third day of opening the Khalīj dam, huge numbers of Christians and Muslims congregated around the Maqs barrage in front of the Maqs church, where tents were pitched for drinking and playing, and where people remained until the end of the day. The Prince of the Believers, al-Ẓāhir li'-I'zāz Dīn Allāh Ibn al-Ḥākim bi-Amr Allāh, rode in a procession to the Maqs where he circled around for a long time, whereupon he returned safely to his palace. Scenes were witnessed, too ugly to be mentioned, of the drunkeness and disgraceful exposure (*tahattuk*) of women, of their mixing with men, and of their being carried away drunken in carriers' baskets. Maqrīzī, *Khitat*, vol. II, 145

Pressured by the exigencies of the social structure, aspects of popular culture continuously undergo a process of mutations. Accordingly, historical periods that witness the emergence of strong political and cultural structures may also witness an increasing pattern of suppression and repression of numerous forms of popular culture. Because of its potential to mobilize collective social action, the festival has been viewed historically with particular suspicion on the part of the authorities as a source of subversion and public chaos, and therefore has often been subjected to official control and censorship. This is especially pertinent to historical contexts in which an indigenous popular culture is subjected to the control of an external hegemonic culture. In this connection, Ibn Khaldūn argues that the conqueror eventually succeeds in imposing his own cultural ideology on the conquered. A twofold process seems to be at work in his analysis: on the one hand, the conqueror uses coercive power to establish his cultural hegemony, and on the other, the conquered gradually adopt the habits of the powerful:

> Domination has other malign effects on peoples. People lose their own customs in imitation of their masters or of those stronger than they, and here the case of the Granadians imitating Castilian and Aragonese dress and other aspects of life, such as erection of statues, is brought to light. Most seriously of all, once a people has fallen under the dominion of another, this invariably heralds its historical extinction that will come with the extinction of *'aṣabiyya* in favour of the stronger one.[1]

[1] Aziz al-Azmeh, *Ibn Khaldun* (London, 1990), 74.

This is only a partial picture of Ibn Khaldūn's thesis on cultural hegemony, for as he has shown elsewhere, conquerors also appropriate the culture of the conquered into their dominant system, just 'as the Arabs took from the Persians habits of luxury which they elevated to even greater heights under the Abbasids, or as the Almoravids took from the Andalusians, or the Turks from the Abbasids'.[2] Ibn Khaldūn, however, does not examine the manner by which this process of cultural domination or appropriation occurs, nor does he address the possibility of conflict between the dominant and dominated cultures. His theory simply assumes that the conquered will readily adopt the customs of their masters, without expressing any form of resistance to such domination. And while he has shown that elements of the conquered cultures are appropriated by stronger ones, he does not discuss the complex process by which certain elements are embraced and others rejected. Under the dominant culture, however, the various dimensions of conquered culture may only reappear in repressed, displaced, or reduced forms. It is this process of cultural transformation that I would like to examine; more particularly the manner by which Egyptian Nile festivals have been recast to accommodate dominant Muslim structures. I would also like to examine the twofold means by which these structures exercised their hegemony: the imposition of state disciplinary restraints, and the articulation of an official discourse that cultivated a hegemonic Islamic identity establishing sharp divisions between what is Islamic and what is not. Such a discourse is prominently illustrated in the Muslim religious treatises on the subject of *bid'a* (corrupt innovations), one which seems to have become increasingly popular with the powerful Sunni religious establishment of the post-Seljuq period.[3] On the subject of Coptic Nile festivals, however, I have chosen to examine Maqrīzī's historical texts, not only because they are richer in historical data, but also because they can be equally used to show that he subscribed to the anti-*bida'*/hegemonic mentality inherent in the *bid'a* discourse. Whereas the *Khiṭaṭ* text is used because it offers one of the fullest treatments of Coptic Nile festivals up to the ninth century AH, the *Sulūk* chronicle is examined to demonstrate how the Coptic festival, as a social or cultural event, is marginalized in the official narrative of the Mamluk state. Rather than attempt to give an exhaustive reconstruction of these festivals throughout the Mamluk period, I would like to focus more on the manner by which Maqrīzī reconstructs their history. Reference to other Mamluk

[2] Ibid., 81.

[3] For more details on the struggle of Sunnī scholars against *bida'* see Subhi Labib's long introduction to his edition of Idrīs ibn 'Abd Allāh al-Turkumānī's *Kitāb al-Luma' fi-'l-ḥawādith wa-'l-bida'* (Cairo, 1986), (hereafter *al-Luma'*. See also M. Umar Memon, *Ibn Taymiyya's Struggle against Popular Religion* (The Hague, 1976). One of the best written treatises on *bida'* is that written by the fourteenth-century scholar Abū 'Abd Allāh ibn Muḥammad al-'Abdarı al-Fāsī, better known as Ibn al-Ḥājj, *al-Madkhal ilā Tanmiyyat al-a'māl bi-taḥsīn al-niyyāt,* (Cairo, 1929), 4 vols. (hereafter *al-Madkhal).* On the revival of Sunnism in Egypt, see Gary La Viere Leiser, 'The restoration of Sunnism in Egypt, madrasas and mudarrisūn, 495–647/1101–1249'. (Ph.D. dissertation, University of Pennsylvania, 1976).

historical texts and *bidʿa* treatises will be also made, but only to supplement and explain gaps or omissions in Maqrīzī's narrative.

For his *Khiṭaṭ* text, Maqrīzī chooses a title and and an introductory framework which reveal a common belief, shared among Muslim historians, that knowledge of history should be used as a lesson from which we must derive wisdom. Thus his title, *Exhortations and Lessons Based on the Account of Districts and Ancient Monuments*, makes use of two Arabic terms, *al-mawāʿiẓ wa-ʾl-iʿtibār*, which underline this didactic approach to the subject of history. This is highlighted further in his introduction in which he explains his historical philosophy: 'The benefit (*manfaʿa*) of this text can be deduced from the intention behind writing it and from its title. Its benefit lies in the fact that a person can survey in a short time the past events and historical changes that take place over long periods of time, so that in reflecting on this, his soul may become refined and his character righteous'.[4] Furthermore, a closer scrutiny of the text reveals his use of history to promote an Islamic hegemonic perspective, for Maqrīzī seems to survey the long progression of Egyptian history in order to document the final triumph of Arabo-Muslim culture. More than any other Mamluk historical narrative, the *Khiṭaṭ* is structured to highlight the defeat of the Copts and the extinction of their culture, for it begins significantly with a long account of how their power was broken by the early Arabo-Muslim state, and concludes with an account of how, after much resistance, they finally became obedient to the Muslims.[5]

Maqrīzī's story of Coptic Nile festivals is one that constructs two cultures in tension with one another: a hegemonic Arabo-Muslim culture versus a declining but resilient Coptic culture. Wishing to mark an official break between Coptic and Islamic Egypt, our historian uses, as a political device, the famous story of ʿUmar I forbidding Nile sacrificial rites. The Maqrīzī story proceeds as follows: when ʿAmr ibn al-ʿĀṣ, the first Arab Muslim governor of Egypt, forbade the paganistic practice of sacrificing a female virgin to the Nile, it showed no signs of increase for three months. Alarmed by the social panic this caused, he wrote to ʿUmar asking him for advice. The pious caliph, we are told, sent an emphatic reply that 'Islam destroys what comes before it', and instead of the sacrificial virgin, he ordered his governor to throw a piece of paper in the Nile, in which he inscribed that

> *Allāh* alone can cause the Nile water to flow. ʿAmr threw the paper in the Nile, one day before the festival of al-Ṣalīb, but in the meantime, the people of Egypt were preparing to depart, because their welfare rested only on the Nile. However, on the day of the Ṣalīb festival, Allāh, the Almighty, caused the Nile to flow, reaching 16 cubits in one night, thus preventing harm from happening to the people of Egypt.[6]

The moral message here is clear: if the 'true' religion is followed, the land will ultimately prosper. This story could also be interpreted to reveal the need, on

4 Aḥmad b. ʿAlī al-Maqrīzī, *Kitāb al-Mawāʿiẓ wa-ʾl-iʿtibār bi-dhikr al-khiṭaṭ wa-ʾl-āthār* (Cairo, Bulāq edition, n. d.) (hereafter *Khiṭaṭ),* vol. I, 4.
5 Ibid., vol. I, 76–86, vol. II, 492–501.
6 Ibid., vol. I, 58.

the part of the Muslim historian, to depict the early triumph of Islamic truth over pagan or Coptic falsehood. It serves a double political purpose: to announce the displacement of Coptic culture, and to articulate the hegemony of a new one. It is no coincidence, therefore, to find that Maqrīzī's introduction to his narrative on Coptic festivals commences with another of ʿUmar's interdictions: 'Keep away from the feasts of the Jews and Christians, for discontent descends on them during their congregations, and do not learn their gibberish-like language lest you adopt some of their behaviour'.[7] Warning Muslims against the cultural contamination of un-Islamic practices, this ʿUmarī statement manifests the manner by which official Islam constructs a sharp division between Muslims and their non-Muslim subjects. Moreover, Maqrīzī's text on Coptic festivals is cast in a hegemonic language hostile to their popular practices, for it commences with the ʿUmarī warning against cultural contamination, and concludes with an account of the ultimate decline of Coptic festivals under Muslim rule.[8]

Ruling over their Coptic subjects, early Arab rulers, in exchange for economic and political profit, seem to have adopted a pragmatic tolerance towards the indigenous culture. The fragmentary historical evidence we have for this early period suggests that, as long as the taxes were paid, Arabo-Muslim governors interfered but little in the expression of popular culture. Furthermore, those governors who wished to establish an independent stance from Baghdad went so far as to patronize important Coptic festivals. Later, when Egypt became the seat of imperial states such as those of the Fatimids and Mamluks, the Egyptian school of Muslim historians documented their history in superb detail. Maqrīzī is heavily indebted to this rich historical narrative in constructing his *Khiṭaṭ* account of popular festivals in the Egyptian capital. This historical evidence suggests that the increasingly centralized state in Egypt often adopted a more restrictive stance towards public festivities. Both the Fatimids and especially the Mamluks, subjected Coptic Nile festivals to intermittent periods of censorship, and sometimes to outright prohibition. It seems, however, that repressive restraints on these festivals were more closely associated with periods of political crisis or consolidation. These repressive policies are particularly noticeable during the occurrences of droughts or other similar disasters. Here, it is the official chronicle of the state, the *Sulūk*, which, as we shall see, is more informative on the state's policies of prohibitions and restraints.

Even though the *Khiṭaṭ* narrative offers the fullest description of Coptic festivals during the Fatimid and Mamluk periods, the Ayyubid period seems to be omitted in Maqrīzī's account. Generally, this festival narrative centres on several themes: historical origins, popular rituals and state restraints, but each festival story seems to be structured around the theme of its decline. In contrast, Maqrīzī's *Sulūk* chronicle is notable for its omissions in recording such Coptic cultural events. When festivals such as the Nawrūz or the Ṣalīb are

[7] Ibid., vol. I, 264. [8] Ibid., vol. I, 264–9.

mentioned, they are simply used as official markers in registering seasonal fluctuations of the Nile.[9] Moreover, the few times when the celebration of Coptic festivals is mentioned, they are depicted negatively. These celebrations seem to be described in order to justify or announce their abolition by the state, as in the case of the feast of the Martyr.[10] Thus in contrast to Muslim festivals, which are registered regularly in the Mamluk chronicle, Coptic festivals are considered unworthy to be inscribed in the official history of the Muslim community. This is a significant ideological point, because it demonstrates how Coptic culture is marginalized in Mamluk historical texts: it was either omitted or criticized.

To understand the nature of Nile festivities in Egyptian culture, we cannot overlook the centrality of the Nile in the everyday life of Egyptians. Historically, it was known to be a river of a sufficiently erratic nature to inspire cultural rituals of revelry and anxiety. Thus, the Egyptians anxiously observed the annual performance of the Nile, inventing their earliest official calendar to mark the seasonal cycles of the Nile. Not surprisingly, the Egyptian New Year – the first of the Coptic month of Tūt – was fixed to coincide with that stage of the Nile cycle when the flood waters crested. The most important festivals, therefore, were developed to celebrate crucial aspects of the river's behaviour. As we shall see, Coptic culture in Egypt retained, in Christianized form, many of the earlier pagan festival rituals, which underwent further historical transformations under Arabo-Muslim hegemony.

Although Egyptian festivals receive more detailed descriptions in Maqrīzī's *Khiṭaṭ*, it is the *Sulūk* chronicle that documents the Nile's omnipotent presence in Mamluk state and society. Given the whimsical nature of the Nile's behaviour, it was crucial for the state to measure its cycle of rise and decline, and for this the earlier Egyptians had invented the Nilometer. Measuring the Nile water became a tradition that was followed religiously by subsequent states, not the least of which was the Mamluk state. During the Abbasid caliphate of al-Mutawakkil, the Copts were deprived of the privilege of announcing the rising waters of the Nile. Instead, an Arab Muslim family, the Ibn al-Raddāds, was appointed to fulfill this crucial function, and it continued to do so throughout the Mamluk period.[11]

The centrality of the Nile in the life of society made it important for Maqrīzī, as well as other Mamluk historians, to record the crucial stages in the Nile cycle in their chronicles. And in contrast to other historical events normally recorded according to the hegemonic Muslim calendar, Nilotic fluctuations are recorded in both the Coptic solar and Muslim lunar calendars. Thus,we learn from the *Khiṭaṭ* and the *Sulūk* that the rising of the Nile's waters

[9] On these references see A. b. ʿAlī al-Maqrīzī, *Kitāb al-Sulūk li-maʿrifat duwal al-mulūk*, ed. Muḥammad Muṣṭafā Ziyāda (Cairo, 1958) (hereafter *Sulūk*), vol. I, 119, 136–7, vol. 4, 618, 669.

[10] Ibid., vol. II, 926. For other cases, see ibid., vol. I, 119, 136, 142. See also Abū ʾl-Maḥāsin Yūsuf ibn Taghrībirdī, *Ḥawādith al-Duhūr fī Madā al-ayyām wa-ʾl-shuhūr* (Cairo, Dar al-Kutub edition, 1963) (hereafter *Ḥawādith*), vol. III, 472.

[11] *Sulūk*, vol. IV, 745.

occurs during the Coptic summer months of Abīb, Masrā and Tūt. However the commencement of measuring the 'arms of completion' (*qiyās adhruʿ al-wafāʾ*) seems to begin two months earlier, during the months of Bashans and Ba'ūna. Tradition had it that the first 'drop of increase' takes place during the month of Bashans, which coincides with a most important Coptic festival that celebrates the prospective increase of the Nile. This is ʿĪd al-Shahīd (Festival of the Martyr). On the twenty-fifth of the Coptic month of Baʾūna, which coincides with another Coptic feast, ʿĪd Mikāʾīl, the Nile bed is measured in order to make an early prediction of the river's behaviour.[12] From that day on, 'the Judge of the River', one of Ibn al-Raddād's titles, keeps a daily record of the water measurement, which is disclosed only to the highest officials of the state.[13] In the following month of Masrā (August), both people and state anxiously wait for the Nile to fulfil its 'promise of completion', for it is during this month that the river is expected to reach the 16 cubits minimum. The Egyptians, therefore, called Masrā the wedding period of the Nile (*ʿurs al-nīl*), during which the most important festival of the Nile takes place: the Wafāʾ al-Nīl. The process of measuring the water level, however, continues until the following month of Tūt, when the Nile waters have crested (*nihāyat al-ziyāda*) and begin to recede (*ibtidā' al-naqṣ*). This period coincides with the last two important Coptic festivals, ʿĪd al-Nawrūz and ʿĪd al-Ṣalīb.[14] My analysis of these festivals will follow the cyclical stages of the Nile. Thus, I would like to start with the Coptic feast of the Ghiṭās, which celebrates that point in the Nile cycle when the river's water is at its purest and its lowest.

ʿĪd al-Ghiṭās: 11 Ṭūba

Except for this feast, the most important Nile festivals normally coincided with the period of rising waters. The Copts, we are told, attach a special religious significance to this feast, for it commemorates the sacred events of Christ's baptism and his unity with the Holy Spirit. And hence the Ghiṭās is considered as one of the greatest seasonal festivals in Coptic Egypt, and the second most important Coptic religious festival after that of the Nativity. The date of the festival coincides with an important seasonal transition, for it takes place shortly after the winter solstice, when the sun is at the point of commencing its spring career and when the Nile water is most pure. (11 Ṭūba – 18 January). The Arabic name *al-Ghiṭās* illustrates that the focal ritual performed during the festival is that of submersion into the Nile, a ritual attested in other ancient river cultures. In addition to this ritual of water purification, other ancient rituals such as fire illumination and popular indulgence in revelry, so typical of pagan festivals, seem to have still been performed publicly during the Ghiṭās celebrations throughout the Fatimid and Mamluk periods. It therefore seems likely that this is an ancient seasonal festival onto which a Christian

[12] *Ḥawādith*, vol. III, 677. [13] *Khiṭaṭ*, vol. I, 476. [14] *Sulūk*, vol. VI, 620.

one was grafted; a hybrid festival, in which earlier pagan features reappear in Christianized form. The Ghiṭās celebrates with special rites of passage the transition from winter to spring, from death to life.

By Maqrīzī's time, the Ghiṭās no longer appears to have been one of the capital's great festivals, and thus the *Khiṭaṭ* narrative depicts its festivities as an event of the past. Maqrīzī's description of the festival makes use of al-Masʿūdī's account during the Abbasid period, one which describes the event in admirable terms:

> The Eve of al-Ghiṭās in Miṣr was a great occasion for its people; no one slept that night. The amir Ikhshīd . . . ordered that 1,000 torches be lit on the shores of the Island and al-Fusṭāṭ. This is in addition to the numerous torches and candles that the people of Miṣr lighted. Thousands of people, both Muslims and Copts, thronged the banks of the Nile. Some were in boats, and others in houses overlooking the river. No one disapproved of the excessive display of food, drink, clothes, gold, silver, jewels, entertainment, music playing and revelry. It is truly the best of nights in the city offering the greatest pleasure, during which the roads remain open all night.[15]

This *Khiṭaṭ* narrative takes us back to the Ikhshīdid period, when al-Fusṭāṭ was still a provincial capital. The Ghiṭās is described as an occasion of popular festivities in the capital. Everyone, Copts as well as Muslims, participated in the festival. Along the banks of the Nile, immense city crowds shared the spontaneous and intense mood of celebration. And as al-Masʿūdī surprisingly remarked, no one disapproved of such public excesses on this special night. Rituals of public revelry such as drinking, dancing and music were performed with the typical indulgence and spontaneity expected on such occasions. Everyday social restrictions were reversed: night was transformed into day, Copts and Muslims celebrated together, women were out in their best attire, roads were left open all night, no one slept, and no one disapproved! These festivities celebrate the seasonal transition from winter to spring. Subsidizing the expenses of illumination, the local Ikhshīdī amir seems to have assumed the role of both protector and patron of the city's festival. Given that Egypt was still largely Coptic during this period, the amir's patronage of such an important feast should be viewed as a co-optation of popular culture by the state, and as a strategy to re-enforce its legitimacy in the eyes of its subjects.[16]

According to the *Khiṭaṭ* account, the Ghiṭās, like many other Coptic feasts, was subjected to a series of repressive policies from which it finally emerged in reduced form. The first Maqrīzī report of state repression takes us back to the period of Fatimid hegemony. In 367 AH, just two years after his succession to the throne, Caliph al-ʿAzīz ordered the prohibition of the festival, and decreed

[15] *Khiṭaṭ*, vol. I, 265.

[16] On Coptic conversion during the Mamluk period, see D. Little, 'Coptic conversion to Islam under the Baḥrī Mamluks, 692–755/1293–1354'. *Bulletin of the School of Oriental and African Studies*, 39 (1976), 552–69. See also M. Gervers and R. J. Bikhazi (eds.), *Conversion and Continuity, Indigenous Christian Communities in Islamic Lands, Eighth to Eighteenth Centuries*, Papers in Medieval Studies, vol. IX), (Toronto, 1990).

the banishment from public office as punishment for Coptic officials who defied the order. This point may be important for its political implications, for why is it that Maqrīzī calls attention only to the punishment decreed against Coptic officials? It is tempting to read this as a political statement, manifesting the tension existing between Coptic officials and the Muslim state, and, at the same time, illustrating Maqrīzī's bias on the issue of Coptic-Muslim conflict of power.[17]

When the Fatimid caliph al-Ḥākim came to the throne, however, these restraints were relaxed, popular celebrations were allowed, and even Coptic high officials were permitted to participate publicly in the festivities.[18] But his tolerance was short lived. For beginning with 401 AH, in the midst of much political turmoil in Egypt caused by wars, a series of bad Niles, high prices and food shortages, the same caliph took serious measures to tighten his grip on the affairs of state and society. All Coptic popular celebrations were banned, bureaucratic corruption was censured, the property of the rich and powerful was confiscated, and tight restrictive measures were imposed against everyone – particularly against vulnerable social elements such as women, Copts and Jews, as well as entertainers. Al-Ḥākim did not just ban the collective ritual of submersion, but in the years 403 – 405 AH, he actually ordered the banishment of Copts and Jews to Byzantine territory.[19] It should be remembered, however, that these harsh discriminatory measures occurred at a time when the Fatimid and Byzantine states were at war with one another.

Fourteen years later, the Ghiṭās festival was to flourish again under the rule of Caliph al-Ẓāhir, who posed as the official patron of the feast. Not only did he subsidize the expenses of illumination, but he also ordered a royal tent to be pitched on the banks of the Nile, so that he and his family could watch the public religious procession of Coptic priests, holding their crosses and chanting their hymns.[20] A crucial development, however, is said to have taken place, for when the moment of collective submersion arrived, Copts and Muslims were ordered by the authorities to do so separately.[21] Thus, if the festivities were to take place under Muslim state patronage, Muslims and Copts were asked to maintain two separate spaces. Such an official stance may be interpreted as an example of how the Muslim state tried to enforce a mode of social division between Copts and Muslims, a process necessary for cultivating a Muslim hegemonic presence.

According to the *Khiṭaṭ* narrative, the Fatimid caliphs seem to have continued in their role as patrons of this important Coptic festival as late as 517 AH. Thus, we are told that under the long reign of al-Mustaʿlī 'the ruling elite distributed to its officials (*ahl al-rusūm*) loads of citrus fruits, sugar cane and mullet fish, everything in accordance with the rates fixed by the *dīwān* for

[17] *Khiṭaṭ*, vol. I, 265. [18] Ibid., vol. I, 265–66.
[19] Ibid., vol. II, 495. For more details on al-Ḥakim's discriminatory policies towards the Copts, see ibid., vol. II, 495–7. [20] Ibid., vol. I, 266. [21] Ibid.

everyone'.[22] The Ghiṭās festival, therefore, seems to have been still of sufficient social and political significance to be worthy of appropriation as a state festival that could be used to articulate Fatimid authority. This last point is important, not only because it illustrates the continuation of Coptic official influence in the Fatimid state, but also because of what it may reveal of possible Coptic resistance to such restraints. It would seem that when conditions became more favourable, Copts could put pressure on the state to allow these festival celebrations.

The *Khiṭaṭ* narrative on the Ghiṭās ends abruptly with the Fatimids and we are left to wonder what happened to the festival during the Mamluk period. The *Sulūk* chronicle is no help here, for as we already know, it rarely describes the celebration of Coptic feasts. In this regard, Ibn al-Ḥājj, a scholar who lived one century earlier than Maqrīzī and author of an important treatise on the *bidʿa* of Egyptians, can be of more use. On the celebration of the Ghiṭās feast in fourteenth-century Mamluk Cairo, he reports that all Copts, old and young, male and female, and even babies, plunged into the Nile on this night. Displaying a hostility that is commonly shared by other Muslim religious scholars to such popular practices, he tell us that 'one of their most awful practices is the public procession in which they carry sugar canes topped with lit candles and with fruit'.[23] In addition to his repugnance with the public display of such rituals, Ibn al-Ḥājj is most outraged by Muslims' participation in the festivities: 'Not only do Muslims increase their expenses to please their children on such a joyful occasion, but some, who are steeped in ignorance, like to perform the plunging as the Copts do on such a night'.[24] While Ibn al-Ḥājjs description of the festival demonstrates that it was still a popular Coptic feast in his day, it does not seem to have been as great a festival as when al-Masʿūdī described it three hundred years earlier. By contrast, Ibn al-Ḥājj's description makes it look more like a Coptic festival, during which only a few Muslims participated. Representing official Islamic ideals, Ibn al-Ḥājj, like Maqrīzī, vehemently denounces the public display of these un-Islamic rituals as corruptions of the past. For them, the display of such practices is viewed as a sign of moral vice that must be eradicated from the Muslim community. And while Ibn al-Ḥājj is not advocating that Copts should convert to Islam, he is certainly demanding that they should not be allowed to display their religious rituals in public, because of the contagious harm that such practices may have on Muslims. We can thus understand why he is so outraged that some Muslims perform the submersion with the Copts during the Ghiṭās. For it is certainly a practice that contradicts Islamic teachings which explicitly forbid *dhimmīs* from displaying their religious rituals in Muslim territories, and which stress the maintenance of sharp social divisions between them and Muslims.[25] It is important to point out here the spatial construction underlying this hegemonic perspective: whereas the expression of Coptic rituals may only be per-

[22] Ibid. [23] *Al-Madkhal*, vol. II, 59. [24] Ibid. [25] See *al-Lumaʿ*, 296.

mitted in the private space, the expression of Muslim rituals may be displayed freely in the public space.

Even if we accept Maqrīzī's statement that the Ghiṭās in fifteenth-century Cairo was no longer the great feast that it used to be, it is still tempting to ask why the *Khiṭaṭ* and *Sulūk* narratives are silent about the Ghiṭās festivities during the Mamluk period. As I argued earlier, this is probably a narrative strategy that deliberately marginalizes Coptic culture in the official historical discourse. Clearly, the Ghiṭās was not banned outright as a religious feast, for it is still celebrated by the Coptic community in Egypt today. Induced by the pressures of a growing hegemonic Muslim culture, the festival must have undergone a process of mutation: from a popular religious feast that had been celebrated by the whole city, it has become a more private Coptic feast in our time, in which its most important ritual, plunging into the Nile, came increasingly to be performed within the precincts of the church.[26] Through this process of accommodation, popular Coptic rituals seem to have been displaced from public to private space. Most importantly, the Ghiṭās has been dissociated from its earlier links with the seasonal festivals of the Nile. Pressured to shed its popular pagan vestiges, it grew to be a more exclusively Coptic religious event.

ʿĪd al-Shahīd: 8 Bashans

The Coptic festival of the Martyr (ʿĪd al-Shahīd) was to meet a more dramatic fate. In contrast to other Coptic festivals in the *Khiṭaṭ*, usually dealt with in the special section on them, this one appears in those sections describing the wondrous nature of the Nile, thus appropriately situating ʿĪd al-Shahīd as a Nile festival *par excellence*.[27] Once again, Maqrīzī casts his account of the festival in terms of the past: 'ʿĪd al-Shahīd is one of those festivals which used to be celebrated in Miṣr, and during which the greatest spectacles *(furja)* were witnessed in the city'.[28] This is the longest of all the *Khiṭaṭ*'s accounts of Coptic festivals, for as we shall see, it details a long struggle of power between the two opposing cultures of Copts and Muslims.

We are told that the feast is celebrated on the eighth of the Coptic month of Bashans (May), approximately three months after the winter solstice feast of the Ghiṭās. This is a spring festival, and also linked closely to the Nile cycle. For the ancient Egyptians, the beginning of spring was normally considered as a period of high expectations, of uncertainty and fear, when revelry and sacrificial rites were performed in order to appease the evil forces of nature and ensure a plentiful inundation of the Nile. Like the Ghiṭās, this feast marks another seasonal transition, the beginning of spring. As with ancient spring festivals which called for sacrificial objects, ʿĪd al-Shahīd is also centred

[26] See E. William Lane, *Manners and Customs of the Modern Egyptians* (London, 1954) (hereafter *Manners and Customs*). [27] *Khiṭaṭ*, vol. I, 68–70. [28] Ibid., vol. I, 68.

around a sacrificial rite. In this case, it is a festival of sacrifice transformed through historical experience. The name *al-shahīd* itself indicates that the focal aspect of the feast is a sacrificial object, which is symbolized here by the finger of a male martyr. Displaying his hegemonic mentality, Maqrīzī casts these beliefs in doubtful terms, for he tells us that the Copts of Egypt claim (*yazʿamūn*) that when the finger of al-Shahīd is thrown into the Nile during the spring season, the river's future inundation is ensured. A similar sceptical stance can also be detected in al-Turkumānī's more revealing narrative on the character of the martyr: 'The Copts claim that the Martyr refers to a Copt who converted to Islam and then apostasized. They claim that, having been wronged, he died unjustly, and is thus considered a martyr'.[29] As we have seen, the sacrificial object of this feast is no longer a human figure, but reappears instead in the degenerate form of a finger that belongs to a male Coptic martyr (*iṣbaʿ al-Shahīd*).[30] Even though the figure of this martyr could be interpreted as symbolizing the historical experience of collective Coptic martyrdom under the earlier oppressive rule of the Byzantines, this signification seems to have undergone a transformation more specific to the historical experience of Copts under Muslim hegemony. For by the Mamluk period, the figure of the Shahīd was believed to have stood for the Coptic martyr suffering from the oppression of Muslim hegemonic power. Here, the figure of al-Shahīd symbolizes a specific act of martyrdom experienced under the dominance of Muslim culture: it is the figure of the subversive Copt who, after conversion to Islam, commits the sin of apostasy, thereby deserving elimination from the Muslim community.

The *Khiṭaṭ* narrative offers rich details, not only on how ʿĪd al-Shahīd was celebrated, but also on how it was ultimately suppressed by the Mamluk state. During this festival, the priests of the Shubrā church in Cairo seem to have been the prime actors, for it was they who orchestrated the ceremonial rituals of sacrifice that were believed to bring about the inundation of the Nile. Throughout the year, they kept the finger locked in a wooden box in their church. 'And on the 8th of the Coptic month of Bashans, the priests meet in the Shubrā church and they take the 'finger' out of the box to wash it in the Nile at a specific spot in Shubrā, claiming that the annual increase of the Nile does not happen until this 'finger' has been thrown into the river'.[31] The ritual of throwing the finger seems to have been performed amidst a great procession. The priests of Shubrā placed the finger in a wooden coffin, and then carried it to be thrown into the Nile, a public ceremony watched by immense

[29] *Al-Lumaʿ*, 311.

[30] It is worth noting here that the symbolic language of Mediterranean festival culture has for long interpreted the finger of a man as a symbol of generative power, and thus if used as a sacrificial object, it is believed to ensure fertility and prosperity in the land.

[31] Muḥammad b. Aḥmad ibn Iyās, *Badāʾiʿ al-Zuhūr fī waqāʾiʿ al-Duhūr*, ed. Muḥammad Muṣṭafā (Cairo, 1984) (hereafter, *Badāʾiʿ*), vol. I, 564.

crowds on both sides of the river. Maqrīzī offers a detailed description of the festival during the reign of the Mamluk sultan al-Nāṣir Muḥammad:

On this day, Copts come from all the villages to watch the ceremony. They ride horses and perform acrobatics on top of them. Residents of al-Qāhira and al-Fusṭāṭ from all classes proceed to the banks and islands of the Nile to pitch their tents. All male and female singers, entertainers, prostitutes, effeminate males and reprobates of all types eagerly participate in the festival. Infinite numbers of people congregate, only the Creator can estimate them. Countless sums of money are spent, and numerous sins are performed in excess. Chaos errupts and some people get killed. Over one hundred thousand silver dirhams worth of wine is sold on this day, of which five thousand gold dinars are appropriated as tax. One merchant sold what is worth twelve thousand silver dirhams of wine. The congregation of festivities always took place in Shubrā, one of the districts of al-Qāhira. Thus the peasants of Shubrā paid their *kharāj* tax to the state from the revenue which they procured from the sale of wine on the feast of the martyr.[32]

If Maqrīzī was silent about state participation in this festival, the sixteenth-century Muslim historian Ibn Iyās was more informative: 'Amirs and other state officials (*al-mubāshirūn*) pitched their tents along the banks of the Nile, while Coptic notables from the state bureaucracy took boats to watch more closely the ceremony of throwing the finger in the Nile'.[33] Based on such accounts, the feast of the Martyr, at least up to the middle of the eighth Hijri century, still appears to be one of the most important popular Coptic festivals that remained closely connected to the Nile festival culture. True, there is no mention of official Mamluk or even Fatimid patronage of this feast, but some state presence can certainly be detected.

Like the Ghiṭās, ʿĪd al-Shahīd is reminiscent of pagan festivals of revelry in which public excesses were displayed freely during a period characterized by scholars as a time of temporary reversal of the social order. This was a time of intense collective energy, when drunkenness, playing, entertainment, and incidents of death could occur. (These festival martyrs should also be viewed as sacrificial objects of ʿĪd al-Shahīd.) Understandably, such patterns of popular excesses were the cause of much consternation on the part of Mamluk historians, including Maqrīzī. They typically complained that such popular chaos was checked neither by ruler nor governor. Our Mamluk historians construct the festival as a period of social rupture, one in which boundless social chaos prevails (*bimā yazīd ʿan al-ḥadd – bimā lā yuḥtamal*).[34] Clearly, this anti-festival narrative must have served to pressure the state to uphold its duty to safeguard the moral integrity of the Muslim community against the dangers of social chaos. But as the narrative ironically demonstrates, the substantial state tax on wine sales must have been one of the important reasons behind the

32 *Khiṭaṭ*, vol. I. 69. 33 *Badā,iʿ* vol. I, 566.

34 For more details on this subject, see Boaz Shoshan. *Popular Culture in Medieval Cairo*, Cambridge Studies in Islamic Civilization (Cambridge, 1993) (hereafter *Popular Culture*) 40–51.

survival of this feast of sacrifice. A close relation between state discipline and popular spontaneity is observed: popular revelry may be displayed in exchange for a disciplinary tax. But here the piety of the Muslim historian appears to be in conflict with the pragmatic policy of the state.

Maqrīzī's first report of prohibition is dated around 702 AH, during the unstable early reign of Sultan al-Nāṣir Muḥammad, who was still under the tutelage of his grand amirs, Baybars al-Jāshinkīr and Sayf al-dīn Salār. We know from al-Turkumānī, however, that the festival had been suspended temporarily during the earlier reign of the powerful sultan al-Ẓāhir Baybars, after which, much to al-Turkumānī's disgust, it was revived.[35] Maqrīzī's later story of prohibition identifies Baybars al-Jāshinkīr as the amir who banned the feast. He issued a decree announcing that 'no finger is to be thrown in the Nile and no festival celebrations are to be allowed on the occasion'.[36] Moreover, he ordered the governor of Cairo 'to forbid people from congregating at Shubrā according to their custom. Messengers were sent to the Egyptian provinces with written decrees addressed to governors, so that they could announce publicly that no Copt should come to the capital to celebrate 'Īd al-Shahīd'.[37] Here, explicit Coptic resistance is reported to have taken place, the details of which serve to demonstrate how the Copts used their official connections in the state to pressure the ruling elite against prohibiting their festivals. Maqrīzī tells us that 'all the Copts of Miṣr were grieving, both those who remained Coptic, as well as those who converted to Islam and claimed to be Muslims (*al-musālima*)'.[38] They tried their utmost to negotiate with the state. Recognizing that Baybars' own Coptic employee, Tāj ibn Sa'īd al-Dawla, would be their most important connection, they asked him to convince his employer. Tāj put forward the most powerful arguments: that the *kharāj* tax would be greatly reduced; that if the feast rituals were not performed, the Nile would not rise; that Egypt itself would be destroyed. Baybars, according to this Maqrīzī report, seemed determined: 'If the Nile does not rise except with this 'finger' then let it not rise, and if Allāh is the one who really decides this, we declare the Copts liars'.[39] Once again an oppositional construct is revealed here: while Copts are denigrated as liars, Muslims are privileged as the possessors of the truth. We should also call attention to the narrative similarity between this dialogue and the earlier one taking place between 'Amr Ibn al-'Āṣ and Caliph 'Umar I on the sacrifice of the virgin bride. Both stories illustrate the underlying hegemonic perspective inherent in Mamluk historical narrative, one which systematically invalidates pre-Islamic popular rituals as corruptions of the past (*bida'*) of which the Muslim community should be cleansed.

According to the *Khiṭaṭ*, the prohibition of 'Īd al-Shahīd lasted thirty-six years, until it was revived again in 738 AH by al-Nāṣir Muḥammad, when he was a more mature and independently wealthy sultan. Maqrīzī provides an

[35] *Al-Luma'*, 312. [36] *Khiṭaṭ*, vol. I, 69. [37] Ibid. [38] Ibid. [39] Ibid.

amusing justification for this, for he tells us that in order to divert his favourite amirs, Yalbughā and Alṭunbughā, from hunting, al-Nāṣir said to them: 'We will revive the celebrations of 'Īd al-Shahīd, the sight of which you will find to be more pleasing than hunting'.[40] The sultan's offer seems to have been readily accepted, and messages were immediately sent out to the provinces announcing the revival of the festival. The usual feasting frenzy lasted for three days, and all forms of public licentiousness were displayed once again. The amirs were on their barges in the middle of the Nile, gazing at the splendour of the people's festivities. They too indulged in their own excesses, and the most sumptuous banquets, offering the widest variety of food, were laid out for them.[41] But there is more to this story of revival than just gratifying the whims of the sultan's favourite amirs. For it is also quite possible that al-Nāṣir, in order to increase his state revenues, was seeking to reintroduce the state tax on the sale of wine during such festivities. Whatever the state's reasons may have been, the narrative can also be read to illustrate Maqrīzī's attitude of ridicule towards Coptic religious festivals: these were simply viewed as sources of entertainment for the Mamluk elite.[42]

The festival continued to be celebrated without interruption until the fateful year of 755 AH, dramatically described by Maqrīzī as the year of Coptic tribulations (*miḥnat al-aqbāṭ*). It was during this year that 'Īd al-Shahīd was to receive its death blow from the Mamluk state.[43] This historical moment representing Muslim triumph against Coptic political and cultural presence, receives the fullest treatment not only in the *Khiṭaṭ*, but also in the *Sulūk*. Serving as a narrative of the state, the *Sulūk* documents in great detail the historical circumstances surrounding the abolition of this great festival, marking it as a point of Coptic defeat in relation to Muslim hegemony. Both narratives allow us to understand better the manner by which such festivals were subjected to prohibition by the state. A dramatic picture is constructed here, for we are told that the state was in disarray and bankrupt, while the bedouins of Upper Egypt were rising in rebellion. Last but not least, Coptic officials were becoming more and more influential in the Mamluk bureaucracy. Here, the textual juxtaposition constructed between the growing power of the Copts, on the one hand, and other factors constituting social and political disintegration, on the other, shows that Maqrīzī construed the increasing power of the Copts as a disruptive factor threatening Muslim hegemony. Thus, we are told, an edict was issued by the sultan, forbidding any Jew or Copt from working in his *dīwān*. Another was issued to investigate the *waqf* property of Coptic churches and monasteries. This was readily undertaken and relevant documents were submitted to the treasury, identifying a total of 25,000 *faddāns* as *waqf* property. These were confiscated by the sultan and conveniently assigned

[40] Ibid. [41] Ibid.

[42] For other situations in which the state imposes taxes on wine drinking and entertainment, see ibid., vol. I, 105, *Sulūk*, vol. II, 642–6.

[43] See Ibn Iyās who gives a later date, in *Badā'i'*, vol. I, 564; *Khiṭaṭ*, vol. I, 69, *Sulūk*, vol. II, 906.

as *iqṭāʿ* property to Mamluk amirs. Moreover, several churches were destroyed, including the Shubrā church, where the 'finger of the martyr' had been kept safely.[44] Expressing gratitude to Allāh for this Muslim triumph against Coptic *bidaʿ*, Maqrīzī states:

> The finger of the martyr was taken in a box to al-Malik al-Ṣāliḥ to be burnt in front of him in the *maydān*. He then ordered that its ashes be thrown in the Nile, so that the Copts would not be able to take it back. From that day on, ʿĪd al-Shahīd was discontinued until this period. To Allāh we owe gratitude and strength.[45]

But the Copts' tribulations did not end here, for we are told that when their difficulties multiplied and their property diminished, the Copts decided – apparently in great numbers – to accept Islam. Maqrīzī uses the Arabic term *fashā* to emphasize that conversion to Islam spread widely among the Coptic commoners in the land of Egypt. This he demonstrates in numerical terms: in one day a total of 450 Copts converted to Islam in Qalyūb, and likewise in other places. He viewed such conversions with the usual suspicion of an orthodox Muslim: these are to be viewed as part of Coptic trickery,which would allow them access to official posts and Muslim women. Thus, as a result of such conversions, Maqrīzī regretfully remarks, lineages became confused in Egypt.[46] This attitude is quite consistent with the prevalent Muslim hegemonic perspective, for it was widely believed that Copts who converted under such pressures were not 'true' Muslims, and therefore do not deserve to be part of this privileged category. Lest they be confused with 'true' Muslims, they were classified, in Mamluk historical and *bidaʿ* narratives, by the distinctive but pejorative term '*al-musālima*'. For Maqrīzī, these mass conversions constituted a threat to authentic Muslim identity, for they blurred the distinction, so crucial for the construction of a dominant Muslim identity, between Copt and Muslim.

The final abolition of the spring festival of the Martyr, or of any Coptic festival for that matter, cannot be viewed simply as a manifestation of Muslim repugnance at non-Islamic popular practices. For such dislike was often used as justification by the Mamluk state and its religious establishment for taking drastic measures that would curb the economic and political power of a potentially threatening group such as the Copts. As we have just seen, the urgent need on the part of the Mamluk state to confiscate the immense property of Coptic religious institutions and officials, in order to relieve its bankruptcy, must be considered as one of the prime causes leading to the final suppression of this festival. Links between the state and Coptic popular spontaneity were dramatically severed by the act of burning the sacrificial object of the feast; Coptic power was perhaps too weakened to resist these violations. Moreover, such state strategies must be viewed as a reflection of the conflict between Coptic and Mamluk state officials, for the latter were to gain much more from these confiscations than from the wine tax collected on such occasions.

[44] *Khiṭaṭ*, vol. I, 70. [45] Ibid. [46] *Sulūk*, vol. II, 927.

Wafāʾ al-Nīl: Kasr al-Khalīj – Masrā ?

An old Egyptian saying goes: 'If the Nile does not fulfill its promise in Masrā, wait for it the next year'.[47] No one knew for sure when the Nile would reach the crucial 16 cubit measure on the Nilometer. The Egyptian populace, and even more urgently the government, waited anxiously for this to happen around the middle of the Coptic month of Masrā (August), more than two months after the festival of the Martyr. Whereas the *Sulūk* narrative offers a systematic reference to the annual date of Wafāʾ al-Nīl, when the river has reached its 16 cubit mark, only cursory reference is made to Mamluk state ceremonials of the Wafāʾ festival. In the *Khiṭaṭ*, however, Maqrīzī gives us the most detailed account of the state's celebration of such an event. But while ten pages of the Būlāq edition are devoted to the most minute descriptions of Fatimid state ceremonials of Wafāʾ al-Nīl, only a short passage is provided on the celebration of such an event during the Mamluk period. Similarly, al-Qalqashandī's Mamluk narrative, *Ṣubḥ al-Aʿshā,* offers only a summary account of how the Mamluks celebrated Wafāʾ al-Nīl.[48] The *Subḥ* narrative, however, confirms what could not be firmly established on the basis of Maqrīzī's narrative: unlike the Fatimid caliphs, Mamluk sultans were reluctant participants in the ceremonial rituals of Wafāʾ al-Nīl.[49]

Based on a large number of contemporary Fatimid sources, Maqrīzī constructs a glamorous picture of Fatimid ceremonials during this festival. This depicts the Fatimid caliph as an awesome and sacred figure of power and wealth, celebrating with his Egyptian subjects the most decisive stage in the river's behaviour, upon which the fate of both people and state depended: 'Wafāʾ al-Nīl was of great importance for them, and they celebrated it with excessive joy, for it was the cause of the land's prosperity and the creatures' harmony before Allāh's grace. This explains why the caliph paid much greater attention to it than any of the other festivals.'[50] Moreover, Maqrīzī depicts the caliph as a focal, almost deified figure in the ceremonials of the festival.As we shall soon discover, nowhere in the *Khiṭaṭ* or the *Sulūk* does Maqrīzī describe the Mamluk sultan with such dazzling metaphors. It may be worthwhile quoting how this Arabian Nights caliphal figure is constructed in the *Khiṭaṭ*:

> Dressed in flowing robes that dazzle the eyes, the caliph goes out in the costume of the caliphate, the costume of dignity and honour. He puts on an Arabian style turban that is adorned with rubies and emeralds, reserved only for such festival celebrations, and described as the turban of dignity (*shaddat al-waqār*). When he is dressed in such a fashion, flags flutter, speech is avoided, and he is feared.[51]

Ibn al-Raddād is depicted as another focal figure in these ceremonials. We are told that when the Nile water is close to reaching the 16 cubit mark, he is

[47] Ibid., vol. IV, 614.
[48] Shihāb al-dīn al-Qalqashandī, *Ṣubḥ al-Aʿshā fī ṣināʿat al-inshāʾ*, (Cairo, al-Maṭbaʿa al-Amīriyya, 1913–19) (hereafter *Ṣubḥ*), vol. IV, 47–8. [49] Ibid. [50] *Khiṭaṭ*, vol. I, 476.
[51] Ibid., vol. I, 473.

ordered by the caliph to carry ten loads of bread, meat and sweets, as well as ten candles, to the Nilometer (*al-miqyās*). Koran reciters and the religious heads of important mosques are ordered to spend the night in the Nilometer mosque. And as is customary in many of these Egyptian festivals, the rituals commence with banqueting. Candles are lit after performance of the last evening prayer, followed by Koranic recitation and chanting, and concluding with the Koranic *khatma.* When the Nile water reaches the 16 cubit mark, Ibn al-Raddād informs the vizier, and preparations are made for the performance of the ritual of anointing the Nilometer (*takhlīq ʿamūd al-miqyās*), an important symbolic ritual, signfiying the desire to bring life to the Nilometer, hence the Arabic term *takhlīq*. Riding in solemn procession, the caliph leaves his palace the next morning in order to attend the festival rituals. After riding through the magnificently decorated streets of Cairo, the caliph takes his royal boat towards the Maqs gate where the anointing of the Nilometer takes place:

> The caliph, his entourage, and the vizier enter the fountain area, and when they have performed the prayers, the machine (*al-āla*), containing the saffron and musk is brought to the caliph, who hands it over to the treasurer, who in turn hands it to Abū'-l-Raddād. The latter throws himself in the fountain . . . where the Nilometer column is close to the steps, and proceeds to *anoint the column.* Meanwhile, on the opposite side, reciters are reciting the Koran in turns. After this the caliph returns in his boat to the palace or the Maqs mosque.[52]

In contrast to the Nile festivals of the Ghiṭās and the Shahīd, which, up to the Mamluk period, were still closely linked to Coptic religious culture, the Wafāʾ festival seems to have undergone a fuller process of Islamization. Thus, whereas the religious rituals of the Ghiṭās and the Shahīd were orchestrated by Coptic priests, the Wafā' rituals appear to have been performed exclusively by Muslim religious officials. Likewise, its rituals seem to be predominantly Islamic: prostrations, Koranic recitation and chanting, as well as exaltations of Allāh. Nonetheless, we can still detect some pagan retentions. This can be readily observed in the rituals of lighting candles and banqueting, but most importantly, in the ritual of *anointing* the Miqyās column with perfume and plants, a ritual that is performed in close association with Koranic recitations and exaltations of Allāh (*al-takbīr*). Thus Wafāʾ al-Nīl seems to have been displaced as a Coptic festival, only to reappear as an official Muslim event. Notorious for their patronage of popular religious festivals, it is quite possible that it was the Fatimids who pushed for the Islamization of the Wafāʾ rituals.

Two more important state rituals, serving to assure the populace of the capital that the Nile has reached the 16 cubit mark, bring about close articulation between people and state. Here, Ibn al-Raddād performs the crucial political function of officially announcing to the public the anxiously awaited sign of the Wafāʾ. Proceeding from the royal palace, he is dressed in the Wafāʾ golden robe of honour (*al-khilʿa al-dhahabiyya*), and in a public procession

[52] Ibid., vol. I, 476.

accompanied by drums and trumpets, he rides along the road of Bayn al-Qaṣrayn, announcing the attainment of 16 cubits.[53] However, the climactic point of the festival is the ritual of opening (*fatḥ*) the Khalīj dam, which is attended by the caliph and all the important state officials, including the chief judge and other Muslim religious notables. Huge tents are pitched for the occasion, where Koranic reciters and poets perform before the caliph. When this is over, the latter proceeds to his panoramic palace overseeing the Khalīj to watch the ritual of opening the dam, which is also performed amidst Koranic recitation and exaltations of Allāh. This is then followed by magnificent banquets lasting until noon prayers, after which the royal procession returns to the palace.[54]

These festival images are but a tiny fraction of the *Khiṭaṭ* narrative recounting the Fatimids' elaborate ceremonials of the festival. If anything, it certainly reveals Maqrīzī's admiration for the ceremonial culture of the Fatimid caliphs. But I would like to note here that whereas this festival narrative provides the most detailed documentation of how the Wafā' was celebrated by the Fatimids, it is almost silent on the manner by which the populace of the capital celebrated the event. Once again, this illustrates Maqrīzī's bias against popular festivities in general, for he prefers to depict the Wafā' as an official state festival, uncontaminated by the popular abominations so typical of such Egyptian festivities. This Maqrīzīan stance is demonstrated in a short but revealing passage which constructs an opposition between popular and high culture. In describing the climactic ritual of opening the dam, the *Khiṭaṭ* narrative constructs two opposite spaces: the western and the eastern banks of the canal. Thus while the western bank is described as a space privileged by caliphal presence, Koranic recitation and exaltations of Allāh, the eastern bank is denigrated as a dusty space contaminated by the playing and dust of the commoners (*rahaj wa-laʿib*).[55]

Similarly, Maqrīzī displays little interest in recording Mamluk ceremonials of the Wafā' festival. In vain does one look in the *Khiṭaṭ*'s encyclopaedic narrative for a depiction of the manner by which sultans participated in the festival. There appears to be only one short reference to the Wafā' celebrations hidden in the entries describing the Nile barrages. But even here, no mention is made of how the Mamluk sultans participated in the ceremonials. This is an omission which may also be read as an indication of the Mamluks' relative indifference to popular festivities. Here the narrative depicts the Mamluk elite adopting a distant and coercive stance toward the Wafā' festivities:

And during the 'days of the Nile', people rode boats in the Maqsī and Nāṣirī canals, where they went beyond the limits because of the exceedingly disgraceful behaviour

[53] Ibid.
[54] Ibid., vol. I, 470–9. Paula Sanders has worked extensively on Fatimid ceremonials: see her *Ritual, Politics, and the City in Fatimid Cairo* (Albany, 1994).
[55] *Khiṭaṭ*, vol. I, 474.

> and pleasures they exhibited. But after al-Malik al-Ashraf Shaʿbān was killed . . . and following the orders of amirs Barqūq and Baraka, as well as al-Shaykh Muḥammad, better known as Ṣāʾim al-Dahr, the boats of spectators were forbidden from passing through the canal. A *fatwā* was requested from al-Shaykh al-Bulqīnī, who decreed that they must be forbidden because of the excessive breaking of taboos, and the public performance of the obscene and the forbidden. Thus a decree was issued by the two amirs, forbidding boats of spectators to enter the canal, and in the year 781 AH, a chain was built to block the Maqsī barrage. Spectator boats continued to be forbidden from passing through the canal until the end of al-Ẓāhir Barqūq's state in 791 AH, after which they were permitted to enter, and this still continues until our time.[56]

This depiction of the Mamluks should be contrasted to that of the Fatimid caliph who is pictured as a focal state figure articulating his authority through magnificent ceremonials. But we should remember that the above Mamluk prohibitions took place during an unstable transitional period, when al-Ẓāhir Barqūq had not yet consolidated the Circassian hold over the Mamluk state. Thus, ten years later, when this was more or less accomplished, restrictions were once more relaxed. However, the need on the part of Mamluk amirs to procure the co-operation of the religious establishment in order to legitimize such an unpopular policy may be indicative of the state's fear of popular resistance. Here, the Mamluk state and its religious establishment are seen hand in hand, suppressing the disruptive aspects of popular culture. Such restraints must have been approved by Maqrīzī, who never tires of using the power of language to denounce popular excesses. The subsequent revival of these festivities, despite a long period of prohibition, should be viewed not only as a form of popular resistance, but also as a sign of a more stable government that could accommodate festival excesses.

A different account of Nile behaviour appears in Maqrīzī's *Sulūk*, which, like other Mamluk chronicles, meticulously records both the increases and decreases of the water's flow during the period of Ayyām al-Nīl. Several entries are devoted to the behaviour of the Nile every year, the most important being that which documents the date of the Wafāʾ. Except for drought situations, the length of these entries is normally one or two lines. For example, the *Sulūk* entry on the festival of the Wafāʾ would simply record that 'when Wafāʾ al-Nīl reached the 16 cubits mark, the sultan rode as usual to witness the anointing of the Nilometer, then he opened the dam, and returned to the citadel'.[57] Here the chronicle account is succinct, almost like a standard formula that is used to describe an official annual event. Often the entry does not even specify who, from among the Mamluk elite, attended the rituals of the festival. Thus the entry would simply state that 'on 26 Masrā, the Nile reached the 16 cubits, and the dam was opened according to the custom'.[58] What is important for the official record here is to document when the Nile reached the 16 cubit mark, a most crucial event for the prosperity of both state and society.

[56] Ibid., vol. II, 150. [57] *Sulūk*, vol. IV, 68. [58] Ibid., vol. IV, 397.

According to the *Sulūk*, Mamluk sultans often appear to have delegated their important amirs to observe the ceremonials of the festival, thus showing a preference for remaining distant from such events. The political implication underlying this reluctant presence during the ceremonials cannot be overlooked. This is clearly illustrated in the case of Sultan Faraj, who, during the turbulent year of 806 AH, decided to absent himself from the festivities for fear of social violence *(khawfan min al-fitna)*. In his place he delegated his powerful amir Yashbak.[59] However, in the year 811 AH, when conditions may have been more stable politically, Sultan Faraj is seen celebrating in person the rituals of the festival. In connection with this, it should be mentioned that the great sultan, al-Ẓāhir Baybars, is singled out by Ibn Iyās as the first to establish the precedent of participating in the festival rituals. The last was al-Ẓāhir Khushqadam (872 AH), after whom, we are told, no sultan attended the rituals. Although Ibn Iyās does not explain the sultans' indifference to the festival; this may be read as an indication of the political turbulence of the later Circassian period.[60] The Mamluks, however, seem to have introduced a new ritual to the festivities of Wafā' al-Nīl. Not surprisingly, theirs was a martial contribution: for three consecutive days, the sultan and his amirs held daily military processions in the more confined space of Bāb al-Lūq square, where they showed off their talents in the art of polo.[61]

The *istisqā'* rituals of anxiety

Unlike festivals, which normally take place at fixed annual intervals, the rituals of rain prayers (*al-istisqā'*) occurred only when the Nile showed signs of a drought. The *Sulūk* narrative offers long descriptions of these drought occurrences, and the resultant social panic that usually took place in the capital. During such catastrophic occurences, rituals of anxiety displaced the rituals of revelry normally displayed when the Nile did fulfil its promise of 'completion'. Both these sets of rituals, however, should be viewed as rites of passage tuned to Nilotic fluctuations. The communal performance of rain rituals may be said to express a collective desire to pass from a state of sin to a state of virtue, in order to bring about divine forgiveness and mercy, thus effecting a reversal of the drought situation. Underlying the performance of these rituals is the common belief that natural catastrophes are caused by human transgressions of God's laws, which may be reversed only if people repent of their sins. Such beliefs are inherent in Maqrīzī's narrative, for he systematically juxtaposes the popular display of abominations (*iẓhār al-munkarāt*) with the occurence of disasters. We can recognize his moral message: in order to reverse such disasters people are not only admonished to return to virtue, but they should also be prevented from committing sinful behaviour. For Maqrīzī, it is the

[59] Ibid., vol. IV, 68. [60] *Badā'i'*, vol. I, 324.
[61] *Sulūk*, vol. I, 444. For more details, see *Ṣubḥ*, vol. IV, 47.

state that is expected to exercise the authority of forbidding such sins. This belief is readily demonstrated in the narrative structure describing the incident of Nile decrease in the year 810 AH: 'The Nile water stopped increasing for three days, beginning Thursday, and several amirs rode in order to attack the sites where people congregated for rejoicing. They were forbidden from committing abominations, so it started to increase on Sunday, and the increase continued'.[62] Similarly, on another occasion of Nile delay, Maqrīzī states: 'The sultan forbade the people from congregating along the banks of the Nile in anticipation of Wafā᾽ al-Nīl. Thanks be to Allāh, people were prohibited from committing the ugly abominations which normally take place there, and He the Almighty came to the rescue of his slaves, and caused the Nile to flow, after they had almost despaired'.[63] As in the first narrative, Maqrīzī constructs this one to demonstrate the presence of a vigilant God who is not only omnipresent in daily life, but who is ready to show immediate signs of mercy if people are prevented from committing sinful deeds.

But it was when the Nile exhibited signs of a prolonged drought that we get more detailed coverage in the *Sulūk* chronicle, for this is tantamount to a social catastrophe, when collective fear of famine, pain, death, disease and strife is heightened. One of the best documented *istisqā᾽* accounts in the *Sulūk* is the one that occurred in 823 AH, during the reign of the pious sultan al-Mu᾽ayyad Shaykh.[64] The text reveals the juxtaposition between collective abstention from vice and the reversal of the drought:

The Nile stopped increasing for several days. Grain prices rose and merchants stopped selling it. People's worry increased. They were called upon to stop committing what Allāh forbade, and instead to commit themselves to virtue. They were asked to fast for three days and to go out to the desert. Many people fasted the next day, including the sultan. So it was announced that there was an increase of one digit (*iṣbaʿ*). Then it was announced that the next day, they should go out while they were fasting to the mountain. The following day Shaykh al-Islām Qāḍī al-Quḍāt al-Bulqīnī left his house early, and riding in his ordinary clothes with a group of people, he reached the mouth of the valley, close to Qubbat al-Naṣr. There, a pulpit was constructed, and he recited *sūrat al-anʿām*. In the meantime, people were arriving in great numbers from all directions, until there was a huge crowd. Two hours after sunset, the sultan arrived alone riding his horse. He was dressed in the costume of the sufis. Neither his saddle nor his horse were adorned with any gold or silk, and when he dismounted his horse, he sat on the ground without any carpet. Leading the people in prayers, the chief judge performed two prostrations. Then he mounted the pulpit and gave two speeches, in which he admonished people to repent, to perform good deeds, repeatedly warning and forbidding them from committing bad deeds. After this he faced the *qibla* and began a long invocation of Allāh. All this while, the sultan was weeping, and rubbing his forehead against the sand during his prostrations. When the speech was over, people left. And

[62] *Sulūk*, vol. III, 1021. [63] Ibid., vol. IV, 479, *Khiṭaṭ*, vol. I, 488.

[64] On the puritanical policy of al-Mu'ayyad Shaykh, see *Sulūk*, vol. IV, 522. See also Ibn Taghribīrdī, *al-Nujūm al-Zāhira fī Mulūk Miṣr wa-᾽l-Qāhira* (Cairo, Dār al-Kutub edition, 1963) (hereafter *Nujūm*), vol. XV, pp. 396, 424–5; see also *Badā᾽iʿ*, vol. I, 124.

as the sultan was mounting his horse, the commoners surrounded him from all four directions, praying for him until he returned to the Citadel.[65]

Clearly, this is not a narrative that is simply used to recount factual events, for Maqrīzī cleverly uses his imagery to play on the pious emotions of the reader. This becomes obvious in his concluding remarks on this historical moment of reversal: 'Watching the 'almighty of the earth' (*jabarūt al-arḍ*) behaving thus, produces humility of the heart and induces praying for the mercy of the Almighty of the heavens'.[66] Clearly, our historian uses the sultan as an example to be followed. The *Sulūk* narrative depicts beautifully this atmosphere of collective anxiety and repentance that ensues in the event of such a cosmic catastrophe. And nowhere else is the government's fear of popular festivities more clearly illustrated than during such periods. Here the government moves quickly to impose restraints on all forms of popular festivities. Thus we are told that during one of these drought periods

the state ordered the forbidding of sins and prevention of their public display. Immediately, the governor rode to the direction of Būlāq, in order to execute his orders. When he arrived at Būlāq, he proceeded to seize the spectators whom he found. Then he went down to the Jazīra, where he found a crowd, so he seized a great number of women and men, mounted them on donkeys, and made a public display of them, all the way from Būlāq to Cairo.[67]

Moreover, the state appears to have adopted other strategies to contain the social panic and chaos that might arise under such circumstances. Thus, through the use of frequent public announcements, people are reminded of divine punishment, and are admonished to repent their sins and return to virtue; they are ordered to fast as an act of purification, and to pray to Allāh that He may bring back life to the Nile. During a similar period of Nile drought, the notorious Fatimid caliph al-Ḥākim went so far as to prohibit the inhabitants of the capital to go out after darkness in order to contain the social chaos that might erupt in the city.[68]

Maqrīzī depicts the Muslim religious establishment as playing a crucial role during the rituals of rain prayers, for it is the chief judge himself who takes on the responsibility of conducting these solemn rituals. They are primarily conducted outside the city, in the mountains or the desert – an ancient custom that appears to have persisted under Muslim culture. A spatial opposition is constructed here: whereas the desert is used to signify a space of purity where the Almighty might be more receptive to human supplication, the city is a contaminated space conducive only to sin. In the desert space, signs of high social status seem to be discarded; whether chief judge or sultan, practices of urban refinement and social hierarchies are to be left behind. Being orchestrated by the Muslim religious establishment, the rituals of rain prayers appear to be

[65] *Sulūk*, vol. IV, 531–2. [66] Ibid. [67] Ibid., vol. III, 429.
[68] For a detailed account on the martial laws that al-Ḥākim imposed on the inhabitants of the capital see *Khiṭaṭ*, vol. II, 286.

predominantly Islamic, consisting of the usual prostrations in Muslim prayers, Koranic recitations and the pious admonitions by Muslim religious officials, all performed to appeal to the mercy of the Creator. Muslims appear to be united in collective repentance, prayer and voluntary poverty. This return to innocence, expressing hope for divine intervention, is further dramatized in Maqrīzī's construction of the sultanic figure, for he is pictured as a solitary figure, dressed in symbolic clothes of poverty, rubbing his head and body against the naked earth, and weeping, like everybody else, for Allāh's mercy. This narrative describes the sultan in reversed terms, for the 'almighty of the earth' is not depicted as a figure of power and haughtiness, but as one of humility and weakness. Clearly, this paradoxical image is manipulated by our pious historian in order to admonish the unrighteous to return to virtue.

The dramatic narratization of Nile droughts is not a peculiar feature of the *Sulūk*, for other Mamluk historians, such as Ibn Taghrībirdī and Ibn Iyās, describe these events in similar fashion. Their narratives use powerful apocalyptic imagery depicting scenes of mass exodus: barefooted children, men and cattle proceed in great numbers to the desert. Most of the Cairene community, high and low, seem to have shared these rituals of anxiety: Mamluk state officials, the caliph, chief judges, *ʿulamāʾ*, Sufi saints, *fuqarāʾ* and the commoners. Even members of the Christian and Jewish communities, carrying their sacred texts, are mentioned as having been present during these solemn rituals. However, their presence has been omitted from Maqrīzī's narrative. This silence about *dhimmī* participation is all the more glaring when we learn that it seems to have been standard practice during such occasions. It is tempting, therefore, to interpret this omission as a desire on the part of Maqrīzī as a pious Muslim to depict this event as an all-Muslim affair, one which is orchestrated by Muslims, and uncontaminated by *dhimmī* presence.[69] Here he may be implicitly reminding us that these two exclusive religious spaces should not be allowed to overlap, even in times of social rupture.

A more notable absence in the *istisqāʾ* narrative is that of women. And whereas only Maqrīzī excises *dhimmī* presence, none of the three Mamluk chronicles that I have consulted mention anything on the participation of women in the rituals of rain. Whether this is a real or ideological absence, it must be read as some kind of metaphorical rejection of female presence/temptation (*fitna*) during the performance of such sacred religious rituals. This interpretation becomes more convincing if we recall that Mamluk narratives always depict a powerful female presence in festivals. Once again an oppositional construct emerges here: the sacred space of purity, where rituals of rain are performed, is opposed to the corrupting temporal space of the festival, where popular abominations are unashamedly displayed. In the sacred

[69] *Nujūm*, vol. III, 429; vol. XV, 396, 429; *Badāʾiʿ*, vol. I, 124, 690. For evidence on the participation of Christians and Jews in the rain rituals in eighteenth century Cairo, see ʿAbd al-Raḥmān al-Jabartī, *ʿAjāʾib al-athār fī-ʾl-Tarājim wa-ʾl-Akhbār* (Beirut, n.d.) (hereafter *ʿAjāʾib*), vol. III, 310–11.

space, woman is made absent; in the temporal, she is an integral part of it. Thus in order to effect the desired link between the spiritual and the temporal, ensuring the transition from divine wrath to divine mercy, the presence of women is eliminated.

The chronicles of Ibn Taghrībirdī and Ibn Iyās illustrate the performance of additional rituals of reversal. These may be observed in ritualistic gestures expressing loss of social status, performed in the hope of bringing about a reversal of the drought situation – as when the preacher of the ʿAmr ibn al-ʿĀṣ mosque uncovered his head and turned his garment back to front, a gesture that was collectively followed by the male congregation. Another such ritual shows the *ʿulamāʾ* committing an act of blasphemy, for in their panic they carried the Prophet's relics (*al-āthār al-sharīfa*) to the Nilometer, where they preferred to perform their supplication rituals. Once again, the mention of this ritual is omitted in Maqrīzī's narrative, who may have felt reluctant to depict religious scholars committing an act that is degrading to their social status.[70] Scenes of plundering, robbery and collective flight, typical of such conditions of social chaos, are graphically depicted in Mamluk historical narratives, and should also be viewed as manifestations of social reversal. So powerful are these images of collective anxiety in the chronicles that we can almost see and hear people crying out loudly, begging the Creator to bring life to the Nile.[71] We must applaud the Mamluk historian for having played his role of edifier with such exceeding cleverness, for there could be no more powerful inducements to piety than those that involve great human suffering.

The Egyptian Nawrūz: 1 Tūt

Because the Nile is the life-giving force of the Egyptians, they fixed the beginning of their calendar during the autumn month of Tūt, when the river's inundation cycle was completed. Thus, the first day of Tūt became the occasion for celebrating the New Year, which the Copts called the Nawrūz.[72] Maqrīzī's *Khiṭaṭ* contains two separate textual entries on this festival, for it is classified both as a Coptic feast and as one of the important official Fatimid festivals. As a Coptic feast, Maqrīzī delves into questions of its historical and religious origins, identifying it as a hybrid feast of Persian inspiration.[73] But as a Fatimid festival, the Nawrūz is depicted more as an official celebration used by the caliph to bestow generosity on his officials and their families. This Maqrīzī documents with his usual passion for detail, specifying the size of state expenses, types of garments and textiles, kinds of food and fruits and, most importantly, identifying the beneficiaries of such state generosity.[74] The Fatimids' decision to patronize the Nawrūz as a state festival may be explained

[70] *Nujūm*, vol. III, 429; *Badāʾiʿ*, vol. I, 124. [71] *Badāʾiʿ*, vol. I, 124.

[72] On the origins of Nawrūz, see *Khiṭaṭ*, vol. I, 268, and Shoshan who has written extensively on the Nawrūz as a carnival of reversal, *Popular Culture*, 46–7.

[73] For more details, see *Popular Culture*, 40–2. [74] *Khiṭaṭ*, vol. I, 493.

by the fact that during the month of Tūt the Nile waters reach their peak. Moreover, it appears to have been a seasonal date during which important dams were opened for irrigation, and tax collection was normally levied on the producers.[75]

At the Amīriyya barrage . . . the Nile water is blocked after the Khalīj dam has been opened when the Nile has completed 16 cubits. The water remains blocked at al-Amīriyya dam until the day of the Nawrūz. The governor of Cairo goes out to ensure that the Shaykhs of the vicinities (*mashāyikh al-ḍawāḥī)* have blocked the irrigation canals in their lands. Then when this dam is opened the water flows until it reaches the dam of Shībīn, which is in turn blocked, until the land in these area is irrigated. The water remains blocked at the Shībīn dam until ʿĪd al-Ṣalīb, the seventeenth day after al-Nawrūz, after which it is opened, and the irrigation water covers all the land in the area.[76]

Like other Coptic Nile festivals, the Nawrūz also celebrates the Nile's transition from one cyclical stage to another. Thus it may be viewed as another example of a hybrid Coptic festival grafted onto a pagan one. But whereas the Wafā' seems to have undergone a fuller process of Islamization under the hegemony of the Muslim state, the Nawrūz was still primarily viewed as Coptic. Despite its close connection to important state concerns, this did not save its popular rituals of revelry from repeated state repression and ultimate suspension. Maqrīzī's narrative on the Nawrūz tells yet another story of a Coptic festival in decline. Typically, he commences his account of the festival's customary rituals of revelry as things of the past: 'The first of Tūt is their New Year, and in past days and during bygone dynasties, that is the Fatimids, it used to be one of their seasons of idleness and times of error, during which forbidden acts (*munkarāt*) were visible and abominations (*fawāḥish*) were obvious'.[77] In denouncing such public abominations as acts of outright defiance to the moral integrity of the Muslim community, Maqrīzī criticizes the Fatimid caliph for posing as the patron of the festival:

Effeminate males (*al-mukhannathūn*) and dissolute women (*al-fāsiqāt*), playing their musical instruments, would congregate under the Pearl Palace so that the caliph could watch them. Voices become loud, and wine, as well as beer is drunk publicly among them, and in the streets. People splash each other with water mixed with wine and dirt, so that if a chaste person makes the mistake of going out of his house, he is met by someone who splashes him, ruins his clothes and ridicules his sanctity.[78]

For three days, he tells us, all business activities are suspended, markets are closed, and the streets of the city and the Nile banks are appropriated by the populace as public spaces for revelry. As Shoshan argues, the Nawrūz, as well as other Nile festivals for that matter, should be viewed as carnival periods, during which the social order is temporarily disrupted, and the world is turned upside-down. The focal figure here is the mock prince or *Amīr al-Nawrūz*, who is chosen by the commoners, and temporarily licensed to issue injunctions to

[75] Ibid., vol. I, 270–4. [76] Ibid., vol. II, 148. [77] Ibid., vol. I, 269; 493.
[78] Ibid., 493.

both high and low. Public drinking, fire illumination, water splashing and street combats were also common features of the Nawrūz. And as in all festivals of revelry, social violence caused a few casualties. Maqrīzī typically complains that such acts of violence remained unpunished by the government, thus failing to uphold its duty of forbidding evil.[79]

The earliest report of Nawrūz prohibitions takes us back to the year 363 AH, during the reign of Caliph al-Muʿizz li-dīn Allāh who established the Fatimid dynasty in Egypt. Al-Muʿizz did not ban the festival, but only prohibited some of its disruptive rituals, such as the illumination of fire on the eve of the Nawrūz and splashing of water on Nawrūz day. However, the following year, 'people's playing with fire and water increased, and the merchants of the markets organized elephant processions, and exhibited their games in Cairo for three days'.[80] Sensing popular resistance to his prohibitions, al-Muʿizz decided to impose stricter restraining measures, so he sent out another decree prohibiting the play with fire and water, and punished transgressors by imprisonment and public exhibition.[81] Apart from these reports, the Fatimids appear to have continued to act as patrons of this festival throughout. Despite its Coptic and pagan connections, the Fatimids seem to have regarded the Nawrūz as second in importance only to Wafāʾ al-Nīl. The Nawrūz abominations persisted, Maqrīzī tells us, until as late as the 780s AH, when Barqūq, the founder of the Circassian sultanate, banned the festival altogether and threatened transgressors with severe punishment. Closer examination of the prohibition narrative, however, shows that the festival appears to have been banished only from the capital and its major markets. People displayed their usual resistance to such restraints, for we see them celebrating Nawrūz rituals in the more peripheral spaces of the city, away from the surveillance of the new government: in the canals, lakes, parks, alleys and in the home. Thus as with the feast of the Ghiṭās, the Nawrūz festivities were banished from the public areas, only to be celebrated within the more private precincts of the city. And if such private celebrations were of less concern to the government, they were not so for Maqrīzī who denounces them in his usual hostile language: 'These reprehensible acts continue to be performed in the alleys and houses of losers'.[82] Ibn al-Ḥājj shared this hostility to Nawrūz revelries. But whereas Maqrīzī seems to be more concerned about the display of such abominations in the public space, the former appears to be more obsessed with those that take place within the private space.[83] Ironically, in denouncing these practices, Ibn al-Ḥājj offers us exclusive information on how Muslim families celebrated the Nawrūz at home:

[79] Ibid.
[80] Ibid. For more details on forms of medieval entertainment, see Samuel Moreh, *Live Theatre and Dramatic Literature in the Medieval Arab World* (Edinburgh, 1992). [81] Ibid.
[82] Ibid., 494.
[83] See my article on Ibn al-Hājj entitled 'Manners and customs of fourteenth century Cairene women, female anarchy versus male Sharʿī order in Muslim prescriptive treatises', in N. Keddi and B. Baron (eds.) *Women in Middle Eastern History* (New Haven, 1991), 91–121.

On this occasion, many women play in their houses, mingling with women, men, young men, and virgins. They wet each other's clothes with water, and thus appear as though they were almost naked . . . Among their nasty habits is that male and female neighbours are not ashamed of one another; the same goes for cousins, in-laws, and friends of the husband . . . And pretending that they play and joke with one another, they take pleasure in all of this. They exhibit such lack of modesty on this day, that they behave as though they were all women.[84]

Once again, we see popular practices in conflict with official Islamic ideals. Contrary to the strict rules of sexual segregation sanctioned by official Muslim ideology, festival rituals allow freer intermingling between the two sexes in both the private and public spaces, an intermingling that is viewed by the religious establishment as one of the most disruptive acts against the Muslim social order. An analogy should be drawn here between how Copts and women are viewed within this hegemonic discourse. Here a parallel mode of social division is articulated, one which privileges Muslim over Copt, and male over female.

ʿĪd al-Ṣalīb: 17 Tūt

This feast is said to have been initiated by Helena, mother of the Byzantine emperor Constantine, who, in order to re-enforce Byzantine Christian presence in Jerusalem, built the Church of the Holy Sepulchre there.[85] Despite its 'foreign' origins, ʿĪd al-Ṣalīb follows the same calendar pattern observed in other Coptic festivals, for it takes place on the seventeenth of the autumn month of Tūt, a date that coincides with the end of the rise of the Nile's waters. This is another hybrid Christian feast which seems to have displaced yet another pagan feast linked to the Nile cycle. Moreover, like the festivals of the Wafāʾ and the Nawrūz, this one coincides with the opening of important dams, such as Abū ʾl-Munajjā and Shibīn.[86] Maqrīzī says that ʿĪd al-Ṣalīb is another great Coptic festival of revelry that used to be celebrated in the past, during which 'people displayed abominations of various forbidden acts and committed excesses (*mā yatajāwazu ʾl-ḥadd*)'.[87] The Copts apparently, did not celebrate this feast in the city, for they went out to the outskirts of al-Fusṭāṭ to join celebrations with the Banū Wāʾil tribe, who resided there. The *Khiṭaṭ* is silent about why the Copts celebrated this feast with the Banū Wāʾil, but we do know that the latter served as guides in the trade route between the Ḥijāz, Syria, and Egypt in the pre-Islamic era, and eventually became close Christian allies of Byzantium.[88] Given the Byzantine origins of ʿĪd al-Ṣalīb, this may explain why the Banū Wāʾil, who may have still retained some of their earlier Christian practices, celebrated the feast together with the Copts. This last point is important for what it reveals about why this feast, unlike other Coptic feasts, was so short lived under the Fatimids.

[84] *Al-Madkhal*, vol. II, 51–2. [85] *Khiṭaṭ*, vol. I, 267.
[86] Ibid., vol. I, 270; *Sulūk*, vol. IV, 1021. [87] *Khiṭaṭ*, vol. I, 267.
[88] See ʿAbdallāh al-Birrī, *al-Qabāʾil al-ʿArabiyya fī Miṣr* (Cairo, 1967), 162.

The first mention of a repressive policy in the *Khiṭaṭ* narrative goes back to the Fatimid caliph al-ʿAzīz, who, on his accession to the throne in 381 AH, ordered the proscription of ʿĪd al-Ṣalīb festivities. Thus people were forbidden to go to the tribe of Banū Wāʾil, and roads and alleys were blocked to ensure that no transgressions were committed. Despite such restraints, the Copts showed signs of resistance. For in the following year, they still went out to join the Banū Wāʾil, where they stubbornly pursued their usual customs of excessive playing and revelry (*al-laʿib wa-ʾl-lahw*).[89] This went on for twenty years, we are told, until the reign of al-Ḥākim, who is credited by Maqrīzī with final suppression of the festival in 402 AH. The *Khiṭaṭ* narrative here is useful on how the Ḥīkīmā state exercised its measures of prohibition: several caliphal decrees were registered and read out in the ancient mosque of Fusṭāṭ as well as the roads of the city. 'The Ḥākimī decree forbade the Christians from congregating, from exhibiting their adornments, and from approaching their churches'.[90] These measures appear to be much harsher than earlier Fatimid restrictions, for the Copts were not just forbidden to make public expression of their rituals, but were also prevented from entering their churches. An explanation for this harsh attitude should be sought in political factors. The years between 400 and 406 AH witnessed a worsening of relations between al-Ḥākim's regime and Byzantium, culminating in the break-up of commercial relations and the destruction of the Holy Sepulchre by the former's orders. ʿĪd al-Ṣalīb, among other Coptic feasts, was thus conveniently banned during this period. However, whereas other Coptic festivals were only temporarily suppressed, ʿĪd al-Ṣalīb, perhaps because of its Byzantine origin, seems to have been the only Coptic festival sentenced to an early death during the Fatimid period. In his concluding statement, Maqrīzī tells us that 'it became obsolete (*baṭula*), and is *almost* completely unknown in the regions of Egypt today'.[91] But it is uncertain to what extent we can believe Maqrīzī, whose narrative seems always to express a desire for the death of such festivals of revelry.

There is no simple answer to this question, for elsewhere in the *Khiṭaṭ* and *Sulūk* narratives, we still find reference to ʿĪd al-Ṣalīb in the Mamluk period. This is primarily because it coincided with the occasion of opening important dams.[92] In neither account, however, does Maqrīzī describe any celebrations of al-Ṣalīb. As with other Coptic festivals in the *Sulūk*, it is simply mentioned as a seasonal marking in the cycle of the Nile's rising waters.[93] However, it is important to observe here that the occasion of opening the important dam of Abū ʾl-Munajjā, formerly coinciding with the festival of ʿĪd al-Ṣalīb, was celebrated during the Mamluk period as a festival in its own right. Thus, popular festivities appear still to have taken place during the same seasonal period. This may be viewed as another instance of displacing Coptic festival culture from its close connection to the Nile cycle. Most probably this is what hap-

89 *Khiṭaṭ*, vol. I. 267. 90 Ibid. 91 Ibid.
92 Such as the dam of Abūʾ-l-Munajjā: see *Sulūk*, vol. I, 119.
93 ʿĪd al-Ṣalīb appears to have been used as a seasonal date in the cycle of Nile increase until the nineteenth century: see *Manners and Customs*, 504.

pened to the Wafā' festival, which also coincides with the opening of the important Khalīj dam, but is no longer associated with a specific Coptic festival. This process of displacement should be viewed as a result of a deliberate policy on the part of the hegemonic Muslim state to separate Nile festivities from their earlier Coptic connections, making them more easily assimilated to a secular or Islamic Nile culture. Through such a process, the ʿĪd al-Ṣalīb festival eventually came to be displaced by that of Abū 'l-Munajjā, which continued to be celebrated until the crucial year of 806 AH, a date which Maqrīzī uses to mark the beginning of decline of all forms of urban prosperity and refinement in the Egyptian territories. We are told that much of the festival culture in Egypt, Coptic or otherwise, was discontinued. Here, the causes of decline are primarily attributed to economic and demographic factors. 'People are too distracted by the burdens of daily life'.[94]

Four out of our five Nile festivals have become almost obsolete today. Two are still remembered by Egyptians. The Ghiṭās continues to be commemorated by the Coptic community, but only as an exclusively Coptic religious event. The Wafā' survives vaguely in our collective memory. In its present form, it is a folkloric event appropriated by the Egyptian cultural bureaucracy to evoke popular nostalgia for an exotic past. However, if we are searching for cultural continuities, we will have to turn to the popular *mawlid* culture of the Egyptians. Here, earlier forms of revelry have been recast to adapt to Muslim hegemonic culture. But this is another festival story.

[94] *Khiṭaṭ*, vol. I, 487–8. For other references in the *Khiṭaṭ* to the year 806 AH as a year marking the decline of economy and culture in Egypt, see ibid., vol. I, 5; vol. II, 162, 164.

CHAPTER 18

Marriage in late eighteenth-century Egypt

AFAF LUTFI AL-SAYYID MARSOT

Marriage among elites was a matter of alliances and conveniences, which should come as no surprise since it was so in any elite society. As with any society, sometimes the emotional element crept in and marriages were negotiated for other reasons, as we shall see.

It was customary in Mamluk society for the Mamluks to marry within their own social group, that is, to marry daughters or sisters of other Mamluks or else to buy slaves and either have them as concubines or manumit and marry them. These women were therefore married off at a young age and represented by a guardian (father, brother, slave-dealer). Often a grandee would buy a slave-woman and give her as a gift to one of his men who would then manumit and marry her. For example Murād Bey gave his concubine, who had borne him a son, Ayyūb, as a wife to Muḥammad Bey. Many of the documents registering sales would describe the female buyer as *maʿtūqa wa-zawja* of such and such a bey, or would list "ʿArīfa Khātūn, daughter of ʿAbdallāh al-Bayḍā' (a euphemism meaning that she was a white slave), freedwoman of the deceased Sulaymān Katkhudā Mustaḥfiẓān and wife of Yūsuf al-Jābī',[1] or "ʿArīfa Khātūn daughter of ʿAbd Allāh al-Bayḍā', freedwoman of the amir Ḥusayn al-Kabīr al-Qāzdughlī, wife of Maḥmūd Katkhudā Ḥusayn al-Qāzdughlī'.[2]

Grandees negotiated wives for their men just as a father would for his sons, and these negotiations served to build networks among the grandees and create alliances just as any marriage among landowners or nobles would in another society. As Jack Goody has pointed out, when a society transfers property to a woman through marriage or inheritance, 'a premium is placed upon in-marriage'.[3] Lévi-Strauss added that in such cases women became objects 'with which men seek to initiate and solidify relationships with one another'.[4] Thus we have the example of ʿAlī Bey al-Kabīr who, accompanied by two of his men, visited Khalīl Bulghia and asked for the hand of Khalīl's

[1] Dār al-Wathā'iq, Maḥfaẓa 7, *ḥujja* 302. [2] Dār al-Wathā'iq, Maḥfaẓa 7, *ḥujja* 350, 352.

[3] J. Goody, *Production or Reproduction* (Cambridge, 1976), 114.

[4] Claude Lévi-Strauss, *The Elementary Structures of Kinship*, ed. Rodney Needham (Boston, 1969), 480.

sister for one of his men. Khalīl accepted. ʿAlī Bey then asked for the hand of Khalīl's daughter for his other retainer, but Khalīl politely refused and when pressed said, 'I will be ruined, I cannot afford to marry off two at the same time'. ʿAlī Bey then promised to help him out financially and the dual marriage was accepted.

This incident shows that a wife, coming from a Mamluk household entered a marriage with a respectable dowry, enough to ruin a father or guardian. It also points out the close relationship between a grandee and his men so that the grandee might be willing to finance his retainer's marriage out of his own pocket.

Marriages were equally common among Mamluks and widows or daughters of grandees. In the first instance, since widowhood was commonplace, given the level of infighting among Mamluk factions in that half century, the widow was frequently married either to her former husband's *katkhudā* or his *khāzindār*. This would allow that individual to take over the headship of the household. Frequently the grandee would negotiate such a marriage for his daughter during his lifetime to ensure the smooth succession of leadership after his demise. Ismāʿīl Bey al-Kabīr gave his daughter in marriage to his treasurer, Ibrāhīm Agha. Muḥammad Bey Abū ʾl-Dhahab gave his daughter to Yūsuf Bey. Muḥammad Shalabī married one of his three daughters to his treasurer; when Shalabī died, Ibrāhīm Katkhudā, his patron, *ustādh*, gave Muḥammad's widow to Ibrāhīm's treasurer, Maḥmūd Agha. Maḥmūd Agha eventually died and the woman was married off to another retainer, Ḥusayn Agha. Such carefully negotiated in-marriages allowed wealth to remain within the household. Wives were dowered, or when widowed, inherited a portion of their husbands' private wealth. It was therefore not uncommon for women married to Mamluks to have up to three husbands successively. Hānim, the daughter of Ibrāhīm Katkhudā, ʿAlī Bey's patron, was married to ʿAlī Bey's treasurer Ismāʿīl Bey. When he died she married Aḥmad Agha, another of her father's men, and when he died she married Muḥammad Agha al-Bārūdī, her deceased husband's treasurer. The widow of a grandee was a great prize. ʿAlī Bey al-Kabīr had had four wives. ʿĀʾisha Ḳadin, his chief wife, had been a slave of Ibrāhīm Katkhudā, ʿAlī's patron. When ʿAlī Bey died she married Muḥammad Bey Abū ʾl-Dhahab, his *katkhudā*, and also his usurper. Another of ʿAlī Bey's wives, the famous Nafīsa Khātūn, so respected by al-Jabartī, was later married to Murād Bey. Ibrāhīm Bey, who was duumvir with Murād, had married the sister of his patron, Muḥammad Bey Abū ʾl-Dhahab, who gave Ibrāhīm one of his own favourites, Āminat Allāh Khātūn, in marriage.[5]

A widow could always refuse to marry the proposed suitor, either because she already had her eye on another suitor, or for any other reason. Ismāʿīl Bey, brother of ʿAlī al-Ghazzāwī, *katkhudā* of Muḥammad Bey Abū ʾl-Dhahab, married Fāṭima Khānim, the daughter of an earlier duumvir, Riḍwān

[5] A. al-Sayyid Marsot, *Women and Men in Late 18th Century Egypt* (Austin, 1995), 41ff.

Katkhudā, who had ruled with Ibrāhīm Katkhudā in the middle of the century. She had been engaged to be married to ʿAlī Agha, one of her father's Mamluks. The marriage contract having been signed (*katb al-kitāb*), she was legally considered his spouse although the marriage had not yet been consummated. ʿAlī Bey then went to Iraq, but his wife was reluctant to join him and petitioned to have the marriage dissolved, which it was according to the Mālikī school of jurisprudence, which allowed a woman to divorce an absent husband on the grounds of prejudice, or *ḍarar*. She then married Ismāʿīl. Later on Ismāʿīl wished to marry one of Riḍwān's former concubines, a certain Sālūn, who had been Ismāʿīl's sister-in-law, married to his brother ʿAlī. When ʿAlī died Ismāʿīl asked for her hand but she refused. Ismāʿīl went to his patron, Abū ʾl-Dhahab, and recounted his luckless attempt at marriage. His patron explained that Sālūn may have not wanted to marry him out of a sense of propriety since he was already married to the daughter of her former master, and could not set herself up as a fellow wife with the daughter of her patron. Whether true or not, at Ismāʿīl's insistence, Abū ʾl-Dhahab interceded with the woman and she finally agreed to marry her former brother-in-law. By then Ismāʿīl's first wife was already ill and dying.[6]

That incident makes clear that Ismāʿīl had known Sālūn and had fallen in love with her, hence his insistence on marrying her. Cynics might assume that Ismāʿīl simply wanted to get his hands on her inheritance from his brother, but since Ismāʿīl would have been his brother's heir, we can assume that more than greed was involved in the affair.

When a grandee died after having lost a battle, the victor could dispose of the grandee's widow, and either marry her himself, as in the case of Abū ʾl-Dhahab marrying ʿAlī's widow, or give her in marriage to one of his men, thereby increasing his retainer's wealth. Jabartī recounted an incident where members of the Qāzdughlī faction, after defeating their opponents, married the widows and installed themselves in their houses. He regarded that as reprehensible behaviour, but it seems to have been a time-honored practice.

Jabartī, who was generally uninterested in women, went into details regarding Mamluk marriages because such marriages reinforced ties between members of the same household, or ties across households, cementing alliances, and expressing power relationship as well. Because the marriage of a woman from one household reinforced the ties to her second household, it was viewed as a means to an end in political terms, for the woman kept close links with her former households and its harem, while the patron–client relationship between the men was reinforced.

Mamluk women often married off their own slaves to other Mamluks and to grandees. Jabartī claims that Nafīsa Khātūn had married off her slave-women to every grandee. That was one sure way of establishing powerful net-

[6] Ibid., 43; ʿAbd al-Raḥmān al-Jaborti al-Jabartī, *ʿAjāʾib al-āthār fī ʾl-tarājim waʾl-akhbār* (Būlūq, 1879–80), 7 vols., vol. II, 20.

works, which served her well, for she was always protected throughout her lifetime, save during Muḥammad ʿAlī's regime. Thus networks developed not only among Mamluk grandees and retainers, but among Mamluk women within the harem. The importance of such networks has not been sufficiently accentuated, but we cannot afford to overlook the influence that a woman or a favourite concubine had on her husband or master, for she could obtain benefits for her friends' husbands from him, or allay his anger towards them when it was roused. Seeking favours from each other was not limited to harem women but was and is a time-honoured practice in Middle Eastern societies to the present day. Where a man might find it demeaning to ask a favour of a colleague, in case his request might be refused, he finds it perfectly natural for his wife to request the same favour of his colleague's wife, seeing nothing degrading in women talking to each other over such matters, for if the request is denied he can claim lack of knowledge that it was ever proferred.

Marriages of relations of powerful Mamluks were celebrated with great pomp and circumstance, thus honouring the households that were being united or allied. Such celebrations in themselves show the importance the Mamluks generally attributed to the creation of new networks. The best example was the wedding of Hānim, the daughter of Ibrāhīm Katkhudā, *ustādh* of ʿAlī Bey al-Kabīr. To show respect and to honour their patron's name, the Mamluks who had been part of his household celebrated the event for a month, during which time the gates of Cairo remained open day and night, to allow anyone to enter the city and participate in the celebrations. As Jabartī pointed out, 'each amir invested by Ibrāhīm Katkhudā considered himself a host in that wedding, for the bride was the daughter of their deceased patron'.[7] Such incidents revealed that Mamluks who had lost their blood ties invented new ones for themselves in the patron–client networks, recreating family bonds they had lost when taken from their blood families. Mamluks did bear legitimate children, but these did not inherit the headship of a house or the father's position within the Mamluk hierarchy. They simply inherited the father's private wealth, and merged with the population, becoming known as *awlād al-nās.*

While close linkages existed between a patron and his Mamluks, treachery between them was not uncommon. But this is frequently the case among families who are tied by bonds of blood, so there is little reason to suppose that Mamluks would behave otherwise. Mamluk women, too, developed close linkages among themselves, although we know little about them since the subject of women was of little interest to the commentators of the period. This, however, is a subject that needs to be studied further.

One of the myths that abounded about Muslim societies was that men preferred to marry virgins, yet among the Mamluks we note that the virginity of the wife was of little consequence. Her age was equally unimportant, so that

[7] Al-Jabartī, *ʿAjāʾib*, vol. I, 251.

men married women who were older simply to consolidate relationships or in order to benefit from their wealth. Those who wished to marry or acquire virgins could always buy themselves a slave-woman.

We might assume that Mamluks behaved differently from other people simply because their system seemed to be an unusual one, yet when we look at other social strata we notice great similarity. The native elites, *ʿulamāʾ* and *tujjār*, also tended to contract marriages with wealthy women – divorced, widowed or virgin; it did not seem to matter much. Or perhaps marriage to younger women was so commonplace that it did not merit a mention in what was, after all, a work of *ʿajāʾib*. We notice that wealthy *tujjār* married women from their field, as did the *ʿulamāʾ* although both professions often intermarried.

Shaykh Sharqāwī, rector of al-Azhar, had married the daughter of another shaykh, ʿAlī al-Zaʿfarānī; Shaykh ʿUmar al-Baqlī married the widow of Shaykh Aḥmad al-Maqdisī who, through her wealth, allowed her husband a life of ease. The same shaykh later remarried, taking another daughter of a shaykh, Maḥmūd al-Kurdī. Within Jabartī's own family, we find marriages between daughters of *ʿulamāʾ* and among as well. For instance, Jabartī's great-grandmother, Maryam, had been widowed and married the amir ʿAlī Agha, *bāsh ikhtiyār* of the Mutafarriqa regiment. Ḥasan al-Jabartī had married the daughter of ʿAlī Agha and then the daughter of an *ʿālim*, Yūsuf al-Khashshāb.[8]

Just as marriage was a process of cementing relationships among Mamluks and networking among households, so was it, to a lesser extent among *ʿulamāʾ*. After all, it made perfect sense to marry daughters or female relations of men whom you knew and had befriended, just as it made sense to marry widows of friends or relations who were known to have inherited wealth.

The same applied to the *tujjār* who married within their profession, or women from among the *ʿulamāʾ* strata, or even, if extremely wealthy, from among the Mamluks. For example, Sharāʾibī men married women of their family. Muḥammad Çorbaci (al-Dāda's son) had married Ṣafiyya. When he died Ṣafiyya married his brother Qāsim. Another of Dāda's sons, Aḥmad, married his cousin, while a nephew married Dāda's daughter. Such in-marriages existed in all social strata, but especially among those with property, for it made sense to keep the patrimonial wealth within the family.

From a *waqfiyya* we learned that a Maḥrūqī had married into the shaykhly family of al-Qawuqjī, who had married into the family of Shaykh Shihāb al-Aḥmadī. The second generation found the daughter of that Maḥrūqī marrying the son of a *ṣarrāf*, while her brother's daughter married her husband's nephew (i.e. her father's sister's husband's nephew). The two families in question brought together a *ṣarrāf*, a *rūznāmjī*, and several *tujjār* as well as shaykhly families. The Shuwaykh family had within two generations allied themselves by marriage to four other *tujjār* families. Occasionally they inter-

[8] Al-Sayyid Marsot, *Women*, 77ff; Jabartī, vol. IV, 161; vol. I, 388ff.

married with Mamluks: thus Amīna al-Shuwaykh married Sulaymān Bey al-Shābūrī; and Zaynab, daughter of a merchant in the Ghawriyya district of Cairo, Muḥammad al-Ḥilw, married ʿUthmān Bey Zāda, son of Yūsuf Bey al-Jazzār.[9] The most famous of Mamluk–*tujjār* marriages was between Shuwaykār, the daughter of a rich merchant, Muḥammad al-Bārūdī, and Ibrāhīm Katkhudā, the early duumvir. Jabartī commented that using his wife's money, Ibrāhīm was able to become the top grandee in the country.

It was also common for Mamluks and wealthy *ʿulamāʾ* to marry slave-women. Muṣṭafā Jaʿfar, a merchant, had married two freedwomen, ʿĀʾisha Khātūn and Fatḥiyya Khātūn. When Jaʿfar died he left a *waqf* in favour of four people, his son, his two wives and his freedman, Ḥājj Sulaymān. Fatḥiyya then married Sulaymān.

Women of the artisanal classes married men who came from the same guild as their men, or who came from ancillary guilds. Just as often they married men who came from very different guilds.

In the rural milieu rich peasants married into families of rich peasants, as one would expect, and poor peasants married poor peasants.

The interesting thing to note in eighteenth-century marriages in general is the degree of leeway that women had as to what they could inscribe in a marriage contract. It would seem that whatever was inscribed was recognized as legally binding, so long as it did not contravene any clearly stated religious injunction. Thus a woman would insert clauses specifying that if her would-be husband married another woman after herself she could divorce him. She could also inscribe that her husband had to follow the inclinations of her family (as Nelly Hanna has shown in her work). She could specify how often her family could visit her, or how often she could visit her family. Thus women seemed to be cognizant of their judicial rights and took full advantage of them to protect themselves.

When it came to the question of property, the registration deed would sometimes bear the notation that said property was paid for 'from her own money', so that her *wakīl*, her husband, could not claim that he was co-proprietor. Women sued husbands, if they defaulted on loans given by the wife, and would just as frequently win such cases, especially when they had proof of tendering such a loan.

One supposes that for every canny businesswoman (and there were plenty in that period as the *awqāf* show, when nearly 40 per cent of all such registrations were made by women) there was a woman content to turn her wealth over to her husband. But we have no way of knowing the percentage of those who did and those who did not. What we clearly note is that many women were entrepreneurial, and bought and sold exactly the same things as men, that they protected their wealth, and went to court to do so, and that they disposed of their wealth as they pleased.

[9] Al-Sayyid Marsot, *Women*, 86.

During the late eighteenth century under the Mamluks, government was chaotic and decentralized, wealth was generated by trade and commerce, or through land, and there was a close relationship between the women and the *ʿulamāʾ*, who supported their rights. Within a society where women controlled wealth, *ʿulamāʾ* allowed them leeway in cases of divorce. For instance, the Mālikī school of jurisprudence allowed for easy divorce, using *ḍarar* as a reason. In brief, when women have a free hand in the market, they seem to have an easier time and to be freer from ample controls (within reason, of course).

Index